THE WILLIAMIT

The Williamite Wars in Ireland, 1688–91

John Childs

hambledon
continuum

Hambledon Continuum is an imprint of Continuum Books
Continuum UK, The Tower Building, 11 York Road, London SE1 7NX
Continuum US, 80 Maiden Lane, Suite 704, New York, NY 10038

www.continuumbooks.com

First published 2007

British Library Cataloguing-in-Publication Data
A catalogue record for this book is available from the British Library.

ISBN 978 1 85285 573 4

Typeset by Egan Reid, Auckland, New Zealand
Printed and bound by MPG Books Ltd, Cornwall, Great Britain

Contents

Maps

(Maps drawn by David Appleyard, School of Geography, University of Leeds.)

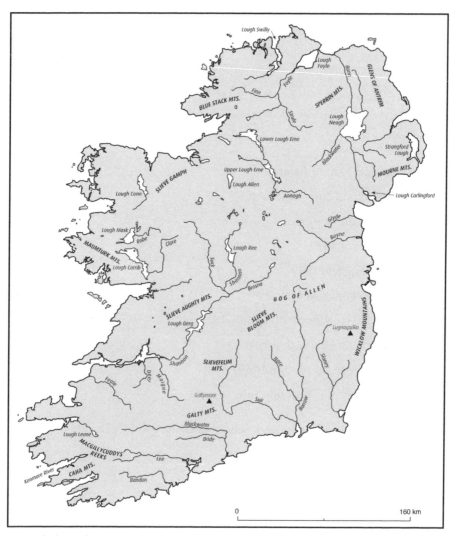

General physical map of Ireland

Principal towns and cities of Ireland

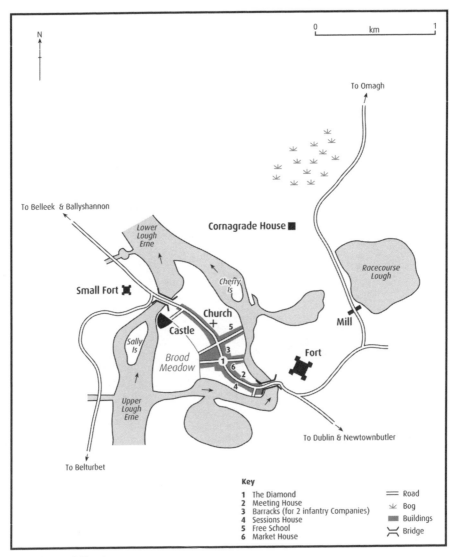

Plan of Enniskillen in 1689

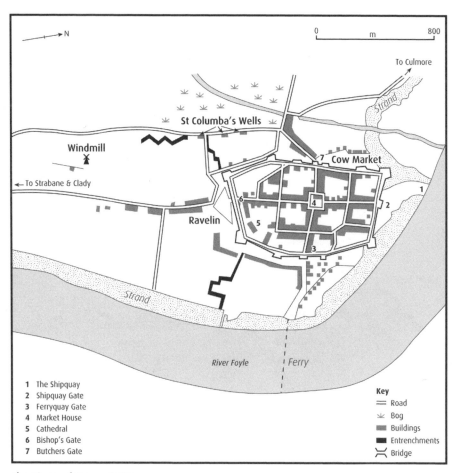

The Siege of Derry, 1689

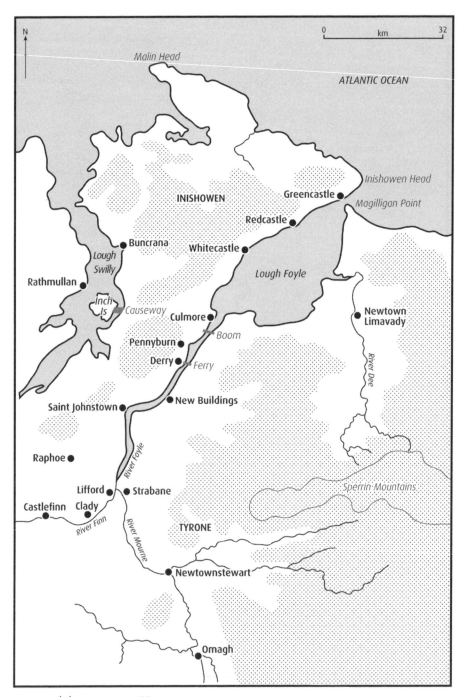

Derry and the Laggan, 1689

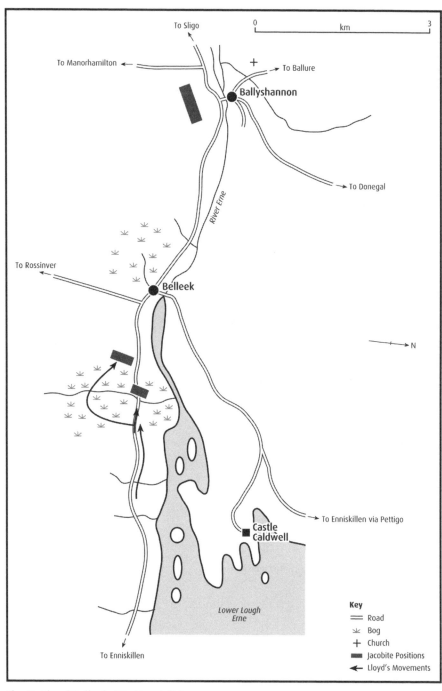

The Battle of Belleek, 7th May 1689

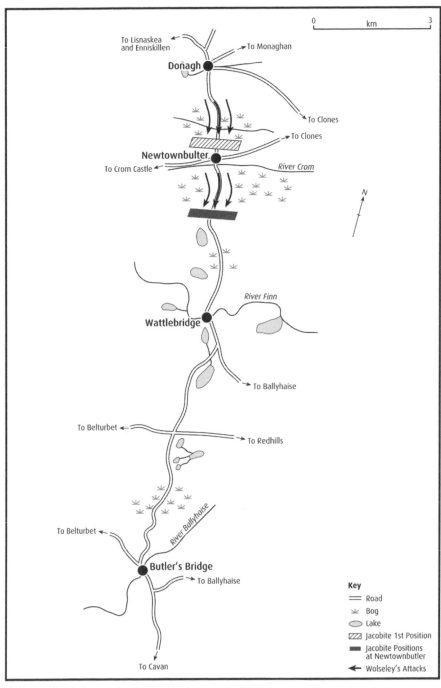

The Battle of Newtownbutler, 31st July 1689

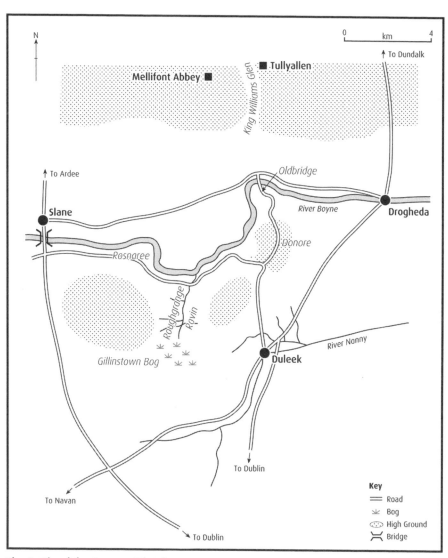

The Battle of the Boyne, 11th July 1690

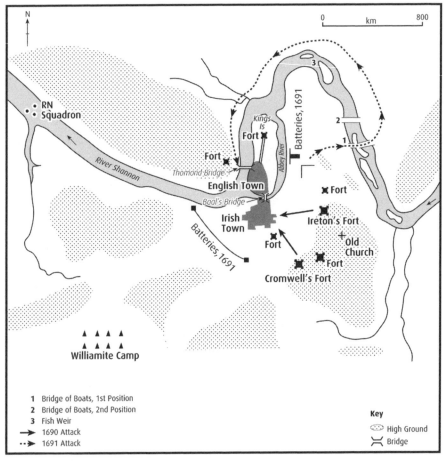

The Sieges of Limerick, 1690 & 1691

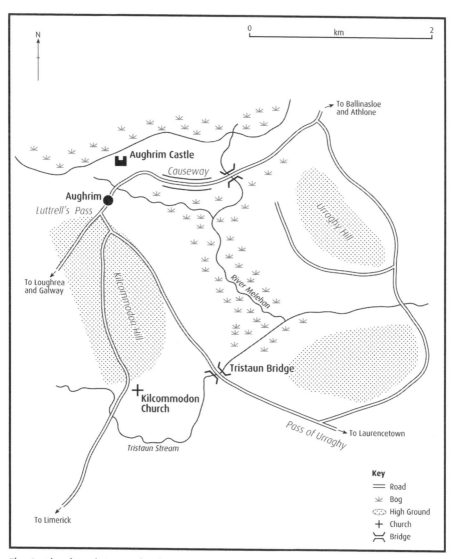

The Battle of Aughrim, 12th July 1691

For Cesca

Abbreviations

Add. MSS.	Additional Manuscript
BL	British Library
Bod. Lib.	Bodleian Library
Bt.	Baronet
CSPD	*Calendar of State Papers Domestic*
CTB	*Calendar of Treasury Books, 1689–1692*
CTP	*Calendar of Treasury Papers, 1557–1696*
Dalton	Charles Dalton, *English Army Lists and Commission Registers, 1661–1714*
Dalton, *Irish Army*	Charles Dalton, *King Charles II's Irish Army Lists, 1661–1685*
Dalton, *Scots Army*	Charles Dalton, *The Scots Army, 1661–1688*
D'Alton	John D'Alton, *Illustrations, Historical and Genealogical, of King James's Irish Army List*
DCRO	Dorset County Record Office, Dorchester
DNB	*Oxford Dictionary of National Biography*
FIC	*Franco-Irish Correspondence, December 1688–February 1692*
HMC	*Reports of the Royal Commission on Historical Manuscripts*
JP	Justice of the Peace
LBRT	'The letter book of Richard Talbot'
Luttrell	Narcissus Luttrell, *A Brief Historical Relation of State Affairs from September 1678 to April 1714*
MSS.	Manuscript
NA	National Archives, London, previously the Public Record Office
NCO	non-commissioned officer
n.s.	new series
o.s.	old series
RN	Royal Navy
SP	State Papers, National Archives
WO	War Office Papers, National Archives

Notes

NOTE ON DATES

The Gregorian Calendar (English Old Style), which was ten days behind the Julian Calendar (Continental New Style) during the seventeenth century, has been used throughout. The New Year has been taken to begin on 1 January instead of Lady Day, 25 March.

NOTE ON DISTANCES

Distances are presented in km and metres according to the International System of Units. An English mile – the Elizabethan Statute Mile established in 1593 – measured 1,760 yards (*c.* 1,609 metres) and an Irish mile, 2,240 yards (*c.* 2,048 metres).

NOTE ON SPELLING AND PUNCTUATION

All spellings in contemporary quotations have been modernized. Similarly, punctuation has been altered in those instances where the meaning of the original was not immediately apparent when read at normal speed.

NOTE ON MAPS AND PLACE NAMES

Where towns and villages are known by both Gaelic and English names, the latter have been employed.

Because it is impossible to produce sufficiently detailed maps, the reader is advised *either* to follow the campaigns in one of the following modern road atlases:

The Complete Road Atlas of Ireland (Ordnance Survey of Ireland: Dublin, 1998)

Michelin Motoring Map 405: Ireland (Clermont-Ferrand, 1996)

Michelin Motoring Atlas: Great Britain and Ireland (Clermont-Ferrand, 1990)

AA Road Atlas: Ireland (Windsor, 2004)

or one of these historical atlases:

Speed, John, *The Counties of Britain: A Tudor Atlas by John Speed*, intr. Nigel Nicolson (London, 1995)

Taylor, George and Skinner, Andrew, *Maps of the Roads of Ireland* (2nd edn, Dublin, 1783, repr. Shannon, 1969)

The Rev. George Story produced a number of clear, contemporary maps and plans in *A True and Impartial History of the Most Material Occurrences in the Kingdom of Ireland during the Last Two Years* (London, 1691), and *A Continuation of the Impartial History of the Wars of Ireland, From the Time that the Duke Schonberg Landed with an Army in that Kingdom, to the 23rd of March 1691/2 when Their Majesties' Proclamation was published, declaring the War to be ended* (London, 1693). These are available over the world-wide web via Early English Books On-Line (http://eebo.chadwyck.com).

Preface

Seventeenth-century wars were usually determined by sieges and myriad minor operations – reconnaissances, attacks on supply lines, patrols, raids and occupation of captured regions by small garrisons – rather than great battles. Warfare was attritional, territorial and positional, complicated in Ireland by the widespread involvement of both Protestant and Roman Catholic irregulars. Although much has been written about the siege of Derry, the Boyne, the Treaty of Limerick and, to a lesser extent, Aughrim, few books have treated the entire War of the Two Kings. Whatever their public justifications, authors usually write the books that they personally would have found useful and interesting. Thus, the following is both a detailed chronicle of military operations, a companion piece to *The British Army and the Nine Years' War, 1688–97: the Operations in Low Countries* (Manchester, 1991) and a work of effrontery and impertinence. An Englishman coming late in his career to the history of Ireland is constantly aware of his ignorance.

Preliminaries, 1688

Between April and June 1688 Prince William III of Orange Nassau, Stadholder and Captain-General of the Dutch Republic, decided to intervene in English affairs to protect the inheritance of his wife, Mary, King James II's elder Protestant daughter, by ensuring that England did not slide into a military alliance with France in the imminent Nine Years' War. The invitation from Lord Macaulay's 'Immortal Seven' reached The Hague early in July and conspiracies in the English Army, the Royal Navy and the court of Princess Anne of Denmark, James's younger Protestant daughter, began to fashion themselves.

William landed at Brixham on 5 November 1688 heading an expeditionary force of around 15,000 men. As the Dutch advanced on London, James's field army, riven with disloyalty and uncertainty, fell back from its advance base at Salisbury and disintegrated. With William's connivance, James slipped away from Rochester on 22 December, landing in France on Christmas morning; within three days he had been reunited with his wife, Mary of Modena, and infant son, the future James III, the 'Old Pretender'.

Pro-Catholic policies and disregard for the property and political interests of the English, Anglican élite had ruined James. Rather than governing through and with the landed gentry and aristocracy, rewarding them with largesse and patronage, James had failed to oblige the monarchy's natural supporters and, instead, promoted Protestant Dissenters and Roman Catholic co-religionists to high positions in local and national government and the armed forces. Most of the gentry and aristocracy – only a small number, no more than a couple of hundred, were actively involved in the Dutch-controlled conspiracies – stood aside to await the course of events in November and December 1688. Few actively assisted their sovereign, the majority indifferent to his fate: many knew of the plots but, whilst personally unwilling to engage in treason, said nothing. Summoned to solve the resulting political conundrum the Convention Parliament determined that James's 'flight' constituted an abdication leaving the throne vacant. With his army occupying London, William was the only conceivable choice to fill the void if England was not to revert to a republic. Several days of political manoeuvring were required to enable small compromises to salve some of the more delicate consciences before, on 13 February 1689, the Earl of Halifax, as presiding officer in the House of Lords, offered the crown jointly to William and Mary.

The War of the Two Kings was a direct consequence of this Glorious Revolution in England. Whereas James had grown increasingly unpopular in England, the reverse was the case in Ireland where the majority of the native population was Roman Catholic and had fought for James's father, Charles I, during the Irish Rebellion in 1641 and the consequent Confederate Wars, 1642-9, in the hope of securing toleration for their religion and freedom from government by the English Protestants sitting in Dublin. Defeat by Oliver Cromwell, 1649-53, was followed by severe punishment in the form of the confiscation of the estates of Roman Catholic landowners and penal legislation against the free practice of Roman Catholicism. Despite high expectations, when Charles II was restored to his throne in 1660 he did little to alleviate their condition but the accession of his brother, James, in 1685 brought a change of fortunes. As in England, James was determined to advantage his Roman Catholic subjects but his lord deputy in Ireland, Richard Talbot, Earl and then Duke of Tyrconnell, drove the policy of 'Catholicization' – the legal toleration of Roman Catholicism and the replacement of Protestant public officials with Irish Roman Catholics – hard and fast, probably a good deal more aggressively than James had intended. Tyrconnell was representative of the 'Old English', the descendants of the English, Welsh and Norman settlers who had come to Ireland following the conquest during the twelfth century. Until the Nine Years' War, 1594-1603, and the Cromwellian Reconquest confirmed English Protestant domination, they were the dominant class and many of Ireland's rulers had been drawn from amongst their aristocracy but continued adherence to Roman Catholicism brought dispossession and replacement during the seventeenth century by Protestant 'New English' settlers. Tyrconnell was determined to re-establish the dominance of the Old English at the expense of both the New English and the native Irish.

Irish Protestants and Roman Catholics were prepared for organized violence in the winter of 1688-9. During the summer of 1687 a disquieting report had reached Tyrconnell: 4,000 Scots-Irish Ulster 'fanatics', inspired by a preacher imported from Scotland, had held a field conventicle of several days' duration during which there had been talk of 'many things tending to sedition and rebellion'. The cleric was arrested and deported but later escaped to Holland,[1] the sanctuary of numerous British religious refugees. As a precaution, when the Irish standing army of 8,938 men broke up from its summer training camp at the Curragh, Thomas Sheridan, one of Tyrconnell's secretaries, recommended that the infantry battalions of John, Lord Forbes, and William Stewart, 1st Viscount Mountjoy, should assume winter quarters in Ulster.

In Ireland, the Protestants received notice of the Prince of Orange's intentions during September; at least, that was when the Protestants in Counties Armagh, Monaghan and Antrim began to arm themselves and form military associations.[2] The decision of some of the leading Ulster Protestants to exploit a Dutch military expedition against England to make preparations to counter a Catholic menace in Ireland came after five years of increasing tension and unease caused by an accelerating policy of de-Protestantization.[3] Between 1685 and 1688, 7,000 Protestant soldiers were sacked from the Irish Army on the grounds that they were either 'Old Cromwellians' or just old and Protestant, and replaced by Roman Catholics. Only the infantry battalions of Forbes and Mountjoy retained significant Protestant components: in 1688, the former contained 130 from a total of 780 privates, 78 NCOs and 41 commissioned officers. Forbes had managed to retain so many Protestants largely through force of character. He was a 'young man of much heat and spirit [who] was continually jarring with the Popish officers' but Tyrconnell 'did not care to disoblige him.'[4] The judiciary and both central and local government were similarly purged. Tyrconnell was rapidly dismantling the English and Scottish Protestant hegemony.

To strengthen his forces in the face of the Dutch threat, James ordered the better elements of the Irish Army into England. One regiment of dragoons, a battalion of the Irish Foot Guards, and Anthony Hamilton's and Lord Forbes's battalions of line infantry, a total of 2,964 men, sailed to Chester during September and early October. To make good the loss, Tyrconnell raised four new infantry regiments, one each from Connaught, Munster, Leinster and Ulster. The latter unit, commanded by Alexander MacDonnell, Third Earl of Antrim, was intended to enter the field by 20 November. Mountjoy's battalion was in garrison at Derry, which felt reasonably secure because of the Protestantism of the colonel and a number of his soldiers and officers. Tyrconnell, on the other hand, did not want an unreliable battalion in such a key post so, on 23 November, he ordered it to England via Dublin. The replacement was to be Antrim's new, Catholic battalion but a fortnight elapsed before it was ready to march north: recruitment had been slow because of rumours that the battalion was destined for England. Without the two-week hiatus, during which Derry was ungarrisoned and in the uncertain care of deputy mayor John Buchanan, 'a person of no good reputation in the town' who remodelled the city militia 'as he saw fit', there may well have been no war. A rebellion might have occurred, probably centred on Enniskillen, but it could not have prospered without Derry.

A constant undercurrent of rumour that the Catholics were on the verge of desperate measures made the Derry Protestants uneasy, many having experienced the Great Massacre of 1641. An inflammatory sermon preached by a friar to Mountjoy's Catholic soldiers during October had already caused apprehension: some Protestants had attended out of curiosity and were thoroughly alarmed by what they heard. Throughout November and December, the Protestants were aware that local Irish blacksmiths were busy producing half-pikes and skeans[5] and priests were urging their flocks to arm. When, in mid-November, news of William's landing at Brixham reached Derry, the better-informed and educated realized that if serious trouble occurred England would be in no position to offer immediate help. Reports of James's misfortunes reached Dublin at much the same time resulting in Catholic agitation against Protestants, the burning of William in effigy and the invocation of divine assistance through fast days.[6]

A letter was delivered on 3 December to the house of Hugh Montgomery, Second Earl of Mountalexander, at Comber, County Down. It was unsigned and written in a style typical of 'the meaner sort of the natives'.

> Good my Lord,
>   I have written to you to let you know that all our Irish men through Ireland is sworn that on the ninth of this month they are all to fall on to kill and murder man, wife and child. And I desire your lordship to take care of yourself and all others that are judged by our men to be heads, for whosoever of 'em can kill any of you they are to have a captain's place. So my desire to your honour is to look to yourself and give other noblemen warning and go not out either day or night without a good guard with you and let no Irishman come near you whatsoever he be. So this is all from him who was your father's friend and is your friend and will be, though I dare not be known as yet for fear of my life.[7]

Copies of the 'Comber Letter' were widely distributed – they appeared in Dublin from 4 December – and read from pulpits by Dissenting ministers. Several Dublin Protestants tried unsuccessfully to discuss its contents and the general situation in England with Tyrconnell. Eventually Edward Brabazon, 4th Earl of Meath, obtained an audience but the lord deputy denied knowledge of the letter and opined that Catholics were in more danger than Protestants, a response that awarded the Comber Letter undeserved credence. William Cunningham of Belfast gave a copy to George Canning who forwarded it to Alderman John Tompkins in Derry. Another copy reached Enniskillen and most of the Protestant gentry of County Fermanagh on 7 December. Rekindling memories of 1641 the impact was considerable because several Protestant leaders were ready and willing to exploit the opportunity. Coming on the heels of the billeting orders to Derry and Enniskillen, the 'Comber Letter' was sufficient to convince many Protestants of the existence of a grand Catholic plot aimed at their massacre and extirpation. Across Ireland, Protestants gathered ancient swords and muskets from attics, cellars and the walls of baronial halls and prepared for a combination of revenge and self-defence.

On 6 December, Tyrconnell instructed the 'seneschal' of Donore, County Meath, to accept a regiment in garrison. Seeking reciprocity, Lord Meath requested that the Protestants be allowed to take weapons from local militia armouries to provide for their own security but Tyrconnell replied that there were insufficient arms for the standing army, certainly none to spare for Protestants; besides, his request smelled of rebellion 'and were it not for the respect he had to his family, he would commit him'. Many Protestant Dubliners decided to leave for England: eight ships sailed on 7 December, seven on 8 December and 18 on 9 December, mostly packed with women and children.[8] 'Those with more courage' armed themselves and occupied places of potential strength, such as Trinity College, or fortified their houses. Although bent over his desk signing commissions for raising 20,000 men, Tyrconnell found time to order three cartloads of weapons to the mass house in St Francis Street whilst the regular soldiers in the capital were re-equipped with muskets instead of pikes and ammunition was stocked at the main guard. Sensing that the situation was rapidly deteriorating, during the evening of 8 December Tyrconnell assured the Protestant Archbishop of Dublin, Francis Marsh, of the safety of his flock. Marsh responded by causing an ameliatory address to this effect to be read in all Dublin churches on the following morning. On 9 December an embargo was placed on ships leaving for England and, that night, Tyrconnell reassured the leading Protestants that their religion was secure and denied all knowledge of a planned massacre. Although this was restated in a proclamation on 10 December trust was already forfeit whilst those sailing to England took with them predictions of impending catastrophe.[9]

Antrim's battalion, variously described by the Protestants as 'dreadfully starved' and 'a numerous swarm of Irish and Highlanders',[10] had reached Colonel George Philips's colony at Newtown Limavady, 20 kilometres from Derry, by 6 December. Philips sent an express letter to Alderman Samuel Norman warning of Antrim's approach and suggesting that he explain to 'the sober people of the town' the danger 'of admitting such guests among them'. Philips intimated that not only were there between six and eight companies of Catholic Irish and Scottish soldiers but they were accompanied by the customary swarm of women, children and camp followers. Philips's message reached Derry on 7 December, the courier adding that he had passed Antrim's advance guard only 3 km from the east bank of the River Foyle, at much the same time that Alderman John Tom[p]kins received the Comber Letter. Later that day Philips dispatched a second note advising Derry to shut its gates, adding the assurance that he would arrive with 'his friends' on the following day (8 December). Assuming that Antrim's soldiers were the most likely agents of massacre, a decision had to be made. The middle- and working class members of the population, discreetly supported by Tompkins and the Bishop of Derry, Ezekiel Hopkins, were opposed because barring the entry of the king's troops into a royal garrison was treason. A number of the town council were in favour but had no desire to become personally involved. Egged on by a non-conformist minister, the Reverend James Gordon, the hot-headed younger men favoured a show of resistance. By this time, three of Antrim's companies, commanded by a lieutenant and an ensign, had reached the east bank of the Foyle. Ostensibly to seek forage for their men, the two officers were ferried across and welcomed into the city by deputy mayor

Buchanan and the sheriffs. Sheriff Kennedy suspected that there was a design to shut the gates and sought to forestall it by stating publicly that the soldiers would camp that night on the east bank of the Foyle before entering the city on the morning of 8 December but his statement was quickly discredited when Antrim's troops began to cross the river coming ashore at the landing place within 300 metres of the Ferry Gate. Seeing this, nine young men, quickly reinforced by at least four others, drew their swords, ran to the main guard, seized the keys 'without any great opposition', and dashed to the Ferry Gate. They hauled up the drawbridge, slammed the gate and locked it: Antrim's leading elements were within 60 metres. The other three gates were then barred.

The precipitate action of the 'apprentice boys', although connived at by several eminent townsmen, alarmed many who had no wish to experience a Catholic garrison but were equally fearful of the consequences of its forcible exclusion. Antrim's two officers, the deputy mayor, sheriffs and Catholic inhabitants, plus a few Protestants, met the apprentices in the market place and tried to persuade them of the error of their ways. The situation was still redeemable because there had been no violence. Whilst attention was attracted to these discussions, some of the more conservative townsmen hastened to secure the municipal magazine in the Tower House but were beaten to the door by a crowd of people, the apprentices in the van. Whilst running towards the magazine, Henry Campsie, one of the original nine apprentices, was shot by Militiaman Linegar, a suspected Catholic. He was lucky to be thrown into gaol rather than lynched but the wounding of Campsie increased the determination and independence of the mob. Both the bishop and the deputy mayor tried argument and reason but failed to make an impression. Meanwhile, Antrim's soldiers were loitering outside the Ferry Gate. Leaning over the rampart, James Morrison told them to go away, or words to that effect, but they made no move until, in a very loud voice, he shouted 'Bring out a great gun here,' whereupon they hurried back to the boats and recrossed the river. During the afternoon of 7 December Councillor David Cairns came into town and, after expressing his approval of what had transpired, encouraged the men by inspecting the walls and main guard. After Cairns had assumed unofficial command, waverers became more supportive of the actions of the apprentice boys. Messages were dispatched to local gentry seeking assistance but most were found to be either averse to developments or, at best, equivocal, several writing to Tyrconnell to exonerate themselves by blaming the intemperance of the mob.

Protected by a 'good guard' upon the walls, during the night of 7–8 December an inventory was taken: just 300 men were capable of bearing arms whilst the magazine contained nine barrels of gunpowder, 150 weapons in decent repair and 1,000 'very much out of order'. Prolonged resistance appeared impractical. During 8 December Bishop Hopkins left for England[11] but many Protestants came into Derry from the surrounding countryside, frightened of massacre and

Antrim's ill-behaved soldiers infesting the road from Newtown Limavady to the banks of the Foyle. Conversely, many Catholics departed the city and a convent of Dominican Friars was 'packed off'. Lord Antrim lodged with George Philips in Newtown Limavady on the night of 8–9 December. On the day of the supposed massacre (9 December) Philips took Antrim in his coach towards Derry but the atmosphere was inauspicious. Derry fired two cannon to celebrate the news that Prince George of Denmark and the Duke of Ormonde had joined the growing list of those who had deserted James II. George Cook, a butcher, assembled between 50 and 60 boys on the Ferry Quay, whom the Irish soldiers on the far side of the Foyle mistook for soldiers, whilst Alderman Tompkins and the Reverend Gordon drew up between 30 and 40 horsemen on a nearby hill. Uneasy before this show of strength, the Irish soldiers began to drift back towards Newtown Limavady, meeting Antrim and Philips on the road. Having listened to the frightful tales, Antrim asked Philips to travel ahead to acquire some accurate information.

Because he had been in Antrim's company, Philips was initially treated with considerable distrust but he was able to convince the townspeople of his Protestant credentials. After excusing his delay in Derry, Philips wrote to Antrim discouraging him from venturing further. Already nervous and uncertain, Antrim retired to Coleraine where he reassembled his dispersed troops. Suspicions assuaged, Philips was offered the governorship, which he accepted. News of William of Orange's progress and the absence of the better Irish regiments in England encouraged the Derrymen; judging by the quality of Antrim's battalion, Tyrconnell's replacement units were weak, badly trained and scarcely disciplined. Captains John Forward and William Stewart brought between 200 and 300 horsemen into Derry on 10 December, whilst John Cowan of Saint Johnstown produced a company of foot. The supply of potential soldiers was greatly augmented by a stream of refugees and Governor Philips organized the able-bodied into six infantry companies under Captains Samuel Norman, Alexander Lecky, Mathew Cachen, Warham Jemmet, John Tompkins and Thomas Moncrieff. Some of these citizen-soldiers possessed a modicum of martial expertise from militia service but most were completely untrained and undisciplined and there was an acute shortage of ammunition and modern, serviceable weapons. Philips dispatched David Cairns to England on 11 December to explain the situation to whatever government he discovered at Whitehall and request urgent assistance. Although Derry was in open revolt against King James and in the van of a generally deteriorating situation across Ireland – Protestants continued to take passage for England and Scotland; Protestant associations had appeared in Ulster, Connaught and Munster; whilst many in Leinster abandoned their homes and journeyed north towards Ulster – Philips asked Mountjoy to intercede with Tyrconnell.

When news from Derry reached Tyrconnell 'he burned another wig'. Mountjoy's battalion, which had already trudged 176 km and was within three days' march of Dublin, was ordered to turn round and recapture the town with musket and pike. Mountjoy and his lieutenant colonel, Robert Lundy, hurried back with six companies whilst friends in Dublin sent express letters warning Derry not to accept them. On reaching Omagh, Mountjoy asked Derry to send representatives to meet him at Raphoe. Captain Samuel Norman and the town clerk, John Muckeridge, were appointed. Following an initial meeting they reported that Mountjoy possessed full powers to negotiate the submission of the city and pardon all acts of rebellion. Mountjoy requested a second conference with two fully empowered commissioners near Ballindrait, County Donegal. On 20 December, Governor Philips, Captains Alexander Tompkins and Horace Kennedy, Lieutenants William Crookshanks and James Lennox duly attended. After listening to Mountjoy's proposals, the commissioners replied that they could only agree to receive a Protestant garrison, liberty to keep their arms and a free and general pardon under the Great Seal.

Mountjoy replied that this was beyond his powers and so, in obedience to Tyrconnell's orders, he rode to Derry on the morning of 21 December and demanded admittance before the Bishop's Gate inducing a fierce debate within the town but resources were so strained that negotiation was the only realistic option. Eleven commissioners, headed by Governor Philips, secured a promise from Mountjoy that a free and general pardon would be issued within 15 days until which time the companies of Lieutenant Colonel Robert Lundy and Captain William Stewart, containing only Protestant soldiers, would be quartered within the city and its liberties. Thereafter, until 1 March 1689, any additional companies from Mountjoy's battalions going into garrison would comprise 50 per cent Protestant personnel. Individual pardons were duly granted and Lundy was appointed governor, receiving the keys to the gates and magazine.

Observed by officials from Derry, Lundy halted at Strabane and reorganized the six companies so that his own and that of Captain Stewart became wholly Protestant. These proceeded into Derry whilst the remaining four were billeted in Strabane, Newtownstewart and Raphoe. Derry's citizens felt sufficiently reassured to allow George Philips to resign the governorship in favour of Lundy. In private, Mountjoy quietly advised the authorities to repair their arms and equipment, re-mount the cannon and prepare to defend themselves.

There were no municipal funds available to meet these unexpected charges so a general meeting in the Guildhall agreed to seek voluntary donations from the more substantial citizens. Over £100 was collected, a significant portion contributed by Sir John Skeffington, Second Viscount Massarene, and James Hamilton accordingly travelled to Scotland where he used some of the money to purchase 42 barrels of gunpowder. Aware that the Catholics might surprise the city, a regular correspondence network was established with neighbouring counties to exchange intelligence and organize mutual assistance. Although he knew by

10 December that the gates had been closed and Antrim defied, Tyrconnell was unable to respond because his new mass army was not yet ready allowing Derry a period of relative quiet.[12]

The Comber Letter was received in Enniskillen and by most of the County Fermanagh Protestant gentry on 7 December. Several were so agitated that they promptly sent their valuables, best furniture and personal papers into Enniskillen Castle for safe keeping. Determined not to allow their throats to be cut, throughout 8 and 9 December the Enniskillen Protestants kept guard 'with what sort of weapons they had'. During the night the guardian of Enniskillen friary, Anthony Murray, a 'cunning, subtle fellow', had noticed these sentries. In the morning he slipped away to hear a sermon, at the end of which he described to the congregation how he had seen many armed Enniskilleners patrolling the streets, led by William McCarmick, 'a great rebel', and therefore concluded that Enniskillen was in rebellion. Sensing the imminence of serious trouble, several friars left Enniskillen but the *agent provocateur*, Murray, remained.

McCarmick subsequently believed that Murray's exaggerated stories of a Protestant rising were instrumental in Tyrconnell's decision to send two companies from Sir Thomas Newcomen's infantry battalion to garrison Enniskillen. Almost certainly, this was not the case. A letter from William Ellis, another of Tyrconnell's secretaries, was delivered to Paul Dane, the provost of Enniskillen, on 11 December 1688 instructing him to prepare billets for two companies of foot, commanded by Captains Nugent and Shurloe [Shirlo]: a communication from Murray was unlikely to have reached Dublin and been acted upon within such a short interval. Indeed, had Ellis not sent letters to Derry and Enniskillen announcing the imminent arrival of troops, both would probably have accepted Irish Army garrisons; inadvertently Ellis provided both the centres of potential Protestant resistance with just enough time to organize hostile reactions. However, although a Protestant, Ellis was loyal to James and there is no suggestion of collusion in the resistance of Derry and Enniskillen.

On receipt of Ellis's letter the townspeople of Enniskillen gathered to discuss whether to admit the two companies. Views were evenly divided but the shortage of arms and ammunition and the attitude of a very well-respected local gentleman, Colonel James Corry, tilted the balance in favour of admittance. Dissatisfied, the firebrands – William Browning, Robert Clark, William McCarmick, James Euart and Allen Cathcart – convened privately in a traditional smoky back room where they resolved to stop the two companies and defend the town. At midnight on 11 December, express letters went to all the Protestant gentry who lived close to Enniskillen to acquaint them with their resolution and seek assistance and support. In particular, they requested up-to-date information on the progress of the two companies and what road they were following.[13]

At midnight on 12 December, Daniel Eccles relayed urgent intelligence to McCarmick that two troops of Irish dragoons had quartered in Armagh on 8 December. They had been offered free fire, candles and salt but told that they would have to pay for anything else. When the Protestant population went to church on 9 December, two guards armed with flintlock muskets were posted on the steeple with orders to fire and ring the bells if the dragoons offered any violence. More important, Eccles wrote that two foot companies under Captain Nugent were marching towards Enniskillen. That night, Nugent and his officers would be lodging at Clones, County Monaghan, whilst their men quartered at Drum, from which Eccles deduced that they would approach Enniskillen via Newtownbutler, Lisnaskea and the north shore of Upper Lough Erne. McCarmick waited on the provost and other prominent townspeople and urged them to continue repairing the damaged drawbridge. On 13 December he rode to Cornet Gustavus Hamilton, who lived 8 km west of Enniskillen, to sound his opinions and those of his neighbours. Several, including Gustavus Hamilton, accompanied McCarmick back to Enniskillen. *En route* McCarmick received a letter from Dane saying that, during his absence, Corry had come to town. He had immediately ordered the carpenters to cease work on the drawbridge and instructed the provost to assemble the townspeople with a view to admitting the soldiers and providing them with billets.

McCarmick and his supporters returned to confront Corry. A heated debate in the open street found a majority, including many from the east of Enniskillen towards Upper Lough Erne, in favour of admitting the soldiers arguing that the Irish troops were well armed and the Dublin government possessed all the magazines, weapons and garrisons throughout the kingdom, except those in Derry. More particularly, there were no trained soldiers in Enniskillen and any hastily raised militia would break and run when confronted by trained soldiers. Several from Lower Lough Erne and west of the town were more militant but, despite being a minority, their opinion eventually prevailed and work restarted on the drawbridge. Religion was also a factor in the division of opinion. Corry and Sir Gerard Irvine were Royalists and members of the Episcopalian Church of Ireland whereas McCarmick and the wilder young men were Presbyterian. Accepting defeat gracefully, Corry 'gave some quiet assistance'. The Reverend Robert Kelso, a Presbyterian minister and one of McCarmick's more committed associates, then exercised his influence to persuade men to come into Enniskillen and support the resistance, promising free lodging and stabling. On 14 December the Catholics were expelled from the town and Friar Murray imprisoned in the castle from which he eventually escaped with the aid of a rope before making off in a boat.[14]

Captain Nugent travelled in a very leisurely manner allowing McCarmick and the more virulent time to prepare themselves. He was still 29 km away at Clones on 14 December, not moving until 15 December when he marched 16 km to camp at Maguiresbridge. James Baird and James Johnston were sent from Enniskillen to reconnoitre Nugent's approach. Returning on Sunday 16 December, they reported that Nugent was at Lisbellaw, 8 km distant. Most of Enniskillen was in church but the male members of the congregation left immediately to collect their weapons and assemble. They numbered about 200 infantry 'not near half armed', commanded by Captain Malcolm Cathcart, and around 150 horsemen 'such as they were' under Captain William Browning and Lieutenant Christopher Carleton. Gustavus Hamilton stood in support with an additional 100 mounted 'soldiers'. It had been agreed that a small party should approach Nugent and attempt to persuade him to turn back but it appears that the entire body of undisciplined infantry and cavalry set off towards Lisbellaw. Their efforts were not required. Nugent's officers were being entertained to dinner by Corry in his home at Castle Coole, leaving their soldiers under the supervision of NCOs. On the road Nugent's men encountered some of the expelled Catholics who described the martial preparations and determination of the Protestants in lurid terms and greatly exaggerated their numbers. Their officers absent, the soldiers lost heart and turned back towards Maguiresbridge. When the dining officers spotted Hamilton's ramshackle cavalry approaching, they left the table, dashed to their horses and galloped away. The Enniskilleners wanted to give chase in order to seize the cartloads of weapons and ammunition that had accompanied Nugent's column but Corry had given the Irish officers his word that they would not be harmed whilst in 'his country' and managed to dissuade the horsemen from pursuit; the infantry were furious at this lost opportunity. That night, Nugent's companies stood at Maguiresbridge before falling back to Newtownbutler on 16 December where William Browning, Corry and another gentleman infiltrated their billets to discover their precise numbers and intentions. Nugent retired to Cavan on 17 December to await instructions from Dublin. There had been neither violence nor bloodshed but armed defiance still constituted rebellion.

Sensible that the Irish were arming – Nugent's wagon-loads of munitions had been intended to equip local irregulars – the Enniskilleners organized the volunteers into companies, collected weapons and maintained a careful watch. A full town meeting on 18 December elected Gustavus Hamilton of Monea governor in the absence of Sir Michael Cole, the proprietor. Hamilton, a JP for County Fermanagh, was the son of Ludovic Hamilton, nephew of Hugh Hamilton, First Baron Glenawly, and grandson of Malcolm Hamilton, Archbishop of Cashel. Despite both his father and uncle having served as colonels in the Swedish Army during the Thirty Years' War, Gustavus boasted only very limited military experience having held a cornet's commission in his uncle's cavalry troop in the peacetime Irish Army. A victim of Tyrconnell's purge, he had never witnessed active service. Although he did not attend the meeting, Hamilton accepted the governorship and moved his family into Enniskillen Castle. He immediately gave orders to raise two foot companies, under Captains Allen and Malcolm Cathcart, and recruited a troop of horse and a company of infantry from his own estates. However, the decision to resist was not universally accepted amongst the Protestants. Irvine and Corry, whose attitude remained equivocal, seized William Browning whilst at the head of a party of horse and flung him into gaol for appearing in arms. Gustavus Hamilton and the pro-resistance faction immediately released Browning before sending Lieutenant Smith, a JP and 'an ancient gentleman', to explain to Corry and Irvine that the Enniskilleners did not wholly approve of Browning's arrest and that they might care to consider leaving town. Corry sailed for England in March but Irvine subsequently underwent a change of allegiance.

Enniskillen, the only settlement of military significance on Upper and Lower Lough Erne, commanded a key route between Ulster and Connaught, and had been held as a Protestant bastion throughout the Rebellion of 1641. It was a small, open village of no more than 80 houses which derived its strength from its location on an island in the Erne River between Upper and Lower Lough Erne and the fifteenth-century castle. Lacking any modern fortifications it was incapable of enduring a siege and could only be defended successfully by keeping an enemy at a distance, a strategy greatly assisted by the local topography. As long as Derry held out, the road from Omagh in the north was an unlikely avenue of attack whilst that from the west was secure provided that Ballyshannon, Belleek and, to a lesser extent, Sligo, remained in friendly hands. The only practical road into Enniskillen ran from Cavan north of Upper Lough Erne via Belturbet, Newtownbutler, Donagh, Lisnaskea and Maguiresbridge. However, the defence was complicated by the division of the road north-west of Lisnaskea, one branch running close to the lough and the other looping to the north before rejoining at Tamlaght within 5 km of Enniskillen.

On 15 December, the Reverend Kelso wrote to David Cairns in Derry.

> After an alarm of intended massacre, there are two foot companies sent to be quartered in this small place, and though we be deserted by our magistrates, yet we intend to repulse 'em. You are therefore entreated in this common cause to look on our condition and if we come to be made a leading card, sit not still and see us sink.[15]

Around 20 December, Gustavus Hamilton reinforced Kelso's letter by sending Captain Allen Cathcart and Lieutenant McCarmick to Derry to explain the situation and seek assistance. Only verbal assurances resulted but contact between the twin centres of Protestant resistance in Ulster was thus established. On 21 December, Cathcart and McCarmick delivered a letter from Governor Hamilton to Mountjoy at Newtownstewart. He reacted publicly by counselling caution, not wanting the hotter heads in Enniskillen to pre-empt war and bloodshed. Privately, Mountjoy wished that Enniskillen had accepted a royal garrison but, appreciating that events had now moved beyond possible compromise, promised to come to Enniskillen. Before he could do so, however, he was summoned to Dublin by Tyrconnell. When McCarmick and Cathcart returned empty-handed from both Derry and Mountjoy, the Enniskilleners realized that they would have to rely solely on their own resources. However, additional foci of Protestant resistance were developing which, to some extent, would temporarily relieve pressure on Derry and Enniskillen. A Protestant association was formed in Connaught, led by Robert King, Second Baron Kingston, which resolved to secure the town of Sligo as a refuge in the event of adverse Roman Catholic activity emanating from Counties Roscommon and Mayo towards Boyle and County Sligo. Ballyshannon became another Protestant base, blocking the coastal route from County Sligo into Donegal. Forming an association under the leadership of William O'Brien, Second Earl of Inchiquin, and Captain Henry Boyle, the father of Henry Boyle, First Earl of Shannon, the Protestant gentry of Munster resolved to seize Cork and Bandon, the places of greatest military and Protestant consequence in the south-west. Across much of Ireland, the Protestants were harried, their goods stolen and their abandoned houses plundered and burned. In the absence of legal redress from Roman Catholic magistrates they emigrated into Ulster with what little they could carry, making for Sligo, Ballyshannon, Derry and, principally, Enniskillen.[16]

2

Practical matters

Armies could not begin to campaign until there was enough new grass to feed the horses. Because of the severe winters experienced during the 1680s and 1690s, the Irish growing season did not start until June in the north and May elsewhere; by October the autumnal rains had arrived and so effective campaigning was normally restricted to June, July, August and September.[1] Small-scale operations – raids, patrols, reconnaissances, punitive expeditions – were possible during autumn, winter and spring but only by light forces for short periods. Although the warmth of the Gulf Stream and the prevailing westerly to south-westerly winds produced a mild, temperate climate, it was extremely damp. Rainfall was fairly evenly spread throughout the year, with a slight peak between August and the beginning of February. The wettest period was during December – an average rainfall of 90 mm – whereas April and June were the driest with an average of 50 mm. Averages, of course, are misleading. The west and south-west, where it rained on two days out of every three, was much wetter than the midlands and east, the south-east receiving the least precipitation. Persistent rain terminated the first siege of Limerick in 1690 and nearly caused the premature conclusion of the second in 1691. Contemporary diaries and journals are peppered with references to the difficulties caused by heavy, persistent rain. The average July temperature was 18°C whilst the coldest month, January, averaged 8°C. Whilst freezing to death in Ireland was unusual, the omnipresent damp severely affected soldiers who spent most of the campaigning months living in leaky canvas tents, crude huts, covered ditches or the open air: disease killed at least 20 times more people than military action.

Ireland is 486 km long and 275 km across the broadest expanse of its midriff: tramping a daily average of 13 km a seventeenth-century army would have taken 37 marching days to travel from one end to the other and 21 to cross from east to west. It was a small theatre, although larger than the Spanish Netherlands and the Bishopric of Liège, the seat of the principal campaigns of the Nine Years' War. Having gouged numerous troughs and hollows that later formed lakes, at each pause in their retreat the glaciers of the last Ice Age laid down 'eskers', terminal moraines of sand, clay and gravel. Eskers generally run in bands from east to west and provide firm ground on either bank of the principal Shannon crossings at

Athlone, Shannonbridge and Banagher. The ice sheets also deposited swarms of 'drumlins', low mounds in a belt from the Ards Peninsula to Donegal Bay. Their crests are often occupied by villages which creep down their slopes towards the reedy, boggy pastures in the depressions between the hillocks. The drumlins divided the English in the Pale from the Gaels in Ulster. The engagement known as the 'Break of Dromore' was fought amid drumlins, which prevented Sir Arthur Rawdon from appreciating the full extent of the Jacobite deployment.

Irish rivers, constituting a total length of 26,600 km, are of two types: fast-flowing streams lead from the mountain ranges directly into the ocean and those draining the central lowlands which are slow-moving, wandering between low, boggy banks and frequently spilling on to flood plains. On meeting glacial depressions, they broaden into lakes: Lough Neagh on the River Bann and Loughs Allen, Ree and Derg on the Shannon. In the seventeenth century, from October to May, the Shannon was but the central channel in a huge flood plain. The middle Shannon, which falls only 2.5 m during its 43-km journey from Athlone to Meelick, could not accommodate the winter rainfall from 12 counties and regularly broke its banks. In winter, the Shannon and the midland bogs were almost impassable obstacles. The 'line of the Shannon', behind which the French advised James to withdraw after the Boyne, was actually a wide inundation. For most of the year, the river could only be approached along the eskers which, naturally, carried the major roads.

Marshy, ill-drained land covered much of Ireland. Blanket bogs occurred where average annual rainfall exceeded 1,200 mm and were thus usually found amidst the mountainous regions on the western seaboard. Raised bogs, up to 12 m deep, stretched across much of the central midlands where the average annual rainfall was between 800 and 900 mm. Many were of considerable extent. The Great Bog of Allen extended for 64 km from east to west, reaching to within 19 km of Dublin, numerous wooded islands rising from the mire. Astride Williamite lines of communication from Limerick to Dublin in 1690 and 1691, it became infested with raparees, highwaymen, bandits, tories, deserters and renegades. Irish main roads were generally better built and maintained than their English counterparts. Sometimes paved with stone – Andrew Hamilton mentioned that the road between Newtownbutler and Wattlebridge was 'for the most part … all paved' – they crossed bogs via causeways, usually wide enough for two horsemen to pass abreast, raised on oak piles and surfaced with logs and packed earth, and rivers and waterways by permanent bridges or well-established fords. However, even major routes were narrow and generally had to be reserved for the movement of artillery, wagons and baggage; infantry and cavalry usually marched through adjacent fields and along the verges. Because the weather and landscape obliged armies to move along the major roads, the line of operations was usually predictable. Along the limited number of available routes all the defiles and river crossings – 'passes' in contemporary parlance – were well-established and thus potentially defensible. Passes that allowed roads through hills or mountains were of the utmost operational importance, especially the Moyry Pass that carried the road from Newry to Dundalk through the Slieve Gullion thus linking Ulster with Leinster.

O'Callaghan estimated the Irish population at 1,200,000 whereas modern demographers suggest around 1,700,000 in 1672 rising to about 2,300,000 in 1712. J. G. Simms followed Sir William Petty's estimate: 850,000 in 1652 and 1,300,000 in 1687. In comparison, Gregory King calculated that, in 1688, England contained about 5,000,000 inhabitants.[2] Assessing the numbers belonging to the Protestant and Catholic groupings is even more difficult. Encouraged by the Plantation of Ulster after the Elizabethan War, perhaps as many as 30,000 Lowland Scots had migrated to Ireland by 1641 concentrated mainly in the south of County Antrim, the north of County Down and the Laggan region of north-west Ulster. A further 10,000 joined them between 1660 and 1688, reinforced by another 70,000 during the 1690s. There were probably about 70,000 Lowland Scots in Ulster at the time of the War of the Kings, nearly all Presbyterian.[3] Overall, there were about four Roman Catholics for every Protestant, only one-third of the latter adhering to the Episcopalian Church.

Population density was insufficient to produce the agricultural surplus necessary to feed parasitic soldiers. Consequently, the economic and commercial infrastructure required to support campaigning armies, whether friendly or hostile, was absent. These two factors informed the English strategy: if they were to be victorious, all supplies had to be imported. In the wars since the late sixteenth century, the English were initially repulsed because insufficient resources were brought to bear but, once this had been rectified, improvements followed. Persistence, the maintenance of large forces and the occupation of all major towns and ports were the keys to English victory. Naval supremacy was essential. Communication between England and Ireland had to be maintained because, after 1689, nearly all supplies and reinforcements came across the Irish Sea. Command of the sea and occupation of Irish ports allowed the English to employ coastal shipping for the movement of troops, supplies, ammunition and cannon. Because the first strategic dimension, space, was lacking, the Irish maximized the second, time, by employing a Fabian strategy. Their intention was to make war so costly that the English would eventually abandon attempts at reconquest. The customary method was to seek foreign assistance from either France or Spain; preserve their own forces; trust to attrition from wet weather, disease, desertion and hunger; and hope that the English would suffer a major defeat in another theatre.

An army enjoying regular provisions and pay was more likely to be disciplined, in good spirit and effective. On the European mainland, the Dutch Army, the

British Corps and the Imperial forces on the Rhine were victualled by civilian contractors. Army provisioning was big business, monopolized by Sephardic Jews. From their office on the Lange Voorhout in The Hague, Antonio Alvarez 'Moses' Machado and Jacob Pereira had first supplied bread to the Spanish and Dutch armies during the French War of 1672–8. Their efficiency secured the contract to supply William of Orange's expedition to England in 1688 and their reappointment for the duration of the Nine Years' War was a formality. Machado and Pereira provided a complete service from the purchase of the cheapest grain; its storage, milling and baking into bread and biscuit; and transport of the finished product by road and water, using their own fleets of wagons and barges, directly to regiments in the field.[4] The British commissariat in 1689 was much less sophisticated. Because the political chaos caused by the Glorious Revolution rendered English naval command of the English Channel and the Western Approaches uncertain, the Irish Protestant irregulars at Derry and Enniskillen lived off plunder and their own reserves. Schomberg's corps went to Ireland without an effective commissariat, a fact that was obvious even before he left England. Whilst Solomon Richards's infantry battalion waited to be shipped from Liverpool and Chester, 'corrupt victuals' made 300 men ill and killed several.[5] Schomberg had to issue each regiment with 500 new muskets because their original weapons were either antique or shoddily made. John Shales, the commissary-general of the expeditionary force, was supposed to have inspected all armaments but accepted bribes for the receipt of inferior products and the new soldiers broke many weapons through incompetence and inexperience.[6]

Once in Ireland, the men subsisted initially from the plentiful standing corn but, as they advanced south through Newry to Dundalk, they entered a region devastated by the retreating Jacobite Army and had to rely upon direct supply from England. As the corps had neither wagons nor horses and the supply ships persisted in docking at Carrickfergus and Belfast instead of going forward to Carlingford Lough, Schomberg's supply situation grew critical. He complained to Portland on 13 September that absence of bread had halted his march for four days, a state of affairs for which no official accepted responsibility. Schomberg did all he could but the three commissaries sent by Richard Carter to help were inexperienced, 'like children'; they had even sailed to Ireland without ready money.[7]

John Shales became the obvious scapegoat, Schomberg ordering his arrest and the seizure of his papers and account books, but the warrant was executed in a very leisurely fashion. Shales wintered quietly in Belfast and not until May 1690 was he finally sent to England and confined to Chester Castle. Although an official inquiry into his conduct was initiated by the Treasury no action against him appears to have been taken and he was allowed to continue in his second office of Auditor of the Crown Lands.[8] He was indeed both corrupt and incapable but several other parties were equally culpable. The officers of the army in Ireland were 'ignorant, lazy and timorous' and there was much 'roguery' amongst the Board of Ordnance resulting in ill-cast cannon, badly made muskets, and improperly charged bombs. The Treasury was disorganized and failed to release sufficient funds; the army itself was divided in loyalty and did not give Schomberg its full backing; Parliament was ignorant of the needs of war and voted inadequate moneys; William was more interested in the campaigning in the Low Countries and failed to take the necessary measures to support his general whilst his developing dislike of Schomberg became an obstacle.

The real villain, however, was Shales's superior, William Harbord, paymaster of the forces in Ireland. His death from a malignant fever at Belgrade on 31 July 1692 *en route* to take up the seals as English ambassador to the Sublime Porte prevented a Parliamentary investigation into his public accounts which showed a deficit of £406,000. In Ireland, Harbord made money from false musters, defrauded the hospital, cheated the artillery and withheld pay from the troops. One reason for the considerable loss of life at the Dundalk camp was his refusal to fund additional apothecaries. Schomberg had become acquainted with him in the Netherlands in 1688 and, initially, had thought him a man of business but his eyes were soon opened. When told that Harbord had fallen from his horse and immediately been set upon by five or six Enniskillen troopers who started to strip and rob him ignoring his loud protests that he was an important man, Schomberg failed to hide his delight.[9]

Shales having been removed, on 24 April 1690 Bartholomew Vanhomrigh, a rich, influential and well-connected Dublin merchant, and the engineer and architect, William Robinson, were appointed joint commissaries-general of the provisions in Ireland. However, Schomberg had commented on 4 November 1689 that the only long-term solution was the appointment of civilian victualling contractors. Isaac Pereira, the son of Jacob, signed an initial six-month contract on 9 April 1690 to provide the Williamite Army with 36,000 1½ lb (*c.* 675 g) loaves of bread *per diem*, at a daily charge of 1¼d. If necessary, 1 lb (450 g) of hard biscuit could be substituted. The commander-in-chief was to ensure that the paymaster-general, still Harbord at this point, deducted 1¼d. from the daily pay of every soldier in receipt of the ration. He was enjoined to account with Pereira every month, usually through his agent in London, Mr Bridges. By January 1691, Pereira was employing 340 horses and 250 wagons. The contract did not always run smoothly – it was much more difficult to bake, transport and distribute bread in Ireland than in the Spanish Netherlands whilst the contract obliged Pereira to import all wheat and grain from England, rarely the cheapest source – but worked well enough for the remainder of the war. The contract was terminated on 10 January 1692. The Danes remarked on 24 August 1691 that the men never had to go more than two days without bread and plenty of beans and potatoes were always available as substitutes. Of course, no logistic arrangements could have prevented the soldiers from marauding, plundering, robbing and commandeering, especially when Roman Catholic Ireland was treated as a foreign, occupied country and devastation of the countryside, ostensibly to deny resources to an opponent, was regarded as a legitimate operational device.[10]

Civilian contractors and army commissariats only provided bread, or hard biscuit, for the men and winter feed for horses. Other dietary items were requisitioned, purchased on the march or bought through markets set up by local producers and traders when the army went into camp. Whilst at Ardee, observing Schomberg at Dundalk, the Jacobite Army established a daily market to which farmers and peasants brought their surplus produce. As a result, pillage and plunder were much reduced and the 'country people' became actively associated with the Jacobite cause. Military markets were of considerable economic importance to the local Roman Catholic farmers and small-holders because the departure of numerous Protestants from the towns had substantially reduced demand. Similar markets were created by Schomberg and Ginkel whenever their troops camped for any length of time.[11] Licensed traders, sutlers, were allowed to march behind the army and sell comestibles and alcohol to the soldiers. For this privilege they were subject to military discipline and could, on occasions, find themselves in some danger but the rewards from selling to a captive market were enticing. Senior officers tried to set maximum prices for sutlers' commodities but the vagaries of supply and demand undermined their best endeavours. When the soldiers' pay was in arrears, considerable tension could develop between sutlers and troops resulting in theft, refusal to pay, the running up of credit and violence. In the rear of the sutlers came an unholy gaggle of wives, children, prostitutes, chancers, card sharps, criminals, refugees and vagrants. These creatures of the military half-light hovered on the fringes of camps sheltering in ditches, out-houses and ruins, an unremarkable aspect of campaign life rarely mentioned in contemporary sources. On 23 May 1691, the Lords Justices of Ireland issued a proclamation forbidding any camp follower from brewing beer under hedges because it made the soldiers ill and, more importantly, evaded excise.[12] Much of the pillaging attributed to soldiers was actually carried out by these professional vultures. As he marched south from Belfast to Dundalk, Schomberg became so enraged with their stealing and ill-behaviour that he issued a general order forbidding anyone from following his army or plundering the countryside through which it passed: the provost marshal could treat all camp followers as robbers, except licensed sutlers and servants.[13] Before the Battle of the Boyne had been concluded, a market was established on the battlefield selling weapons, clothing, equipment and personal effects stripped from both Jacobite and Williamite wounded and dead. The Jacobites probably suffered more from this disease because, as they abandoned ever larger tracts of Ireland, increasing numbers of refugees clung to their field army. In 1691, after the Jacobites had been pushed back over the Shannon, the soldiers were greatly outnumbered by the camp followers. Licensed sutlers also served the Jacobites. During the winter of 1689–90 in Dublin a number of official 'sutling houses' were allowed to display a sign which read, 'Ale to be sold at two pence the quart, by the King's order, paying ready money.' Soldiers were instructed to respect these establishments, behave well and not accumulate debts.[14]

The Jacobites also employed civilian victualling contractors. A Frenchman, Monsieur Aufroy, assisted by Pierre Alexandre, the commissary and paymaster of the French Brigade in Ireland, undertook to provide 'ammunition bread' to the army between 6 June and 31 December 1689 but lost heavily and was still owed 11,000 *livres tournois* in October 1694; James agreed to pay off outstanding interest on the debt at 550 *livres tournois* per quarter until the capital had been repaid.[15] Thereafter there was no money for bread contractors. Rowland White was mentioned on 14 September 1689 as Superintendent General of the Victuals for the field army concentrating at Drogheda; by 13 June 1690, his title had been altered to Commissary-General of the Victuals but it was probably the same position. White also appears to have undertaken contracts for the delivery of hay. Like their opponents, the Jacobite Army also began the war with no supply organization. Orders were given late in January 1689 to build up magazines of oatmeal, meat, salt, butter and cheese at Carrickfergus, Charlemont, Athlone, Galway, Waterford, Cork, Limerick and Fort Charles at Kinsale but shortage of money hamstrung this initiative. A month later, on 24 February 1689, Tyrconnell opened a public subscription to help pay for corn and equipment.

As Richard Hamilton advanced towards Coleraine and Derry in the spring of 1689, he issued a general order for the country people to bring foodstuffs to his army in return for payment in ready money, at reasonable prices, and protections for their goods and persons.[16] Supply by these methods grew increasingly inadequate during 1689 and 1690 necessitating ever greater inducements to the country people to present their produce for sale at army markets: royal protections, guarantees against plundering, plus exemption from taxes, customs and excise. The Jacobite supply situation steadily deteriorated and assistance was required from France which was already heavily committed to land campaigns in the Low Countries, the Rhineland, northern Italy and Catalonia. The French Navy in 1688 deployed 150 ships compared with between 166 and 174 Royal Navy vessels, a disparity exacerbated by the need to deploy vessels in the North Sea, Mediterranean, Atlantic, English Channel and Irish Sea, whereas the Royal Navy could, until 1694, commit all its strength to home waters. During 1689 and 1690, in two major convoys, the French provided the Irish with 2,500 firearms, 19,000 swords, 100,000 lb (45.3 tonnes) of gunpowder and over 1,000,000 lb (453.6 tonnes) of miscellaneous supplies. Although a considerable help, it was not enough to enable the Irish to confront the English on anything approaching equal terms.[17] Tyrconnell sent a mournful letter to Queen Mary on the 22 October 1689 listing the shortages. He required 10,000 tents, or canvas for such, 18,000 shirts, 40,000 hats, enough cloth to uniform 30,000 infantry, 3,000 cavalry and 3,000 dragoons, 40 cannon that could be melted down to mint brass money and a quantity of steel to make muskets.[18]

During the winter of 1690–1, the Jacobite Army was reduced to extensive plunder. In the aftermath of the first siege of Limerick, Sarsfield's men robbed merchants' warehouses in Galway and Limerick and seized cargoes from foreign ships that were unfortunate enough to put into west coast ports; the ravaged merchants and ship-owners were compensated in worthless brass money and paper tickets.[19] A further problem, particularly after the Jacobites had been forced behind the Shannon, was a general shortage of military manpower caused by the shrinking recruitment pool: the chronic shortage of money made the hiring of mercenaries impossible. In some of the lands reconquered by the Williamites, insufficient local population remained to gather the harvest. The Lords Justices responded by granting protection to anyone who returned to his farm within 15 days but this had little impact and much of the harvest was left to rot. However, too much can be made of this. In an age when an average of one harvest in every seven failed, people were accustomed to food shortages and famine. Soldiers subsisted on the most meagre and nutritionally inadequate diets for considerable periods yet continued to fight effectively. For military administrations, the essential point in providing adequate supplies of basic foodstuffs was to lower the incidence of plundering and thus improve discipline but the extent to which either was achieved should not be exaggerated.[20]

A well-equipped late seventeenth-century army contained one horse for every two men. William's armies were generally well-enough provided with cavalry and dragoon mounts, both taken up locally and imported from stud farms and breeders in England, but there was a constant shortage of draught horses which caused some of Schomberg's supply difficulties in 1689 and delayed the arrival of the heavy siege cannon at Limerick in 1691. Although Protestant gentlemen and nobles around Dublin offered their coach horses the only answer was impressment, although every effort was made to avoid the seizure of horses employed in agriculture or listed for the militia. The Jacobite Army experienced a continuous and insoluble dearth of all types. During the summer of 1689 it was regular practice for soldiers in the Dublin garrison to stop travellers on the roads and seize their mounts regardless of passes and protections. Horses were requisitioned from civilians travelling to fairs, despite the death penalty for soldiers and dismissal for officers found guilty of this offence. By September, even plough and cart horses had become targets. When a French convoy arrived at Cork in March 1690, major difficulties were experienced in moving the cargoes because of the shortage of horses: 'chief gentlemen and ablest persons' in the counties abutting Cork were ordered to send their best steeds without delay. Sarsfield attempted to replenish the equine stock in the winter of 1690–1, mostly by theft from Williamite garrisons. The final device was to order all gentlemen volunteers from the counties still under Jacobite control, to parade mounted on King's Island, Limerick, on an appointed day 'pretending to confer marks of honour and distinction upon the forwardest'. The gullible volunteers were then instructed to dismount and hand over their horses to the army.[21]

Feeding thousands of horses was a major problem. In areas where an army intended to campaign, efforts were made during the winter and spring to prevent the grass and hay being devoured by local, agricultural horses. During 1690, the Jacobite Army was not permitted to graze its horses within enclosed meadows, allowing them to become 'magazines of hay' for later military use, and country people were encouraged to bring forage to the various garrisons in return for full payment. In those regions where cavalry and dragoon regiments took winter quarters there were constant disputes over the division of forage and pasture between the soldiers and local population. The Jacobite administration attempted to resolve this during the winter of 1689–90 by establishing set prices for the sale and purchase of forage and trying to ensure that its mounted soldiers were fully paid. On campaign, when the enemy was not close, horses could be turned out to graze but, obviously, this could not be done if the enemy was near at hand. Generally, the cavalry and dragoon horses were tethered in 'horse lines' in camp and fed with forage gathered locally by the troops. The 'grand forage', in which large sections of an army went out to the flanks and rear of a camp to mow the hay, was a major operation of war and occurred every three to four days. Contractors pressed and baled forage with 'engines' for horses in winter quarters but, on campaign, responsibility for sustaining the horses was passed to the army.[22]

Perversely, regimental surgeons were well equipped, by the standards of the time, to deal with battle casualties, which formed only a small fraction of their workload, but almost entirely unprepared to tackle sickness and disease. Typhus, typhoid, malaria, plague, smallpox, pneumonia, influenza, dysentery and food-poisoning were the more prominent soldier-killers. Schomberg's corps possessed a medical service inadequate for a campaign in a country well known for the high rates of medical attrition it inflicted upon English armies. On the strength of each regiment should have been a surgeon but not all the positions had been filled by the time of arrival in Ireland. It mattered little. No contemporary military medical organization could have coped with the scale of disease suffered at the Dundalk camp. The sick were left to die in their tents, bodies lay unburied and the small, tented hospital was soon full to overflowing. Towards the end of September, the sick were shifted to Carlingford with a view to shipping them to Belfast and

Carrickfergus. Quite how many died at Dundalk is unclear but the epidemic continued throughout the winter and not until the spring of 1690 was the army reasonably clear of infection, Schomberg reporting to William on 14 March that there were fewer than 300 men in the Belfast hospital.[23] The Jacobite Army also suffered considerably whilst encamped at Bridge of Fane and Ardee opposite Schomberg. James's medical service was bedevilled, in common with his entire military effort, by lack of funds. In August 1689, several 'good and pious persons' asked the king for a licence to make collections' for sick and wounded soldiers. Permission was duly granted, Luke Hore, a Dublin merchant, acting as collector, and James invited similar initiatives in other parts of the country.[24]

Various theories were offered to explain the epidemics. The Duke of Württemberg, commander of the Danish Corps, blamed 'the fresh, warm, unwholesome beer' for an outbreak in May 1690 that rendered 300 men *hors de combat*. In July, it was a combination of 'long marches and the bread, which is not sour but too sweet and our soldiers are quite unaccustomed to it'. Whatever the cause, contemporary medicine was largely helpless. Most of the Danish sick were transported to Dublin in empty returning bread and ammunition wagons and those surviving the journey were housed in Kilmainham Hospital, which also served as the principal accommodation for men wounded at the Boyne, and private houses adapted into temporary sanatoria.[25] Reform of the medical services was urgently required. Colonel Samuel Venner, the Governor of Kilmainham Hospital, proposed to the Lords Justices on 21 January 1691 the creation of a 'marching hospital' to accompany Ginkel's army into the field. It would consist of 25 four-bed tents, lined with old tents of which Kilmainham had an abundant supply. They were to be designed so that they could be joined together to form one long marquee housing 200 men in 100 beds. Twenty-five male servants would pitch and strike the tents, fetch water, clean, drive wagons and undertake basic nursing. They would also be trained as soldiers and equipped with flintlock muskets to defend the hospital, should the occasion arise. There would be ten washerwomen. A train of 12 carts would carry the tents, doubling as field ambulances, whilst eight, four-horse, heavy wagons would convey the beds, medicines and other equipment. The Lords Justices accepted Venner's suggestions and combined them with their own plan for the wider reorganization of the army's medical services. A hospital in Dublin would serve as a central medical depot, Venner's marching hospital would accompany the soldiers and a fixed hospital would be established in the most convenient town nearest to the army when it was in action. Each of these three hospitals would employ a resident physician. A master-surgeon would always be stationed at the fixed hospital with the surgeon-general accompanying the marching hospital. Eighteen surgeons' mates would be disposed in proportion to need. A master apothecary was to be attached to each hospital and six apothecaries' mates distributed according to requirements. A purveyor would be attached to each hospital; a clerk, cook and butcher to the marching hospital; whilst a central pool of 40 nurses or 'tenders' and 20 washers would be distributed as required. Venner's marching hospital duly went on campaign in 1691, usually set up so that the large tents formed a quadrangle. The inmates enjoyed the luxuries of 'quilts and conveniencies' and the attentions of the Physician-General, Dr Thomas Lawrence,[26] and Surgeon-General, Charles Thomson, surgeon-general to the Irish Foot Guards until 1688. Reverend Story noted on 30 June that the new arrangements boosted morale, the soldiers knowing that they would be properly looked after if they were wounded or fell sick.[27]

William's soldiers usually lived in tents on campaign. Central stores contained 4,000 in January 1691 and Captain Lovet of Chapelizod offered to provide more, enclosing his patterns and terms in a letter to the Lords Justices. The Jacobite Army was always short of portable lodgings and lived mostly in the open air or makeshift huts built from branches and turf.[28] How many men were there to take advantage of such luxurious accommodation? Having sent the core of the Irish Army to England, during December 1688 Tyrconnell issued commissions for raising 50,000 men in 60 regiments.[29] It was probably the Brobdingnagian size of this force that dissuaded William from launching an early assault upon Ireland but, had he been in receipt of accurate intelligence, he might have acted differently. Tyrconnell lacked everything with which to equip these recruits and the whole enterprise was far beyond Ireland's financial, human and economic resources. In addition, the remnant of the Irish standing army could not furnish a large enough cadre around which to mould and train the levies. Some of the new regiments contained 45 companies and, in return for their commissions, the officers were expected to pay the recruits from their own pockets for the first three months. Meagre financial reserves were quickly exhausted obliging an undisciplined, untrained, marauding soldiery to resort to either plunder or desertion, a gift to the Protestant propagandists. The Dublin Protestants joked that the new levies had a string tied round one wrist to help them distinguish their right hand from the left. Another merry jape insisted that the Jacobite soldiers loaded their muskets with the charge uppermost. A more reliable story told how a grenadier, whilst in Castle Street, tamped down his pipe with the small end of his powder flask and was horribly disfigured by the resulting explosion. During 1689 the army was reduced and rationalized. A French estimate of 16 June 1689 put the Jacobite Army at 40,000 new levies whilst a list from later that year gave a grand total of 34,253 men in 42 regiments of foot, eight regiments of dragoons, and eight of cavalry. The effective field army, as opposed to the total military establishment, was much lower: a second French account, dated 2 September, gave a total of 20,840 which had fallen to 17,701 on 27 September. Diarmuid and Harman Murtagh estimate that, at the end of 1689, the total

Jacobite Army contained 45 regiments of foot, eight of dragoons, seven of cavalry and a Life Guard. Thereafter, the paper establishment did not alter significantly for the remainder of the war although the strength of individual units steadily atrophied giving grand totals of 45,000 in April 1690; 28,400 in November 1690; and 30,500 in the spring of 1691.[30]

Three extra-mural elements boosted the Jacobite Army. On 13 March 1690, six French regiments, initially numbering 6,000 men, arrived at Cork. Except for covering the withdrawal from the Boyne, the Frenchmen's contribution was thoroughly disappointing and they were not missed when they departed for France in the aftermath of the first siege of Limerick.[31] The second addition was the corps of Hugh Balldearg O'Donnell. Descended from the chiefs of Tyrconnell in Ulster, O'Donnell had been brought up in Spain and achieved the rank of colonel in the Spanish Army. He claimed to be the real Earl of Tyrconnell and was thus resolutely opposed to the current incumbent, Richard Talbot, the defender of the Old English interest. Arriving at Kinsale a few days after the Boyne, he carried a personal recommendation from James which Tyrconnell could not ignore. He bore the nickname 'Balldearg' or 'red spot' following an ancient tradition that the true Earl of Tyrconnell bore such a mark on his body and his popularity was enhanced during the siege of Limerick by a suspiciously timed revival of a legend foretelling that an O'Donnell sporting a red spot would deliver Ireland from the English. O'Donnell himself simultaneously spread another fable forecasting that the English would be victorious until they reached a well on Singland Hill outside Limerick but after that they would be defeated and driven from the country. Vindicated by the successful defence of Limerick, this nonsense helped to raise both Jacobite morale and O'Donnell's prestige. Tyrconnell allowed him to raise a private army of 13 weak regiments of infantry and one of cavalry from amongst the Ulster and north Connaught Gaels, which was said to have numbered 10,000 but probably, even at its peak, never exceeded 5,000.

A report from either November or December 1690 said that, at the most, 2,000 of his men were equipped with firearms. Nevertheless, his army was a complication that Ginkel could not afford to ignore and made some contribution to the Jacobite cause helping to defend the line of the Shannon near Jamestown during the winter of 1690–1 and by complicating operations around Galway and Sligo in 1691. Aware of O'Donnell's growing popularity with the native Irish, Tyrconnell confiscated eight of his better regiments and incorporated them into the main Jacobite Army – Lord Merrion's cavalry regiment was redeployed into County Kerry – leaving O'Donnell with a rump but no maintenance, Tyrconnell refusing to donate a single brass farthing or an ear of corn to this ill-armed, poorly equipped and half-trained force. As a result, O'Donnell's men lived off the land through plunder and pillage. The rivalry between Tyrconnell and O'Donnell grew so intense that Jacobite loyalties were further divided. Tyrconnell also played cleverly on the rivalry between O'Donnell and Brigadier Gordon O'Neill, who was descended from another branch of the chiefs of Tyrconnell. O'Donnell's response was to change sides ending the war in the vicinity of Sligo having vaguely agreed to join his army with that of Ginkel.[32]

Irregulars constituted the Jacobites' final supplement. There was no clear distinction between the various pikemen, tories, bandits, highwaymen and raparees who were endemic even in peacetime Ireland. Raparees were members of the rural population armed with half-pikes, skeans, scythes and ancient muskets; the word 'raparee' means a half-pike. Some called them 'creaghts', after the little, moveable huts built from hurdles and turf that frequently comprised their field accommodation. According to Anthony Hamilton, priests were largely responsible for recruiting country people into the irregular bands; it was rumoured that an unarmed man was not allowed to attend mass. Deserters from the regular Irish Army and escaped prisoners of war frequently joined the raparees. Weapons intended for the army sometimes found their way into the raparee hands through the carelessness or connivance of officers. To some extent, raparee activity was an expression of popular Jacobitism but it also masked much naked lawlessness and criminality. By April 1691, Lord Longford had identified five varieties:

> the general Irish raparees; secondly, some of the Irish Army; thirdly, some of the English Army; fourthly, some of the militia; fifthly, some of the Englishmen that fled from the County of Limerick.

So diverse in origin and intention were the raparees that Longford found it impossible to come to an understanding with all of them about the protection of property.[33] In other words, by the middle of the war, 'raparee' was a collective noun for criminals, bandits, deserters and aggrieved persons intent on pillage. Raparees quickly seized upon the opportunities presented by civil war. Almost as soon as disorder broke out in the winter of 1688–9, long before any engagement between opposing armies, raparees were robbing and pillaging Protestants' houses and attacking travellers. Charles Leslie, the Protestant Jacobite from Glaslough,[34] argued that the raparees rather than the Irish Army were responsible for much of the material damage committed in Ulster between March and August 1689. The sometimes semi-disciplined raparees operated mainly across the Midlands and the south and south-west; they were largely absent from the Pale and had been removed from southern Ulster by the late autumn of 1689. Although they could not affect the course of the war between the main armies, they were a great nuisance attacking stragglers and couriers, intercepting mail bags, and raiding outposts and small garrisons. They were notably active in the months when the regular armies had drawn into winter quarters. Sometimes the raparees acted in concert with elements of the Irish Army, particularly in Counties Kerry, Cork and Waterford. They thrived in the mountains and, especially, the midland bogs, the eastern segments of the Bog of Allen housing the 'White Sergeant' and his gang which operated towards Kildare. 'Galloping' Daniel Hogan was based in County Tipperary and raparee activity was intense in Counties Cork and Kerry in the second half of 1690 and 1691. When in receipt of support from the local population, raparees could assemble, strike and melt away leaving few traces, after the manner of modern guerrillas.[35]

To some extent raparee attentions were focused upon Roman Catholic Irish who had taken Williamite protections but they were equally likely to attack both Protestants and their own, natural supporters. With rare exceptions, like Longford, the Protestants and Williamites did not bother to distinguish between varieties of raparee, or indeed between raparees, civilians and enemy soldiers. In the movie, *Full Metal Jacket*, as a United States Marine Corps helicopter skims across rural South Vietnam, its vaguely uniformed machine gunner fires indiscriminately at everybody in sight, despite the fact that they are all obviously civilian, drawling, 'if they run they're VC; if they stand still they're disciplined VC'. The attitude of William's English, Dutch, French and Danish Protestant soldiers towards the native Roman Catholic Irish was identical: anyone in arms, or not demonstrably opposing the irregulars, was regarded as a raparee to be hunted down and killed. Punitive expeditions against raparee concentrations occupied much of the Williamite Army during 1690, a duty largely assumed by the new Protestant militias during the following year. James II was partly to blame. When he arrived in Dublin in March 1689 he was unable to halt the considerable raparee activity in southern Ulster and so deliberately chose to incorporate it into his overall strategy. In a proclamation of 5 August, he encouraged the Catholic Irish to arm themselves and assist the royal army to expel the invader by attacking the property of rebels.[36]

The rival armies fought in much the same manner following the tactical doctrine enshrined in the 1686 edition of *The Abridgement of English Military Discipline*, which favoured French practices over Dutch.[37] This was a transitionary period when West European armies were switching from matchlock muskets and pikes to flintlocks and bayonets. The Grenadier (First) Foot Guards and the Coldstream (Second) Foot Guards had been entirely re-equipped with flintlock muskets in 1683, the Royal Fusiliers followed in 1685, and all the infantry battalions raised after 1689 were intended to carry the more modern firearm. However, severe shortages resulted in some being equipped with what was available rather than desirable – in 1693 there was still one matchlock for every two flintlocks among the English infantry. Denmark had re-armed its foot soldiers with flintlocks during the Scanian War, 1674–9. In addition to loyalty and competence, its modern, homogeneous armaments recommended the Danish Corps for leading roles in most minor and major operations in Ireland during 1690 and 1691. In the Jacobite Army, the matchlock was the dominant firearm throughout the war, flintlocks being comparatively rare. Even the French Brigade was armed mostly with matchlocks, Louvois's army being one of the slowest in Western Europe to change to modern weapons. Similarly, the pike was rapidly being replaced by the socket bayonet – the Danish Army was in the process of switching from pike to bayonet when Württemberg's corps was in Ireland – which allowed musketeers to protect themselves against mounted troops. In 1678, one-third of every English battalion was armed with pikes and two-thirds with muskets; by 1691, several battalions possessed entire companies armed with flintlock muskets and socket bayonets. At the end of the Nine Years' War in 1697, most British battalions had three bayonet-equipped musketeers for every pikeman. Each battalion possessed a grenadier company entirely equipped with flintlocks and small hand grenades, hollow shells of cast iron filled with gunpowder and ignited via a fuse and touch-hole. Grenades were used in siege operations and assaults on field fortifications but rarely in open battle. Grenadiers were élite infantrymen and both sides frequently grouped them into task forces to lead dangerous and difficult assignments.

Because dense, well-laid hedgerows could turn a ball fired from low-muzzle-velocity muskets they offered effective field fortifications to infantry and tactics reflected this fact. Leases stipulated that a tenant had to enclose his fields with a ditch, a metre wide and one-and-a-half metres deep, the spoil to form a bank topped with a thick hedge. Since it was almost impassable for cavalry in formation and channelled or canalized attacking foot soldiers, the resultant 'bocage' landscape was ideal for infantry ambushes and close-quarter fighting. However, enclosed landscapes were restricted to the more fertile and agriculturally developed regions, particularly near cities: the southern approaches to Limerick were substantially enclosed.[38]

Battlefield formations, which had evolved slowly since the days of Gustav II Adolf, were in transition between the 'thick battalions' of the later Thirty Years' War and the thinner, linear deployments of the early eighteenth century. Except for the very few wholly armed with flintlocks and bayonets, infantry battalions fought in three 'wings': two of 'shot' flanking the pikemen in the centre, the grenadier company occupying the position of honour on the battalion's extreme right.[39] In 'matchlock regiments' the musketeers formed six ranks, the pikemen five, files three paces apart to enable the men to handle their unwieldy weapons. The grenadiers stood in three ranks. Amongst battalions which had switched from matchlock to flintlock but retained an element of pike, the musketeers stood in four, occasionally three, ranks.

From flank to flank, a battalion occupied a minimum frontage of roughly 200 m and a depth of about 10 m. The basic concept was for the pikemen to protect the musketeers from cavalry attack whilst the main issue was decided by a fire fight between rival musketeers. Pikemen gave a cutting edge to a charge, although the clumsy pike was usually discarded in favour of the hanger, or short sword. In Ireland, pikes proved particularly useless. Many Williamite officers commented that they could be dispensed with altogether and called for their total replacement by flintlock musketeers equipped with socket bayonets. Both sides, when defending hedgerows and ditches or sending out detachments for specific operations, always employed flintlock musketeers, 'firelocks' as they were often known. When firing in both attack and defence, the musketeers fired volleys by rank, each standing in turn to give fire before kneeling to reload. The battalion had to be stationary – firing on the march was impossible – and so battles tended to be determined by static battalions firing at distances of between 40 and 60 m, the musket's maximum effective range. It was a prudent system because only one-sixth of a battalion fired simultaneously leaving the majority of its musketeers loaded and ready to fire. However, it was inefficient because the cheaply manufactured muskets were horribly inaccurate and there was no point in asking the men to take aim. Consequently, volley fire produced no appreciable weight of shot and inflicted commensurately light casualties. This feeble firepower was partially augmented by two three-pounder 'infantry guns' attached to each battalion in battle but these were rarely available in Ireland. Late seventeenth-century infantry was insufficiently motivated and disciplined to trade volleys at 50 m for any length of time, even though they would scarcely have been able to see their opponents through the dense, grey-white clouds of black powder smoke; one side normally broke after a few exchanges of fire.

Usually, a battalion advanced, brought the three rear ranks of musketeers forward to fill the intervals between the files in the front three to form three dense ranks, delivered a whole-battalion volley and then charged home with sword, bayonet, clubbed musket and pike: identical to the tactics employed by the Swedes in Germany between 1630 and 1634. Frequently, one side assumed the defensive either 'lining' hedges and ditches or, if there was time, erecting field fortifications, usually known collectively as 'breastworks'. Although soldiers were instructed to begin movements with the right foot, there was no provision for a cadenced step. Battalions approached a battlefield in column of companies, the frontage varying between six and ten files according to the width of the road. Once at its designated place a battalion deployed into line of battle, a process that could be protracted because each company marched with its three wings of shot and pike in separate blocks whilst the battalion formed up with all pikemen in the centre and the musketeers on either side.

In the British, French and Dutch armies, roughly one-third of the available troops were mounted, either as cavalry or dragoons. Away from the battlefield, the mounted troops escorted provision, artillery and ammunition convoys, formed raiding parties, and were heavily employed in reconnaissance and patrolling. In battle, provided that their intervention was timed correctly, cavalry could decide the outcome. Cavalrymen were armed with pistols and carbines for reconnaissance and patrol work but, in battle, they fought with the sabre. They formed in three ranks, roughly 6 m apart, but, in the charge, the second rank filled the intervals in the first and the horsemen went forward at the trot, not the gallop. The third rank served either to reinforce success or provide support in the event of a repulse. Dragoons, properly infantry who travelled on horseback but fought on foot, combined cavalry and infantry tactics. They wore long, heavy riding boots, which strictly limited their utility as marching infantry, and rode lighter, cheaper mounts than the regular cavalry. When employed as cavalry, they formed in three ranks and trotted home with the sword. In infantry mode, the horses were tended by every tenth man, the 'linkman', and stood in three ranks to fight with flintlock musket and socket bayonet, in a manner similar to grenadiers. Only *in extremis* were dragoons employed as substitutes for regular, line infantry; with their heavy armament of musket, bayonet, sword and pistols, dragoons were much more useful as multi-purpose mounted troops finding their forté in the 'little war' of patrols, ambuscades and posts.

Apart from the very light infantry guns, artillery was unimportant on the battlefield. Medium field guns were employed at the Boyne and Aughrim – six-, eight- and 12-pounders – but they were extremely heavy and cumbersome, could only be moved by teams of horses and were effectively immobile once they had been initially positioned. Their rate of fire was very low. Artillery's principal rôle was at sieges where the bombarding cannon – 18- and 24-pounders – and mortars dismounted the defenders' guns, wrecked buildings to induce civilians to pressurize the garrison into surrender and breached the outworks and ramparts.

Armies usually adopted a standard battle deployment. The infantry occupied the centre, the battalions normally arrayed in two lines with about 60 m separating their flanks, sufficient space for friendly troops to withdraw 'through the intervals'. The second line stood about 300 m to the rear, echeloned so that its units covered the gaps between the battalions in the front line. Should sufficient troops be available, a third, reserve line might be added. Mounted troops, usually a mixture of dragoons and heavy cavalry, were positioned on the flanks in two lines corresponding to the infantry deployment. Cavalry did not fight in regiments – these were administrative organizations too large to be controlled in battle – but in handier and more flexible squadrons commanded by a captain. The first task of the cavalry in battle was to protect the flanks of the infantry lines from the opposing cavalry and, should the enemy became 'disordered', to charge and exploit the confusion. Some generals, particularly those schooled in French methods, placed companies of musketeers between cavalry squadrons to support them in case of a reverse and fire on opposing cavalry to 'disorder' them, thus creating a situation that their own cavalry might exploit through a well-timed charge.

Many of the general officers in Ireland were experienced in European warfare and adapted conventional methods to the requirements of the Irish countryside and the nature of their opponents. Because the Williamites were usually better disciplined and trained than the Jacobites, in the major battles at the Boyne and Aughrim they employed approximations of the tactics outlined in the *Abridgement*. Some sieges, especially the two sieges of Limerick and Galway, were recognizably European although orthodoxy was compromised by topography and weather. The operations at Derry and Sligo, however, resembled blockades rather than sieges 'in form'. The currency of seventeenth-century warfare, though, was not great battles and sieges but the occupation, domination and exploitation of territory. Success in battle and siege might remove the enemy from an area – Newtownbutler and Derry cleared Ulster; the Boyne freed Leinster and parts of Munster; Aughrim and Galway secured central Connaught – but the newly acquired territory had to be held, occupied and defended by garrisons. Often very small and based in old castles or small open towns and villages reinforced by a few trenches, breastworks and fortified houses, garrisons patrolled their hinterland, seized provisions for their own maintenance and ensured that the local population remained loyal to the occupiers and did not aid and abet the raparees. Raids and counter-raids between garrisons comprised the most numerous operations of war, exacerbated by endemic cattle stealing. Infantry battalions and cavalry regiments rarely operated as unified wholes: for most of the war, individual troops and companies were the largest combat units and, very often, soldiers fought in even smaller detachments or 'selections'. The *Abridgement* was silent on the conduct of the small war. Parties of a few tens of infantrymen seconded by, perhaps, 20 or 30 cavalry or dragoons, clearly did not fight in formal lines; their tactics resembled those of skirmishers, tirailleurs and light infantry. Flintlock musketeers fired from cover – thickets, bushes, hedges, houses and walls – using individual initiative. They advanced and, ultimately, charged, in groups and rushes. Parties of supporting cavalry probably did charge in short lines before separating into the mêlée and pursuit. Possibly, the troops of both sides received special training in irregular and light tactics. Did officers discuss and pass on tips and useful devices? Did the Williamite regulars learn and imbibe the methods used by the Ulster Protestants? Historians usually know least about the routine and everyday.

3

Towards war, 1689

AT Uxbridge in mid-December, the royal army, including the four regiments from Ireland, was disbanded by James's commander-in-chief, Louis de Duras, First Earl of Feversham; many of the demobilized Irish soldiers began to make for the west coast ports to find passage to Ireland. The movement of so many hated Irish gave rise to the 'Irish Alarms' and, consequently, on 14 December the Assembly of Lords at the Guildhall ordered the demobilized Irish soldiers to report back to their original regiments where they would receive pay but remain unarmed; a surprisingly large number complied. When the four Irish regiments had thus partially reassembled, Protestant officers purged all Roman Catholics, a process that reduced Lord Forbes's infantry battalion to 130 men. The re-dismissed Roman Catholics were then herded into quarters in Sussex before being marched to Portsmouth where all remaining Protestants were extracted from the four regiments and transferred into the Irish Foot Guards, which thus became a wholly Protestant unit; the displaced Roman Catholics were shifted into the remaining three regiments. Numbering about 1,500 men these units were then shipped to the Isle of Wight which served as an internment camp. Although guarded by ten foot companies and a few small Royal Navy patrol vessels, some 300 escaped. The remaining 1,200 were sold to the Holy Roman Emperor for service in Hungary. Packed aboard transports, on 24 April they sailed for Hamburg where many deserted to join the French Army.[1]

Because the first acts of overt defiance had occurred before the Convention Parliament had formally offered the crown to William and Mary, Tyrconnell was in no doubt that the Ulster Protestants were in open rebellion against the legitimate government of James II. The position of the Protestants was more complicated because, although their property had indeed been attacked, they blamed the raparees rather than Tyrconnell's army. Ignorant of the confusion in Whitehall, a minority advocated doing nothing provocative until assistance arrived from England but the majority sought to induce an immediate confrontation believing that aid would rapidly follow. The reality was that the English Army, having been wrecked by the Glorious Revolution, was slowly being cleansed of Roman Catholics, reorganized and augmented. William's priority was to assemble 10,000 British troops for Georg von Waldeck's Grand Alliance Army in the Spanish Netherlands. This had been achieved by the end of May – Marlborough led them into the field in July – but only scraps remained for Ireland.[2] This was not a matter of great concern to William who was unenthusiastic about opening a major theatre of war in Ireland because the Royal Navy was deemed politically unreliable and could not be trusted with the twin tasks of transporting troops and protecting their communications whilst Parliament had yet to provide sufficient money to fund an additional strategic liability. William's initial response was to negotiate with Tyrconnell.

John Keating, one of the few remaining Protestant judges in Ireland, wrote to Sir John Temple, the Irish solicitor-general and the brother of Sir William, the diplomat who was well known to William, reporting that Tyrconnell was speaking openly about his readiness to disband the Irish Army and resign the government provided that the Roman Catholics might be allowed to return to the political, religious and constitutional position they had enjoyed in 1685. The contents of the letter were taken seriously and Major General Richard Hamilton, who had come to England with the Irish Corps and subsequently been placed under arrest, was released on parole to talk with Tyrconnell. On arrival in Dublin, around 8 January, Hamilton disobeyed his instructions and urged Tyrconnell to resist, citing the chaos in England. Tyrconnell, a pragmatic fellow, had only expressed fleeting interest in a negotiated settlement in order to secure an interlude in which to train and equip his augmented army. By the time of Hamilton's arrival, Tyrconnell had received assurances of assistance from France and his interest in negotiation had evaporated.

Whilst Tyrconnell prepared his army, the more militant Protestants decided to seize Carrickfergus although it was not explained how this was consistent with a desire to 'defend' themselves against assault from Catholic 'bandits'. Aggressive, impetuous, hot-headed and messianically anti-Catholic, Sir Arthur Rawdon Second Bt., nicknamed the 'Cock of the North', quickly emerged as the leader in Counties Down and Antrim. As a preliminary to a *coup de main* against Carrickfergus and an attack on Newry, Rawdon intended to disarm Sir Thomas Newcomen's battalion stationed in Lisburn in order to block the Dublin–Carrickfergus road and open Belfast Lough to receive assistance from England. At the appointed hour on 4 January 1689, Rawdon and Sir John MacGill led 500 foot and mounted volunteers from Moira towards Lisburn whilst four of Newcomen's Protestant officers – Captain Joseph Leighton, Captain George Bermingham, Lieutenant Barnes and Lieutenant John Tubman – apprehended the Catholic soldiers and placed them under guard, assisted by the arrival of Captain O'Bray with a small party of volunteer cavalry. The plan then unravelled. Rawdon and MacGill were met on the Lisburn–Belfast road by James Hamilton who informed them that the unenthusiastic Protestant gentlemen of Belfast had received insufficient notice of the enterprise, Hamilton not having delivered details until 21:00 on the previous evening. Rawdon and MacGill abandoned the attack and sent their men home whilst James Hamilton went to Lisburn to seek Sir Thomas Newcomen's aid in the common defence of the Protestants but his unhelpful response was to barricade the streets and dispatch a warning to Carrickfergus. The Carrickfergus garrison contacted the Earl of Antrim's regiment in Coleraine, which duly marched south to reinforce Carrickfergus along with a detachment from Colonel Cormack O'Neill's regiment. Shortly afterwards, sensing that a Protestant rising in Counties Down and Antrim was imminent and anticipating that his exposed and vulnerable command would be cut off, Newcomen took the opportunity presented by a great meeting of the Ulster gentry at Mount Alexander on 7 January to slip out of Lisburn by night and make for Newry, leaving behind his disloyal officers and 110 Protestant soldiers. He was only just in time and his soldiers were harassed and bullied on the march by the local Protestants.[3] It is not clear if shots were fired during these activities or any casualties suffered but the Protestants had acted in a concerted and aggressive manner advancing the possibility of war.

Even the meanest intelligence could have predicted Tyrconnell's reaction and, on 7 January, some of the leading Protestant gentry and aristocracy of Ulster established defence associations. Counties Down and Antrim banded together and their first thought was to offer the position of commander-in-chief to Lord Mountjoy but, following his removal from Ireland by Tyrconnell, their second choice fell upon Lord Mountalexander. Unfortunately, Mountalexander proved an ineffective leader who was unable to control his subordinates so he was later replaced by Clotworthy Skeffington, the son Viscount Massarene. Counties Armagh and Monaghan elected William, Third Baron Blaney, whilst Counties Derry, Donegal and Tyrone chose Lieutenant Colonel Robert Lundy, the Governor of Derry, and Major Gustavus Hamilton[4] as his deputy. Each association was directed by an executive committee and central leadership was provided by a General Council of the Union, known as the Council of Five or the 'Junto', comprising Rawdon; Sir Robert Colvill of County Antrim; James Hamilton of Newcastle, County Down; James Hamilton of Tullymore, County Down; and John Hawkins from County Down, who acted as secretary. Headquarters were in Sir Arthur Rawdon's house at Moira but the Council of Five met more often at Hillsborough, where the Dublin–Carrickfergus road was guarded by a fort.[5] The association committees appointed their own field officers and encouraged clergymen to exhort their congregations to recruit volunteers. In the absence of public funds, the officers raised and armed troops from their own pockets but, later, taxation payable to Dublin was intercepted and diverted.

Captain Baldwin Leighton sailed from Belfast on 10 January to apprise William of developments. On the same day the Council of Five ordered the levying of troops in Counties Antrim and Down: two cavalry regiments (Colonels Lord Mountalexander and Lord Blayney); two of dragoons (Rawdon and Skeffington);

and ten infantry battalions (Sir William Franklin, Baldwin Leighton, Arthur Upton, William Lesley, William Montgomery, Francis Hamilton, Sir John MacGill, Sir Robert Colvill, James Hamilton of Tullymore and James Hamilton of Newcastle). In County Antrim, 300 unregimented infantry were recruited by Colonel Edmondston whilst Captain Francis Annesley levied additional horse and foot from County Down. Leighton returned on 10 February conveying William's approval of the Ulstermen's actions, commissions for the new officers but neither money nor arms. According to the contemporary understanding of the constitutional position in England, these formal commissions from the Prince of Orange created a new, Protestant, Irish army thereby translating rebellion into an undeclared state of war. The Jacobites regarded these commissions as invalid because, in their eyes, James was still king even though William had been entrusted with the exercise of the civil and military government by the Lords at the Guildhall on 29 December 1688.[6]

Unrest also developed in south-west Ulster. During a quarter sessions in Cavan, where the bench included a number of Irish Catholic justices, Captain Robert Sanderson rode into town at the head of 80 horsemen. He burst into the court and demanded to know by what authority they were in session. They replied, 'that of King James', whereupon Sanderson declared that this was no longer valid and ordered them to go home. Some of the bolder justices started to argue whereupon Sanderson swept them off the bench with his cane and the sessions broke up. News soon reached Tyrconnell who threatened to send some cavalry into County Cavan to restore order: the local Protestants responded by organizing for self-defence.[7] Incidents multiplied during mid-January as many Protestants fled with their families and belongings to England and the Isle of Man. Despite the opinion of a Dublin diarist that nearly all Protestants had already left the Irish Army, on 18 January 'over 40' Protestant soldiers 'with an officer or two' deserted from Mountjoy's regiment in Dublin, complete with their weapons, drums and colours, and set out for the north. They had reached Navan in County Meath before being overtaken by two troops of cavalry, one riding into position ahead of the deserters whilst the other took station in the rear. Surrounded, they were captured, escorted back to Dublin and clapped in irons.[8]

Bearing out A. J. P. Taylor's observation that most wars begin and end in confusion, both sides thrashed about in ignorance, blindness and apprehension. The Ulster Protestants feared the imminent arrival of a great Catholic army whilst Tyrconnell positioned mounted scouts 70 to 80 km north and north-west of Dublin to give warning of the expected approach of a Scots-Irish Protestant multitude intending to overwhelm him in Dublin before his new army was ready. Some commentators thought that if Protestant forces, however ramshackle, had marched on Dublin during December and January, Tyrconnell, who had insufficient loyal, trained troops to oppose them, would have retired to France.

However, with the exception of Sir Arthur Rawdon and his acolytes, most Protestants still regarded self-defence as the priority and were reluctant to make overtly hostile moves. As Ulysses S. Grant observed in 1861, during the early stages of a war both sides are equally scared of each other.[9]

Lord Mountjoy had been ordered from Ulster to wait on Tyrconnell in Dublin. Despite the entreaties of his associates to disobey, Mountjoy remained a loyal subject. There he talked with Tyrconnell about granting Derry and the Ulster Protestants favourable terms which, in Mountjoy's opinion, might have halted the escalation. Convinced that he had achieved a *modus vivendi*, Mountjoy sent letters into the north announcing that Tyrconnell had agreed to issue no more weapons from the stores, no further commissions to levy troops would be granted, all newly raised forces would remain in their quarters, no one would be arrested for attending a meeting or assembly, no private dwellings would be used as billets and no gentleman's house would be turned into a garrison, reassurances that partially quelled the hysteria. In the meantime, Tyrconnell took the opportunity to rid himself of Mountjoy, an experienced soldier who enjoyed considerable prestige amongst the Ulster Protestants and was a potential leader of rebellion. Along with Sir Stephen Rice, a senior judge, he was sent to France under the pretence of interesting James II in a negotiated settlement in Ireland. Unknown to Mountjoy, Rice carried secret instructions and on arrival in France Mountjoy was arrested and committed to the Bastille. Tyrconnell hastened to complete his army and awaited the arrival of three vessels from France carrying money, ammunition, weapons and some professional officers. Fearful of an invasion from England, he garrisoned Drogheda, Dundalk and, more importantly, Newry, guarding the Moyry Pass. Having secured Dublin and the Pale, Tyrconnell was in a position to move into Ulster but the unfortunate experience of Sir Gerrard Irwin induced caution. Sir Gerrard, lieutenant colonel of Lord Granard's projected cavalry regiment, entered County Fermanagh with several cartloads of weapons and equipment for his recruits. Daniel French and Henry Gwillyms marched from Belturbet to Cavan with 60 horsemen, seized the arms and accoutrements and took Irwin prisoner. From Belturbet, Irwin was sent to Enniskillen where he was detained in the castle. At much the same time, Cavan gaol was broken open and all Protestant inmates released.

Lieutenant Aspel commanded a troop of Irish dragoons in Armagh, one of several small units stranded in garrisons scattered about Ulster. Noticing how rapidly and efficiently the local Protestants were arming and organizing, Aspel prepared to depart as quickly and quietly as possible but his intentions were discovered and, on the appointed morning, Protestant townsmen surprised the officers in their billets and seized all the horses and weapons they could find. About ten of the dragoons who had been on guard during the night barricaded themselves into the court house. After some firing, during which a sergeant was shot in the arm, they were rushed and forced to surrender. The whole troop was then locked inside the church, their horses and weapons distributed amongst the Protestants. After a few days, they were released and allowed to march on foot for Dublin. *En route*, they partially reimbursed themselves by plundering the house of Captain William Blaney, stealing his horses and some household effects.[10] Wishing to concentrate his available strength, Tyrconnell recalled to Dublin the two companies of Mountjoy's regiment in Derry and the other four in Strabane. When this order reached Derry, the town authorities persuaded some of the officers to purge their commands of all remaining Roman Catholics and join the rebels thereby considerably augmenting the existing garrison of six companies of citizen volunteers. Dublin responded by forbidding all 'British' in the north from organizing themselves into troops and companies but the situation had deteriorated too far for this to have any effect. Letters of support from the leading figures in Counties Antrim and Down encouraged Derry to continue with defensive preparations. Some of Robert Lundy's decisions caused disquiet. Against the advice of the Committee for the City, he appointed Mr Norman lieutenant colonel and Mr Hill major of Mountjoy's Protestant companies. Lundy also refused to allow the six volunteer companies to be issued with ammunition and forbade them to stand guard. Following a protest, the latter order was rescinded but only to the extent of allowing one city officer on each watch.[11]

Catholic letters intercepted by the Enniskilleners talked of 'hellish designs against the poor Protestants'. One in particular, addressed from Sligo to John Delap in Ballyshannon on 27 December 1688, revealed that the Catholics in Counties Mayo and Roscommon were arming themselves with a view to falling upon Boyle.[12] On receipt of this information via Enniskillen, the Protestant gentry of County Sligo met on 4 January and elected as commander-in-chief of their association Robert King, Second Baron Kingston, who owned extensive estates in Counties Cork and Roscommon and had been a cavalry captain during the reign of James II. Captain Hon. Chidley Coot, an officer previously purged from the Irish Army by Tyrconnell, was appointed his deputy. They arranged the volunteers into troops and companies and deployed them to guard the borders of Counties Sligo and Leitrim and the route from Connaught into Ulster and County Donegal via Sligo and Ballyshannon. A garrison in Grange, on the coast road between Sligo and Bundoran, helped to maintain communications between Sligo and Derry. Newtown (now Parkes) Castle on Lough Gill and Manorhamilton were occupied to maintain links with Enniskillen. Fortified houses at Collooney guarded against incursions from the direction of Boyle and Ballymote whilst troops in Crockets Town watched the frontier towards County Mayo where the Irish were already active; the Bishop of Killala had been forced from his palace and a servant of Sir Arthur Gore, appropriately named Tremble, had been murdered by some of Captain Walter Bourke's soldiers.

Despite a reminder that the Protestant garrison of Sligo allowed free passage to all Catholics who wished to quit the Protestant enclave and journey towards Boyle or Athlone, Colonel MacDaniell, commanding at Boyle, refused to reciprocate by giving Protestants leave to travel towards Sligo. Kingston and Coot gathered a body of volunteer horsemen and infantry and marched towards Boyle with the intention of demanding free passage for Protestants. Even though MacDaniell's regulars outnumbered Kingston and Coot by five to one, they assumed defensive positions in Lord Kingston's house and walled garden in Boyle. After a stand-off MacDaniell agreed to grant free passage although he reneged after Kingston and Coot had withdrawn. Some Sligo cavalry, under Captain Arthur Cooper of Markree, occupied the castle at Ballymote after defeating Captain Terence MacDonagh's garrison company in the open field. Around the same time, between 500 and 600 Irish appeared before Dr Lesley's house in Ballintogher but Lesley produced about 30 horsemen and 40 infantry, at the sight of which the attackers dispersed. In the meantime, Kingston and Coot were fortifying their base at Sligo. A 'sod fort'[13] was thrown up and the 'stone fort' repaired, officers providing the money and common soldiers the labour. As if to confirm that Ireland was still in a state of high tension rather than open war, Sligo continued to hold an open market frequented by both Catholics and Protestants. A group of English was approaching the market with supplies of meal and cattle when they were set upon and their goods seized by some Irish who lodged in an old castle belonging to Captain Henry Crofton. As soon as news reached Lord Kingston, he ordered out Captains William Ormsby and Francis Gore with a mixed detachment of horse and foot. Although fired on 'briskly' as they approached, the two captains set fire to the gate and smoked out the garrison. Inside they found 17 muskets belonging to the Irish Army plus several half-pikes, daggers, swords and stores of meal and other provisions. Early the next morning, Kingston left Sligo with reinforcements and was met on the march by Cornet Charles Nicolson who reported that Ormsby and Gore had already been successful. Kingston retained both the stolen goods and the military stores, paying the previous owners compensation at the market rate. Several letters were sent to Lundy asking for gunpowder but there was no response until a supply ship reached Derry from Scotland. Lundy then consented to allow Sligo three barrels, and Ballyshannon one, at a cost of £5 per barrel. A bill of exchange for £20 was tendered but no powder was delivered.[14]

Truth and accuracy were the customary first casualties. A letter from Hillsborough stated that Kingston commanded 2,000 armed men in Sligo and a recent muster at Enniskillen had counted 4,000 soldiers. A further 1,200 had, apparently, gathered at Augher, County Tyrone. When the Protestant army assembled, continued the writer, it would number 20,000 'and can be as many more as we please'. Fantasy was further extended by the confident assertion that the assembled 20,000 would receive arms from the Prince of Orange.[15] In reality, the Ulster Association's forces were weak, untrained, undisciplined, unpaid and numbered in the hundreds rather than thousands. Although enthusiastic, especially about plundering Roman Catholic Irish, these *ad hoc* volunteers were incapable of resisting a professional army.

Enniskillen was the natural centre of defence and protection for Protestants from a radius of between 50 and 60 km, volunteers flocking into the tiny village. During January, some troops of horse and 12 companies of infantry were raised, the latter regimented under Governor Gustavus Hamilton as colonel. Of Welsh descent, Thomas Lloyd was a third-generation settler who came to Enniskillen with his family during January 1689, a refugee from his estate in County Roscommon. Lloyd had served as a cornet in Richard Hamilton's regiment of dragoons during the reigns of Charles II and James II and was acquainted with Gustavus Hamilton. Desperately short of men with any military experience, on 4 February 1689 Hamilton appointed him lieutenant colonel of the Enniskillen regiment of foot and he quickly proved his worth. Nicknamed 'Little Cromwell', he resembled Oliver in that, relatively late in life, he discovered war to be his true *métier*. His great admirer, William McCarmick, gushed:

> [that] under his command we never failed accomplishing what we designed but, without him, could not, or never did anything ... For Lloyd was a good sort of man: he was vigilant, careful, active, of a great soul, very observing, slipped no opportunity that offered to gain his end and, besides, a man of unwearied industry and good intelligence, and for his personal valour few went beyond him.[16]

In addition, Sir John Hume, Second Baronet, one of the richest landowners in County Fermanagh, recruited and equipped two foot companies and a troop of horse, a total of 300 men. Instead of joining these directly with the Enniskillen forces, he employed them to fortify and garrison his own house, Castle Hume, which lay 5 km from Enniskillen, across the River Erne on the road to Belleek. This outpost became invaluable in blocking any attack on Enniskillen from the south obliging potential attackers to take the longer route via the northern shore of Upper Lough Erne through Newtownbutler and Lisnaskea. It also extended Enniskillen's control over a considerable hinterland towards Belcoo and Manorhamilton. Hume was too old and infirm to take the field himself – he died in 1695 – and so sent for his son, who had served for three or four years in the English Army, to come to Ireland and assume command.

During the first half of 1689 both Tyrconnell's army and the Protestants had more men than arms. After receiving letters of support and reassurance from Mountalexander, Rawdon and Lord Massarene, the Enniskilleners spent January regimenting and equipping the volunteers: captured and commandeered firearms were repaired, pike staffs shaved, scythe blades beaten flat and, by the end of the month, nearly all soldiers possessed a weapon, however crude. More were required, however, if schemes to organize the rural Protestant population into a militia of last resort were to be realized. Enniskillen's strong natural advantages were improved by simple field fortifications and all the potential crossing points and fords on the River Erne between the Upper and Lower Loughs were covered by bulwarks, redoubts, entrenchments and breastworks. A number of officers conferred every day, under the chairmanship of the Reverend Kelso, to devise a series of regulations and standing orders to secure the safety of the town and ensure the best use of scarce resources: musters and lists were taken of the country people who could be called up in an emergency; as far as possible, all the boats on the Upper and Lower Loughs were collected and moored close to Enniskillen Castle; stocks of provisions were garnered in case of siege; a cavalry patrol scoured the surrounding countryside every night to uncover ambushes and attempts at surprise attacks; and Roman Catholics were allowed to enter the town, unarmed, only on market days. At the end of January, Hugh Hamilton and Allen Cathcart were sent via Scotland to England bearing an address to the Prince of Orange and full powers to negotiate for money, arms, ammunition and commissions. They also took letters from the Protestant Association in Down and Antrim.[17]

Tyrconnell issued a proclamation on 25 January ordering all 'fiery spirits' who had taken warlike measures to disperse, disarm and return home. Failure to obey would be treated as high treason. 'We are galloping in the highway to destruction,' prophesied Lord Longford on 28 January. None of the terms of Tyrconnell's earlier 'agreement' with Mountjoy was observed; commissions were signed to levy four more regiments and weapons continued to be issued from local armouries. Tyrconnell, however, remained hamstrung for want of money, ammunition, modern weapons 'and some expert and brisk officers from France'. Accurate reports that the Jean-Bernard-Louis Desjean, Baron de Pointis, had arrived at Cork from France on 23 January and left from Waterford six days later, suggested a reconnaissance to enable King Louis XIV to determine the appropriate level of assistance. Whilst impressed by the clergy-induced enthusiasm of the newly raised Irish soldiers – despite the absence of pay and uniforms, the men were following a rigorous training programme – Pointis reported that only about half the levies were armed with matchlock muskets and rotten pikes, the remainder making do with nail-tipped sticks. Tyrconnell's greatest need was money and he asked James to approach Louis for a gift of 500,000 crowns, which, when added to his own resources, might support the army for a year.[18]

Dungannon, commanding the routes to Derry and Coleraine via Omagh and Cookstown, was deemed an important post by the Council of Five. Also, it lay close to the fort at Charlemont on the River Blackwater, one of the strongest positions held by the Irish Army in Ulster. Dr George Walker, since 1674 the

Church of Ireland rector of Donaghmore, County Tyrone, 3 km north-west of Dungannon, was entrusted with finding a Protestant garrison. Educated in Glasgow and Dublin, he was descended from a Yorkshire family that had migrated to County Tyrone after the Restoration. Walker quickly raised a regiment and began to provision the town but there was a shortage of gunpowder and morale was low. Colonel Gordon O'Neill of the Irish Army sent his chaplain into Dungannon to find out what was going on. It was explained to him that there were so many armed Irish in the countryside that the Protestants felt obliged to defend themselves. Walker rode to Derry to ask Lundy for help. Satisfied that Dungannon was worthy of defence, he sent two files from Mountjoy's battalion followed by two troops of volunteer dragoons and infantry companies from Counties Tyrone, Derry and Donegal.[19]

At the beginning of February, Lundy held a series of consultations in Derry with leading figures from Counties Derry, Donegal, Tyrone and Cavan, resulting in orders for the Protestant volunteers in these counties to arrange themselves, first into formal troops and companies, and then into regiments, after the manner of Antrim and Down. In an emergency, everyone agreed to submit to Lundy's leadership 'who was in great reputation with us for conduct and experience in military matters' and the senior regular officer in Ulster, even though his commission was in the name of James II. The Protestant gentlemen of County Fermanagh convened and decided to raise two battalions of infantry and one regiment of cavalry but these failed to materialize returning the onus to Gustavus Hamilton and Thomas Lloyd in Enniskillen where, throughout February, work continued on improving the fortifications and establishing reliable communications with Sligo. Kingston continued to strengthen Sligo's defences and his main problem was shortage of ammunition. Lundy urged Kingston to abandon Sligo and fall back to reinforce Derry where he would find accommodation and provisions for both his men and horses. Initially, Kingston ignored these suggestions but when they became firm orders he had no option but obedience.[20] Despite the degree of mutual protection offered by the triangle Sligo–Ballyshannon–Enniskillen, Lundy presumably considered Sligo too far in advance of the main Protestant positions to be tenable in the event of a major attack. However, should Kingston retire on Derry he would leave open the Sligo–Ballyshannon route into Donegal and the Laggan. It may have been in Lundy's mind that, should a major Irish attack develop, Enniskillen and Sligo would be unable to keep in touch and co-ordinate their operations and be defeated in detail. In that case, it made sense to concentrate the West Ulster forces in the Laggan. The different strategic emphases adumbrated by Lundy and Kingston may simply have reflected the fact that the former anticipated a defensive campaign in response to an offensive by the Irish Army whilst Kingston was thinking aggressively.

On 11 February the Protestant Association of Down and Antrim attacked a unit of the Irish Army. Colonel Cormack O'Neill, 'a professed Protestant', whose regiment was scattered in billets between Carrickfergus and north-west Antrim, received intelligence that Sir Arthur Rawdon planned to seize him in his own house at Broughshane. O'Neill promptly retired into Carrickfergus rather ungallantly leaving his wife, a Roman Catholic, at home under the protection of the Reverend Maurice Dunkin, O'Neill's Protestant regimental chaplain and vicar of Glenavy. The units of O'Neill's regiment in Antrim were already being harassed by forces of the Protestant Association under Clotworthy Skeffington and, fearful of being cut off, marched for the safety of Carrickfergus. Protestant Association forces pursued and caught them crossing the River Bann at Toome ford; O'Neill's soldiers were routed and dispersed, several losing their lives. In the wake of this action, the Protestant Association built a small fort at Toome garrisoned by 60 men. Around or on the same date large numbers of Irish gathered near Stewartstown and Killeen, north-east of Dungannon. Captain Stewart led out 24 cavalry and infantry to watch them. In the ensuing scuffles, 13 or 14 Irish were killed and several taken prisoner. Soon after, a considerable party of Irish soldiers from the Charlemont garrison joined with some 'country people' near Benburb, south of Dungannon. A detachment of horse and foot from the new Dungannon garrison beat them off and seized a considerable number of cattle. Tyrconnell was furious interpreting these incidents as offensive acts of open rebellion rather than defensive measures against 'robbers'.

Hearing of the skirmish at Toome and fearing for her own safety, Mrs O'Neill fled to the residence of the Reverend White, a Presbyterian minister in Broughshane. Protestant Association troops under Mr Adare and Lieutenant John Michelburne[21] passed through Broughshane on 13 February *en route* to attack Carrickfergus and rifled Mrs O'Neill's house as a matter of routine. The Reverend Dunkin tried to intervene but, because he was still in King James's service, he was regarded as an enemy and promptly stripped and robbed. Dunkin's servant and Mr Arthur Dobbing, a gentleman visiting Mrs O'Neill, were similarly humiliated. Fortunately the Reverend White knew Adare and Michelburne and had enough credit with them to be allowed to take Mrs O'Neill in her coach to the protection of Shane Castle, the seat of her relative Rose O'Neill, the Marchioness of Antrim. Adare and his crew then completed the plundering of the O'Neills' home, but only a silver bowl appears to have been stolen.[22] Although a minor incident the hounding of Mrs O'Neill anticipated the character of the imminent conflict. In the first place, it was to be a vicious civil war with few, if any, distinctions drawn between soldier and civilian. Second, the Protestants were divided: in their attitudes towards the Roman Catholic Irish, adherents of the Church of Ireland were generally less extreme than the Presbyterians, the latter regarding the former as frequently equivocal in their loyalties and veering towards crypto-Jacobitism.

Third, the gratuitous destruction of civilian property and cattle raiding would figure prominently; cattle ownership – the dominant breed appears to have been the small, black cow, probably Dexters or Irish Moils – was a measure of wealth and all sides were constantly on the lookout to steal from personal, political and religious enemies. Some cattle raids were associated with the needs of military supply but most were for vengeance and personal gain.

Carrickfergus, a haven for Roman Catholic refugees and major military magazine, remained the principal target of the Down and Antrim Association. Thomas Phillips, the second engineer in the English Ordnance Office and Captain of the Royal Company of Miners, had surveyed Ireland's fortifications in 1685. Carrickfergus, he reported, no longer commanded Belfast Lough because the main channel had shifted 2.5 km towards the County Down shore. Large ships could not dock and even small vessels had to rest on mud for between six and eight hours on every tide. Although the town was not effectively fortified, Phillips thought the thirteenth-century castle worth repairing as a garrison and storehouse.[23] The Council of Five decided upon a surprise attack on the night of 21 February. A first step was to reduce the flow of supplies into Carrickfergus. On instruction from the Council, Colonel Edmondston seized a boat laden with provisions for the Earl of Antrim's family in Carrickfergus at Broad Island and diverted it across Belfast Lough to Bangor. Lord Antrim was incensed and threatened to burn both Bangor and Edmondston's house; Edmondston responded by garrisoning his residence with 100 men and putting a similar number into Bangor. Reflecting that this precipitate action might reveal its intentions, the Council decided to restore the boat and its cargo but Colonel Hamilton of Bangor, the local commander, chose not to obey possibly because he knew, through Sir William Franklin, that the decision to attack Carrickfergus had already been taken.

To reduce the tension, Lord Antrim and his officers met in Belfast with Association representatives. In reply to his questions about the reasons for the seizure of the boat, Antrim was informed that the numerous Roman Catholic refugees and 19 companies of regular soldiers in Carrickfergus constituted a threat. Antrim offered to divide the soldiers between Belfast and Carrickfergus but the Protestants would only agree if they were also disarmed. Refusing to accept this indignity Antrim proposed disbanding the newly levied troops, provided that they were allowed to go home in peace and quiet. This satisfied many Protestant gentlemen but not the aggressive Council of Five which interpreted Antrim's compromise as a sign of weakness justifying the earlier decision to attack Carrickfergus. Colonel Hamilton of Bangor, one of the many victims of Tyrconnell's purge of Protestant officers from the Irish Army, was especially vehement in his opposition to Antrim's proposal fearing that the Carrickfergus garrison might plunder his estate in retribution for his behaviour over Antrim's boat. Sir William Franklin was another incendiary. Suspecting that he was on Tyrconnell's black list, he had already determined to abandon Ireland but, having been given command of a regiment by the Association and his soldiers knowing of his plans to travel to England, he felt obliged to remain on duty. The attempt on Carrickfergus did not enjoy the support of the majority of the local Protestant gentry and aristocracy, Sir Robert Colvill and Mr Upton being particularly vociferous in their opposition. They were confident that it would fail, thereby publicly demonstrating the weakness of the Protestant forces and encouraging Tyrconnell to dispatch a major expedition against rebellious Ulster.

The Carrickfergus Protestants were made aware of the scheme and, on the night of 20–21 February, 1,000 infantry left Belfast commanded by Lieutenant Colonel William Bermingham and Major Henry Baker. Rain turned the road to mud and daylight was well established when, in accordance with the Council's instructions, Bermingham halted the column within 2 km of Carrickfergus where he was to wait until he heard from Mr Henry Davis, a resident of the town charged with inducing intoxication amongst the garrison officers, and four of the Council of Five – Mountalexander, Franklin, Rawdon and James Hamilton of Tullymore – had joined him with additional volunteers. Despite the dreadful weather Franklin and Hamilton with 3,000 infantry reached the rendezvous on schedule but made so much noise that the Carrickfergus sentries were alerted. According to one account, Henry Davis's bar bill was so large that there was scarcely one officer sober and Carrickfergus could have been taken with ease but no attack developed because Bermingham's men had no assault equipment: Rawdon had not wasted time on trifling matters like reconnaissance and preparation – an assault on a major fortress required cannon, mortars, scaling ladders, fascines and numerous other impedimenta – but relied on audacity and speed. Mountalexander and Rawdon then rode in with between 400 and 500 horsemen and expressed surprise that the town had not yet been taken; most of the infantrymen were standing around doing nothing, except for the vanguard which was firing at the walls. Uncertain of what to do, the Protestant leaders conferred providing time for the Carrickfergus officers to sleep off the worst effects of their night's entertainment and convene a council of war. Knowing that Carrickfergus was insufficiently equipped, manned and provisioned to withstand either storm or siege, the garrison officers decided to seek a parley; Lieutenant Colonel Mark Talbot of Antrim's regiment, a natural son of Tyrconnell, was sent to talk with the Protestants. He began by enquiring, politely, why Carrickfergus was under attack. He was told that the military stores in the town had traditionally been under the control of a Protestant governor but, because this was no longer the case, they had come to demand the stores in the name of the Prince of Orange and 'to prevent the insolencies and robberies of the soldiers'. Whilst Talbot was seeking clarifications, the Carrickfergus garrison contravened the temporary truce by manning the walls, lining some hedges beyond the town and plundering the suburbs as a prequel to putting them to the torch. Talbot was allowed to return before the Protestants marched forward in battalions only to discover that scythes and pikes were somewhat ineffective against cannon, muskets and stone ramparts. Demonstrating further incompetence by leaving their men standing in battalia within range of the garrison's cannon, the Protestant leaders retired into a dovecote in the middle of a field of barley. They decided to seek another parley and this bizarre episode concluded with an attacking force that was demonstrably incapable of capturing the town dictating terms of partial surrender to a strong garrison. Lord Antrim's proposals to the earlier meeting in Belfast formed the basis for the settlement. Cormack O'Neill's newly raised regiment, then in Carrickfergus, would disband and the men return to their homes under protection; Carrickfergus would be garrisoned by some of Antrim's soldiers but they were never to have more than a week's provisions in stock; both the Protestants and Catholics in Carrickfergus would be allowed to mount guard in equal numbers; full compensation would be paid for all plundered goods; and letters from the garrison to Dublin would be sent, unsealed, to the Council of Five in Hillsborough, which would censor them before posting them on. These terms were unenforceable although the fifth article was obeyed, at least for a short time, but with unfortunate results. A letter from the Earl of Antrim describing what had happened at Carrickfergus was censored by Mountalexander before being entrusted to Friar O'Haggerty for conveyance to Dublin. O'Haggerty took the opportunity to inform Tyrconnell that the Association forces were far less numerous than had been previously reported; were untrained; possessed few experienced officers; lacked supplies, provisions and the necessary equipment for conducting a campaign; and had very few effective, modern weapons. Having already dithered for three weeks, Tyrconnell listened intently before deciding to crush the rebellion by sending a strong army into the north composed of the best troops under his most experienced and trustworthy commander, Lieutenant General Richard Hamilton.[24]

Two letters from Dublin, dated 22 and 25 February, accurately reported Tyrconnell's intentions but the northern Protestants were arrogant and contemptuous. With airy waves of lace cuffs, the Council of Five dismissed the warnings describing Tyrconnell's actions as an opportunity rather than a threat. They wrote to Lundy asking him to leave Derry with whatever forces he could spare from Counties Derry, Tyrone and Donegal and assume command of the grandiosely titled Protestant Army of the North. Lundy promised to march with a train of artillery and 1,000 men, intending to be at Hillsborough a fortnight before the anticipated appearance of Hamilton's army. Accordingly, the Council gave instructions that Hillsborough be stocked as a magazine. Tyrconnell, they said, was a loud-mouthed, rude, foul-tempered braggart, an ignorant political general whilst his army was an undisciplined, untrained rabble that wanted weapons and equipment. To an extent these reactions were understandable. The Ulster Protestants, especially the Scots, were hard, tough, resourceful, aggressive, fierce men, accustomed to constant hostility as they carved out plantations at the expense of their Irish owners. Living in a hostile environment, carrying and frequently employing weapons, they were used to skirmishes and small actions against raparees, tories, bandits and robbers. As the French were to discover, the Irish seemed able to fight effectively in any cause but their own. Mercenaries from Ireland made significant contributions to the French, Austrian, Dutch, Swedish and Spanish armies during the seventeenth and eighteenth centuries but, for James II and Tyrconnell, the Irish fought with insufficient resolution and commitment. We shall encounter numerous incidents where very small detachments of Protestant Irish or Williamite troops utterly defeated substantially larger Irish parties, both regular and irregular. The Russo-German War, 1941–5, is called to mind where, until the very end of hostilities, small numbers of effectively trained, well-motivated German soldiers were able to defeat ridiculously large Russian forces, mainly because Soviet soldiers were thrown into battle with little or no training under the command of inept subaltern and field officers.[25] In modern military parlance, the Jacobite forces were militarily inefficient whereas the Protestant Irish and Williamites generally possessed a much higher level of combat effectiveness. Why?

Schomberg's, William's and Ginkel's campaigns were headed by a diamond-hard edge of ruthless, religiously motivated Scots-Irish, organized into the Enniskillen and Derry regiments of infantry and horse, who knew the country and frightened the enemy. Second, most of the new regiments and battalions forming Schomberg's expeditionary force contained substantial numbers of Irish Protestant officers and men. Three of the colonels were Irish peers: Cary Dillon, Fifth Earl of Roscommon; Henry Moore, Third Earl of Drogheda; and Adam Loftus, First Viscount Lisburn and, consequently, the majority of their regimental officers also came from similar backgrounds. Many of those cashiered by Tyrconnell between 1685 and 1688 were re-engaged. Edward Brabazon, Fourth Earl of Meath, for instance, took over the colonelcy of Lord Forbes's battalion of foot on 1 May 1689 and filled the vacant commissions with unemployed Irish Protestant officers. Sir Henry Ingoldsby, who had served with Cromwell in Ireland and commanded a troop in horse in the Irish Army under Charles II, was commissioned on 8 March 1689 to raise a battalion in Staffordshire. Again, he appointed officers from amongst his Irish connections. On 28 September 1689 Nicholas Sankey, formerly a captain in the Irish Foot Guards, was appointed colonel of the regiment of cavalry previously commanded by John, Third Baron Lovelace. Aside from the Anglo-Irish forces, much of the Williamite Army in 1690 and 1691 comprised Dutch, Danish and Brandenburg troops, all well armed, trained and effective. With time, even the English troops that Schomberg found so unsatisfactory in 1689 improved in quality and performance.[26] Supporting the Williamite regular army was the Protestant militia which devoted itself with wholehearted devotion to hunting Catholic raparees and irregulars. Third, the Williamite Army represented a government that was revolutionizing public finance and thus making the English state increasingly proficient in making war. Whilst Irish resources were scarce and finite, the Williamites possessed the economic resources to persist with a series of attritional campaigns until success was eventually achieved. Fourth, Jacobite soldiers were demoralized from the outset: defeated before Derry by a rag-bag of regular soldiers and civilians in arms; smashed at Newtownbutler by the dreaded Enniskilleners; deserted by their king after a half-hearted rearguard action on the Boyne and then forced back behind the Shannon into Connaught. Even the Association's abortive attack on Carrickfergus revealed an Irish Army anxious to avoid confrontation. From the outset, the Jacobite Army was concerned only with staving off ultimate defeat for as long as possible but even this strategy was dependent upon French aid. The Williamites would come again and again with their huge navy, their supply convoys, their endless streams of reinforcements and their wagon-loads of money until the Irish were either crushed or surrendered. Morale was temporarily lifted following small successes – Dundalk, Ballyneety and the first siege of Limerick – but overall there was a steady decline in morale and élan.

In Dublin, rumours were spread that James II was about to return to Ireland with 30,000 French troops; bonfires illuminated the streets and church bells clanged throughout the night. At 09:00 on 24 February, after the commotion had subsided, units of the Irish Army assembled inside and outside Dublin, and sentries were placed on all the gates. No one, except soldiers, was allowed to enter or leave the city and, away from the centre, only the military was permitted to move from street to street. When all was ready, on 25 February the soldiers began a systematic search for weapons and horses. The Lord Mayor toured the streets shouting that anyone not sending their arms to the collection points at Christ Church or St Werburgh's would feel the displeasure of the soldiers, a sufficient threat to persuade most Protestants to comply. Everyone, male and female, was searched for weapons, even small pocket pistols, as they went in and out of the city or walked about the streets. Trinity College was turned upside down, trunks and cupboards broken open and ransacked, and even almshouses were violated. Finally, at midday on 26 February, the search was called off. Next day (27 February) the Protestants discovered that Tyrconnell had received three letters from James asking him, in the nicest possible way, to be kind to his Protestant subjects. The rumours of a French landing at Youghal had clearly been a deliberate smokescreen to enable the disarming of the Dublin Protestants.

Soldiers were billeted in Protestants' houses, the armoury was restocked with several thousand additional weapons and the predominantly Protestant city was placed firmly under Tyrconnell's control.[27]

Across Ireland, law and order were disintegrating. In the last week of February, dragoons from the Irish garrison of Newry ambushed a Protestant party foraging from Loughbrickland killing its leader, Captain Daniel Poë, and eight of his men. Lord Blayney, at the head of a detachment of Association soldiers, surprised and disarmed a troop of Irish dragoons near Armagh. Following the bungled attempt on Carrickfergus, which was represented as a victory rather than a humiliation, Rawdon and his acolytes tried to clear Ulster of Irish Army troops and garrisons before the arrival of Richard Hamilton's field army. Operations against Newry and Charlemont were mooted but no plans materialized. Tyrconnell's army was ready to take the field even though it was exceptionally early in the campaigning season. To secure his principal base, on 1 March he issued a proclamation ordering the seizure of any remaining weapons and serviceable horses in Dublin. A second proclamation followed on 7 March explaining that every peaceful method to stop the trouble in the north had been essayed but the Protestant rebels had continued to kill, imprison and humiliate members of the Irish Army and had demonstrated scant regard for private property. Even though it was likely to result in the 'total ruin and destruction' of Ulster – no violence would be offered against women, children, aged or decrepit men, labourers, ploughmen and tillers of the soil – Tyrconnell had ordered an army under Lieutenant General Richard Hamilton to suppress the rebellion. Disaster could still be avoided and the rebels pardoned provided they laid down their weapons, surrendered their serviceable horses and submitted to either General Hamilton or Colonel MacDaniell in Boyle: only Lord Mountalexander, Lord Massarene, Lord Kingston, Clotworthy Skeffington, Sir Robert Colvill, Sir Arthur Rawdon, Sir John MacGill, John Hawkins, Robert Sanderson, James Hamilton and Sir Francis Hamilton were exempted. William responded by issuing a counter-proclamation requiring the Irish to lay down their weapons by 10 April. With nothing to lose, during mid-March Sir Francis Hamilton and Captain Robert Sanderson were very active in County Cavan.[28]

4

The Break of Dromore and the retreat to Coleraine

Captain Baldwin Leighton returned on 9 March from his second trip to England bearing a letter from William to Mountalexander intended for circulation amongst the local gentry and aristocracy. It explained that William approved the measures they were taking and gave assurances that relief was coming: some cannon and ammunition had already been shipped whilst 15,000 men were on notice to embark.[1] The day before, 8 March, Alexander Osborn had been granted an audience with Tyrconnell following which he was given a pass to travel to Ulster. Reaching Hillsborough on 9 March he told the Protestant Association that the lord deputy took no pleasure in the imminent prospect of bloodshed and devastation but the Protestants were in open rebellion. When Richard Hamilton's army advanced into Ulster the raparees in Counties Cavan, Monaghan, Tyrone and Derry would probably prove uncontrollable and massacres might result. However, Tyrconnell was willing to take Ulster back under royal protection provided that the rebels surrendered their weapons and serviceable horses to General Hamilton. Tyrconnell was even prepared to accept the surrender of the ten gentlemen omitted from the free pardon offered in the proclamation of 7 March, if they could demonstrate that they had initially taken up arms in self-defence. Unless these terms were promptly accepted, Hamilton's army would reach Newry around 11 March before progressing through Ulster to restore order. Inadvertently, Tyrconnell let slip to Osborn the route of Hamilton's advance – Newry–Belfast–Coleraine–Derry – solving the conundrum of whether he would travel east or west of Lough Neagh. Mountalexander, who was with his troops at Loughbrickland, wrote to the leading gentlemen of northern Ulster on 9 March, enclosing Osborn's report, and repeating his earlier request to Lundy to come south and assume command of the army: Lundy replied that he would leave for Dungannon within a couple of days. Along with a copy of Mountalexander's letter and Osborn's report, Lundy sent a warning to the Enniskilleners that they would probably come under pressure from subsidiary Irish forces in order to inhibit them from rendering assistance to either Newry or Derry.[2]

Hamilton's army left Dublin on 8 March. Hamilton himself commanded the infantry whilst the English Catholic, Dominic Sheldon, led the cavalry. A train of artillery, consisting of seven brass and two iron guns, followed on the next day (9 March). As soon as patrols reported Hamilton's arrival in Newry on 11 December to the headquarters in Loughbrickland, Rawdon asked the Council at Hillsborough for reinforcements but was told that none was available and advised to retire on Dromore. Scouts indicated that Hamilton would reach Loughbrickland on the morning of 12 March although he did not arrive until the evening, his progress slowed because the Protestants had burned the forage and destroyed the countryside before abandoning their homes to join Rawdon. Unwisely, Rawdon detailed many of the available infantry to escort these refugees to the coast via Belfast leaving the force at Dromore top-heavy with cavalry. Hamilton's march flanked the small post at Rathfriland, north-east of Newry, obliging the Protestant garrison and inhabitants to quit the village and retire on Dromore. Rawdon received further reinforcements when Captain Hugh MacGill brought in a troop of 80 dragoons, which he had raised in the Ards Peninsula. In a second message to the Council at Hillsborough, Rawdon asked for 100 'good' musketeers but the cupboard was bare.[3]

On 24 February the townspeople of Bandon, a walled town and long-established refuge for Munster Protestants, attacked Captain Daniel O'Neill's Irish garrison of two infantry companies and a troop of horse, a sergeant and two soldiers losing their lives. Tyrconnell in Dublin, however, had received advance warning and dispatched Major General Justin Macarty with six companies of infantry to investigate. Equipped with the garrison's weapons and horses, Bandon's inhabitants closed the gates as Macarty approached. At the same time, the Earl of Inchiquin was active in County Cork at the head of a considerable body of Protestant insurgents whilst, at Castlemartyr, west of Youghal, Henry Boyle had fortified his house and was determined to defend it with the help of 140 followers. Macarty's strategy was to separate and isolate these three risings and defeat them in detail. He preferred persuasion to force and attempted to reason with the leaders of Bandon who, in turn, attempted to win him over to their side. Not yet prepared to risk an open confrontation at Bandon, Macarty blockaded Boyle's house at Castlemartyr before moving his main force to occupy Cork in the name of the Irish government. When he heard of Boyle's plight, Sir Thomas Southwell and other Protestant gentry from County Limerick travelled south to attempt to relieve the blockade. *En route*, they heard that Castlemartyr had fallen and so turned north with the intention of reaching Lord Kingston's Protestant enclave at Sligo. They had reached Loughrea, County Galway, before being overtaken and captured on 1 March by a troop of Irish horse and a company of foot under Captain Thomas Bourke. Macarty then turned on Bandon. Taking his six companies, a body of cavalry and two or three cannon that he had found in Cork, he obliged the Protestants to open the gates and submit. They were fined £1,000 and forced to demolish the walls, which were never rebuilt. By pursuing a strategy of restraint, backed up by a minimum of violence, Macarty had defeated the Protestant rebellion in County Cork. After a small cell of Protestant resistance at Kilowen House in County Kerry had been overcome, Munster was cleansed of insurrection and ready to receive King James II.[4]

James, who had suffered a nervous breakdown when his army concentrated at Salisbury to face the Dutch invader in November 1688, was not anxious to sail to Ireland. His 'abdication' had been God's punishment for an iniquitous early life and failure to return England to the Roman Catholic faith. Providence, the notion that God directly influenced man's earthly activities according to the justness of either the cause or individual, had abandoned him. A broken man, James would have contentedly spent the rest of his days at the gloomy palace of St Germain-en-Laye immersed in devotion, prayer and self-castigation but his host, protector and paymaster, Louis XIV, was not prepared to waste a useful asset. Contrary to French expectations, the Glorious Revolution had failed to foment a civil war in England but a satisfactory substitute, which France could exploit, was about to occur in Ireland. By sending James to Dublin with just enough military and financial assistance to keep his supporters interested, Louis hoped to profit from the subsequent weakening of the armies of the Grand Alliance in Flanders and Germany. Should Ireland be reconquered, then it would serve as a base from which James could invade Scotland and England, thus putting William under further pressure. Because the two previous major conflicts in Ireland had lasted for nine years and 12 years respectively, even failure was likely to induce protracted civil strife. Should William make a major military effort to settle Ireland rapidly, then he would only be able to do so at the expense of operations in the Netherlands, Germany and northern Italy. If James was quickly defeated Louis would have forfeited little.

A reluctant James took coach from St Germain on 15 February, drove to Brest and embarked for Ireland. The French escorting squadron of 13 ships-of-the-line, six frigates and three fire-ships sailed on 7 March conveying some of James's English, Irish and Scottish supporters; a handful of French officers; miserly quantities of arms and ammunition; and James's two natural sons, James Fitzjames, Duke of Berwick and Henry Fitzjames, the 'Lord Grand Prior'. The English included the Duke of Powys, Lord Thomas Howard, and Thomas Cartwright, the titular Bishop of Chester. John Drummond, Earl of Melfort, secretary of state for Ireland, was the most prominent Scotsman. Amongst the Irish were Judge Sir Stephen Rice and Colonels Patrick Sarsfield and Roger MacElligott. Leading the French contingent were ambassador Jean-Antoine de Mesmes, Comte d'Avaux, one of Louis XIV's leading diplomats particularly well acquainted with Anglo-Dutch politics, and General Conrad von Rosen, who bore the brevet title of Maréchal d'Irlande. Also on board were some French general officers: Lieutenant General Claude-François de Vauvré, Comte de Girardin-Léry; Lieutenant General Jacques de Fontanges, Marquis de Maumont; Major General Jean Le Camus, Marquis de Pusignan; Major General Alexandre de Rainier de

Droué, Marquis de Boisseleau; and Pointis, the military engineer, artillerist and sailor. The squadron arrived at Kinsale on 12 March. James travelled to Cork to be met by a 'gallant troop' of nobility that conducted him in style to Dublin where he made a ceremonial entry on Palm Sunday, 24 March. A Protestant observer noted that James entered his capital 'with far less splendour than the Lord Deputy was used to ... his two base sons riding on each hand of him. He was very courteous to all as he passed by. It is said that he wept as he rode into the Castle. His apparel was red, though rusty'.[5]

Well-connected Irish Protestant refugees in London lobbied for prompt English military intervention. Richard Cox of Kinsale, a lawyer and future Lord Chancellor of Ireland, published *Aphorisms Relating to the Kingdom of Ireland* in January 1689[6] and pressed copies upon members of the Convention Parliament. Cox thought that a field army maintained at a constant strength of between 10,000 and 12,000 men was sufficient to retake Ireland. Because of the high rates of attrition, this target could only be achieved by dispatching 20,000 soldiers in the first instance followed by a regular supply of reinforcements. The campaigns – Cox advocated an invasion of Munster – could be self-financing, costs being met from the confiscation of the estates of James's Irish supporters.[7] Sir John Broderick sent a paper to the Committee for Ireland, which had been formed on 14 February, proposing the recruitment of a regiment from among the distressed Protestants in County Cork.[8] On 20 February King William adopted the substance of Cox's argument: 10,920 existing troops were earmarked for Ireland and recruiting orders were issued for raising 13,260 new soldiers in 17 new battalions of foot, a theoretical total of 24,180.[9] On 1 April, the War Office produced a distribution list of the British Army: 25,652 men were garrisoning England; 10,972 were serving in the Netherlands; and 22,290 were detailed for Ireland.[10] It was noted on 30 March that, eventually, the Irish expeditionary force would amount to 23,070 but the new regiments would not be ready before 1 May.[11] There was clearly an expectation that the Ulster and Munster Protestants would raise considerable local forces to complement the English regulars. Sir William Franklin arrived from Belfast on 25 March to assure the Committee for Ireland that the Protestant Association in Counties Antrim and Down had already listed between 13,000 and 14,000 men. This may have been technically correct but bore no relationship to the numbers deployed to fight Richard Hamilton's army.

In the interim, the 780-man infantry battalions of Colonels John Cunningham, recruited in June–July 1685, and Solomon Richards, raised in October 1688, were ordered to reinforce Derry. Cunningham, the brigade commander, received William's orders on 12 March, including a packet of sealed instructions for Lundy. As soon as shipping arrived at Liverpool and had been provisioned, he was to embark. Provided that Derry remained in Protestant hands and conditions were propitious, Cunningham was to put his brigade ashore and place it under Lundy's command. However, no risks were to be taken and if he judged the situation too uncertain he was to sail to Belfast Lough and attempt a landing at Carrickfergus. Should this prove impossible, Cunningham was to investigate Strangford Lough. If none of these destinations was safe, he was to return to Liverpool. Cunningham's ships carried some spare weapons plus £2,000 in cash to pay the soldiers and meet incidental charges. Frequent reports were to be sent to England noting in particular what Protestant forces had been raised locally so that reinforcements from England would not be sent unnecessarily. Above all, Cunningham was to be cautious: England was short of troops and he was not to throw away two precious battalions by landing at Derry unless it was secure.[12]

The Council of Five had chosen Lord Blayney to command the Association forces in Armagh, Monaghan and Glaslough, and Captain Francis Hamilton, a deserter from King James's Irish Army, to direct those in Counties Cavan and Fermanagh which lay beyond the orbit of Enniskillen.[13] Blayney, who led about 1,800 ill-organized and untrained troops, established headquarters in Armagh whence he could observe the garrison of 3,000 'very insolent' men at Charlemont. When the Catholic soldiers began to plunder Protestants' houses between Armagh and Charlemont, skirmishing broke out and a stream of refugees fled initially into Monaghan Castle. On 13 March, Blayney heard that his own house in Monaghan had been seized and the Protestants in Monaghan Castle had withdrawn further to Glaslough where they were surrounded. Sir Nicholas Acheson, Fourth Baronet (c.1655–1701), arrived on the same day to inform Blayney that Rawdon had withdrawn from Loughbrickland. Blayney held a council of war which resolved to relieve Glaslough but, if this could not be accomplished, the Armagh forces would move through Dungannon, cross the River Bann at Toome and join Rawdon in County Antrim.

No sooner had the refugees from Monaghan reached Glaslough Castle than they were surrounded by Colonel John McKenna with 600 of the Charlemont garrison. From Armagh, Blayney sent 'expresses' ordering 'the country' to march to relieve Glaslough but the local Irish soon learned of these movements and set ambushes along the approach roads. Captain Matthew Anketel, of Anketel Grove, County Monaghan, 'a person of undaunted courage', and Captain Richardson led forward seven files of infantry and a handful of dragoons on 13 March to flush out the ambushes and reopen the lanes, the Irish losing six dead before the remainder dispersed. Anketel proceeded into Glaslough which was further reinforced on the morning of 14 March by Captain Cole leading one troop of horse and two foot companies. Anketel and Cole initially decided to break out of Glaslough but when they received intelligence that a detachment of Irish foot was advancing they changed their minds and sought battle. Discovering that the Irish had occupied an old Viking earthwork within 1 km of the town, Anketel formed up all the serviceable cavalry plus 100 musketeers and advanced. The Irish fired a volley at too great a distance to have any effect and some of their number then sallied but Anketel's horsemen pressed on rapidly in a close, tight formation and forced them back into the fort. Seeing some of their comrades killed and others ridden down, the remainder abandoned the fort despite outnumbering Anketel's men by five to one. According to Protestant accounts, which usually massively over-estimated Irish casualties, between 89 and 180 Irish were killed, including Colonel McKenna, four captains, six lieutenants and six ensigns. The sole loss to the Protestants was Captain Anketel, shot during the aftermath of the action by 'a rogue' lurking under a bush. Pursuit was impossible because the Irish had retreated through a bog and the Protestant soldiers had only enough ammunition for one more reload, and that had to be reserved for the march away from Glaslough. Anketel's victory also gained enough time for Lady Blayney, along with two troops of horse and three companies of foot, to escape from Armagh to Derry.[14]

Richard Hamilton moved out of Loughbrickland on 13 March along the Belfast road towards Dromore. Rawdon's men were very poorly armed, their muskets of numerous calibres few of which could use the ammunition sent from Hillsborough. During the night of 13–14 March, Major Henry Baker brought four companies of foot into Dromore but they were ill-equipped and did little to replenish Rawdon's supply of infantry. An express arrived early on 14 March ordering Rawdon to fall back to Hillsborough where additional Protestant forces, gathering at Lisburn, had been ordered to rendezvous. To make sure that he could withdraw safely, Rawdon sent out scouts to reconnoitre Hamilton's position and they soon encountered three or four troops of Irish cavalry riding towards Dromore, a threat that had to be cleared before the retreat on Hillsborough could begin. The scouts' report indicated to Rawdon that the Irish horsemen were an advance guard or reconnaissance patrol and he decided to force them to break contact in order to ensure an uninterrupted withdrawal on Hillsborough. Rawdon's total force amounted to about 500 men. Assisted by Major Baker, he drew up the horse and dragoons in the main street of Dromore and deployed Baker's four companies of foot in supporting positions at the southern entrance to the village. The mounted troops then went forward intending to scatter the Irish horse. Had Rawdon pushed his own scouts around the flanks of Dominic Sheldon's vanguard he would have discovered the main body of Hamilton's army behind a large drumlin. Before Rawdon had engaged the Irish vanguard, the main army came into view and was obviously far too strong for 500 Protestant irregulars. Baker's four companies promptly fled through Dromore towards Hillsborough, closely followed by their mounted comrades. Sheldon's cavalry vanguard pursued almost to Hillsborough, killing several Protestants and seizing a good deal of plunder. The pursuit was then halted in case a larger Protestant army was in the vicinity, and the vanguard regrouped and waited for the main army to close up.

As Rawdon was breaking from Dromore, in Hillsborough every effort was being made to gather reinforcements. Mountalexander, James Hamilton of Tullymore and Colonel Arthur Upton, on hearing the news of Hamilton's advance, drew out all the men present at Hillsborough and set off for Dromore. They had reached the edge of the town when the first fugitives galloped into sight, closely followed by Rawdon himself. They tried to stop and rally as many as they could while Rawdon rode through Hillsborough to bring forward the 4,000 men concentrated at Lisburn but the rapid advance of the Irish Army terrified the poorly armed and untrained Protestant irregulars and few at Hillsborough were prepared to stand. The headquarters of the Protestant Association was thus abandoned along with its stores and the archives of the Council of Five. Some brave souls garrisoned Hillsborough Fort but, realizing that they had been abandoned, later surrendered to Sheldon and Hamilton. In the absence of reinforcements from England and other parts of Ulster the Association leaders, meeting at Lisburn, could not agree on a course of action and the troops began to desert. About 4,000 men, including Lieutenant Colonel Thomas Whitney, Major Tubman, Colonel Arthur Upton, Colonel Edmondston, Major Joseph Stroud, Captain Clotworthy Upton and Major White from Belfast, remained together under Rawdon and marched east of Lough Neagh for Coleraine. Other Association colonels either went to England or accepted protections from Hamilton: Colonel William Lesley took protections before making a profit out of supplying the Irish Army before Derry with victuals; Mountalexander rode to Donaghadee, 'the ready port for England', and departed the kingdom. [15] Rumours circulated 'amongst the vulgar' of Derry and Omagh that Blayney, Rawdon, Lieutenant Colonel George Maxwell and several other leaders of the Protestant Association had accepted protections. To counter the stories, on 21 March these gentlemen and several others signed a Declaration of Union in which they vowed to fight and denied that there were rifts between those who wanted to continue the struggle and those who had taken protections. [16] Despite the fine words, this was precisely what happened; worthless protections or flight into England were the only feasible options available to those who were not marooned in Derry or Enniskillen. Hamilton and Sheldon offered protections to anyone who was prepared to stay at home and the majority of the Protestant rural population in Counties Down and Antrim accepted rather than join the exodus to the north. They also gave blanket protection to the town of Belfast. Unfortunately for Hamilton, the countryside of County Down was infested by raparees and half-pikes who had stolen into the vacuum created by the withdrawal of the 'army' of the Protestant Association. These people took no notice of Hamilton's orders or protections. He did not have enough men to protect all villages and settlements and the local people were reluctant to defy the well-armed, aggressive raparees because it was unclear whether such action might be construed as rebellion against the king. Hamilton gave instructions that any raparee who did not hold a legitimate commission from King James could be arrested. Should he resist, he could be killed.

As Hamilton moved slowly north, securing County Down, instead of honouring his earlier commitment to march south, Lundy remained in Derry and ordered the Dungannon garrison to retire into the Laggan. There was considerable reluctance to obey because the town was strongly situated and well provisioned but, eventually, Lundy's instructions were followed. The regiment of ten companies left on 14 March and had reached Strabane by 17 March where it received a written order from Lundy to go to Omagh, presumably to keep open communications with Enniskillen. A fortnight later, about 31 March, the regiment was requested to march back north to Saint Johnstown, 10 km from Derry.[17] The evacuation of Dungannon was the signal for the majority of the rural Protestant population in Counties Monaghan and Tyrone to escape northwards into the Laggan. Governor Gustavus Hamilton of Enniskillen received a letter from Lundy on 16 March. After painting a very dark picture of affairs, he explained that Derry's council of war had advised him to ask all forces, including the Enniskilleners, to withdraw behind the River Finn where they could be supplied from the city. The Enniskilleners held a meeting at which they decided not to comply arguing that the abandonment of the town would allow the Irish in Connaught to flood into Ulster. Enniskillen and Derry were sufficiently distant from one another to oblige the Irish to mount separate military operations to subdue them whereas the voluntary abandonment of Enniskillen would permit the Irish to concentrate all their forces against Derry. On the other hand, distance prevented Enniskillen and Derry from providing direct mutual support although they might maintain communication.[18]

Apart from the Enniskilleners, the Derrymen and the retreating Protestant Association Army in County Antrim, Lord Blayney's 300 soldiers in Armagh constituted the only remaining organized Protestant force in Ulster: 1,500 of his initial 1,800 men had taken protections. Lundy had been expected to reinforce Armagh to cover the approaches to Enniskillen and Derry and protect the flank of Rawdon's men falling back towards Coleraine but he took no action. Isolated and vulnerable, Blayney executed the earlier decision to march to Dungannon, cross the River Bann at Toome and join Rawdon. Learning of these intentions, on 16 March the garrison of Charlemont sent 1,200 men north to Ardtrea Bridge over the Ballinderry River to block his path whilst another 500 fell upon his rear. Blayney only just escaped the trap, reaching Ardtrea Bridge a mere 15 minutes before the blocking force, which, thwarted, descended on his rearguard and opened fire. Immediately he deployed into battle order and sent two companies back towards the bridge to clear the Irish away from the road. On the first volley the Irish broke and Blayney was able to complete the march to Coleraine without further interruption.[19]

Around 20 March, 'in pitiful stormy weather', the roads deep in mud and scarcely passable, the Protestants of County Cavan abandoned their homes in obedience to a supposed order from Lundy and trailed into Enniskillen 'in a most distracted and confused manner'. First came three or four troops of horse, followed by three or four companies of foot, 'then the whole inhabitants with their women and children [up] to their middle in clay and dirt, with pitiful lamentations and with little or no provisions to sustain them'. Many were starving and most were 'in a deplorable condition … filling all corners' of the tiny town. Two hundred families squeezed into the church whilst the school and court house were converted into temporary hostels. The elders of the Cavan Israelites tried to persuade Governor Hamilton and the Enniskilleners to follow them north; some wavered until Major John Rider 'gave so weighty and forcible reasons of the necessity of holding that place, that he over-ruled all and confirmed several … to be firm in our former resolution'. Close questioning of the Cavan officers revealed that the migration owed little to Lundy's letter, indeed there was no evidence that Lundy had issued orders to Cavan, but everything to the sudden appearance of a regiment of Irish horse and some dragoons under Piers Butler, Third Viscount Galmoy. Accompanied by hordes of the 'rabble of the country', Galmoy had advanced as far as Belturbet. *En route* he had visited the house of the Very Reverend Edward Dixie, Dean of Kilmore, and taken prisoner his eldest son, Woolston, captain of a troop of horse, together with his lieutenant, Edward Charleton, and ten troopers. This small incident had induced panic; volunteer Protestant garrisons broke up, householders set fire to their own property and the country people fled towards Enniskillen, their traditional refuge in times of danger.

Rather pleased with himself for securing most of County Cavan through the arrest of two officers and ten soldiers, on 21 March Galmoy advanced from Belturbet to besiege Crom Castle, Enniskillen's 'frontier garrison towards Dublin' on the north shore of Upper Lough Erne, about 26 km distant, covering both the water and land approaches. Having no infantry Galmoy had to use imagination. A pair of ersatz cannon was produced, both nearly 1 m long with 15-cm bores, strongly bound with small cord and covered with a 'sort of buckram'. Each was dragged towards Crom by eight horses 'making a great noise as if they were drawn with much difficulty' and as soon as they were in position Galmoy summoned the governor to surrender. On his refusal he threatened to batter down the walls and fired one of the cannon but the breech burst killing the gunner. The garrison returned fire with rather more effective weapons and accounted for several Irish. Galmoy continued the siege on 22 and 23 March and even had the effrontery to include Enniskillen in his summons to surrender. Governor Hamilton convened a meeting of officers that quickly resolved to defend the town and fight Galmoy should he approach any closer. During the afternoon of 23 March the Cavan men were invited to join the Enniskilleners but, pleading the imperative of Lundy's order, they mostly refused and prepared to depart in the direction of Derry. In response Hamilton announced that all the Cavan men who left Enniskillen must take their wives and children with them: any families left behind would be turned out of the town. Enough men to form three or four companies of foot changed their minds but the rest disappeared towards Omagh and Strabane, including a number of potential officers. Following the agreed policy that it was preferable to fight the enemy at a distance rather than suffer a siege, later in the afternoon Hamilton drew up the horse and foot on the 'common hill' outside the town where they stood to arms until dark, expecting Galmoy to come into view at any moment. Scouts then reported that Galmoy had ventured as far as Lisnaskea, 16 km to the south-east, but had retired to resume the siege of Crom on learning that the Enniskillen forces had deployed. On leaving Lisnaskea, 'a curled fellow, one Kemp, with some of the rabble of the country [as] his consorts, burned that pretty village, to the great loss of the inhabitants and the worthy gentleman that owned it': Enniskillen was already short of accommodation for refugees and troops and Lisnaskea was big enough to have housed a regiment. During the night of 23–4 March Hamilton sent 200 of his best men by water to force an entry into Crom Castle during the hours of darkness but they did not arrive until after daybreak. Galmoy's soldiers fired volleys to prevent them landing but they were poor marksmen and only hit an old boatman whilst the return fire, although from floating platforms, accounted for several. Coming ashore close to the castle, they joined the garrison in a sally that drove Galmoy's troopers from their trenches, killing between 30 and 40, and captured the two cannon. Particularly valuable were the firearms of the dead and wounded Irish. One of the cannon was left to reinforce Crom and the other was taken to Enniskillen.[20]

In the wake of the relief of Crom occurred the first reported savagery committed by the Irish Army, as opposed to incidents perpetrated by raparees. Captain Brian MacGuire had been captured by the garrison during the siege and Galmoy sent an express on 25 March to Captain Abraham Creighton, the owner and governor of Crom Castle, proposing the exchange of MacGuire for Captain Woolston Dixie. Galmoy suggested that Dixie be returned on receipt of MacGuire and this was acceptable to Creighton so he sought official clearance from Enniskillen, which was promptly granted. Creighton then sent MacGuire to Galmoy, asking that Dixie be returned according to the agreement. However, as soon as MacGuire arrived at Galmoy's camp a council of war was summoned that found Dixie and Lieutenant Edward Charleton guilty of levying soldiers on the strength of commissions from the Prince of Orange, which had been found in their pockets, and sentenced them to death. They asked for a stay of execution until the next day to prepare themselves. Great efforts were made to persuade them to convert to Roman Catholicism and join King James's army but, although young, they refused. MacGuire was deeply concerned and begged Galmoy not to destroy his reputation by such a gross breach of good faith and the conventions of war. He offered himself as a hostage for the lives of Dixie and Charleton but his entreaties had no effect and they were hanged from 'Mr Russell's sign post in Belturbet'. Their corpses were then carried into a nearby kitchen where the heads were cut off and tossed into the street for soldiers to use as footballs. Later, they were impaled on the Market House. Whether events occurred in quite the manner reported by the Protestant sources is uncertain but this was the version that reached Enniskillen and contributed to a hardening of attitudes.[21]

HMS *Jersey* (Captain John Beverley RN) and the merchantman *Deliverance* entered Lough Foyle on 21 March carrying Captain James Hamilton and a mixed cargo: 500 barrels of gunpowder; 1,500 old, rusty weapons 'and half of those unfixed'; £1,000 for the use of the garrison; a royal commission for Lundy appointing him Governor of Derry; and assurances that more supplies were on their way. Before leaving Chester, James Hamilton had been instructed, on reaching Derry, to summon the mayor and all civil and military officials aboard the *Jersey* to witness Lundy qualifying himself for public office by taking the Oaths of Supremacy and Allegiance. However, according to Mackenzie, 'most of the gentlemen on board were desired to withdraw on pretence of private business: so that, if Lundy was sworn, "'twas very privately"'. To allay suspicions, on 22 March the Committee of Derry asked Lundy to repeat the oaths publicly in their presence but he declined because he had already done so. To set an example, the mayor, sheriffs, aldermen and all civil and military officers then swore the oaths in public before the Bishop of Derry.[22]

On either 18 or 19 March Lundy asked Kingston whether Sligo would be able to hold out should Derry succumb. Kingston accordingly held a council of war on 20 March which failed to reach a consensus; on the next day (21 March) a second session agreed, by majority vote, to abandon Sligo, destroy all surplus stores and retire on Ballyshannon. The infantry and baggage set off in pouring rain early on 22 March, covered by a cavalry rearguard, along the coast road via Grange and Bundoran. Kingston and a small mounted party lingered at Sligo to smash the trunnions on some of the lighter cannon and spike the heavier pieces. The smallest field guns were dispatched to the north by sea but the vessel was later wrecked off the Donegal coast. Behind the troops trudged the refugees. Most struggled through the wet mud and fast-flowing rivers, some took to open boats whilst the more fortunate secured passage on a ship in Sligo harbour. An uncorroborated report says that Lieutenant Colonel Sir Connell Ferrall led 180 Irish musketeers from the Boyle garrison and about 500 raparees and country Irish to break down the bridge over the River Bundrowes at

Bundoran in advance of Kingston's column but was driven off by an advance guard of 50 Sligo horsemen. Kingston's forces, numbering about 1,000 men, had reassembled at Ballyshannon by 24 March. Either on the march or shortly after arrival, Kingston received another communication from Lundy telling him that there was insufficient forage at Derry to support his forces; instead, he was to continue at Ballyshannon and secure the crossings of the River Erne between the coast and the Lower Lough. Lundy's decision to encourage Kingston to halt at Ballyshannon was logical. Standing on a steep slope above the north bank of the Erne estuary, the bridge protected by a tower and gateway, it was a tighter and stronger position than Sligo from which to defend the route into County Donegal and the Laggan and was within supporting distance of Enniskillen by either road or water. An Enniskillen garrison under Captain Henry Folliott already occupied Ballyshannon. When Kingston was safely north of the Erne, Folliott sunk the ferry boat and burned all the buildings on the south bank of the river, including his father's house, to prevent them from being used to cover an approach to the bridge. At Belleek, 7 km to the east, a second arch of the bridge was pulled down and a garrison installed commanded by Major [Bethell?] Vaughan and Lieutenant Arthur Cooper. Mullick, the house of Lieutenant Walter Johnson situated at the western extremity of Lower Lough Erne, was occupied by Captain William Smith, Captain Francis King and Lieutenant Toby Mulloy. As a fall-back position a body of troops under Captain Francis Gore and Captain Edward Woods was placed in Donegal town. These garrisons must have been small but they were sufficient to render unattractive the westerly route to Donegal and the Laggan and ensured that any attack on Enniskillen would probably develop through Belturbet, Newtownbutler and Lisnaskea, enabling Governor Hamilton to concentrate his forces.[23]

Assuming control of strategy and policy from Tyrconnell, James issued two proclamations on 25 March. In the first he extended religious toleration and freedom of worship to all Protestants who had fled to England and Scotland on condition that they returned within 40 days to resume their vital economic activities. The second recognized that irregulars, raparees and half-pikes were in action against the Protestants. Provided that it was directed solely at known rebels and not against loyal neighbours, their rapacity was condoned and encouraged. James also summoned the Irish Parliament.[24]

News of Captain James Hamilton's arrival in Derry reached Enniskillen on 25 March. Governor Hamilton sent Nicholas Westby and Andrew Hamilton, escorted by 24 men, bearing written requests, addressed to both Captain Hamilton and Lundy, for a share of the arms and ammunition. The former was ready to oblige but Lundy greeted the emissaries very coldly and refused to give them a single working weapon: his generosity extended to just 60 antique musket barrels and five casks of powder, the only external supplies to reach Enniskillen until the coming of Major General Percy Kirke. Munitions and equipment were otherwise either manufactured within the region or seized from the Irish. The Enniskillen party returned safely with its meagre ration but local craftsmen soon cleaned the barrels and affixed furniture. Although the Enniskilleners blamed Lundy for failing to support their efforts they were in no position to object because they had deliberately disobeyed his earlier orders to concentrate in the Laggan. Also, the emissaries probably did not realize that the cargo of the *Jersey* and *Deliverance* consisted solely of old and broken weapons whilst Lundy, who was expecting an imminent confrontation with Richard Hamilton's army, was unlikely to waste valuable gunpowder on a disobedient outpost. At Lifford, on his journey back to Enniskillen, Andrew Hamilton met the Reverend Dr George Walker. They established a secure method of communication between Enniskillen and Derry; couriers would carry an agreed token and only if it could be produced on demand was their information to be given credence. During the period when Derry was blockaded rather than besieged, the Irish allowed numerous people in and out enabling a steady exchange of news with Enniskillen. Only after the implementation of a closer siege did communication virtually cease.[25]

No one appeared anxious to accept the overall command of the remnants of the Protestant Association Army as it filed north through County Antrim; Rawdon was discredited; Mountalexander had left for England; Blayney was fully occupied in County Monaghan; so Gustavus Hamilton (1639–1723), created Viscount Boyne in 1715, assumed the task. The leading elements reached Coleraine on 15 March where they were joined by local volunteers and *ad hoc* units from Belfast, Lisburn and County Antrim. Richard Hamilton and Dominic Sheldon followed at a distance, plundering the countryside. There were only two bridges across the River Bann between its estuary and the exit from Lough Neagh: Portglenone and Coleraine. The Association troops broke down Portglenone Bridge and burned as many boats as possible on Loughs Neagh and Beg and along the Bann but many were overlooked and fell into Richard Hamilton's hands as he moved north.[26] However, these hurried and incomplete measures restricted Hamilton's strategic options. If he wished to march into Counties Derry and Donegal, he had either to capture Coleraine Bridge or retrace his steps and take the longer, more difficult route around the south and west of Lough Neagh, via Charlemont and over the Sperrin Mountains, which would have consumed valuable time and left Coleraine and County Antrim as a Protestant enclave behind River Bann. Hamilton set about quashing the rebellion in Ulster according to a logical sequence: defeat the Association Army and then reduce and occupy the centres of Protestant resistance: Coleraine; then Derry; and, finally, Enniskillen.

On arrival in Coleraine, the Association officers immediately contacted Derry and several rode to Newtown Limavady[27] on the following day (16 March) to meet Lundy and escort him to Coleraine. Pursuing his strategy of concentrating all resistance at a single point that could be supplied by sea, Lundy advised them to abandon Coleraine as soon as it came under pressure and bring their troops into Derry where there were already provisions sufficient for 12 months even before the local corn and hay had been gathered. He supported this instruction by arguing, first, that there were only 40 barrels of powder in Derry – there were nearly 500 – and none could be spared for the defence of Coleraine and, second, that the alternative approach of defending as many places as possible, understandably favoured by the Protestant Association, had resulted in disaster at Dromore and the loss of Counties Down and Armagh. The cavalcade entered Coleraine and Lundy inspected the defences. Not dissatisfied, he was leaving when the 'commonalty' raised the drawbridge and waved some muskets and pikes in his direction fearful that he was abandoning the town. Indeed he was but Lundy was not a fool and stayed until 18 March. Before departing finally, he formally appointed Lieutenant Colonel Gustavus Hamilton to manage operations in and around Coleraine: Lieutenant Colonel Thomas Whitney was then ordered to guard the drawbridge in case the townspeople tried to detain him and he crossed the Bann without interference.[28] Short of provisions, ammunition and trustworthy officers Coleraine could not offer prolonged resistance. Many of the 'rabble' and townspeople not yet prepared to submit to the Irish quit the town, most making for Derry in a disorderly mob, a perfect prey for raparees. Only Association soldiers and those prepared to accept protections remained in Coleraine. Gustavus Hamilton held a council of war on 24 March to explain that there was insufficient ammunition to mount a defence and advised abandonment and an orderly retirement on Derry before the town came under pressure. During the session, two squadrons of Irish horsemen, Richard Hamilton's vanguard, came into view and everyone rushed to the ramparts. Before retreating out of sight, they approached so close that one trooper was shot dead by a soldier on the walls. This ended thoughts of evacuating the town, 'which else had been done', because it was beyond the capabilities of amateur troops to execute such an operation in the face of a numerically superior opponent. When a fire broke out close to the magazine at 0200 on 25 March, treachery was suspected and terrified townspeople and soldiers dashed to the ramparts but the blaze was rapidly extinguished, no enemy appeared and quiet resumed.[29]

Coleraine, on the right bank of the Bann, was defended to the north, east and south by a high earthwork rampart and ditch; water guarded the west side. Richard Hamilton informed Gustavus Hamilton on 26 March that he would advance in force on the following day. Expecting an easy victory, he came into view at 08:00 on 27 March with only five light field guns and about 1,000 infantry, cavalry and dragoons. Behind hedges and along ditches Hamilton's infantry filed towards the Blind Gate, on the south side adjacent to the river, and the King's Gate to the east. There had not been enough time for the garrison to level and burn all the suburbs, houses, barns, ditches, hedges, mills and rubbish heaps beyond the fortifications that gave cover to attackers, normal procedure when a town was threatened. Two guns were deployed, under the protection of cavalry, opposite the King's Gate and a battery of three cannon was positioned, covered by dragoons, to fire on the Blind Gate and the bridge over the Bann with the intention of breaking it down to hinder the escape of the garrison towards Newtown Limavady and Derry and inconvenience relief attempts. The infantry was drawn up in between. A shot split the beam anchoring the chain of the drawbridge but Captain Hugh MacGill arranged a temporary repair. The easterly battery concentrated on harassing fire to lower morale but bringing down a few chimneys and shattering some roof tiles proved ineffective. Not heavy enough to damage the walls, the artillery bombardment became even less efficacious after Hugh MacGill shot an Irish gunner. Between 30 and 40 grenadiers gained a position in a water mill, close enough to fire on the troops lining the ramparts. Musketry continued all day but the Irish were unable to create an opening. They also became aware of a detachment of horse and foot under Lord Blayney that appeared on a hill outside the town. Late in the afternoon, under cover of a sudden and heavy snow squall, Hamilton withdrew his infantry, followed by the cavalry and dragoons. Seeing the Irish retreating in some disorder, bolder members of the garrison thought to pursue but they could not release the gates which had been reveted with timber, earth and rubbish. Nevertheless, some enthusiasts jumped from the ramparts and seized several prisoners and a few weapons. The garrison lost three men killed but Irish casualties were not known because the retreating soldiers carried them away: it was later reported that the Irish had cremated their dead in a house. Hamilton made just one attack, hoping that a quick assault would carry Coleraine, because he lacked the resources necessary for the conduct of a siege: heavy artillery, iron cannon balls and provisions. The scorched-earth tactics employed by the Association forces as they withdrew through Counties Down and Antrim had achieved their objectives. Few, if any, supplies reached Hamilton from Dublin because of distance, the absence of a wagon park and Tyrconnell's failure to make logistical arrangements. Hamilton was supposed to live off the Protestant countryside but, as it had been partially destroyed, he could neither linger nor operate for any length of time within that theatre. He withdrew to Ballymoney to await promised reinforcements, presenting the Protestant Association with its first military success.[30]

A detachment from Coleraine garrison foraged to within 3 km of Ballymoney on 27 March and brought in some cattle. Confident that Hamilton would not try again at Coleraine but seek other routes across the Bann, Gustavus Hamilton installed a garrison of 3,000 men – the regiments of Sir Tristram Beresford and Colonel Francis Hamilton plus several *ad hoc* units – and redeployed the majority of his command to guard the line of the river above Lough Neagh. He ordered Rawdon's regiment to Moneymore, north-east of Cookstown, to observe Colonel Gordon O'Neill who was said to be making for Coleraine with 2,000 men; Clotworthy Skeffington's regiment stood in support at Bellaghy, north-east of Moneymore. Establishing his headquarters at Bellaghy, Skeffington placed garrisons at Castledawson and the Bann fords between Portglenone and Toome. Lieutenant Colonel Charles Houston was detailed to cover the ford at Toome with one battalion but his men had great difficulty in approaching because the weather was very wet and the Bann in spate; having struggled into position, inundations hindered the regular relief of the guard. Another detachment of Skeffington's, commanded by Major John Michelburne, defended Newferry ford at the northern extremity of Lough Beg, where the flooding was less severe and access easier. Colonel Edmondston watched the pass at Portglenone with instructions to interfere with any attempt to repair the damaged bridge. Colonel Canning's regiment went to Magherafelt, between Moneymore and Bellaghy, to stiffen the open southern flank of the Protestant deployment. To Kilrea, roughly midway between Coleraine and Toome, travelled Sir John MacGill's infantry in order to guard the middle reaches of the river: MacGill was entrusted especially with gathering and sinking all the boats in his sector. It was probably a detachment of MacGill's that drove back an attempt by some of Richard Hamilton's soldiers from Ballymoney to cross the Bann at Agivey Bridge. Rawdon's infantry reached Magherafelt on 2 April where plenty of provisions were discovered. Conversely, at Portglenone, Edmondston entered a stripped and ravaged countryside and asked Rawdon to share his abundance; a supply convoy reached Edmondston on the night of 5 April. Rawdon was impressed by Edmondston's defensive preparations. His trenches were so well designed that they were impervious to fire from across the river and he had broken down most of what remained of Portglenone Bridge. Richard Hamilton's men had closed up to the line of the Bann and were probing to find an inadequately defended crossing. There was, noted Rawdon, continual firing from both sides around Portglenone and, using red-hot shot, Edmondston had burned most of the town denying the Irish accommodation in the cold, wet weather.[31]

The weakness of Gustavus Hamilton's position was not the line of the flooded Bann but the open, southern flank and it was only a matter of time before it came under pressure. At 02:00 on 7 April, intelligence was received that Lord Galmoy and Colonels Gordon O'Neill and Art MacMahon had reached Dungannon with 3,000 infantry and 1,000 cavalry. Some of these forces came from the Charlemont garrison but James had also sent Pusignan with reinforcements from Dublin. Rawdon was ordered to take the bulk of his regiment forward from Magherafelt to reinforce the garrison at Moneymore. Setting off with Major Henry Baker, Captain Hugh MacGill and Captain Dunbar, Rawdon had not ridden more than 2 km when he received a report that the Irish, in five or six 'great boats', had avoided Skeffington's outposts and Edmonston's entrenchments and crossed the Bann 1 km south of Portglenone. Indeed, the report suggested that the Irish were already infiltrating into the rear of Edmondston's position. Rawdon immediately dispatched riders with urgent warnings for Edmondston at Portglenone and Major Michelburne and Lieutenant Colonel Thomas Whitney. One company of Edmondston's regiment, which was billeted in houses near the Bann, had advanced to the river bank and fired on the Irish boats until their ammunition was expended. Having established a bridgehead, the landing party of between 30 and 40 men was quickly reinforced by two or three companies of grenadiers under Colonel William Nugent, the son of the Earl of Westmeath, increasing the strength to about 200 men.[32] Some local raparees and country people also swelled Nugent's ranks. He then waded through a bog to storm Edmondston's main entrenchments, manned by about 120 infantry, from the flank and rear. Edmondston detached 60 men to line a ditch along the edge of the bog at right angles to his trenches to face the advancing Irish, leaving Captain William Shaw with the remaining 60 to guard the trenches fronting the river and watch for further crossings. Edmondston held the flanking ditch until his ammunition was exhausted when he was overrun by superior numbers.

Nugent then noticed the arrival of Lieutenant Colonel Thomas Whitney, Rawdon, Captain Dunbar and five infantry companies so he moved his grenadiers behind a hedge to block the single avenue of approach and welcomed the new-comers with a volley. Whitney instructed three young captains to lead the men forward but, when he realized the size of the Irish force, his nerve failed and he ordered them to fall back. Only Captain James MacGill, ashamed of Whitney's cowardice, pressed on, joined by Rawdon and Dunbar but a second party of Irish had lined the hedges to the rear of the position held by the grenadiers and James MacGill was shot from his horse. Helpless on the ground, a grenadier captain stepped forward and ran him through several times with his sword before a soldier beat out his brains with a clubbed musket. Major Henry Baker and Captain Hugh MacGill then arrived with a few men they had been able to gather on their approach but they only succeeded in stopping and rallying Whitney's men as they withdrew in disorder; Edmondston's original 60 infantry were now trapped in the trenches close to the river, a strong Irish force across their line of retreat. However, Lieutenant Colonel William Shaw and Edmondston escaped from the pocket on the river 'by several ways' and joined Baker, Hugh MacGill and Whitney's demoralized infantrymen. There was little ammunition or match remaining whilst the strength of the Irish was steadily increasing as more infantry were ferried over the Bann. Not only did the Protestant forces lose Captain James MacGill and several soldiers killed but Captain Henley was wounded and captured, Rawdon subsequently succumbed to illness, whilst Edmondston contracted a fever and died on 14 April. A bad position deteriorated further when news was received that Galmoy's force was marching on Moneymore from Dungannon. With the Coleraine–River Bann position pierced and out-flanked, the Protestant forces at Moneymore, Magherafelt, Newferry and Toome set off over the Sperrin Mountains for the sanctuary of Derry. In danger of being cut off, Sir Tristram Beresford evacuated Coleraine and the garrison withdrew through Newtown Limavady towards Derry, joined by the forces responsible for patrolling the more northerly reaches of the Bann. Beresford's troops assembled on the east bank of Lough Foyle, opposite Derry, on 9 April, and patiently awaited the ferry. From the countryside, Protestants packed a few belongings and headed north. Despite the reverse at Coleraine, Richard Hamilton had neatly manoeuvred the Protestants out of County Antrim. His main force had remained encamped at Ballymoney, awaiting promised reinforcements and skirmishing with Beresford's foraging parties, until Nugent had forced the line of the Bann. Although the departing Protestants demolished Coleraine Bridge, Hamilton marched into the abandoned town, repaired the crossing and moved towards Derry.[33]

5

Clady and the Ards Peninsula

Swamped by hordes of refugees, tensions increased within Derry. Adherents of the Church of Ireland were equivocal in their attitudes towards King James whilst the Presbyterians were adamant that William and Mary were the legitimate sovereigns. There was also a racial complication because the Presbyterians were overwhelmingly of Scottish origin whereas the Church of Ireland men were mainly English. Many left Ireland while flight remained possible. Accompanied by his mother, brother, sister and children, Arthur Bushe had fled north with virtually no possessions, reaching Derry early in March. As Richard Hamilton approached from the east and Pusignan and Galmoy from the south, the atmosphere in Derry became so claustrophobic and hopeless that Bushe decided to leave the country. He bought passage to the Isle of Man where he and his family stayed for ten days before proceeding to Whitehaven.[1]

On 10 April Lundy ordered the mounted troops which had retreated from the line of the Bann and Coleraine to quarter in Letterkenny, thus spreading the demand for forage over a wider area. David Cairns sailed into Derry on the same day bearing a letter and secret instructions for Lundy from King William. Cairns witnessed many civilians and several military officers, to whom Lundy had granted passes, taking passage for England, an exodus that did not surprise him because Lundy talked gloomily about the indefensibility of the town and his low spirits were infectious, starting rumours that he intended to surrender upon terms. However, Cairns also brought the cheering news that a relief expedition was already at sea; a council of war was summoned for that evening. Lundy read his letter and instructions aloud and Cairns explained that Derry's defiance had caught the imagination of the English public and the Whitehall government was making substantial efforts to send assistance. Having successfully dissuaded the council from surrendering, Cairns requested, urgently, that an inventory be made of all weapons, ammunition and provisions in the city's stores. Colonel James Hamilton then proposed the signing of an association to commit those present to the defence of the town. The resulting declaration was posted in the market place on the following day (11 April) and read before every battalion and regiment. Some elements of Richard Hamilton's army appeared on the east bank of Lough Foyle but there were insufficient boats to carry troops across to engage and harass them, except the vessel in which Cairns had arrived. As a gesture he gave permission for it to be used as a warship should the Irish soldiers try to cross in their own boats but Hamilton had no intention of launching an attack across a tidal waterway. Already his main body was marching via Newton Limavady to concentrate at Strabane, where he intended to link up with King James, Pusignan, Galmoy and reinforcements from Dublin, in order to cross the Finn by the Tyrone–Donegal fords at Clady and Long Causeway to come at Derry from the south. James moved rapidly: on 14 April, his main corps reached Omagh, via Charlemont, whilst Pusignan led the advance guard into Newtownstewart. Most of James's troops rested on 15 April following a long, tiring march in very bad weather but Rosen, Maumont and Girardin were ordered forward to Strabane with two troops of horse and one of dragoons to assist Richard Hamilton in crossing the Finn. News of James's approach was delivered to Derry on 13 April by the Reverend Dr George Walker, who had been serving with his regiment around Omagh. Lundy ordered all the houses outside the walls along the waterside to be burned. By the time that Walker had ridden back to Lifford, Richard Hamilton had joined with Rosen, Maumont and Girardin around Clady.[2]

A general council of war at 10:00 on 14 April ordered a force to be in place by 10:00 on Monday 15 April to defend the crossings of the River Finn between Clady Bridge and Strabane–Lifford. All officers and soldiers of horse, dragoons and foot

> and all other armed men whatsoever of our forces and friends, enlisted and not enlisted, that can and will fight for their country and religion against Popery, shall appear in the fittest ground near Cladyford, Lifford and Long-Causeway, as shall be nearest to their several and respective quarters, there to draw up in battalions to be ready to fight the enemy.[3]

Everyone was instructed to bring a week's provisions and as much horse forage as he could carry. Utter confusion resulted and the forces that reached or, in most cases, failed to reach Clady, were a disorganized and unarticulated mob, a desperate *levée en masse*: officers had not been given local responsibilities; the men were untrained; a command structure was absent; there was no agreed system of communications; fall-back positions were undesignated and unprepared; reserves were lacking; little ammunition had been issued; and the men were armed with a mixture of matchlock muskets, fouling pieces, antiques from the Confederate Wars, pitch forks, scythes and carving knives. James II's Irish Army was indeed unproven but it was unlikely to be halted by such opposition; it was small wonder that Lundy looked glum and talked about Derry's indefensibility. With the exception of Coleraine, the Protestant Association had been defeated in every engagement and Lundy – moody, shifty, uninspiring and pessimistic – was certain they were about to lose again but the greatest captains of the age could not have held the line of the Finn with the forces at his disposal. Lundy also appreciated that Derry would not be able to withstand a formal siege because the enemy would hold both banks of the Foyle and interdict seaborne supply. Because nearly all ports were already under Irish control, there would be scant possibility of relief. A copy of the council of war's order of 14 April was sent to the Enniskilleners with a covering note from Lundy suggesting that, following the collapse of the line of the Bann, they should consider surrender. Lundy had, however, overlooked the propinquity of the relief expedition, announced by David Cairns; he probably did not believe it would arrive at all, certainly not in time, and, even if it did, would be unable to approach the town.

A Captain Richard Lundy served with Colonel William Herbert's regiment of foot in the New Model Army from 1645 to 1647 but there is no proven connection. Robert Lundy was born in Dumbarton and brought up in the Episcopal Church of Scotland. During the 1670s he served in the Earl of Dumbarton's infantry regiment in the French service until 1678, reaching the rank of captain. After two years in England he went with Dumbarton's, re-named the Royal Scots, to Tangier and was wounded during the action against the Moors on 27 October 1680 receiving £80 compensation in 1683. Lundy married Martha Davies, daughter of the Reverend Rowland Davies, later Dean of Cork, and exploited her connections with the Duke of Ormonde to secure promotion on to the Irish establishment in 1685 as lieutenant colonel of Lord Mountjoy's foot battalion. He avoided prosecution for his conduct in Ireland: despite pressure to return him to Derry for trial, he was saved by the intervention of George Walker who argued, probably to deflect investigation into his own uncertain conduct, that most of the necessary witnesses had already been dispersed and there would be insufficient available to secure a successful prosecution. Gradually, Lundy was rehabilitated through the patronage of the Earl of Galway and the Duchess of Marlborough and was commissioned adjutant general of the English troops serving in the Portuguese Army in 1704, a post he held until 1712. Taken prisoner at sea by the French in 1707, he was exchanged for 20 men two years later. He died before 1717.[4] Lundy's career up to 1689 suggested a competent, career regimental officer who had seen action; what he lacked was experience in independent command.

The council of war on 14 April also ordered Lord Kingston to bring all his forces from Ballyshannon, 50 km distant, to Clady, Lifford and Long Causeway[5] by 10:00 on 15 April. Kingston was placed in some difficulty because he did not receive this communication until 22:00 on 14 April. He immediately convened a council of war which decided, largely because the men were billeted over such a wide area, that it would be impossible to reach the rendezvous within twice the time allowed by Lundy's order. Instead, Kingston would take forward a dozen horsemen to reconnoitre. Early next morning (15 April), Kingston rode out with his escort and came to Stranorlar where he encountered several fugitives from the débâcle at Clady who told him that the Irish were over the Finn and already at

Raphoe, thus severing Kingston's communications with Derry. Seeing that there was nothing he could do and that, with the Irish Army controlling the Laggan, he would be cut off if he remained at Ballyshannon, Kingston decided to demobilize his troops. Returning to Donegal, he disbanded his soldiers. Some went home and took protections from the Irish but most, a total of two troops of horse and six companies of infantry, marched to Enniskillen. Kingston travelled to Killybegs where he took ship for Scotland whence he sent a full report to William.[6]

The infantry battalions of Colonels John Cunningham and Solomon Richards sailed from Hoylake on 10 April and arrived in Lough Foyle on 15 April amidst a crisis. Through telescopes from the higher points in Derry, observers watched Richard Hamilton's battalions move up to the banks of the Finn opposite Strabane on 14 April. Major Joseph Stroud advised Lundy either to garrison or demolish Raphoe Castle; amalgamate weak battalions, companies and troops into fewer, stronger units; block Clady ford with obstacles; and hold the Finn crossings in strength to protect the rich resources of the Laggan but nothing was done. Cairns implored Lundy to take some measures in case the Irish crossed the ford before the Derry forces had reached their rendezvous at 10:00 on 15 April. Again Lundy failed to act because, in all probability, there was nothing he could have done within the time available. Several others told Lundy that, if the men did not march during the night of 14–15 April, the Irish would be across before they were in position but, lacking a command structure, Lundy could not hasten his 'army'. Revised orders would have created yet more confusion so Lundy accepted the risk and adhered to the original scheme. News also arrived on 14 April that ships had been sighted off the coast near the entrance to Lough Foyle but had been forced out to sea again by bad weather. Had Cunningham and Richards reached Derry on 14 rather than 15 April, their two regular battalions might have influenced the outcome.[7]

Richard Hamilton sent a note to James at Omagh stating that 9,000–10,000 rebels were lining the banks of the Finn; also he could see 13 vessels in Lough Foyle, four of which were men-of-war. Therefore he proposed crossing the Finn immediately before the troops that had obviously been brought over in these ships joined the Laggan forces. He suggested that James remain at Omagh whilst, in company with Rosen, Maumont and Girardin, he attempted a crossing of the Finn with three squadrons of cavalry, two of dragoons and 1,000 detached infantry. They would be in position by 10:00 on 15 April. Maumont and Girardin reached Strabane with 700 infantry at midday on 14 April but found the crossing well guarded by Protestant troops who had erected a small fort, positioned some cannon in Lifford and entrenched the river bank. Hamilton joined Pusignan at Clady ford but their force comprised only 600 cavalry and 350 infantry. A small detachment moved further west and attempted to force the river at Castlefinn and, although repulsed by elements of Clotworthy Skeffington's regiment, usefully served to keep the defenders guessing as to where the main attack would develop.

In reality the Finn crossings were scarcely defended. Lundy's forward concentration was not scheduled for completion until 10:00 on 15 April and suffered considerable delays, most 'soldiers' not leaving the city until between 08:00 and 09:00. The total of the Derry forces may have approached 10,000 but, when the decisive action occurred at Clady, most were on the road from Derry: according to Ash, Lundy himself did not leave the town until midday. There was a bridge at Clady but some of the arches had been broken down about a week before and a breastwork built on the north side, which was manned when Hamilton approached but its small garrison lacked ammunition, resolute command and instructions. A Jacobite source suggests that Lundy had already assembled 7,000 men at Clady – Captain Thomas Ash notes that the attackers were outnumbered five to one by the defenders – who subjected Hamilton's troops to a brisk fire but this was probably a substantial over-estimate. Both the Jacobites and the anti-Lundy faction in Derry had every reason subsequently to exaggerate the numbers manning the Finn defences. Hamilton began the action by ordering his infantry and field guns to shoot at the troops gathering along the north bank. About 30 dragoons of Colonel Stewart's regiment, commanded by Captain Adam Murray, stood and returned fire until their ammunition was expended but could then do no more because the wagons carrying replenishments were caught in traffic 7 km back along the Derry road. Major Joseph Stroud, who appears to have been the senior officer in the vicinity of Clady, tried to draw up the cavalry that had arrived but they lacked arms and ammunition and he could not move to support Stewart's dragoons without running a gauntlet of heavy flanking fire. Noting the 'scattered condition' of the defenders, Richard Hamilton took a calculated risk and ordered his cavalry to ride through the ford with infantry hanging to the horses' saddles, manes and tails. The water level in the Finn was high – Major Richard Nagle and a trooper were drowned – and the soldiers reached the shore with hardly a dry charge of powder between them; had the Derrymen been organized, the Irish would have been vulnerable to a prompt counter-attack. Instead, shouting 'To Derry! To Derry!' they turned and fled north. When news of the crossing reached Lundy, instead of deploying his marching forces into blocking positions, he ordered a withdrawal. Hamilton, whose cavalry pursued for about 5 km before halting to regroup, thought the campaign finished.

An infantry detachment at Lifford under Captain Hugh Hamill and Major Richard Crofton had been firing on the Irish in Strabane but was called back before it was cut off. It retreated to the defile at Long Causeway allowing Girardin's infantry and cavalry to swim from Strabane to Lifford. At Long Causeway, assuming that Lundy would come to his support from Raphoe, Colonel Francis Hamilton rallied Hamill's and Crofton's soldiers deploying them to cover the northern exit from the pass. However, the Irish cavalry took the road to Raphoe, their passage but mildly inconvenienced by Major Stroud commanding a small mounted rearguard. Colonel William Montgomery's foot regiment stood at Raphoe and would have been destroyed if the men had not broken ranks and taken to the marshes to escape the Irish horsemen. Francis Hamilton's *ad hoc* units remained at the head of the Long Causeway defile until evening when, fearing that the Irish around Raphoe would infiltrate behind them, they withdrew. Lundy had no control over the retreat. Although there were a number of passes and choke points between Clady and Derry that could have been held by relatively few men, if well supplied with ammunition and regularly relieved, his sole thought was to reach Derry, probably the correct course of action because the shattered, disorganized and demoralized soldiers could not have conducted a fighting retreat. On reaching Derry Lundy ordered the gates barred obliging many gentlemen and volunteers straggling back from Clady to spend the night of 15–16 April outside the walls. Lundy later explained that he had done this to protect the food magazines which were sufficient to support 3,000 men for three months.[8]

At 10:00 on 15 April Colonel John Cunningham, in his cabin on HMS *Swallow* lying off Greencastle at the entrance to Lough Foyle, wrote to Lundy announcing his arrival and asking for orders. A second message followed at 14:00 when the ship was opposite Redcastle; having heard that Lundy had taken the field, Cunningham informed him that two well-disciplined battalions were on board and could be ashore and ready within 48 hours. They would, said Cunningham, be of great use in any type of service but especially in the encouragement of raw and untrained men 'as I judge most of yours are'. He assumed that Lundy would hold on the Finn for long enough to enable him to link up before offering battle, should that be necessary. Finally, he apologized for being free with operational advice because he was, by commission, Lundy's subordinate.[9] The first of these letters was delivered by Major Zachariah Tiffin (Cunningham's battalion) and the second by Captain Wolfran Cornwall RN, the commander of the *Swallow*, both of whom remained in Derry awaiting Lundy's reply. No replies were forthcoming so, still anchored off Redcastle, Cunningham wrote again at 21:00 requesting orders.

Late in the evening, Lundy sent Major Tiffin, Captain John Lyndon and Captain Cornwall RN to HMS *Swallow* with a reply to Cunningham's three letters. With delightful understatement, Lundy explained that he had returned to Derry rather sooner than he had expected. After placing 'numbers' on the banks of the Finn he had gone to a pass, probably the Long Causeway, 'where a few might oppose a greater number than came to the place'. Unfortunately, as he arrived, the defenders were already running before 'the enemy who pursued with great vigour' and pressed on towards Derry. Lundy asked Cunningham to land his men immediately and march them overnight to Derry, taking care to maintain good order in case they were surprised by the Irish. Billets were plentiful in the city. There were two postscripts. In the first, Lundy ordered that if the men had not already come ashore then they were to do so immediately and march to the city. Then Major Tiffin entered the chamber to impart further dismal news causing Lundy to add to the postscript that if Cunningham's two battalions could not reach the city on 16 April, then 'it will not be in your power to bring 'em at all' because, without an immediate supply of money and provisions, Derry would fall very quickly. After referring to information that would be delivered verbally by Tiffin, Lundy penned a second, contradictory postscript. There were now, apparently, supplies in Derry sufficient to support 3,000 men for only ten days, a remarkable revision of the estimate made earlier that evening, even if useless mouths were expelled and private stores requisitioned. Accordingly, Lundy ordered Cunningham to leave his men on board but to come with Colonel Richards and his other officers into Derry for a conference on 16 April.[10]

Cunningham, Richards, Cornwall and ten army captains attended, all ignorant of the state of affairs in Derry and the north of Ireland. Lundy, James Hamilton, Chidley Coote and Lord Blayney represented the defenders; Colonels Francis Hamilton and John Chichester, Lieutenant Colonel William Ponsonby and Major Richard Crofton sought admittance but were refused. No civilians were allowed to attend, except Mr Muckeridge, the town clerk. Lundy explained that he had sent for Sir Arthur Rawdon but he was dying, which was less than truthful although his health was poor. Lundy opened proceedings by presenting a pessimistic appreciation leading to the conclusion that the city should be abandoned because its supply area was occupied by 25,000 Irish troops and the city would have consumed its food reserves long before resupply arrived. Most of the officers from England assumed that the governor was well acquainted with the details of his command and did not question his evaluation. Only Richards, realizing that evacuation would mean the end of Protestantism and the English interest in Ireland, argued against this defeatism but he received no support. The council resolved not to land the two battalions and the expedition was ordered to return to England carrying the Association officers on Tyrconnell's black list; the removal of these gentlemen would make it easier for Derry to surrender upon acceptable terms. The council expected that James, whose troops had advanced to Saint Johnstown, would deal leniently with Derry granting a general pardon and restoring plundered property. Some gentlemen were sufficiently persuaded to sign a document seeking to know on what terms James might accept the surrender of the city but others refused and threatened to hang Lundy and the entire council of war. Captain White was sent to James to hear his response to the council's proposals whilst Richard Hamilton agreed to keep his troops 7 km distant.[11] Cunningham and his officers then returned to their ships which had fallen down just to the south of Redcastle. In agreeing not to land, Cunningham was following orders, although in a rather pusillanimous manner, but he was disobedient in returning to England rather than attempting Carrickfergus or Strangford Lough.[12]

Ignorant of the council's resolutions, when the meeting broke up a group of townspeople pressed Lundy to allow the two battalions to land and join with the local troops to form a field army to preserve 'that corner into which the provisions and wealth of three or four counties was crowded' before Richard Hamilton could bring up cannon and mount a formal siege. He replied, in public, that it had indeed been decided to disembark the two battalions immediately and then open the gates to allow all able-bodied persons to combine in the defence of the city. To mask the truth further, Lundy instructed the sheriffs to tour the city arranging billets for the regulars. At this point, in an aggressive and ugly mood but 'tolerably good order', the majority of the soldiers from Clady and Lifford arrived before Derry to find the gates shut. A captain in Skeffington's regiment shot a sentry and called for fire to burn them down. All four were then flung back and the troops entered, including those who had been locked out overnight. To have announced to these men that the council had already decided to surrender the town would not have been prudent and confirmed Lundy in his mendacity. Because there was little forage around Derry, the cavalry was sent north to Culmore and some of the infantry ignored the city altogether and marched into the Inishowen Peninsula. The actual resolution of the council of war was not made public until 18 April, although it was privately conveyed to those blacklisted, principally Colonel Francis Hamilton, Captain Hugh MacGill and the ailing Sir Arthur Rawdon, so that they could take refuge aboard Captain Cornwall's squadron. Many others, witnessing Lundy's ambivalence, also assumed that Derry was a lost cause and during 17 April made their way towards the ships. Others rallied around Captain Adam Murray and resolved to resist.

After bringing his forces to Saint Johnstown on 17 April, James sent the Reverend Whitlow to Derry to investigate whether a capitulation on honourable terms could be arranged. The ground had already been partially prepared. On 16 April, Whitlow had met an acquaintance, Cornet Nicholson, who told him that Derry intended to surrender by Saturday 20 April. William Blacker and an ensign from the garrison at Charlemont had then gone to Derry to 'amuse' the townspeople with stories of James's clemency and the strength of his army. Before Blacker was arrested and clapped in gaol he sent a letter to James that was intercepted. It implicated Captain Darcy and Mr White, the Collector at Strabane, as working for the Jacobite cause; both were dismissed. Amidst the confusion, many volunteer soldiers were appalled that some of their officers were deserting and escaping to England. Captain Bell was shot dead and another officer wounded as, with several others, they boarded a tender to row out to Captain Cornwall's squadron. Lundy was coming to be viewed as, at best, a defeatist and possibly a traitor. Captain Cole was sent to offer the governorship to Colonel Cunningham but he explained that he was under the king's orders to obey Lundy.[13]

James was fairly confident that, on his approach, Derry would submit. Accordingly, on 18 April his entourage marched from Saint Johnstown with colours flying, drums beating and trumpets braying and halted on the beach below the windmill to await the city's response. However, James was slightly hesitant and hung back on the south side of Derry Hill under the protection of a detachment of cavalry 'the more safely to observe what salutation his forces had from the garrison'. In Derry, orders were given that there was be no firing until James's demands were made known and a messenger was dispatched to the king for this purpose. Seeing Richard Hamilton's army approach closer than the previously agreed minimum of 7 km, some of the men on Derry's ramparts ignored their officers and opened fire, killing Captain Troy. To the garrison's delight and the embarrassment of Richard Hamilton and James, the Irish Army became 'disordered' by the spasmodic gunfire, some men running away and others diving for cover. Lundy and the council were furious but their authority was so compromised that they could take no preventive action. Fearing serious repercussions – the firing had been an act of open rebellion that had placed the king in physical danger – some of the more moderate council members sent the Archdeacon of Raphoe, the Reverend James Hamilton and Mr Neville to apologize to James for their inability to control the 'tumultuous and intractable rabble' but, as soon as he reached the Irish camp, the archdeacon deserted and sought protection. If, suggested the two remaining envoys, the army drew back and provided evidence of the royal presence, which some in Derry doubted, then their comrades might be persuaded to behave more respectfully.

Derry needed a credible and popular leader. Having fought on the Finn, Captain Adam Murray, a Presbyterian of Scottish descent, had retreated with his cavalry to Culmore Fort and assumed command. Hearing of the approach of James's army, he brought 400 horsemen into a field below Penny Burn Mill and stationed 1,500 infantry supports at Brook Hall. The council sent one of Murray's relatives to ask him to hide his forces out of sight behind a hill. When he queried these bizarre orders it was explained that Lundy and the council were about to surrender the city to James and the appearance of his troops would disrupt proceedings. Murray realized that immediate intervention was required. Leading his troopers directly on the city, despite a brief exchange of fire with some Irish dragoons, he came to the Ship Quay Gate. The council sent the Reverend Dr Walker to negotiate who suggested the wondrous expedient of lifting Murray over the walls in a basket. Even the meanest intelligence could appreciate that this was a device to separate Murray from his troops and Captain James Morison, the guard commander, personally took the decision to open the gate and admit Murray's entire party. He paraded through the streets giving assurances that he would uphold the Protestant interest and defend the city and asked his supporters to identify themselves by sporting a white band on their left arms.

Although Murray's presence gave new heart to the common people and soldiers it caused Lundy and the defeatists to hasten arrangements for submission, the council quickly producing an instrument of surrender, which all members signed. The council summoned Murray and suggested that he add his signature but he refused, causing Lundy to ask why he held such a low opinion of him. Murray replied that Lundy was either a fool or a knave. Again, Lundy asked why. Because, said Murray, Lundy had failed to defend the crossings at Lifford and Clady and the passes at Long Causeway and Carrigans when he had available between 10,000 and 12,000 men. Murray urged him to resume the field but he demurred because the men were demoralized and untrained. Murray was of the opposite opinion and refused to sign the surrender document. Confident that the bulk of the rank and file was strongly opposed to surrender he then went outside to explain to the public what had happened in the meeting, adding that he would be unable to hold Culmore Fort if Derry capitulated. During the evening, the town clerk, no doubt a supporter of Murray, released an account of the proceedings of the council of war on 16 April resulting in a heightening of tension, tempers and the propensity towards violence amongst the common soldiers, particularly against Lundy and members of the council.

Displaying some moral courage, Lundy and the councillors continued with their agreed policy and decided to send 20 men to carry the instrument of surrender to James. Before the meeting adjourned, Lundy asked for some non-conformist ministers to attend, who he hoped would feel able to advertise positively the council's proceedings and put a gloss on the strategy of surrender, but only one responded. Intending to intimidate the defeatists, Murray led a rabble of soldiers and townspeople to the main guard, seized the keys from Captain Wigston, and placed his own men on both the walls and gates. Frightened, Lundy withdrew to his lodgings which he ringed with regular soldiers from Mountjoy's regiment. In the evening, James withdrew his army to Saint Johnstown where he remained until 20 April. Many felt that nothing more could be achieved in Derry and, despite some personal risk because intolerance of deserters was increasing, left for Culmore to board the ships in the lough. Amongst them was the ailing Sir Arthur Rawdon although he had spoken out against the council's policy. It was not so easy for Lundy to escape. A new council was appointed which sent the Reverend George Walker and Major Henry Baker to ask Lundy to continue his government with the full support of the new council but he refused to have anything more to do with Derry. It was in the interest of neither the city nor the new council to sacrifice King William's commissioned representative to the mob so he was allowed adopt disguise, throw a load of match across his back, slip into a boat and row to the safety of Cornwall's vessels.[14]

Now that the Irish Army controlled the Laggan, reliable communication between Derry and Enniskillen became vital, especially if false information should be broadcast that either had fallen. Around the middle of April, news reached Enniskillen of the arrival in Lough Foyle of Captain Cornwall's convoy. Governor Hamilton dispatched Andrew Hamilton and Anthony Dobbin, a County Fermanagh JP, to seek a share of the supplies on board but, on discovering that Cunningham had landed nothing, made their way back towards Enniskillen. *En route* they were captured on 25 April by a quartermaster of Irish horse and taken to Richard Hamilton's main camp. Fortunately, James had just issued his conciliatory proclamation that all men should have liberty to return to their former dwellings and so Hamilton was able to secure a pass to travel to his house at Kilskeery, north-east of Enniskillen. Whilst in the camp, he succeeded in paying a messenger, identified with one of the previously arranged tokens, to go into Derry and inform Dr George Walker that he should disbelieve any report that Enniskillen had fallen unless signed by Governor Hamilton. Similarly, Enniskillen would believe nothing of Derry unless it bore Dr Walker's signature. This was timely because, although Derry had been under pressure for only a week, the Irish were indeed spreading rumours of its surrender.[15]

Whilst waiting for their passes to be completed, Hamilton and Dobbin encountered Lieutenant Colonel Sir Connell Ferrall, Lieutenant Colonel Thomas Nugent and his father, plus several others from County Longford. Andrew Hamilton owned some lands in County Longford and was well known to these gentlemen. Very civilly, they offered to help him in any way that they could. Whilst talking, they heard some shots from close by and spotted a soldier coming from the direction in which the firing had occurred. Ferrall asked him to account for the firing. He replied that some soldiers had captured an English or Scottish witch who was trying to cast spells upon the Irish horses. The soldiers had fired about 20 shots but had failed to kill her. Suspecting that the soldiers were simply torturing someone, Hamilton asked his acquaintances to intervene. They arrived to see a woman of about 70 years of age slumped on the ground, wounded, her left breast bare. At that moment, an Irish soldier walked up, held his gun against her exposed chest and shot her dead. Hamilton was disturbed and sought more information. Apparently, she was an old country woman from near Derry who had been robbed of all she possessed by Irish soldiers. Hearing that there were supplies of meal in the Irish camp and that the soldiers were 'civil', she had arrived early that morning. As she begged amongst the tents, a man had passed her carrying a bag of meal which promptly burst, some of it falling amongst horse dung. The man gathered up what he could and then the old woman had set about retrieving the remainder, separating the meal from the dung. On seeing this, an Irish soldier shouted out that she was gathering manure in order to bewitch the horses on behalf of the defenders of Derry. Soldiers then gathered and used her for target practice. So bad was their aim that they only succeeded in injuring her until she was dispatched by the final, close-range shot. This incident illustrates one of the reasons for the resistance of Derry. The country Protestants who had sought refuge in Derry knew that had they surrendered, accepted protections and repaired to their own dwellings, everything would have been plundered by the soldiers and half-pikes and they would have been at the mercy of the Irish. Already, the depredations of the raparees and the Irish soldiery had provided the Derry garrison with a high level of motivation.[16]

Despite protections taken from Richard Hamilton, the Protestants and law-abiding Roman Catholics of Counties Down and Antrim were molested and harassed by both raparees and Irish soldiers. Henry Hunter, a servant of Sir George Archison of County Armagh, had been made a captain by the local Protestant Association. Taken prisoner near Antrim in March during the chaotic days following the Break of Dromore, in mid-April he escaped and journeyed to the Ards Peninsula in County Down. Although the population mostly comprised Scottish Presbyterians, nearly everyone in this rich and agriculturally productive region had taken protections from Richard Hamilton and lived quietly and peacefully under the eye of Captain Conn Magennis's infantry company in Newtownards. Hunter, though, was a trouble-maker and demagogue who persuaded a 'great rabble' of the poorer people to follow him although 'the wiser sort dread[ed] the consequences of this wild uproar, after they had taken protection from the king'. Determined to manufacture an incident, around 13 or 14 April, 3 km from Newtownards, this aggressive mob assaulted Magennis's men, several of whom were killed, wounded and stripped and the remnants driven from the peninsula. In response, Lieutenant Colonel Mark Talbot left Carrickfergus with about 100 musketeers on 15 April, tramping through Belfast to reach Newtownards on the following day. Sensing that the disorder was probably over, but wary of the large number of Scots he saw 'rolling about', Talbot marched back towards Carrickfergus on 17 April.

The Hunterian virus, however, had already spread beyond the Ards Peninsula, across Strangford Lough to the mainland. Sir Robert Maxwell, then living at Killyleagh Castle, wrote to John Stuart, an apothecary in Downpatrick, enclosing a letter for Captain Patrick Savage of Lord Iveagh's regiment,[17] inviting him to bring his company to quarter in Killyleagh town to secure it from the rabble. Savage arrived and, finding a large and unruly mob, was afraid that his men might be surprised and overcome should they lodge in the open town of Killyleagh. He asked Maxwell if they might quarter in Killyleagh Castle. Maxwell's response was unexpectedly chilly and, during the next two days, he prevaricated whilst sending one Gavin Irwin to find Hunter and bring him to Killyleagh. Clearly, Maxwell had enticed Savage into a trap. Hunter arrived and, at the head of the local rabble, seized Savage and his lieutenant in their billets before falling on the guard, killing three men and wounding six or seven. Savage complained loudly that he had been betrayed by Maxwell. Because he objected strongly to Maxwell and Hunter's dishonesty and bullying, the Reverend Clulow, the Church of Ireland minister in Killyleagh, took Savage into his house where, although still a prisoner, he enjoyed a degree of protection. Iveagh, who was marching towards Downpatrick with elements of his regiment 'newly raised in the upper part of the County of Down (of mere wild Irish)', wrote to Maxwell asking for the safe return of Savage and his lieutenant. Hunter made an uncouth reply on Maxwell's behalf: he would fight Iveagh. Promptly, he gathered all the local people who would follow him, extracted the Protestant soldiers from Savage's company and marched out to do battle. Outnumbered, Iveagh retired to Clough Bridge, south-west of Downpatrick, where he tried to make a stand but Hunter pressed on, forced the position and drove Iveagh's raw recruits southwards along the beach at Dundrum into the Mountains of Mourne.[18]

Hunter returned to Downpatrick in triumph and appointed himself the local satrap governing the region in an arbitrary and ruthless manner, treating the leading Protestants as severely as the native Irish: if a deeper purpose justified Hunter's rebellion it may have been to express the discontent of the poorer Protestants against larger landowners. When news of this humiliation reached James before Derry, characteristically he ordered Iveagh's regiment to be disbanded;[19] in Dublin, Tyrconnell reacted in a more positive manner. Determined that a local incident should not be allowed to ferment into a wider Protestant rising, he ordered Major General Thomas Buchan of Auchmacoy to end the nonsense.[20] Buchan, an Aberdeenshire Catholic convert and a highly experienced soldier who had seen much active service with the French and Dutch armies, gathered troops from the garrisons of Carrickfergus, Antrim and Lisburn: the infantry battalions of Tyrconnell and Cormack O'Neill, the latter with its attendant troop of dragoons; a troop from Lord Galmoy's cavalry regiment; and Captain Charles Fitzgerald's dragoon troop. Assembling the horsemen into an advance party, Buchan pushed ahead leaving the infantry to make its best speed. The response was remarkable, the foot marching 'sixteen long Irish miles' from Lisburn to Killyleagh on 30 April to join the horsemen within 3 km of the enemy at 17:00. Estimates of the size of Hunter's force vary between 400 and 3,000, a difference probably explained by the fact that many of his followers did not join his 'army' facing Buchan but watched from the surrounding hills and waited to see what happened. Following James's instructions to try to end the rebellion without further bloodshed, Buchan advanced within sight of his opponents and sent a trumpeter to seek a meeting with Hunter. Evidently not understanding the conventions of war, Hunter's men fired on the trumpeter so Buchan immediately attacked and routed them. During the action and pursuit, about 60 of Hunter's followers were killed. The Protestants claimed that, during the following days,

Buchan butchered between 500 and 600 people but a Catholic source denies this saying that Buchan gave quarter to the Protestant garrison of Killyleagh Castle and kept his men on a very tight rein. His infantry, despite their long march and evening battle on 30 April, was not allowed to billet in Killyleagh on the night of 30 April–1 May but made to camp on neighbouring hills. On the morning of 1 May, Buchan marched north to Newtownards, a thoroughly Protestant town owned by Sir Robert Colvill. Again, not allowing his soldiers into the town for fear of what they might do to the Protestants, Buchan entered accompanied by a few of his officers. Not a single Protestant, says the Catholic source, was harmed. Buchan then released all his prisoners on oath not to bear arms again against King James. The infantry was ordered back to garrison while Buchan took the mounted troops on a pacification sweep south through the Ards Peninsula to Portaferry. Having settled the area, Buchan returned his cavalry and dragoons to their garrisons; as they crossed Belfast Bridge, the troopers were searched by their officers to make sure that they carried no plunder.[21] According to Roman Catholic sources, Buchan's careful and cautious conduct was a model repacification.

A different story can be constructed from Protestant accounts. In return for Richard Hamilton's protections, the Protestants of every parish in County Down and the Ards Peninsula had to gather quantities of oatmeal and grain and deliver them to the garrisons in Carrickfergus and Charlemont: 'contributions', in all but name.[22] No sooner had the supplies been delivered than Lord Iveagh's newly raised regiment entered and plundered the Ards Peninsula violating the protections. Henry Hunter, one of seven Protestant captains who had been disarmed near Antrim in March, was in County Down when he heard of the outrages committed by Iveagh's soldiers. Arguing that it was legal to kill anyone who continued to rob and plunder after a protection had been granted, he persuaded the local people to make a stand against the 'common plunderers'. Within a few days, Hunter had gathered 3,000 'poor, oppressed Protestants', determined to defend their region until the mythical relief army appeared from England. Hunter commandeered Sir Robert Maxwell's house at Killyleagh for his headquarters, no doubt with the owner's permission, adding some martial dignity by mounting at its entrance an ancient, iron cannon that had lain for some years rusting in Downpatrick. When news of these events reached James he ordered Lord Galmoy's cavalry, the Royal Regiment of Foot, and the infantry battalions of Sir Maurice Eustace and of John Bellew, First Baron Duleek, all encamped before Derry, to join with infantry billeted in Belfast, Carrickfergus, Antrim and Lisburn. Major General Buchan and Lieutenant Colonel Mark Talbot were placed in command. Buchan moved rapidly, cut Hunter's communications and fell upon his force on 28 April at Conlig, midway between Bangor and Newtownards. In the ensuing rout and pursuit, about 300 of Hunter's followers were killed and many wounded and taken prisoner. Hunter escaped in a small boat to the Isle of Man. The Irish Army lost Cornet Lock, a Protestant, supposedly shot in the back by his own men. Following the collapse of the rebellion, Iveagh's regiment returned and continued its regime of plunder, turning many Protestants out of their homes. Lord Bellew's foot chased these refugees to Donaghadee and even forced some into the sea. One Agnew, whose small, four-gun ship was anchored off Donaghadee, saw what was happening and fired two cannon at the Irish. They drew back and Agnew took 68 unfortunates on board. He landed them in Scotland, charging not one penny for the passage.[23]

Although the same episode is recognizable in both accounts, there are numerous contradictions in detail, causation, chronology and place. Charles Leslie places the final battle near Killyleagh on 30 April: the Protestant source says that the action occurred two days earlier at Conlig, 20 km further north. Leslie describes a peaceful region disturbed by Hunter and his accomplices, whereas the Protestant source places the blame firmly on plundering Irish soldiery and interprets Hunter's rebellion as a legitimate and aggrieved reaction to the breaking of the protections. After the battle, Leslie has the Irish Army quietly pacifying the region: the Protestant source describes a resumption of plundering ending with Protestant refugees physically driven into the Irish Sea. There are also differences in mood and expression. Leslie fails to explain either why Hunter began his movement or how he acquired substantial support so rapidly, and places the blame, as he does throughout his book, on raparees beyond the control of the Irish Army. Some details about the Irish Army presented in the Protestant source are wrong: Eustace and Bellew commanded infantry regiments not cavalry and dragoons respectively. Leslie's moderate tone and language are more persuasive making his narrative appear even-handed and believable: the Protestant source is more hectic in expression and pace, resembling an anti-Catholic tract. These differences prevent the historian from either determining the course of events in eastern County Down or explaining its precise cause. The Ards Rebellion presents in microcosm the problems of having to rely upon partisan sources to reconstruct the history of a civil war.

6

The defence of Derry and Enniskillen

In County Kerry there were not twenty Englishmen remaining and none of them had more than 6*d.* to his name. Stocks of food had been destroyed and famine threatened.[1] By the time that Captain Cornwall's squadron dropped down Lough Foyle from Redcastle to Greencastle on 18 April, sailing for England on the following day, the English military presence in Ireland had been whittled down to the defence of Derry and Enniskillen. Cornwall carried so many aristocrats and gentry that the Protestant hierarchy was seriously eroded obliging Derry's defenders to seek leaders amongst the middling tiers of society. Many in England thought the situation both 'sad' and unnecessary: a little timely help might have prevented the string of disasters. Adam Murray, the new hero, was the popular candidate for the vacant governorship but he demurred. Instead, on 19 April the remodelled council offered the position to Major Henry Baker of Dunmahon, County Louth. Formerly a lieutenant in the Irish Army under Charles II, Baker had been dismissed by Tyrconnell in 1686 and had proved himself subsequently in the major engagements of the Protestant Association. Following an acceptance speech he asked the council to employ the Reverend Dr George Walker as joint-governor with specific responsibility for the stores, a key office during a siege.[2]

Baker's first task was to organize and discipline his citizen soldiers so that they could work effectively alongside the regulars from Mountjoy's battalion. Walker depicts a smooth and well-ordered process whereby he and Baker selected regimental colonels before dividing the men evenly between seven regiments of infantry and one of cavalry, the latter under Adam Murray. John Mackenzie's *Narrative* describes a less formal procedure. After appointing the colonels, the council allowed the men to decide on their own company and troop captains who then chose the regiment in which they were prepared to serve; that the regiments contained between 12 and 25 companies supports this version of a popular, decentralized regimentation. Some regiments were formed around the core of old Protestant Association units, others were new constructions. Each company contained 60 men, making a total of 7,020 soldiers commanded by 341 officers.

Around this time, about 1,000 old people, women and children departed to accept Jacobite protections, prelude to a persistent, daily trickle of escapees. At the beginning of the blockade Derry was packed with so many refugees huddling in cellars, doorways, porches, churches and makeshift shelters that it was impossible to calculate the total military and civilian population: estimates varied between 19,000 and 36,500. Few, however, displayed much useful military experience or knowledge and there was a dearth of engineers and gunners. Beneath the tensions – 'covetousness, ambition and factions' split the city – developed an awareness that survival lay through co-operation. Religion played a vital, sustaining role in justifying resistance, raising spirits and reinforcing common purpose. In rotation, 18 Church of Ireland ministers conducted daily prayers and preached sermons while seven non-conformist ministers were 'equally careful of their people'. Governor Walker asked the Reverend John Mackenzie to serve as chaplain to his regiment, the majority of the officers and soldiers being Presbyterian. He discovered that non-conformist chaplains received neither pay nor additional allowances from the public stores as recompense for these additional duties, unlike their Episcopalian colleagues who received both extra food and a weekly wage of one shilling and sixpence. To add insult to injury, the stocks of provisions held by several non-conformist ministers were confiscated and moved into the central warehouse.

Carrying a satchel containing royal protections and full pardons, Claude Hamilton, First Earl of Abercorn, rode up to the walls on 20 April to discuss terms of surrender. Murray, who went out to talk with him, was offered a colonel's commission in James's army and a gratuity of £1,000. Whilst they were in conversation the garrison noticed the Irish moving cannon into firing positions, chicanery that confirmed the wisdom of resistance. Abercorn was asked to leave immediately and Mr Bennet was dispatched to England to broadcast Derry's resolution to defend itself. To create verisimilitude, the garrison fired at the departing Bennet to give the impression that he was a deserter. The Jacobites disposed three infantry battalions and nine squadrons of mounted troops at Saint Johnstown and a further four battalions within 3 km of Derry, led by Brigadier Robert Ramsay. Brigadier John Wauchope commanded on the east bank of the Foyle with two battalions, some cavalry and a few light field guns. Later that day, a detachment of Irish horse and foot marched past Culmore Fort into the Inishowen Peninsula where they robbed many Protestant refugees awaiting passage to Scotland. Two battalions moved towards Penny Burn (sometimes Penny Brook) Mill (sometimes Mills), about 2 km to the north, and camped across the direct road between Derry and Culmore Fort. These developments precipitated the surrender of Culmore, whose guns controlled the sea passage to Derry by commanding the narrows where the River Foyle debouched into the lough. The garrison of 300 men under Captain Jemmet was already demoralized because there was little ammunition, eight of the cannon had been sent into Derry and, as he was making his escape, Lundy had sent a message into Culmore that Derry had already surrendered. The severing of communications with

Derry was sufficient to persuade Jemmet to surrender on terms that permitted the garrison to depart for England. The Catholic commentator, Charles Leslie, said that the articles of capitulation were faithfully observed and the garrison was 'used with civility and humanity'. Protestant sources disagreed. According to the surrender, the soldiers had to forfeit their firearms but were allowed to keep swords and baggage. On the march through Coleraine, Ballymena and Antrim, they were robbed by the 'rabble' of their swords and possessions because Lieutenant General Richard Hamilton failed to provide an escort. Following the fall of Culmore, which Hamilton garrisoned with 100 men, about 7,000 troops were positioned in an arc from Saint Johnstown to Culmore, the headquarters situated at Brook Hall. The infantry was encamped closest to Derry whilst the cavalry and dragoons were mostly around Saint Johnstown and Carrigans. A further 3,000 were camped on the east bank of the river, supporting a battery that was being raised in Strong's Orchard to the north-east of the city, opposite the end of Ship Quay Street. By 23 April, this battery mounted seven medium cannon which subjected the city to a low-level bombardment. Several people were subsequently injured, walls and garrets battered and it became unsafe to live upstairs. A wooden 'blind' or barrier was erected across Ship Quay Street 'to preserve the people' whilst the cannon on the walls attempted counter-battery fire. 'An experienced old soldier' advised Baker to have the paving slabs lifted to reduce the hazard from splinters when the Irish started to fire explosive mortar rounds. All the timber salvaged from demolished buildings outside the walls was distributed along the ramparts so that it could be hurled at attackers in the event of an assault. An outpost of 60 musketeers occupied Windmill Hill.

On 21 April a demi-culverin (twelve-pounder) in Strong's Orchard fired over 40 rounds across the river, a distance of around 1,000 m, damaging the market house on the Diamond and killing one man. Adam Murray, now officially designated the 'commander of sallies', viewed the Irish presence at Penny Burn Mill as a serious impedance to the defenders' operational freedom and resolved to attack. According to Walker, no friend of Murray, the sally of 21 April was disorganized. Murray ventured out with 'as many as pleased, and what officers were at leisure, not in any commendable order, yet they killed above 200 of the enemy's soldiers'. A detachment of Irish cavalry counter-attacked furiously forcing them to retire. Murray, commanding 50 horsemen, was pressed back to the city gates and Walker found it necessary to mount a horse, rally the cavalrymen and rescue Murray who was surrounded by the Irish 'and with great courage laying about him'. The Derrymen lost four privates and Lieutenant MacPhedris killed. Murray's admirer and fellow Presbyterian, Mackenzie, witnessed a better-organized operation. Three hundred horsemen were divided into a vanguard under Major Nathaniel Bull, a main body commanded by Murray and a rearguard directed by Captain Cochran. They were accompanied by four companies of infantry, about 240 men, whilst Lieutenant Colonel John Cairns stood upon an adjacent hill with an infantry reserve. Irish sentries sounded the alarm and two battalions of foot and two detachments of horse formed up outside the Penny Burn Mill camp and prepared to give battle. Murray charged one section of the Irish horse and broke through but Bull's vanguard fled before coming into action whilst Captain Cochran, bringing up the rear, led a few men forward until his horse was shot. During this charge, Murray is supposed to have struck down, with his own hand, Lieutenant General Maumont. The infantry exchanged fire with the Irish but, seeing most of their own horsemen racing back to Derry pursued by Irish cavalry and only a few troopers keeping company with Murray, they moved towards the riverside and lined some hedges and ditches to flank the victorious Irish horse as it returned along the beach on blown mounts. Thomas Ash merely notes that there was a 'hot skirmish ... our men were compelled to retreat; for this the cavalry were blamed'.[3]

However, there is a fourth description, sober, impersonal and altogether more credible containing neither Walkerian heroics nor Murray fighting the whole Jacobite Army single-handed. During the night of 20–21 April, Murray ordered 500 musketeers to leave the city in batches to take up positions in the hedges and ditches between the city and Penny Burn Mill. Murray and Captain Nathaniel Bull then marched out with two parties of horse. Irish sentries sounded the alarm and a detachment of Irish cavalry advanced towards Murray's vanguard. Realizing that he was substantially outnumbered, Murray halted and sent orders back into Derry for a further 500 musketeers to march out and assume a supporting position on adjacent higher ground. As the two battalions of Irish infantry at Penny Burn Mill drew out in battle formation, the Irish cavalry advanced along the beach and charged Murray's horsemen, receiving 'some prejudice' from the musketeers previously concealed in the ditches and hedges. Despite this harassing fire, the attack was pressed home and most of the Derry troopers broke at the first caracole and raced for the city leaving Murray, Bull and a few braver souls isolated. Murray and Bull promptly turned and counter-charged through the Irish cavalry to reach safety. Some 15 Irish cavalrymen chased the Derry horse, slashing and 'pistolling', to within carbine shot of the Butchers' Gate but, as they retired, 13 fell to the musketeers lining the hedges and ditches along the Culmore road. Receiving notice that Lord Galmoy's regiment of cavalry and Sir Maurice Eustace's battalion of foot were marching with the intention of cutting them off from the city, the musketeers in the hedges and ditches and their supports disengaged and made their way back into the town. Covered by the cannon on the ramparts which deterred Galmoy's and Eustace's leading elements, this was successfully accomplished for the loss of seven men and one lieutenant. Lieutenant General Maumont was amongst the Irish dead along with nine other officers and 60 men. Murray, it was said, had designed the operation to 'blood' his soldiers but he was also trying to re-open a route to Culmore Fort.

From the Jacobite perspective, the action resembled that described in the fourth Derry account. Colonel John Hamilton, on Ramsay's orders, marched with 200 infantry to take possession of Penny Burn Mill. Observing this small party pass within sight of Derry, the garrison sallied with 1,500 foot and 300 horse. Hamilton took up defensive positions, lining some hedges and occupying the houses in Penny Burn and sent a messenger to Ramsay asking for immediate assistance. Most of the Jacobite cavalry was out foraging and the only mounted troops immediately available was the standing guard of 40 troopers and 40 dragoons who rode for Penny Burn as quickly as possible under the command of the Duke of Berwick. They arrived to find the Derry infantry facing the Jacobite foot and their cavalry drawn up on the right of their line towards the river. Berwick formed his 80 troopers into two squadrons and charged the Derry cavalry, which broke and was pursued along the beach until close to the town. Seeing their cavalry worsted, the Derry infantry withdrew back into the town without molestation. In addition to six or seven dragoons killed, nearly all the Jacobite horsemen involved were either wounded or lost their mounts. The garrison of Penny Burn Mill was increased to 500 infantry.[4]

An immediate consequence of the loss of Culmore Fort and the failure to remove the Jacobite blocking force at Penny Burn Mill was the denial of adequate grazing beyond the walls for the garrison's horses. Most were set free and six of the eight troops in Murray's cavalry regiment were relegated to infantry; for the time being only Murray's own and Nathaniel Bull's troops remained mounted. A survey of the provisions and available fighting men by the city authorities revealed enough food in store to maintain 12,000 men for between ten and twelve weeks although stocks would become more elastic when the garrison began to diminish through disease, injury, desertion and battle casualties. Civilians would have to fend for themselves. Opportunities occasionally arose to acquire additional supplies. Around 22 April reports were received of 60 tuns of salmon in a nearby warehouse owned by Lord Massarene and 20 barrels were secured. Conversely, a hay stack within 400 m of the city was ignored 'although it might easily have been brought in'.[5]

On 25 April Murray led a sally, comprising mostly infantry plus the few remaining cavalry, to press back some Irish troops who were using the ditches to approach unhealthily close to the walls. Having achieved their objective, some of the foot soldiers pushed on too far and were surprised by a detachment of Jacobite horse that appeared from behind a hill, forcing them to retire on their supports. The reunited infantry then lined a ditch along the road and by weight of fire forced the Irish cavalry to withdraw. They pursued as far as Penny Burn Mill putting the Irish troopers under such pressure that their supporting dragoons had to dismount and sustain them. Thus far Murray had suffered no casualties and remained at Penny Burn Mill until evening when he began to withdraw. Guards lining the ramparts of Derry spotted a detachment of Irish cavalry, each trooper carrying a musketeer behind the saddle, advancing to interfere with Murray's retreat; a party of foot under Major Parker left the city to cover the withdrawal. Although he successfully kept the Irish at bay whilst Murray withdrew into Derry, Parker was slow and negligent in bringing his own soldiers from the field, exposing them to unnecessary risk and danger. For this incompetence he was threatened with a court-martial but he slipped away during the night and deserted to the Jacobites. Irish casualties were light, although Major General Pusignan received a wound which proved mortal, but the defenders lost Cornet Brown and three others killed and eight or ten wounded.[6]

Following the successful sallies on 21 and 25 April, Baker, Walker and Murray were satisfied that Derry could be defended with the troops and resources at its disposal so they set about organizing the defence in a more professional manner. All the houses and buildings 'clear round the town' were burned and the rubbish heaps and ditches levelled 'so that the enemy might not skulk in them and gall the men on the walls'. This included the fruit trees of Alderman Tompkin's orchard. Eight cannon had been brought up from Culmore Fort and two were mounted on the church roof commanding a wide field of fire as far as the Irish battery in Strong's orchard. The enceinte was divided into eight equal sectors and a garrison regiment permanently assigned to each so that the men became familiar with their segment of the ramparts, outworks and external topography. Each regiment was billeted adjacent to its station and two stood guard every night. On an alarm, regiments would automatically man their sections of the ramparts and await orders. All regimental drummers were billeted in the same lodging to enable them to receive instructions simultaneously before proceeding directly to their regiment's headquarters to beat the orders 'without the least disorder or confusion'. Regimental adjutants were likewise housed in one location. Tippling and drinking were forbidden after 20:00 as was the lighting of candles so as not to attract enemy fire. A weekly ration comprised one and a half pounds of salmon, two pounds of beef, and four quarts of oatmeal. Innkeepers were not allowed to charge more than one penny per quart for beer because the soldiers were unpaid. To lessen the dangers from fire and treachery, the ammunition was shifted from the grand store to four separate magazines. Keys to the four gates were held at the main guard and were not to be delivered to anyone beneath the rank of captain. Two captains were to attend at each gate every night. To reduce the risk of soldiers breaking into vacated shops and cellars, the goods of merchants who had left Derry were brought into the common stores and inventories taken. Finally, in order to conserve ammunition, no soldier was allowed to discharge his firearm unnecessarily. On 27 April, Lieutenant Colonel

Whitney sold some stolen horses to a Captain Darcy. He was court-martialled, found guilty of horse stealing and imprisoned resulting in a re-structuring of the command hierarchy. In addition to the eight incorporated regiments, there were about 5,000 non-regimented volunteers who performed useful service, in particular, Captain Joseph Johnston, 'who was very careful to have good patrols kept', Mr David Kennedy and Captain William Crooks, who was later mortally wounded in the leg by bomb shrapnel.[7]

By 25 April the Irish had placed mortars in Strong's Orchard and opened fire but the 18 light bombs fell mainly in the open streets and did little damage although one fell on Mr Long's house killing Mrs Susannah Holding, a gentlewoman of 80 years of age, who lived in the garret. Presently, larger bombs were thrown. The first pierced the roof of a house, passed through a bed and the floor of an upper room in which several officers were dining, before exploding on the lower storey. The landlord was killed and one side of the house blown out. As Walker laconically remarked, the dining officers were able to leave the house through the breach 'instead of the doors' which the explosion had blocked.[8] Of more concern was the general feeling of abandonment. Colonels Cunningham, Richards and Lundy would, it was feared, have already spread pessimistic predictions about the likely fate of Derry sufficient to discourage relief attempts. In addition, Culmore Fort had been lost and it would be extremely difficult for assistance to reach the city by sea. A council of war decided to send a messenger through the Irish lines to take ship for England from the nearest open port. A volunteer was found and, again, as he left the town some of the Windmill Hill garrison fired at him to make it look as though he was a common deserter. He reached England via Scotland and presented an account of the situation. Further to foster good will and harmony, Governor Baker ordered that, on Sundays, followers of the Church of Ireland and non-conformists should enjoy equal access to the cathedral.

Between 25 April and 12 May the situation in and around Derry was quiet. Short of necessities and awaiting resupply from Dublin, the Irish had concluded that a blockade, rather than a close siege, would produce the desired results because the defenders wanted competent commanders, provisions and fresh water. Their camp was shifted slightly closer and the ditches from which the Derry musketeers had been such a nuisance during the actions on 21 and 25 April were levelled. Determined to conduct an active defence, Governor Baker and Colonel Murray constantly harried the besiegers with small patrols that rarely returned without inflicting damage. A few Irish who infiltrated through Alderman Tompkin's orchard into the meadows and parks around the city to seize the garrison's horses were killed by the defenders. Colonel Ramsay led a detachment of Irish to secure a small rivulet, from which they mistakenly thought that the town drew its supply of fresh water, but was beaten off.

On 28 April, a sally towards Penny Burn Mill killed several Irish but was forced to withdraw when pressed on all sides by cavalry: two defenders were sacrificed and some eight to ten wounded.[9] Late in April, Governors Baker and Walker again examined the stores and decided to move everything into a central warehouse, which was carefully supervised throughout the remainder of the siege by the brothers Joseph and Samuel Harvey. Cellars were scoured for foodstuffs which were confiscated and transferred to the central storehouse, a fruitful exercise because many gentlemen and wealthier burghers had amassed considerable reserves. Fearing that potential traitors might use basements adjacent to the walls to 'start' mines, Governor Baker and William Mackie, 'one of the citizens who was very active and industrious for the defence of the town', made a thorough search but found nothing.[10]

On 24 April, shortly after reinforcement by the majority of Lord Kingston's men,[11] Enniskillen received information that the Irish garrison in Omagh had occupied Trillick, 15 km north along the Derry road. Governor Hamilton and his advisers believed 'they would be but unneighbourly guests' and decided to uproot them 'to prevent their settling there'. Commanded by Lieutenant Colonel Thomas Lloyd, the Enniskilleners marched at night, arriving before Trillick very early in the morning only to notice, in the distance, an Irish detachment marching towards them. Lloyd, a thrusting, energetic, aggressive and driving commander, dismounted and led on foot 'through the bogs and mountains, the nearest way he could'. Observing these offensive movements, the Irish began to withdraw, abandoning their cattle and baggage, but Lieutenant William McCarmick went forward with 100 musketeers to pin them and gain enough time for Lloyd to bring up the main body. However, the countryside was so saturated that the cavalry could only move on the roads and neither Lloyd nor McCarmick was able to approach sufficiently close to engage.

After a chase lasting six hours, the Irish force broke up 'every man shifting the best way he could for himself'. Lloyd's men then scoured the area, collecting a considerable amount of booty that was divided between them. In the aftermath of this victory the governor, officers and private soldiers all swore an oath to defend Enniskillen and the Protestant religion. To confirm their defiance, Governor Hamilton ordered the building of a strong fort on the 'common hill' towards the eastern end of the town, which was later completed at his own expense. It was a regular, polygonal earthwork, designed and laid out by Majors Hart and Rider, 'both good mathematicians', with the latter responsible for construction. Work was finished during June, complete with a communication trench back to the East Bridge. It commanded the whole town and 'clears the roads leading to it on that end'.[12]

News then arrived on 27 April that the Irish had established a garrison at Augher Castle, about 29 km from Enniskillen on the road to Charlemont. Augher

Castle's defences were fairly strong, comprising a substantial bawn wall and flankers at the angles. Lloyd journeyed overnight and came to Augher early on the morning of Sunday 28 April. Despite the 'private' march, the Irish garrison had learned of Lloyd's approach and departed, taking what they could with them. Lloyd razed the castle to the ground, levelled the fortifications, and seized as many cattle and sheep as possible. He marched south on Monday 29 April, through the Slieve Beagh to Clones with the intention of saving from plunder and destruction the home of Daniel Eccles, 'the gentleman that first gave us notice of the two companies' approach to Enniskillen'. Lloyd also wished to garrison the house as a trip-wire position. He moved to within 3 km of Clones during the night of 29–30 April before allowing his weary men to rest for three or four hours, 'being toiled with our long march and the bogginess of the mountains', intending to attack at daybreak. He was too late: the Clones garrison, having received notice of Lloyd's approach from the country people, had burned Eccles's house to the ground and fled. Lloyd pursued eastwards into County Monaghan but could not overtake. Instead, he gathered supplies from County Monaghan and part of County Cavan before returning to Enniskillen on 2 May loaded with meal, malt, wheat, oats, butter, bed clothes and a huge 'prey' of sheep and cattle. Provisions were never short in Enniskillen because it was not besieged but Lloyd's raid created such a temporary abundance that a good milk cow could be purchased from the soldiers for as little as one shilling and four pence.[13]

A Jacobite appreciation argued that Enniskillen's strength lay in its location between Upper and Lower Lough Erne and propinquity to Derry. Lacking artificial fortifications, Enniskillen could resist only as long as Derry survived and it was just a matter of time before the latter succumbed. Jacobite confidence waxed, many thinking the war virtually over, and landowners anticipated reclaiming their forfeited estates.[14] Such optimism was further encouraged by the Battle of Bantry Bay. Having landed James II and his entourage at Kinsale, Jean de Gabaret took the French fleet back to Brest to embark weapons, ammunition, money, Jacobite soldiers who had found their way to France and some French officers. For political reasons, the professional seaman, Gabaret, was replaced by Admiral François de Châteaurenault, who had never before held a senior naval command. With 24 warships, Châteaurenault was off Kinsale on 29 April when five English men-of-war were sighted. The wind was blowing from the wrong direction for making Kinsale in the face of hostile forces, so Châteaurenault set course for Bantry Bay, 64 km to the west. Admiral Arthur Herbert had been cruising off the Irish coast during early April and had then put into Milford Haven for a partial refit. Although England was not yet at war with France – a formal declaration did not occur until 7 May – a *de facto* state of hostilities already existed because France was an active auxiliary in Ireland. Herbert had intended to sail from Milford Haven to Brest, having received intelligence that the French fleet was about to put to sea, but the wind was easterly so he made for Kinsale, which he knew to be Châteaurenault's intended destination. When his scouts sighted Châteaurenault on 29 April, Herbert's main objective was to prevent him from making Kinsale. This was achieved but at the cost of losing contact. In vain Herbert looked into Baltimore Bay before, on the evening of 30 April, discovering Châteaurenault in Bantry Bay where he had been there since morning and had already disembarked the stores and 3,000 soldiers. Despite commanding the smaller fleet – 18 ships of the line, a frigate and three fire-ships – Herbert entered Bantry Bay on the morning of 1 May: Châteaurenault's vessels raised their anchors, got under way and engaged. French fire forced the English to withdraw westwards, closely pressed. The battle continued from 11:00 to 17:00, by which time the fleets were 32 km out to sea. Fearing that Herbert was deliberately drawing him away from his unprotected transports and cargo ships in Bantry Bay, Châteaurenault broke off the action and put back whilst Herbert made for the Scilly Isles. No ships were sunk, although Herbert's vessels suffered considerable damage to their sails and rigging and lost 96 killed and about 250 wounded. French casualties were 40 killed and 93 wounded.

Both sides claimed victory but the French had greater justification: Châteaurenault had landed his men and stores, fought off the English fleet without losing a vessel and returned safely to Brest. Herbert had neither intercepted nor interrupted the disembarkation. More important, he had failed to dominate the sea communications between France and Ireland and had only succeeded in demonstrating that the French Navy was at least his equal, if not superior, in the Western Approaches. When news of Bantry Bay reached James in Dublin, even though he ordered a *Te Deum* to be sung, the bells of Dublin to ring and bonfires to be lit in the streets, he was deeply saddened: his old command and first love, the Royal Navy, had been beaten even though that defeat improved his chances of regaining the throne of Ireland. The real problem, though, was that Châteaurenault was not prepared to remain in Irish waters to exploit his success. James wanted him to sail north to transport heavy siege cannon to Richard Hamilton at Derry and discourage any Williamite relief expedition. He also wished Châteaurenault to sweep St George's Channel clear of the Royal Navy preparatory to convoying 10,000 Irish troops into Scotland. D'Avaux said that Châteaurenault had orders from Versailles simply to land troops, money and arms in Ireland and then return to Brest. Still James persisted, asking Châteaurenault to convoy troops to Anglesey but, by then, the French admiral had departed for France. Three troops of Colonel Nicholas Purcell's dragoons were convoyed by three French frigates from Carrickfergus to Scotland where they joined army of John Claverhouse, First Viscount Dundee, just before the Battle of Killiecrankie, in which they performed good service. This was the sole strategic benefit to accrue from Bantry Bay, apart from limited quantities of materiel, but Châteaurenault's decision to obey his orders rather than sail for the north coast of Ireland was probably wise if frustratingly cautious; lacking a local dockyard, he could not have operated for long in Irish waters.[15]

A vicious war of 'posts and ambuscades' continued around Enniskillen. Two men from the Irish garrison of Omagh entered Kilskeery parish on 1 May and, during the night, stole between 20 and 30 cows. Next morning (2 May) the owners noticed tracks leading northwards and asked some of their neighbours to help recover the livestock. Eight men, riding poor horses and lightly armed, overtook the raiders within a few kilometres of Omagh, the thieves promptly abandoning their prey to the Enniskilleners who turned for Kilskeery. About halfway home they were overtaken by 24 well-mounted Irish dragoons. Three rode off into a great bog whilst the remaining five, thinking that recovering their own property was not a crime, surrendered and were granted quarter. Leaving a guard with the five men, the remainder of the Irish dragoons pursued the other three into the bog but they had a good start and escaped over the hills. On the return of the pursuing dragoons the party marched towards Omagh. At some point the dragoons murdered the five Protestants, cutting off their heads and mutilating their faces and bodies so severely that, when discovered, their acquaintances could scarcely recognize them.[16]

Following the rebuff given to Lord Galmoy on 24 March, James attempted to bring more concerted pressure to bear on Enniskillen by ordering Patrick Sarsfield to seize Sligo. Since Lord Kingston's departure, Sligo had been ungarrisoned and Sarsfield entered unopposed on 1 May to be greeted by one-eyed Terence 'Blind' MacDonogh, leader of a detachment of local irregulars whose tiny force had been unable to make any impact on the Protestant defensive line along the Erne. Sarsfield's arrival presented new opportunities. Theoretically, Enniskillen and its hinterland were now threatened on three sides: Sarsfield at Sligo menaced Ballyshannon; the army before Derry hovered on the northern flank; and forces were gathering in Cavan. Even though his information was out of date, Enniskillen patrols having prevented his scouts from approaching the town, MacDonogh advised Sarsfield that Ballyshannon was an easy target. Leaving a garrison in Sligo, Sarsfield marched via the coast road through Bundoran to appear before Ballyshannon on 4 May but scouts had already reported his movements to Governor Henry Folliott. Sarsfield tried to block all the roads leading out of Ballyshannon but was unable to intercept Folliott's messengers who informed Governor Hamilton that a considerable force of infantry and cavalry had advanced out of Connaught and summoned both the town and castle to surrender. Speedy relief and reinforcement were requested. Hamilton sought to form an expeditionary force by ordering all the garrisons under his command to send as many men as they could spare. Troops hurried into Enniskillen on 5 and 6 May, finally amounting to 12 companies of infantry and a few troops of cavalry, before leaving for Ballyshannon under Thomas Lloyd early on the morning of 7 May by the road along the south shore of Lower Lough Erne.

MacDonogh's intelligence was erroneous: Ballyshannon was strong. The castle was protected by two thick outer walls ringed by a wet moat, 3 m deep, within which was an inner keep surrounded by a broad ditch. Additional earthworks had been thrown up and a drawbridge guarded the single entrance. The church had been converted into a secondary strongpoint, circled by a strong wall, whilst the Erne Bridge was covered by a tower and gateway. Sarsfield had committed his forces to a major operation upon MacDonogh's vague ramblings and taken with him only two small field guns for use against shipping on the Erne rather than the walls of Ballyshannon. Folliott refused Sarsfield's summons to surrender, fairly confident that reinforcements were on their way from Enniskillen and certain, from the information provided by his scouts, that Sarsfield lacked the equipment to conduct a siege.

Sarsfield blockaded Ballyshannon but had to detach troops to protect his eastern flank against 400 well-equipped men based in Castle Caldwell, led by the owner, the eponymous Sir James. Caldwell's soldiers guarded the northern exits of all the fords on the River Erne between Ballyshannon and Lough Erne, the more likely crossings protected by earthworks. About 8 km to the east of Ballyshannon, straddling the river, stood Belleek, where a broken bridge carried the Enniskillen road over the Erne. Belleek, whose northern segment was occupied by Caldwell's soldiers, was almost encircled by marsh and water. Sarsfield split his forces, leaving most of his infantry to watch Ballyshannon and sending nearly all his cavalry and dragoons, plus the remainder of the foot, to Belleek. 'Blind' MacDonogh was exiled to Fish Island in the Erne estuary, along with the two field guns and 60 infantry, to interrupt shipping on the river and, occasionally, fire into Ballyshannon to remind the inhabitants that they were, technically, besieged.

South from Belleek stretched an extensive bog through which the road to the Erne bridge ran along a causeway parallel to the river bank. Sarsfield's troops barricaded the road and broke down a bridge across a small stream that flowed from the bog into the Erne just in advance of their position. Dismounted dragoons and infantry manned the barricade while the cavalry, a mixture of regulars and MacDonogh's volunteers, stood on higher ground to the rear. Arriving late in the afternoon of 7 May, reconnaissance reports suggested three possible courses of action to Lloyd: file along the causeway, exposing his men to Irish musketry; a frontal assault across the quagmire; or move to the left, try to find the edge of the bog and turn the Irish right flank. The first was most unattractive whilst the third would take time although he dispatched an officer to reconnoitre. Even though the infantry would become disorganized and harassed by musketry during the traversal of the bog and be vulnerable to cavalry attack as they formed into line of battle on the firmer ground beyond, Lloyd chose the second option and ordered brushwood to be collected to make fascines. 'God Almighty [then] sent a man from whence I know not' who contacted the officer searching for the southerly limit of the bog claiming to know a path and offering to act as guide. This man was produced just as Lloyd was about to order the infantry forward into the unpromising frontal operation, which was immediately abandoned. Captain Acheson took a company to check the feasibility of the route, subsequently followed by the rest of Lloyd's command. Initially, the Irish thought that the Enniskilleners were filing off to the left to leave the field so they jeered and 'made great Huzzas … inviting us to come on and fight them'. However, on realizing that Lloyd's men were moving in column diagonally across the bog to outflank the barricade, the cavalry trotted southwards to block their progress but they were too late: Lloyd had already been allowed sufficient time to form up his men on dry ground whilst 300 of Caldwell's soldiers from the northern segment of Belleek had crossed the Erne in boats to threaten the Irish rear. Outnumbered, the Irish foot were ordered to withdraw but they panicked and ran. The cavalry stood whilst Lloyd's horsemen prepared to charge before breaking, wheeling left and running for Ballyshannon without firing a shot. None of the Irish fought except one called Fitzgerald who was overtaken by Lieutenant Moyle. Moyle fired three shots but Fitzgerald's armour resisted the bullets and they fell to with swords until more Enniskilleners came up and took the wounded Fitzgerald prisoner. Because of his bravery, Fitzgerald was carried to Enniskillen and nursed back to health. The Irish cavalry lost about 190 men during the pursuit which possibly reached as far as Bundoran. Sarsfield ordered the troops besieging Ballyshannon to retire and regroup at Sligo: most succeeded although some were run down by the Enniskilleners. Terence MacDonogh, his 60 men and two field guns on Fish Island were all captured. The 'beggarly' Irish camp was plundered yielding some serviceable horses and small quantities of arms and ammunition. Lloyd had no dead and only Cornet King wounded. The 'Break of Belleek' gave the Enniskilleners renewed hope and confidence because they had defeated, not irregulars, but a substantial detachment of the regular Irish Army under its most charismatic leader, Patrick Sarsfield.

Having reorganized his army at Sligo, Sarsfield encamped with 6,000–7,000 men at Manorhamilton 'in a stone deer park belonging to Sir William Gore'. He proposed an exchange of prisoners so that he might regain the services of some of those taken at Ballyshannon and Belleek. Although this appeared to be an opportunity to secure the release of Sir Thomas Southwell, remembering Lord Galmoy's earlier treatment of prisoners, Governor Hamilton replied cautiously asking Sarsfield to send a list of those he wished to exchange. This placed Sarsfield in a quandary because he did not have sufficient Williamite prisoners to make an equal and fair exchange. There were some Protestant prisoners in

Galway and Ballinrobe but not enough. So, delaying his response for a month, he acquired some bargaining counters by throwing into Sligo gaol numbers of local Protestants who had been given protections by the Irish, telling them to petition the Governor of Enniskillen for their release. Sarsfield then sent a list of their names to Enniskillen. Omitted from this list were the names of Sir Thomas Southwell and others who had been held in Galway, Sarsfield explaining that these gentlemen had already been sent to England in an earlier exchange. Suspecting fraud, Governor Hamilton refused to proceed further replying that those on the list had not been taken as prisoners of war but had been forced from their dwellings simply as a device for freeing Irishmen. Sarsfield retaliated by treating the Protestants in gaol very badly, denying them sufficient food, and sending some of their wives to Governor Hamilton with petitions and letters begging him to relieve their husbands. At length, Hamilton gave way. Captain Francis Gore, with a detachment of musketeers, took the Irish prisoners 13 km towards Manorhamilton where they met a party of Irish soldiers escorting the Protestants, which Gore then escorted back to Enniskillen. Among them was Captain Jackson, who raised a company of infantry from among the released prisoners. Relations between the Enniskilleners and the Irish were not improved.[17]

Intelligence was received late in May that the Irish in County Cavan had garrisoned Redhill House and Bellanacargy, threatening Enniskillen. Consistent with the policy of always taking the offensive and never allowing the town to suffer a siege, Thomas Lloyd went to dislodge them. *En route* along the north shore of Upper Lough Erne, Lloyd was joined by the garrison of Crom Castle giving him a total force of around 1,300 infantry and 200 cavalry. The Enniskilleners expected to contest the crossing of the River Finn at Wattlebridge because the bridge had been broken down and the water ran deep but the only Irish in sight were some videttes on the far bank who promptly withdrew to an adjacent hill allowing Lloyd to pass unopposed. Pressing on, Lloyd came to 'the strong and large' Redhill House, the property of Francis White. Although they left a garrison in Redhill House, the main Irish force offered it no support and retired south-east on Bellanacargy. Late in the evening, Lloyd drew up before Redhill House and the garrison surrendered 'upon mercy'. The soldiers were stripped of their arms and the house was preserved 'out of tenderness' to Francis White, then in England, whose brother commanded a company of Enniskillen foot. Next morning, Lloyd moved towards Bellanacargy Castle, 'a very strong house, well vaulted, that had held out for a long time in the former war in Ireland'. Standing just to the south of the River Annalee, Bellanacargy Castle was a powerful fortress. Its ramparts were very high presenting an almost insuperable obstacle to a force lacking heavy cannon. At 16:00, Lloyd arrived and summoned the garrison, which promptly surrendered upon condition that the soldiers were allowed to go free, along with their women and children, in their 'wearing clothes', in other words leaving behind their martial equipage: they were accordingly escorted to safety in company with the soldiers from Redhill House. In the castle Lloyd found some pikes, about 30 muskets, a few cases of pistols, very little ammunition, plentiful provisions, household goods and much general plunder. Because it was too far advanced into enemy territory for the Enniskilleners to garrison, after everything useful had been removed masons were summoned to undermine the castle's walls, which were then set on fire. Within a few hours it had collapsed into a heap of rubble. Having thoroughly cowed the Irish Army in Counties Cavan and Monaghan, Lloyd scoured the countryside as far as Kells and Finnea, within 50 km of Dublin. Rumours that 15,000 Enniskilleners were about to attack threw the capital into great consternation. Instead, probably recognizing that a raid by 1,500 men was unlikely to end the war, Lloyd turned back, content with a plunder of 3,000 cattle, 2,000 sheep and 500 horses loaded with meal, wheat and malt. He had no casualties.[18]

Before Derry, on the night of 5–6 May Brigadier Ramsay drove the guards out of a small earthwork built during Lundy's governorship and occupied Windmill Hill. By dawn, his soldiers had traced the line of an entrenchment across the hill from the bog to the river and begun to construct a battery overlooking the city from which their light and medium cannon would be able to batter the walls and harass the population. Governor Walker drew out ten men from every company of infantry and 'after putting them into the best order their impatience could allow', sallied 'with all imaginable silence' at 04:00 from the Ship Quay Gate. Once again, Mackenzie's account was slightly different. Walker rapidly lost control of the ill-disciplined troops who rushed out of the Bishop's and Ship Quay Gates to charge Ramsay's advance guards in the ditches and behind some old stone walls in front of the embryonic entrenchment. The headlong assault with clubbed muskets first drove these men back into the entrenchment and then forced Ramsay's main body to abandon the entire Windmill Hill position. Ramsay and some officers tried to rally the panic-stricken men but he was killed in the attempt. Around midday, the attackers returned to Derry. Walker and Mackenzie agree that 200 Irish lost their lives, 'most of which were shot through the head or breast' and 500 were wounded, 60 per cent dying from their injuries within a few days. Both report three or four Protestant dead and about 20 wounded. Governor Baker dispatched a drummer on 7 May to ask the Irish to appoint a fatigue party to bury their dead, 'which they did perform very negligently, scarce covering their bodies with earth'.[19] As rumours and tall tales spread, the action on Windmill Hill grew into a major victory. By the time the story reached Whitehaven, the Irish had made a great assault on Derry and the Protestant counter-attack had pursued the Irish for over 3 km subsequently filling 12 coaches with the 'chiefest' of the Irish dead. In retaliation, the Irish had murdered most of the Protestants in Counties Down and Antrim, only a few managing to escape, 'the men without noses and the women without breasts'. Governor Baker decided to occupy Windmill Hill in greater strength. During the week following 7 May, an entrenchment was traced from the bog to the banks of the Foyle. Workmen soon completed the excavations and the 'line' was strengthened by redoubts to both flanks, particularly important on the Foyle side where the Irish could enfilade the line from the east bank of the river. This new position was guarded by strong detachments day and night. Small sallies and actions continued over the next few weeks along with numerous 'little parleys' to arrange for doctors to attend sick or wounded prisoners, such as Lord Netterville and Captain Talbot.[20]

Whilst the Enniskilleners gained tactical victories that maintained their operational freedom, gradually increasing pressure was brought to bear upon Derry. Among the city's many weaknesses was the supply of drinking water. The wells within the walls had become muddied and dirty through over-exploitation and many preferred to use the three wells of St Columba situated just beyond the fortifications on Windmill Hill but close enough to be covered by fire from the new entrenchment. As the blockade tightened visits to the wells grew increasingly dangerous and frequent skirmishes occurred: one gentleman had a water bottle shot from his hand as he was raising it to his lips. Had a significant effort been made to capture the wells, the siege would have been rapidly concluded.[21] Around 11-12 May, the principal Irish camp was moved forward from Saint Johnstown to Ballingry, 3 km south-south-west of Derry, the main position having always to remain south of Derry to cover possible interference from Enniskillen and keep open communications with Dublin. A secondary encampment was established at Penny Burn Mill and a third in an orchard on the east bank of the Foyle, allowing the Irish to guard both banks of the river and deny the garrison intelligence and freedom of movement. Having completed these adjustments, at dusk on 12 May the Irish fired all their cannon and muskets, possibly to strike terror into the hearts of the defenders, but probably to demonstrate the extent of the ring around the city. Next, the Irish dug an entrenchment and a redoubt on a 'heathy hill' near Penny Burn Mill, on which they positioned some light cannon. On 18 May, Captains Noble, Joseph Cunningham and Archibald Sanderson, accompanied by some volunteers, took about 100 men out into the open fields to attack the new fort but a detachment of cavalry rode down and cut their retreat, capturing Cunningham, who was initially granted quarter but subsequently murdered. Noble and Sanderson led back the remaining men but at the cost of 15 or 16 casualties. 'In order to surprise the enemy's camps', on 26 May 300 men sallied from the trenches on Windmill Hill, half moving towards Ballougry and the remainder marching on Penny Burn Mill. The former achieved nothing but the latter conducted a fire fight with the garrison of a small redoubt. Four Derrymen were wounded and two killed.[22]

The non-conformists held a solemn fast on Tuesday 21 May accompanied by sermons preached at two places in the city, as well as the cathedral, at which several collections were taken for the poor 'who begun to stand in greater need of them': the Episcopalians kept an equally solemn fast shortly afterwards. In a small, blockaded city, with an engorged population divided between rival versions of Protestantism and not everyone wholeheartedly supporting the defence, cliques, cabals, ill-feeling, pettiness and all manner of accusations and personal attacks were bound to develop. Towards the end of May many officers had grown suspicious of Governor Walker and drew up a list of charges which were lodged with Colonel Hamill. He had held a secret conclave with unidentified persons around 18 April which had agreed to send a messenger to James armed with proposals for surrender. The courier had been arrested on his return but Walker had secured his release before sending him over the walls to Culmore Fort, which had surrendered shortly afterwards. At the end of April, Walker consulted with more unnamed parties with a view to shutting the gates when a large proportion of the garrison was involved in a sally. He had embezzled the stores and offered to sell Derry to James for £500 cash and a pension of £700 *per annum*. Walker abused officers who went to the stores and there were other items 'relating to personal vices, I shall not mention', which rather whets the appetite although probably referred to a fondness for the bottle. Witnesses were examined before Colonels Hamill, Murray, Crofton and Monro. Lieutenant Colonel Fortescue, Captains Noble and Dunbar plus a further 100 officers, then signed a motion to prosecute Walker and remove him immediately from any position of trust relating to the army and the stores. Governor Baker had no option but to agree and placed the management of the stores into a commission of 14, with himself as president. Having granted this concession, Baker then successfully urged the petitioners not to proceed further. After Walker's death at the Boyne, the charges were revived, his autocratic conduct following the death of Governor Baker causing the number of accusations to be increased to 14. Walker's arrogance no doubt contributed to the campaign against him and there was probably a small flame beneath clouds of smoke. Thereafter, whenever a sally in force was made, a substantial guard was always retained in the city under either Lieutenant Colonel Cairns or Captain James Gladstanes, prudent and reliable officers. Also, an order in council required the storekeepers not to accept a note from Walker unless it bore the countersignature of either Governor Baker or Major Adams.[23]

7

General Kirke

Enniskillen received intelligence on 3 June that Richard Hamilton's army was grazing many of its horses on waste land near Omagh. On the following day (4 June) Governor Hamilton requested Captains Francis Gore and Arnold Cosbie to take two troops of horse to Captain Mervyn's house at Trillick. Two companies of infantry under Captains Henry Smith and Robert Corry which were billeted in Newport, 6 km from Trillick, joined the cavalry before the combined force marched towards Omagh on the evening of 6 June. At around 08:00 on 7 June they returned to Trillick with about 160 dragoon mounts, 150 draught horses and 300 cattle. Not only were three troops of enemy dragoons thereby dismounted but the Enniskilleners were able to create an equal number of horse soldiers.

The Duke of Berwick commanded a 'flying army', no more than a weak brigade, camped to the south of the Derry cantonments, charged with testing the Enniskilleners' defences and preventing them from trying to break the siege. Berwick's force was quite sufficient because, on 28 May, Lord Melfort in Dublin had forwarded to Richard Hamilton very accurate intelligence about the strength and condition of the Enniskilleners: they had no more than 1,500 infantry; between 900 and 1,000 cavalry; provisions and ammunition were scarce; and there was a general lack of firm command because 'the rabble dominate there'.[1] Initially, Berwick tried unsuccessfully to co-ordinate operations with Brigadier Hugh Sutherland at Belturbet, which would have produced a force of about six infantry battalions, four cavalry regiments and two of dragoons. Instead, obliged to act independently, around 4 June Berwick edged south through Omagh but the Enniskilleners received prompt intelligence and marched out forcing him to draw back to Trillick in some haste, burning Mr Andrew Hamilton's house *en route*. For as long as Berwick remained around Trillick, the Enniskilleners maintained strong patrols and guards on the roads through Kilskeery Parish. Shortly afterwards, Berwick moved against the north-western flank of the Enniskillen hinterland, marching through the Blue Stack Mountains via the Barnesmore Gap, to appear early one morning before Donegal, occupied by a garrison of 300 men under Captains Edward Johnston and Hugh Cudwell. Berwick proved too strong and, following a short resistance, Johnston and Cudwell abandoned the town and retired into the castle. Having suffered several fatal casualties, Berwick decided not to press the attack but burned the town and withdrew into the Laggan.[2]

Before Derry, on 4 June, 400 of the Irish Army launched another assault on Windmill Hill. At low tide, three squadrons of horse advanced along the beach, whilst two detachments of infantry, holding faggots in front of them to deflect bullets, attacked the entrenched line. The cavalry drew up in three lines, the first, commanded by Captain Edward Butler, son of Richard Butler, Fifth Viscount Mountgarret, comprising mostly gentlemen who had sworn to penetrate the enemy's positions. One infantry grouping was detailed to advance on the trenches stretching from the windmill to the river whilst the other, composed of grenadiers under Captain John Plunket, struck at the Bogside between the windmill and the city. Derry received considerable advance notice enabling the precise location of reinforcements. The defenders formed up in three ranks inside the entrenchment 'so advantageously that one rank was always ready to march up and relieve the other, and discharge successively upon the enemy'. In the redoubts, the ranks were four or five deep 'so that they were in a posture to fire continually', a tactic that apparently surprised the Irish even though it had been in common European usage for over a century; evidently, they expected to fall upon the Derry infantry as they were reloading following the discharge of a single, massed volley. Captains John and James Gladstanes, Andrew Adams, Francis Boyd, Robert Wallace, John Maghlin and William Beatty commanded in the trenches and redoubts closest to the river. True to their oath Edward Butler's men charged 'furiously' with 'loud huzzas' but they probably came on at no more than a gentle trot because they carried fascines with which to bridge the trenches. Light field guns from around the windmill and long, accurate fowling pieces kept up a steady, but ineffective, fire until Captain Crooke noticed that the cavalrymen were wearing armour and instructed his musketeers to aim at the horses. The cavalry's route along the strand outflanked the two-metre-high dry bank that constituted the defenders' position next to the river. Quickly appreciating the danger, Captains John and James Gladstanes left the lines and rushed to the beach to fall on their exposed flank with muskets, pikes and scythes, killing several, driving many into the river and capturing Butler. Observing the fate of the élite first line, the second rank stood its ground and refused to advance.

Simultaneously the foot moved forward 'after the Turkish mode' with the 'most dreadful shrieks and howlings'. The detachment directed to attack between the river and the windmill was greeted by rolling fire instead of the anticipated single volley. Despite the psychological protection offered by the fascines only a few brave individuals reached the entrenchments whilst the remainder were unable to stand and wheeled about draping dead and wounded comrades over their shoulders as shields against bullets fired at their backs. The grenadier party concentrated on the 'new' fort, which anchored the Bogside flank of the lines and was commanded by Colonel Monro. Between the fort and the Bogside stood an infantry company that faced the grenadiers with great resolution, even when their commander, Captain Michael Cunningham, was wounded by shrapnel. Throughout, Governor Baker maintained overall control sending out reliefs and reinforcements to points under particular pressure. The women also excelled, carrying ammunition, match, bread and drink to the men 'and assisted to very good purpose at the Bogside in beating off the grenadiers with stones, who came so near to our lines'. Irish casualties were heavy – the Jacobites admitted to 120 wounded – particularly amongst the officers, but the defenders lost only six men and one officer, Captain Thomas Maxwell, whose arm was broken by a cannon ball, a wound which proved mortal within three weeks. Two of the casualties were felled by a shot from a gun in Strong's Orchard which enfiladed the Windmill Hill entrenchment from across the river.

The failure to capture Windmill Hill led to a change in tactics. Numerous small bombs had already been thrown into the town many of which had failed to explode because the rush of air during flight extinguished the fuses. On the night of 4–5 June, heavier mortars were deployed. Bombs weighing 273 lb (124 kg), propelled by 17-lb (8 kg) charges of powder from tubes positioned in Strong's Orchard, began to plough up the streets and demolish houses. Remaining indoors or wandering the streets became equally hazardous, the sick, old and injured confined to their homes being particularly vulnerable. One bomb fell into the house of Captain Thomas Boyd, burying him beneath a collapsed wall; Alexander Lindsay, a surgeon, was killed; Major Breme was felled by a cannon ball; whilst mortar bombs accounted for Henry Thompson, a burgess, plus a further 24 people and set fire to some barrels of powder in 'a back house'. Another went through the Diamond House dropping within 2 m of a dry well which contained 47 barrels of precious gunpowder. The safest places were the western and northern sectors that lay beyond the mortars' effective range, at the base of the walls and on the ramparts. Civilians also crowded on to Ferry Gate Quay, Windmill Hill and the ravelin outside the Bishop's Gate. At night the light from the fuses revealed the flight of the bombs making it easier to take avoiding action but this was much more difficult during daylight. The cannon and mortar barrage, when added to general fatigue and increasing shortage of food, rendered the inhabitants and garrison more prone to disease and lowered morale.[3]

Early in June Enniskillen received several highly coloured descriptions of conditions in Derry – 'a dog's head and pluck at that time … yielding two shillings and sixpence, all the horses they had being already eaten, with old hides, tallow, starch and what else of that nature they could purchase' – but Governor Hamilton could not afford the luxury of verification because, should Derry fall, Enniskillen would receive the full attention of the Irish Army. Accordingly, despite just two barrels of powder remaining from the five so grudgingly provided by Lundy, a shortage of effective weapons, and the presence of only 2,000 soldiers and two light field guns, Governor Hamilton decided to sustain Derry. A full-scale, military relief was impossible because he would inevitably be defeated by numerically superior forces and the entire war would be forfeit. However, Enniskillen was well stocked with provisions, particularly sheep and cattle, so he proposed marching a supply train down the east bank of the Foyle before ferrying over the stores. He knew that the main weight of the Irish Army lay on the Derry side of the Foyle whilst the east bank was held by light forces which could be 'beaten up' and, if all went well, there was always the option of crossing to 'give the enemy a brush'. Against almost unanimous advice – his strengths lay in administration, co-ordination and organization and he had never acted as a field commander – Hamilton decided to conduct the expedition himself. In his absence, Lieutenant Colonel Thomas Lloyd, a proven raider and light cavalryman *par excellence* rather than a garrison governor, would command in Enniskillen. Nevertheless, he insisted and proposed committing the majority of the 2,000 available men to this airily planned, desperate enterprise which exposed the weaknesses rather than exploited the strengths of both senior officers.

On the evening and night of 10 June, Hamilton marched 14 km to Trillick. During the afternoon of 11 June, he moved northwards and camped overnight within 2 km of Omagh, having been informed that its garrison had already departed. *En route*, local Protestants and 'British', mostly freebooters and general riff-raff on the lookout for plunder, joined the column doubling Hamilton's numbers although they were not under military discipline and a damned nuisance. These irregulars rode ahead of the soldiers in order to enter Omagh first and steal the choicest loot. Within 5 km of their objective they were ambushed in a hollow by a detachment from the Omagh garrison. They managed to fall back on to the vanguard, which was 1 km behind, except for one Rowland Batty who fired his pistol and then fell off his horse whilst wheeling. He was taken prisoner and later murdered. Omagh was an open town and Governor Hamilton marched in during the morning of 12 June, the retreating garrison having set fire to all the buildings along or near the Omagh–Trillick road. However, the retiring Omagh garrison had left a rearguard in Captain Mervyn's house, which was 'pretty strong' and surrounded by a bawn wall. Hamilton drew up the main body of his infantry within musket range, whilst the vanguard under Captains Acheson and Galbraithe occupied the nearby ditches, gardens and ruins of the burned-out buildings. They opened fire but an equally heavy fusillade was returned against both the vanguard and the main body of Enniskillen infantry standing in the open. The Irish were summoned to surrender but their commander replied that he knew of no authority by which the Enniskilleners appeared under arms and any future trumpets would be attacked. Enniskillen cavalry scouted around Omagh and seized five prisoners on the Dungannon road; interrogation revealed that they belonged to a force of two infantry battalions, one dragoon regiment and one of cavalry, led by Donough MacCarthy, Fourth Earl of Clancarty, which had camped the night before at Dungannon and was marching, via Omagh, to reinforce the army before Derry. Clancarty planned to be in Omagh by 15:00 that afternoon. At much the same time, Governor Hamilton received expresses warning that Sarsfield was approaching Ballyshannon with 6,000–7,000 men and Brigadier Sutherland was forming another army in Belturbet. A council of war was summoned. As the majority of the officers had families in Enniskillen, the debate was short and the only possible decision taken: to return immediately. Some wished to burn the strategically important town of Omagh but because it belonged to Captain Mervyn, a 'good Protestant', it was spared. Except to consume precious gunpowder, Governor Hamilton's expedition achieved nothing except to undermine his credibility causing the garrison to regard Thomas Lloyd as the natural leader.

They returned to Enniskillen on 14 June receiving intelligence on the following day that Brigadier Sutherland's corps at Belturbet was increasing daily as it absorbed local forces and volunteers. More precise information arrived on 16 June from Lieutenant Colonel Creighton in Crom Castle and Captain Wishart, who maintained at his own expense a troop of horse patrolling the eastern borders of the Enniskillen hinterland, that Sutherland was marching with a powerful force along the Enniskillen road via the northern shore of Upper Lough Erne. Reverting to the strategy of never allowing the enemy to approach close enough to besiege Enniskillen, Governor Hamilton ordered Thomas Lloyd to take as many men as he could muster against Sutherland. Lloyd set off in the evening of 16 June reaching Lisnaskea that night but he was spotted by an Irish scout. Sutherland's force comprised two foot battalions, a dragoon regiment, some troops of horse and a few light field guns although he had brought from Dublin sufficient arms and accoutrements to equip two infantry battalions that he hoped to raise from amongst local volunteers plus plentiful supplies of biscuit, wheat, flour, malt and general provisions. The intelligence received by both sides was sheer hyperbole. Sutherland was led to believe that he was facing 15,000 terrifying Enniskilleners whilst Lloyd received exaggerated estimates of Sutherland's strength.

Rain poured down on 17 June and Lloyd remained at Lisnaskea allowing Sutherland to retire on Belturbet, an open town lacking defensible buildings except for a church and walled churchyard too small to contain his whole force. Sutherland's first thought was to preserve his command against what he thought were overwhelming odds. Whilst the main body marched for Monaghan and Charlemont, Lieutenant Colonel Edward Scott was left to hold the ecclesiastical perimeter with a rearguard of 80 dragoons and 200 infantry until Sutherland returned with reinforcements. The weather on the next day, 18 June, was fine and Sutherland slipped away down the Monaghan road. Lloyd advanced to Newtownbutler where he allowed his men to rest. During the halt a man named Vitch arrived from Belturbet and presented an accurate description of Sutherland's recent movements. Lloyd summoned a council of war to discuss whether to attack Sutherland's main force or the rearguard at Belturbet. During the conference, a troop of horse returned which had been sent at the gallop to discover Sutherland's exact position. They reported that, by now, Sutherland was approaching Monaghan after a forced march so rapid that a number of carts and carriages had been abandoned by the roadside. Monaghan was 25 km distant so Lloyd proceeded towards Belturbet taking advantage of the continuing fine weather.

Two troops of dragoons led Lloyd's column, commanded by Captains Robert Vaughan and Hugh Galbraith, followed by most of the cavalry; then came Lieutenant William McCarmick with an advance guard of 100 infantry; eight companies of foot under Major Wood and 14 companies under Captain Francis Gore comprised the main body; whilst two troops of horse brought up the rear. Within 2 km of Belturbet, the vanguard encountered a troop of Irish dragoons, which had dismounted and lined the roadside hedges. Their fire initially drove back the leading dragoons but the cavalry were close in support. The dragoons dismounted and worked along the inside of the hedges, flushing out the Irish dragoons, whilst the cavalry, advancing slightly behind the dragoons, cleared the road. Having lost some men and under pressure from Lloyd's cavalry, the Irish dragoons withdrew into Belturbet to join their comrades in the church and churchyard. Lloyd followed them into the town with his cavalry and dragoons and threw a cordon around the churchyard. Realizing that the ring of mounted troops was ridiculously thin and Edward Scott might sally at any moment and break out, 'express upon express' was sent to Wood and Gore to hasten the arrival of the hard-marching infantry. When the sweating foot soldiers reached their destination, the Irish welcomed them with heavy but inaccurate musketry. Lloyd ordered the infantry into all the houses around Scott's position, including the tall residence of the Archbishop of Dublin that overlooked the churchyard. Under cover of a two-hour exchange of musketry, Lloyd worked his soldiers into position to storm. A trumpeter was then sent to summon Scott to capitulate: on condition that the officers were not stripped and each was allowed to retain ten pounds cash, he agreed to surrender his force as prisoners of war.

Lieutenant McCarmick was entrusted to enter the churchyard and execute the terms of the surrender. The officers were personally disarmed whilst the men paraded before grounding their weapons and stepping back. The Irish rank and file, amounting to about 300, were taken into the archbishop's house where they were stripped of their red coats. The 16 officers, including Edward Scott, were put under guard in another house where they remained for the night of 18–19 June. On the following day, 19 June, Lloyd released 200 of the 'meanest of the common soldiers' along with their women and children because of the cost of their maintenance. The remaining 100 were marched to Enniskillen where they were given subsistence in return for labouring on the new fort. The officers travelled to Enniskillen by water. The booty was considerable: 700 muskets, allowing all the Enniskillen forces to be well armed with sufficient left over to equip two additional companies of infantry; two large barrels of powder, doubling the supplies available in Enniskillen; 53 dragoon mounts complete with horse furniture; sufficient provisions to last until the harvest; and enough red coats to clothe two companies of infantry. Lloyd did not lose a single man.[4]

The issue of prisoners was also a headache for Governor George Walker who had personally agreed to ransom Lieutenant Colonel 'Wicked Will' Talbot for £500 but the matter was further discussed at 'a sort of council' convened in Governor Baker's lodgings within the Bishop's House. Baker, whose health was beginning to fail, concluded that the majority opinion was against the deal because it would be ill-received within the garrison. Walker, however, urged acceptance of the arrangement 'with some violence and threats against those that opposed it'. Ignoring the decision of the meeting, Walker ordered the 'bier' that was to convey Talbot to be brought to his lodging that same day. The more active citizens, particularly the Presbyterians, were so enraged by this autocratic behaviour that they set fire to the bier as it stood outside the main guard before trying to find Walker but he had sensibly sought sanctuary in Baker's apartment. Frustrated, they seized all the prisoners they could find – the officer and gentlemen prisoners were on parole and thus at liberty – and threw them into the main gaol. Walker's house was the next target. After breaking in, they seized his beer, ham and butter but they still could not find Walker. Finally, they discovered him skulking in Baker's apartment: some threatened lynching, others offered to shoot him through the windows whilst the more moderate would have been content with sending him to prison. At length Baker, 'to whom they paid a great deference', came out to pacify them saying that there would be neither ransom nor prisoner exchange and asked them to overlook Walker's indiscretion. With some difficulty, the mob was persuaded to accept these conditions and disperse, although 'what construction the multitude put on this practice by Mr Walker, I think not fit to mention'. Paroled prisoners were freed and allowed to return to their lodgings. A little later Baker offered Talbot's release in exchange for permission to send a messenger to Kirke's ships in Lough Foyle but this was refused; Talbot's death shortly after put an end to the matter. Walker's *True Account* simply mentions that the defenders agreed to ransom Talbot for £500 but the request was rejected by the Irish.[5]

Walker's unsuccessful dabble in private enterprise came at a time when the blockade was beginning to have a serious impact. Sickness and disease, mostly caused by semi-starvation and malnutrition, multiplied to the extent that 15 officers died on one day. Some public-spirited citizens asked Captain Alexander Watson, commander of the gunners, whether his men might search for foodstuffs that were being hoarded or had previously been overlooked. By 'digging up' cellars and other likely hiding places, the artillerymen found much that had been spirited away as well as stores belonging to people who had left the city. Others were shamed into surrendering their private reserves. Iron for casting cannon balls was in short supply so William Brown, the adjutant to Governor Baker's regiment, fashioned ammunition out of lead wrapped around a core of brick, both commodities readily available from the numerous ruined houses. Captain Gregory and some workmen built carriages to mount all the available gun barrels.

William wanted the corps destined for Ireland to rendezvous at Milford Haven so that it might be diverted, if the opportunity arose, to descend on the French coast. Indeed, according to the Marquis of Halifax, William said 'he had a great mind to land in France and that was the best way to save Ireland'. Perhaps not fully cognizant of the difficulties of campaigning across the Irish Sea, William hoped that the war could be concluded in 1689 and the troops then redeployed in an amphibious assault on northern France to distract French attention from the Spanish Netherlands.[6] William had invaded in 1688 with the full support and backing of the States-General, to prevent England from falling into a French alliance and secure the considerable English financial, military, naval and economic resources for the service of the Dutch Republic and the Grand Alliance in their war with Louis XIV. William's inclination was to treat England as a vast fund of credit to repay the Dutch Republic for the huge investment that had been made in 1688. France was the principal enemy and the corollary of her defeat or humbling would solve most of the outstanding political and military problems. Ireland was just a nuisance. The only dissonance in this logical international reasoning was the fact that William was now king of England and the interests of the Protestant majority had to be respected. More important, James II was in Ireland where a victory would provide him with a base and troops with which to mount an invasion of England. However reluctant he was to accept the compromise, William could not ignore Ireland and was forced to fight a war on two fronts. Not until 16 April 1689 did the English House of Commons resolve to support the king in a war with France and a formal declaration of hostilities occurred on 7 May. The Lords and Commons had not acted out of concern for William and Dutch strategic interests but because James had personally returned to Ireland, sponsored by France, giving a new dimension and imperative to the conflict. As Parliament understood the matter, Ireland had to be reconquered to safeguard the Glorious Revolution and subsequent Revolution Settlement.

Finding troops for Ireland was difficult. The English Army was in disarray following the Glorious Revolution and its disbandment at Uxbridge by the Earl of Feversham. Nevertheless, despite disloyalty, faction and incompetence, a corps of 10,000 troops commanded by the Earl of Marlborough was dispatched to the Netherlands during March, April and May according to the 'Articles Separés' included in the Anglo-Dutch Mutual Defence Treaty of 3 March 1678. Soldiers also had to be found for Ireland. On 29 April 1689, orders were issued for an infantry brigade of four battalions to assemble at Liverpool ready to sail to the relief of Derry; their supply convoy would load and sail from Topsham, near Exeter. The battalions of John Cunningham and Solomon Richards were again involved, although their colonels were sacked on 1 May and replaced by William Stewart and the Irishman, Sir George St George, in company with Sir John Hanmer's battalion and that of the expedition's commander, Major General Percy Kirke. Son of George Kirke (d. 1675), a Scottish immigrant who rose to become Gentleman of the Robes to Charles I and Keeper of Whitehall Palace under Charles II, Percy Kirke was a professional soldier very well connected at court, through both his father and marriage, at some time before 1684, to Lady Mary Howard, the daughter of George Howard, Fourth Earl of Suffolk. Born around 1646, Kirke was first commissioned as an ensign in the Lord High Admiral's Regiment, the Duke of York's own, in 1666 during the second Anglo-Dutch war. Four years later, he was appointed cornet in the Royal Horse Guards commanded by his brother-in-law, Aubrey de Vere, Twentieth Earl of Oxford. In February 1673, Kirke went to France as a lieutenant in the Royal English Regiment, commanded by James Scott, Duke of Monmouth. His excellent combat performance resulted in promotions to captain-lieutenant in February 1675 and major in June. Following the death of his father, Kirke returned to England to settle his affairs before returning to France where he appears to have continued until the withdrawal of the British troops from French service in 1678. During his sojourn abroad, Kirke retained his commission in the Royal Horse Guards, rising to captain-lieutenant in March 1675, captain in May 1679 and lieutenant colonel in June. Kirke sailed to Tangier in 1680 as lieutenant colonel of the newly raised Second Tangier Regiment, commanded initially by the Earl of Plymouth. From 1682 until the evacuation of Tangier in 1684, Kirke was colonel of the Second Tangier Regiment and governor of Tangier. It was here, viewed through the censorious eyes of a middle-aged, sober and slightly hypocritical Samuel Pepys, that Kirke's reputation for roughness, vulgarity, crudity and hard drinking was confirmed, although he was probably no worse than anyone else in a garrison noted for insobriety, immorality and constant danger: Admiral Arthur Herbert acquired a similar character when leading a Royal Navy squadron in the western Mediterranean between 1678 and 1683. Pepys developed a great dislike of Kirke and, subsequently, there has been no attempt to challenge the Pepysian portrait. Some, perhaps most, of Pepys's loathing may have stemmed from his obsession with Lady Mary Kirke, 'a lady I have long remarked for her beauty'.

Ogling Lady Kirke was the only thing that made hot, horrible and tedious Tangier endurable.[7]

Kirke's posthumous reputation was further besmirched by the conduct of his Tangier infantry battalion, renamed the Queen Dowager's Regiment, during the aftermath of Monmouth's Rebellion in 1685 when it accompanied Judge George Jeffreys on his assize circuit, forming the guard at many of the subsequent hangings. Gilbert Burnet in the *History of His Own Time* said that, amongst a number of army units that treated the West Country like an occupied territory following the Battle of Sedgemoor, Kirke's was egregious and frequently hanged prisoners without trial. Burnet suggested that they learned their particular brand of savagery when fighting the Moors around Tangier. This, however, was all *ex post facto* malice – Kirke's soldiers were no worse than other units and there was a notable absence of contemporary complaint about the conduct of either Kirke or Jeffreys – and James continued to patronize his career promoting him to brigadier later in 1685 as a reward for his conduct. In his use of the army to push forward the policy of repealing the Test Acts and the Penal Laws, Kirke was just the type that James required: apolitical, amoral and a professional soldier whose first loyalty was to his superior. Neither did he evince any deeply held religious attachments. During a 'closeting' by James, in 1686 or 1687:

> the king, after he had told him a great many things, spoke plain unto him, and told him he would have to change his religion. Upon which the colonel began to smile, and answered him thus – 'Oh, your majesty has spoke too late. Your majesty knows that I was concerned at Tangier, and being oftentimes with the Emperor of Morocco about the late king's affairs, he oft desired the same thing of me, and I passed my word to him that if ever I changed religion I would turn Mahometan'.

A good story but written by a third hand seven years after the event: Abraham de la Pryme heard it on 3 September 1693 while at St John's College, Cambridge, from a man who had been Kirke's servant between 1680 and 1689.[8] There is no record that Kirke ever met the Emperor of Morocco. Unquestionable is the fact that he was a leading figure in the conspiracy that arranged for substantial elements of the English Army to desert to William of Orange on his landing in November 1688, even though James promoted Kirke major general that same month. Despite the availability of senior officers from the Netherlands, Germany and the Anglo-Dutch Brigade, William evidently thought Kirke capable of relieving Derry, probably thinking an Englishman more suited to navigating the intricate racial, political and religious delicacies of Ulster. In truth, the choice amongst British officers was not extensive: Marlborough and Thomas Talmash were attached to the corps in the Netherlands and most of the others were incompetent, untrustworthy, or both. Whether Kirke was entirely dependable was another matter but, in addition to his proven combat record, he had participated in the pro-Williamite conspiracy and, when the direction of the wind had clearly set, deserted, services that begged some reward. However, like Lundy, he had never held an independent command.[9]

Kirke's problem was simple but the solution problematical: to relieve Derry by water he had to pass Culmore Fort. Commanded by the Third Engineer of the Ordnance Office, Captain Jacob Richards, advised by four Huguenot technicians,[10] a reconnaissance expedition left Hoylake on 13 May, comprising HMS *Greyhound* (sixth rate, Captain Gwillam), HMS *Kingfisher* (ketch, Captain Edward Boyce) and a merchant ketch, the *Edward and James* (Master Mr Meers). Richards was instructed to study both the lough and river to within cannon-shot of Culmore Fort to locate batteries, booms, sunken vessels and all other obstacles that might hinder a water-borne relief. Bad weather, high seas and contrary winds delayed the ships and not until 29 May did they meet Captain George Rooke's squadron which was patrolling St George's Channel to interdict Jacobite communications between Scotland and Ireland. Rooke informed Jacobs that the fourth rate HMS *Portland* (Captain Thomas Lee RN) was awaiting them in Lough Foyle. Captain Gwillam passed Greencastle on 1 June and made the two-hour run up to Redcastle. Bad weather forced him to anchor off Redcastle until 7 June[11] when he took advantage of slightly improved conditions to 'kedge and warp' past Whitecastle to within 5 km of Culmore Fort. Information from the inhabitants confirmed the presence of a boom near Brook Hall. In a north-westerly gale, Gwillam took the *Greyhound* up to Culmore on Saturday 8 June. Somewhat surprisingly, he was engaged by just one field gun and one heavy cannon, the barrel of which burst with the first shot. The *Greyhound* then anchored and bombarded Culmore for 45 minutes. Richards climbed to the maintop and, through his telescope, saw what looked like a boom stretched across the river from Charles Fort and noticed that the Irish were moving cannon to cover both ends. Having seen enough, although not entirely certain of his observations, Richards asked Gwillam to sail the *Greyhound* back into Lough Foyle from where the *Kingfisher* would convey a report to Kirke. In attempting to wear, the *Greyhound* ran aground and lay stranded, heeled over on the mud as the tide retreated. The Irish brought up several cannon and 17 shots damaged the *Greyhound* below the water line, flooding the hold with 1.5 m of water. Three or four battalions of Irish infantry assembled ready to board but were held off by musketry from the *Greyhound*'s decks. Soldiers from the *Kingfisher* rowed in longboats to reinforce the *Greyhound* and Captain Boyce, despite suffering from a stomach wound, assumed command after Captain Gwillam had been hit by several musket balls. Boyce decided that the *Greyhound* could not be saved and had begun to transfer the crew to the *Kingfisher* when the wind shifted to south-south-east: enough sailors remained on board to set sail and bring her clear on the rising tide. However, she had shipped a great deal of water and had to be run aground. Fortunately, she was not attacked again and repairs were made during the night of 8–9 June sufficient for her to depart in the morning on a hazardous voyage to Greenock. The *Kingfisher's* report of this dispiriting episode, delivered to Kirke whilst at sea, permitted an exaggerated impression of the strength of Culmore and the Jacobite positions in general and inclined him to think that Derry could not be relieved by naval action alone.[12]

Kirke had sailed from Hoylake at 15:30 on Thursday 30 May, the four battalions packed aboard 24 transports escorted by three warships, HMS *Swallow*, *Bonaventure* and *Dartmouth*. The convoy reached Ramsey Bay on the Isle of Man at 12:00 on 1 June and sailed again at noon on 5 June, anchoring in Red Bay, north of Garron Point, off the east coast of County Antrim early on Friday 7 June where it rendezvoused with Rooke's squadron from the Mull of Kintyre. Shepherded by Rooke, Kirke's ships sailed under Rathlin Island and, on Sunday 12 June, arrived under Inishowen Head.[13] Receiving Captain Richards's report via HMS *Kingfisher*, Kirke decided first to establish a secure base for both ships and soldiers and link up with local forces – including the Enniskilleners – before attacking the Irish siege lines. From the outset, Kirke regarded his position somewhere between disadvantageous and hazardous because he was short of men and resources and lacked clear, reliable intelligence and local knowledge. Possibly also, officers from Cunningham's and Richards's old battalions whispered in his ear about the potential difficulties.

As Derry anticipated relief, the spirits of the besieging army correspondingly sank; some of the soldiers pulled down their tents ready to strike camp and the country people reported that many had thrown away their red coats and deserted. However, Kirke dithered allowing the Irish to recover their confidence and take measures to counter his progress towards Derry, moving cannon to Charles Fort to cover the end of the boom and constructing batteries along the river banks. The first boom, which had been distantly observed by Captain Richards, was started between 4 and 8 June when the Derry garrison noticed the Irish pulling timber down to the shore and a number of boats busy on the water, although the country people reported that it was not completed until around 15 June. It stretched from Charles Fort on the west bank to a battery, Grange Fort, on the east at a point 3 km north of the city where the river narrowed as it emerged from the Crook of Inver, a broad bend-cum-bay. Designed by Pointis, it comprised oak beams linked by iron chains with a 300-cm cable wrapped around for reinforcement but it sank to the riverbed and was soon smashed by the force of the tides. A second version, in which spruce replaced oak, floated and served its purpose well enough.

Walker says that Kirke's ships were not spotted until 15 June, after they left the head of Lough Foyle and sailed up to Redcastle, but Ash reports a sighting at 18:00 on 13 June. Signals were made to the ships, which were acknowledged, but because there was no common method of signalling between land and sea, the sailors thought that all was well and there was no need for emergency measures whereas the city hoped that the sailors had comprehended their desperate condition. Finally, around 25 June, two messengers, James Roche and a Scotsman named Cromy[ie], slipped ashore and made their way through the Irish lines and down the east bank of the Foyle. Roche then swam across to Derry and delivered information about Kirke's expedition. As an agreed sign that Roche had successfully reached Derry, four rounds were fired from the cathedral roof. Cromy, however, could not swim and after waiting all night hoping to find a boat in the morning, he was taken by the Irish and 'turned', agreeing to verify a re-written message differing considerably from that which Roche had already taken into Derry. The Irish then hung out a white flag, indicating a wish to parley. They explained that the defenders had been misinformed about Kirke: the expedition was weak, he was thoroughly confused about what action to take and the city could hope for nothing, as was proved by Cromy's 'new' message. This remarkably prescient fraud was unmasked by Lieutenant Colonel Blair who asked Cromy why his account of affairs varied so much from that of Roche. He replied, 'he was in the enemy's camp, Roche within the walls of Derry'. Roche tried to return to Kirke but was forced back by Irish sentries along the waterside.

The leaders in Derry were perturbed about the inability to establish effective communication with Kirke. One MacGimpsey approached Adam Murray on 15 or 16 June and volunteered to swim down river. Murray sought the approval of Lieutenant Governor John Michelburne, who had recently been appointed to take over duties from the ailing Baker, but he could not make up his mind and so Murray, after consulting with Captain James Gladstanes and Lieutenant Colonel Cairns, accepted both responsibility and MacGimpsey's offer. A letter for Kirke was placed in a small bladder, weighted with two musket balls, and slung round MacGimpsey's neck. If he ran into trouble, he could slip the string and the musket balls would sink the bladder to the bottom of the river. Whether MacGimpsey, who was offered a considerable reward if successful, was drowned or captured alive was never discovered but, within a couple of days, a man was hanged on a gallows on the east bank of the river and the Irish informed the garrison that it was their messenger. Lieutenant Crookshanks tried a more obvious approach and supervised the construction of a boat, powered by eight oars, and set off to make contact with Kirke but had to turn back in the face of heavy enemy fire. During July, a little boy brought two dispatches from Kirk, one tied in his garter and the other folded within a cloth button. Two replies were sent, one 'within a piece of bladder in the shape of a suppository and the same way applied to the boy', and the other in 'the folding of his breeches'. He was arrested and swallowed the second letter but, after a short confinement during which his captors literally tried to get something out of him, he was released and reached Kirke, by then at Inch Island.[14]

At least three other letters were sent to Kirke between 15 and 16 June all of which were intercepted. From these the Irish learned that the garrison was reduced to eating horsemeat whilst food for the 20,000 population would run out within eight to ten days; the Irish trenches were approaching uncomfortably close to the walls and mines were feared; and, if Kirke could not push through supplies, James's offer of peace and free pardon might have to be accepted. In the garrison's opinion, there was nothing to stop Kirke sailing down river. Rosen had moved most of the Irish cannon from the river to concentrate on the west side of the city except for one field gun and 'a few little drunken dicks' at Culmore Fort. All Kirke had to do was send through one or two small vessels loaded with biscuit, cheese and butter and the city would survive. Fuel with which to cook was also scarce and so Kirke was asked to send coal. Even more important for the Irish was the knowledge that the numerical and physical strength of the garrison was daily falling through disease, death and desertion: able and competent leaders were in particularly short supply.[15]

Kirke's version of these events differed in fact, emphasis and understanding. His interpretation of Captain Richards's advice predisposed him against relief by water so he was committed to an overland option. The fleet 'lay off' Redcastle on the night of 15 June and a 'diver' was sent into Derry to inform the garrison of Kirke's arrival and arrange a system of signalling between the ships and the cathedral tower. On the next day, Kirke examined the signals from the cathedral tower through a telescope and thought they indicated that all was well. The diver returned to the ships on the night of 16–17 June, having apparently swum the whole distance, and reported that, in places, the river was so narrow that he was within pistol-shot of either bank. He also observed that the shores were lined with cannon and musketry emplacements. Via the swimmer, the governor informed Kirke that he had no immediate need of succour as the garrison numbered 13,000 and he had provisions for two months. He advised Kirke that, unless he had direct orders from the king to 'come in', he should hold off beyond the reach of the enemy cannon until he received reinforcements. Then he might make 'a more prosperous attempt' by land, especially as 10,000 Scots-Irish were ready to join him, which the garrison would support with a major counter-attack. The swimmer also brought news that the Derry garrison had made a small sally some nights before during which they had seized many horses, 'an hundred of which they killed and barrelled up in case, after two months time, the garrison should be put to any extremities for want of provisions'. The diver went to Derry again on the night of 17–18 June, returning with information that reinforced the already optimistic assessment. Weapons, apparently, were the only items in really short supply and Kirke decided to send 10,000 arms but changed his mind when he discovered how difficult it would be for even a small vessel to run the gauntlet along the Foyle. As always in the evaluation of intelligence, Kirke interpreted it to support his preconceptions. A full council of war on 19 June weighed all the evidence gleaned since arriving in Lough Foyle and resolved to wait until reinforcements were received from England because the garrison was not *in extremis*, the river too narrow and the defences too strong. At least Cunningham and Richards had decided to run away; Kirke did nothing.[16]

During the night of 17–18 June, Colonel Murray; Captains Noble, Dunbar and Holmes; two lieutenants; and 20 men ventured 6 km up-river in the one remaining boat ostensibly to rob a fish-house on 'the isle' but actually to land a couple of boy messengers in Dunnelong Wood who would try to make contact with Enniskillen. The Irish saw what was happening and, as the boat passed Evan's Wood, fired a heavy cannon which only just missed the target, followed by sustained musketry from both banks. On arrival at Dunnelong Wood, the boys were so frightened that they refused to go ashore. In the dim light of the pre-dawn, the crew spotted two Irish craft full of dismounted dragoons in pursuit. The Derrymen turned and rowed towards the Irish boats, firing as they approached. After both sides had expended their ammunition, the Irish tried to come alongside in order to board but found that they had 'catched a tartar' when the Derrymen counter-boarded one of their boats, forced some of the dragoons into the water, killed three or four and captured 13, one of whom was injured by Irish fire as the boat made its way back to Derry. Seeing the fate of their comrades, the crew of the second boat rapidly pulled away. The Derrymen received no casualties although Murray suffered a bruised head and concussion after a shot hit his helmet. Having landed the prisoners near the city, the boat party took to the water once more to attack the battery at Tamnimore. Its defenders fired at the approaching boat but fled when the crew disembarked. They chased the gunners to the top of a hill but had to beat a rapid retreat when an Irish detachment attempted to cut them off. The captured boat was offered to the Irish in exchange for permission to send a messenger to Kirke but this was declined.[17]

8

Endurance

Schomberg received a letter from Kirke on 21 June giving assurances that, having arrived at the head of Lough Foyle, he would do everything possible to effect a relief but was apprehensive about passing the cannon in Culmore Fort. Kirke's difficulties were elaborated in a letter sent into Derry by a boy messenger early in July. The neck of the lough was narrow and deep but its natural guardian, Greencastle, was a weak position. Eight kilometres further along the west bank lay Redcastle but here the channel was wide rendering Redcastle unable to protect shipping. Another 5 km brought the traveller to White Castle at Quigley's Point but, located 1 km from the water, it was also of scant military value. Below, where the lough tapered into the River Foyle – which was so shallow that large vessels could only enter on spring tides – stood Culmore Fort. Built 5 km above Derry during the siege of 1649, it was not a particularly strong position and no new fortifications had been added in the interim. In 1649 the attackers had constructed Charles Fort to anchor the western end of a boom stretched across the river to Grange Fort and these earthworks had been revivified by the Jacobites. Kirke therefore declared that the passage of the river could not be forced so he had decided to relieve Derry by land operations. First, officers, arms and ammunition had been sent by sea to Enniskillen while, second, a detachment under Colonel William Stewart had gone to Inch Island in Lough Swilly to see whether an overland threat to the rear of the Irish Army might be developed. Once Enniskillen had been relieved and reinforced, Kirke intended to attack the Irish Army with his own four battalions from Inch whilst the Enniskilleners drove up from the south. Kirke also believed that 6,000 reinforcements from England had already been at sea for eight days.[1]

Having been sent by James to support Richard Hamilton, the arrival of General Conrad von Rosen around 20 June with substantial reinforcements marked the opening of the close siege and the defenders made frantic attempts to contact Kirke, firing cannon and raising and lowering the standard flying above the cathedral tower.[2] Horrified by the amateurism and incompetence, beginning on the night of 20–21 June Rosen began to galvanize the Irish Army through a series of intemperate statements, entreaties, threats and curses. He also made several redeployments. The various encampments on the west bank of the River Foyle were moved closer to the city and the artillery was realigned. Three mortars and several cannon were shifted from the east to the west bank on to the hill above the bog whilst two battering cannon[3] were positioned to shoot at the Butcher's Gate, which he had identified as the most vulnerable sector. Rosen began to excavate a trench running from Bog Street across to the eastern side of the bog whence he could start mines beneath the gate. Rosen also caused additional trenches to be dug so that attackers might approach closer to the defenders' lines in order to harass such routine activities as the relief of guards and the fetching of water from St Columba's Wells. He also maintained strong, permanent trench guards ready to exploit any weakness or negligence displayed by the defenders. Encouraged by Lieutenant Governor Michelburne, the garrison responded by working every night to dig counter-mines before Butcher's Gate. Captain Michael Cunningham, Captain Schambroon and Mr William Mackee, who paid the men out of their own pockets and even fed them meat from their own stocks, supervised the works. By these means, Rosen's new trenches were prevented from reaching quite to the eastern extremity of the bog making it impossible for mines to be started. Civilians, rewarded from the proceeds of a special collection, erected a blind in front of the Butcher's Gate to cover the workmen and protect the gate from cannon fire although not before some damage had been done.

Richard Hamilton sent a letter into Derry on 27 June. First, he clarified any misunderstandings about the command structure within the Irish Army: he remained in overall command and, despite contrary appearances and statements, General Rosen was subordinate and charged solely with keeping General Kirke at bay. It was, said Hamilton, in King James's interest to reach a peaceful accommodation in order to have access to the services of all his subjects, both Catholic and Protestant, and he offered full protection to any who wished to return to their former homes. Colonel Neill O'Neill was appointed plenipotentiary to treat with the garrison. Similar terms were extended to Enniskillen. Hamilton's approach coincided with a deterioration in the situation in Derry where the diet now consisted of horses, cats, dogs, rats, mice, tallow, starch, salted and dried hides and 'greaves[4] of a year old' and there were murmurs in favour of making a positive response. However, despite discussions between Colonel O'Neill and Colonels Lance and Campbell on 27 June, the majority remained resolved to eat the Irish first and then each other rather than surrender.

On 18 June, Lord Clancarty brought his party of about 1,500 men, which had brushed with the Enniskilleners at Omagh, to reinforce the besiegers. At 22:00 on the evening of 28 June, under cover of a bombardment, Lieutenant Colonel John Shelton led forward Clancarty's regiment, strengthened by detachments from other units, to attack the outworks and blinds outside the Butcher's Gate. Shelton approached quietly and managed to introduce a few miners into a cellar underneath the weakly garrisoned half-bastion with the intention of filling it with gunpowder, lighting the fuse and withdrawing to watch the outwork, and probably much of the Butcher's Gate, sail through the air. During their approach, a mortar bomb fell short and exploded clearly illuminating the advancing infantrymen. The alarm was sounded and immediately confirmed when an Irish officer rode towards the gate and called for fire to burn it down. Captains Noble, Holmes and Dunbar gathered between 60 and 80 men, slipped out of the Bishop's Gate and crept along the foot of the wall until they came upon the enemy's flank guards, who spotted them and fired, but they made no reply until they had arrived at 'the right distance, and then thundered upon them'. This was sufficient, when supported by musket fire from the walls and cannon firing case shot from the half-bastion, to drive Shelton's men back towards their own lines leaving behind the miners and about 30 dead, including a French lieutenant colonel. Noble's force lost one killed and one wounded. Walker suggests, probably correctly, that the Irish soldiers had been fuelled by liquor.

On 30 June 1689 Governor Baker died, a judicious, resolute and firm leader who had steered a *via media* between the religious extremes. Already, on 21 June, Baker and a council of war had agreed that Lieutenant Governor John Michelburne should become acting governor although there was no subsequent formal confirmation of his appointment following Baker's death.[5] Born in 1648 at Horsted Keynes, Sussex, the son of Abraham Michelburne, he had been brought up in Kilcandra, County Wicklow. During the 1670s he had served in the Earl of Dumbarton's regiment seconded to the French Army, probably as a sergeant, but was able to buy a lieutenant's commission in 1678; Teague O'Regan, his opponent at Sligo in 1691, also fought in this unit. Probably returning to England in either 1678 or 1679, Michelburne was commissioned lieutenant in the Second Tangier Regiment, commanded by Percy Kirke, and he served on that station from 1680 until the evacuation in 1684. Here he came into contact with Robert Lundy. Transferring to the Irish establishment in 1684, he was first lieutenant of the grenadier company in Mountjoy's Foot, effectively under Robert Lundy's command, and found himself in Derry when Mountjoy's Protestant soldiers garrisoned the city. He did not stay long in Derry on that occasion, joining the forces of the Protestant Association in Counties Down and Antrim and fighting in the retreat from Dromore, to Coleraine, along the line of the River Bann and back into Derry. He received a major's commission from William of Orange on 5 February 1689 and, on 19 April, was appointed by Governor Baker colonel of the infantry regiment that had formerly belonged to Clotworthy Skeffington. After Derry had been relieved, Kirke appointed him colonel of Skeffington's old regiment, which was merged with that of Richard Crofton, and sole governor of Derry. He paid a heavy personal price: his wife, Susan, and seven children succumbed to disease during the siege. Michelburne continued to live in Derry until his death on 1 October 1721 devoting time and slender resources to continuing the memory of the siege and writing a play, *Ireland Preserv'd: or, the Siege of Derry* (1705), effectively a personal memoir in dramatic form. He was buried in Glendermot churchyard.[6]

A message to the city from General Rosen on 30 June illustrated the divisions within the Irish high command. Rosen said that if Richard Hamilton's proposals were rejected and Derry had not surrendered by 18:00 on Monday 1 July, he would send orders as far as Ballyshannon, Charlemont, Belfast and the Inishowen Peninsula, that all protected and unprotected Protestants either related to anyone under siege or belonging to their faction would first be plundered and then herded to Derry and driven into the no-man's-land between the walls and the trenches to starve unless relieved by the garrison. He also threatened to burn and devastate the countryside on the first sign that troops were coming to relieve the city. This was his only offer and, if rejected, no quarter would be given, regardless of gender or age, when the city fell. Should surrender be chosen, the inhabitants and garrison would receive protection and Rosen's 'favour'. To ensure wide dissemination, copies were delivered via an empty mortar shell and addressed personally to senior officers. Orders to gather all men, women and children related to anyone in Derry and Enniskillen and bring them to Derry went to the governors and commanders of the Irish forces in Coleraine, Antrim, Carrickfergus, Belfast, Dungannon, Charlemont, Belturbet and Sligo; Sarsfield's 'flying army' around Manorhamilton; Colonel Sutherland in County Cavan; and the Duke of Berwick guarding the line of the River Finn.[7]

The appointed hour, 18:00, on 1 July passed and, in the absence of any signs of surrender, Rosen executed his threat. On the following day the Irish began to drive 'the poor Protestants' – men, women and children – towards the walls. During their journeys they were 'stripped and guarded in dirty pounds and rotten houses' and many 'tender people' and pregnant women died. At first, the defenders thought it was a detachment of the Irish Army advancing so they opened fire but no one was hit and the mistake discovered. How many Protestants were herded towards the walls is uncertain. Rosen's letters to Derry and his theatre commanders were written on 30 June and most would not have been delivered until 1 or even 2 July. Within such a short time, only the Protestants from the immediate vicinity of Derry and adjacent parts of the Laggan and Inishowen could have been collected. Walker reported that there were 'some thousands' whilst Mackenzie said that the round-up affected a 16-km radius. Captain Ash, rather more credibly, says that 'about two hundred' were driven to the walls on 2 July followed by a further 1,000 on the following day. Although 'much moved with this pitiful sight' the garrison did not know how to respond. It was decided to keep the refugees in the open outside the entrenchments on Windmill Hill but, for the first night only, they were allowed within the trenches. Further embarrassment was caused when some of these unfortunates implored the garrison to hold out and not to surrender on their account.

Michelburne and his officers decided to reciprocate with equally stern measures and erected a gallows on the bastion closest to the Irish camp on which they threatened to hang all Jacobite prisoners in Derry if the Protestant hostages were not allowed to go home. In readiness, the 20 prisoners were collected from their lodgings and put into gaol. Lieutenant Colonel Campbell and Captain the Reverend Christopher Jenny, a Church of Ireland minister, prepared the prisoners for death. Under supervision, they wrote to Lieutenant General Hamilton beseeching him to intercede with General Rosen to obtain their release otherwise they would all die on the morrow, 3 July. Hamilton replied that the fate of the Irish prisoners rested in the hands of Derry's defenders but, if the prisoners had to die, then their sacrifice would be avenged by many thousands of Protestant lives. Despite Hamilton's callous, probably Rosenian reply, on 4 July the poor Protestants were allowed to depart. In return, the gallows were dismantled and the prisoners allowed to return to their usual lodgings. However, the garrison, which now numbered 5,709 men, was presented with an opportunity to rid the town of 500 useless mouths or *gens faibles*, mostly women and children, by mingling them amongst the departing hostages. An old hand like Rosen had met such tricks before and ordered a strict search 'with Argus eyes' and a number were turned back, betrayed by the condition of their faces and legs. However, some managed to slip away. Conversely, a number of able-bodied male hostages were persuaded to join the defenders. Rosen's draconian tactics were counter-productive. First, many of the detainees held protections from either James or Richard Hamilton and Rosen's action demonstrated that the Irish could not be trusted, strengthening the garrison's determination to resist and reject terms. Second, the episode had given the garrison an opportunity to enhance both its fighting strength and supply position. Despite this, there was still a trickle of people prepared to risk accepting a protection rather than suffer in the seemingly inevitable fall: Andrew Robinson left around 3 July but he was stripped and turned back 'because of some imprudent expressions'. Captain Beatty, sick of a 'violent flux', returned to his house at Moneymore to recover his health. There was no question of Beatty's integrity because he had fought in all the major actions and 'ever behaved himself with great integrity and valour'. George Walker received several hints from a friend in the Irish camp that some mischief against him was intended by his enemies within Derry. Soon after, rumours circulated that he was hiding provisions in his house but Walker countered by arranging for his house to be thoroughly searched and suspicions were temporarily dampened.[8]

On 4 July a letter was received in Enniskillen from Archdeacon Brown, the chaplain of the frigate HMS *Bonaventure* (Captain Thomas Hobson RN), which had reached Killybegs on the previous day from Kirke's squadron in Lough Swilly. Brown wanted to know the Enniskilleners' condition, whether they required supplies and, indeed, if they were still in existence because Irish propaganda insisted that they had been long since erased. Brown asked some officers to come to Ballyshannon, where the *Bonaventure* had sailed on 4 July, to give a first-hand account to Captain Hobson. Governor Hamilton asked Lieutenant Colonel Lloyd, Captain Francis Gore, Captain Hugh Montgomery and Lieutenant Andrew Hamilton to ride immediately for Ballyshannon with an escort of horse and foot to bring back as many supplies as possible. News of Hobson's arrival boosted morale and, that night, bonfires were lit and volleys fired 'which was more than we could well spare of ammunition'.

Two hours after they had left for Ballyshannon, Berwick brought some troops of horse and two regiments of foot to Andrew Hamilton's home which they searched but, finding him absent, burned it along with the dwellings of his tenants declaring that 'if they had got him himself, they would have made him meat for their hawks': the Irish held Hamilton principally responsible for the raid on Omagh on 11–12 June. Berwick then camped at Trillick. On the night of 4–5 July, Governor Hamilton marched to the ruins of Hamilton's house but, finding Berwick gone and not having enough men to beat up his camp, retired to Enniskillen placing strong guards on the roads. At Ballyshannon, Captain Hobson listened to Lloyd's account, promised that Enniskillen would soon be relieved from England and handed over 30 barrels of powder plus some muskets. It was agreed that two Enniskillen officers, John Rider and Andrew Hamilton, would sail with Hobson to ask General Kirke for commissions, arms, ammunition and some experienced officers 'of which we had great want' to train, instruct and lead the levies. Rider and Hamilton boarded the *Bonaventure* on 8 July, reaching Lough Foyle four days later. For two days, from 12 to 14 July, Kirke quizzed them about the state of affairs at Enniskillen. They reported that there were 17 troops of horse and a few of dragoons, all poorly equipped, and 30 well-armed infantry companies. Kirke had few surplus cavalry arms but gave them 600 dragoon flintlocks, 1,000 muskets with which to equip additional foot companies, bullets, match, eight small cannon and a few hand grenades. He also signed commissions for a regiment of horse of 16 troops, each of 50 men; a regiment of dragoons, with 12 troops of 50 men apiece; and three regiments of infantry, each with 18 companies of 60 men, two of which were to be composed of grenadiers, plus an independent troop of horse permanently attached to its establishment for scouting, patrolling and support in action. Kirke said that although he could not spare any soldiers he had available some very good officers. Lieutenant Colonel William Wolseley was appointed commander-in-chief of all the Enniskillen forces and colonel of the regiment of cavalry with Captain William Berry as his lieutenant colonel and Captain Charles Stone major. Captain James Wynne, 'a gentleman from Ireland', then a captain in William Stewart's battalion of foot, would become colonel of the Enniskillen dragoon regiment. Governor Gustavus Hamilton was to be appointed colonel of one of the infantry regiments, whilst Thomas Lloyd and Zachariah Tiffin were to be promoted to command the other two. Captain Thomas Price, who already commanded a troop in what would become Wolseley's regiment of horse, was to be appointed adjutant general. Captain James Johnston, who held a company in Stewart's, was appointed engineer. Kirke was most helpful, demonstrably loyal and enthusiastic; he could have taken the opportunity to off-load some of his more questionable officers but sent the best. Indeed, according to Hamilton, he seemed genuinely ignorant of affairs in Enniskillen 'and no man could have shown more zeal for their Majesties' service, and preservation of the Protestants'. Rider, Hamilton, the new officers and the supplies left Kirke in Lough Swilly on Sunday 20 July but contrary winds delayed their arrival in Ballyshannon until 26 July. They reached Belleek on 27 July and Enniskillen the next day.[9]

On Windmill Hill the opposing soldiers were close enough to converse. The garrison discovered that the Irish hated the French, who strutted around in jackboots grabbing all the promotions, key positions and best provisions. Disease was gradually reducing the garrison's numbers. On 8 July the muster strength was 5,520: by 25 July, it had fallen to 4,892. Morale was also declining. On 6 or 7 July, some Irish troops were seen forming up near their principal camp so Governor Michelburne sent a couple of patrols to investigate. One advanced as far as the old ditches beyond Windmill Hill and engaged in a short fire fight, whilst Colonel Barker took a dozen men towards the strand. Two Irish companies marched from the camp to reinforce their lines near the beach but it was growing dark and the desultory business petered out. Mistaking the word of command, there was some confusion as the Derrymen withdrew. Barker was shot in the hand, a wound from which he later died. The zip, enthusiasm and aggression of the garrison were diminishing but the spirits of the besiegers were also depressed and the Irish commanders decided to make no more attacks but to wait until starvation produced victory.[10] However, James remained sufficiently confident of victory to dispatch Brigadier Alexander Cannon, a Scot from Galloway who had spent most of his career in the Anglo-Dutch Brigade, with 400 raw recruits from Colonel James Purcell's dragoon regiment, plus 75 unattached officers, to assist Viscount Dundee's rebellion in Scotland. Following an eventful passage they landed at Lochaber on 17 July.[11]

On 11 July, the Irish called for a parley and sent a trumpet to enquire whether Derry would negotiate. As most of Kirke's ships had disappeared, 'we knew not whither', and provisions were approaching danger level, the garrison sought to gain time by taking advantage of a renewed offer of terms which Richard Hamilton had issued on 10 July. Both sides appointed six commissioners, whose names were to be exchanged by 12 July, with a view to holding an initial meeting on 13 July. There was some disagreement as to whether the commissioners represented the Council of Fourteen or Governors Walker and Michelburne.

Nevertheless, the Derry envoys travelled to the Irish camp on 13 July and talked long into the night; they returned bearing inflexible conditions. The Irish would permit a capitulation no later than 12:00 on Monday 15 July and hostages would be housed in Derry during subsequent negotiations. When it came to the formal act of surrender, only the officers and gentlemen of the city would be allowed to carry arms. After much argument, the commissioners secured 12:00 on 14 July as the deadline for a response. Whilst these discussions were continuing, Walker received a message, via a 'little boy', from Lieutenant David Mitchell on board Kirke's ships. Mitchell said that Kirke had moved to Lough Swilly and landed some men on Inch Island but Walker edited the contents to read that 4,000 cavalry and 9,000 infantry had disembarked.[12] At the Council meeting on 14 July, Walker amazingly used the revised figures to argue in favour of accepting the terms of surrender when, by any logic, they supported the opposite stance. He then admitted to having altered the letter; John Mackenzie thought he had taken leave of his senses. Accordingly, before 12:00 on 14 July the Council of Fourteen replied that they would not surrender unless the deadline was extended to 25 July and hostages might be secured on board Kirke's vessels. Negotiations were terminated.[13]

When HMS *Bonaventure* came into Lough Foyle from Killybegs on 12 July, Captain Hobson carried not only Andrew Hamilton and Major Rider but also some Donegal gentlemen who wished to propose to Kirke that, given arms and officers, they could recruit 8,000 infantry and 1,200 cavalry. Kirke seems to have gained the erroneous impression that these troops already existed and would join him on Inch Island. It was midnight on 19 July when HMS *Swallow*, bearing Kirke, hove into Lough Swilly and fired 13 guns, the battery on Inch Island saluting with nine. Instead of 8,000 infantry and 1,200 cavalry from Donegal, Kirke found on Inch only a rabble of Protestant refugees huddled together to escape the storm of depredation, burning, looting and killing that was devouring Inishowen and northern Donegal. Across the lough, smoke from the ruins of Rathmullan drifted on the breeze. He received also a factual and informative letter from Governors Walker and Michelburne; clearly, delay was no longer an option and Kirke had to reconsider his approach. Colonel William Stewart and an advance party of 600 men had already converted Inch Island into a firm base. A redoubt mounting 22 cannon covered the causeway to the mainland, only a musket-shot in length and fordable at low tide, whilst additional fire support was available from naval vessels lying off-shore. One thousand cattle had been driven on to the island and Stewart had armed about 1,000 of the male refugees. He was in touch with the Enniskilleners and hatched vague plans for them to march north but nothing could be expected in the near future because they were coming under pressure from Berwick, Sarsfield and Justin Macarty. Kirke's four battalions had been on board ship for some time and their health was deteriorating. Confident that Inch was a strong position and Berwick would not move north to attack because he was fully occupied with Enniskillen, Kirke disembarked his men and left them under Stewart's command. Refusing to contemplate major land operations until reinforced from England, on the night of 20 July Kirke sailed back to Lough Foyle having finally decided that the only way to relieve Derry was by naval action against the boom.[14]

Kirke seems to have been unaware of developments in Enniskillen. On 13 July, Berwick's 'flying army' started towards Enniskillen from its camp at Trillick. Thomas Lloyd was absent in Ballyshannon and operational leadership devolved upon the lesser talents of Governor Hamilton. Scouts brought the news before dawn and every available man stood to arms, even the governor 'getting on horseback'. Lieutenant William McCarmick's company paraded in the main street and Governor Hamilton ordered him to secure Cornagrade House standing on a hill 400 m from the town and adjacent to the road which Berwick would take from Trillick. It was untenable: the roof was thatched, the bawn wall lacked loopholes and was too high for the men to fire over, and the internal courtyard was full of hay, straw and other combustibles. In McCarmick's view, one pistol shot would set the whole place ablaze. On his own initiative and without reference to Governor Hamilton, McCarmick pulled back to Enniskillen Mill 'a very straight pass and under the cannon-shot from the fort'. Governor Hamilton rode to McCarmick's new position accompanied by the cavalry troops of Captains Hugh Montgomery and Francis King plus 30 infantrymen from Captain Hudson's company, under Lieutenant Robert Starlin and Ensign Williams. Hamilton took McCarmick by the hand and asked him to join his men with those of Lieutenant Starlin and lead the infantry as far as the hedge along the left hand side of the road down which the two troops of horse would charge when Berwick appeared. McCarmick replied that 92 men were insufficient, especially as one-third were pikemen and unsuitable for this type of fighting. McCarmick added that he had scant confidence in the cavalry who were likely to desert or run if engaged. Hamilton replied to this insubordination – he appears to have ignored McCarmick's earlier non-compliance – by personally guaranteeing the loyalty of the cavalry and promising to send strong infantry reinforcements. McCarmick graciously consented to obey but reminded Hamilton of his undertaking to hasten support.

McCarmick then met Lieutenant Campbell who said that the Irish were at hand. He sent Campbell, who was mounted, to prompt Governor Hamilton about the pledged infantry support but Enniskillen was packed with troops and he had trouble in locating the governor. When he did, it was clear that Hamilton had either deliberately or accidentally forgotten his earlier undertaking and had completely lost control of the situation. After Campbell had explained that the Irish were almost upon McCarmick, Hamilton told him to return and instruct

McCarmick to disengage, withdraw towards the lough and he would send boats to bring him off. Governor Hamilton then went into Enniskillen Castle, which was overflowing with troops, where Captain Webster also reminded him of the commitment to McCarmick so he instructed Webster to go to Captain Henry Smith, who was marching his company to Portora Castle on the other side of the lough and was already 3 km from McCarmick, to order him to turn around and march to McCarmick's relief. Meanwhile, McCarmick remained at Enniskillen Mill in full view of the Irish neglecting Hamilton's orders to move forward and line the hedges alongside the road. Berwick's vanguard of 600 dismounted dragoons supported by two troops of cavalry, commanded by Colonel Simon Luttrell, advanced towards McCarmick's position but the defensive fire was so rapid and effective that they faltered, lost momentum and fell back. Taking advantage, the two troops of Enniskillen horse charged down the road. Although initially successful, they soon ran into Berwick's main body and, without McCarmick's infantry manning the hedgerows in support, turned and fled back into Enniskillen. Luttrell shouted, 'They run, they run. Their horse are fled' at which the dragoons rallied, reorganized and began to advance once more on Enniskillen Mill. A sharp fire fight ensued until two troops of Irish horse rode along the road, turned McCarmick's flank and attacked the rear of his position. Surrounded and out of formation, McCarmick's infantry suffered severely. Ensign Williams and 50 privates were killed whilst Captain Fulton, Lieutenant McCarmick, 'who had his eldest son killed at his side', Ensign Pickering, two sergeants and 20 men were taken prisoner. Governor Hamilton sent no support. Lieutenant Fort, a cavalryman, met the governor and offered to lead a detachment of horse to sustain McCarmick but his reply was 'very peevish: "Don't you see the enemy before you? Can't you go and fight?"' Fort responded, equally unhelpfully, 'If that be your answer, I'll fight none today.' Captains Atkinson and Robert Corry heard that McCarmick was engaged and seeing the cavalry come flying back, marched without orders to his assistance but the action was over before they arrived and Luttrell had withdrawn. Fortunately for Governor Hamilton, Berwick considered Enniskillen too strong to be attacked directly and was content with his small tactical victory. During and after the Battle of Enniskillen Mill, Governor Hamilton ordered the burning of the houses of Captain Corry, Mr Paul Dane, the Provost of Enniskillen, and Mr Lautournal because he feared that the Irish would garrison them and establish permanent positions close to Enniskillen. McCarmick and his fellow prisoners were well treated – Governor Hamilton wrote to Berwick threatening dire vengeance if they were harmed – and quietly exchanged a few days later for Lieutenant Colonel Edward Scott, taken at Belturbet, the Enniskilleners' principal bargaining counter.[15]

McCarmick's defeat revealed much about Enniskillen. There was neither a clear chain of command nor effective discipline; officers questioned orders and were openly insubordinate whilst lieutenants gave orders to captains and captains told the governor what to do. Governor Hamilton appeared indecisive, possessed limited martial aptitude and, in a crisis, demonstrated neither grip nor leadership. In the absence of Thomas Lloyd, as McCarmick admits, the Enniskilleners were disorganized and fragmented. Lloyd must have been an extremely effective natural leader because his authority over the Enniskilleners was absolute and, given the rickety rank structure, must have commanded by force of personality and charisma. The evidence from 13 July suggests that he was the key element in the town's successful resistance.

However, the action convinced Berwick that Enniskillen was too strong to be taken by assault and the route to victory was starvation, which could best be achieved by interrupting the passage of boats into Lower Lough Erne through Ballyshannon and Belleek. Accordingly, Berwick instructed Sarsfield to advance from Manorhamilton, via Bundoran, against Ballyshannon with 3,000 infantry and 200 cavalry, whilst Berwick attacked from the north. Sarsfield duly moved to Bundoran but Colonel William Stewart's appearance on Inch Island pulled Berwick's attention back to the Derry theatre. Falling back, he remained at Trillick until Monday 15 July when he moved to Omagh. He reached Castlefinn on 16 July and, the next day, shifted 5 km to a deer park at Convoy, where he left his cavalry and dragoons because there was insufficient forage further north. On Friday 19 July, Berwick marched his infantry to Letterkenny and, on Saturday 20 July, to Rathmullan, where he engaged some of Stewart's scouts before burning the town. With Berwick's detachment no longer threatening from Trillick, the Enniskilleners were clear to turn against Sarsfield; in Lloyd's continuing absence, Sir Gerald Irvine, of Castle Irvine, County Fermanagh, was chosen to command the expedition. During the early days of Enniskillen's resistance, Irvine, who had fought with Charles II at Worcester in 1651, had applied to Dublin for arms and equipment stating his intention to raise 100 cavalry to help reduce the town. The weapons were seized by local Irish forces as the wagons travelled through County Cavan and their non-delivery seems to have shifted Irvine's allegiance. At his own expense he fortified and garrisoned his house at Trillick but was driven out by Berwick. Later, he raised a troop of horse and served under Schomberg at Dundalk, where he died from disease. On 18 July Irvine led forward a force of about 1,500 men, divided into two wings, one entirely of cavalry and the other of horse and foot, but Sarsfield had taken up a strong defensive position at Bundoran, supported by three cannon. Irvine felt unable to attack and returned to Enniskillen. Without Lloyd, the Enniskilleners had suffered two setbacks within a week.[16]

A small party of Irish attacked and took possession of the temporarily unmanned demi-bastion and entrenchments outside the Butcher's Gate at Derry on 15 July but were driven out by the weight of musket and cannon fire from the walls, supplemented by the hurling of heavy stones. This was probably a feint, intended to divert the defenders' attention from the principal effort against Windmill Hill by two infantry regiments. Encouraged by Michelburne, the garrison went out in considerable numbers to line the trenches but the Irish only advanced as far as the middle of the hill before withdrawing. The Derrymen raised a cheer, waved their hats and politely invited the Irish to come back and fight. Adam Murray then took 12 men and, in an act of unnecessary bravado, rode to the end of the Irish trenches before the Butcher's Gate and disturbed them with enfilade fire but the cost was heavy. James Murray was killed whilst Adam was shot through both thighs, serious wounds from which he did not recover until November. About this time, the Irish redeployed their heavy cannon to Brook Hall to cover the boom. This cheered the garrison as did a culinary discovery. James Cunningham, a merchant, demonstrated how to make pancakes by mixing starch, of which there was a ready supply, with tallow. These horrible things proved not only edible but also sufficiently costive to help some recover from diarrhoea and dysentery caused by bad diet.[17]

Still working on the assumption that Kirke would relieve Derry and, by extension, Enniskillen, William III continued to prepare a major expeditionary force of 10,000 men for Ireland. The Committee of the Privy Council on Ireland instructed the Secretary at War, William Blathwayt, to advance £12,000 to Chester for the reception and transport of the troops.[18] On Thursday 18 July, the Dutchman, Major General Adam van der Duyn, Heer van Scravenmoer, quartermaster-general of the expeditionary force for Ireland, arrived in Chester and, on Friday 19 July, laid out a camp to the south of the city. Lieutenant General Hendrik Trajectinus, Graaf van Solms-Braunfels, a cousin of King William and commander of the Brigade of Dutch Foot Guards, reached Chester on Saturday 20 July at 14:00, closely followed by one of his battalions. At 22:00 on the same day, Herman von Schomberg, the commander of the expeditionary force, entered Chester to be received by the mayor and aldermen in their scarlet 'and all their formalities, attended by several companies with their flags carried before them'. The trained bands of the Chester militia met Schomberg at the 'Bars' and escorted him to his lodging at Alderman Mannering's house. Schomberg held a meeting with Solms and Lord Gerrard of Brandon, the Governor of Chester, on Monday 22 July before inspecting the shipping that had been gathered at Liverpool, Hoylake and Neston to convey the troops to Ireland. The plan was for 8,000 infantry to encamp at Chester on 22 and 23 July whilst 4,000 cavalry assembled at Whitehaven. Execution lay a little behind expectation but, by 31 July, seven infantry battalions were encamped at Chester and the supply convoy, sailing from London, was expected daily. On 30 July, Schomberg put each battalion through its paces. The original intention had been to reinforce Kirke in either Lough Foyle or Lough Swilly but events in Northern Ireland moved so rapidly during the last week of July that, by the first week of August, plans required revision.[19]

Everyone attending the council of war in Derry on 24 July was sworn to secrecy. At 03:00 on 25 July, 500 men assembled in Ship Quay Street with the intention of seizing some of the Irish Army's cattle that were grazing close behind the entrenchments within reach of the city. One party of 100 (Captain Blair, Captain Dixon and Lieutenant Boyd) was to exit the Bishop's Gate, man the ravelin to watch for a possible Jacobite attack on Windmill Hill, and act as a reserve. The main assault was to be conducted by two detachments each of 200 men, one leaving via the Ship Quay Gate (Captain Wilson, Lieutenant Moor and Sergeant Neely) and the other from the Butcher's Gate (Captain A. Hamilton, Captain Burley and Captain Thomas Ash). The besiegers were taken by surprise, 'for most of their matches were out, quite unprepared for an attack'. Sir John Fitzgerald's regiment, which was manning the trenches near the Butcher's Gate, deployed in good order but its musketeers had only three matches alight when they were attacked and overrun, the Derrymen claiming 300 killed. More might have been accounted for but the soldiers were severely malnourished and lacked the strength to pursue, 'some falling with their own blows'. As reinforcements began to move towards the site of the action, the raiders were forced to retire without any cattle although abandoned Jacobite knapsacks provided some oatmeal loaves and cold mutton. An alternative, although ludicrous, approach was tried. The one remaining cow in Derry was tethered close to the walls and set on fire, in the hope that the cattle in the Irish lines would come to her aid. They began to move and lifted their tails in readiness but the unfortunate bait managed to break free.[20]

9

The relief of Derry and Newtownbutler

Having finally made up his mind that the boom had to be forced even if ships might be lost, Kirke had returned to Lough Foyle in HMS *Swallow* accompanied by three victuallers: the *Mountjoy* of Derry (Captain Michael Browning), the *Phoenix* of Coleraine (Captain Andrew Douglas), and the *Jerusalem* (Captain Pepwell). Kirke was off Greencastle on Sunday 21 July where he met HMS *Portland* (Captain Sir Thomas Lee RN), who told him that Sir George Rooke's squadron was cruising off Carrickfergus. Kirke sent Lee to Rooke to ask for the loan of the frigate HMS *Dartmouth* (Captain John Leake RN). On 22 July, Kirke sailed into Lough Foyle, sending the three victuallers to lie off Culmore Fort. The *Dartmouth* and the fourth rate HMS *Deptford* came up to Kirke on 25 July and he instructed the former to join the victuallers off Culmore and proceed up-river with the first fair wind. The wind continued unfavourable until Sunday 28 July when at 18:00, a 'moderate gale' blew from the north-north-west, probably a squall. The *Dartmouth* and the *Mountjoy* weighed anchor: the *Phoenix* was not to follow until the *Dartmouth* had engaged Culmore whilst the *Jerusalem* was to wait for a signal from the *Dartmouth* that the boom had been broken. Accompanying the leading ship was the *Swallow*'s longboat, its nine-man crew charged with cutting the boom. Leake worked the *Dartmouth* into a position between Culmore Fort and the boom before anchoring to cover the *Mountjoy* and *Phoenix* from the fort's fire as they proceeded towards the boom. Kirke said that the *Dartmouth* fired six cannon in reply to every one from the fort.

By 27 July the Derry garrison had fallen to 4,456 men: a cat cost four shillings and sixpence, a rat one shilling, a mouse sixpence and a quarter of a dog, fattened by eating dead Irishmen, five shillings and sixpence. The last 16 cows and 12 horses had been slaughtered and morale was low. On Sunday 28 July, with the wind veering between north and north-west, the flag on the steeple was raised and lowered twice to indicate the garrison's distress and eight cannon were fired to reinforce the message, 'to say, if they came not now, the wind blowing fair, they might stay away for ever'. Six cannon were fired in reply from the ships, 'which intimated that when the tide answered they would endeavour to relieve us'. At 19:00, about an hour after sermon,[1] lookouts on the cathedral tower noticed two provision ships, led by an escorting frigate, making towards Culmore. Cheers broke out when it was perceived that the ships had successfully passed the Culmore cannon.

As Captain Leake anchored the *Dartmouth* to provide covering fire, the *Mountjoy* and *Phoenix* were seen to sail on towards the boom. Under cannon and musket fire from both banks, the *Mountjoy* hit the boom, recoiled and ran aground. The already light wind dropped away stalling both ships and, through gun smoke and fog, the Irish were seen swarming about the shore readying boats to board the stranded vessels. Spirits in Derry sank but recovered when, on the flooding tide, the *Mountjoy* fired a broadside and floated clear. Probably, the *Mountjoy* did not break the boom; this was the work of the seamen manning the *Swallow*'s longboat who hacked through the cables with hatchets. A slight tidal rush resulted, sufficient to push through the *Mountjoy* and the *Phoenix* but subsequent progress was painfully sluggish in the light airs. So slowly did they move upriver – they were propelled by the incoming tide rather than any wind and the *Mountjoy*, a much larger ship than the *Phoenix*, had to be towed by the *Swallow*'s longboat – that the Irish were able to redeploy their cannon to keep up a desultory running fire.

Eventually, at 22:00 the *Phoenix* reached the quay and immediately began to discharge her cargo of 800 barrels of meal from Scotland, the *Mountjoy* close behind carrying 135 tons of beef, peas, flour and biscuits. To protect the unloading from Irish fire, blinds made from hogsheads and casks filled with earth were erected along the quay. There was only one fatal casualty, Captain Browning of the *Mountjoy*, shot when his vessel ran aground.[2]

The relief had been greatly assisted by Kirke's move to Inch, only 10 km to the west, which had obliged the Jacobites to move a considerable portion of their army away from the siege lines. The contribution of the Enniskilleners was also important, obliging Richard Hamilton to secure his rear areas by maintaining garrisons at Strabane, Lifford, Castlefinn, Clady, Newtown Stewart, Castlederg and Omagh. Consequently, the banks of the Foyle were weakly defended; only 'an inconsiderable party' and two cannon covered the boom. When the *Dartmouth*, *Mountjoy* and *Phoenix* sailed upriver the relief was effected so quickly that the Jacobites had no time in which to redeploy their forces. Culmore was a weak position, largely denuded of its cannon. In addition, Gilbert says that the gunners were drunk on brandy and could not shoot straight whilst it has been suggested that they had been bribed from the secret service fund administered by Thomas Coningsby, the paymaster-general of the English Army in Ireland. Stevens referred to them contemptuously as 'blind gunners'.

The boom was equally feeble. There is an old military maxim that a defensive obstacle is only effective provided that it is covered by adequate fire: when the boom halted and grounded the *Mountjoy* there was insufficient local firepower available to take advantage. Sinking a few old ships would have created a much stronger barrier, something frequently suggested by James's French advisers, but he demurred on the grounds that it would have proved extremely difficult to clear the passage of the river after Derry had fallen rendering useless a port through which French supplies and aid might later have been channelled into the north of Ireland.

Following the joyous welcome, the leaders of Derry went aboard HMS *Swallow* and informed Kirke that they wanted neither men nor ammunition, only provisions. They also asked him to continue Walker as governor because he 'had been so successful' and the imposition of a new commander might induce 'grumbling'. They suggested that Kirke's soldiers should not be landed at Derry but continued at Inch whence land and sea communications with Enniskillen, Ballyshannon and Derry could be maintained. Flushed with victory, which they attributed to their own resourcefulness rather than assistance from England, the Derry leaders failed to grasp that their independence had ended. They were now under the command of the Williamite Army, and General Kirke in particular.[3]

Even had hulks been sunk in the narrows, Derry would probably have survived. Kirke's promised reinforcements, in the form of Schomberg's expedition, were only a fortnight away and would have put into Lough Swilly instead of Belfast Lough. Also, the letter from Walker and Michelburne to Kirke had, probably deliberately, considerably exaggerated Derry's plight. Mackenzie and Walker both agree that, although supplies were low, following an issue of rations on 27 July some foodstuffs, mostly tallow, shilling and dry hides, remained in the stores. To the very end, officers enjoyed better fare than the soldiers. On 26 and 27 July, each officer received 1½ lb (680 g) of horsemeat, 1½ lb of barley and ½ lb (227 g) of tobacco. The real problem was the non-military population, which was close to starvation by the end of July and it was not unknown for malnourished civilians to rebel against the military government and demand surrender. It is impossible to calculate accurately the casualties suffered by Derry. The ration strength of the regimented soldiers fell from 7,020 men and 341 officers at the beginning of the siege to 4,508 soldiers and 252 officers on 30 July. In other words, 36 per cent of the troops and 28 per cent of the officers died, deserted or left Derry. Estimates of the number of civilian deaths varied between 7,000 and 8,000.

Because the attackers lacked heavy cannon to enfilade and breach the fortifications, the walls remained largely intact. Many buildings were damaged although, by contemporary European standards, the bombardment had been desultory; between 24 April and 22 July, 261 light and 374 heavy cannon balls and mortar bombs were received, an average of seven per day: over 300 projectiles per day had been fired into 's-Hertogenbosch in 1629 whilst over 60,000 bombs and shot had rained down on Namur in 1692.[4] Following his visit to Derry on 4 August, Kirke wrote to the Duke of Hamilton that

> Since I was born I never saw a town of so little strength, to rout an army with so many generals against it … The houses are generally broke down by the bombs, there having

been five hundred and ninety-one shot, shot into the town. The walls and outworks are not touched.[5]

Cannon fire continued until 31 July when Irish troops began to set fire to the neighbouring countryside, interrupted by some patrols from Derry. During the night, they burned their own huts and tents and, before daylight on 1 August, marched south to Lifford and Strabane where they camped to await news of Macarty's progress against Enniskillen. Colonel Stewart received orders from Kirke to embark all his men and guns and sail to Derry but delayed executing his instructions because of the need to protect the numerous Protestant refugees from the fury of a defeated enemy. On 1 August some Derry officers travelled to Inch, where Kirke had arrived during the night, and unsuccessfully sought permission to take 300 men into the field to protect local Protestants' houses and bring in some cattle. Within a week, Irish 'stay-behind' parties had burned Newtown Limavady and several gentlemen's residences towards Coleraine: when Captain Thomas Ash visited his farm on 1 August he found that 'the roof of my house was smoking in the floor, and the doors falling off the hinges'. Colonels William Stewart and Jacob Richards arrived on 2 August to congratulate Derry on its deliverance and then, on Sunday 4 August, Kirke was formally received by the governors and garrison. Walker offered the keys but he would not accept them. The following day, the governors and several officers dined with Kirke on Inch Island where Walker, wishing to return to his ministry, resigned the joint governorship and his regiment. Kirke confirmed his client Michelburne as sole governor.

Kirke's attitude to the Ulster Protestants was ambivalent. He issued a proclamation that all people not in arms who had taken refuge in Derry were to return home leaving behind their goods and chattels unless specifically instructed to the contrary. No corpse was to be buried within the walls. Considerable numbers of cattle, belonging to both neighbouring Protestants and the Irish Army, were driven in from the countryside and herded close to the walls. It was impossible to determine ownership so Michelburne supervised their sale 'at a good rate' to local butchers and merchants, the proceeds presumably lining the pockets of Kirke and his officers; many local Protestants thereby forfeited their principal means of livelihood. An address to the king was prepared but, to the discontent of many, Kirke selected Walker to be the emissary. Many did not fully concur with the compliments to Kirke contained in the document but no one was willing, at this juncture, to cause disquiet by protesting publicly. Later, on 24 September when the army was in camp at Dundalk, a formal council of war considered Sir Henry Ingoldsby's assertion that Derry might have been relieved much sooner 'with a great deal more to that purpose; but it came to nothing and was no more talk'd of'.[6]

Kirke's battalions reached Derry on 6 August, except for a small garrison of 150 men under Captain Thomas Barbour left to garrison Inch. Reinforced and backed up by his own English soldiers, Kirke set about the task of demobilizing the Derry forces. They were paraded outside the city that same day and rumours spread that Kirke was about to distribute £2,000. Instead, Richard Crofton's regiment was disbanded and its remaining men incorporated into Michelburne's 'Antrim' regiment. Walker's was amalgamated with Hugh Hamill's, who was dismissed, Robert White taking over the combined remnants. White died in September 1689 and was replaced by John Caulfield. Henry Monroe's and T. Lance's regiments were dissolved into one, Monroe losing his place, whereupon Lance was made colonel but he died in September. It was intended to merge the late Governor Baker's regiment with that of Adam Murray but most of the men refused to comply and went off in a huff taking with them their carbines and pistols. Thereupon, Kirke seized the horse furniture of Murray's regiment, which had been assiduously preserved throughout the siege. What was left of Baker's and Murray's formed a new regiment under Colonel Thomas St John, a regular soldier with an excellent record and currently major of Kirke's infantry battalion. Having created four battalions, Kirke appointed the captains and allowed the men to select their own lieutenants and ensigns. This reorganization was enormously resented. Many captains who had raised, armed and paid their own companies were dismissed whilst others, whose performance during the siege had not been unduly distinguished, were elevated into lucrative, regular commissions. Lieutenants and ensigns fared no better than captains. To make matters worse, Kirke removed men from their home companies and drafted them into different units to balance the new regiments. Captains with under-strength companies were informed that their commands would be disbanded if they could not immediately fill the ranks. The final affront was to place the new Derry regiments on the Irish establishment ensuring lower rates of pay than comparable English units. Regimenting and regularizing the Derry forces, as well as disarming and demilitarizing the citizen-soldiers, were necessary because Kirke was short of troops and needed every available reliable soldier whilst the conduct of the operations had to be removed from militias and transferred to the regular, professional armed forces. Unfortunately, Kirke's *modus operandi* was tactless, arbitrary and insensitive. Sentries at the gates, who came from Kirke's four regular battalions, were ordered to confiscate the weapons of anyone who tried to leave the city bearing arms, a great insult to men who had been fighting in the Protestant cause. Weak and sick soldiers were not allowed extra subsistence from the stores but were forced to leave Derry and beg in the depopulated countryside, many dying as a consequence. In his customary charming manner, Kirke's reaction to complaints was to point towards the new gallows that had been erected on the ravelin.

The ill impression created by Kirke was partly rectified by a letter from King William to Walker and Michelburne thanking them for the loyal service performed by Derry and assuring them that the crown would provide adequate compensation for its services and suffering. On receipt of this letter, Michelburne – Walker was already in England personally reaping the glory – ordered a 'day of joy' on 17 August. The drums beat and the citizens assembled on the Diamond where Michelburne read the royal epistle. All the cannon on the walls and ships in the river then fired and a volley of musketry accompanied every health drunk from the barrels of ale in the Market House. As an earnest of his good intentions, William gave financial help to the widow and children of the late Governor Baker but Walker's assertion that William also gave 'due consideration to every officer and soldier in the garrison, giving them commissions, money and clothes, to the great encouragement of these poor men, as well officers' was untrue.[7]

Although short of provisions, money and ammunition, Major General Justin Macarty slowly gathered a new brigade at Belturbet ready to attack Enniskillen via the north bank of Upper Lough Erne. Macarty, the third son of Donagh Macarty, Third Earl of Clancarty, was an experienced soldier who had served both France and Denmark. By 27 July he had assembled 3,600 men in three complete infantry regiments (2,418), two of dragoons (1,086) and two troops of horse (96). In addition, there were seven brass field guns and one heavy, iron cannon. Ranged against him were 30 companies of Enniskillen infantry (2,216 men), 17 troops of horse (950) and three troops of dragoons (180), a total of 3,346, supported by six field guns. The coming contest appeared even in quantity but not in quality; the spirited Enniskillen tenant farmers and yeomanry were hardy and resourceful, individually and collectively superior to the native Irish troops. The only prospect of success lay in Sarsfield at Bundoran and Berwick in the north co-ordinating their offensives with Macarty, forcing the Enniskilleners to split their forces, but Berwick had already attacked and vanished back into northern County Donegal. Sarsfield failed to move until well after Macarty enabling the Enniskilleners to take advantage of interior lines and deal with the Irish in detail. Also, as Macarty advanced towards Crom Castle, at the western extremity of the Lough Erne assistance for Enniskillen was sailing into Ballyshannon.

John Rider and Andrew Hamilton, together with the officers commissioned by Kirke, left Inch Island on Wednesday 24 July, disembarking from their ketch 5 km from Ballyshannon two days later (26 July), although variable winds delayed the vessels transporting the arms, ammunition and equipment for a further three or four days. The Ballyshannon garrison fired several welcoming volleys before escorting them into the town where they were greeted by news that Macarty was marching from Belturbet. The party rode to Belleek on Saturday 27 July and took to the water, reaching Enniskillen on Sunday 28 July. When Colonel William Wolseley and his officers came ashore they found the infantry parading from the castle 'to the far point of the island'. An honour guard received them and three volleys echoed from the castle walls, heard above the cheering of the women and children who mobbed these *dei ex machina*. That night a courier galloped in bearing an express from the governor of Crom stating that Macarty was raising a battery against the castle. The regular officers quietly assumed control, supreme authority automatically passing to Wolseley because Governor Hamilton was *hors de combat* with fever, thus avoiding potential disputes between governor and senior field commander.

Wolseley was the fifth son of Sir Robert Wolseley, First Baronet, of Wolseley, Staffordshire. Born around 1640, he chose a military career and was patronized by Henry Somerset (1629–1700), Marquis of Worcester and, after 1682, First Duke of Beaufort. Wolseley appears to have entered the army in 1667 as captain-lieutenant of Worcester's infantry regiment. When this unit was disbanded later that year, he was found a billet as lieutenant of an independent company in Chepstow Castle, of which Worcester was both captain and governor. On the re-raising of Worcester's Foot in 1673, Wolseley was again captain-lieutenant, returning to his Chepstow bolt-hole when the regiment was disbanded in the following year. When Beaufort's was again recreated in 1685 and joined the permanent English establishment, Wolseley was listed as a captain. Promoted major in late June 1688, he demonstrated increasing unhappiness with James's religious policies and was active in promoting the interests of William of Orange. Sir John Hanmer was commissioned colonel of this regiment on 31 December 1688 and, when it was selected as one of the four battalions comprising Kirke's force for Ireland, Wolseley was ideally placed to be appointed to command the Enniskillen forces and the Enniskillen regiment of cavalry on 20 July 1689. Wolseley was advanced to brigadier in 1693 and became a Lord Justice of Ireland after 1691. He died in 1697. Like Thomas Lloyd, when given the opportunity of independent command, Wolseley hardly made a false step: Percy Kirke was a sharp judge of military talent.[8]

On the morning of Monday 29 July, another express galloped into Enniskillen from Crom Castle, stating that Macarty had begun to batter the walls and was starting approach trenches. Although the garrison's musketry had accounted for a number of Irish infantry there was no means of resisting cannon and prompt relief was requested. Wolseley sent back the messenger with a note saying that he would gather his men and come as quickly as possible, aiming to arrive on the morning of 31 July. Orders to concentrate went to all the outlying stations, including Ballyshannon where only a skeleton force was left to watch Sarsfield at Bundoran, releasing the cavalry and 500 infantry to march the 32 km to Enniskillen, those billeted outside Ballyshannon having to trudge an extra 5 or 6 km. On the evening of Monday 29 July, further information arrived that Macarty had left a small force to prosecute the siege and taken the main body towards Lisnaskea, 16 km from Enniskillen. All of Wolseley's available troops reached Enniskillen on the night of 29–30 July and were prepared to press on, without resting.[9]

On the morning of Tuesday 30 July another Kirke client who had come with Wolseley, Lieutenant Colonel William Berry,[10] led four troops of horse, one of dragoons, and two companies of infantry, about 400 men, towards Lisnaskea Castle: if tenable, it was to be occupied; if not, he was to burn it. Berry did neither. On arrival he found Lisnaskea Castle 'so out of order' that it was neither fit to garrison nor of any conceivable use to the enemy so he ignored it and continued forward to camp about 10 km from Macarty's leading elements. Macarty captured some outlying entrenchments at Crom Castle during 30 July but his ill-disciplined soldiers disobeyed orders and tried to rush the walls, suffering between 75 and 80 casualties. During the night of 30–31 July, Macarty erected a battery closer to the walls with a view to launching a general assault on 31 July but he also received intelligence that 4,000 men were marching from Enniskillen to lift the siege. The ground about Crom was unsuitable for offering battle and so he withdrew 3 km to Newtownbutler. The following morning, 31 July, Brigadier Anthony Hamilton with the advance guard comprising the Regiment of Dragoons of Daniel O'Brien, Third Earl of Clare, numbering 540 men, and a single troop of cavalry commanded by Captain Murrough O'Brien, was ordered towards Lisnaskea to drive in any hostile forces they might encounter before seizing and holding a pass where it was said that 100 men could stop ten times as many. Hamilton set off early on the morning of 31 July encountering Berry's out-guards at 06:00 around Donagh, 3 km south-east of Lisnaskea.

Reports of the contact were passed to Berry as he was marching along the Lisnaskea–Newtownbutler road; probably sensible that he was already acting beyond his orders, he began to withdraw on Lisnaskea. *En route*, from some rising ground, Berry caught sight of Anthony Hamilton's detachment and concluded that he was outnumbered by two to one. Berry also assumed that Macarty's main army was close behind Hamilton's vanguard and so he decided against fighting in the open but sought a strong, defensive position from which he might delay the Jacobite advance. Once through Lisnaskea, the rearguard came under pressure and Berry sent an express to Wolseley explaining that Macarty had raised the siege of Crom and was advancing with all his forces on Enniskillen via Lisnaskea. Already on the march from Enniskillen, Wolseley responded to Berry's express by sending forward some reinforcements. Berry 'faced about' several times with his mounted troops, obliging the pursuing Irish to deploy into line of battle on each occasion thus gaining time for the infantry to hasten their retirement. Without these rearguard actions, Macarty's men would 'certainly have routed us to Enniskillen'. On a morning when it was *à la mode* to ignore orders, Anthony Hamilton neglected to halt at the selected pass but continued after Berry.

Two routes ran from Lisnaskea to Enniskillen: an old track to the north, via Maguiresbridge, and a new, more southerly road through boggy ground beside Upper Lough Erne replete with a number of useful defensive positions. Accordingly, Berry took the latter and, about 1½ km from Lisnaskea towards Enniskillen, reached a deep, boggy defile 'below one Mrs Lenard's' where the carriageway crossed a river on a causeway, about a musket-shot in length and the width of a pair of underfed horses. The banks of the stream were coated in undergrowth, providing cover for musketeers: here an inferior force might readily delay a superior. Berry was conscious that his detachment's cohesion was fraying under the pressure of the long retreat: the Enniskillen Horse, which had recently acquired a reputation for unreliability after failing to support Lieutenant McCarmick at Enniskillen Mill, appeared particularly anxious. As a newcomer who did not yet know his men, Berry decided to leave matters to the Enniskillen officers. Having crossed the causeway to the far bank of the rivulet, Captain Martin Armstrong, one of the best troop leaders in the Enniskillen Horse, and Captain Malcolm Cathcart, a prominent infantry officer, persuaded 120 of the foot to halt, rally and take up defensive positions in the bushes. Cathcart then challenged the officers of the Enniskillen Horse to let him know whether they would run or support his musketeers. Should they stay, Cathcart guaranteed that the Irish would be beaten. Insulted, the cavalry officers replied that of course they would stand, a bravura bolstered by the timely arrival of the reinforcements from Wolseley amounting to one company of foot, four troops of horse and one of dragoons, raising Berry's strength to about 800 men so that he outnumbered Anthony Hamilton. Berry left Cathcart to deploy the foot and dismounted dragoons. Twenty flintlock musketeers were placed in a thicket east of the river to flank the road with strict orders not to fire until the action had been opened by the main body on the far side. Cathcart placed his main body on the west bank, utilizing as much cover as possible, to enfilade the road. Berry held the cavalry and mounted dragoons close either to support the foot in case of withdrawal or exploit a tactical success. The word for the day was 'Oxford'.

Anthony Hamilton arrived before the causeway at 09:00 and, unaware that Berry had been reinforced, estimated his opponent's strength at five troops of horse and two companies of foot. Four hundred metres from the river, Hamilton, his dragoons and the troop of horse dismounted and advanced pausing from time to time to fire, wounding between 12 and 14 Enniskilleners. Cathcart maintained control over his men and fire was not opened until Hamilton was within 40 m of the river bank. Enfiladed from right and left, 20 dragoons were killed and wounded, including Hamilton who was shot in the thigh: he hobbled to the rear to mount his horse, instructing another officer to take over command. That officer and several more soldiers were felled by the cross-fire and as no senior officer remained to lead the advance, Hamilton instructed Captain

Peter Lavallin (Francis Carroll's Dragoons) to order 'a wheel to the left' to shift the men out of the damaging musketry by moving to the left, possibly with a view to working around the Enniskilleners' flank.[11] Either misunderstanding or mishearing – perhaps Hamilton, in shock and pain, did not express himself clearly – Lavallin ordered 'to the left about', i.e. 'turn round', which the dragoons interpreted as an order to retire. Seeing this, the Enniskilleners 'huzzaed' and the horsemen trotted across the causeway whilst the infantry waded through the bog on either side. As the Irish dragoons withdrew, the 20 flanking musketeers, who had been waiting patiently in cover on the east bank, added their fire turning retreat into rout. Despite Hamilton's best efforts, Clare's Dragoons were broken, losing between 106 and 230 men, and so many weapons and horses that the regiment had, subsequently, to be reformed. Berry suffered between 12 and 14 men wounded. Cathcart pursued for 5 km 'all which way the road was filled with their dead bodies'. At this point, the Enniskilleners began to come into contact with advance elements of Macarty's main body so, tired and disorganized, they withdrew to Lisnaskea Castle where they met Wolseley who had arrived with the principal force via the old road.[12]

The soldiers who had marched from Ballyshannon had enjoyed little time to eat and rest whilst the main force had left Enniskillen in such a hurry that no food had been brought. Gathering his officers, Wolseley thanked them for a good morning's work and explained that they must reach a decision quickly: press on immediately to fight Macarty or return to Enniskillen for supplies. The officers agreed that the former was the correct course of action and, when this was put to the men, they unanimously concurred. Because there had not yet been time to reorganize and regiment the Enniskillen forces, the foot was formed into three loose battalions, commanded by Colonels Thomas Lloyd, Zachariah Tiffin[13] and Wolseley himself. The advance guard rode about 1 km before the main body which comprised the five or six companies of Tiffin's battalion, seconded by some horse; Lloyd's battalion, of much the same size, also with cavalry support; the three troops of dragoons organized into two parties 'to assist the flanks' in battle; and Wolseley's battalion accompanied by the remainder of the cavalry under Berry. Major Charles Stone brought up the rear. In this extended formation about 2,000 men – 16 troops of horse, three of dragoons and 21 companies of foot, 'besides some that were not under command' – advanced from Lisnaskea to Donagh where they learned that Macarty had raised the siege of Crom and assembled near Newtownbutler. Just south-east of Donagh, the advance guard made contact with Macarty's scouts who immediately fell back.

On being informed of Wolseley's advance, Macarty had collected his men and guns from before Crom and withdrawn to a strong position just to the north of Newtownbutler. His situation was not encouraging: the rout of Anthony Hamilton's force at Lisnaskea had erased half his cavalry whilst Wolseley's confident approach seemed to confirm that neither Berwick nor Sarsfield had made any threatening move towards Enniskillen. Macarty deployed on a steep, north-facing slope above a bog across which the Newtownbutler road was carried on a standard, two-horse-wide causeway. With his men approaching the limit of their endurance, Wolseley had no time to manoeuvre and attacked frontally. Tiffin and Lloyd were directed to take their battalions through the quagmire to the right and left of the causeway respectively, the dragoons equally divided in support. When these assaults had reached firm ground and secured the flanks, Berry was to lead the cavalry across the causeway. Wolseley held back his own battalion to feed in reserves and reinforce local success. As Wolseley came on, Macarty torched Newtownbutler and some neighbouring country houses before opening a desultory fire at extreme range. Once within effective musket-shot, Tiffin and Lloyd's infantry fired two or three volleys, at which the Jacobites filed away and resumed their withdrawal towards Newtownbutler. The stand-off had lasted about 30 minutes. From an advantageous position on higher ground to the rear Wolseley could see that Macarty was retiring in good order, probably with the intention of either drawing the Enniskilleners into an ambush or seeking a more advantageous deployment but, at a lower level, some of the foot sensed that Irish cohesion was weakening and grew over-excited. As their commanders struggled to maintain discipline, Wolseley sent orders that no man was to leave the ranks to pursue until it was absolutely certain that the Irish had broken.

Having brought their more hot-headed soldiers under control, Tiffin and Lloyd advanced steadily; their progress periodically checked by the retreating Irish whose rear ranks faced about from time to time to give fire. The withdrawal continued through and for 2 km beyond Newtownbutler until Macarty reached the far side of a bog, nearly half an Irish mile (1,024 m) wide, which the road crossed on another two-horse causeway. The two field guns were placed at the end of the causeway and the infantry was drawn up, under cover, immediately to the rear, a number of musketeers placed as skirmishers in the undergrowth fronting the bog. The cavalry was positioned on a rise to the right. Wolseley could have swung round Macarty's right flank but the men were tired, footsore and hungry whilst he feared that, at any moment, news might arrive that Sarsfield had moved against Ballyshannon. In that event, he would be unable to turn round and march back to Enniskillen because Macarty would fall on his rear. There was no alternative but to attack immediately and frontally without reconnaissance or preparation, despite the strength of Macarty's position.

Wolseley employed only his musketeers, between 700 and 800 men, the ineffectual pikemen, who comprised nearly half the infantry, remaining in the rear to guard the colours. Because the topography was similar, the same battle plan that had been used against Macarty's earlier deployment was readopted: Tiffin took the bog to the right and Lloyd the left, both supported by Colonel

James Wynne's Enniskillen Dragoons, whilst Berry and Stone led the cavalry along the road in the centre. As soon as the horsemen approached the end of the causeway, Macarty's two field guns fired accurately and vigorously, preventing Berry's men from advancing. Despite brisk defensive fire from the musketeers in the undergrowth, Tiffin and Lloyd's infantrymen worked their way through the bog on either side of the causeway. When within musket-range, they returned fire at the puffs of smoke emitting from the thickets before closing with sword and bayonet to flush out the skirmishers. Almost simultaneously, they reached the two field guns, seized them and killed the cannoneers – a soldier who had come to Enniskillen from Lord Kingston's force apparently dispatched seven or eight with a hatchet – before pressing on towards the main body of Macarty's foot. As soon as Berry saw that the Irish battery had been put out of action, he sent his men across the causeway, inducing panic amongst Macarty's cavalry and dragoons who wheeled about, deserting their infantry, and departed towards Wattlebridge where the Cavan road crossed the River Finn. Macarty's foot stood its ground until the Enniskillen infantry began to deploy into line within musket-shot. Then, seeing their own horse disappearing, they panicked and fled but, instead of running east towards open country, they crowded to the west into a bog, about 2 km long, that stretched towards Upper Lough Erne, 'most of them throwing away their arms into turf pits'.

In a landscape littered with marsh, pools, ponds, water courses and small loughs, Berry's horsemen had to keep to the road, which was mostly paved, following the retreating Irish cavalry and dragoons in a long column. They placed a strong guard at Wattlebridge and then patrolled the road back to the head of the Newtownbutler causeway so that 'not one of their foot could pass them'. The infantry chased the Irish foot into a wood close to Lough Erne and began to hack down the virtually defenceless soldiers, unless they were officers. About 500 took to the waters of the lough and tried to swim to safety but only one man was known to have avoided drowning, despite the Enniskilleners amusing themselves by using his bobbing head for target practice. A further 600 or 700 came to Wattlebridge where they drew up in a meadow and advanced but some Enniskillen infantry joined the cavalry guard to break up the attack, forcing most of the Irish into the river. All night the Enniskilleners beat the bushes for fugitives and their officers were unable to regain control until around mid-morning on 1 August, by which time scarcely an Irishman who had fled towards Lough Erne was either alive or at liberty.

Desperate to retrieve some honour from the humiliations suffered at Lisnaskea and Newtownbutler, Justin Macarty and five or six mounted officers retired into a small wood close to the position of the Irish battery. After a short while, Macarty charged out and attacked the 100 men under Captain George Cooper who were guarding the captured guns. Seven or eight Enniskilleners levelled their muskets at Macarty. Several bullets bounced off his armour but two entered his right thigh, another went into the lower back and a third, which fragmented when it hit Macarty's watch, caused a slight wound in the groin. As he fell, an Enniskillener clubbed his musket ready to beat out his brains but one of his aides called to him to stop or he would kill General Macarty. Captain Cooper was informed and Macarty was duly granted quarter and taken that night into Newtownbutler. Together with several captured Jacobite officers, Macarty was taken by water to Enniskillen while 300 other captives had to march overland. When asked by his captors why he had thus hazarded his life, Macarty replied that the Jacobite cause was lost because King James's army had been wrecked before Derry and his own force, which was the best that the Jacobites possessed, was ruined: following the actions at Crom, Lisnaskea and Newtownbutler, at least 2,000 were dead and 300 captured, including 50 officers. The Enniskilleners seized seven cannon, 12 or 13 barrels of powder, all the Jacobite colours and drums, numerous weapons, and several carts and wagons. Wolseley lost 12 soldiers killed, including Captain Robert Correy and Cornet William Bell, plus a further eight from amongst the irregulars, camp followers and hangers-on. Between 50 and 60 were wounded. Once the main Enniskillen army had departed on 1 August, the local Protestants continued to hunt for Jacobite fugitives amidst the woods, thickets and bogs and accounted for several hundred more.

Wolseley was most impressed: he had never commanded better infantry and the musketeers were excellent marksmen. However, he was conscious that the rough-and-ready Enniskillen military organization needed to be improved because bread was in short supply and the men wanted both money and uniform. Without a proper logistical structure, the men could not be kept together for more than two or three days at a time before they had to be allowed home to find food, 'which is of very ill consequence now we are surrounded by enemies; this place and Ballyshannon are of no strength'. There was also a dearth of surgeons and medicines, although Enniskillen casualties had usually been infinitesimal, and no beer, wine or ale. Wolseley, a realist, added that these deficiencies had always been present at Enniskillen and had not yet impaired its military effectiveness. He asked Kirke to provide 500 experienced infantry to leaven the enthusiastic, ferocious, poorly disciplined local material but the request was ignored. Wolseley also advised Kirke that pikemen were ineffectual in Ireland and should be completely replaced by musketeers. Locally, this advice was followed; Lloyd's and Tiffin's Enniskillen battalions contained no pikes when reviewed in Dundalk on 18 October 1689. Even the cavalry had been of scant use during the fighting and only partially justified its expensive existence during the pursuit.

The remnants of Macarty's army straggled back to Dublin. From a position of virtual domination, within a week the Jacobites had suddenly lost Ulster. Had the Enniskilleners marched on Dublin immediately after Newtownbutler, as the

Jacobites feared, then larger consequences might have ensued because James had very few armed men in his capital and both field armies had been badly mauled. However, the Enniskilleners could not exploit their success in such a dramatic fashion because, in Macarty's pocket, had been found a letter to Sarsfield from which it became clear that the Jacobites had attempted a concerted strategy against Enniskillen. Macarty had intended to seize Crom Castle before advancing via Lisnaskea and the shore of Upper Lough Erne, whilst Sarsfield attacked Ballyshannon and the Duke of Berwick brought down some of the Derry forces through Omagh. Not until these threats had been removed could wider strategies be considered.[14]

On Thursday 1 August, Wolseley returned to Enniskillen and held a council of war which decided to march to Ballyshannon on the following day with a view to engaging Sarsfield somewhere between that town and his camp at Bundoran. *En route*, they received an express from Captain Folliott stating that Sarsfield had learned of Macarty's defeat at Newtownbutler, raised his camp and withdrawn to Sligo. Folliott added that the arms and ammunition sent by Kirke had arrived at Ballyshannon. Even more encouraging was the return of prisoners taken during the action on 13 July who brought the welcome news that Derry had been relieved. Whilst Wolseley turned round most of his men and headed back to Enniskillen, Tiffin and Lieutenant Colonel Francis Gore, commanding a mixed detachment of horse and foot, were dispatched to Ballyshannon to secure that town against Sarsfield's return and convoy the arms and ammunition to Enniskillen. Arriving back in Enniskillen on 3 August, Wolseley sent a troop of horse under Lieutenant William Charlton to observe the movements of the Jacobite Army as it fell back from Derry via Omagh, fearing that it might invade Enniskillen territory. Charlton rode as far as Castlecaulfield, 3 km west of Dungannon, where he saw that, although burning and destroying the countryside, the Jacobites were clearly hastening southwards towards Dublin via Charlemont and posed no danger to Enniskillen. Having watched the tail of the Irish Army until it was out of sight, Charlton returned to Enniskillen on 5 August. All was quiet and a day was set aside for thanksgiving.[15]

10

A tired old man

As in 1649, wrote Dr Robert Gorge[s], a fellow of St John's College, Oxford, once again Enniskillen and Derry had proved the only effective English garrisons in Ulster. Embarking at Milford Haven, Oliver Cromwell had originally intended to land at Cork but switched to Dublin Bay after hearing of Michael Jones's victory at Rathmines. A proclamation had then been issued offering full protections to any Irish who laid down their arms and went home; the response had been encouraging. After the Scots had secured Carrickfergus and occupied Counties Antrim, Down and Armagh, Sir Charles Coote had marched the Derry garrison into County Donegal before advancing through Ballyshannon and Sligo into Connaught. Supplied by sea, Coote had captured and fortified Inishbofin to serve as a magazine to service north-west Ulster and the western parts of Connaught. Coote had then besieged Galway and Athlone. In the meantime, Cromwell took Drogheda, Wexford and Waterford whilst Cork, Youghal and Kinsale, rebelling against the Earl of Inchiquin, had dispatched reinforcements over the Shannon to assist Coote, ensuring the surrender of Galway and Athlone. Only Limerick remained to the Irish and this soon capitulated. The process of scattering the Irish Army and capturing the major garrisons had taken 18 months.

Gorges, who was to serve as the Duke of Schomberg's secretary during the 1689 campaign, advocated that, as far as possible, the Cromwell–Coote strategy should be emulated. Having established that large forces and abundant supplies would be necessary, he noted first that both Cromwell and Coote had operated close to the coast and had been successfully provisioned by sea. Second, co-ordinated thrusts from Dublin and north-west Ulster had served to overwhelm the Irish Army. He therefore suggested that Schomberg's main force should land at Cork while a secondary corps, possibly from Scotland, disembarked either at Carrickfergus or within Strangford Lough. A third detachment of 2,000 infantry should land around Sligo and seize Inishbofin as an offshore base and magazine. The garrisons of Derry and Enniskillen might march into Donegal, where they would be joined by the Scot Corps from eastern Ulster, and invade Connaught from the north. Gorges was very enthusiastic about employing as many of the Irish Protestants as possible: formed into regiments of cavalry and dragoons, the gentry and farmers would provide reliable intelligence and fight well in defence of their own property and estates. Finally, attention would need to be paid to the pacification of Ireland following the formal termination of hostilities. After the fall of Limerick the Irish Army had scattered into the woods, mountains and bogs where they formed guerrilla bands that became a great nuisance. Accordingly, Ireland had been divided into several 'precincts', each under a governor. These governors arrested any Irish guilty of murder; seized Irish landowners who refused to relocate voluntarily into Connaught; established 'lines of protection' within which the protected Irish lived peaceably – those who chose to remain without the lines were treated as enemies; and bodies of cavalry were employed to establish and maintain rapid communications with Dublin. These methods had quieted Ireland within three years.[1]

News of Derry's relief was current in England by 4 August[2] and Schomberg's expeditionary force gathering around Chester and Neston was free to assume an offensive strategy. About 10,000 strong, it embarked at Hoylake on 8 August but contrary winds delayed departure for four days. A council of war was convened aboard the *Cleveland* yacht on 11 August to determine where to disembark. The landing had to be on the east coast of Ulster: Derry and the whole north shore were too distant from England and only reachable via the dangerous North Channel. One general expressed a preference for Carlingford Lough so as to start the campaign as close to Dublin as possible but the majority supported a point nearer to Derry, Enniskillen and Kirke's camp on Inch Island to allow all the Protestant forces in Ulster to unite before starting the southward advance. The naval officers favoured a protected anchorage for subsequent resupply vessels and transports and so the decision was made to sail for Belfast Lough. Should bad weather prevent this landfall, the fleet was to shelter and reassemble in Loch Ryan, Galloway. Finally, on Monday 12 August the wind shifted to east-south-east and, at 04:00, Captain Hobson in HMS *Bonaventure* fired a gun and hoisted a lantern in the main topmast shrouds to signal the fleet to weigh anchor. By 06:00, 80 provision ships and troop transports carrying eight English, three French Huguenot and two Dutch battalions of infantry, escorted by the frigates *Bonaventure*, *Princess Anne of Denmark* and *Antelope*, the *James Galley* and the yachts *Monmouth* and *Cleveland*, were under way. Forty artillery, horse-boats and miscellaneous transports and merchantmen, escorted by three frigates, would follow, Schomberg having arranged to rendezvous with them in Ramsey Bay on the north-east coast of the Isle of Man. Because the weather and wind stayed fair, it was decided not to put into Ramsey Bay but to make straight for Ireland and a message was sent to the artillery convoy explaining the change of plan. At daybreak on Tuesday 13 August, the fleet came within sight of the Mountains of Mourne and, by 10:00, drew abreast of Copeland Island, Mew Island and Light House Island. Here they were met by Captain George Rooke, with HMS *Deptford*, HMS *Portland* and the *Henrietta* yacht, who had already cleared Belfast Lough of

French shipping. At 16:00, Schomberg came to anchor in Bangor Bay opposite Carrickfergus.

Schomberg immediately hung out his flag on the main yard arm of the *Cleveland*, signalling his troops to land. Preceded by an advance guard of 200 infantry to secure a lodgement the disembarkation proceeded without interruption and the men camped that night in the fields next to the beach. There were numerous unsubstantiated warnings and rumours of approaching Jacobites so the troops lay upon their arms and musketeers lined the hedges and approach roads but nothing occurred; some thought that Schomberg deliberately manufactured these alarms to test the soldiers' loyalty and reliability. If the adjacent garrisons in Carrickfergus, Belfast and Bangor had attacked, Schomberg might have been embarrassed but the local Jacobites could not possibly have co-ordinated such a manoeuvre in so short a time. The artillery convoy sailed at 08:00 on 12 August, reaching Ramsey Bay during the following morning. There was no sign of Schomberg's fleet or any orders so they patiently waited. On the morning of 15 August, HMS *Antelope* returned from Belfast Lough with orders for the artillery convoy to sail with all possible speed and join Schomberg in Bangor Bay. By the end of August, reinforcements comprising one French Huguenot and five English regiments of cavalry plus nine English battalions of infantry had arrived in Belfast Lough.[3]

On the Day of Thanksgiving in Enniskillen, 7 August, Andrew Hamilton travelled to Inch Island to congratulate General Kirke on the relief of Derry. Kirke was on his best behaviour and received him civilly. Two days later, 9 August, Hamilton returned carrying orders for Wolseley to dispatch 500 cavalry and 200 dragoons to escort Kirke's four infantry battalions, which had been instructed to march to Belfast Lough to join Schomberg. Kirke also asked Wolseley to bring 200 of the Irish prisoners taken at Newtownbutler to Derry to unload stores and clean the city because the population, still suffering from disease and malnutrition, was incapable of hard, manual labour. The Enniskilleners reached Derry on 15 August and, within a couple of days, the cavalry rode to Newtown Limavady to await Kirke's infantry escorted by the 200 Enniskillen dragoons. Hearing that the terrible Enniskillen Horse and the fearsome General Kirke were marching towards them, Sir Charles Carney evacuated Coleraine and led the garrison south to seek refuge in Charlemont Fort. Wolseley accordingly pressed ahead to occupy Coleraine and organize an impressive formal reception for his patron. The Enniskillen Horse then proceeded to lead Kirke's column until it joined Schomberg at Carrickfergus.[4]

Colonel Tiffin, in command at Ballyshannon, seeing no sign that Sarsfield intended to move, sent forward Lieutenant Colonel Francis Gore with three troops of horse and 150 infantry to reconnoitre as far as Sligo to ascertain the enemy's strength and dispositions 'for he did not think it fit to let an enemy lie so near our borders'. By a ruse, Gore managed to convince Sarsfield that he was leading the vanguard of a force of 20,000 men, comprising all the Enniskilleners plus Kirke's detachment, which would be before Sligo on the morrow. In some haste, Sarsfield decamped and fell back, disorganized, to Athlone and Gore occupied Sligo unopposed.[5]

Throughout 14 August, Schomberg remained in camp on the shore of Bangor Bay, landing stores and organizing his men for their first task, the reduction of Carrickfergus. Time was short. The Irish campaigning season was already well advanced and Schomberg aimed to seize Dublin before the onset of winter. The Jacobite garrison of Carrickfergus, anticipating a siege, set fire to the suburbs beyond the walls, which burned throughout the night of 14 August and all the next day. Responding to reports that the retreating Jacobite forces had threatened to burn Belfast and Lisburn, on 15 August, Schomberg sent Lieutenant Colonel Sir Charles Feilding (Earl of Kingston's infantry battalion) with 250 cavalry to reconnoitre Belfast and any adjacent Jacobite positions. After his return in the evening to report that the Jacobites had vacated Belfast and retired towards Lisburn, Schomberg ordered Colonel Henry Wharton's infantry battalion to take possession of Belfast. Another reconnaissance was carried out on 16 August when Lieutenant Colonel Toby Caulfield (Earl of Drogheda's infantry battalion) was sent with 300 men through Belfast towards Antrim. They arrived on the following day to find the town deserted: the Jacobite garrison had quitted Antrim on the night of 15–16 August and withdrawn to the small fort at Toome. Caulfield returned to the main army on Tuesday 20 August, having left Captain Arthur Ormesby and Lieutenant Wallis with 50 men to garrison Antrim town and castle.

While Schomberg cleared his flanks, reconnoitred and organized his forces, the Jacobites attempted to repair their position. Informed of the imminence of Schomberg's departure from Hoylake, on 30 July James's government in Dublin took emergency measures to counter the threat of invasion. Lords Lieutenant, their deputies and commissioners of array were appointed to each county and charged with raising a militia from all males aged between 16 and 60 who had not already been taken into the army. Upon the first appearance of enemy shipping, people living by the coast were instructed to move themselves, draught horses, cattle, money and provisions at least 16 km inland. The Dublin militia was to assemble on St Stephen's Green at 09:00 on 2 August with 'such effective horses and arms that they have'. Three days later, James reviewed the regular troops in Dublin amounting to about 2,000 infantry and five or six troops of cavalry, all billeted in empty houses. The king ordered a general rendezvous at Swords for 5 August and warned everyone to be ready to face an invasion from the north. All horses in Dublin were requisitioned and the main Jacobite army was moved from Rathmines to encamp on the north side of Drumcondra Bridge on the road to Finglas. According to a French list, at a date between 5 and

19 August James's forces comprised approximately 16,200 infantry, 2,000 cavalry and 1,100 dragoons. Of these, 5,600 foot were in garrison at Athlone, Galway, Limerick, Kinsale, Cork, Waterford, Wexford, Castledermot, Kilkenny, Carlow and Carrickfergus, leaving only 10,600 available to form a field army.[6]

Intelligence from Ulster was discouraging. The precipitate retreat of the besiegers of Derry and the remains of Macarty's army from Newtownbutler had left Ulster open and allowed Schomberg to land safely and unopposed in Bangor Bay with a powerful army and considerable train of artillery. Brigadier Thomas Maxwell, commanding the remaining Jacobite forces in the north, considered himself too weak to interfere with Schomberg and fell back to Newry, leaving in Carrickfergus only the battalion of Colonel Charles MacCarthy More and nine companies of Colonel Cormack O'Neill's regiment to hold up Schomberg by making the longest possible defence.[7] To support Sarsfield, efforts were made to improve Athlone's prospects by dispatching three cannon, three mortars and 80 cartloads of ammunition. Morale was poor, desertion heavy, there were many sick and numerous wounded from Derry, Lisnaskea and Newtownbutler, whilst the few troops in and around Dublin were inadequately disciplined and many unarmed. Tyrconnell, the driving force behind the Jacobite war effort, was in poor health and on sick leave during most of August. On 27 July the Scottish Jacobites under John Graham of Claverhouse, Viscount Dundee, routed Major General Hugh Mackay's force of 4,000 men at the Pass of Killiecrankie. Despite the tactical success, Dundee was killed and the Scottish Jacobites rendered leaderless. Mackay gained his revenge at Dunkeld on 21 August and the Jacobite war in Scotland was virtually over leaving William free to concentrate on the reduction of Ireland.

Having sent an advance guard of 200 foot on 14 August to secure Belfast, Schomberg followed on the next day with the main army. He remained in Belfast until 19 August sending patrols into the countryside to apprehend numerous Irish who had been reported robbing and plundering. Belfast, probably an open town,[8] was garrisoned to secure communications with the fleet base in Bangor Bay and, on 20 August, Schomberg marched five battalions to Carrickfergus followed next day by a further seven. *En route*, Schomberg was joined by 16 troops of the Enniskillen Horse, which had marched ahead of Kirke's column 'and at that time they were acceptable enough, there being no horse landed out of England'. The trenches were formally opened and musketry duels between Williamite infantry and MacCarthy More's defenders marked the beginning of the siege. By beat of drum, Schomberg summoned Carrickfergus to surrender at which the garrison requested a parley. Lieutenant Gibbons accordingly brought 'propositions in writing' and Schomberg retired into his tent to read them; they asked for time in which either to send to James for help or seek his formal permission to surrender. Schomberg rejected such obvious time-wasting tactics, bidding Gibbons 'to be gone'. The garrison immediately fired cannon directly at Schomberg's tent but the wily old general had already left for another part of the camp. Schomberg directed his gunners to fire on Lord Donegal's house, within the town, on which two cannon had been mounted whose fire was disturbing the camp. During the night of 20–21 August, the trenches were advanced several metres and the garrison responded with some 'warm firing'. A Jacobite drummer escaped over the walls and brought news that Schomberg's cannon and mortars had already caused 30 casualties, including two officers. Throughout 22 August the saps edged closer whilst four cannon and two mortars bombarded the town and the demilune to the right of the castle. Reinforcements – four battalions of infantry, one regiment of dragoons and John Coy's cavalry regiment – landed at the White House, between Belfast and Carrickfergus, from a convoy of 50 vessels. 'Smart firing' punctuated the night of 22–23 August. The garrison sought a second parley at 15:00 on 23 August. Discussions revealed that they were prepared to surrender if granted the full honours of war but Schomberg would only allow capitulation as prisoners of war. Because a parley was always accompanied by a cease-fire, Schomberg took the opportunity to visit his trenches and inspect closely the walls of the town and castle. The fruits of this reconnaissance brought a redirection of artillery fire when hostilities resumed following the failure of the talks: the mortar battery on Windmill Hill aimed at the castle from the west whilst the other battered the North Gate. A large mortar was positioned under the walls to shoot at Lord Donegal's house whence Jacobite cannon were continuing to incommode the attackers. Up to this point Schomberg had not caused his gunners to fire directly on the castle, no doubt wishing to preserve it for his own use.

During the night of 23–24 August, First Engineer Captain Jacob Richards, who was conducting the siege, suffered three wounds and was carried from the trenches to Belfast. By daybreak on 24 August, Carrickfergus was cloaked in dust and smoke and, through the haze, several houses were observed to be on fire. At 14:00, a Mr Spring escaped and reported to Schomberg that the soldiers of the garrison had taken up permanent positions on and under the walls so that the bombardment was only affecting Protestant civilians. He also conveyed the useful information that the garrison was ready to surrender and was prevented only by the opposition of Colonel Owen MacCarthy and Governor MacCarthy More. The defenders were running short of gunpowder and, should Schomberg attack the town, had already decided to retire into the castle, which was well stocked with corn, beef, salt and other provisions. During the afternoon, soldiers were seen working on the roof of the castle, presumably to mount cannon, but it was later discovered that they were ripping off the lead in order to make bullets. Breaches had now been created in the ramparts. These were widened during 25 and 26 August, particularly to the east of the North Gate.

During the hours of darkness, the garrison did its best to repair the damage and excavate retrenchments in the rear of the breaches. Methods were ingenious. Cattle were driven up the rubble behind the breaches, as far they could be made to go, soldiers keeping close behind them. Several of the beasts were killed and the troops then threw earth, stones and timber over them and so, to some extent, filled the holes in the walls. Realizing that their position was desperate and no relief possible, on 26 August the garrison requested a further parley but Schomberg refused. Instead, he increased the pressure by ordering a line of naval vessels to contribute to the bombardment of the town and castle. This was decisive. At 18:00 on 27 August, the garrison hung out the white flag and Schomberg, anxious to leave Carrickfergus as quickly as possible, invited the garrison to submit their proposals. During the final parley, Henry Wharton's battalion of infantry stood before the major breach, near the castle, ready to storm. This time Schomberg agreed to an honourable surrender. The garrison could march out to Newry, the nearest Jacobite garrison, with their arms and some baggage. As soon as the capitulation had been concluded, Williamite officers entered the town and were entertained to wine in the castle by some of the garrison's officers. They discovered several hundred barrels of beef, pork, peas, wheat, malt and oatmeal in the stores but very little gunpowder. Schomberg lost about 200 men, whilst around 150 of the 500-man garrison were killed. Carrickfergus town had been reduced to rubble and ruins but, except for the garrisons at Toome and Charlemont, Ulster had been cleared of regular Jacobite forces.

At 10:00 on 28 August, the garrison – 'lusty, strong fellows, but ill clad, and to give them their due they did not behave themselves ill in that siege' – marched out, accompanied by wives, children and camp followers under the escort of a detachment of cavalry commanded by Captain Sir William Russell (Colonel John Coy's regiment of horse). According to the capitulation, Schomberg was obliged to escort the garrison for 5 km towards Newry but within less than 2 km of Carrickfergus order disintegrated. In revenge for the plundering and despoliation previously committed by the Carrickfergus soldiers and furious with Schomberg for not having ordered their massacre, both sexes of the local Protestant population set upon the inadequately protected column stripping the women naked and seizing arms and equipment from the men. It was said that some of Schomberg's soldiers joined in although no one was later punished. Schomberg was forced to ride into the mob, pistol in hand, to prevent the mass murder of the helpless garrison which eventually sought refuge amongst the drawn-up Williamite battalions 'else the country people would certainly have used them most severely'. To compound an ugly occasion, contrary to the terms of the articles of capitulation, several of the garrison's officers were detained as prisoners of war.[9]

Leaving Sir Henry Ingoldsby's battalion to occupy Carrickfergus,[10] Schomberg marched towards Belfast on 28 August. That night, he camped 2 km south-west of Belfast and, over the following three days, incorporated recently disembarked reinforcements, including the cavalry regiments of Henry Booth, Second Baron Delamere, and William Cavendish, Fourth Earl of Devonshire, plus Sir Thomas Gower's battalion of infantry. When mustered on Saturday 31 August the army amounted to four regiments of cavalry, one of dragoons and 18 infantry battalions. On 1 September, a trumpeter delivered a letter to Schomberg from Berwick, commanding James's advance guard at Newry, which was returned unopened because it was addressed to Count Schomberg instead of Duke.[11] Anxious to press on along the Dublin road as fast as he could, Schomberg discovered only obstacles. He grumbled to William on 27 August that he was obliged to attend to everything himself – provisions, shipping, artillery, horse supply, accounts and even, as a result of Captain Richards's injuries, the conduct of the siege of Carrickfergus – because he was surrounded by idle and incompetent officers, particularly those of the artillery who were 'ignorant, timorous and lazy'. He despaired of ever finding sufficient reliable officers to assume all these duties. Materiel was also of poor quality: badly made bombs; ill-cast cannon that split and exploded; and small arms of faulty construction. Much, in Schomberg's opinion, was the fault of Mr John Shales. Had he marched instead of grumbling, Berwick was firmly of the opinion that he could have walked into Dublin virtually unopposed.[12]

Preceded by the two battalions of the Royal Regiment of Foot and 70 cartloads of arms, ammunition and supplies, James left Dublin for Drogheda on 26 August escorted by the Troop of Life Guards and 200 horsemen from Colonel Parker's cavalry regiment. At Drogheda he found already assembled seven regiments of foot and a few troops of horse. Tyrconnell commanded the main army around Finglas and dispatched it north by detachments to encamp to the south of Drogheda with a view to defending the line of the River Boyne should Schomberg drive suddenly and rapidly towards Dublin. Although Tyrconnell's heroic efforts had improved morale and the men appeared keen to advance towards the enemy, they remained raw, badly disciplined, ill-clothed and inadequately armed despite several days of intensive training and the distribution of small quantities of serviceable equipment. Only the cavalry seemed ready for the field but they were not numerous. James was already looking over his shoulder; the most valuable royal baggage was moved to Athlone, handily positioned for escape via Galway. Uncontrolled popular military activity hindered rather than helped the main field army. By his proclamation of 5 August 1689, James had encouraged Catholic subjects to arm themselves and assist the royal forces against the invader. These irregulars gathered in considerable numbers on the borders between Leinster and Ulster but, although only supposed to raid Protestants' lands and attack invaders and rebels, they robbed and plundered indiscriminately.[13]

Schomberg found plentiful standing corn around Belfast Lough but the advance south towards Dundalk brought the army into a desert created by the retreating Jacobites: the only solution was supply direct from England. Unfortunately, Schomberg's army was accompanied by neither horses nor wagons whilst the provision ships docked at increasingly distant Carrickfergus rather than Carlingford Lough. Before leaving the Belfast camp on 2 September and marching through Lisburn, 'one of the prettiest inland towns in the north of Ireland, and one of the most English-like places in the kingdom', to encamp 3 km beyond, Schomberg ordered that his artillery horses, still at Chester, be shipped to Carlingford Lough. Next day, 3 September, the army proceeded through Hillsborough, pausing briefly to hang two deserters by the roadside, to camp outside the deserted town of Dromore where Schomberg received intelligence that Berwick was at Newry with about 1,000 infantry and 600 dragoons, plus two troops of horse. Newry was a key position on the direct road from Belfast to Dublin, protecting both the passage of the River Clanrye and the entrance to the Moyry Pass through the Slieve Gullion, separating Ulster from the plains of Meath. To the north, Sir Henry Ingoldsby at Carrickfergus received news that 800 Irish had gathered in a threatening manner in the glens of County Antrim, inland from Glenarm. Captain Stewart was sent with a detachment to deal with the problem, which he accomplished quickly, seizing a number of cattle in the process.

The army marched from Dromore to Loughbrickland on 4 September and encamped in two lines, the usual formation, on the side of a hill south of the town. Like Dromore, except for a beggarly quantity of corn rotting on the ground, Loughbrickland was empty. Throughout, the Enniskillen cavalry and dragoons rode point, scouting, reconnoitring and driving back the Jacobite videttes, normally operating about 5 km in advance of the main body. Curious to meet these fabled warriors, the Reverend George Story, chaplain to the Earl of Drogheda's Foot and later Dean of Limerick, rode out from the Loughbrickland camp to find them. They pointed out Berwick's patrols ranged across the hills to the south, remnants of a troop of horse pushed north to make contact with Schomberg but which had withdrawn back into Newry on encountering the feared Enniskillen Horse. Story urged them to attack but they explained that their instructions were to keep in touch with the enemy scouts but not to attempt anything more ambitious. Story noted that they appeared extremely dissatisfied with this, muttering that 'they would never thrive so long as they were under orders'. Schomberg likened the mounted Enniskilleners to a band of Tartars or Croats from the military frontier in the Balkans. They rode wiry little nags and wore an approximate uniform of grey coats, pistols and sabres dangling from their belts. They always fought in white shirts, throwing off their coats before going into action. A host of wives, children and camp followers meandered in their rear. Although they must have deeply offended Schomberg's professional sensibilities, he recognized that they knew the country and its ways and, like all bullies, could terrorize an inferior force. In battle, as demonstrated in the actions at Enniskillen Mill and Lisnaskea, they could be unreliable but were invaluable in the little war of posts and ambuscades.[14]

Berwick was alarmed to learn of the propinquity of the enemy, far closer than he had anticipated, and expected Schomberg to come into view at any minute. He made ready to depart immediately but, when the enemy failed to appear – Schomberg had encamped at Loughbrickland – took the opportunity to plunder Newry before putting it to the torch. On receiving news of this gratuitous destruction, Schomberg wrote to Berwick warning that, should there be a repetition elsewhere, then the officers taken prisoner at Carrickfergus would be executed. Berwick left Newry at sunset and, marching through the night, arrived in Dundalk on the morning of 5 September, a distance of 13 km, his men breaking up the causeways *en route* in order to delay Schomberg's progress.[15] Without fighting or making any show of resistance, Berwick had abandoned both the crossing of the River Clanrye and the Moyry Pass. Dundalk, however, was an open town and Berwick decided to continue the withdrawal back on to the main army assembling at Drogheda. Berwick's feeble leadership caused morale within his detachment to collapse, many officers losing faith in the Jacobites' ability to resist the Williamite Army. His opponent also had critics. Story thought that, had Schomberg not constrained the Enniskilleners, they could have prevented the destruction of Newry, pressed against Berwick's rearguard and relayed the vital information that the crossing of the River Clanrye at Newry Bridge was undefended and the Moyry Pass wide open.

In ignorance, Schomberg assumed that Berwick would defend both. Accordingly, he formed an *ad hoc* detachment of 1,200 infantry, plus cavalry, dragoons and four field guns, under Colonel Henry Wharton. He was to attack the defenders of Newry Bridge 'at the end of the town', where there was an old church and several useful defensive positions. Schomberg could have manoeuvred to outflank Newry to the west by crossing the Clanrye at Jerrettspass or Poyntz Pass but this would have taken him wide through the Slieve Gullion and wasted precious time. It would also have presented Berwick with an opportunity to raid his sole supply line to Belfast and Carrickfergus. Wharton departed at 03:00 on 5 September, Schomberg following with the main body at 06:00. On the march, Schomberg received intelligence from a Mr Humphrey of Belfast that Berwick had retired from Newry and burned it. Schomberg hurried forward and found the flames 'not quite extinguished'. It had been a pretty town but only an old stone tower and five or six houses had been left standing.[16] Escorted by Richard Leveson's regiment of dragoons and some Enniskillen horse, Schomberg rode 3 km beyond Newry but saw no sign of Jacobite troops. He gave orders for the army to camp 2 km north of Newry, where the line of the river protected against any surprise from Berwick. The weather was bad – rain and strong winds – making it difficult to pitch tents and there was insufficient food for the cold, wet soldiers because the countryside had been ruined by the retreating Jacobites and Schomberg was short of horses to work his supply train. Sickness was already breaking out amongst the soldiers, mostly the 'bloody flux' occasioned by the incessant rain, sodden clothing and tents, drinking stagnant bog water and relying upon raw and innutritious food: raw cabbages were often the only items available. Belatedly, the Enniskillen Horse was sent ahead through the Moyry Pass and they reached close to Dundalk, seizing 150 cattle, several sheep and much oatmeal and butter. The army rested outside Newry on 6 September. Story rode into the country and, for miles around, saw nothing but deserted houses and corn either rotting on the ground or shaken by the wind, there being no one to take in the harvest. All the people had gone: the Protestants had fled north in March and the Roman Catholics were now withdrawing southwards accompanied by their livestock, some through fear whilst others had been forcibly evacuated by the Jacobite Army. In the evening, Schomberg sent a detachment of 520 infantry and some cavalry, commanded by Colonel Lord Lisburn, forward towards Dundalk. They arrived on the morning of 7 September and found the enemy departed but the buildings intact.

Garrisoning Newry with 50 men under Captain Hugh Palliser, Schomberg marched for Dundalk on 7 September. Near Four Mile House, in the midst of the Moyry Pass, he came across a potentially strong defensive position. The main road ran along a causeway through a bog in the bottom of a narrow valley between two steep hillsides before narrowing to cross a stream via a stone bridge, the exit of which was covered by two mutually supporting redoubts. Had these been manned and their garrisons seconded, Schomberg would have experienced some difficulty. Rosen had built them earlier in 1689 as a second line of defence in the event of an enemy forcing the passage of the Clanrye at Newry. Three kilometres further on stood Moyry Castle, again undefended. Having traversed the pass, later in the day Schomberg's army marched into camp 2 km north of Dundalk, which comprised a single street stretching southward from the tip of the Kilcurry estuary for perhaps 400 m: the modern town was laid out by James Hamilton, First Earl of Clanbrassil, during the 1740s.

It was a promising position covered to the west, south and east by the line of the River Kilcurry and its estuary, and to the north and north-east by bogs and the Newry-Carlingford mountains. In addition, the estuary made a 'pretty good haven for small ships to bring him necessaries from England'.[17] Schomberg made his headquarters in the town, guarded by the Enniskillen horse, dragoons and foot. No sooner had they arrived than 2,000 sheep belonging to Lord Bellew, an infantry colonel in the Jacobite Army, were driven into camp. This was timely because bread was in very short supply and, that evening, Schomberg ordered every regiment to send an officer and a small group of men back over the Moyry Pass to collect their soldiers who had collapsed on the march from hunger, fatigue and sickness. Initially, Schomberg had no intention of lingering at Dundalk but intended to press on towards Dublin as rapidly as possible. However, the supply ships had not yet arrived in Carlingford Lough, as ordered, and so the artillery and train horses were sent back towards Belfast to fetch bread. Compounded by the acute shortage of provisions resulting from the inadequate logistical arrangements and the ravaged countryside, the long, hard marches from Carrickfergus in bad weather had rendered Schomberg's soldiers in poor physical condition on arrival at Dundalk. Because the main Jacobite field army was at Drogheda and the exact whereabouts of Berwick unknown, the first task was to entrench the camp. As soon as a lengthy stay was indicated, Schomberg ought to have secured the magazine at Ardee. Although James had decided initially to defend the line of Boyne, Drogheda acting as the flank anchor, when he realized that Schomberg was not immediately advancing from Dundalk he sent a detachment to occupy Ardee, 13 km to the north, a Protestant settlement that had gathered considerable quantities of provisions in the expectation that Schomberg would come marching through. Instead, the Jacobite soldiers evicted the Protestants, most scattering north towards Dundalk, and seized their possessions and the magazine. Scouts and patrols then pushed northwards and came into contact with outposts of the Enniskillen Horse reconnoitring southwards towards Ardee. Skirmishes occurred, especially around Mansfieldstown where control of the bridge across the River Glyde was contested: in one action, Williamite scouts killed nine Jacobite soldiers for the loss of one Enniskillen horseman and one dragoon. General Kirke arrived at Dundalk on 8 September with his own battalion of foot and those of Sir John Hanmer and Brigadier William Stewart, three-quarters of the Derry relief force. Schomberg's army thus comprised two regiments of cavalry; three of dragoons; 16 British infantry battalions, three Dutch and three Huguenot. No sooner had Schomberg halted at Dundalk than problems arose. The soldiers were forbidden to stir outside the confines of the camp on pain of death to prevent them straggling to plunder and murder the few remaining local people: some marauders had already been lynched by raparees. During the afternoon of 9 September, Reverend Story rode to the little seaside town of Carlingford, 13 km from Dundalk. It had mostly been burned at the same time as Newry, only five old, ruinous 'castles' still standing along the shore, and there was no sign of the supply ships from Belfast. Carlingford Castle was already in use as the principal hospital where the sick were given straw, blankets and two bowls of gruel per day.[18]

On 7 September, a Jacobite deserter provided Schomberg with the seemingly reliable intelligence – the man was an engineer – that most of James's army had assembled at Drogheda but, even when concentration was complete, it would comprise less than 20,000 men; many regiments were still actively recruiting. Following Derry and Newtownbutler, morale was low. In addition, they were labouring under the delusion that Schomberg was well equipped and supplied and had double the number of troops that he actually possessed. Rosen was most concerned about the poor state of affairs and advocated the abandonment of both Drogheda and Dublin preparatory to a withdrawal on Athlone and Limerick behind the line of the Shannon. Tyrconnell, lying sick at Chapelizod, strongly disagreed and boasted that he would produce an additional 20,000 men in next to no time. This he achieved by recruiting from the militia and draining the Munster garrisons. When Rosen learned that Schomberg had halted at Dundalk, he reversed his earlier appreciation and recommended a more forward concentration.[19]

Schomberg chose to disregard this maverick intelligence, probably because it contradicted his preconceptions, and continued in his belief that the Jacobites outnumbered him by at least two to one and possibly numbered as many as 35,000 men.[20] He was uncertain about what to do. Colonel John Coy, commanding 200 cavalry, was dispatched in the afternoon of 9 September to scour the countryside to the south but he encountered no hostile troops. However, on 12 September Schomberg issued some basic standing orders to regulate camp life, suggesting that he had decided to continue at Dundalk for at least the immediate future. Amongst this list was an instruction to gather the forage from the countryside south of the camp towards the enemy. Accordingly, on the following day, foraging parties of cavalrymen went out, covered by a few of Leveson's Dragoons, and were busy tying rolls of hay on to their mounts when a party of Jacobite horse appeared in the distance. They threw their bundles to the ground, mounted, formed up and advanced but the enemy cavalry disappeared. The men returned to foraging only for the same thing to happen again and then a third time. This caused a commotion in the camp so Schomberg rode out to see what was happening and deduced that the Jacobite cavalry pickets were reconnoitring his position as a prelude to an advance by their main army. Plans to consume the forage between Dundalk and Ardee were promptly abandoned allowing the Jacobites freedom to operate in relatively unmolested countryside.

Schomberg had read the tactical situation accurately. The Jacobite Army completed its concentration at Drogheda on 13 September and marched the next day in fine, dry weather on a good road through green fields to encamp west of Ardee along the south bank of the River Dee: the vanguard pushed on to Bridge of Fane, 5 km from Dundalk. That night, most of the Irish infantry lay in the open, having arrived too late to build shelters, but the weather remained fair though cold. Lacking sufficient cavalry to hold back the main body, Schomberg ordered earthworks to be constructed at the southern extremity of Dundalk's long street covering the head of the Drogheda–Ardee–Dundalk–Newry road as it emerged from a bog immediately to the south of the town. Entrenchments were also excavated at the mid-point of the street to defend the approaches to the more vulnerable western side of the camp. Six hundred infantrymen began work on 16 September with spades and shovels, creating an entrenched camp strong enough to resist any Jacobite efforts to force Schomberg into accepting battle. Eight field guns were subsequently mounted in these positions which were permanently manned by two battalions of infantry. A fortified house belonging to Lord Bellew, about 1 km north-west of Dundalk, was also garrisoned. According to intelligence reports reaching Schomberg, James had brought 40,000 men to Ardee but only 30,000 were properly armed, the remainder carrying skeans and half-pikes. Schomberg possessed nothing approaching these numbers. Although he commanded a total of 28 battalions of foot, four regiments of dragoons and 11 regiments of cavalry, a number of these units were either in garrison at Derry, Enniskillen, Sligo, Belfast, Carrickfergus and Newry or weakened from providing detachments to defend the lines of communication. Lives had been lost at Carrickfergus, many lay sick in hospital at Belfast whilst Kirke's, Hanmer's and Stewart's battalions were in poor condition having endured a long period on board ship prior to the relief of Derry followed by a demanding march. At Dundalk Schomberg directed no more than 2,000 horse and dragoons and 12,000 infantry. Even the arrival of Colonel Edward Villiers's cavalry regiment on 14 September scarcely improved the situation because many of its horses had been lost at sea. Opposed by superior numbers to the south, his supply fleet still in Belfast, and his sick-list growing, Schomberg gave orders for timber to be cut to build stables for the cavalry horses and huts for the troops; within a couple days nearly all the surrounding woods had been felled. Although Schomberg had decided to remain until the situation clarified, to maintain morale the rumour was allowed to spread that he was awaiting the arrival of the mercenary corps from Denmark before resuming the march towards Dublin.

Now that the main Jacobite Army was fully occupied by Schomberg, Enniskillen could only be threatened from the west and south. Wolseley instructed Colonel Lloyd to take charge of the western sector and he reached Sligo on 10 September with three troops of horse. Here he found three dragoon troops, two of horse and five companies of infantry, commanded by Sir Albert Conyngham, colonel of the Enniskillen Dragoons. Lloyd was 'hourly alarmed' that the Jacobite forces around Boyle under Colonel Charles O'Kelly were about to surprise Sligo so he determined to act pre-emptively. Leaving a strong garrison in Sligo, on Thursday 19 September he marched with the remainder of the troops – about 200 cavalry, 100 dragoons and 150 infantry – and camped that night within 2 km of Ballinafad, at the southern tip of Lough Arrow. In the morning (20 September), headed by an advance guard of 20 infantry and a troop of dragoons under an ensign, Lloyd crossed the Curlew Mountains, surprising the Jacobite outposts on the tops, killing one and taking three prisoners, although enough escaped to raise the alarm in Boyle at the foot of the mountains. From the heights Lloyd overlooked the town and watched a detachment of Jacobite infantry march out and deploy about 500 m up the slope of the mountain whilst another party lined the wall of a deer park in advance of the main position flanking the route of the Enniskilleners' advance. Instead of the reported 3,000 or 4,000, there were, at the most, 600 foot. O'Kelly's cavalry, composed of 300 'Irish gentry', formed on a 20-man front on the road at the foot of the mountain with the wall of the deer park on their right and a ditch to the left. The approach to the Irish position was narrow and rugged and Lloyd's men would have to attack on a frontage of only three or four men and risk being outflanked. O'Kelly was strongly posted.

Taking advantage of an early morning mist, at daybreak Lloyd ordered Conyngham to lead the dragoons into the deer park and take the flanking musketeers in the rear, which was easily achieved, the Irish falling back on the main body of infantry. Lloyd then split his foot into two bodies each of about 40 musketeers, under Captain George Cooper on the right and Captain Archibald Hamilton on the left. Lloyd supported Cooper with the cavalry. Because of the rough terrain, Hamilton and Cooper could not attack simultaneously but this mattered little. A few shots from Cooper's musketeers and the sight of Lloyd's cavalry persuaded the Irish infantry to break and run through a nearby bog and across open country into a wood. Lloyd ordered the dragoons to fall upon their flank whilst the infantry pressed on the rear. As soon as they saw their foot disintegrate the Irish horsemen retreated through the town, then split into three groups and withdrew rapidly before Lloyd's cavalry which pursued for 11 km cutting down about 50 although most escaped because their horses were fresh whereas Lloyd's were tired after a long march. At least 200 Irish infantry were killed. The majority of Lloyd's foot consisted of pikemen commanded by Major Wood but, as at Newtownbutler and Lisnaskea, they played no part in the action although they advanced and formed a reserve in case the Irish might rally. Captain John Aughmounty commanded a small rearguard of horse which was also not engaged. Lloyd had intended to occupy both Boyle and Jamestown but he had insufficient forces and bands of raparees and military fugitives criss-crossing the region made the countryside between Boyle and Sligo insecure. Instead he resolved to hold only Sligo and Boyle. When news of this success reached Schomberg on 27 September, he ordered three salvoes to be fired from all the cannon and complimented the Enniskillen troops in camp.[21]

However, when he heard that the Irish had garrisoned Jamestown with 80 men, Lloyd changed his mind and marched from Boyle intent on taking this not 'inconsiderable pass upon the River Shannon' through which a Jacobite force could have advanced on either Sligo or Enniskillen and, more importantly, moved to endanger communications between Boyle and Sligo. On his approach, the Jamestown garrison fired but did little damage apart from killing a horse and wounding one man in the leg. Lloyd positioned his infantry as close to Jamestown as possible, so as to occupy the garrison, before marching his cavalry 2 km eastward along the bank of the Shannon to a fortified manor house at Drumsna. Here he found two boats and was about to cross the river and fall on the rear of Jamestown when some local Protestants came to tell him that it had been evacuated by the Irish. Lloyd duly retraced his steps and took possession, gathering a large prey of cattle, sheep and horses. Because the three newly captured positions – Boyle, Jamestown and Drumsna – were beyond effective supporting distance from either Enniskillen or Sligo and there were insufficient men to provide appropriate garrisons, Lloyd was uncertain about the best course of action so he wrote to Schomberg seeking instructions. The general replied that every inch of ground gained should be held and promised reinforcements and supplies. Accordingly, Lloyd garrisoned Boyle, Jamestown and the house at Drumsna before returning to Sligo.[22]

On 15 September, detachments from the Irish regiments at Ardee gathered wood and straw and spent the rest of the day constructing huts. At midnight the drums beat 'to arms' but it was a deliberate false alarm to see how quickly the army could assemble in an emergency. On the following day James went forward with the cavalry and dragoons to join the advance guard at Bridge of Fane whence he reconnoitred Schomberg's position. The main army moved forward to Bridge of Fane on 17 September; because the new campsite was devoid of trees, every soldier was obliged to carry timber to build huts but many could not be bothered so they had to lie in the open that night and spend the next day searching far and wide for building materials. The camp was in two lines on the south bank of the River Fane to the west of the bridge, James lodging in a simple cottage.[23]

Expecting to be attacked in his camp, Schomberg recalled all detachments except for the vital garrison at Newry. Wolseley at Enniskillen was ordered to send Colonel Wynne's regiment of dragoons and the infantry battalions of Colonels Lloyd and Tiffin to Dundalk.[24] When these materialized on 18 September, they amounted to four troops and 24 companies. Only one battalion, plus Wolseley's troop of horse and the forces in Ballyshannon, Sligo, Boyle and Jamestown, remained within the Enniskillen theatre of operations. Schomberg also dispatched his sick to Carlingford. As the advance guards and outposts came into regular contact and skirmished, Schomberg spent a good deal of time forward inspecting the Jacobite dispositions. On 20 September, he received intelligence that the enemy numbered between 30,000 and 40,000 and had sent a detachment of 2,000 infantry and 1,500 cavalry around his western flank, through the Slieve Gullion, to attack Newry, 'no ill project' because it was garrisoned by only 50 men, although Sir Henry Ingoldsby's battalion, a few Huguenot detachments, and Lord George Hewett's cavalry regiment were then in temporary redsidence *en route* to Dundalk.[25] Had Newry fallen, Schomberg's land communications with Belfast would have been severed and, had the main Jacobite army then attacked the front of the Dundalk position, his situation rendered perilous. The Reverend Story thought that the Jacobites had missed an excellent opportunity. Indeed, such a detachment was out but it was marching to Athlone to reinforce Sarsfield's projected counter-attack on Sligo.[26] At 10:00 on 20 September a party of Jacobite horsemen appeared in sight of Dundalk and several battalions of infantry were observed drawn up in front of their camp. Alerted by this show of activity and in receipt of intelligence that the Jacobites intended to attack on the morrow, Schomberg pushed forward a detachment of cavalry but the Irish troopers retired on their infantry supports. Reserving the forage to the north to sustain a retreat, Schomberg's soldiers foraged eastwards towards Carlingford, operations to the west being no longer viable in the face of the Jacobite Army. Story rode to Carlingford and on his way back to Dundalk in the evening observed a small party of horsemen, in no great haste, cross the road in front of him. He discovered later that this was an Irish party from the Bridge of Fane camp raiding into the Carlingford Mountains where it had killed five Huguenot and two Enniskillen foragers. In the afternoon, the first ammunition and provisions ships sailed into Dundalk from the anchorage in Carlingford Lough. That night heavy rain fell.

The morning of 21 September dawned clear and sunny. Around 07:00 several bodies of Jacobite cavalry were seen advancing towards Dundalk and, between 09:00 and 10:00, there was sufficient activity to cause Schomberg concern. James's standard was unfurled and his whole army, along with the field artillery, marched out. The troops formed up quietly, smoothly and efficiently along a line of hillocks, running from south-east to north-west, to the south-west of Dundalk, about 1 km from the entrenchments at the south end of the main street. James and Rosen adopted an orthodox deployment with cavalry on each wing and two lines of infantry in chequer-board formation, the battalions in the second line covering the intervals between those of the first line. James commanded the centre; Rosen the left; and Tyrconnell, elevated to captain-general, the right. The armies were separated by the boggy valley of a stream, across which ran the main road plus several narrow, minor paths. James's cavalry advance guards were stationed on some hummocks to the south of the bog facing Schomberg's outposts; the extreme right of the line lay within cannon-shot of Schomberg's entrenchments. Standing in the sunshine, the good order and discipline of James's army were apparent but that same bright light also reflected off the scythe blades with which the majority of the infantry were armed. Schomberg rode down to observe and ordered Colonel John Beaumont's battalion into the trenches, reinforced one hour later by that of Colonel Thomas Erle. Many of Schomberg's senior officers advised inducing a battle and urged the recall of the cavalry, most of which had gone on a foraging expedition into the Carlingford Peninsula. Schomberg, much less enthusiastic, replied, 'Let them alone, we will see what they will do.' From the outset, Schomberg was fairly confident that the Jacobites were making a demonstration and had no intention of fighting. He was half right: James and Tyrconnell were appalled by the notion of assaulting an entrenched camp whereas Rosen thought it feasible and worth risking. So many supported him, arguing that the longer the war continued the stronger the Williamite position would become, that James and Tyrconnell had to acquiesce and agree to make the demonstration.[27]

Attended by D'Avaux, James watched as 60 cavalry volunteers commanded by the Englishman John Carey, Fifth Viscount Hunsdon, rode straight down the Ardee–Dundalk road to the point where it entered the bog. Although infantry and dismounted dragoons were already manning the trenches, Schomberg ordered 300 of Tiffin's Enniskillen Foot to advance to the exit from the pass on the Dundalk side, whilst all the entrenchments back to the main camp were lined with musketeers.

Schomberg's earlier confidence that James did not intend to force an action faltered. Lieutenant General James Douglas was sent back to the main camp with orders for the cavalry to continue foraging until they heard three cannon-shots, when they were to return immediately, whilst the foot was to stand by. In a theatrical demonstration of *sang froid*, Schomberg then dismounted and lay down. Optimists suggested that he was pondering tactics; pessimists thought a tired old man had gone to sleep. Douglas was greeted enthusiastically by the infantry in the camp who would have welcomed escape from the 'sad place, which they begun already to be weary of'. Noting Schomberg's dispositions, James pushed some dragoons ahead of Hunsdon's squadron to line both sides of the road thus flanking Schomberg's men should they try to attack through the pass. In addition, he positioned grenadiers in some little wooden huts close to the road inside the bog, within musket-shot of Schomberg's most advanced positions. There was some desultory firing and both sides suffered a few casualties. Three hours of posturing, cheering and shouting failed to persuade Schomberg to venture across the bog, so at 14:00 James ordered his army to march off by the left – the left wing forming the vanguard – back to its camp along the River Fane. James stayed with the right wing, now the rearguard, expecting Schomberg to push cavalry across the bog to observe his march 'but not a man of them stirred'. This was not quite accurate. Leveson's Dragoons killed four or five Irish during the withdrawal and some Enniskilleners could not contain themselves and dashed forward, killing two or three Irish but taking casualties themselves. That evening Lord Lisburn and Colonel Wolseley approached Schomberg with a plan to beat up the Jacobite guards during the night but permission was refused: he would receive blame if it failed but no plaudits for success. To emphasize his reasoning, Schomberg ordered all infantry battalions not detailed for guard duty on 22 September to take advantage of the rare fine weather by undertaking some firing practice because 'he knew most of his men had never been in service, and therefore he would have them taught as much as could be'. Rosen decided to leave Ireland.[28]

To add to Schomberg's troubles, James had issued a proclamation offering pardons to all foreigners and native Irish who deserted the Williamite service. Copies of this proclamation littered the Dundalk mud causing Schomberg to reflect that most of the Irish troops who had been recruited indiscriminately in England had already deserted. He began to lose faith and confidence in his soldiers and grew more concerned with improving internal security than advancing on Dublin. Everyone, on pain of death, was ordered not to venture outside the perimeter without formal permission whilst the provost marshal was encouraged to prowl about the camp and rewarded with money for every deserter apprehended. Since arriving in Ireland, Schomberg had suspected the loyalty of the recently recruited Huguenot cavalry regiment and three infantry battalions, which contained numerous deserters from regiments in the Dutch Army.

On 22 September, a conspiracy was uncovered. A captain in one of the Huguenot infantry battalions was informed by one of his men that four soldiers and a drummer, all of whom were Roman Catholic, planned to desert to the Irish garrison at Charlemont. They were immediately arrested and the captain who had initially received the information subsequently found letters addressed to D'Avaux amongst the possessions of one of the accused. During interrogation this man revealed that he also had letters from one Du Plessis, another Roman Catholic, then serving as a private soldier in Colonel François de Cambon's Huguenot regiment. Du Plessis had previously been a captain of horse in the French Army but had been obliged to resign his commission after committing murder. Du Plessis was seized and confessed under 'examination' that he had written to both James and D'Avaux telling them that there were many Catholics in the Huguenot regiments and promised to bring them over to the Irish Army on condition that he might be pardoned by Louis XIV and rewarded with a commission. Another account says that Du Plessis had promised the desertion of over 400 Roman Catholic soldiers from the Huguenot regiments and hinted that there were also numbers of native Irishmen amidst the ranks of the Huguenots, a statement corroborated by D'Avaux. A third report says that Du Plessis was arrested with a map of the camp in his pocket, complete with data about unit strength, the state of supply, dispositions and the numbers of sick. A fourth narrative tells that on 22 September, two Huguenot grenadiers were arrested as they attempted to desert. Next morning, 23 September, 21 Huguenot soldiers were apprehended and on their persons were found several letters from Du Plessis addressed either to D'Avaux or James II. James's answer to Du Plessis's letters was brought to Dundalk by a Frenchman who concealed a red and white cross under the folds of his sleeve and clutched a bottle of brandy. By prior arrangement he promenaded, conspicuously, up and down the Huguenot lines shouting, 'Brandy wine, brandy wine', until approached by a soldier who said to him, whilst simultaneously turning back the brandy seller's sleeve in search of the red and white cross, 'God bless you friend, how do you sell your brandy?' When this had been satisfactorily accomplished, the letter from James was handed over. This part of the operation proceeded without incident but the brandy seller was arrested during the return journey to the Irish camp and allowed his freedom in return for informing on Du Plessis. Together with five accomplices, Du Plessis was tried, sentenced to death and hanged on 26 September. When Schomberg was first informed he ordered a proclamation to be read at the head of every regiment to the effect that all Catholics were to declare themselves. Anyone who did not do so immediately and was later discovered to be Catholic would be instantly executed. Until further notice, no Huguenot was permitted to leave the Dundalk camp without a pass. Upon this, 150 men surrendered themselves and were sent under escort for Carlingford and England. This new breed of Catholic-Huguenots was not wasted. They were dispatched to the Dutch Republic where they were transferred to the pay of the States-General and used to garrison fortresses.[29] The colonels of the three Huguenot infantry battalions then conducted an investigation into how many Roman Catholics they were harbouring but no more seem to have been found.

> Most of these had deserted the French service this summer and, passing to Holland and thence to England upon report that three French regiments were levying here, had listed themselves in the same, the officers raising their companies in so much haste that they had not time to examine them very strictly.[30]

James knew of these intended desertions and had timed his advance on 21 September in the expectation that Schomberg's corps would be both physically weakened and psychologically damaged. Du Plessis had arranged for his conspirators to fire on the rear of Schomberg's army prior to deserting, to sow confusion. Colonel Wolseley ran an agent in Dublin who had given advance warning that the Jacobite Army placed great store in a revolt by the Huguenot troops. This information had been relayed to Schomberg before 21 September but he refused to believe that his co-religionists could behave in such a manner. Only the production of evidence changed his mind.

The Huguenot infantry colonels did not over-exert themselves in the search for secreted Roman Catholics – Du Plessis had named 400 potential deserters but only 150 were uncovered – because they were too short of men to indulge in such luxuries. Thereafter the Huguenot regiments remained unclean.[31] On 30 June 1690, during the march south towards the Boyne, the Reverend George Story reported that there were still Catholics in the Huguenot regiments. Feeling very unwell after drinking contaminated water, a French soldier stumbled out of his column and collapsed on to the side of the road. Fearing for his life he started fingering his rosary beads and muttering Catholic incantations. One of the Protestant Danish soldiers noticed this and promptly shot him dead probably justifying his action, if anybody had bothered to enquire, by reference to Schomberg's proclamation.[32] When the Huguenot infantry battalions and Galway's Horse were redeployed into the Spanish Netherlands in 1693 they became natural magnets for both Catholic and Protestant French deserters. In preparation for the voyage from Flanders to Ireland in November 1697, the Huguenot colonels cleansed their commands of Catholic soldiers. Their ranks were accordingly 'decimated' and as many as 700 Roman Catholics were evicted.[33] In this, of course, the Huguenot regiments were no different from many other corps in contemporary armies, most of which took whatever soldiers they could from whatever source. Niceties of nationality, religion and motivation were not the concern of the recruiting party.

A French ship had scarcely cleared Dublin when five British warships accompanied by four smaller vessels appeared from behind Howth Island and chased her back into harbour. Two of the pursuers even crossed the bar but the Frenchman took cover under Ringsend Point. Uncertain of what was happening at Dundalk, the aggressive activities of the Royal Navy frightened the Dublin authorities. Fearing invasion, they closed the gates, marched soldiers to Ringsend Point and generally alerted the city's defences. Scholars were evicted from Trinity College to make room for a Catholic garrison. Schomberg ensured that such minor victories were duly celebrated at Dundalk in order to provide some encouragement for his increasingly lacklustre soldiers.[34]

On 23 September, its morale high after the face-off against Schomberg, part of the Jacobite Army moved back to the Ardee position leaving a substantial portion at Bridge of Fane to reap, burn and destroy all the forage between the River Fane and the Dundalk camp but Schomberg refused to send out cavalry to disrupt them for fear of ambush.[35] The weather was unusually fine, so Schomberg again set his men to musketry practice. Many of the new recruits were equipped with matchlocks but experienced such difficulty in attaching the match to the serpentine in the correct manner that hardly one man in four could fire his gun. Lieutenant General James Douglas, on 29 September, attempted to teach the battalions of the first line the intricacies of platoon fire but, when it was regarded as a considerable feat just to fire a gun, not much could have been achieved. Schomberg's reluctance to fight and dependence upon the Enniskilleners was thereby increased.

He wrote to William on 27 September justifying his defensive posture. Convinced that James was intent on bringing on battle before the end of the campaigning season, Schomberg, who believed himself heavily outnumbered, had decided to remain on the defensive whilst waiting promised reinforcements from Scotland and Denmark. Just as the bog to the south of Dundalk constricted James's avenues of advance, so it inhibited his own offensive deployment whilst the Jacobite camp at Bridge of Fane was strong, its front covered by a little river and some hills. Around this time, certainly no later than the army muster on 25 September, sickness was first noted as a serious problem. The health of the army was declining, explained Schomberg, because of 'new beer' and a shortage of clothing and shoes. To compound his problems, the weather turned: violent wind and heavy rain on 28 and 29 September; the next day was fine but cold; followed by rain from 1 to 3 October.[36]

11

Sligo and Dundalk

Following the successes at Boyle and Jamestown, Schomberg sent Colonel Theodore Russell, an experienced and capable Protestant Irish regular officer who had seen active service in the Portuguese and French armies before being dismissed from his colonelcy in Ireland by Tyrconnell,[1] with reinforcements for Thomas Lloyd at Sligo comprising a detachment of cavalry; Colonel James Wynne's Enniskillen Dragoons; 200 infantry from Colonel Isaac de Monceau de La Melonière's Huguenot battalion, commanded by the Captain of Grenadiers, de St Sauveur; and 100 foot from Colonel Henry Wharton's battalion, led by Captain Richard Smith. James feared for the safety of Connaught but sensed that the Enniskillen advanced positions would remain exposed and vulnerable until Russell's arrival. To pre-empt Russell, he ordered Sarsfield to retake Sligo with a detachment comprising the infantry battalions of Colonel Oliver O'Gara and Colonel Charles Moore, Colonel Sir Neill O'Neill's dragoon regiment and Colonel Henry Luttrell's cavalry regiment. Setting off from Athlone with around 3,000 men at the beginning of October, Sarsfield gathered on the march an additional 2,000 irregulars, deserters and fugitives. On reaching Roscommon (2 October), assuming that the Enniskillen garrisons in Boyle, Jamestown and Sligo would receive intelligence of his approach and retire on Sligo, Sarsfield forwarded a detachment of 90 horse and 80 dragoons, led by Luttrell, to harry their withdrawal and prevent the burning and plundering of vacated villages. He also sent Major Ulick Bourke to occupy the pass across the Curlew Mountains, cutting communications between Boyle and Sligo, and another party under Colonel Charles O'Kelly to block the road between Jamestown and Boyle. Luttrell's party disturbed 200 Protestant horsemen commanded by Captain Weir, convoying 1,000 stolen cattle, who quickly scuttled into Boyle. That night Weir tried to break out towards Sligo but lost his own life and those of 15 of his men when they encountered Bourke in the Curlew Mountains. Via a circuitous route to avoid O'Kelly's blocking party, the remainder returned to Boyle and then made for Jamestown where they reported to Colonel Theodore Russell, who had beaten Sarsfield in the race for Sligo before going forward to take charge of the frontier posts.

On the next day, 3 October, Thomas Lloyd twice attempted to break through to Boyle from Sligo but was unable to dislodge Bourke from the Curlew Mountains.

Aware of his isolation, Russell decided to abandon Jamestown and retire on Sligo, hoping to evade Sarsfield's main body. On the morning of 4 October, he led out 400 men but they were soon spotted and Irish cavalry closed in and pressed them hard across country. Russell extricated the bulk of his men and eventually reached Sligo but they were reduced in number and somewhat disorganized. Behind this aggressive cavalry screen, having gathered in the detachments of Bourke and O'Kelly, Sarsfield marched rapidly through Boyle towards Sligo, covering 54 km in one day. Reaching Collooney, 12 km from Sligo, on 5 October his scouts reported that the Protestants had broken down the bridge over the River Owenbeg at Ballysadare, about 3 km further north, and on the far bank stood Lloyd who had arrived that morning with a small force. Well served by local guides, Sarsfield dispatched Henry Luttrell with 300 infantry, 100 dragoons and 70 cavalry along 'a very private way about by the mountain foot [probably Union Wood]' to take the Enniskilleners defending the smashed bridge in the rear. Whilst Luttrell executed the flank march, Sarsfield moved up the main body to occupy and distract Lloyd. Some firing occurred, and Lieutenant Colonel Talandier of O'Neill's fell wounded in the groin. Luttrell's march took him further towards Sligo than had been intended. As he came down to the main road between Ballysadare and Sligo, he found himself between a detachment under Colonel Theodore Russell – he had arrived back in Sligo only a few hours before – marching from Sligo to Ballysadare to reinforce Lloyd, who, realizing he had been flanked, was retiring towards Sligo. Luttrell had only his cavalry to hand, the infantry and dragoons lagging some way behind having been delayed in traversing a long defile.

Luttrell charged and scattered Russell's troops, killing 50 and pursuing the remnants to within sight of Sligo: this cleared the road and allowed Lloyd to reach Sligo relatively undisturbed. In the meantime, Sarsfield repaired Ballysadare Bridge with planks and joists and hurried to support Luttrell. Manning barricades at the town's southern entrance, Russell and Lloyd delayed Luttrell and Sarsfield until their ammunition was exhausted. Realizing that Sarsfield was too strong, Russell led all the Enniskillen mounted troops back to Ballyshannon, advising the infantry to follow.[2] However, Sarsfield was already too close to allow disengagement giving Lloyd no option but to remain and fight with the Enniskillen Foot, supported by Captain de St Sauveur's Huguenots. As Sarsfield entered the southern end of Sligo, Lloyd counter-attacked but was heavily outnumbered and repulsed.

Sligo was an open town defended by an old ruinous Fitzgerald castle in the centre and two Cromwellian forts, one a square, earthwork sconce to the north of the River Garavogue and the other of stone construction to the south of the river. Lloyd – a cavalryman whose forté was the offensive – had neither repaired nor improved these fortifications. Falling back into the town, the Huguenot foot sought refuge in the castle whilst Lloyd occupied the earth fort with about 300 infantry. Sarsfield immediately sealed off both positions. During the night of 5–6 October, abandoning St Sauveur in the castle, Lloyd evacuated the earth fort and escaped to Ballyshannon. Quickly realizing that Sligo Castle was indefensible, in the darkness St Sauveur led his men through the town, having sufficient time to collect some provisions, to the stone fort in which he discovered three barrels of powder. Sarsfield, although he had 5,000 men to St Sauveur's 400, lacked heavy artillery to batter down the walls of the fort but sought a rapid conclusion because, at any moment, a counter-attack might develop from Ballyshannon. Fearing that the Irish would approach the fort under cover of darkness, St Sauveur ordered his men to collect 'fir-deals', which were then dipped in tar, ignited and hung over the walls. Their light revealed the Jacobites bringing up a timber 'sow', or crude siege tower, covered with wet cow hides. It was as tall as the fort's rampart and internal stairs allowed attackers to gain the top of the wall under partial cover. Once the sow had been hauled into position, every effort was made to set it on fire and its unfortunate designer was killed by musketry. A Huguenot soldier tipped a bucket of wood shavings around the base and lowered a comrade equipped with a match. Illustrative of the unintensive nature of many of these actions, having ignited the shavings the soldier refused to return until he had stripped a Jacobite corpse. His colleagues then hauled him up but Sarsfield's men shot through the rope and he tumbled to the ground. Whilst waiting for a second basket, the soldier filled in the time by stripping a second dead body before being pulled to safety along with his booty. At dawn, the musketry from the garrison forced the Irish to abandon a field gun planted in the main street. However, such heroics could not endure indefinitely because there was no water supply in the fort and St Sauveur surrendered on 10 October, the fifth day of siege, marching for Enniskillen with the full honours of war on the next day. As the garrison crossed the bridge, Sarsfield stood with a purse full of money offering a horse and five gold guineas to any man who would serve King James. One accepted but deserted within 24 hours; even the stragglers and those who had been captured during Russell's retreat from Jamestown refused to accept. Colonel Henry Luttrell was appointed governor of Sligo to command a garrison comprising his own regiment of horse, Sir Neill O'Neill's regiment of dragoons and 3,000 infantry. He improved the fortifications by excavating a retrenchment around the town which incorporated the earth fort. Luttrell also constructed a redoubt to cover the Ballyshannon road on the north-west side of the town. Blamed for the loss of Sligo, probably with some justification, Lloyd was ordered to Dundalk where he died from the camp sickness, his reputation severely damaged. This, as William McCarmick noted, 'ended the actions of the Enniskillen men'.[3]

The only other significant Jacobite post in northern Ireland was Charlemont

Fort, threatening the western flank of Schomberg's line of communications between Belfast and Dundalk. Built in 1602 by Charles Blount, Lord Mountjoy, the Lord Deputy of Ireland, to restrain the raiding of the Earl of Tyrone from Dungannon, it was a simple, square sconce built around an old tower-keep, with four triangular bastions at the angles, each mounting three cannon, surrounded by a dry ditch, palisaded counterscarp and glacis.[4] The four-acre site enclosed a guardhouse, magazine and well. Charlemont's unfounded reputation for strength rested upon its location on the east bank of the River Blackwater, where it covered the bridge carrying the Armagh–Dungannon road. Corseted to the west and north by marshland and water meadows, the fort stood on slightly higher ground which extended south to include the small eponymous village. Unfortunately it was too small to contain sufficient stores or house an adequate garrison and was overlooked by higher ground. Increasingly aware of the enormity of his mistake in not garrisoning Derry with loyal troops at the time of the Glorious Revolution, Tyrconnell took especial care over Charlemont appointing to the governorship Sir Teague O'Regan, a veteran of Louis XIV's wars, to command a garrison of four foot companies and two cavalry troops. James thought Charlemont might serve as a base for autumn and winter raids into Ulster. Accordingly, he dispatched infantry reinforcements and, as soon as they arrived, O'Regan sent an expedition towards Dungannon which seized a considerable booty. Concerned about the increasing activity, during October Schomberg ordered Lieutenant General James Douglas, with three battalions, to observe and blockade the fort.[5]

Following the confrontation on 21 September, Schomberg was fully occupied in trying to maintain the health and discipline of his troops. A muster taken on 1 October revealed 11,651 infantry, 457 dragoons and 1,995 cavalry, a total of 14,103 effectives, but there were also 3,291 sick and 1,914 'wanting'. Sixty-four cavalrymen lacked mounts.[6] On that day, a 'good quantity' of brandy was delivered to every regiment and officers were enjoined to take good care of their men. The weather was 'exceedingly bad' and regiments that had pitched their tents upon 'wet, low ground' were given permission to move to drier areas. On 14 September Schomberg ordered his men to abandon their sodden, leaky, draughty tents and build huts. Although the Huguenot and Dutch soldiers promptly complied, the British troops took no notice and it was over a fortnight before Schomberg realized that his order had not been universally obeyed. The number of sick increased steadily. Schomberg made money available and instructed bread, cheese, brandy, beef, peas and meal to be provided for the sick but delivery was difficult amidst the chaos of the supply train. Fit men were supposed to collect ferns to make beds for the sick. Apart from the dreadful weather and the general shortage of food, the principal cause of ill-health was indiscipline. The men were lazy, could not be bothered to collect ferns for themselves or their comrades, failed to keep themselves and their clothes clean becoming lousy, indifferent, listless and sullen, whilst the officers were ignorant and irresponsible. Lack of action, or even a prospect of action, added to the ennui. A market was established in Dundalk town to which local people brought foodstuffs but they charged high prices and there was the constant danger that sensitive information about the state of the Williamite Army would be passed to the Jacobites.

Despite the garrison of a captain and 50 men in Moyry Castle, 10 km north of Dundalk, the countryside between Newry and Dundalk was insecure. Parties of raparees attacked, murdered and mutilated individual soldiers and small detachments and seriously embarrassed the regularity of supply convoys, so much so that most provisions were delivered by ship from Belfast and Carrickfergus directly into Dundalk harbour. On 3 October, Schomberg wrote to William that, in a few days, he would have to send the cavalry back into County Down because all the available forage had been consumed. In an emergency, they could rejoin the infantry at Dundalk within two days, sooner if they came via the ford at Narrow Water Castle, above Carlingford. In the meantime Schomberg was confident that he could hold Dundalk with infantry. Part of the problem was that the English cavalry officers did not ensure that their men took care of the horses, allowing them to ride at a full gallop and not knowing how to conduct forages. Consequently, there was never more than two days' stock of horse-feed.

Schomberg had based his campaign on false expectations and assumptions. When halting at Dundalk to rest his men and allow supplies and rear services to catch up, he did not anticipate that the rapid Jacobite concentration at Drogheda would be followed by a swift push north to Ardee. Probably, he thought that the Jacobites would remain around Drogheda or even retire west of the Shannon, giving him time to refit before advancing to take winter quarters in and around Dublin. Instead, his poor and unreliable army unexpectedly faced superior numbers.

Never ranked amongst the élite of French marshals, Schomberg was 73 years of age, tired, over-cautious and pedestrian, tendencies illustrated by his failure to secure the magazine at Ardee, tardiness in beginning to consume the forage between Dundalk and Ardee and failure to observe that the British soldiers had ignored his orders to 'hut'. He had acted decisively and quickly to seize Carrickfergus and move south to Dundalk but his nerve faltered when opposed by a supposedly superior force. There is some suggestion that Schomberg was baffled by Ireland. He had never seen such a country before: the weather was atrocious, there were hardly any roads, what passed for a town would have been described as a miserable village in other parts of Europe, the countryside consisted of a succession of impassable mountains, rivers and bogs and an absence of modern fortresses constrained his operational approach. Schomberg found it difficult to adapt and the discovery of the conspiracy within the Huguenot regiments wrecked his scant remaining confidence.[7]

An improvement in the weather on 4 and 5 October allowed the Jacobites to undertake some limited operations. On 2 October a party of 150 infantry commanded by Lieutenant Colonel Stapleton and Captain Hugh McNamara was ordered to rescue the Roman Catholics who had been recently cashiered from the Huguenot regiments and were held under a light guard at Carlingford. Stapleton and McNamara had to work their way around the Dundalk camp, which involved a detour of 50 km through the mountains, until coming to a valley within 10 km of Carlingford. Whilst resting to clean their arms and cover the priming pans against a sudden shower of rain, they were surprised by a Williamite patrol. When challenged, Stapleton replied that they were Williamites but he was immediately contradicted by his men who promptly compounded their error by firing a volley. In the subsequent action, 14 Williamites were killed and eight captured but the rescue attempt had to be abandoned.[8]

The forage around Bridge of Fane had been consumed and a council of war decided that it was too risky to make another attempt on Schomberg's camp so, on 5 October, orders were given to march the next morning at dawn. At 01:00 on 6 October, the army moved back to Ardee, the cavalry forming a rearguard. Because all the huts and any remaining forage were burned, the soldiers marched amidst a cloud of smoke, which turned to fog in the thick, wet, heavy weather, causing some regiments to lose cohesion. It was expected that the retirement to Ardee would be the signal for Schomberg to break up the Dundalk camp and go into winter quarters. Whilst encamped at Bridge of Fane, the Jacobite Army had remained in much better condition than its rival. Plentiful local corn and straw provided food, bedding and roofing for huts – the Jacobites had few tents – and there was abundant horse fodder. Punctually paid in brass money, the rank and file took advantage of a well-stocked daily market. Only beer was relatively scarce, costing 3d. per quart. Shortage of arms and equipment was the major problem for the Jacobites. Tyrconnell wrote to Queen Mary at St Germain-en-Laye to hasten the dispatch from France of 10,000 tents; 72,000 shirts; 40,000 hats; uniforms for 30,000 infantry, 3,000 cavalry and 3,000 dragoons; and steel for the manufacture of flintlock muskets.[9]

Under pressure from William to act before his army mouldered away and the enemy was reinforced from France, the Jacobite withdrawal allowed Schomberg to review his strategy. Perhaps, he mused, a march for the Shannon would draw the Jacobites into a battle. Indeed, he would leave for the Shannon tomorrow (7 October) but the generals were against it because half the men lacked shoes and the footwear of the remainder would disintegrate within two days. In addition the wagons had not arrived; the few transport horses at Dundalk were in poor condition because Commissary Shales had used them as draught horses at Chester; and the 120 artillery horses were still in Cheshire. William wrote again on 6 October urging Schomberg to press the Jacobites. Easier said than done, replied Schomberg, in a country where it was only possible to move via 'two or three great roads, the rest being divided by bogs and mountains'. Additional reasons for doing nothing were produced: he was outnumbered by two to one; the Jacobites were better armed, disciplined and fed; many of his new regiments raised from amongst Ulster Protestants by Irish lords consisted of mere boys, cheap to pay, clothe and feed; there was a shortage of shoes; the officers were generally lazy and incompetent; the cavalry officers did not take care of their troopers' horses and were so accustomed to lodging overnight in inns and taverns whilst on the march that they were unprepared for field service; there were not enough wagons and provisions for an advance; and the front of the Jacobite camp at Ardee was covered by a rivulet. Had Schomberg attacked and been obliged to fall back, then this rivulet might have endangered the safety of the army.[10] William, himself prone to impatience and rashness in military operations, found his disenchantment with the elderly, timorous, indecisive and supine Schomberg fermenting into dislike.

Forage and firewood were extremely scarce and the weather remained adverse: Commissary Shales was ordered to provide each regiment with two tuns of coal. Units released from Scotland arrived in Belfast on 9 October – the Royal Regiment of Dragoons (Colonel Anthony Heyford), the cavalry regiments of Colonels John Lanier and Thomas Langston, and the infantry battalion of Colonel Ferdinando Hastings, the latter comprising less than 300 men – giving rise to speculation that the advance on Dublin was to be resumed but they moved directly on Clones and Armagh to form the basis of a force for the siege of Charlemont.[11] Several Irish deserters came into the Dundalk camp on 10 October reporting that serious sickness, occasioned by the heavy rains, had also appeared amongst the Jacobites at Ardee. Schomberg was becoming increasingly vexed by William's impatience and refusal to understand the particular difficulties of campaigning in Ireland with a green army. Indeed, said Schomberg, had he attempted something ill-considered and failed then James might now be master of all Ireland. What good would be the promised Danish troops if Schomberg had lost a major battle before their arrival? Why could not the superior Anglo-Dutch navies mount a proper guard on the east coast of Ireland and stage a diversion in the form of an amphibious operation? Then he reverted to more familiar territory: ignorant colonels more interested in defrauding the paymaster through false musters than in caring for and remunerating their men; corrupt commissaries; broken and badly made weapons; shortage of officers and many more requesting leave under pretence of illness. Even the plan to relocate the cavalry in County Down had to be abandoned when Count Solms pointed out that the Irish would be able to manoeuvre between the cavalry and Dundalk and thus split Schomberg's force. So they remained at Dundalk, fed on oats landed from the ships. Not once did Schomberg question his own rôle and responsibility: in Field Marshal Lord Alanbrooke's famous phrase, he never demonstrated 'grip'.[12]

Schomberg gave an order on 13 October to ship all sick soldiers at Carlingford or Dundalk for transfer to hospital in Belfast but it was not executed for three weeks, regimental quartermasters inspecting the hospital transports as a prelude to embarkation on 31 October. Officers were again instructed to make sure that the men built huts – evidently this still had not been done – whilst quartermasters were reminded of their basic duty to provide the soldiers with shoes, clothes, bread, cheese, brandy and coal. Regimental surgeons met with Dr Thomas Lawrence, Physician-General to the Army in Ireland, to discuss measures to contain and control the flux and fever, 'which were then very violent'. Schomberg, whose sources of intelligence in a hostile country were unreliable, received information that the Jacobites were entrenching the Ardee camp, suggesting that they intended to remain for a considerable time. Although this turned out to be incorrect – they were actually fortifying the town of Ardee in order to leave a garrison when the army drew off into winter quarters[13] – it further constrained his freedom of manoeuvre and increased his reluctance to evacuate Dundalk. On 16 October, all the cavalry, except the Huguenot regiment, the Enniskillen Horse and Leveson's Dragoons, marched towards Carlingford where some forage was still available. Even officers were dying. Captain Paul Gore of the Earl of Drogheda's Foot was buried in Dundalk churchyard on 17 October, followed shortly after by Colonel Sir Edward Dering. Colonel Sir Thomas Gower died on 28 October and Colonel Henry Wharton on 29 October: both were interred in Lord Bellew's family vault in Dundalk church. The Reverend Story did not know the total numbers of sick but his own regiment, the Earl of Drogheda's Foot, had 67 men incapable of marching the 400 m to the new camping ground: they were left behind under the charge of a captain and 12 rankers and he visited once a day always finding fresh corpses. The healthy were reluctant to bury the dead because their bodies were useful as mattresses and draught excluders.

Around 23 October fit soldiers began to leave the main camp with its huts full of sick, dying and dead and disperse into satellites – near the artillery park, in Dundalk town, close to Lord Bellew's house, towards the harbour – but this had a further deleterious effect because they returned to cold, wet, leaking tents. The officers were ordered to account regularly for their numbers of sick and deliver the weapons of deceased soldiers into the train of artillery; there appears to have been a secondary epidemic of damaged weapons, scarcely one in ten muskets being serviceable. Funeral volleys were forbidden lest their frequency encouraged the Jacobites. A muster of the infantry, taken on 27 October, listed 10,510 effective men, 4,340 sick, and 2,415 already dead.[14] Murmurs were heard in the camp blaming Schomberg for the fiasco. If he had not stopped at Dundalk they would be in Dublin by now; Schomberg sought to protract the war for his own benefit and profit; he did not care how many men died; he was too old and unfit for command in the field; if he ever rode into camp, within two or three hours he had forgotten why he had come; and more men had been lost to disease than would have been killed in fighting the Irish. Interestingly, Reverend Story did not counter these allegations, confining himself to platitudes about the impossibility of great men being able to please everybody.

In an effort to shake off the general lassitude, on 27 October Schomberg authorized some offensive action, sending Cornet Charles Green with 200 of Leveson's Dragoons towards Tallanstown to reconnoitre a Jacobite outpost in the Earl of Louth's house, which had a frontal courtyard surrounded by a stone wall. The garrison comprised a captain, two lieutenants, an ensign and 60 men, rotated weekly. Of these, 20 men and one officer were on detached duty about 220 m from the house in an old, loopholed mill guarding a bridge over the River Glyde. However, the river was also fordable in several places. Green seized a large herd of cattle before reporting to Schomberg who, sensing an easy victory, decided to send a detachment of 1,000 cavalry, under Lord Maynard, to attack the position on 29 October. As Maynard came on, the party at the mill fell back on the house. A sergeant, who was slow to get away, was taken along with some cattle. Some of Maynard's men then advanced towards the house but a lieutenant was killed and two men wounded. Leaving the dead man behind, Maynard retired and turned back towards Dundalk. Had the main Williamite army been in support, mused Lieutenant John Stevens (Lord Grand Prior's Foot) who was a member of the garrison, and moved on the main Jacobite camp Schomberg may well have been successful because 'not the fourth part of our men could be found at their arms; the rest, the day being fair, were ranging the country for provisions, straw and other necessaries'. On the following morning (28 October), 80 grenadiers from Kirke's battalion, commanded by Lieutenant Robert Layton, were mounted and left the camp to escort the returning cavalry which had but one prisoner and some cattle and horses to show for its efforts.[15]

Recognizing that Schomberg would not quit Dundalk whilst he continued at Ardee, James decided that nothing more could be gained from the campaign and, anxious to spare his men before the onset of winter made conditions intolerable, on 1 November ordered the army to disperse into winter quarters. James himself returned to Dublin. To cover and observe the retirement, Schomberg ordered that two grenadiers from every English and three from each Huguenot infantry battalion be mounted and assemble at the White House early on the morning of 2 November, a reflection of how few fit cavalry and dragoons remained at Dundalk. Sick soldiers who were not *in extremis* were to assemble at 07:00 in the artillery park where officers would issue a week's pay before a detachment escorted them via Newry to the hospital ships at Carlingford. Several died as they were carried down to the roadside and the rest were bundled into carts, 'which was the most lamentable sight in the world, for all the roads from Dundalk to Newry and Carlingford were next day full of nothing but dead men who, as the wagons jolted, some of them died and were thrown off as fast'. The more seriously ill were conveyed by wagon to transports in Dundalk harbour on 3 November.[16] Even Schomberg, who spent most of his time in and around Dundalk church, rarely visited the camp and did not appear over-concerned about the soldiers' welfare, rode to the assembly point at Dundalk Bridge and was extremely annoyed that the regimental field officers had disobeyed instructions to be in attendance. As soon as the ships had filled with sick they cleared Dundalk harbour, gained deep water and sailed for Belfast. On board, sodden, rotten tents were the only available bedding.

On hearing that Jamestown, Boyle and Sligo had fallen, the Enniskillen regiments of horse and foot in Dundalk were instructed to reinforce western Ulster. By 5 November it had been confirmed that the Jacobite Army was dispersing into winter quarters from Ardee. At this, Schomberg finally decided to evacuate Dundalk and marching orders were given to 14 infantry battalions on 6 November: four were to go to Newry; seven to Armagh; whilst Percy Kirke's and the two Dutch battalions were destined for Antrim. Bread for six days and a fortnight's subsistence pay were issued. As tents were being struck on 7 November, rumours started that the Jacobite Army was approaching. Morale was surprisingly high and there was no panic but fortunately – because even the fit men were very weak and their performance would probably have been unimpressive – the threat dissolved into a small Jacobite reconnaissance party that seized two or three stragglers. As the heads of the columns marched on 7 November, the higher hills were white with snow whilst rain poured down in the valleys. The enfeebled fell out to die in the gutter and that night's lodgings amongst the ruins of Newry were 'indifferent'. So anaesthetized had the soldiers become to suffering, death and hardship that those who expired during the hours of darkness were used as seats by those still alive in the morning. The remainder of the army departed 'fatal Dundalk' on 9 November and all stores and equipment that could not be carried away were burned. Some sick soldiers had to be left behind to the mercy of the enemy who entered Dundalk within an hour of Schomberg's departure. A small party of Jacobite horsemen followed the rearguard as far as Moyry Castle, where they killed the adjutant of Lord Kingston's regiment and some stragglers. A detachment of Williamite horse went back to drive them off and they withdrew into Dundalk. Through cold and wet the winter marches killed yet more of the already weakened soldiers but arrival at their allotted billets brought scant alleviation: provisions remained in short supply, the countryside had been largely devastated and even firewood was sometimes hard to find. Discipline and organization partially collapsed as the men left the ranks to forage before drifting slowly towards their winter quarters.[17]

Between 1,600 and 1,700 soldiers died at Dundalk but even more succumbed in winter quarters. Of the 1,970 sick taken by ship from Dundalk harbour and Carlingford Lough, only 1,100 were landed alive at the main hospital in Belfast largely because no arrangements had been made for bringing the men ashore and they lay untended off Carrickfergus for several days. Between 1 November 1689 and 1 May 1690, 3,762 died in Belfast hospital – nothing more than a motley collection of rented and requisitioned houses – whilst many lost toes, feet, legs, fingers and hands to trench foot, gangrene and frostbite. At Dundalk and in winter quarters, Schomberg sacrificed half his strength.[18] After army headquarters had been established in Lisburn, 'Lisnagarvy' to the English, the winter line, or 'frontier', ran from Newry, around the north of Charlemont, to Cavan and Belturbet. The battalions of Colonels John Beaumont and William Stewart were placed at Rostrevor and Greencastle, County Down, to guard the north bank and entrance of Carlingford Lough. Newry, holding the mouth of the Moyry Pass and covering the road to Belfast, was occupied by Richard Ingoldsby's battalion. Should a Jacobite raiding detachment succeed in passing Newry, Sir Henry Bellasise's battalion and some of Leveson's Dragoons were stationed at Tandragee, south of Portadown. Some Huguenot infantry protected the headquarters in Lisburn, the battalions of the Earl of Drogheda and the late Sir Edward Dering held Armagh, whilst Clones and Monaghan were garrisoned by Ferdinando Hastings's battalion and some Enniskilleners, the latter also controlling the long sector from Clones to Ballyshannon.

When the Jacobite Army withdrew from Ardee, eight regiments remained in camp. As soon as Schomberg had abandoned Dundalk, a detachment of 1,700 infantry and six troops of cavalry and dragoons was formed from amongst these troops with the aim of crossing the Moyry Pass, seizing the bridge at Newry and then rolling up the Williamite frontier garrisons before they had become established, 'which at that time had been no difficult task to have performed'. Commanded by Major General Alexandre de Rainier de Droué, Marquis de Boisseleau, assisted by a brigadier and three colonels, the detachment marched through the night of 23–24 November and arrived at daybreak on the west bank of the Clanrye River opposite Newry. The town was occupied by the remnants of Sir Henry Ingoldsby's battalion, led by the governor, Lieutenant Colonel Tobias (Toby) Purcell. On hearing of Boisseleau's approach, Purcell dispatched a captain and 60 men south to Narrow Water Castle; a sergeant and 12 soldiers to Fathom, a ford on the Clanrye just upstream from Narrow Water Castle; and a considerable party to Poyntz Pass, a ford halfway to Portadown. Purcell was reasonably confident that he had covered all the likely avenues into County Down but just 60 men remained to garrison Newry, only 40 of whom were sufficiently fit to carry a musket. Keeping his main body west of the Clanrye, Boisseleau sent 100 men, probably commanded by Captain Christopher Plunkett of Lord Louth's regiment, to ford the river north of Newry Bridge before advancing on the town from the north-east. Meanwhile, under cover of this diversion, 200 infantry made a frontal attack across the bridge, which was watched by two sentries, 100 paces apart. Spotting the approaching Jacobites, one shouted three challenges before raising his gun, which misfired; he was rushed and killed. The other sentry also issued a challenge and managed to fire, alerting the garrison. Unopposed, the Jacobites pressed over the bridge, down a straight street and into the centre of the town. The main guard, comprising a sergeant and 12 men, ran out of the castle into the street, formed up and fired, before retreating behind some ruined walls to reload and offer a second volley. This gained enough time for the remainder of the garrison, those who were well enough, to assemble in the market place along with the few remaining townspeople. Boisseleau's two forces – Plunkett from the north and the principal party along the main street – entered the market place, opened fire and inflicted some casualties. Members of the garrison who were too ill to leave their lodgings shot from the windows, whilst others staggered outside and propped themselves against ruined walls in order to present their muskets. The Jacobites possessed good intelligence and knew where the officers were billeted: 'hit squads' were dispatched to deal with them. Captain Thomas Whitfield was killed as he left his quarters, Captain Michael Miller was cut down in the street and Lieutenant William Stroud was shot in the thigh, a wound from which he later died.

Several exchanges of musketry caused the Jacobites to think the Newry garrison numerically stronger than originally supposed and they began 'to shrink'. Sensing that the Irish were losing momentum, the garrison 'huzzahed' and they began to withdraw despite their officers' entreaties to stand, many wading up to their necks through high tide in the Clanrye. A captain and a few soldiers followed cautiously as far as the bridge but Purcell's invalids were in no condition to pursue. Two Jacobite prisoners taken in Newry reported that morale in Boisseleau's force was poor, to the extent that the main body could not be persuaded to attack across the bridge and Purcell's men had faced only the advance guard. The Irish lost a lieutenant colonel and six men killed and an unknown number of wounded. Ingoldsby's suffered two captains and six men dead whilst a lieutenant and an ensign were injured. It was thought odd that a crucial position like Newry had neither cavalry nor field artillery in close support but their absence was probably explained by the lack of accommodation, the general shortage of forage and the disorganization amongst the frontier positions.

Following this action, Schomberg arranged for detachments from Edward Villiers's and John Coy's regiments of horse, and other mounted regiments nearby, to do duty in Newry according to a rota. In addition, the bridge at Newry was demolished and a battery built to cover the ford to the north. On 29 November, Brigadier William Stewart received information that the Earl of

Antrim's regiment, billeted in Dundalk, intended to renew the pressure on Newry. Taking 250 cavalry and infantry, Stewart advanced and encountered Antrim's on the march through the Moyry Pass: he turned them back, killing 30 and taking 17 prisoners, 100 cattle plus several small horses. Thwarted, the Jacobites tried to invade Ulster through Belturbet but Colonel William Wolseley, commanding at Enniskillen, received notice of this intention and occupied Belturbet, virtually without opposition, on 4 December.[19]

Colonel François du Puy de Cambon travelled to view the fort at Charlemont on 26 November, escorted by 60 of Leveson's Dragoons. Irish scouts spotted them when they were about 3 km distant and the garrison rushed musketeers to line the hedges. The dragoons dismounted and drove back the musketeers but between eight and ten grew over-confident and advanced beyond the support of their comrades. They were surprised, taken prisoner 'and most of them died before they could be relieved'. At the very end of November, a party from the Charlemont garrison attacked and burned Dungannon, 8 km to the north-west. Charlemont, standing at the head of a salient pointing into Ulster, had become a nuisance under O'Regan's energetic governorship. The Huguenot battalion of Colonel Charles de Massue de La Caillemotte had taken winter quarters along the Blackwater, southwards from Milltown and Magher on Lough Neagh, specifically to watch and constrain Charlemont. Lieutenant General James Douglas made a tour of inspection of the frontier garrisons early in December, his principal purpose being to ensure that everything possible was being done to inhibit supplies and relief from reaching Charlemont. Williamite raiders ventured close to the fort, endeavouring to carry off livestock grazing outside the walls. On 12 December, Schomberg himself rode to reconnoitre Charlemont and was welcomed by cannon fire.[20]

Although settled into winter quarters, neither army was in good condition. Tyrconnell reported shortages of copper, ammunition and weapons, especially flintlock muskets; the sole source of resupply was France but the Jacobites had no money and Louvois was anxious to reduce expenditure on Ireland. Only the fact that many of the sick soldiers were recovering and rejoining the ranks added a little cheer.[21] Operations wound down and the time had arrived to take stock of what had been achieved. Primarily, the capture of all Ireland for the Jacobite cause had been prevented and, due largely to the efforts of local levies in Derry and Enniskillen, Ulster had been recaptured and secured. Charlemont remained the only Jacobite outpost in Ulster and its eradication would form the next major operation. However, plans to end the war in 1689 by an advance on Dublin had been thwarted. Following the defeats at Derry, Newtownbutler and Carrickfergus, the Jacobites had stabilized the situation by the end of the campaign retaining Leinster, Munster, Connaught and a small part of Ulster, three-quarters of Ireland: Schomberg's march on Dublin had been stopped and turned back; Boyle,

Jamestown and Sligo regained; and Williamite winter quarters were restricted to the Protestant heartland.[22]

On 27 December, the aged general penned his final apologia to William. Had he risked battle at Dundalk against a more numerous and well-positioned enemy, he might have lost all Ireland leading to grave consequences in Scotland and England. All alone, isolated, surrounded by incompetent officers and thus obliged to assume myriad minor duties that a commander-in-chief would normally have delegated, Schomberg's health had suffered. One of the more surprising revelations had been the discovery that members of the English Parliament seemed to think that one raw, English recruit was equal to six Irishmen. Schomberg had neither sought nor found any personal profit but had risked his health entirely in the king's service.[23] Some mitigation for Schomberg's conduct of operations can be offered. Story had arrived in Chester a week after Schomberg landed in Bangor Bay and was witness to the fact that most of the artillery and wagon horses were still in England and did not arrive in Ireland until the army had been at Dundalk for some time. Schomberg was indeed hamstrung by shortage of transport. The devastation of the countryside between Carrickfergus and Dundalk by the retreating Irish compounded the problem; at Newry, even the dignified Story had been obliged to dig potatoes for his own dinner. Robert Ayleway, commissary of the stores to the train of artillery, explained to Story that he had no option but to use his few artillery horses to haul bread for the soldiers. It was most irregular and Ayleway had never known such a thing before, but Schomberg had said that he would prefer to break conventions than see his men starve. Because of his lack of horses, Schomberg had re-embarked the siege train after the fall of Carrickfergus and ordered both the artillery and provision ships to rendezvous with the army at Carlingford. Despite favourable winds, the ships took ten days to clear Belfast Lough and only after Schomberg had been at Dundalk for a week did four ships come into Carlingford Lough. It was rumoured that the man entrusted with delivering Schomberg's instructions to the ships 'went somewhere with them and the ships lay still for want of them'. Clearly, the incompetence, ill-will and questionable loyalty of many of Schomberg's subordinates further constrained his operations.

When he left England, Schomberg seems to have laboured under the misapprehension that a second army would land on the west coast of Ireland, splitting the Jacobite defence and opening his route to Dublin. This may have been a misunderstanding of the rôle to be played by Percy Kirke's four-battalion relief force after it had secured Derry. It was also possible, although unclear, that Schomberg believed his essential task was to protect Ulster by confronting the main Jacobite field army. If this was the case, then he was successful. Schomberg's march from Belfast to Newry was unopposed because the road lay through mountains, drumlins and bogs making it impossible for the Jacobites to deploy their advantage in cavalry. The only missed opportunity was the Irish failure to defend Newry and the Moyry Pass. South of Dundalk the country was open and Schomberg would have found himself disadvantaged by the Jacobite cavalry and his communications with Belfast and Carlingford embarrassed. In Leinster, Schomberg was operating in hostile territory and his sources of intelligence were poor and unreliable resulting in the belief that he was heavily outnumbered. Advancing on Dublin in the face of a superior enemy, without adequate logistics, would have been extremely hazardous. By remaining at Dundalk the main road into Ulster via Newry was covered and supplies could be delivered by sea, whilst the Enniskilleners protected the frontier to the west. Even if he had intended to push south from Dundalk, before he was ready the main Irish Army had arrived in force and blocked the path. Schomberg was a stranger to Ireland. He lacked a professional, efficient staff and had neither authoritative nor trustworthy advisers. He was an old man, on his own, without help or support. He 'had the whole shock of affairs upon himself, which was the occasion that he scarce ever went to bed till it was very late, and then had his candle, with a book and pencil by him'. Story argues that Schomberg was correct in declining action on 21 September. His strength was known to the Jacobites – they accurately estimated that he had no more than 14,000 men, mostly infantry – because they had been observing the camp for a week, whilst the treachery within the Huguenot regiments effectively rendered the Williamite Army temporarily *hors de combat*. To approach the Jacobites and give battle Schomberg would have had to thread his men through a bog across open causeways and then deploy in the face of an enemy army already in line of battle. This would have been suicidal. The men were willing enough and, before sickness reached epidemic proportions, morale was reasonably high but poor leadership had left them insufficiently trained and unprepared for action. Had these men been caught in the open south of Dundalk by Jacobite cavalry, disaster may have resulted. There was, of course, the obvious point that the Jacobite Army was no better but Schomberg could not have afforded to test that hypothesis. Story does not even censure Schomberg for the ill-health within the Dundalk camp because, by the time that an epidemic became apparent, he was trapped at Dundalk unable to move away. At the beginning of the sojourn at Dundalk, he could have retired north to occupy a position at Newry but this option dissolved as the army grew weaker. It would also have surrendered the Moyry Pass, necessitating a major preliminary operation in the spring.[24] Even meteorology acted against Schomberg. The campsite at Dundalk may have harboured a particularly inauspicious micro-climate, caused by its location in a basin at the foot of the Slieve Gullion and Carlingford Mountains. Apparently, it often rained at Dundalk when not a drop fell on the Jacobites at Ardee and Bridge of Fane. Wet weather added to the problem caused by the camp's location on the low, wet, marshy estuarine plain whereas the Jacobite camps were situated on higher, drier ground. However, the better health of the Jacobite Army did not endure and, as the campaign stretched into late autumn and early winter, the numbers of Irish sick began to rival those at Dundalk and the Jacobite Army suffered from poor health throughout the coming winter.

If Schomberg the tactician and strategist may be excused, in his rôle as a commander, manager and administrator he can be heavily criticized: he demonstrated a lack of 'grip', failed to ensure that his orders were carried out, and lost control over his men. The resulting indiscipline eroded the army. The English, says Story, were idle, lazy, careless and vulnerable to the Irish climate and their regimental surgeons were ill-provided with drugs. He compares their fate to that of a Dutch regiment, which built such effective huts that they lost only 11 men through sickness. The English ignored repeated orders to construct huts but, again, Schomberg should have made certain that his instructions were obeyed. Finally, Story states that the army's general state of health at Dundalk was reasonable until Percy Kirke's battalions arrived from Derry. Did they bring the seeds of disease?[25]

James and Tyrconnell were not without critics. Whilst the self-contradicting argument – by disbanding the new levies because they could not be maintained the Jacobites were short of troops before Derry – can be dismissed, the accusation that James failed to demonstrate sufficient aggression against Schomberg at Dundalk bears closer attention. He could have attacked on 21 September 1689, at moderate cost. If successful, Schomberg would have been thrown out of Ireland and William would have been unable to launch another invasion in 1689 or even 1690. In the meantime, James could have mastered all of Ireland and deployed the army to invade Scotland or England, although this would have required French naval command of the Irish Sea and the Western Approaches. At the very least, James might have waited at Ardee for Schomberg to decamp first and then harassed the rear of his weakened and disease-ridden army. By allowing Schomberg to leave the field last, the technical victory, albeit pyrrhic, was handed to Schomberg and such questions of prestige mattered greatly. For the Jacobites, whilst the campaign in Ulster had been humiliating, the later operations against Schomberg had been a qualified success, sufficient to raise spirits and morale. However, even after his losses at Dundalk, Schomberg still commanded 12,000 men and, when added to the Enniskillen forces and other local levies, the Williamites remained formidable.[26]

12

Winter operations, 1689–90

The Whitehall government needed to assume the strategic initiative in 1690. Sir Robert Southwell, shortly to be appointed secretary of state for Ireland, submitted a memorandum on 31 January. Ireland had to be reduced quickly: better to spend two million pounds in one year than one million pounds *per annum* over seven. Where possible, Irish Protestants should be employed because they were committed, trustworthy and inured to the climate, a point well illustrated by the performance of the Enniskillen troops and Schomberg's reliance upon them during the march to Dundalk. Between 1,500 and 2,000 new cavalry should be raised from amongst the poor, Irish, Protestant gentry to counter the opponents' principal arm. Southwell estimated that the Jacobites, who had recourse to about 120,000 Roman Catholics of effective military age, had nothing to lose and would seek to prolong the war. In the long run they could only be subdued by famine and disease unless William made a substantial military and financial commitment. Thus, a Munster port should be captured – perhaps Kinsale, although Cork would be preferable – to squeeze the Irish from both north and south and interdict supplies and reinforcements from France. Always, advised Southwell, hound and harass the main Irish army, lay waste the countryside and avoid sieges. It was, in essence, a modern version of the old Cromwell–Coote strategy earlier advocated by Robert Gorges.[1]

The essence of this advice was followed. Remembering his own successful amphibious attack in 1688 and exasperated by Schomberg's dismal campaign, William appreciated that he would have to divert his full attention to securing the Jacobite bastion of Ireland from which James could launch attempts to regain the Scottish and English thrones. Continuing political instability in England, where many of the politicians, soldiers and sailors who publicly served William and Mary were in covert communication with James, increased the need for a prompt solution to the Irish problem. Pressed by both the English House of Commons and members of the Grand Alliance to turn his full attention to fighting France in Europe, William knew that he would be unable to comply until Ireland had been reduced. The States-General was of the same opinion and urged him to take personal command of operations in Ireland in order to bring that war to a speedy conclusion. William was hugely assisted by the fact that he was virtually sole director of anti-French strategy through his rôles as king o⁴ England, *de facto* leader of the Grand Alliance, and captain-general and stadtholder of the United Provinces. During 1690, he was to add to these burdens by assuming the field command in Ireland.[2]

The Jacobite leadership evinced no such clear priorities and James and his sole patron and supporter, Louis XIV, were at cross-purposes. D'Avaux had argued during 1689 that the primary objective was to secure Ireland and then convert it into a French-client state under James. However, there was no urgency because the longer the war, the greater would be the advantage accruing to France in distracting William and British resources from the main theatres in the Spanish Netherlands, the Bishopric of Liège, the Middle Rhine, and Piedmont-Savoy. Ultimate French-Jacobite victory in Ireland would create a permanent threat to England obliging William to maintain large home garrisons commensurately reducing the British contribution to the armies of the Grand Alliance in Europe. James though, from the moment of his appearance in Ireland in March 1689, had been in a quandary. He had joined his army at Derry on 18 April 1689 partly because he feared the harm that would be done to his Protestant subjects if they were left to the tender mercies of French generals and the Catholic Irish. Also he had expected Derry to submit as soon as the rebels caught sight of the royal person and was rather disappointed when the garrison welcomed him with cannon fire. James sought to unite Ireland by appeasing his Protestant subjects, whereas the native Irish faction sought to erase English domination to achieve an independent, Catholic state. Frustrated before Derry, James retired to Dublin where he spent the summer in consultations and sessions of the Irish Parliament (7 May–18 June), which were entirely pointless unless he could re-conquer the country. He could not be persuaded to repeal the Elizabethan anti-Catholic laws for fear of alienating his Protestant subjects on both sides of the Irish Sea. It was only at the insistence of the French that James reluctantly agreed to reverse the legislation of Charles II that had confirmed the Cromwellian confiscation and distribution of Catholic lands amongst English Protestant settlers and soldiers. James was heavily influenced by the Scottish secretary of state, John Drummond, First Earl of Melfort, who was anxious for an invasion of Scotland to restore his family fortunes and argued that Ireland was a waste of time and money. Although this attitude attracted opprobrium from every quarter, events ultimately proved his assessment. James fled from Ireland in 1690, Tyrconnell died in 1691, and Lauzun and the French troops were recalled. Melfort's arguments, coupled with James's indecision, convinced many Catholic Irish that their sovereign intended to cut some sort of a political deal with William. James was certainly fixated on using the Irish Army to invade England or, as a poor alternative, Scotland. Thus intent on regaining his English crown and dissatisfied merely with the throne of Ireland, he was unwilling to make concessions to the Catholic Irish that might undermine or alienate his potential future support in England. Because

James enjoyed executive authority and had already proved his incompetence by mishandling a strong position in 1688, the French felt that he would misuse and squander any resources committed to Ireland. Hence, their support was lukewarm and Louvois extremely reluctant to expend French troops and money. When finally persuaded, in exchange for a like numbers of Irish troops, only 6,000 were sent under instructions not to risk their own destruction. Indeed, the French brigade appeared to have three objectives: landing, fighting as little as possible and returning home safely.

Tyrconnell argued in a letter to Queen Mary early in 1690 that the Jacobite cause would best be served by landing James in England, where everything appeared auspicious for a restoration. William's announcement that he intended to lead the Irish campaign in person in 1690 was interpreted by Tyrconnell to mean that he intended to keep James in Ireland and not give him the opportunity to invade England either directly or via Scotland. The French agreed with this analysis suggesting that by prosecuting the war in Ireland, William and his ministers hoped to prevent the outbreak of civil war in England. Given the resources that William would commit and the parlous condition of the Jacobite forces, unless James invaded England Tyrconnell did not think the Irish could survive the campaign of 1690, a view repeated in April.[3]

Control of the sea and major ports was vital to the survival of any army in Ireland; in its absence it was impossible to receive supplies and reinforcements from abroad, or *in extremis*, escape. Jean-Baptiste Colbert, Marquis de Seignelay, the French minister of marine, could have conducted a strategy of interdicting English communications across the Irish Sea from temporary bases in Dublin and the southern Irish ports. This would have made a greater impact than sending 6,000 troops but the Irish Sea was rough, stormy and unpredictable whilst the Royal Navy was operating in home waters backed by established ports from Bristol to the Clyde. Instead, Seignelay preferred to gain control of the Western Approaches and the Channel prior to an invasion of the English mainland. French strategy thus boiled down to three principles: to divert William and English resources away from the Netherlands; to use Ireland as a recruiting ground for Roman Catholic manpower; and to trade French wines, fruit and salt for Irish wool, hides and meat. To some extent, these objectives were realized. Ireland did serve as an important strategic diversion; Irish Catholic soldiers were secured following the Treaty of Limerick; and eight major convoys sailed from France to Ireland between 1689 and 1691. Nevertheless, more might have been achieved if the French Navy had concentrated on interdiction operations in the Irish Sea, St George's Channel and the Western Approaches but this was probably well beyond its capacity and ability.[4]

English operational strategy within Ireland initially concentrated on the recapture of Dublin, a city of 41,000 people whose manufactories and wealth, largely the product of English Protestants, maintained the Jacobite Army – it billeted 20,000 troops over the winter of 1689–90.[5] Governor Simon Luttrell told D'Avaux that if the Protestants were turned out of Dublin the Jacobites would also have to leave: quitting Dublin would mean the abandonment of Ireland. The Jacobite Army did not employ the non-campaigning months profitably. As Schomberg removed his sickly soldiers from Dundalk, buried the dead and put the survivors into quarters, James and his officers spent the winter in revels, gaming and 'debauches'. Virtually nothing was done to prepare for the coming campaign: the troop numbers were not augmented; little training or exercising took place; no great efforts were made to find extra sources of clothing and armaments; strongholds were not victualled; and no town or fortress was refortified. Seemingly unconcerned about William's preparations in England the Jacobite Army rested on the laurels of its success against Schomberg, forgetting the lessons of Derry and Enniskillen.

James pursued an operational plan as internally contradictory as Jacobite and Irish political thinking. Seeking a decision by battle was the obvious strategy for William whereas James's best option was to delay and prolong. Instead, he decided to accept battle and precipitated it by advancing north. He would have been better advised to have retired on Dublin, destroying the countryside, forcing William to subsist from devastated Ulster and a vulnerable naval supply line, a scenario that might have been realized following the victory of Maréchal Anne-Hilarion de Cotentin, Comte de Tourville, over the Anglo-Dutch fleet off Beachy Head on 30 June 1690, after which the French Navy could have gained control of the Irish Sea and cut William's communications with England. Seemingly intent on inducing a decision as quickly as possible, James instead played directly into William's hands but even that strategy was not consistently applied. James knew that William would march on Dublin via the coastal route because it was the quickest and shortest and he had to rely on seaborne supplies. Therefore, it made sense to hold Newry and the Moyry Pass but he stopped short at Dundalk. Also, when seeking battle, even a general of modest abilities would have sought to maximize the strength of his field army but James left many infantry battalions in unnecessary garrisons. Compounding the mistake, not enough of these battalions occupied the key strategic towns and fortresses, which were thus inadequately garrisoned so that there were no effective secondary points of resistance should the battle be lost. Consequently, with strength in neither the field army nor the vital fortresses, in the event of a major defeat James stood to lose battle, campaign and war.[6]

Whilst the Jacobites played, the war continued along the frontier. On about 1 January 1690, Lieutenant Colonel William Berry (Enniskillen Horse) ranged across the south of the Fermanagh lake country from Clones to Sligo but met no Jacobite forces, returning with 1,500 cattle, plus sheep and garrons. A week later, 60 Irish horses and 150 sheep were seized by a party from Colonel Thomas St John's (Derry) infantry battalion in garrison at Armagh. At about the same time, Brigadier William Nugent, Jacobite Lord Lieutenant of County Longford, besieged Mosstown House at Keenagh, County Longford, the home of Sir Thomas Newcomen. Only his wife, Lady Sarah, was at home but she gathered 200 of her 'British' tenants into the house and prepared to defend herself. Although 32 km from the nearest Williamite garrison, several attacks were beaten off and only the arrival of field guns on 13 January finally persuaded Lady Sarah to surrender. Her military prowess so impressed Nugent that he granted the most generous terms. The house was spared from destruction and Lady Sarah was allowed to continue in residence with her servants. The 200 tenants who had been in arms were given permission to leave for Enniskillen under military escort, if they so wished, but were also free to remain at Keenagh: the latter, though, would have been highly dangerous and nearly 100 departed to enlist in Sir John Hanmer's infantry battalion whilst the remainder travelled to Lisburn where they were provided for by Schomberg.[7]

Brigadier William Stewart led a detachment of 500 cavalry and infantry from the garrisons in Rostrevor and Newry, over the Moyry Pass towards Dundalk and Carlingford, burning all the Irish cabins they encountered and seizing considerable numbers of cattle. On detecting the approach of a Williamite raiding party, the local Irish lit prearranged signal fires. Stewart discovered this from a prisoner and so, on three or four occasions, caused bogus beacons to be ignited. Because no raids followed, the Irish grew blasé and began to ignore the signals. Consequently, when Stewart sallied again, on 22 January, no signals were made adding greatly to the efficacy of the operation. In retaliation, the Irish attacked small groups of soldiers billeted in isolated houses and cabins. Following the kidnapping of five or six of Lord Drogheda's infantrymen, all troops were ordered to lodge within their main garrisons. A party of 100 infantry from Drogheda's battalion, plus 20 dragoons and 60 local Protestant volunteers, marched from Tandragee and Markethill to surprise two companies of Irish foot camped near the Slieve Gullion protecting a large herd of cattle. The Irish received intelligence of the Williamite approach and, initially, considered fighting but then thought better of it and melted away. Seventeen hid in a bog, from which a Lieutenant Murphy and four men were taken prisoner and another killed. The prize was 500 cattle, a vital acquisition at a time when the Williamite Army remained short of provisions.[8]

Between 7 and 9 February, information was received that the Jacobites were accumulating forces and supplies at Dundalk prior to attacking the frontier garrisons. Six regiments of horse and five battalions of foot were already at Dundalk, said the report, another five battalions were on the march and over 20 lighters, or 'gabbards', loaded with hay, oats, butter, cheese, bacon and biscuit had already arrived in Dundalk harbour from Drogheda. Schomberg, who had just returned to headquarters following a tour of the frontier posts, alerted Brigadier Stewart and Lieutenant Colonel Purcell at Newry and sent a warship from Carrickfergus into Dundalk harbour to destroy some of the gabbards. After observing in a letter to William that the enemy's march 'at this time of year must be ruinous to their troops', Schomberg rode south to Dromore to observe developments and ordered Colonel Sir John Lanier and Colonel de La Melonière forward to Carlingford but they reported only three Jacobite regiments in Dundalk, the usual garrison. Jacobite operations, however, were more subtle. As Schomberg's attention was thus drawn towards Dundalk, Berwick was marching to Cavan to lead a substantial force north towards Belturbet with a view to raiding deep into Ulster.[9] Colonel Wolseley learned that the Jacobites had reinforced their troops at Cavan and decided to pre-empt any attack on Belturbet.

Forming a detachment of 700 English (from the battalions of Percy Kirke and Richard Brewer), Dutch and Enniskillen infantry, plus 300 cavalry and dragoons, Wolseley left Belturbet at 16:00 on 10 February intending to surprise the Cavan garrison, which he estimated at about 1,000 men, 30 minutes before daybreak. Aware of Jacobite scouts at Butler's Bridge where the main road crossed the Annalee River, Wolseley tried to disguise his movements during the 11-km journey by taking a more easterly road near Bellanacargy. Unfortunately, he was spotted by the garrison of Bellanacargy Castle which passed the information to Cavan via a prearranged sequence of musket fire and beacons. Wolseley was over the Annalee by 01:00 on 11 February but the roads were bad and the defiles through the drumlin country so numerous that they did not come within sight of Cavan until 30 minutes after dawn. Berwick admits that Wolseley's sudden advance took Brigadier Wauchope, the governor of Cavan, completely by surprise but, in turn, Wolseley did not know of Berwick's arrival in Cavan the night before with 1,500 foot and 200 horse, which when added to Wauchope's garrison, gave him around 2,500 soldiers. Cavan was an indefensible, open town and so, when warned of Wolseley's approach, Berwick put his men into line of battle to the north along the ridge of Tullagh-Mongain Hill just in advance of Tullymongan Castle. His strength was rather more than Wolseley had anticipated but it would have been too dangerous to withdraw so he delivered a pep talk and advanced. Even so, although confident of the troops' high morale, he only committed 750 foot and 220 horse leaving 250 infantry and 80 cavalry in reserve to sustain a possible withdrawal. A reconnaissance party of dragoons was sent forward but they were charged by a numerically superior body of Irish horse and forced back on to the supporting English infantry whose musketry dropped seven or eight riders, at which the remainder withdrew. Simultaneously, Wolseley sent his remaining infantry up the slope of the ridge in a frontal assault. When fairly close, the Irish line fired a 'whole volley' and 'huzzahed' but shot too high to inflict serious damage. Wolseley's men pressed on until they were within pistol-shot, at which point they halted, dressed their ranks and gave a volley. Their fire was low and effective, shattering the Irish line which ran pell-mell for Cavan and the safety of an earthwork fort, Wolseley's troops following closely.

Berwick's version is somewhat different. Although Wolseley commanded 3,000 infantry and 300 cavalry, Berwick ordered Brigadier William Nugent to attack and the Enniskilleners were beaten back from hedge to hedge. Officer casualties, however, were high and when Nugent was wounded the troops panicked: the horse fled and the foot rushed back into the earthwork fort. At this point – the action had lasted about 60 minutes – the Williamite infantry began to plunder Cavan, indiscipline possibly fomented by the Enniskilleners. Taking advantage, 1,500 Irish erupted from the fort led by Wauchope. Although surprised, Wolseley had to hand the reserve of 250 infantry and 80 cavalry and, when they appreciated what was happening, a number of the pillagers returned to their duty. After containing the counter-attack, Wolseley then drove the Irish foot back into the fort 'like sheep' whilst their cavalry escaped to the south. Having gathered a useful supply of shoes, provisions and £4,000 in brass money, Wolseley ordered his horsemen to burn the town and what remained in its magazine – one source says that this was the only way in which Wolseley could persuade his ill-behaved infantry to stop plundering – before drawing off his tired soldiers and returning to Belturbet. Berwick lost 500 killed and wounded, including Brigadier Nugent and 13 officers. For some days afterwards, wounded Irish soldiers trudged south from Cavan and the roadside ditches were reported full of discarded weapons. Wolseley's casualties amounted to some 50 dead and injured, including Major Treherne, Captain Armstrong and Captain Mayor of the Enniskillen Horse 'who were killed by pursuing too far'. Berwick estimated Wolseley's casualties at 300.[10]

A gradual recovery in his soldiers' health allowed Schomberg to shift to more active defence. News of the Battle of Cavan revealed the extent and success of the Jacobite deception so Schomberg, still at Dromore, ordered most of the troops from Rostrevor and Newry back to their garrisons except for 500 infantry plus 500 horse and dragoons under Sir John Lanier who was instructed to reconnoitre as far as Dundalk. Leaving Newry on the evening of 15 February, he arrived before dawn to discover that Dundalk had been partially fortified and garrisoned by 2,000 men but he was not under orders to attack the town. He drew up his infantry on the slope where the Newry road dipped towards the River Kilcurry, within musket-shot of the bridge, pushing his mounted troops closer to the river on the right-hand side of the road. On the alarm, the garrison filed out but, observing Lanier's dispositions, promptly withdrew into Dundalk to maintain incessant musket fire throughout the remainder of the engagement. Keeping his main body north of the river, Lanier sent Brigadier Stewart with a detachment of horse and dragoons across the bridge to burn the suburbs on the western and south-western sides of the town. His work completed, Stewart retired having lost one lieutenant and two privates to musketry. Simultaneously, a second detachment, drawn from Leveson's Dragoons, attacked Lord Bellew's Castle which was occupied by an ensign commanding about 20 soldiers and ten 'country fellows'. From the cover of a bawn wall their fire had no effect on the approaching dismounted dragoons so they retired into the castle. The dragoons rushed the gate, forced it open and broke into the lower part of the house discharging their muskets upwards through the floor, wounding an Irishman. Threatened with having the house burned down around them, the defenders hung out a white handkerchief but their request to be allowed to leave honourably was refused so they surrendered as prisoners of war and were later marched under guard to Lisburn. Here, in the garden where 'he commonly used to walk before dinner', Schomberg interviewed the ensign. The dragoons' casualties amounted to one lieutenant and three or four troopers.

Although there were other targets that Lanier might have attacked, the Dundalk garrison outnumbered him by two to one and Jacobite cavalry was encamped at Ardee. Unwilling to take further risks, he fell back through the Slieve Gullion to Newry, capturing 1,500 cattle *en route*. Thereafter, Schomberg maintained a line of outposts within 7 km of Dundalk and a Royal Naval vessel took station off the entrance to Dundalk harbour preventing further gabbards from stocking the magazine. Schomberg continued to pester William: weapons from Ordnance stores in the Tower of London were faulty; he had been obliged to borrow money to pay the artillery; the army was owed six weeks' subsistence pay; the men had no overcoats; the hospital at Belfast was in a sorry state; the cavalry were in lamentable condition; Brigadier Edward Villiers was unfit for command and merely feathered his own nest; reinforcements, particularly infantry, were urgently required; and where were the Danes? Such negative communications did not improve the opinion that William had already formed of his general.[11]

It is possible, although by no means certain, that another operation against Dundalk was executed in early March. Major General Kirke lay 13 km distant with 600 cavalry and a battalion of foot, about 1,000 men in total. Kirke drew out 400 horse and 400 infantry and ordered a party of dragoons to drive 30 oxen in front of the detachment. Oxen riding point, Kirke was within 3 km of Dundalk by evening. Having sent his men to camp in the cover of an adjacent wood, he ordered the oxen to be driven a further 2 km towards Dundalk and there left to graze. Kirke instructed his scouts to report any movement of the Irish out of Dundalk. Overnight, the oxen meandered into some rich pasture and at daybreak, 'as their custom is', they began 'to roar', alerting the Irish who looked with relish upon a prey of 30 oxen. A detachment of 300 cavalry and 200 foot left the town, news of which was promptly relayed by Kirke's patrols. In silence his troops drew up in the wood and advanced through the trees until they came to a position flanking the road along which the Jacobites would travel. After a wait of 90 minutes the Jacobites came to the meadow, corralled the oxen and turned for Dundalk. The ambush was so unexpected and successful that the Irish offered no organized resistance and were pursued as far as the town, losing a number of men. Kirke's casualties were light, although one captain was killed, and all the oxen were retrieved.[12]

Colonel Caillemotte's Huguenot battalion had wintered on the River Blackwater close to Lough Neagh entrusted with containing the garrison of Charlemont Fort and interrupting its communications with County Tyrone. They had been relatively successful but the Williamites did not hold the countryside in sufficient strength to prevent O'Regan from raiding up to 16 km from his base. On 8 March, Caillemotte seized a small village within 3 km of the fort, easily turning back a feeble counter-attack by 300 men, and fortified it over the next couple of days. From here and outposts on both sides of the river, he was able to keep Charlemont under close, constant observation. On the night of 12–13 March, Caillemotte led 80 soldiers and 20 officers drawn from his own battalion and that of Colonel Thomas St John, one of the old Derry regiments then billeted in Armagh, with the aim of smashing the wooden bridge to prevent the garrison from making nocturnal excursions across the Blackwater into Williamite quarters.[13] In three boats the expedition sailed down the river to within 2 km of the fort. Leaving a guard on the boats, they marched along the river bank to the bridge and burned it even though the bright moonlight had revealed their presence to the garrison. They then split: Major De La Borde de La Villeneuve's (Caillemotte's foot) group seized a redoubt only 30 paces outside the Armagh Gate to prevent the garrison from sallying whilst Caillemotte's party stormed a second redoubt, between the counterscarp and the bridge, occupied by a sergeant and 15 men, killing six and capturing the remainder. Recombining, they proceeded to plunder and burn abandoned houses right up to the Armagh Gate. During the action, about 20 of the garrison and six or seven of Caillemotte's men were killed. As dawn was breaking, Caillemotte withdrew to the river in style, his drums beating and colours flying but, during disengagement, Major De La Borde was killed by the last cannon to be fired and Lieutenant Colonel Pierre de Belcastel and Captain Paul de Rapin de Thoyras were wounded. Because of the sheer insolence and effrontery – the ramparts of Charlemont Fort were within musket-shot of both the redoubts and bridge – this raid became a *cause célèbre* among the army in Ireland. However, the Charlemont garrison was inconvenienced and embarrassed but not defeated.[14]

The Williamite Army in Ireland required a larger core of solid, reliable, trained troops to augment the Dutch and Huguenot battalions. Equally important was the need for professional and competent officers untainted by English politics.

These could only be acquired from abroad. The Danish Army of King Christian V, comprising 5,500 cavalry and 15,000 infantry in Denmark and 9,000 foot in Norway, enjoyed a good reputation. It was also modern, the infantry having exchanged the matchlock musket for the flintlock between 1675 and 1679 whilst the pike had been abolished and replaced by the socket bayonet.

Following preliminary talks in London with the Danish envoy, Major General Frédéric Henri de Suzannet, Marquis de la Forest, a Huguenot and friend of Schomberg, William sent Robert Molesworth to Copenhagen to negotiate a settlement between Denmark and Sweden over Holstein-Gottorp in order to release elements of the Danish Army for mercenary service in Ireland. By the time Molesworth arrived in mid-June, Christian had already concluded the Treaty of Altona with Charles XI of Sweden, making his task considerably easier. Rather than join the Grand Alliance against France, which would automatically have triggered French support for Sweden, Christian preferred to rent 6,000 infantry and 1,000 cavalry to William III. It was good business to have England pay for 20 per cent of his army and provide them with training through active service, in addition to receiving a generous financial subsidy. The corps commander was a German, Lieutenant General Ferdinand-Wilhelm, Duke of Württemberg-Neustadt, a member of a cadet branch of the ruling family of Württemberg, who had entered the Danish service during the late 1670s and seen much action.

Three cavalry regiments and nine infantry battalions sailed from Denmark on 6 November 1689 intending to make Leith in the Firth of Forth but the weather was bad, the pilots incompetent and the majority of the convoy appeared off the Humber on 15 November. One ship, carrying four companies of the Queen's Regiment, was captured by French privateers who took the troops to France where they were incorporated into the Royal Danish Regiment in the French service, commanded by a natural son of Christian V. Another vessel also fell to French privateers but the 130 soldiers of the Queen's Regiment on board overcame the French prize crew and sailed to the coast of Holland where they were wrecked but managed to scramble ashore, secured passage to Portsmouth and eventually rejoined their regiment. The resultant damage to the Queen's Regiment was so great that its remnants were amalgamated with the Oldenburg Regiment, commanded by Colonel Otto von Viettinghoff, thus reducing the infantry corps to eight battalions. Another ship, with a cargo of 52 horses and 300 men, made for the Tyne. The soldiers landed at Hull took winter quarters in Yorkshire. Württemberg was in London during January and February 1690 solving administrative problems, mostly relating to pay, with the king and William Blathwayt, the Secretary at War. He left Chester on 12 March, reaching Belfast on the following day. The foot regiment that had landed in Scotland embarked at Greenock early in March and another section of the infantry departed from Whitehaven at about the same time. The bulk of the Danish foot sailed from

Hoylake in mid-March. Of the three cavalry regiments, Colonel Christian Juel's travelled from Scotland to Ireland in mid-March but there was some delay before the arrival of the other two regiments completed the Danish Corps. Colonel Jens Sehested's spent 11 days at sea between Scotland and Ireland and the seasick troopers did not step ashore until 11 April.[15]

The arrival of Württemberg and the majority of the Danes boosted Schomberg's confidence. Belfast, the main base and supply depot whence wagon convoys lumbered to the frontier garrisons, was so full of generals, lieutenant generals, major generals, brigadiers and quartermaster-generals that it was nearly impossible for more humble mortals to find accommodation.[16] Württemberg met Schomberg formally on 13 March and found him 'very vigorous, in spite of his great age, so that no business is a burden to him'. The general explained that it would be some time before the army could take the field because the train of artillery contained only three battering cannon and one mortar and the whole army was under-strength and awaiting reinforcements from England. When operations did commence, he said, Charlemont would be the initial target. To help training and acclimatization, the Danish Corps was billeted in County Antrim, Württemberg establishing his headquarters in Galgorm Castle on the outskirts of Ballymena. During January, Schomberg's four weakest battalions – the Earl of Drogheda,[17] the Earl of Roscommon, Colonel Nicholas Sankey and Colonel Sir Henry Ingoldsby – were disbanded and their men drafted to fill vacancies in other units. All four colonels were Anglo-Irishmen whose battalions had been identified by the inspectors at Dundalk on 18 October 1689 as the worst in the army. Recruiting parties from the surviving regiments were then sent into England and, by June 1690, 5,360 replacements had been raised. Volunteers were also gathered locally in Ireland whilst the Huguenot regiments were filled by men who travelled from Switzerland via the Dutch Republic along a well-established series of staging posts in the Rhine valley.[18]

As early as January 1690, Blathwayt and the secretaries of state had identified 30,717 troops – Schomberg's original corps plus reinforcements – who would serve in Ireland during 1690: 1,302 English, 1,417 Dutch and 1,034 Danish cavalry; 1,538 dragoons; and 5,640 English, 5,600 Dutch, 6,466 Danish and 7,720 Scottish infantry. In addition there would be 1,293 baggage horses to service the infantry battalions, plus 3,300 horses to tow the 100 artillery wagons and 450 bread carts.[19] Transport ships gathered at Bideford, Appledore, Barnstaple and Milford Haven during the second week of April. At the opening of the campaign, William commanded about 37,000 men, only half of whom were English, rather more than the January estimate, the difference probably resulting from the inclusion of local levies and Enniskillen forces in the later figure.[20] A review held at Finglas, north of Dublin, on 8 and 9 July 1690 in the aftermath of the Battle of the Boyne, listed a grand total of 30,330 soldiers, excluding officers, in the field army. Undoubtedly, the friction of war accounted for some of the reduction but most was explained by the necessity of leaving garrisons in key positions.

In January 1689, Justin Macarty was discussing with François Michel le Tellier, Marquis de Louvois, the French secretary of state for war, an exchange of French and Irish troops. Louis XIV's wars had taken a heavy toll of French manpower and Louvois was only prepared to furnish troops if a reciprocal number of Irish soldiers went to serve in the French Army. D'Avaux, who personally witnessed the excellent raw military material represented by the Irish, became an enthusiast for the scheme. Initially, James was unenthusiastic not wishing further to encourage French influence, but Derry, Newtownbutler and Schomberg's arrival changed his mind. From the beginning of negotiations, Macarty was the assumed commander, an officer well known and respected in France for his previous service and achievements, but James did not wish to lose him and favoured the appointment of Berwick, his natural son. The French, however, insisted so James endeavoured to mitigate the sacrifice of Macarty by ensuring that the other officers were not of the highest calibre. Shortly after 4 November 1689, James wrote to Louis proposing to exchange five or six regiments of French 'old foot' for a like number of newly raised Irish. Louvois replied favourably and asked James to dispatch five regiments each comprising 16 companies of 100 men. To this end, James commissioned Major General Justin Macarty, now Earl of Mountcashel; Daniel O'Brien, Third Viscount Clare; Arthur Dillon; Robert Feilding; and Richard Butler to raise new infantry regiments. Mountcashel was to command. The Irish Brigade, consisting of 5,387 raw levies, immediately became an integral element within the French Army unlike the Treaty of Limerick troops which, until the Peace of Rijswijk in 1697, constituted the army of James II in French pay.

Having left Brest on 7 March, a convoy of transports escorted by 40 warships under the Marquis d'Amfreville came in sight of Kinsale on 13 March. On board were seven 'French' infantry regiments – Famechou, Zurlauben, Mérode, La Marche, Courvassiez, Forest and Tournaisis – totalling 6,666 men led by Antonin de Caumont, Comte de Lauzun, a great personal favourite of James's queen, Mary of Modena, who enjoyed a thoroughly justified reputation as an injudicious, brainless playboy. The ships also carried between 300 and 400 Irishmen, some English and French volunteers, 22 field guns, 300 bombs, 6,000 grenades, ammunition, and considerable quantities of small arms. The fleet shifted round to Cork where Lauzun had landed his men and equipment by 24 March but an outbreak of disease rapidly killed 500 and the epidemic continued to reduce their numbers during the march to Dublin via Kilkenny. Although superior to Mountcashel's force, the French regiments were not of enormously high quality comprising Walloons, Dutch, Germans, Swiss and other non-Frenchmen, some of whom were prisoners of war taken in the Spanish Netherlands during 1689. When this corps marched north on 16 June 1690 to join James's assembling field army, a Dublin diarist noted that their ranks were so depleted that they had been recruited with native Irish and, even then, their numbers had fallen to 5,000. One report says that as soon as these regiments arrived in Dublin, at least 500 of the Dutch, German and Swiss 'French' attended Protestant churches and tended to sympathize with William of Orange rendering their loyalty questionable. James wrote to Mary of Modena asking her to suggest to Louis, very diplomatically, that future replacements might be proper, upright Roman Catholics, preferably of impeccably French descent.[21]

The ships were then to embark Mountcashel's Irish Brigade plus D'Avaux and Rosen. The latter had grown thoroughly disenchanted with the pusillanimous conduct of the war whilst the former had fallen foul of James, Mary of Modena, Lauzun and Louvois. Before leaving, D'Avaux encouraged Lauzun by explaining to him that, 'you are come to be a sacrifice for a poor, spirited and cowardly people whose soldiers will never fight and whose officers would never obey orders, and therefore they would meet with the same fate his Master's [i.e. Louis XIV's] army met with at the Siege of Candia, that is to be wasted and destroyed'. Colonel Robert 'Handsome' Feilding was charged with embarking the Irish Brigade. Before the reluctant dupes could be enticed on board, possibly as many as 1,000 ran away. At a loss as to how to make good the shortfall, Feilding remembered 120 Protestant prisoners in Galway, Sir Thomas Southwell's troop of horse which had been raised in 1689 to secure County Limerick for the Protestants but had been driven northwards until incarcerated in Galway by the sheriff, James Power. If each Protestant produced eight recruits, proposed Feilding, he would be granted liberty and pardon; in short time, 14 of the prisoners purchased the services of eight mercenaries apiece. Once Feilding and his brigade had been shipped, James ordered the Protestants rearrested because the deal with Feilding had not received royal approval. Another source says that 1,000 Protestants were pressed into Mountcashel's brigade. Whatever the true story, on arrival in Brest the five regiments were so under-strength that the French immediately reformed them into three. Delayed by adverse winds, the fleet sailed on 8 April but the voyage was dogged by bad weather and it took nearly a month to reach Brest.

James had already arranged with Louis that the French brigade would garrison Dublin, despite the objections of Governor Simon Luttrell, the lord mayor and aldermen who said that they did not wish to become subjects of the king of France. Nevertheless, three French battalions marched to Dublin in early May where their rude and overbearing behaviour created considerable difficulties. Having been resident for just two days they murdered some Protestant clothiers who tried to protect their wives from being raped. A country girl, who came to market with her father, was raped openly in the street. The French arrival also polarized opinion amongst the Jacobites. Those who sought to establish an independent, Roman Catholic Ireland, realizing that both James and the French would now be intent on using Ireland as a resource with which to regain the English throne, grew more amenable to reaching a compromise settlement with William. Opposed to this faction was a pragmatic group which recognized that French assistance was essential if the Jacobites were going to stand any chance of defeating the Williamites, whatever the eventual political purpose of any victory. These differences were exacerbated when Lauzun reached Dublin and demanded the keys to both the city and castle, which he received on 4 May.

A reasonably well-informed source listed the Jacobite Army on 9 April as containing 3,163 cavalry in seven regiments and three troops of guards; 2,880 dragoons in seven regiments; and 38,016 infantry in 44 single-battalion regiments plus the two-battalion Royal Regiment. As in 1689, Schomberg hugely over-estimated Jacobite numbers. He wrote to William on 14 March explaining that James had about 40,000 men at Ardee, plus another 15,000–16,000 in Dublin, Drogheda, Cork, Kinsale and along the line of the Shannon. He predicted that the Jacobites would hold Drogheda in strength so that the Williamites would have to cross the River Boyne 10 km inland. He also asked for Royal Naval vessels to patrol the Western Approaches in order to intercept any French troops *en route* for Ireland.[22]

Along the western frontier, Colonel Wolseley maintained high levels of activity. On 21 March, he left Belturbet with 220 men to search for livestock with which to feed his troops. They moved about 10 km south-east of Cavan into the area around the village of Clifferna where they rounded up about 700 cattle. As they made their way back towards Belturbet, one troop of cavalry, a troop of dragoons and three companies of infantry, around 400 men in total, marched from Cavan aiming to cut them off before they had reached the Annalee River. The Irish deployed into line of battle to bar Wolseley's crossing but he immediately attacked, driving them as far as the outskirts of Bellanacargy. Before 4 April, Schomberg decided to blood one of the new Danish battalions, the Funen Regiment under Colonel Hans Hartman von Erffa, by ordering it to Belturbet to strengthen Wolseley.[23] Thus reinforced, he returned to the offensive leaving Belturbet on Sunday 6 April at 20:00 with 700 men – 120 infantry of Kirke's battalion under the major, Richard Billing, and two captains; 120 from Thomas Erle's commanded by two captains; 60 from the Funen Regiment; seven troops of horse and four of dragoons – to attack the Castle of Killashandra, 14 km to the south, dominating the north–south road to the west of the complex of lakes. Its capture would also give the Williamites access to the upper Shannon crossings.

Abraham Creighton, lieutenant colonel of Colonel Gustavus Hamilton's battalion of Enniskillen infantry, took 350 of his men west to Fenagh, both to serve as a diversion and protect Wolseley's western flank from Jacobite forces in Boyle and Jamestown and behind the Shannon. Wolseley arrived before Killashandra at dawn on Monday 7 April and deployed his men in battle order, sending advance detachments to seize the hedges. Meanwhile, an engineer examined the defensive works, which consisted of an outer and inner courtyard, the latter incorporating the walls of both the house and the ruins of an old castle. Wolseley had brought scaling ladders but first the outer courtyard had to be secured. The infantry advanced under cover of the hedges and ditches to within musket-shot of the outer courtyard and then, by working round behind a low wall to the rear of a stable block, was able to approach the walls of the house directly without having to take the outer courtyard. The garrison of about 100 men promptly withdrew into the house and ruined castle whilst the engineer supervised the digging of a mine from the stables underneath the wall of the house. By 11:00 the mine was finished and charged. Wolseley's invitation to the governor, Captain Darcy, to surrender was readily accepted because the house lacked a water supply. The garrison lost three or four wounded and one dead, whilst Wolseley's casualties amounted to three killed and five or six injured. Wolseley put in a garrison of 100, soon reinforced by the Funen battalion, and burned the surrounding country before retiring to Belturbet. The first task of the new garrison was to sink wells.

On 10 April, Colonel Zachariah Tiffin, the governor of Ballyshannon, ordered his lieutenant colonel, Francis Gore, to raid towards Sligo with 200 flintlock musketeers from his own battalion, plus an escort of 20 dragoons. They arrived within 3 km of the town before daybreak on 11 April and seized 400 cows, 150 sheep, 80 goats and 60 horses. Alerted, the Irish pursued with two troops of horse, one of dragoons and three companies of infantry, overtaking the raiders within 5 km of Ballyshannon. Gore immediately deployed and attacked. After an action lasting 30 minutes, he forced the Irish aside, killing a captain and 16 soldiers, and returned to Ballyshannon with his booty. Colonel Gustavus Hamilton took a small detachment from his garrison at Clones on 19 April and raided 20 km into Jacobite territory, bringing back 200 cows, 400 sheep and a number of horses. Although he had to thread his way past a number of Irish garrisons, he regained Clones without incident.[24]

The Jacobites also came under limited naval pressure. Rear Admiral Sir Cloudisley Shovell arrived at Belfast in HMS *Monk* on 12 April escorting a convoy laden with reinforcements, arms, ammunition and money. Acting on information that there were many small merchantmen in Dublin harbour ready to leave for France with cargos of hides, tallow and frieze,[25] Shovell sailed from Belfast and stood into Dublin Bay on the morning of 18 April. Through his perspective glass he saw the *Pelican*, a French frigate of 20 guns which had been captured from the Scottish Navy in 1689, about 2 km inside the bar. Shovell transferred to the *Monmouth* yacht, commanded by Captain Wright RN, and, in company with two hoys, a ketch and some pinnaces, crossed the bar on the flood tide. The *Pelican* promptly shifted into the Salmon Pool in the estuary of the River Liffey, within range of the armament of a small French warship of 12 guns and two or three Irish vessels, loaded with soldiers, which lay aground on the mud. Shovell received cannon and musket fire as he came in but, on seeing him signal for a fire-ship, the soldiers and French crew abandoned the vessels and took to the boats. Shovell's men boarded the Frenchman, heaved unnecessary gear overboard to lighten ship and warped her clear of the mud. As the small squadron began to make its way from the river into the bay, the wind veered easterly and one of the hoys ran aground close inshore; despite considerable efforts, she could not be refloated, and the ebbing tide left her stranded. Shovell's ships launched their boats, crewed by armed sailors, which circled the hoy and ran out her anchor ready to warp when the tide turned. Thousands of Dubliners came down to the sands at Ringsend to watch the fun, including King James. Two Protestants ran out to Shovell's boats and jumped in whilst a Frenchman from King James's Life Guard rode into the water and shouted, in broken English, a number of coarse, insulting remarks and fired his pistols. Shovell's men shot his horse and quickly began to row towards the shore to 'unrig' the beast. The Frenchman slipped out of his heavy, stiff riding boots and ran away. When the tide turned, the hoy was pulled clear and Shovell stood off in Dublin Bay until 20 April. Happening under the eyes of the hyper-critical French, this episode was deeply humiliating to James but Shovell did not stay long enough to prevent the convoy sailing for France. By the end of April, up to 12 merchant ships were entering and leaving Dublin every week. Nor did the Royal Navy appear in strength in the Irish Sea during the remainder of the campaign, 'a great oversight in the English not to guard these coasts, but leave them open to the French'.[26]

Although lack of forage and money, bad weather and the 'horrible' roads argued against an early attempt on Charlemont, Schomberg was determined to attack as soon as possible. On 31 March, army headquarters at Lisburn received reports of Berwick's arrival in Dundalk but Schomberg was confident that he was only there to inspect the frontier garrisons rather than conduct an offensive towards Newry; he was already firmly convinced that the Jacobites would make their main resistance along the line of the River Boyne. By mid-April the situation was improving. Money, horses and an artillery train were on the way and Württemberg and Major General Kirke were visiting all the infantry in garrison in order to muster, pay, inspect and drill them. When Schomberg's son, Meinhard, reached Ireland the cavalry would receive similar attention.

Despite the facts that William did not intend to leave London until 15 May, there would be insufficient growth of grass before mid-May to support major operations, and the few heavy battering cannon had been worn out over the winter through training gunners, on 19 April Schomberg moved on Charlemont. This tidying-up operation would ensure that all of Ulster was in Williamite hands before the advance on Dublin began and, if William so wished, make available an alternative route via Kells. Equally important, Schomberg badly needed a personal success. Tyrconnell, who thought that major operations were impossible so early in the year, was taken by surprise. On 22 April, just prior to Colonel St John's infantry battalion moving to reinforce the blockade, which had been conducted up to that point by 150 infantry from Caillemotte's and Colonel John Cutts's battalions lodged in two or three ruined houses in Charlemont village, Lieutenant Colonel Hugh MacMahon with between 400 and 500 men escorted a small provision convoy across the nearly dry bogs into the fort. Schomberg formed the view that Charlemont was now over-garrisoned and under-provisioned. Therefore, given that Schomberg was not in a hurry because the advance on Dublin could not begin before William's arrival, a blockade was likely to produce results more economically than a formal siege. Governor O'Regan, who shared Schomberg's assessment of Charlemont's supply situation, was anxious for MacMahon to remove his additional, unwanted men as quickly as possible.[27]

Information reached Lieutenant Colonel Joseph Davessein de Moncal of Cambon's Huguenot infantry battalion that some of MacMahon's relief party were about to break out towards Armagh. He arranged three detachments in an ambush under the command of acting Major Jean Ribot, Captain Sylvie de Montaut de Pralou and Captain Nicholas de la Cherois. On the first two nights, 23 and 24 April, the Irish failed to appear but, on 25 April, they came out and marched within range of the weakest of the three parties, Cherois's 40 men. He let the van pass before ordering his men to fire on the main body. Eight men, including an officer were killed, and the remainder fled back to Charlemont leaving behind 110 muskets, six halberds, five drums and 60 hats. At dawn, Cherois was reinforced by the other two parties and they advanced towards the fort coming upon the broken Irish, who had rallied, drawn up on a hill about 2 km from the fort. As soon as they saw the Huguenots approaching, they ran and were pursued as far as the Charlemont counterscarp, losing five prisoners and seven horses. The Huguenots suffered no casualties. On the evening of 25 April, the garrison sallied against an out-guard of about 40 men from Caillemotte's battalion stationed in the remains of Charlemont village. The Huguenots retired on a support of 60 infantry from Cutts's battalion and then counter-attacked, driving the Irish into the fort, killing nine and taking eight prisoners. When Schomberg heard that the garrison had become active, he ordered two additional battalions to reinforce the blockade. Governor Teague O'Regan was furious with MacMahon for having failed to break out of the cordon and swore that his men would neither be allowed into the garrison nor receive provisions. He was as good as his word and MacMahon's unfortunate soldiers were forced to build little shelters in the ditch, trapped 'in a most lamentable condition' between the garrison and the blockaders.

Schomberg wrote to William on 5 May that the blockade was complete and the garrison had been reduced to eating its horses but he had also dispatched mortars and cannon to expedite a conclusion. Charlemont, though, had other uses; Schomberg acclimatized newly arrived battalions by deploying them in the ring. On 11 May O'Regan asked for a parley. When previously summoned to surrender he had been 'very surly' instructing the messenger to tell Schomberg that he was 'an old knave and, by St Patrick, he shall not have the town at all', but the supply position was now critical – 20 salted horses had been consumed and only rats, dogs and hides with hair still attached remained – leaving no option except the white flag. A lieutenant colonel and a captain agreed the articles of surrender on the following day, 12 May. Anxious not to waste any more time sitting before Charlemont because William was expected shortly, Schomberg conceded very generous terms and allowed the garrison to march out with the full honours of war. Everyone in the fort – governor, officers, soldiers, gunners, camp followers and the unfortunate inhabitants of what had once been Charlemont village – was to enjoy quarter and depart with arms, baggage, drums beating, colours flying, matches lit and bullet in mouth. Each officer and soldier was allowed to carry 12 charges of powder, with match and ball proportionable, plus all their possessions and horses and travel to Dundalk at a speed not exceeding 14 km per day. All the sick were to remain in Charlemont until recovered when they might proceed to the nearest Irish garrison. Charlemont's fall meant there was no Jacobite cavalry north of Drogheda and only three infantry regiments at Dundalk plus some companies at Castleblaney. Tyrconnell explained to Queen Mary that the surrender of Charlemont did not really matter: the fort had only been retained over the winter because it housed some artillery and ammunition that could not be brought south until the spring. This nonsense, however, was intended for French consumption: the ammunition and cannon were now forfeit and the capitulation of Charlemont represented a significant defeat.

Throughout 13 May, the country people conducted a market, officers from both sides visited each other's camp and Schomberg ordered a loaf of bread out of the stores in Armagh to be given to each member of the surrendered garrison. Charlemont Fort passed into Williamite control at 08:00 on Wednesday 14 May, three companies from Colonel Philip Babington's infantry battalion taking formal possession. Governor O'Regan duly marched out with 800 men, leaving behind a considerable store of ammunition, 17 brass cannon and two mortars. When the Irish stepped out along the road to Armagh, most of the Williamite regiments in the area of the blockade were drawn up alongside the road to give the Irish an impression of the strength and quality of the army that was forming against them. Schomberg rode from Lisburn to observe the condition of the Irish.

Although the colonel of the Brandenburg regiment was very annoyed that he had travelled so far to fight 'such scoundrels', after the garrison had marched about 1 km down the Armagh road, they drew up into two battalions of about 400 men each: in between were 200 women and children. They created a reasonable impression: their uniforms were in decent repair, they were adequately armed and their morale appeared buoyant. The ancient, hunch-backed warrior O'Regan was perhaps the most interesting item on parade. He sat upon an equally antique stallion, which was very lame but vicious if anyone came within range, dressed in a plain red coat and a moth-eaten, weather-beaten, full-length wig was clamped to his head by a narrow, cocked, white beaver hat. A yellow cravat was so askew that only the string was visible, his boots had a thousand wrinkles and, although it was a hot day, a huge fur muff hung round his neck. He was tipsy from brandy. Thus accoutred he approached Schomberg to pay him a compliment but, because his horse would not stand still, it was a very short compliment that received an equally abrupt reply. Afterwards, Schomberg commented that, 'Teague's horse was very mad, and himself very drunk.' The general then reviewed the two Irish battalions but the men just stared at him as though he was from another planet. On seeing the numerous women and children, Schomberg asked why they had been allowed to stay and consume so many provisions. The trite answer was because the Irish were very hospitable but the real reason was that they could not be made to remain in garrison unless accompanied by their families and mistresses. Before riding off to view Charlemont Fort, Schomberg remarked that love had no place in military affairs.[28]

Continuing with the policy of giving Wolseley free rein to divert the Irish from attempting to relieve Charlemont and keep open the option of taking the road to Dublin via Kells, Schomberg was pleased to hear of another limited offensive in the west. This time the target was the ruins of Bellanacargy Castle, once one of the strongest places in Ireland which the Irish reoccupied during the winter. Bellanacargy stood on a small, rocky island in the Annalee River, and attackers could only approach by wading up to their waists but, lying in drumlin country, it was dominated by higher ground. On Monday 12 May, Wolseley departed from his base at Belturbet with 1,200 men, reaching Bellanacargy early next day. Wolseley spent the morning and early afternoon raising blinds and earthworks to overlook the castle and set his men to making as many fascines as possible. All was ready by 16:00. Colonel John Foulkes led a detachment of infantry into the river and occupied an island near the castle walls on which Wolseley intended to raise some earthworks. Unfortunately, Foulkes lost control of his men who, instead of digging, chased the Irish through the water to their trenches under the castle walls and could not be recalled. Seizing the opportunity presented by Foulkes's disorganization, the Irish rallied and counter-attacked. So serious did the situation appear that Wolseley ordered a diversionary assault against the other side of the castle and this was prosecuted with such vigour that the defenders were expelled from a ravelin before the drawbridge.

As the pressure eased, Foulkes regained a hold over his men and secured the island depriving the Irish of all their outworks. Wolseley then ordered the cavalry and dragoons to bring fascines to the edge of the wet ditch and throw them in. During this action Wolseley was shot in the scrotum, but not seriously, and Foulkes assumed command. As they watched the ditch being filled and having fired a few volleys, the defenders hung out the white flag. Generous terms were promptly offered because, had serious resistance been offered, Bellanacargy's capture would have proved extremely costly and time-consuming. About 200 soldiers were allowed quarter but denied the honours of war and were conducted to the nearest Jacobite garrison. Foulkes initially manned Bellanacargy with 20 Enniskilleners, later increased to 200. The indiscipline amongst Foulkes's detachment made the engagement more expensive than Wolseley anticipated: Colonel Gustavus Hamilton's Enniskillen infantry battalion lost four killed and 16 wounded; the Funen battalion had one ensign killed and one captain and 17 other ranks wounded; and Foulkes's battalion lost the Dane, Captain Louis Gratien Du Bois, three gentleman volunteers and six other ranks killed, and ten men wounded. Following the loss of Bellanacargy, the Jacobites abandoned some other small garrisons in the area.[29]

Minor operations continued along the frontier but both armies were now gathering themselves for the principal campaign. Wolseley raided as far as Kells, 64 km from Dublin, capturing considerable quantities of livestock. However, on 25 May the grass was still not growing and another fortnight would pass before William arrived and there was any prospect of taking the field. The Duke of Württemberg was worried that the war might end quickly, thus terminating his employment: 'I hope they will have the spirit to let us have a bit of a fight, so that we can have some sport.'[30] Anticipating William's arrival, Schomberg moved his headquarters to Belfast on 6 June where he received news that the Jacobites had concentrated 12,000 troops at Kells and were ruining the forage in order to deny that route of advance towards Dublin and also to curb the raids of Wolseley and the Enniskilleners from Belturbet and Clones. In response to these strong suggestions that the Jacobite Army was already in the field, Schomberg issued orders for the partial mobilization of his own forces. The Danish Corps was instructed to leave winter quarters on 10 June to camp at Tandragee whence they would join the main army as it marched from Lisburn to Newry.

13

The Battle of the Boyne

William left Kensington Palace on 4 June, reaching Hoylake eight days later (12 June). He embarked immediately and sailed during the afternoon. Light and variable winds resulted in slow progress but next day the breeze picked up and he arrived off Carrickfergus around 16:00 on 14 June. Schomberg had prepared Sir William Franklin's house in Belfast to receive the royal personage. On receiving notice of William's disembarkation, Schomberg clattered out of Belfast in his coach and met William's party at the White Abbey, halfway to Carrickfergus. Transferring to Schomberg's carriage, William was greeted outside Belfast by a considerable yet silent crowd which simply gaped, never before having seen a king. After a while someone raised a cheer and the rest gradually joined in before following William's coach to the temporary palace. That evening, celebratory bonfires in Belfast and Carrickfergus were repeated across Ulster, in response to prearranged signal guns and beacons, spreading the news of William's arrival. It was advisable to join the merry-making. In Lisburn, George Gregson, a Quaker preacher, neglected to build a bonfire so a group of soldiers broke all his windows, pulled down the garden fence, took his wheelbarrows, shovels, pick-axes, tubs, pitch and tar barrels from his back yard, piled them up before the front door and lit them in a 'stately bonfire'. Had the Reverend Gregson's residence not also been the billet of Lieutenant General James Douglas, the soldiers would probably have pulled down the house as well.[1]

Although William initially observed the necessary courtesies and civilities towards a man of Schomberg's rank and seniority, in professional matters he virtually ignored him. During the Glorious Revolution and the previous year, Schomberg, an obvious Protestant symbol throughout Europe, had proved an immensely useful political tool. Unfortunately, the Dundalk campaign had led the king to form an unfavourable impression of his martial abilities, not that William – a soldier-ruler-politician whose approach to war was to achieve positive results as speedily as possible, even to the extent of rashness, carelessness and inattention to basic principles, the very antithesis of Schomberg's generalship – was a prime judge of such matters. William, an impatient and irascible man who cared little for personal feelings, did not even consult him about which route the army should follow on its march towards Dublin. Hurt and insulted, Schomberg complained to Dr George Clarke, secretary at war in Ireland, that he had spent the autumn and winter of 1689 studying the country and, at the very least, the king might have sought his counsel. Had he done so, Schomberg would have advocated the route through Armagh; he did not know that the Newry road had been chosen until informed by Clarke. Initially William had indeed intended to use the Armagh–Kells route, with Belturbet covering the western flank, but had changed his mind because of the difficulty of maintaining supplies so far from the coast.[2]

Tyrconnell was pessimistic about the forthcoming campaign. First, James could muster only 50 Irish and six French battalions of foot, seven regiments of dragoons, eight regiments of cavalry and two troops of Life Guards. Once infantry had been extracted to garrison the major seaports in Leinster, Munster and Connaught, as well as several inland towns, there remained about 26,000 men to form a field army supported by a train of artillery amounting to 18 cannon, 12 of which belonged to the French Brigade. The Williamites would be far stronger. Second, morale was damaged by watching Williamite supply convoys, with minimal escort, sail uninterrupted up the east coast of Ireland. Third, Tyrconnell appreciated that military events in Ireland could have little impact upon English politics. James could only unseat William if he landed in England with an Irish army, convoyed and then supplied across the Irish Sea by a French fleet.[3] Unless James was to state publicly that he was content to reconquer Ireland and serve solely as ruler of that kingdom, the war no longer appeared relevant to Irish political and religious ambitions. There would be no help for Irish Roman Catholics and no ultimate separation from England; Ireland had already become simply a resource to help James back into Edinburgh and Whitehall and even that remained fantasy in the absence of a major, sustained commitment from the French Navy. William, ultimately, would succeed through attrition. Most of James's followers were fighting, and would continue to fight, because they were rebels against the Williamite regime and had nothing to lose. Their strategy sought to prolong the contest for as long as possible in the hope that William might become more amenable to a moderate settlement through which the Catholic religion and lands might be partially preserved.

William had available 22,000 infantry in 46 battalions, around 14,000 mounted men in two troops of Life Guards, 23 cavalry regiments and five of dragoons, supported by a well-equipped train of artillery. It was a typical, polyglot seventeenth-century army, a mixture of Scots, English, Protestant Irish, French Huguenots, Dutch, Germans and Danes, reasonably trained, effectively armed, and irregularly paid. The senior commanders were similarly international. From Denmark came Prince George, the husband of Princess Anne; from Germany the Duke of Württemberg, the Prince of Hesse-Darmstadt, the Duke of Schomberg and his son Meinhard, Count Schomberg; from the United Provinces the Count of Nassau, Baron Ginkel, Count Solms, Major General Overkirk, Major General

Scravenmoer and the Earl of Portland; from Scotland Lieutenant General James Douglas; from Ireland the Duke of Ormonde; from England Percy Kirke, the Earl of Scarborough, the Earl of Manchester, Lord Sidney and the Earl of Oxford.[4]

A reconnaissance of the road between Newry and Dundalk revealed that all the bridges and causeways had been broken. Schomberg ordered the road from Lisburn to Newry and from Newry to Dundalk to be repaired and for a major forward magazine to be established at Armagh. During 15 and 16 June, William busied himself with administration and the tedious round of sermons and receptions. James had decided to concentrate at Ardee and ordered a camp to be marked out. On 16 June he left Dublin accompanied by the 5,000-strong French Brigade the Royal Regiment of Foot and four regular regiments. Dublin was garrisoned by 6,000 militia.[5] The Jacobite Army moved from Ardee to Dundalk on 18 and 19 June, occupying Schomberg's old camping grounds. Had James pushed half his army 6 km north to Four Mile House in the centre of the Moyry Pass, where Rosen's pair of 1689 redoubts covered the defile of the main road, the whole Williamite multitude might have been forced into a wide detour via Armagh and Castleblaney. James could then have taken advantage of interior lines to deploy his regulars and militia to impede and delay William in a desolate, devastated countryside where he would have found insufficient maintenance. To fantasize further, William might even have been forced to march west and come through Connaught or re-embark his army and land on the Leinster coast, either of which would have consumed the entire campaigning season. This would have placed William under enormous pressure within the Grand Alliance and the Dutch Republic as he would have been obliged to extract military assets from the Netherlands' theatre in order to commit increased resources into Ireland in 1691.[6] However, James remained at Dundalk nervous about advancing into a defile where he could have been trapped had William swung round through Armagh.

The Protestant population of Dublin represented a security risk. Effectively prisoners of war, the Protestants' main fear was that, in the event of James suffering a defeat, they would be plundered, their property burned and the city razed. Dublin, however, remained unfortified and so there was no question of a siege. The disarmed and constrained Protestants could do nothing except hope that William would win the coming battle and occupy Dublin before either the Jacobites or the French had the opportunity to inflict serious damage. Initially, the Dublin Protestants thought that the Irish would be dispirited by news of William's arrival but it appeared to have the opposite effect. Rather, they argued that William had placed his neck in a noose: the French fleet would cut him off from England where, behind his back, a Jacobite insurrection would break out. The Protestants, who were rounded up and imprisoned on 19 June, held a very jaundiced view of the capabilities of the Jacobite Army and attributed this seemingly unwarranted optimism to an unknown third factor, such as a plot to assassinate William.[7]

William travelled from Belfast to the headquarters at Lisburn on 19 June where he dined with Schomberg. That evening he continued to Hillsborough from where, on 20 June, he issued orders for the army to march into the field: units that had wintered in central and northern Ulster were to concentrate at Tandragee, under Lieutenant General James Douglas; the Danish Brigade was to gather at Armagh; those which had occupied the frontier garrisons towards Newry were to join on the march south; whilst the remainder were to concentrate at Loughbrickland, whence William proceeded on 22 June. During the previous few weeks, a series of patrols from Newry had kept the Moyry Pass under observation to check that it remained open and unoccupied. One such, ordered out by Major General Kirke, comprising some dragoons from Leveson's regiment under Captain-Lieutenant James Crow and infantry from Brigadier Stewart's battalion commanded by the captain of grenadiers, Captain Farlow, in all about 200 men, set out on 22 June to see whether Schomberg's instructions to repair the road and bridges had been carried out. The Irish in Dundalk were expecting a reconnaissance and received advance notice. A mixed party of 400 cavalry, dragoons and infantry, commanded by Colonel Sir John Fitzgerald and Lieutenant Colonel Lawrence Dempsey (Lord Galmoy's Horse), entered the Moyry Pass and set up an ambush at Four Mile House near Jonesborough, at the southern end of the causeway through the bog. They placed some infantry in one of Rosen's redoubts but held the remainder and the horsemen further back. The morning was foggy. Most of Farlow's infantry had cleared the causeway and Crow's dragoons were 200 m beyond when the Irish musketeers fired into their flank from the redoubt and, simultaneously, Dempsey's cavalry charged. Many of the dragoons were raw recruits and gave way, falling back behind the infantry, but most were rallied by their officers and subsequently led forward. Having also reorganized, Dempsey advanced in a caracole manoeuvre in which ranks of cavalrymen and dragoons trotted up to the Williamite infantry and discharged their pistols before wheeling away. Farlow's infantry responded with a volley, seriously wounding Dempsey and seven troopers and killing an equal number of horses. The disordered Jacobite cavalry retired and their place was taken by the infantry, having reloaded, which advanced very close to the Williamite foot, gave a volley and then charged home with swords, bayonets and clubbed muskets.

In this 'pretty sharp' action, the Williamites lost about 22 killed and Captains Farlow and Jones were captured. Crow assumed command and, unable to ascertain whether the Irish had hidden reserves, ordered a general retirement along the causeway to the northern edge of the bog where he deployed into line but he was not followed. Ten Jacobites lost their lives and Dempsey died three days later at Oldbridge on the Boyne. The death of this veteran professional who had served in the Portuguese and French armies 'was regretted because he had been a good horse officer'. Both sides, of course, claimed victory but, although the Williamites were clearly repulsed, the pass remained open and they also gained an unexpected and accidental advantage; when interviewed in Dublin Farlow declared that the Williamite Army was 50,000 strong confirming James's suspicion that he was massively outnumbered. Tyrconnell wrote to Queen Mary on 24 June that William would lead about 40,000 against only 25,000 Jacobites.[8]

In dry, windy weather William spent the day at Loughbrickland reviewing his regiments 'very critically', and his evident interest helped to raise morale. The Reverend Story was worried lest the dust triggered William's asthma but he remained in good health. Both William and Prince George of Denmark had their 'moving houses' set up in the camp and these remained their lodgings throughout the majority of the coming campaign. The great difference between the campaigns of William in 1690 and Schomberg in the previous year was speed: William was in a hurry to engage the main Jacobite Army, defeat it, occupy Dublin, and end the war before dashing to the Netherlands. Hearing of the misfortunes of Farlow and Crow, on the evening of 22 June William directed Major General Scravenmoer to take 500 cavalry, plus a strong detachment of infantry under Lieutenant Colonel Toby Caulfield, to scour the Moyry Pass and advance as close as possible to Dundalk. On reaching the outskirts of Dundalk, Scravenmoer sent a trooper to a hill beyond Bellew's Castle whence he could see a considerable distance south towards Knockbridge and had clear sight of Jacobite columns heading for Ardee. This was later confirmed by information from deserters who explained that the aggressive patrolling southwards from Newry had persuaded the Jacobites to retire. Scravenmoer returned on the evening of 23 June and reported to William, who had ridden forward during the day. Certain now that both the Moyry Pass and Dundalk were secure, William ordered the army to continue its march and instructed Douglas, commanding the troops at Tandragee, to join him at Dundalk.[9]

James's army arrived at Ardee from Dundalk on the evening of 23 June. It was obvious to Tyrconnell that William was trying to bring on a battle and equally obvious that the Jacobites should avoid one. It was not worth fighting for Dublin, said Tyrconnell, because he who controlled Ireland automatically controlled Dublin although apparently, the inverse did not apply. His next point made better sense: the Jacobite Army should adopt a delaying strategy to tie William down in Ireland whilst James, assisted by the French fleet, led an Irish army into England. Unfortunately, there were insufficient troops for both operations whilst their quality remained very uncertain – between 24 and 26 June much time was spent in camp at Ardee 'teaching the men to fire, which many of them had never been used to before' – whilst the essential co-operation of the French Navy was highly improbable. Had French warships been stationed in the Irish Sea since the beginning of May, William would have been unable to reinforce Ireland or, indeed, supply the troops already there confounding his entire strategy. As Tyrconnell observed, a French fleet in the English Channel was useless to the Irish. After victory over the Anglo-Dutch fleet off Beachy Head on 30 June, Tourville dominated the Channel for nearly two months but all he achieved was to land a few men at Brixham, which he deemed symbolically important, burn the strategically irrelevant village of Teignmouth and retire to Brest in August, his crews decimated by disease. Also, on 21 June Maréchal François-Henri de Montmorency, Duc de Luxembourg, utterly defeated the army of the Grand Alliance, commanded by Georg Friedrich, Graf von Waldeck, at Fleurus near Charleroi. There could have been no more persuasive argument for the Jacobites and French to adopt a delaying strategy in Ireland but news of Fleurus did not travel fast enough.[10]

The main army regrouped at Newry on 25 June crossing the Moyry Pass on the next day – the dead from the action on 22 June were lying, unburied, by the roadside – their march observed by several Irish skulking close to the road. Some of Lord Meath's men chased them off into the mountains, killing one and taking prisoner a Frenchman who had deserted from the Williamite Army at Hillsborough three weeks before. The camp that night was at Dundalk, 2 km to the south-east of the 1689 position, where the arrival of Douglas's corps completed the field army; in contrast to the previous year, the supply fleet promptly sailed into the harbour. During the afternoon of 27 June a detachment from Colonel Abraham Eppinger's Dutch regiment of dragoons sighted a party of Irish horse, which quickly withdrew towards the camp north of Ardee. This was regarded as unusual because, although the Jacobites always maintained cavalry contact, normally they employed horsemen who knew the country well enough to remain out of sight. When William weighed this minor observation with intelligence from other sources he formed a view that the Jacobites intended to embarrass his advance guard so decided to launch a pre-emptive attack against their mounted troops north of Ardee that night or early the following morning. During the evening of 27 June William took 1,500 horse and dragoons and reconnoitred as far as Ardee believing the Jacobites to be still in camp to the north of the town. Before departure, William ordered all the cavalry and dragoon horses to be saddled at the picket and their riders ready to mount at the sound of the trumpet; by 21:00, every man 'was booted and had his horse in his hand'. William's assessment proved inaccurate and his troopers only encountered a rearguard covering a Jacobite withdrawal to a new position 7 km south of Ardee. Whilst resting at Dundalk on 28 June some soldiers amusing themselves during the afternoon by lynching an Irishman and woman accused of endeavouring to poison the camp's water supply with 2 lb (907 g) of arsenic. The Jacobite Army retired 8 km on 28 June to within 5 km of Drogheda, 'along corn fields, gardens and meadows, a place very irregular for a camp, with the River Boyne on our backs'. Around midnight, there was a general alarm and the soldiers were drawn out into line of battle but calm had returned by dawn.[11]

Having stood to arms all night the Jacobite Army filed off in two columns at daybreak on 29 June, the infantry crossing the Boyne via the bridge in Drogheda and the cavalry through the ford at Oldbridge, to encamp along the south bank in two lines. The left lay towards Bridge of Slane and the right, dominated by the royal pavilion, within 5 km of Drogheda. Because the Jacobites thought themselves heavily outnumbered by higher-quality troops, they considered that they had insufficient strength to face the Williamites in open battle. The operational concept was thus to hold Drogheda and strengthen the exits from the fords at Oldbridge with field fortifications and cannon in order to equalize the odds. Many thought this feasible but James was less certain. Captain Farlow's report that William commanded 50,000 men had undermined his fragile confidence and he believed that the army should fall back on Dublin, although he failed to indicate how an open city might be defended. James ordered Sir Patrick Trant, first commissioner of the Irish revenue, to ride from Dublin to Waterford on Monday 30 June to 'prepare ships' in case James needed to leave Ireland in a hurry. In Dublin, desperate measures were taken. All Roman Catholics were ordered to appear on Oxmantown Green on 29 June, on pain of death, to be harangued and exhorted to take up arms. They were told that the Williamites had hanged everybody in Dundalk and they must expect no mercy should Dublin fall but few were persuaded to volunteer.[12]

William went forward to view the ground and at 02:00 on 29 June the army tramped to Ardee which had been thoroughly wrecked, nothing remaining but bare walls, and depopulated except for a few old, sick and bedridden. A Scottish soldier and a woman were hanged for murdering four of these unfortunates in cold blood. In four columns, the army departed for the north bank of the River Boyne very early on 30 June. Sir John Lanier commanded the advance guard and Jacobite pickets remained in contact falling back 'very regularly'. For much of the march the troops enjoyed the distant sight of their supply fleet sailing south. Within 3 km of Drogheda, William, who was riding with Lanier's men, rode to the summit of a hill whence he surveyed the Jacobite positions. An impromptu conference with Schomberg, the Duke of Ormonde, Count Solms, Scravenmoer, Sidney and other senior commanders determined the outline of preliminary operations. Scravenmoer thought the Jacobites 'une petite armée' as he could count only about 45 regiments but William suggested that more were probably sheltering within Drogheda as well as behind a hill to the south-west. Lanier's horsemen were now pushing hard towards the ford at Oldbridge and, from his vantage-point, William saw Jacobite troopers hurrying to bring in their grazing mounts and organize a cavalry screen.[13]

As they traversed the low hills to the north of the Boyne, 'some of the poor country people flying before them', the Williamites were silhouetted against the dawn sky. They pitched camp, their tents partially hidden amidst the folds of the hills making it difficult for the Jacobites to gauge their strength. About midday, William set out on a reconnaissance riding parallel to the river and, whilst inspecting some old houses, came under fire from a battery of six Irish field guns. He paused within musket-shot of the Oldbridge ford to observe the Jacobite dispositions. A small body of horse stood on the south bank and behind them, on rising ground, were several hedges and some cottages, one of which was built of stone and boasted a courtyard enclosed by a wall: this natural strongpoint was already garrisoned. Musketeers also lined the hedges. Some light breastworks had been thrown up to the west of the ford. Because Oldbridge blocked the direct route to Dublin, some time was spent in examining the lie of the land and determining the most advantageous locations for field guns. After a while, William rode another 200 m to a point almost opposite the western extremity of the Jacobite camp, before he sat down on a hillock and took refreshment. He remained for about one hour.

Captain Thomas Pownall of Leveson's Dragoons led a party of cavalry and dragoons to reconnoitre the route towards Bridge of Slane but, before departure, the troopers took their horses to drink from the river. The Irish brought up two long-range muskets to drive them off; fire was returned but no casualties were reported. A detachment of about 40 Irish cavalry then took station in a ploughed field across the river from William's picnic site where they remained, inactive, for about 30 minutes before turning and retiring. The purpose of this strange manoeuvre, which some took as an attempt to intimidate the king, was soon revealed. Two six-pounder field guns had been smuggled down amongst the horsemen and positioned behind a hedge bordering the field. They waited until William and his entourage had remounted and were riding slowly back to the east. The initial shot killed two horses and one man within 100 m of the king; the second ricocheted off the bank of the river, lifted and grazed William's right shoulder, tearing his coat, waistcoat and shirt and abrading the skin on the shoulder-blade drawing 'near half a spoonful of blood'. A third shot broke the butt of one of the Duke of Württemberg's pistols in his saddle holster and deprived his horse of its whiskers. Thomas Coningsby applied a handkerchief to the wound and William was quickly led away from the river. Despite his staff being 'in some disorder', William did his best to appear unconcerned. After allowing his shoulder to be roughly bandaged and changing his coat, he quietly rode back towards the camp. In fact, the incident had affected him considerably and when he returned to his tent at 16:00 to have the wound properly dressed, he was clearly exhausted by shock and had to be lifted down from his mount. Revived by some dinner and a change of clothes, he was soon back in the saddle supervising the march of the rear of his columns into camp around Tullyallen. William, whose general health was poor, had been almost continuously active since 01:00 on 30 June and physical fatigue plus the shock caused by his wound may well have affected his subsequent judgement.

During the late morning of 30 June William had ordered most of his English and Dutch cavalry, commanded by Lieutenant General James Douglas, to dismount and form a line close to the river bank before Oldbridge. Two Irish field guns at the cottages promptly engaged the passive cavalry and, together with another battery of six eight-pounders, subsequently fired over 200 rounds, killing at least 20 men and 40 horses. Around 15:00, Melonière's battalion escorted field guns into position opposite Oldbridge to support the cavalry with counter-battery fire: they dismounted one Irish eight-pounder and demolished some tents adjacent to those occupied by James and Lauzun. Having endured the cannon fire for four or five hours, at 17:00 William said, 'Now I see that my men will stand,' and ordered the horsemen to draw back and take cover in a fold in the ground. Possibly, this deliberate exposing of the Anglo-Dutch cavalry to sustained cannon fire was intended to test their loyalty, training, discipline and endurance but there were also sound tactical reasons: William was either covering the front of his campsite against interference while the infantry filed in or trying to induce the Jacobites to launch an attack. A great shout from the Irish camp followed the withdrawal of the Williamite cavalry and several squadrons of horse made a demonstration of aggression by deploying in the plain towards the river but at a point where the depth of the water and the height of the bank rendered them completely safe from harassment. After this show of bravado, they withdrew into their camp. The remainder of the afternoon and early evening was spent in a desultory cannonade. Deserters from both sides added to the fog of war by providing contradictory information concerning numbers and morale; one Protestant swam the Boyne and reported that the Jacobites numbered 25,000 and were determined to fight. 'The Boyne', observed Robert Southwell, 'is the walls of Dublin.'[14]

Between 20:00 and 21:00, William held a council of war. Schomberg and some English generals recommended attacking that night. A feint in the direction of Oldbridge would draw the Jacobites' attention, whilst the majority of the army marched upstream to cross the river and descend on their left flank and rear, trapping them in the bend of the Boyne. When this was rejected, they advocated pushing some regiments across the river that evening to test what degree of resistance might be offered. Again, William disagreed, perhaps because he had a superstition of never undertaking anything on a Monday, and announced his intention of crossing the following day. Count Solms, second in seniority behind Schomberg, favoured a mass frontal attack by the whole army across the Oldbridge fords. Seeking a compromise, Schomberg then suggested sending part of the army at midnight to cross the Boyne at or near Bridge of Slane, about 5 km to the west, to establish a block between the Boyne and the pass at Duleek, 6 km south of the Irish camp. In the dark, under officers who did not know the country and without reliable guides, such a manoeuvre would probably have ended in confusion but, retimed for daylight, Schomberg's concept offered possibilities. The problem of guides was partially solved when Colonel Lord George Hamilton, the future Earl of Orkney, who had taken over Thomas Lloyd's Enniskillen infantry battalion, produced four or five of his officers who were well acquainted with the Boyne and its fords enabling a modified version of Schomberg's plan to be adopted. A detachment under Count Meinhard Schomberg comprising 4,000 cavalry and dragoons and 3,000 infantry would leave the camp early in the morning and cross at Bridge of Slane before marching into the Irish left flank and rear. Meanwhile, when this attack had developed sufficiently for the Irish to react, the left wing of the cavalry would pass the river between Drogheda and the right of the Irish camp whilst the main body of the foot launched a frontal assault at Oldbridge ford.[15]

That evening, the Jacobites also conducted a council of war. Lieutenant General Richard Hamilton advised sending a detachment of dragoons to a ford below Drogheda, of which the Williamites were actually ignorant, whilst the rest of the mounted troops defended Bridge of Slane and the ford at Rosnaree. The infantry would cover the Oldbridge ford. James replied that he would send only 50 dragoons to the Drogheda ford but was resolved to defend all other negotiable crossings. In his 'memoirs' James claimed that he had firmly resolved to fight because another withdrawal could only have ended in Connaught where there were no magazines and insufficient provisions to support an army of 20,000 men for more than two months. Also the morale of his raw, inexperienced troops would have been undermined by another retreat.[16] In reality, his determination was less certain. James was muddled and confused, torn between Tyrconnell's and Lauzun's advocacy of delay and the heroic alternative of battle. This was the first land action in which James, who enjoyed a wholly unearned reputation as a warrior-monarch, acted as commander-in-chief; previously he had always been subordinate. Even during the campaign in England in November–December 1688, James had sheltered behind the Earl of Feversham's meagre abilities. James's nerves had been permanently shattered in 1688 and he really wanted to disengage from the Boyne and fall back on Dublin, not through a sudden conversion to Fabianism, but because he could not face the responsibility of directing a battle.[17] Tyrconnell, who provided most of James's missing vertebrae, was suffering from heart disease and had lost much of his former energy and drive whilst Lauzun was under orders not to commit the French Brigade to battle; several of his cannon were still in Cork. To the rear, the situation in Dublin was 'chaos equal to that in Genesis before the creation of the world'. Little had been done to create field fortifications at vital points along the Boyne nor was the probable course and conduct of the battle fully discussed. Clearly revealing his continuing preference for slipping away behind a rearguard, James ordered the baggage and most of the cannon to be drawn off during the night and sent back along the Dublin road but William had advanced to the Boyne much more rapidly than had been expected and complete withdrawal was now impossible. If he was not intending to fight on the Boyne then James should have decamped on the morning of 30 June, before William's army had arrived or, at the very latest, during the night of 30 June–1 July. Having viewed the ground and Jacobite dispositions, many of William's senior generals thought that this was precisely what James would do. In the great world of might-have-beens, had James made up his mind to fight then he should have fortified the exits from the fords forcing William into either a costly frontal assault or a wide out-flanking sweep through Navan. Commanding the smaller, handier army and possessing the advantage of interior lines, James might have responded to the latter by breaking down Navan Bridge, keeping his army in being thus drawing William further into Ireland and away from his seaborne communications. Such a strategy would also have given time for 15,000 militiamen from Counties Meath, Dublin and Kildare to have joined the Jacobite Army. James did not finally decide to retire from the Boyne until the evening of 30 June but the order could not be executed before 08:00 on 1 July. The army was instructed to march by the left, that is swinging up towards the Boyne before turning left and marching through Duleek to Dublin. To cover the open right flank of the marching columns the Earl of Antrim's and the Earl of Clanrickard's infantry battalions were to form a rearguard amidst the walled gardens of Oldbridge to prevent the Williamites from crossing to exploit this potential opportunity. The dragoon regiment of Sir Neill O'Neill was posted at the ford of Rosnaree, a little below Bridge of Slane. With their rear and flank guards in place, the Jacobite Army prepared to decamp.

Around midnight, a deserter reported that the Jacobites had struck their tents and sent off the baggage, clear evidence that they were retiring, leading William to expect to encounter only thin rearguards in the morning, greatly reducing the risks previously associated with the planned frontal assaults. To make certain, Count Schomberg's flanking manoeuvre via Bridge of Slane and Rosnaree would unhinge the weak Jacobite front at Oldbridge and, possibly, establish a blocking position around Duleek cutting off their retreat. The Jacobite tents were indeed thrown down very early in the morning and the baggage train started towards Duleek but, later in the night, fallacious information reached James that the Williamites had beaten off O'Neill's dragoons at Bridge of Slane, seized the crossing and were advancing their entire right wing that way. Realizing the débâcle that would ensue if his army was attacked as it wheeled and marched, at the last possible moment James countermanded the withdrawal orders and adjusted them to effect a partial redeployment to meet the developing threat. Accordingly, the Jacobite left continued to move along the bank of the river, its right flank under fire from Williamite cannon 'without intermission, yet to little effect', but its purpose was now to extend the Jacobite line to counter William's movement towards Bridge of Slane. This allowed the main body of infantry to come into position opposite Oldbridge. These last-minute adjustments and changes of orders meant that the Jacobite positions were unbalanced and approximate, a situation exacerbated by the absence of a clear plan.[18]

Late in the evening the cannon fire died away. In the Williamite Army orders were given for the soldiers to receive a good stock of ammunition and for everything to be ready by daybreak. All the baggage and greatcoats were left behind under the guard of a small detachment from each regiment and every man attached a green bough or sprig to his hat band as a distinguishing mark; the Jacobites were identified by pieces of white paper. The password was 'Westminster'. At midnight, William rode through the camp between Mellifont and Tullyallen by torchlight.[19] Having woken at 02:00 it was not until 05:00 on a clear, bright morning that Count Schomberg, assisted by Lord Portland and Hendrik van Overkirk as maréchaux de camp, set out towards Bridge of Slane with Brigadier Charles Trelawney's brigade of infantry, two cavalry brigades, three regiments of dragoons commanded by Colonel Eppinger, and five field guns. As soon as this movement was confirmed, the Jacobites continued to draw out their left wing towards Bridge of Slane and Rosnaree where O'Neill's regiment of dragoons was the sole covering force. Now that William had openly committed the martial sin of splitting his forces in the face of the enemy, the Jacobites could have advanced on Rosnaree and Oldbridge in two big wings but the army was not effectively arrayed for battle so the opportunity could not be seized. Had this proved possible, the benefit of interior lines might have allowed them to deny both crossings and defeat the Williamites in detail because Count Schomberg's corps quickly passed beyond supporting distance of William's centre and left. Less significantly, the Jacobite artillery enjoyed the advantage of firing from the lower, southerly shore of the Boyne whilst the Williamite cannon, located on the higher northern bank, were unable to depress their muzzles sufficiently to fire effectively. Instead, the majority of James's army stood around for most of the day watching a minority of their comrades fighting briefly at Oldbridge and Rosnaree, whilst a sizeable section of William's men spent their time marching to Rosnaree. Through bad planning, generalship and staff work, neither army brought to bear more than a minority of its available forces.

Despite orders to cross at Bridge of Slane, although the bridge had long since been demolished, the Enniskillen guides advised Count Schomberg to use two fords closer to the camp, no doubt seeking to save time – it had already taken three hours to march 6½ km – and abbreviate the dangerously long flank march.

At about 08:30,[20] Schomberg's 100-strong advance guard of cavalry and dragoons – the infantry and field guns were lagging behind – slithered down a steep bank towards the crossing at Rosnaree. O'Neill, who had taken one look at the broken Bridge of Slane and decided that the Williamites were much more likely to attempt to cross at Rosnaree, trotted down from heights above with 480 dragoons. They dismounted, lined the bank and opened fire delaying Schomberg for 60 minutes until his field guns came into action. Having suffered only five or six casualties and his mission accomplished, O'Neill fell back towards the French Brigade which was hurrying to his support under Lauzun. During disengagement, O'Neill's thigh was smashed by a cannon ball, a wound which proved mortal. Schomberg brought his men across the river and advanced cautiously to find Lauzun drawing up in two lines on the eastern slope of Roughgrange Ravine, about 2 km distant, his right resting on the Boyne and cavalry covering the left towards Gillinstown Bog. Sarsfield and Thomas Maxwell led in reinforcements during the late morning. When James joined around midday two-thirds of the Irish Army had been committed on the left. Count Schomberg was worried. According to his understanding of the situation, he had evidently arrived and crossed at Rosnaree before William had attacked at Oldbridge and thus drawn the main Jacobite force upon himself. His own foot was clearly outnumbered by the Jacobites, although he held an advantage in mounted troops, but faced with the prospect of a formal action rather than the expected brush with flank or rearguards he sent an express to William asking for immediate infantry support. In the meantime he adopted a defensive posture deploying in two lines on the western side of Roughgrange Ravine, separated from the Jacobites by a boggy stream flowing between two steep banks, a distance of 'half a cannon shot'.[21] Lord Portland advised him to mingle the mounted troops amongst the infantry – squadron next to battalion – an old Swedish deployment of the Thirty Years' War, also frequently adopted by Turenne to provide maximum mutual defensive support. James, who had observed Schomberg's march and could see reinforcements moving towards Rosnaree, assumed it to be William's main effort. Earlier, he and Tyrconnell had inspected the deployments around Oldbridge and thought them adequate to cover the withdrawal of the baggage train along the Dublin road. When the baggage train had progressed far enough to be safe from attack, James expected the troops at Oldbridge to reinforce the left at Roughgrange. He probably reasoned that there might also be a holding attack at Oldbridge but this could be contained by light forces: the main danger was developing to his left. The lie of the ground on the north bank of the Boyne opposite Oldbridge encouraged James's delusion because the low hills partially screened Williamite movements and he was unable to appreciate that, although half of William's army had indeed been deployed towards Rosnaree, the remainder was about to descend on the Oldbridge fords. Fortuitously, William had achieved numerical superiority at the decisive point, one-half of his army facing one-third of the Jacobite. William, who had observed the lion's share of the Jacobite Army march towards their left, grew concerned and, before the arrival of Schomberg's express, had already ordered Lieutenant General James Douglas to take 12,000 reinforcements.[22] Douglas reached Schomberg around mid-morning enabling him to assume a more conventional deployment comprising the cavalry on the right and the foot on the left. The adjustments took a considerable time and were still incomplete when news arrived that William had launched the main attack at Oldbridge. Now that the right of his line overlapped the Jacobite left, Schomberg began to edge cautiously around the Gillinstown Bog.

The cavalry of the Irish right wing and some seven or eight battalions of infantry moved downhill from Donore, close to the Oldbridge ford. Their mission was to cover and delay any Williamite attacks, which were expected to be light, in order to gain time for the artillery and baggage trains to make good progress down the Dublin road. An advance guard of musketeers lined the cottages, walled gardens and hedges in and around Oldbridge and seven battalions stood in the rear of a long ridge running 150 m behind the village. The Jacobites would have been better advised to place their best infantry, the French Brigade, at Oldbridge but the Irish Guards refused to yield precedence. Supporting the infantry were two troops of Life Guards, four troops from Tyrconnell's Horse, some of Sutherland's regiment and four of Parker's troops. William had no knowledge of the obstacles facing Schomberg and Douglas and launched his frontal attack when he estimated that they had crossed the river and were moving on the Jacobite rear. Three infantry crossings were made: Sir John Hanmer's brigade to the left; the Huguenots in the centre; and the three battalions of the Dutch Blue Guards, commanded by Count Solms, leading the assault on the right. Between 08:00 and 09:00, the field guns opened fire on two houses 'with yards walled about' on either side of the road that led from Oldbridge ford. Having assembled beyond Jacobite observation in King William's Glen and approached the river via a sunken road, at about 10:00 the Dutch Blue Guards stepped out in column of companies, eight to ten files wide, their drummers beating a march until the front ranks entered the Boyne around 10:15. In mid-stream the water rose to their waists – clearly the attack was delivered well after ebb tide when the Boyne was only calf-deep – the passage of so many men creating a human dam that noticeably increased the downstream depth. When the Dutch were halfway over, the Jacobite advance musketeers opened fire from behind their walls and hedges: one Dutchman fell and another staggered. Leading the column was a lieutenant of the Dutch grenadiers who, on reaching the far bank, deployed two files of musketeers and ordered them to fire over his head into the first hedge, which was only 14 m distant. The Irish musketeers abandoned the hedge and scattered into the next field giving the Blue Guards enough time to clear the water and form in line of battle within a small bridgehead. At the optimum moment, before the third battalion of the Dutch Guards had cleared the river, five supporting Jacobite battalions advanced from behind the shelter of the low banks: 'one would have thought that men and horses had risen out of the earth'.

The Dutch Guards slowly pushed up the road through Oldbridge but both their flanks were unsupported. From the north bank William could see a squadron of Tyrconnell's Horse preparing to charge. Those close by heard him mutter softly, 'My poor guards, my poor guards, my poor guards', but the charge, delivered at the trot, was beaten off by disciplined, flexible musketry. On the first advance, only the front rank fired before lying flat on the ground to reload. At the second charge, the three rear ranks gave a volley. The third charge was met by a second volley from the reloaded front rank, which had got to its feet, reinforced by those in the second rank who had reloaded. Covered by enfilading fire from the third and fourth ranks which had formed two platoons, one to the right and the other to the left, the first and second ranks then fixed their plug bayonets and drove off the horsemen. William was heard to 'breathe out, as people use to do after holding their breath upon a fright or suspense'. Major General Kirke commented that the thoroughly up-to-date Dutch Guards, equipped throughout with the flintlock musket and plug bayonet, would have benefited from a few pikemen.

At much the same time Colonel Thomas St John's Derry infantry battalion and two Huguenot battalions also reached the south bank, the former 100 m east of the Dutch. After the Dutch Guards had repulsed the first cavalry charge, St John's battalion moved closer to protect their open flank whilst the Dutchmen reloaded and reorganized. Two hundred metres further to the east, Major General Kirke led over Sir John Hanmer's battalion, and Count Nassau's and Zachariah Tiffin's Enniskilleners. There were, thus, wide gaps in the Williamite front which Lieutenant General Richard Hamilton, who commanded at Oldbridge, hastened to exploit ordering the Earl of Antrim's battalion to advance and attack the exposed flank of Hanmer's and Nassau's battalions but the men refused to obey orders. His dignity and authority compromised, Hamilton had to watch as the Williamite infantry was allowed time to deploy and gradually extend their lines to form a continuous front.

Jacobite hopes now rested on the cavalry. A squadron of Jacobite horse charged the Huguenot battalions, which also lacked pikes, and about 40 troopers broke through Caillemotte's ranks, badly wounding the colonel, but as they wheeled left to regain their own lines suffered heavy casualties from Dutch and Enniskillen flanking fire and only seven or eight survived. Sensing that affairs had reached a critical point and realizing that the Huguenot Brigade now had no commander, the Duke of Schomberg crossed the river to rally the wavering Frenchmen riding into a mêlée of slashing swords and indiscriminate firing; Major General Kirke was fairly certain that the carbine shot in the neck that killed the old man came from his own men. Another account says that Schomberg was shot by the pistols of Trooper Brian O'Toole of the Irish Horse Guards, who fell in the act. He was certainly shot in the neck and suffered three sword cuts over the head and one in the face. He fell without speaking and Captain Henry Foubert was shot in the arm as he helped to recover the body. Dr George Walker, some said going to Schomberg's assistance, had just reached the south bank when he was shot dead. As the Irish cavalry threatened the left and right flanks of the small Williamite bridgehead, the Dutch Blue Guards at the apex of the salient advanced driving the Irish musketeers from the second hedgerow to a third, where they rallied. Another body of Irish horse descended upon the Dutch. Instead of forming behind an adjacent hedge they met the horsemen in the open, taking such close order that it proved impossible to break them, their platoon fire driving off the assault. Some of the Huguenots and Enniskilleners had now reached the ploughed field whence the two Irish six-pounders had wounded William the day before. From here, their musketry halted the advance of another Irish cavalry squadron. Berwick's troop of Life Guards charged Hanmer's battalion almost as soon as it had emerged from the river but was beaten off. Despite its courage and offensive spirit, the Irish cavalry was uncoordinated attacking in small parties rather than combining into a series of powerful and potentially overwhelming charges. At 11:00 the Irish drew back to some rising ground to reorganize.

A squadron of Danish cavalry had crossed with the initial infantry assault but advanced too far too quickly and was driven back over the river by a charge of 60 Irish horsemen. The absence of cavalry was a serious impediment and the infantry could not make significant progress away from the river because close formation had to be retained to counter the constant threat from mounted troops. The attack appeared in danger of stalling. Although the view from the north bank was obscured by smoke and dust, it was assumed that the infantry had established a bridgehead of sufficient depth to allow the cavalry to cross. On the Williamite left wing, the Danish, Dutch and Huguenot cavalry, Wolseley's Enniskillen Horse and some dragoons passed the Boyne at a very difficult ford. The Danish infantry and Colonel John Cutts's battalion crossed a little above them where the water was deeper, coming up to the soldiers' armpits and chins. After landing, they had to climb a steep slope. Colonel Lord Henry Sidney and Major General Kirke appear to have acted as roving senior officers, moving from place to place as attacks unfurled. William led the left wing of cavalry through the water although his horse became mired on the south bank and he had to alight until a gentleman helped to release his mount. Once free, he drew his sword, despite pain and stiffness in his injured shoulder, placed himself at the head of the cavalry and advanced towards the Jacobites who, following their withdrawal and reorganization, were showing signs of renewing their attack on the Williamite infantry around Oldbridge which, outnumbered by two to one, urgently required assistance. When the approaching Irish horsemen were within musket-shot of the infantry at Oldbridge, William's cavalry was observed moving towards their right flank. They halted, faced about, and withdrew up a hill to a little church called Donore, nearly a kilometre above Oldbridge. William followed steadily until the Irish turned and charged. Even though the king was leading them the left wing squadrons gave ground so he rode over to Wolseley's Enniskillen Horse and asked whether they could help him. After an officer had identified the short gentleman and explained the honour that was being paid them, William placed himself at the head of the Enniskillen Horse and received a Jacobite volley before he wheeled left to leave the horsemen a clear field for a return of fire. Unfortunately, the troopers failed to appreciate what he was doing and followed him thereby falling back 100 m until, realizing the mistake, they rallied and came forward once more by which time William had lost patience and transferred to some Dutch horse. On the left of William's cavalry grouping, Lieutenant General Ginkel charged along a lane with a small detachment of horse but was heavily outnumbered and forced back in some disorder. Noticing Ginkel's distress, a party from Sir Albert Conyngham's regiment of dragoons, commanded by Lieutenant Colonel Robert Echlin, and another from Leveson's Dragoons, under Captain Brewerton, ordered their men to dismount, line a hedge and occupy an old house flanking the lane whence their fire sufficiently impeded the Irish cavalry to allow Ginkel to disengage. These actions against the Irish cavalry lasted for about 30 minutes at the end of which Tyrconnell decided that the battle was lost and ordered the forces at Oldbridge to make their way back through Duleek towards Dublin. Lieutenant General Hamilton was ordered to delay William's advance with the remains of the cavalry, a task which he performed until wounded in the head and captured.

Count Schomberg and Douglas's infantry had initially tried to march straight through the Gillinstown Bog before extricating itself to follow the cavalry and dragoons around the southern edge towards the open Jacobite left flank. Around 14:00 James and Lauzun heard of the collapse before Oldbridge. The king's initial reaction was to order an immediate offensive against Schomberg and Douglas. Brigadier Hocquincourt placed himself at the head of the French Brigade, dragoons moved into the intervals between the infantry battalions and Lauzun prepared to lead the attack. Sarsfield and Brigadier Thomas Maxwell went forward to reconnoitre the ground but returned with the depressing news that 'two double ditches, with high banks, and a little brook betwixt them, that run along the small valley that divided the two armies' made it impossible for the cavalry to operate. They advised strongly against making an attack. At this point, the broken remains of Tyrconnell's cavalry from Oldbridge ran across the rear of the troops waiting to attack. It was initially assumed that they were

Williamite cavalry which had broken through at Oldbridge; indeed so much damage did they inflict that their allegiance mattered little. Eleven or twelve infantry battalions were, at best, disorganized and, at worst, shattered by their own horsemen. In addition, Lieutenant John Stevens says that many of the Irish soldiers were drunk on brandy – he claims to have seen over 1,000 lying about the Roughgrange position in alcohol-induced stupors – which James had issued to encourage his troops. James's temporary and uncharacteristic bravado thus dispelled and with Schomberg's dragoons beginning to edge around his left flank threatening to sever the route back to the defile at Duleek, James started to retire. The ground was awkward – cornfields surrounded by deep ditches – which made it difficult for the Williamites, who had to advance in line of battle because of the propinquity of the enemy, to maintain their dressings and alignment. They were further slowed by the deep course and wet surroundings of the Nanny Water. The cavalry rode through without too much inconvenience but the foot was seriously incommoded, losing formation and falling well behind the horsemen. As the partially disorganized Williamite infantry emerged from the quagmire, an alert general might have been ready to launch a counter-attack but the Jacobite *mentalité* was entirely defensive so Lauzun continued towards Duleek. Colonel Richard Leveson led some of his dragoons around a flank to interpose themselves between the Irish and Duleek and caused some casualties but the dragoons were isolated and the attack could not be developed. James and Lauzun's troops were the first to reach the Duleek defile, where Tyrconnell commanded, and had mostly passed through before the infantry and cavalry from Oldbridge arrived. The entire Jacobite Army had to cross the Nanny Water via Duleek's single stone bridge, wide enough for only six men to march abreast. On several occasions the sheer press of troops nearly caused the situation to collapse – weapons and equipment were strewn across the countryside – especially when Williamite infantry approached from the south, but the French Brigade formed a rearguard supported by its six field guns. Fortunately the wet, marshy ground to the north of the Nanny Water kept the Williamite infantry at a distance and they were forced to use light cannon to attempt to disrupt the Jacobite retirement. Lords Oxford and Portland advocated sending 3,000 horsemen, each with a musketeer mounted behind him, to fall upon the Irish as they withdrew beyond Duleek but more cautious counsels prevailed. By the time that an adequate body of cavalry had been assembled and moved through Duleek the Irish main body was well along the Dublin road, their foot in the van 'marching with great haste and confusion', whilst the cavalry, French infantry and artillery formed a steady rearguard under the direction of Lord Galmoy. Count Schomberg and Douglas followed for 5 km but were unable to launch an effective attack amidst the difficult and close terrain. William and the foot spent the night at Duleek whilst the majority of the cavalry and dragoons remained under arms, resting where they had abandoned the pursuit. Tyrconnell was deputed to conduct the withdrawal whilst James departed immediately for Dublin escorted by about 200 troopers from Sarsfield's Horse and Maxwell's Dragoons. He reached Dublin about 22:00 to be met at the gate of the castle by Lady Frances Tyrconnell, sister of Sarah Churchill, who asked what he would like for supper. He replied that, after the breakfast he had enjoyed, he had no stomach for supper.

Gilbert described the decisive phase at Oldbridge as an elongated skirmish between nine Jacobite regiments and half William's army, lasting no more than 60 minutes. Following the action on the river bank and the Irish withdrawal on Duleek, the second stage involved a few regiments of Jacobite horse and the French infantry brigade, against the entire opposition. It was a tribute to the motivation and cohesion of the Jacobite Army that the retreat to Duleek was conducted successfully across open ground in the face of a hugely superior enemy. However, once beyond Duleek order amongst the infantry naturally weakened as the men streamed back towards Dublin.[23] According to other Jacobite sources, defeat at the Boyne was simply a function of numbers: James had about 20,000 Irish troops 'newly raised, half-disciplined and half-armed', and 5,000 Frenchmen supported by 12 field guns, six of which were on the road back to Dublin when the battle began. Opposed to them were 45,000 Williamites with over 50 cannon. Charles O'Kelly was scathing in his assessment of James; so rapid was his flight that he was the first man to bring news of his own defeat to France where, instead of seeking immediate help, he explained to Louis, who since the recall of D'Avaux had no reliable source of intelligence in Ireland, that the Irish cause was irrevocably lost. This self-serving version of events persuaded Louis that the Irish had let down James rather than *vice versa* so he ordered Lauzun's troops to be withdrawn and offered refuge to those of the Irish Army wishing to escape servitude. Williamite sources, in contrast, were surprised by the political and strategic magnitude of the victory which was out of all proportion to the scale of the action. Those who toured the battlefield could count no more than 1,600 dead from both sides, 'which is a wonderful thing that so small a loss should disperse the whole Irish Army who seemed to be blown away only by a wind from God'.[24]

The victor, however, was not beyond reproach. In the first place, the Irish Army had not been shattered but remained in being, its numerical strength scarcely dented. William had failed to bring his full resources to bear: Douglas spent a good deal of the day marching whilst the whole of Count Schomberg's flanking corps underperformed in terms of the numbers and effort committed. On the other hand, the terrain over which Schomberg operated had not been reconnoitred and he was delayed by streams, bogs, hedges and ditches, even though he had only a short distance to travel to Duleek once across the Boyne. The Irish retired before him in good order, always threatening to counter-attack if his men faltered in their formation and lost cohesion. The timing of Schomberg's flanking attack was not properly synchronized with the main assault at Oldbridge but these things nearly always fail to go according to plan and, by any standards, the flank attack at the Boyne was reasonably successful. William offended against the military Ten Commandments by splitting his forces in the face of the enemy but he thought that he would only encounter the rearguards of a retiring army. Of the three fords around Oldbridge, two were only passable at low tide.[25] Accordingly, William's infantry crossed at the ebb but the water level steadily rose behind them; even William would not have cut off his own infantry if he had thought that the Jacobites were going to offer substantial opposition. In all these assumptions he was correct but was thwarted by the incompetence rather than the genius of James. Having finally decided that he did not wish to stand on the Boyne James left it too late to escape and enough of his army was still on hand on the morning of 1 July to offer serious resistance to both William's frontal attacks at Oldbridge and Schomberg's flanking manoeuvre via Rosnaree. Neither monarch was fully in command of his army. Opposite Roughgrange Ravine, James had neither knowledge nor influence over the fighting around Oldbridge. William, after biting his nails over the fate of his beloved Blue Guards, forfeited all control when he charged into the mêlée at the head of his cavalry like Alexander the Great. He could have been shot or hacked down by any common trooper and it was inappropriate behaviour for the Stadtholder of the United Provinces, King of England, leader of the Grand Alliance and commander-in-chief in Ireland. *In extremis*, such personal valour had its place but the situation at Oldbridge was in hand although slower to develop than William's impatience might have wished. On the day before, however, his performance in front of both the enemy and his own troops following the wound to the shoulder had been vital in maintaining morale and cohesion. Schomberg was equally foolhardy and lost his life in consequence. So was the Reverend Dr George Walker, but he was a silly, vain man of very questionable judgement.

William also failed fully to exploit his victory. He might have sent 10,000 men towards Athlone, nearly as close to the Boyne as Dublin, Limerick and Galway which would almost certainly have fallen because they were inadequately garrisoned. Without Limerick, Galway and Athlone the Jacobites would have possessed no refuge and been obliged to fight for Dublin; a second defeat would have ended the war. Such a strategy, however, was unrealistic. The French fleet was hovering off the Channel coast so William could neither divide his army in Ireland nor move it far from the Irish Sea ports in case he needed to hurry into England to counter an invasion, a development that would also repair Jacobite morale: intelligence indicated that the Irish believed that Schomberg and William were dead and the Dauphin had actually landed in England at the head of a French army. Already this encouragement has caused the Irish to begin to improve the fortifications of some of their strategic towns and cities. William did not know whether the Irish would rally and offer battle north of Dublin – Swords was the anticipated location – so he required his army complete and undivided. However, he realized the crucial importance of Athlone as a major Shannon crossing and portal into central and northern Connaught: Lieutenant General James Douglas was dispatched on 9 July with a strong detachment to seize Athlone. Once it was clear that the Jacobites would not stand again before Dublin, William followed them to Limerick as fast as he could, bearing in mind the need to pacify and occupy the largely hostile countryside of Munster and Leinster as he advanced.[26]

14

From Dublin to Limerick

Dublin's Protestants were awakened by an alarm early on the morning of 1 July announcing that there was to be a great battle. They found the entrances to the city closely guarded and so, in considerable apprehension, most returned home and stayed out of sight. The firing could clearly be heard and rumours circulated throughout the day: the French fleet was in the bay; the Isle of Wight had been invaded; Dover was under attack; the English right wing had been routed; and the Prince of Orange was a prisoner. Around 17:00 some troopers on tired horses arrived and reported that the Jacobites had been 'much worsted': by 18:00 this had become 'total defeat'. During the evening and into the early hours of 2 July, dusty, exhausted soldiers stumbled into the city accompanied by carriages loaded with wounded officers. James's arrival around 22:00 led the Protestants to conclude that he had been annihilated and the Williamites must be close behind. They were thus much surprised and deflated to witness the well-ordered main body of Jacobite cavalry ride in around midnight to the music of kettledrums, trumpets and oboes, followed, very early on 2 July, by a sizeable infantry detachment and the French Brigade: the scale of defeat was diminishing with every passing hour. Having rested, most of the infantry trudged through the city to the south. At 05:00 on 2 July, James summoned the Lord Mayor of Dublin and the principal citizens to attend him in the castle. A short speech loaded with self-pity and blame for everyone but himself announced his immediate departure for France, his third flight in less than two years. As far as the Protestant citizens of Dublin were concerned, James's speech salved their most immediate fears: Dublin was to be surrendered rather than defended and it was not to be burned by the French. James's route, already prepared by Sir Dominic Trant, lay first to Bray whence pre-positioned horses and coaches conveyed him via Arklow to Duncannon on Waterford harbour. There he took ship for Kinsale where he found a squadron of French frigates, which had recently arrived with orders to scour St George's Channel and the Irish Sea to interdict William's communications with England. James commandeered the entire squadron to convey him to France, thus undermining one prop of a French naval strategy designed to render the Jacobites some effective assistance. The war was to be decided without further reference to James. The sole service that he provided for Ireland was his refusal to listen to French entreaties to burn Dublin: not all of Dublin's inhabitants were rebels, he had replied.[1]

At some point during the evening of 1 July, Tyrconnell ordered the army to reassemble at Limerick. That night most of the soldiers crossed the Liffey at Leixlip, Chapelizod or in Dublin itself, and made for Rathcoole on 2 July. Via Naas, Carlow and Kilkenny, the leading elements trudged across country reaching Limerick about a fortnight later, the soldiers mingling with a host of civilians: gentlemen without military positions, displaced Roman Catholic clergy, farmers and tradesmen, ladies, wives, women, children, criminals, ruffians and camp followers. This throng grew as the troops meandered westwards, many of the inhabitants of Counties Kildare and Westmeath and the King's County having no wish to be governed by heretics: their empty houses were plundered by the Protestants and several murders committed. There was no alternative to this radical retreat. The wasted winter of 1689–90 meant that potential points of intermediate resistance – Wexford, Duncannon, Waterford, Kilkenny and Clonmel – were unsupplied, weakly garrisoned and their fortifications unrepaired. Consequently, defeat in a skirmish on the Boyne resulted in the abandonment of Leinster and eastern Munster forcing a still-adequate army to withdraw behind the line of the Shannon there to rely upon the slender resources of mountainous Connaught and western Munster.

Temporarily, the army was leaderless. Mountcashel, Rosen and James had all left in quick succession whilst replacements, principally Patrick Sarsfield and Berwick, had yet to fill the vacuum. Initially, Tyrconnell, as the Lord Deputy and James's viceroy, gradually assumed control but his authority was neither total nor unquestioned whilst his health was poor and he had been obliged to alter his strategy. James's departure meant that the Old English interest would now best be served by reaching a settlement with William so Tyrconnell began to discourage the Irish from offering further resistance. His first step was to send his wife to France with his and James's disposable assets. After landing at Brest, she spread the story that all Ireland was lost, except for Limerick and Galway. Lauzun, anxious to escape back to civilization, was party to this canard. Tyrconnell, in turn, told the Irish in Limerick that it was foolish to expect further relief from France and the only practical course was to agree a treaty with William. However, this was all in vain because the native Irish did not trust the English and had no wish to enter into a treaty. At a Grand Council in Limerick it was decided to send a pair of envoys to give Louis XIV and his ministers an accurate assessment of the situation and announce a determination to defend their own country. When the true picture was presented, rather than the James–Tyrconnell–Lauzun gloss, Louis would realize that it still served French interests to detain William in Ireland. To counter-balance Tyrconnell, the council decided to appoint Patrick Sarsfield, the 'darling of the army', as second-in-command. Tyrconnell, who did not attend the council, claimed that its decisions were *ultra vires* and regarded Sarsfield's elevation as a personal insult.[2]

By offering terms sufficiently generous to induce individual Jacobites to surrender William sought to exploit these internal divisions but, overestimating the decisiveness of the Boyne, they were too severe to attract the Roman Catholic landowners. Pursuant of the theory of detaching followers from leaders, instead of the other way round, common labourers, soldiers, farmers, ploughmen, cottiers, citizens, tradesmen, townsmen and artificers who surrendered and returned home by 1 August would receive a full pardon and be allowed to live in liberty and enjoy their property whereas 'the desperate leaders of the present rebellion' did not qualify. Had the targets been reversed then the Declaration, published in the army camp at Finglas on 7 July 1690, might have achieved its purpose but William was advised by Irish Protestants and Englishmen whose agenda was the eviction of rebellious Roman Catholic landowners and the reassignment of their estates amongst themselves. So meagre was the fruit that the Declaration was reissued on 1 August, from the camp at Chapelizod, extending the deadline to 25 August and including foreign soldiers.[3]

On the night of 1–2 July, William's army lay in the open around Duleek, its tents and baggage still at Tullyallen. In the morning, Brigadier Melonière was sent with 1,000 cavalry and dragoons, 300 infantry and eight cannon to capture Drogheda. The governor, Lord Iveagh, received the first summons 'very indifferently' but was informed that if the cannon were obliged to open fire then no quarter would be given. Believing that the Irish Army had been totally routed on the previous day, Iveagh allowed himself second thoughts and surrendered on condition that the garrison of 1,300 men was allowed to march to Athlone with full honours of war. The brigadier replied that he had orders only to allow them to leave without arms and the governor must decide quickly whether to accept these terms. To hasten his decision, Melonière began to build two batteries, which would be ready by dawn on 3 July. Iveagh's immediate response was to gather all the Protestants in the town and drive them under the section of wall earmarked for bombardment but, following a hurried consultation, the garrison officers prevailed upon the governor to capitulate and a gate was handed over. The garrison marched out towards Athlone between 13:00 and 14:00 on 2 July, the officers having been graciously permitted to retain their swords. The terms stipulated that the sick and wounded Irish troops in Drogheda would be cared for by the Williamites and, when recovered, returned to the Jacobite lines, equipped with the requisite passports. Instead they were neglected and starved and the survivors retained as prisoners. Whilst Melonière attended to Drogheda, William pitched camp 2 km south of Duleek. During the afternoon, five Jacobite troops of horse and three infantry battalions came within sight to the west, *en route* from Munster to join the main army. Two scouts were sent to ascertain the character of the encamped army, who were seized and hanged, but the detachment was allowed to march away without interference. Riding out the Reverend Davies found a little corn to feed his horse but, otherwise, the countryside had been stripped bare. In the evening, William Sanders came to Duleek from Dublin with the welcome news that the Jacobite Army had departed towards Munster and released all its prisoners. He found William's army in arrogant, confident mood, the Danes regarding the war as virtually concluded.[4]

Throughout 2 July officers and leading Roman Catholic citizens and officials left Dublin in their carriages heading south and west followed by dust-stained, weary stragglers from the direction of the Boyne. The entrances and the castle were still guarded by the Catholic militia which threatened to burn the city before they left. At about 16:00 the Jacobite cavalry re-entered followed by the French Brigade and the infantry rekindling fears that Dublin was to be destroyed but they marched through the streets to the south side where they were reviewed by Tyrconnell before trudging off. Governor Simon Luttrell made some bellicose noises about taking several hundred Protestant hostages to Limerick but he slipped away, alone, when rumours began to spread that an English detachment had landed in the harbour and was approaching the outskirts. Protestants peeped around their doors and, seeing the city virtually deserted, began to venture forth. A group entered the castle and found it deserted apart from Captain John Farlow, who had been a prisoner since his capture in the Moyry Pass, and a few other detainees. Early on the morning of 3 July the Protestants began to act more confidently, a rabble touring the streets to disarm dispirited Roman Catholics; most handed over their weapons without argument. At 06:00, those with sufficient *noblesse* to *oblige* began to assume responsibility. Dr William King, Dean of St Patrick's cathedral, the Bishop of Meath and other leading Protestants formed a committee to administer the city until William arrived. As well as publishing proclamations ordering the citizens to maintain order, they decided to establish a Protestant militia. They also sent a message that Dublin was clear of the enemy: this found William as the army was marching south from Duleek in two lines towards a camp site at Balbriggan, expecting to encounter the Jacobite Army at Swords. At 20:00 William sent an officer escorted by a troop of dragoons to take charge of any stores in Dublin city.

> It was impossible, the King himself coming after this, could be welcomed with equal joy to this one troop. The Protestants hung about the horses and were ready to pull the men off them as they marched up to the castle.

William then dispatched Overkirk and the Duke of Ormonde with 1,000 cavalry to secure Dublin and they arrived during the morning of 4 July and reported to Captain Farlow, the acting governor. Two battalions of the Dutch Blue Guards marched in around midday.[5]

William remained at Balbriggan on 4 July, marching forward to camp at Finglas on the next day. *En route* news was received that the Protestant citizens had seized the port of Wexford and declared for William. When Colonel Walter Butler, the lord lieutenant of County Wexford, heard that James was heading for Duncannon, he ordered the governor of Wexford, Captain Kelly, first to fire Wexford Castle and then march his single infantry company to a rendezvous at Duncannon. Through the intervention of one Mr Chaplin, only the first part of the Butler's order reached Kelly. When he had left, the Wexford Protestants rose, disarmed James's supporters and seized the castle. Two messengers were sent to William asking for some troops – one cavalry regiment would be enough – to secure the town, which was protected only by an undirected wall. William acted promptly dispatching Brigadier Eppinger, assisted by Lieutenant Colonel Henry Boyle (Lord Cavendish's Horse) and Captain Sir Purey Cust, with 1,000 cavalry and dragoons and an infantry battalion on 10 July to take formal possession. Eppinger marched that night to Castleknock, west of Dublin, before proceeding south via Bray. On 6 July, William rode into Dublin and attended divine service in St Patrick's cathedral where Dean King preached on the text, 'of which, that which seemeth to us greatest upon earth, mighty armies was a faint shadow', in other words, 'on the power and wisdom of the providence of God in protecting his people and defeating his enemies', returning to camp for dinner. No soldiers were allowed to enter Dublin, except for essential guards and sentries. At Finglas, William heard reliable information that a squadron of French frigates had sailed into Cork and Kinsale charged with challenging the Royal Navy in the Irish Sea. William was extremely concerned for the safety of his provision ships from England, most of which were sailing from Chester, Hoylake, Liverpool and Whitehaven, making landfalls off Belfast and Carlingford Loughs before coasting down to Dublin. George Clarke and some general officers were sent from Finglas to Dublin to investigate how the provision ships sheltering in Dublin harbour could be better protected. They recommended sinking gabbards in the harbour entrance but this was never carried out.[6]

Williamite morale was further raised by rumours that the Jacobite Army was disintegrating on its long retreat to Limerick. The whole army was apparently 'in great disorder' especially the French regiment of Zurlauben, the Duke of Württemberg reporting that 500 of its men had deserted and returned to Dublin, where 100 had been recruited into the Danish Brigade. William reviewed and inspected his army on 7 and 8 July. On the latter day, the hyperactive William was in the saddle for 14 hours, dismounting only for 15 minutes to snatch something to eat and drink. Satisfied that his army was in reasonable condition, on 9 July William ordered a march from Finglas, round Dublin, to Kilmainham, west of the city. When in camp, news reached William that the Anglo-Dutch fleet under Admiral Lord Torrington had been defeated off Beachy Head by Tourville. Should Tourville exploit his victory to enter the Irish Sea, the presence of the French frigates in Cork appeared an even greater menace, although, unknown to

William, they had been commandeered to escort James back to France.[7]

Before leaving the camp at Finglas on the morning of 9 July, William divided his army. He was to take the main body towards Limerick, via Kilkenny; a small detachment was already marching to Wexford; and a corps commanded by Lieutenant General Hon. James Douglas was to capture Athlone, 125 km to the west. Given William's decided preference for Dutchmen, Germans, Huguenots and Danes, the choice of a Scotsman might have seemed slightly surprising but Douglas was one of the godly who had served with the Anglo-Dutch Brigade in the army of the Dutch Republic and was personally known to the king. The second son of James Douglas, Second Earl of Queensberry, he was originally intended for a career in the law but entered the English Army in 1672 as a captain in Sir William Lockhart's infantry battalion. He served in France with this regiment between 1673 and 1674, before transferring to the Anglo-Dutch Brigade in which he achieved the rank of colonel in 1680. He recrossed the North Sea in 1684 to take up the appointment of Colonel of the Scottish Foot Guards in the rank of brigadier and, in 1688, rose to become commander-in-chief of the Scottish Army. At the Glorious Revolution, Douglas smoothly transferred his allegiance to William of Orange. In 1691, he was switched from Ireland to the Flanders theatre where he died of fever at Namur later that year. He had a reputation as a martinet and Schomberg found him prickly, ultra-sensitive about his dignity, always finding fault, never content and difficult to please. Conversely, a Jacobite source thought him 'an excellent officer'. William must have held a high opinion of his abilities to appoint him to the first major independent command in Ireland during the 1690 campaign.[8] Douglas commanded the cavalry regiments of Thomas Langston, Theodore Russell and William Wolseley; the dragoon regiments of Sir Albert Conyngham and James Wynne; and his own infantry battalion in addition to those of Sir Henry Bellasise, Sir John Hanmer, Philip Babington, Thomas St John, Lord George Hamilton, John Michelburne, Zachariah Tiffin, the Earl of Drogheda and Gustavus Hamilton. It was a potentially effective force, ideally suited to operations in central Ireland: Wolseley's, Cunningham's, Wynne's, Lord George Hamilton's, Tiffin's and Gustavus Hamilton's were all Enniskillen regiments, whilst those of St John and Michelburne were from Derry. On the other hand, these regiments were still poorly disciplined, indeed often lawless and out of control, and always on the lookout for an opportunity to plunder and harass the Irish. A further weakness was the train of artillery – two 12-pounders, ten field guns and two small mortars – too light and too little to attack a fortified town.

Douglas's corps left Finglas on Wednesday 9 July and camped that night at Chapelizod, continuing to Maynooth on 10 July. A journey of 10 km took the corps to Cloncurry on 11 July by which time, despite orders to the contrary from the supposedly fearsome Douglas, serious plundering had started. The troops marched a short distance on Saturday 12 July to Clonard Bridge where they rested on Sunday 13 July allowing Douglas to conduct a thorough inspection and muster to ascertain the exact ration-strength. Openly disobedient, many soldiers strayed from camp to rob the local Irish who, believing the promises made in William's Finglas Declaration, had mostly remained in their homes instead of flying to the hills and bogs as was customary on the approach of a Protestant army. Douglas received numerous complaints but the depredations continued and he seemed either unable or unwilling to discipline his Irish soldiers 'who are very dextrous at that sport'. On the morning of 13 July, Captain John Auchmouty (Wolseley's Horse) took a party of cavalry towards County Longford to reconnoitre and gather provisions returning to rejoin the corps at Mullingar on 14 July. Auchmouty brought in a considerable prey of cattle as well as two Irish messengers, taken whilst carrying letters from Athlone. One instructed a soldier named Tute to protect a number of horses and valuable stores on an island near Mullingar; the other, from an officer in Athlone to his father, stated that the Irish Army would reassemble at Limerick within two to three days. It also presented the latest news: the Dauphin had landed in England; the French had beaten the English and Dutch fleets; Schomberg and William were dead; and James had gone to France, although this was of no consequence because the Irish were better off without him. The writer then advised his father against accepting a protection from the Williamites because the Irish viewed such people as traitors and enemies. After sealing the letter, the writer had added on the outside, 'Just now we have an account by a gentleman that's come to us from Dublin, that Orange is certainly dead, so that all will be well again.' This jumble of fact, fiction and wishful thinking illustrates the sort of information on which Jacobites in Athlone probably based their decisions. The lack of affection for James was later amplified by Sarsfield who said that if he could change kings, he would re-fight the Boyne and win.

Douglas remained at Mullingar on Tuesday 15 July, the inmates of a local friary hurrying for the safety of Connaught. About 500 creaghts arrived from County Longford accompanied by their wives, children, cattle and possessions seeking general protections. These were granted but did them no good because most were plundered shortly after setting off for home. A patrol from Colonel Russell's cavalry regiment pushed on to within 5 km of Athlone during the evening but encountered nothing of interest. On the following day (16 July) Douglas advanced to Ballymore, a long thin settlement stretched along the Dublin–Athlone road comprising about 100 cottages and cabins, three public houses, some almshouses, an old castle and a little church to the north on some rising ground. Probably demoralized, the Athlone garrison had refused several opportunities to delay Douglas's progress at numerous defiles. As he drew closer, the garrison burned English Town on the east bank of the Shannon, because it was difficult to defend being dominated by higher ground, broke down an arch in the stone bridge, and withdrew into Irish Town. Athlone was strategically important because of its central location and permanent crossing of the Shannon. Standing on a narrow neck of land between two bogs, the stone bridge, built by Sir Henry Sydney and repaired in 1663, could only be approached via the town and the river could not be crossed for 15 km to the north and south. It was protected by an earthwork enceinte to which several outworks had been added during the effective reign of James II. On the Connaught, or Irish, side was a thirteenth-century castle which had been partially modernized in the time of Charles II and contained artillery emplacements. Some redoubts housing four cannon covered the exit from the bridge and breastworks had been hurriedly thrown up 200 m north of Irish Town and along the west bank of the river.[9]

Douglas marched from Ballymore on 17 July and camped 400 m from English Town. A drummer sent to summon Athlone to surrender was greeted by a pistol shot from the governor, Colonel Richard Grace, a veteran of the Confederate Wars and the French and Spanish service who had commanded at Athlone since 1687. Grace added that when provisions had been consumed he was prepared to eat his own boots. The three infantry regiments, nine troops of dragoons and two of cavalry, about 2,000 men, supported by additional horse stationed close by, was numerically sufficient to defend the river front of Irish Town. Douglas spent the next day (18 July) constructing batteries close to the river bank and communication trenches running back into the burned-out buildings. Two field guns were in position by evening and engaged the garrison cannon, doing some damage. A battery of six guns, positioned near the end of the bridge, was ready on 20 July and its fire made a small breach just beneath the castle roof. Lieutenant Colonel William Berry (Wolseley's Horse) with a detachment comprising mounted grenadiers commanded by Major John Margetson (Earl of Kingston's Foot) and some infantry led by Captain James Carlisle (Richard Brewer's Foot), reconnoitred towards the Lanesborough Pass at the northern extremity of Lough Ree. They found the bridge guarded by a well-manned fort, supported by four companies of infantry in Lanesborough itself.

Douglas's feeble artillery could achieve nothing against the castle's thick, stone walls especially after Isaac Nelson, the fire-master and most capable gunner in the train, was killed by musket fire on 22 July. It was rumoured that at Finglas Douglas had been given a free hand to select what men, equipment and artillery he thought he would need: if so, then he seriously miscalculated. On the following day, 23 July, it was rumoured that Sarsfield was leading 15,000 men from Limerick to relieve Athlone causing Douglas to send all his sick and wounded back to Mullingar. Further credence was given to this story on the following morning when the garrison hung out a 'bloody flag' from the castle, the signal of defiance and intent to continue resistance. Sarsfield was indeed on his way but not with 15,000 men. He had departed from Limerick on 23 July with five weak battalions of infantry, four field guns and some supporting cavalry. In pouring rain, through unpopulated, desolate, wild country, without tents or many provisions, the infantry struggled through Killaloe, along the shores of Lough Derg, over the Aughty Mountains to Duniry. Meanwhile, Sarsfield led the horse on an easier route via Gort to Loughrea. Here, on 26 July, they heard that Douglas had lifted the siege so returned through Gort and Sixmilebridge, arriving back in Limerick on 31 July.[10]

In the evening, Douglas summoned the regimental colonels to a council of war where he voiced his concern that Sarsfield might interdict communications with Dublin. Some contrary voices suggested crossing the Shannon at a little ford just above the bridge, thus flanking the garrison's earthworks along the river bank. However, Douglas argued that the river was deep and dangerous and the Irish breastworks and redoubts strong and well manned. Even if they did ford the Shannon successfully, a major siege would be needed to reduce the castle and, all the time, Sarsfield was drawing closer. Should both Irish Town and the castle fall, Sarsfield would still be free to manoeuvre against Douglas's communications with Dublin; bread was already scarce. More to the point, the behaviour of the soldiers on the march to Athlone had aroused the local people creating over 100 km of hostile country. Many who had accepted Douglas's worthless protections were in a hopeless position, continuing to be plundered by the Williamite soldiers whilst regarded as traitors and turncoats by the local Irish who had remained loyal to the Jacobite cause. With Douglas about to withdraw even his modicum of theoretical protection, these unfortunates saw no alternative but to trail east in Douglas's wake abandoning their homes, harvest and possessions. As if this was not enough, they continued to be 'hardly used' by Douglas's Ulstermen. Orders were given for the baggage to depart at midnight and the troops at dawn on 25 July; they withdrew in silence, undisturbed by even a single shot. During the day Douglas received orders from William to rejoin the main army on its journey to Limerick and news that James had landed in England at the head of a French army to exploit a conspiracy against Queen Mary. That night, the corps camped at Ballymore where it remained for four days in wet, thundery weather.

On 30 July, Babington's battalion marched towards Dublin whilst the remainder turned south to Stoney Cross. The march was no longer on roads radiating from Dublin and the supply of bread suffered accordingly: there was none for four days and only short rations thereafter. On 31 July, Douglas marched to Ballyboy. Despite ordering that no one should stray from the ranks on pain of death, Douglas spotted five men from his own battalion leaving the column to maraud. They were seized and obliged to dice for their lives, the loser being shot by the roadside. At Ballyboy Douglas received intelligence that a substantial Jacobite force at Banagher Bridge intended to interfere with his progress although, in fact, Sarsfield's detachment had already returned to Limerick leaving only small patrols hanging on Douglas's flank. However, Douglas did not know this so, instead of proceeding as planned to Birr along a route through numerous woods, defiles and narrow passes, ideal for ambushes, he moved to Roscrea on 1 August where the corps rested on the following day. Twelve troopers arrived at Roscrea on 3 August from William's main army, encamped at Golden Bridge, bringing instructions for Douglas – who had not distinguished himself by the speed and length of his daily marches – to hurry because William suspected that he would be short of troops when facing the defences around Limerick. Douglas camped in the lee of Devilsbit Mountain on 3 August, where numerous raparees gathered on the heights but took no action because the Williamites were accompanied by so many refugees, cattle, sheep and horses that it proved impossible to gauge their exact numerical strength.

Resting on 4 August, Douglas was now within reach of William's army and able to dispense with Colonel Wolseley's three regiments. Accordingly, the Enniskillen Horse, and the battalions of Tiffin and St John returned, via another route, to Mullingar where Wolseley established his headquarters with orders to patrol and secure the Midlands between Dublin and the Shannon, in particular interdicting movements from Connaught via the mid-Shannon crossings that might endanger William's communications between Limerick and Dublin. On 5 August, Douglas moved to Holycross Abbey, south-west of Thurles, where he allowed his men to plunder because bread was in such short supply. He marched from Holycross Abbey to Dundrum, north-west of Cashel, on 6 August; to Cullen, north-west of Tipperary, on 7 August; and into William's camp at Caherconlish, within 6 km of Limerick, on 8 July. No more than 30 men were lost in action before Athlone but during the approach and withdrawal, sickness, hard marching, and raparees killed between 300 and 400.[11]

William was in considerable operational difficulty. News from England following the Battle of Beachy Head was so alarming that he had to keep the army within reach of the eastern and southern ports to enable swift embarkation should a discouraging situation deteriorate. On the other hand, he needed to reach Limerick as quickly as possible to prevent the Jacobites regrouping and reorganizing. His compromise secured Wexford whilst taking the main body south to capture Waterford. The army shifted from Kilmainham to Johnstown, north-east of Naas on 10 July. Ten days were scheduled for the march to Waterford, indicating William's reluctance to stray too far from the coast too quickly, but some urgency was injected by pushing the cavalry and the dragoons ahead of the infantry. From Johnstown the mounted troops marched to Timolin on 11 July, 21 km ahead of the infantry encampment at Kilcullen Bridge.[12] The rich and cultivated landscape, although 'interspersed here and there with hills and marshes', was largely empty, most of the local population having joined the exodus towards Limerick and Connaught or taken to the bogs and mountains until the heretics had passed. William was anxious to prevent plundering so the soldiers were forbidden to stray beyond the camp upon pain of death. However, during the march to Kilcullen, as William was passing Naas he flew into a rage and beat with his cane a soldier he caught robbing an old woman. He announced that several others who had been arrested whilst plundering, including two Enniskillen dragoons, would be executed on the following Monday. This may have brought some temporary improvement in the conduct of the infantry, which was under William's personal command, but had no effect on the cavalry and dragoons. On 12 and 13 July the soldiers rested at Kilcullen and Timolin.

After the Boyne the Irish adopted a Fabian strategy, seeking to wear down the invaders through the adverse effects of inclement weather, disease, desertion and hunger reinforced by the judicious application of military pressure. By thus prolonging the war, the Irish increased the human and financial costs to the English whilst maximizing the effectiveness of their own forces, particularly the raparees and irregulars. In the background lay the hope that the English would suffer major defeats in other theatres of the Nine Years' War – the reverse at Fleurus in 1690 offered encouragement – abandon their plans of reconquest and reach a reasonable peace settlement. Such an approach, however, seriously underestimated their opponents' persistence, determination and economic endurance. The English were indeed obliged to maintain large forces in Ireland, although local Protestant recruits and militias were used as far as possible, but, in the absence of French naval activity, their supply line from England through Dublin was reasonably secure. William could therefore destroy Irish agriculture, on which the Jacobites were almost entirely dependent, through depredation and occupation. Ulster was wrecked in 1689, principally by the Jacobites themselves, and the occupation of Leinster and Munster in the weeks following the Boyne pushed the Irish Army and refugee population into the less productive and under-populated mountains, lakes and bogs of County Clare, the south-west peninsula and Connaught. This physical concentration caused crises in both the provision of both manpower and foodstuffs rendering the Jacobites increasingly reliant upon direct supply from France.[13]

During the night of 13–14 July a cavalry patrol under Lieutenant Morton brought in 120 black cattle and 1,500 sheep. Refreshed, the mounted troops rode south from Timolin on 14 July in very orderly fashion without the pillaging that had disfigured the previous day, camping just to the south of Carlow. Mostly from local Protestants who came daily to the camp to express their gratitude and support, William received numerous reports of the chaotic state of the Jacobite Army as well as the welcome information that the garrison of Kilkenny intended to evacuate rather than defend the town. The Jacobite Army was indeed in an ill condition. Having taken a week to straggle across Ireland from Dublin, the Lord

Grand Prior's regiment of infantry gradually reassembled at Limerick. It had been reduced from 800 men to 300, only half of whom had effective weaponry. This, noted Lieutenant John Stevens, had been achieved without really having seen the enemy or received a shot in anger. The officers' baggage had been plundered twice, first by those appointed to guard it at the Boyne and then by dragoons, and the majority of the tents and field equipment had been lost. All units, noted Lieutenant John Stevens, were in a similar condition and a series of regimental amalgamations were carried out to group these skeletal battalions into more effective, tactical formations.[14]

The Williamite infantry marched to Castledermot on 14 July, the columns covered by flanking parties to clear raparees from the adjacent woods and hills, whilst the cavalry moved to Gowran, east-south-east of Kilkenny. Intelligence came in that the Jacobites had abandoned the fort at Duncannon and were concentrating to defend Waterford. William's infantry moved forward 12 km to Carlow on 15 July. There was a rest day on 16 July but welcome news arrived that Brigadier Eppinger had secured Wexford and put in a garrison. The Danish Brigade, which was leading William's infantry columns, reported undiminished pillaging and the execution of 15 guilty English soldiers. They also noted a good deal of sickness, especially dysentery. William's infantry advanced to Kelly's Bridge on 17 July whilst the cavalry moved from Gowran to Kells on the King's River. Deserter interrogations suggested a garrison of about 1,600 men in Waterford and that the troops in Clonmel were preparing to withstand a siege. The army rested again on 18 July; William was now proceeding extremely slowly because of the increasingly gloomy news from England. From the cavalry camp at Kells, a party of one lieutenant, one cornet, two quartermasters, one corporal and 21 troopers raided south-west beyond Callan to within 13 km of Clonmel where they seized a considerable prey of cattle. Without bothering to set sentries or videttes, they settled down for two hours' rest. When they came to, thinking themselves safe, some herded the cattle whilst others 'scampered abroad to get what they could'. The sudden appearance of 120 Jacobite cavalry took them entirely by surprise and the Williamite party was routed, losing the corporal and 11 troopers.

Whilst the infantry moved forward to Bennetsbridge on 19 July, William took the opportunity to dine with the Duke of Ormonde in his home at Kilkenny Castle, which Lauzun had spared from destruction during the retreat from the Boyne although the contents of the wine cellar had been much reduced. William received erroneous information that, on the previous day, Sarsfield at the head of 5,000 men had abandoned the crossing of the River Suir at Clonmel and fallen back to Limerick. On 20 July Count Schomberg took all the cavalry and dragoons, plus four field guns, on a long, fatiguing march from Kells to Clonmel, the baggage not catching up until nightfall. As the horsemen passed under the Slievenamon above Kilcash, they could see groups of Jacobite soldiers and raparees hovering in the mountains waiting for the opportunity to pick off stragglers but Schomberg maintained good route discipline and adequate flank guards. He discovered that the Jacobites had intended to hold Clonmel, whose capture had cost Cromwell 2,000 men, having levelled hedges and razed some of the suburbs but, having extorted £300 from the inhabitants by threatening to burn the town, they had departed.

The infantry reached Carrick-on-Suir, which surrendered on the same terms as Drogheda, its garrison being allowed to march to Mallow. On 21 July a trumpet was sent to Waterford demanding immediate surrender. The governor, Colonel Burke, proposed capitulating with the full honours of war otherwise he would defend the city to the last man. William took exception to such arrogance and was only prepared to offer the same terms that had been granted to Drogheda: the garrison could leave with arms and baggage only and, if the cannon should be forced to open fire, no quarter would be given. Again Burke demurred, returning further 'scruples' on 22 July, whereupon Major General Kirke was detached on 23 July with four battalions – his own, Viscount Lisburn's, Richard Brewer's and François de Cambon's – plus 14 cannon. They found the approaches to Waterford denuded of cover, the suburbs having been razed, the hedges broken, the ditches filled and the gardens levelled, but the garrison's confidence evaporated on the appearance of Kirke's artillery and Burke sent three commissioners to negotiate with William who appointed Colonel Cambon to treat on his behalf. A treaty was signed on the afternoon of 23 July and, on the next day, 'three scurvy regiments' comprising 1,400 men marched out in silence, without beat of drum, carrying their weapons and furled colours – 'sorry, wretched fellows', according to the English; in good spirits but lamentably clothed and equipped, said the Danes – and were escorted as far as Mallow from where they made their own way to Limerick. Kirke took formal possession on 25 July. William's relatively generous terms were partially explained by his 'compassion' for Waterford's 300 Protestant families. The port, however, could not be opened until the reduction of Duncannon Fort, a coastal battery protected by a weak blockhouse on the east shore of Waterford harbour, its 50 cannon in a linear emplacement facing the water: against attack from the landward side it was virtually defenceless. On 25 July the same terms that had been extended to Drogheda and Waterford were offered to governor Colonel Michael 'Brute' Burke who replied that he needed six days' grace to consult his superiors in Limerick. When permission was refused, Burke let it be known that he still intended to take this time, whereupon William ordered up troops and guns. During the evening of 26 July Sir Cloudisley Shovell sailed into Waterford harbour with 16 frigates and assumed station ready to bombard Duncannon; Burke promptly accepted the original terms. Some of these vessels were actually victuallers, escorted by Shovell, but the garrison thought they were all warships and reached for the white flag.[15]

A Williamite reconnaissance patrol of 24 cavalrymen marched almost as far as Golden Bridge on the night of 21 July when, less than a carbine-shot distant, it suddenly came across three squadrons of Jacobite horse supported by infantry and dragoons. They turned and fled but, fearing a trap, the Jacobites did not pursue and the troopers returned safely to the cavalry camp at Carrick-on-Suir on the morning of 22 July. Letters from England described a critical situation in which there was an hourly expectation of a French landing on the Channel coast, so a council of war on 25 July agreed that William should return to Whitehall. He was to be accompanied by 1,200 cavalry and dragoons and five battalions of infantry leaving his cousin, Lieutenant General Solms, to command the army in Ireland. William departed on 27 July reaching Carlow that evening. Here he received letters that presented a more optimistic outlook and his presence in England no longer appeared so pressing. Nevertheless, he continued to Chapelizod where he spent three days hearing petitions, mostly about the outrages and violations of protections committed by Douglas's expedition to Athlone. There were also several complaints about the behaviour of Brigadier Charles Trelawney's battalion garrisoning Dublin, a problem solved by adding the unit to Schomberg's Horse, Matthews's Dragoons, and Hastings's battalion already earmarked to reinforce the army in England. On 27 July, Solms conducted the infantry from its camp at Carrick to join the cavalry at Clonmel.[16]

Between 28 and 31 July, the main army marched from Clonmel to Golden Bridge, 37 km from Limerick, the cavalry again in the van. Bored because his regiment had returned to Dublin, Chaplain Rowland Davies asked Lieutenant General Ginkel if he might form a small party 'to scour' County Limerick. Ginkel agreed so Davies and his friend, Frank Burton, accompanied a party of 30 horse and ten dragoons, under Captain Saunder (sic), 'a Dutchman that spoke Latin but very little English', north to secure Thurles but lost their way in the dark and halted beyond Cashel to await daylight. When they arrived on 30 July Thurles offered no resistance and the soldiers found some wheat, salt and bread, which they sent south to the army, before disarming the Roman Catholics. On 1 August, a party of Danish and Enniskillen cavalry reconnoitred from Golden Bridge to within sight of Limerick. Information arrived on 31 July that Youghal had surrendered. Captain Thomas Pownall, leading 50 of Leveson's Dragoons, was escorting the garrison of Waterford to Mallow, via Dungarvan. On approaching Youghal, Pownall contacted the governor, Colonel Macarthy More, an acquaintance, suggesting that it might be preferable to surrender his small garrison rather than face certain destruction. More asked for time to consider, promising a decision by 22:00. At the appointed hour, three companies of foot marched out and Pownall entered the town. The dragoons found 14 mounted and two unmounted cannon, as well as some provisions, but, significantly, no ammunition. Receiving intelligence on 5 August that the Irish had assembled a mixed body of regulars and raparees to recapture Youghal, William reinforced Pownall with infantry and 600 cavalry.[17]

William's army approached Limerick slowly on account of the poor roads, continuing uncertainty about the situation in England and the notion that, given sufficient time, the Jacobites might defeat themselves. In the latter assumption, there was reason for cautious optimism. Lauzun and Tyrconnell tried to persuade the Irish that resistance was pointless and it would be best to reach an accommodation. On 1 August, Lauzun inspected all Limerick's outworks and fortifications, which were unfinished, and stated publicly that the city was untenable. On the following day, 2 August, he despaired of Limerick and marched his French Brigade, now about 3,500 strong with eight field guns, to Galway, camping under the walls of the town until securing passage to France. Some senior officers were beginning to be swayed by the arguments when Sarsfield returned from leading the expedition to relieve Athlone. Already the darling of the rank and file, whose morale was high because many of the new levies had yet to fight the Williamites – following amalgamation and recruitment, the Lord Grand Prior's regiment now numbered 543 – he was surprised to hear what had occurred during his absence. With Sarsfield in Limerick, the general officers suddenly grew reluctant, if not downright frightened, of acting contrary to the wishes of the common soldiers. Reluctantly, Tyrconnell temporarily supported the war party. Equipped with a renewed resolve, the infantry stood to the defence of the walls whilst the cavalry and dragoons camped close by on the Connaught side of the Shannon.[18]

The Williamite Army waited for a week at Golden Bridge, creating some difficulties with the supply of rations and money, until Lieutenant General Douglas had arrived within supporting distance, Major General Kirke had rejoined with the Waterford and Duncannon detachments (4 August), and William had returned from Chapelizod. Early on 5 August, a Jacobite reconnaissance patrol appeared within sight of the Golden Bridge camp but was driven off by 300 cavalry under the Dane, Major General Hartwig Ahne Schack. Later in the day, a strong scouting patrol comprising 300 horse and 100 dragoons under another Danish officer, Colonel Jens Sehested, rode towards Limerick. William finally left Golden Bridge on 6 August, the infantry marching via Oola and cavalry through Cullen. Around noon on the following day the columns recombined and closed up to Caherconlish, about 11 km from Limerick, where Douglas's corps was expected on 8 August. As they approached, the Irish burned and levelled Limerick's suburbs and many houses, buildings and potential strongpoints in the hinterland stretching to Caherconlish. As the Reverend Davies searched for an intact house in which to lodge, all he could see for miles around was smoke rising from blazing buildings. During the afternoon, several reconnaissance patrols pushed towards Limerick but were unable to penetrate the Jacobite cavalry screen. Frustrated, William himself rode forward but was equally unsuccessful in the dark and rain and came uncomfortably close to a Jacobite outpost. A council of war was summoned in the evening at which it was decided that, on the following morning, Portland and Scravenmoer would take forward 1,000 cavalry and 300 musketeers to locate a suitable campsite from which the army could threaten and, if necessary, besiege Limerick.[19]

Within 8 km of Limerick a defensive landscape had been prepared: the approaches to defiles had been ploughed up to make the ground more difficult for advancing troops; several small earthwork forts and redoubts had been constructed; numerous trenches dug; musketeers positioned behind garden walls and hedges; and felled trees thrown across roads and tracks. At 01:00 on 8 August, Portland, Scravenmoer and Brigadier William Stewart tried to move forward but there was a thick mist and the cavalry did not dare to advance, knowing, from the shouted insults, that the hedgerows were lined with Jacobite musketeers. At 10:00 they were back in Caherconlish with nothing to report. Without awaiting the return of Scravenmoer and Portland, William set off on a personal reconnaissance in company with Prince George of Denmark, General Hendrik van Overkirk, and General Ginkel, escorted by 200 'select' cavalry. The mist having partially lifted, they were fairly close to Limerick when a party of Irish horse advanced upon them. Captain Rowland Selby (Royal Horse Guards), commanding the advance guard, rode forward with a view to charging but the Irish drew back towards Limerick taking cover under the cannon on the walls. Later that day a Protestant clergyman came from Limerick and reported that the French Brigade had sold all its provisions to the Irish and withdrawn to Galway preparatory to evacuation. Because the whole country had come into Limerick, the Irish Army numbered 45,000 but only 25,000 were disciplined, armed regulars, the rest peasants equipped with pitch forks and scythes. He also drew attention to some fords above the city.[20]

Limerick, the third largest city in Ireland after Dublin and Waterford with a population of around 5,000, was the principal port on the west coast and warships of the third and fourth rate and large merchantmen could navigate the 96 km of the Shannon estuary without obstacle or difficulty there being 'not any foul places, rocks, or sands'. The city comprised two separate entities – English Town on the King's Island and Irish Town on the Munster mainland – linked by Baal's Bridge across the Abbey River. English Town was larger, containing King John's Castle and St Mary's Cathedral. Three gates led into Irish Town from County Limerick whilst Thomond Bridge over the main channel of the Shannon linked Irish Town to County Clare. Although the houses were generally solidly constructed in stone, Limerick enjoyed no great military strength, particularly Irish Town which was overlooked by higher ground to the south and south-west. However, any siege was likely to be a two-stage affair because English Town could not be taken until Irish Town had been captured. Engineer Thomas Phillips noted in 1685 that Limerick enjoyed a reputation as the strongest fortress in Ireland to which, in his opinion, it was not entitled. The walls were decayed, largely through the neglect of the city corporation, and the draining of some bogs had made the approaches easier for attackers to negotiate. Phillips recommended constructing a new citadel to command both towns but the cost at £78,310 was prohibitive. He also suggested building defences on Scattery Island, in the Shannon estuary south of Kilrush. De la Vigne, the senior French engineer at Limerick in 1690, contradicted Phillips: the existing wall was well built, being between 8 and 10 m high and 1½ m thick, with a one metre walkway around the top. On 18 July de la Vigne set 1,200 labourers to improving the fortifications of Irish Town. First, to create a field of fire, the suburbs were razed. These were considerable, particularly to the south and at the head of Thomond Bridge, housing more people than the whole of walled Limerick, and so, for the second time in 40 years, the majority of the population was made homeless. Besides excavating a ditch outside the stone wall and employing the spoil to build a counterscarp, covered way, and glacis, two bastions appeared on the east wall, and two demilunes thrown up, one at St John's Gate and the other outside Mungret Street Gate, which was later reinforced by a larger outwork, inaccurately referred to as a hornwork. The counterscarp was palisaded using timber floated down the river from O'Briensbridge in County Clare. Some detached redoubts were constructed on the higher ground to the south and south-west to cover the avenues along which the Williamite horde would advance. De la Vigne demolished the antique citadel within St John's Gate replacing it with an earthwork large enough to mount six heavy cannon. There was also a battery of three cannon by St John's Gate. Even after these hurried improvements, Limerick's defences lacked depth and were puny in comparison with the fortifications found in contemporary Europe. There were hardly any outworks, the palisade was 'a toy' and the rampart too narrow to serve as a gun platform.[21]

Topography rendered Limerick extremely difficult and dangerous to besiege. It could only be surrounded and blockaded if an attacker was prepared to split his army, provided that he had sufficient troops, and operate on both banks of the Shannon. However, communication between the two halves depended upon fords and pontoon bridges, which were vulnerable to raids and fluctuating water levels. Also the defenders were able to operate on interior lines against either section making defeat in detail a constant danger. Failure to operate on both banks meant that Limerick could be attacked but not besieged because Thomond Bridge always permitted access to County Clare enabling reinforcement, resupply and regular rotation of the garrison. William's position, however, was not without some advantages. Usually a fortified town was occupied by a garrison whilst the remainder of the defenders' forces constituted a relief army. In response, the besieger normally employed only a portion of his troops at the siege leaving the majority to form a covering corps to counter any relieving forces. Limerick in 1690 was defended by the entire Jacobite Army and so William was able to employ all his forces in the siege lines. The Jacobite strategy of choice was to split their army between the city and County Clare, Thomond Bridge acting as the line of communication. Having failed in his quest to persuade his comrades to surrender because Limerick was indefensible, Tyrconnell adopted this approach garrisoning Limerick with 8,000 infantry – there were insufficient modern weapons to equip more – leaving the cavalry and the remainder of the foot in County Clare. The ford above Limerick, via which William might divide his army and cut off the garrison from its supports, was entrenched. Major General Boisseleau was appointed governor, assisted by Berwick, Major Generals William Dorrington and Sarsfield, and Brigadiers Henry Luttrell, John Wauchope and Thomas Maxwell. Tyrconnell then travelled to Galway to supervise the departure of the French Brigade.[22]

At 05:00 on 9 August, the Williamite host decamped from Caherconlish and advanced towards Limerick, led by 100 cavalry and 50 dragoons under the Dane, Captain (Rittmeister) La Jarrie. Next was the vanguard of 1,000 infantry selected from all the battalions in the army, commanded by Brigadier Sir Henry Bellasise with assistance from Colonels Lord Drogheda and Thomas Erle. Behind the vanguard came the Dutch Blue Guards. The main infantry body formed five brigades – the Danes; the Danish Guards, resplendent in their orange coats; Brigadier William Stewart's (Stewart, Kirke, Meath, Erle); Sir Henry Bellasise's (Bellasise, Douglas, Lisburn, Gustavus Hamilton, Lord George Hamilton); and Melonière's (Melonière, Drogheda, Cambon, Bellefont, Michelburne, Cutts, Gröben) – and marched in two lines, the first with an infantry brigade on the right and left, whilst the second contained the remaining two infantry brigades plus a cavalry brigade in the centre utilizing the principal road. Bellasise, encountering the first opposition at 06:00 on a hilltop 5 km from Limerick, advanced in line of battle but the Irish quickly retired. About 1 km further on, Bellasise topped some rising ground and saw Limerick but could not visualize an obvious route of advance or locate the enemy because of the close ground littered with hedges, ditches, deep lanes and enclosures. Some Irish musketeers appeared within one of the enclosures so Bellasise's pioneers hacked gaps in the hedges to right and left but, before flanking attacks could be launched, they fell back to another hedge-line allowing Bellasise to edge forward. A similar process was executed on two or three occasions and the advance slowed to such an extent that the main body caught up, William at its head. The king took command, riding here and there delivering orders. Gradually, as the hedges were cut down, the army inched forward on either side of the central lane until, within 1 km of Limerick, they reached a 150-m wide defile between two bogs through which were channelled three lanes.

It contained all manner of useful defensive features: hedges, an orchard, a stone wall, and the smoking ruins of a house by the side of the central lane. Just beyond the ruined house, the Irish cavalry stood astride the middle and widest of the three lanes, the hedges to either side lined with musketeers. Very clearly, this was the main Jacobite defensive position.

Covered by Captain La Jarrie's cavalry vanguard, which advanced close to the Irish horse and exchanged several shots, the pioneers were again sent forward to chop down the hedges. Bellasise's vanguard now formed the centre of the first line of the army between the Danish Brigade on the left, led by Württemberg, and the Dutch Blue Guards and some English battalions towards their right, commanded by Kirke, with Drogheda's battalion in reserve. Cavalry stood behind seconded by the infantry brigades of the second line. William ordered forward two field guns on the left which fired on the Irish cavalry in the defile, forcing them back. Demonstrating either remarkable *sang froid* or the fact that this was low-intensity fighting, whilst the pioneers hacked at the hedges the English infantry, knowing that the Irish musketeers were lurking behind the next hedge, sat chatting about what they would have for breakfast, behaviour which the Danes, who remained in line, regarded as unprofessional and indicative of low morale. However, as soon as the pioneers had opened a hedge, the English got to their feet and pushed forward, despite taking volleys from flanking hedges. On the left, Württemberg employed similar tactics. His advance was led by 50 pioneers who broke down the hedges, supported by infantry platoons and four field guns. Although the Jacobite foot contested each hedge-line, Württemberg said that they did so without determination; the Danes lost only 30 killed and wounded. Within half an hour the defile had been cleared and the Irish pushed back on to Singland Hill, the final height before Limerick, on which stood the Old Kirk and Ireton's Fort, a relic from the siege of 1651. These positions could have been defended for some time and imposed serious delays on the Williamites but the Danish infantry attacked vigorously and drove off the defenders. The whole Jacobite Army then withdrew towards the town to take station under the shelter of the garrison cannon. Up to this point, the heavy cannon on the walls of Irish Town had been silent for fear of hitting their own men, but now they opened fire causing some damage to the attackers. In response, four field guns were dragged into Ireton's Fort whence they attempted counter-battery missions. By 17:00, all of William's army had marched in and encamped within cannon-shot of the town. Württemberg garrisoned Ireton's Fort with the Danish Brigade and Hanmer's battalion, later reinforced by Drogheda's battalion, and stood to arms all night expecting a counter-attack but nothing occurred: Württemberg thought that the Jacobite officers could not prevail upon their men to stand. The day's fighting had apparently cost the Williamites 35 killed, and the Jacobites 250 but the actual figures were probably a great deal lower. Had the heavy artillery been at hand, the demoralized Jacobites might well have surrendered.[23]

Encouraged by information from deserters on 10 August that the garrison was internally divided and suffering from low morale, between 18:00 and 19:00 William sent a trumpeter to summon the town to surrender. Many in the garrison favoured acceptance but Sarsfield, Boisseleau and Berwick, employing a farrago of half-truths and lies, persuaded them to resist. Governor Boisseleau wrote formally to Sir Robert Southwell, secretary of state for Ireland, rejecting the summons. Normally, a besieging army performed two initial tasks: the establishment of an encampment safe from the fire of the defenders' cannon; and the construction of a line of contravallation to protect the camp from sallies. At Limerick, the former was only partly achieved whilst the latter was thought unnecessary in view of the assumed poor morale which rendered offensive action by the garrison highly unlikely. Besides, it would have consumed precious time when the end of the campaigning season was rapidly approaching. The Danes pitched their tents next to the Shannon on the extreme left of the line where, to their great delight, they found an old Viking earth fort, but their position was enfiladed by Jacobite field guns on the Clare shore. Instead of sheltering in the deep, covered entrenchments of a line of contravallation, infantry battalions had to stand in the open, day and night, guarding the key points.

As William closed on Limerick, guerrilla activities began to break out in the army's rear. Between Athlone and Mullingar a mixture of raparees, Jacobite deserters and local supporters, abetted by the garrison of Athlone, had grown so 'insolent' that Colonel Wolseley led out the Enniskillen Horse on a punitive expedition from his headquarters at Mullingar. They broke up the Jacobite groupings, killing 56 and taking several prisoners. It was typical of the operations that were to dominate the coming autumn and winter.[24]

15

The first siege of Limerick

During the evening of 9 August a party of dragoons reconnoitred the ford at Annaghbeg, about 5 km upstream from Limerick, but their report was discouraging: the stream was rapid, the bottom stony and the pass guarded by six battalions of infantry, two regiments of dragoons and three of cavalry strongly posted in Sir Samuel Foxton's house and behind numerous brick walls and hedges close to the river-side. Early next morning, General Ginkel led eight squadrons of cavalry and dragoons, accompanied by three battalions of infantry (Kirke, Meath and Stewart) under Major General Kirke, to Annaghbeg anticipating a hard fight in order to gain a crossing. Even in a dry summer the Shannon was not usually fordable but in 1690 the water level was abnormally low and Ginkel's horsemen crossed without difficulty whilst the infantry waded waist-deep. There was no opposition: the defenders had evacuated their positions during the night. On hearing of the successful crossing, William appeared at 08:00 and ordered Kirke to guard the ford, placing one battalion on the Clare side and two on the Munster bank, seconded by some field guns and a party of cavalry that was to be relieved every 24 hours. Ginkel's expedition was probably intended to secure the ford in case William needed to develop operations in that direction at a later date; much larger forces would have been required to cut off Limerick from its supporting infantry and cavalry. Disturbed by the ease with which the barrier of the Shannon had been forced the Jacobite senior command assumed that Ginkel's reconnaissance in force was indeed the precursor of a major operation into County Clare and ordered the destruction of the forage within a 16-km radius. Tyrconnell took the Irish cavalry to a new campsite at Sixmilebridge 10 km north-west to gain access to new foraging grounds. At 16:00, William sent a mounted patrol under a lieutenant colonel to locate Tyrconnell's position but it was unable to penetrate Jacobite cavalry screens. That evening, Ginkel recrossed the Shannon.[1]

William was accompanied to Limerick by only his field artillery and even this had taken a month to travel from Dublin along the bad roads. The siege train, comprising six 24-pounders, two 18-pounders, 60 ammunition wagons carrying 27,000 kg of gunpowder and 3,000 cannon balls, bridging pontoons, engineering equipment, plus a portable workshop and three days' rations for the whole army, was still on the road from Dublin, escorted by two cavalry troops (Edward

Villiers's Horse) commanded by Captain Thomas Pulteney (Second Troop of Life Guards). A Huguenot gunner deserted from the besiegers on 10 August and provided the garrison with a plan of the camp, including the location of William's tent, and the itinerary of the siege train. It would camp near Ballyneety on the night of 11 August, he said, aiming to reach the siege lines the following day. On hearing this, Sarsfield, who was anxious to delay a close siege of Limerick for as long as possible, rode to the cavalry camp on the night of 9–10 August and offered to lead an expedition to intercept the siege train provided that he could take the very best horsemen. Tyrconnell, who could see little to lose but much to gain, allowed him 600 men, even though this involved denuding the forces at Annaghbeg ford of cavalry support, without which the position was untenable: this was the probable reason for the abandonment of the Annaghbeg defences on the previous night. Sarsfield decided to ride westwards, cross the Shannon as if intending to raid into County Tipperary or reinforce Athlone, before swinging south to reach Ballyneety. Sarsfield departed on the night of 11 August. To avoid the Williamites who held the bridge over the Shannon at Killaloe, Sarsfield used a ford at Ballyvally, 2 km north of Killaloe and out of sight of the bridge. Three km beyond Ballina, Sarsfield was joined by a group of raparees, led by Daniel 'Galloping' Hogan, who knew the country intimately and acted as guides. They led Sarsfield under the mass of Keeper Hill where they halted for a while near Toor to feed and rest the horses, through the mountains and valleys of the Slieve Felim, southwards, via Rearcross. After sunrise, Sarsfield halted for most of the day amidst thick woods around Glengar sending his scouts forward to ascertain the precise location of the siege train. Legend has it that, close to Monard, Sarsfield's scouts came across the wife of a Williamite soldier attached to the siege train who was bathing her tired feet in a stream. They fell to talking and invited her to a tavern in Cullen village where, after a few drinks, she let slip that the password for the camp of the siege train, now at Ballyneety, close to Old Pallas Green village, 3 km from Cullen, was 'Sarsfield'. The scouts returned to the bivouac and preparations were made to attack at 02:00 on 12 August.

Within the space of 15 minutes on the morning of 11 August, about 20 heavy cannon shot fell 'all in a line' amidst the Williamite field artillery park. So accurate was the fire that the guns had to be moved back behind a low hill. More cannon balls fell in the area where William's tent was positioned, a clear indication that the Jacobites had received precise information about the lay-out of the camp. The king had his tents moved to a more secure position but not before two of Prince George of Denmark's 'fine horses' had been killed. Six 12-pounders were dragged from the artillery park on to Singland Hill by Ireton's Fort, whence their fire dismounted one of the Irish cannon by the South Gate and damaged some houses in Irish Town. During the morning, Manus O'Brien, 'a substantial country gentleman', rode into the Williamite camp and said that, during the night,

Sarsfield had crossed the Shannon with a detachment of cavalry and planned 'something extraordinary'. O'Brien told of the arrival of the Huguenot deserter in Limerick and commented that it would have been clear to Sarsfield that should the heavy cannon reach Limerick then the town and the Jacobite cause would soon fall. Sarsfield, surmised O'Brien, was almost certainly intent on destroying the siege train. Initially O'Brien was disbelieved. One officer pooh-poohed his information and enquired about a possible prey of cattle instead causing O'Brien to comment that he was sorry the king's officers were more interested in cattle raiding than operations. Later in the morning, O'Brien was taken to see William. Fairly certain that Sarsfield intended to attack the artillery train, he instructed Solms to arrange for a sizeable detachment of cavalry to meet the guns. In turn, Solms ordered Sir John Lanier to take out 400 cavalry and 200 dragoons but, for some reason, departure was delayed until between 01:00 and 02:00 on 12 August when they rode off very quietly, making several unnecessary halts that caused further delays, until a sudden, bright light in the southern sky accompanied by deep rumbling suggested that they were too late. Lanier, who had been a great favourite of James II, was widely suspected of treachery but nothing was proved and his military career continued until ended by a cannon ball at Steenkirk in 1692. There were also questions about whether Solms had issued the orders to Lanier with the necessary dispatch whilst Lanier said that he had misunderstood Solms's directions.[2]

The siege train made relatively good progress from Cashel on 11 August camping that night on 'a small piece of plain, green ground' bordered by the ruins of Ballyneety Castle and several earthen 'fences'. Had there been any suspicion of danger the wagons and guns could easily have been drawn inside the castle ruins where they would have been safe from attack. Failing this, the wagons might have been laagered, Hussite-style, but no warning had been received from Limerick and the main army was close by. So the train and escort officers placed a light guard, turned the horses out to grass and settled down for an undisturbed night under canvas. Led by raparee guides Sarsfield left his lair at Glengar after dark. Just before midnight scouts reported horsemen approaching Ballyneety from Limerick, 'six, thin troops' of Sir Albert Conyngham's Enniskillen Dragoons, but they passed the artillery camp making for Carrick to escort a supply convoy. Appreciating that he might be discovered at any moment by more troops using the Limerick road, Sarsfield sent Captain James Fitzgerald to place an ambush to intercept Conyngham, should he return, and moved forward to attack the train around 02:00 on 12 August, achieving total surprise. Several local people bringing provisions to the camp, soldiers, wagoners and women were killed before the alarm could be sounded. When he realized what was happening, Pulteney ordered the trumpets to sound 'To Horse' but the animals were grazing and the men detailed to bring them in were either hacked down or did not dare to venture out. Some disorganized resistance was offered before the men were told to shift for themselves and many escaped, although forfeiting their baggage and mounts. Altogether, about 60 men and women lost their lives, including Lieutenant William Bell of Villiers's Horse.

Sarsfield's men filled the guns with powder and rammed their muzzles into the ground before piling on top all the wagons, ammunition, and provisions. They took what they could carry, herded the horses, laid a powder trail, lit the fuse and departed. *Prima facie*, the physical damage was considerable: 120 wagons were destroyed; 500 horses driven off or killed; 12,000 lb (5.5 tonnes) of gunpowder burned along with quantities of match, grenades and bombs; 3,000 cannon balls scattered or lost; three days' supply of bread and flour destroyed; and a few of the 49 'cork and tin' pontoons required for bridging the Shannon were holed. However, only two cannon were completely ruined whilst six remained serviceable, most of the pontoons were 'not much damnified', and a wagon laden with coin was untouched. The Jacobite belief that they had seriously undermined the Williamite siege capability boosted morale improving the chances of making a successful defence. Above all, Ballyneety bought time by delaying the formal opening of the trenches for at least a week. Before galloping away, Sarsfield visited Lieutenant Colonel Robert Freke (Erle's Foot) who was lying sick in a nearby house. Polite and civil, he told Freke that the raid had been risky but worthwhile; had it failed, he would have departed for France leaving Tyrconnell to reach terms with William. Conyngham heard the explosions and immediately turned to investigate. Warned of the ambush by a deserter, Conyngham charged through, killing a major, Captain Fitzgerald and about 15 troopers, and then moved cautiously towards Ballyneety but he was too late to intercept Sarsfield's main body. Lanier's horsemen wheeled left racing for the Killaloe–Ballyvally crossings, Colonel Edward Villiers took another party of horse towards O'Briensbridge whilst Scravenmoer crossed the Shannon to scour the banks between Limerick and Killaloe. Sarsfield used none of these obvious routes, returning around the north of Lough Derg. Apart from the blow to Williamite pride and morale, the real loss was not so much the two heavy guns but the ammunition and horses. One immediate consequence was a letter from William to the Earl of Nottingham asking that a 'good' naval squadron under Rear Admiral Sir Cloudisley Shovell be dispatched promptly to the Shannon to interdict Limerick's sea communications and threaten the French ships at Galway. Shovell, however, was not to take unnecessary risks and should he find a superior French naval squadron in the Shannon he 'is not to make any rash attempt'.[3]

Until the Ballyneety Raid, the Tyrconnell-Lauzun strategy of ending the war by reaching an accommodation with William had been progressing steadily. Tyrconnell had received a letter from James on 24 July announcing that empty French ships would be sailing for Galway to convey to Brest the French Brigade and anyone else who wished to escape. Those who chose to remain were absolved from their oaths of fidelity to James, freeing them to negotiate with William. Tyrconnell and Lauzun were thus rather disappointed at Sarsfield's success and let it be known that they thought it irrelevant to the overall strategic situation and could not, by itself, prevent the eventual fall of Limerick. They stressed that the relatively advantageous terms currently on offer from William would be withdrawn if Limerick fell: within a short while the Irish could lose everything, leaving mercy as the best possible outcome. These arguments began to gain converts because most of the army was already disenchanted with the French Brigade due to its bad behaviour in Dublin and abandonment of Limerick. Sarsfield and the war party countered by arguing that there was no danger of losing Limerick because the Williamites had lost their siege artillery and lacked the numbers to besiege the town on all sides. Provided that aid was received from France, the defence of Connaught was feasible. They also suggested, rather tortuously, that Lauzun had connived at the partial ruination of parts of southern Connaught and the barbarities and irregularities committed by the French in order to alienate the Irish, reduce their ability to prolong the conflict and thus hasten the end of the war. Further support for Sarsfield came from the Roman Catholic bishops who knew that a Williamite victory in any circumstances would lead to the suppression of their church. Along with zealous lay Catholics they favoured sidelining Tyrconnell and vesting Sarsfield with the overall military command. The scheme foundered when Sarsfield did not feel able to accept this level of responsibility and refused to depose the viceroy. However, even Tyrconnell could not ignore Ballyneety. He recommended Sarsfield to James who, five months later, issued a patent creating him Earl of Lucan.

Brigadier William Stewart, commanding a mixed detachment including four field guns, marched early on the morning of 12 August to attack Castleconnell, a place of some strength on the Shannon 12 km above Limerick garrisoned by 140 men under Captain Barnwell, who had refused a summons to surrender from Stewart's advance guard on the previous evening. However, as soon as Stewart's cannon came into view, the white flag was hung out. Castleconnell was then garrisoned until the end of the siege. On 13 August wagons, carriages and horses, including the personal mounts of Württemberg and several senior officers, were sent both towards Waterford, to hasten the arrival of replacement artillery and mortars, and Ballyneety to bring up the undamaged cannon and broken gun carriages. Lieutenant Colonel Toby Caulfield (Earl of Drogheda's Foot) garrisoned Cullen with 300 foot to guard the Limerick road and patrol the surrounding countryside in order to forestall another raid and control the activities of raparees who were 'beginning to disturb us'. The majority of the army spent the day bundling brushwood into fascines. Learning that a number of raparees had gathered at Castlemartyr, about 12 km west of Youghal on the

Cork road, on 14 August Lieutenant Colonel Luke Lillingstone led the Youghal garrison of 50 infantry and 36 dragoons to attack. The dragoons soon left the infantry behind and, near Castlemartyr, encountered 300 raparee horse and foot and promptly routed them, killing 60 and capturing 17. When the foot caught up, the castle was summoned and the garrison surrendered on condition that they were allowed to go to Cork, minus horses and arms, which were distributed amongst the local Protestants. The troops then returned to Youghal.[4]

The Williamite camp was shifted during 15 August to anchor the left flank firmly on the bank of the Shannon, the Danes still entrusted with holding this vulnerable wing. Jacobite cannon inflicted considerable damage on 16 August and infantry sallied towards the river against the Danes, where bushes and thick undergrowth provided cover, but were repulsed by a counter-attack. Württemberg was ordered to open the trenches formally on Sunday 17 August. Accordingly, in the evening he marched seven battalions from the parade ground to the location selected for the first parallel. Eighty-five soldiers from each battalion were detailed as pioneers, the remainder of each battalion waiting behind hedges ready to support the workmen should the garrison sally. The relay of seven battalions was relieved at midnight. During the small hours, 300 paces of trench were excavated and the Irish cleared from two small flanking redoubts, William observing progress from Ireton's Fort. A battery was planted to the right of the trenches below the Two Chimneys Fort and fired throughout 18 August, dismounting some of the garrison's cannon. That night, Douglas's and Stewart's battalions were ordered to support on the right of the trenches but lost their way in the dark and took station within 20 m of the Irish positions. The men were ordered to lie down and many drifted off to sleep. Noticing a lack of alertness, the Irish attacked causing both battalions to fall back in confusion but they rallied and fired, although they had no idea at what they were shooting. The Danes on the left, assuming that Douglas's and Stewart's battalions were Jacobite infantry sallying, also opened fire: in turn, Douglas's and Stewart's mistook the Danes for Irish, and returned the compliment. The Irish fired on both. Several men were killed in this muddle and it was two hours before the mistake was realized, order restored and Douglas's, Stewart's and the Danes all turned on the Irish. Following this embarrassment, William ordered the trenches to be relieved during the day rather than at midnight, even though this involved men having to enter and leave the trenches under observed cannon fire and long-range musketry. Heavily guarded, the cannon from Waterford arrived in camp.

By 20 August the trenches were within 30 paces of the Yellow Fort just to the right of St John's Gate, a V-shaped redoubt, its rear open towards the town, garrisoned by Captain Barrett and 150 men. William ordered an assault. Württemberg gathered an advance guard of 120 grenadiers, drawn from four battalions, under Samuel Foxton, captain of the grenadier company of Colonel

John Cutts's Foot, and Richard Needham, captain of the grenadier company of Lord Meath's infantry. Next came 16 men carrying ladders, escorted by a lieutenant commanding 100 Dutch fusiliers, followed by two captains with a reserve of 100 fusiliers. In the rear waited 400 pioneers carrying woolsacks, fascines, hatchets and shovels, their task to block and fortify the redoubt's gorge. In support were the Danish Guards and Colonel Belcastel's battalion along with Major Cornelius Wood who stood in a lane on the right with 50 cavalry (Byerley's Horse) to deter sallies from the town. At either 14:00 or 14:30, the firing of three cannon signalled the opening of the attack. Under covering fire from the siege lines, Foxton and Needham's grenadiers climbed from the trenches, ran across the open ground and hurled their grenades in the face of heavy defensive musketry from both the town walls and Yellow Fort. Unfortunately the men carrying the scaling ladders fell behind the grenadiers and Foxton was obliged to try to clamber into the fort but he failed and the assault lost momentum. Württemberg ordered up Belcastel's battalion, the colonel himself taking overall command of the assault, and he reorganized the formation, placing the scaling ladders in the front line. A second attempt was successful, the troops mounting the walls, breaking in and driving out the defenders who lost between 60 and 70 men. Cannon fire continued for an hour, some of it directed at Wood's supporting cavalry, which withdrew to a safer position behind a low hill. In the meantime, the pioneers hurried to make the gorge of the redoubt secure against counter-attack. Württemberg had been in possession of the redoubt for about 60 minutes when Lord Kilmallock led forward four infantry battalions and three squadrons of cavalry from St John's Gate. The Danish Guards and Cutts's battalion advanced to flank the fort and a vigorous action ensued, the Jacobite cavalry coming very close until forced back by heavy defensive fire, supported by musketry from the trenches. Wood then advanced, leaping a ditch and breaking one of Kilmallock's squadrons whilst Lieutenant Colonel Hugh Wyndham and Captain Davenport Lucy (both Byerley's Horse), leading some Dutch and Danish horse, beat back the remaining two squadrons almost to St John's Gate. This placed the Williamite cavalry too far forward and they drew fire from the walls as they retired, Captain Lucy losing his life. The engagement did not die down until 19:00 and losses were high, the Williamite infantry suffering 58 men killed and 140 wounded, and the cavalry 21 killed and 52 wounded. Sixty-four cavalry mounts had been destroyed and 57 injured. Captain Needham was shot dead whilst in the trenches on the following day (21 August). Deserters reported that the Jacobites had lost about 300 men.

Because of the high water table, mining was impossible so the only way to breach the ramparts was to blast them with siege artillery firing solid shot from as close as possible. Most of the heavy cannon were dragged forward into a battery within half-a-musket-shot of the east wall of Irish Town on 20 and 21

August; the garrison responded by hanging woolsacks over the parapet to soften the impact of the cannon balls. On 22 August, fire was concentrated against two towers from which snipers enfiladed the trenches: by the end of the day both had been levelled, one collapsing into the Black Bastion burying many of the defenders. During the night of 22–23 August, considerable numbers of bombs and carcasses were shot into the Irish Town starting a number of fires. A truce was arranged in the evening of 23 August to allow the retrieval and burying of the dead from the action at Yellow Fort three days before. Searching amongst the bodies, the Williamites found a wounded French officer, still alive despite having been trapped beneath the carcass of his horse. Mortars continued to shoot bombs and carcasses into the town during the day and night, starting numerous fires including one that consumed a store of hay. Around midday on 23 August, two Jacobite captains, one lieutenant, a priest and 70 soldiers, the garrison of Nenagh Castle, were brought into the Williamite camp. With 1,500 horse and dragoons, a battalion of infantry and two field guns, Ginkel had captured Nenagh Castle after a siege lasting 24 hours. Mounted troops were of limited value in capturing fixed fortifications and the governor of Nenagh, Captain O'Bryan, seeing only cavalry and dragoons initially refused a summons to surrender but promptly waved the white flag when the infantry and cannon arrived and the men began to bind fascines ready for the construction of a battery. From Nenagh, a Williamite garrison could deter Jacobite raids across the Shannon into the Midlands, as well as reduce the risk of further Ballyneety-type operations.

The head of the trenches was now 20 metres from the counterscarp. The dangerous work of sapping was carried out by relays of 30 volunteer infantrymen, who each received two shillings (ten pence) per shift. By 24 August, although sections of the parapet had been shot away, the cannon were still not close enough to breach the wall. During the night of 24–25 August, the guns were moved forward into two new batteries 60 m from the counterscarp, one of eight pieces to fire on Irish Town and the other of two guns to target Baal's Bridge. The Irish, sensitive about the latter's security, planted two cannon outside the walls of English Town to fire on the Williamite battery and flank the counterscarp on the east side of Irish Town. Up to this point, the weather had been mainly fine. Two or three days previously there had been rain for 24 hours and the trenches had flooded to knee-depth but the rains returned on 25 August ending the unusually dry summer. Sections of trench collapsed and a morass developed that effectively interrupted communication between the left and right wings of the Williamite camp: it was imperative to conclude the siege as rapidly as possible. A respectable breach had been created to the east of St John's Gate by the end of 25 August, perhaps sufficient to risk an attack. Indeed, a general assault on the counterscarp before the breach was scheduled for 26 August but postponed after an inspection revealed that it was still too narrow. During 26 August the gap was slightly widened and some of the palisades on the counterscarp beaten down. At a council of war that evening, Colonel Cambon, the quartermaster-general, argued that the assault should be put off for a further two or three days to ensure that the opening was so wide that it would be impossible to defend. In which case, according to the received wisdom of the laws of war, the garrison would be expected to surrender as soon as a lodgement had been secured on the counterscarp, a convention that did not apply if the breach was small and defensible. The breach appeared largely unimpeded by rubble but was only some 12 m wide restricting the attack frontage to between eight and ten files. Should the defenders, who had known for some days where the assault would come, have built adequate retrenchments and breastworks within the breach, success was not guaranteed. When the maximum breadth of breach had been achieved, the textbook asked for a storming column of enough depth to create sufficient momentum for the main body to push through the opening over the corpses of the fallen front ranks. William had insufficient infantry to form such a column. Württemberg belatedly agreed with Cambon, protesting that they should wait until the breach could accommodate a 16-man front: at the very least, fresh battalions should be employed, rather than those who had done duty in the trenches all through the previous night. This, however, would have meant entrusting the attack mostly to Danes and Dutchmen 'and it was desired that the English should do something too, in order to prevent jealousy'. However, ammunition was running low, the weather had turned, and William's customary impatience prevailed: it was decided to attack the counterscarp on the following day (27 August).

Governor Boisseleau had indeed retrenched the width of the breach and manned the position with some infantry companies, supported by two cannon and the duty battalions. The battalions that had been on guard the previous day were held in reserve. In Europe, with a large breach in the walls and a powerful enemy about to attack, a garrison would probably have surrendered but the situation at Limerick was entirely different; rather than being a component within a defensive system, Limerick was the last bastion and stronghold of the desperate Jacobites. The attack by the first line of the army was scheduled for the afternoon under the overall command of Lieutenant General Douglas. The morning was spent bringing up all the impedimenta required for seizing and holding a lodgement on a counterscarp: woolsacks, ammunition, timber and fascines. Under Colonel John Cutts, all the grenadiers in the army, about 500 men, entered the trenches to lead the attack. They were to be supported on the right by one battalion of the Dutch Blue Guards, Meath's, Lisburn's and the Brandenburgers; on the left stood the Danes and Cutts's battalion; whilst Stewart's and Cambon's battalions were in reserve. A body of horse was drawn up to sustain the infantry in the event of a counter-attack. Douglas's troops deployed as soon as they had been relieved in the trenches by seven battalions of the second line under Württemberg. At 15:30, on the signal fire of three cannons, the grenadiers in the angle of the trenches nearest to the breach clambered out and dashed forward, firing their muskets and throwing their grenades. The defenders were fully prepared and alert. They waited for a minute or two until the 'pound was full' before opening fire with musketry and cannon loaded with partridge shot. Within a couple of minutes, the scene was shrouded in dust and smoke, which eventually obscured the peak of a mountain 10 km distant. Between the trenches and the counterscarp, Captain Ludovic Carlisle, leading the grenadier company of Lord Drogheda's battalion, received two wounds but struggled on, before leaping into the dry ditch below the counterscarp where a defender shot him dead; Lieutenant Barton took over and led the grenadiers on to the counterscarp. Sensing defeat, the Irish Foot Guards on the counterscarp threw down their arms and ran back into the town through the breach. Despite orders to take just the counterscarp, the grenadiers pursued them 'pell mell'; within seconds, about half the grenadiers were actually inside Limerick, a few even reaching as far as the main square. The supporting battalions, however, came as far as the counterscarp and halted according to instructions. Some of the Irish troops in and around the breach began to break away towards Baal's Bridge and King's Island but, seeing only a few Williamite grenadiers in the town and their supports halted on the counterscarp, their officers managed to rally them. After the action a deserter reported that Boisseleau had used dragoons to bar the passage of the infantry falling back from the breach and 'persuade' them to return to their duty. Seeing their supports remaining on the counterscarp, the grenadiers wavered, lost momentum and started a confused and uncoordinated withdrawal: some were shot, some taken prisoner and nearly all who escaped were injured. Had the supporting battalions also disregarded their orders and advanced into the breach, Irish Town would have fallen. Had both grenadiers and supports obeyed orders, all would have been well; had they both disobeyed orders the outcome would have favourable; but one obeying and one disobeying was ruinous. Württemberg claimed that he sent Major General de la Forest to William, who watched from his customary post at Ireton's Fort, to explain that it was hard going on the counterscarp but the situation might be salvaged if an all-out attack was launched on the breach. Solms opposed this saying to the king that it was already too late.

Having returned to their posts the defenders laid down a heavy fire on the counterscarp from every gun that could bear. Particular damage was done by the two cannon on King's Island which flanked the counterscarp and the two field guns that hosed partridge shot from within the breach. Women, often closer to the enemy than the soldiers, threw stones and broken bottles. Because nearly all the engineering officers were dead or wounded little was done to reinforce and protect the lodgement leaving the Williamite infantry standing without protection from the fire and missiles. After enduring this for three hours, the troops retired to the cover of the sodden trenches. When the action was at its height, the Brandenburg battalion forced its way into the Black Battery. Precisely what happened is unclear: either the defenders' gunpowder caught fire or the defenders sprung a mine but a huge explosion sent Germans, stones, fascines and guns flying through the air. To facilitate the withdrawal from the counterscarp, Württemberg ordered Colonel Cutts to advance with his battalion and pre-empt an Irish counter-attack from the spur outside the South Gate. Covered by fire from the Danes, Cutts led his men to within half-a-musket-shot of the gate but they were uncovered in the open whilst the defenders were 'secure within the spur and the walls'; Cutts was wounded, several killed and the assault stalled. Because they had been fighting from behind cover, the Irish casualties were heavy, about 500 dead, but lighter than those of the attackers, who lost over 500 killed and 1,000 injured. The defenders also enjoyed the advantage of being able to feed fresh men into the fight. As usual, the infantry officers suffered disproportionately: from the five English supporting battalions, 59 were casualties. By 19:00 the action was concluded and William returned to the camp much concerned.[5]

The trenches that had been damaged as the grenadiers had scrambled from them on the previous afternoon were repaired during the night of 27–28 August. William attempted to arrange a truce in order to bury the dead but the Irish refused. Williamite morale remained high and the soldiers favoured a second attack. The battering cannon continued to fire but rain fell almost without intermission throughout the night of 28–29 August, all the following day and into 30 August. At 22:00 on 28 August, Solms conferred with Württemberg. The latter favoured augmenting the batteries, intensifying the bombardment, enlarging the breach and launching another attack. Solms replied that ammunition was low, particularly solid cannon balls, a result of Ballyneety and the last ammunition convoy which had delivered only unfilled bombs and carcasses, useless for battering stone walls. In addition, the troops were soaked, exhausted and falling sick. William summoned a council of war on 29 August. Suggestions for making a fresh assault with the second line of the army, supported by the first line, were rapidly dismissed. In the first place, should the assault fail, the Irish would be very strong and the Williamites so weak that most of the territorial gains of the campaign of 1690 would be lost: better to lift the siege and consolidate. Second, there had been so much rain, and probably much more would fall, and the condition of the ground was deteriorating so rapidly that soon it would be impossible to drag off the heavy baggage and cannon. The Shannon was beginning to swell and the experience of 1689 had shown the disastrous effects of sustained wet weather upon an English army under canvas. Third, although supposedly demoralized by the Boyne, the Jacobites had fought much better than anticipated.

Fourth, the French might return to Limerick from Galway and encourage the Irish to attack the weakened Williamites. Fifth, there were strong, although false, rumours that Berwick and Colonel Dominic Sheldon had led 3,000 horse through Loughrea into the Midlands and were about to spread mayhem towards Dublin and 8,000 men under the Earl of Clancarty and Colonel Roger MacElligott were raiding through County Cork. The immediate raising of the siege – a rare event in seventeenth-century warfare – was the only sensible conclusion. The withdrawal was undisturbed because the Jacobite cavalry was still at Sixmilebridge and the infantry were still poorly disciplined and unreliable. The heavy cannon were dragged from the batteries and the numerous sick and wounded loaded into wagons and taken towards Cashel and Clonmel. On 30 August, the siege guns were towed back to Caherconlish, escorted by the infantry battalions of Drogheda and Stewart, a difficult exercise because the rain had so softened the ground that oxen had to be employed instead of horses. Passing command to Count Solms, William left the camp heading for Cullen, Waterford, Duncannon Fort and then England: he arrived at Kensington on 10 September.

With hindsight, the Jacobites could have improved their performance by fortifying the approaches between Caherconlish and Singland Hill. They might also have dug an enveloping entrenchment around Irish Town from the Shannon to the Abbey River, reinforced with small forts and redoubts, in order to keep the attacking artillery at a distance from the weak main wall. To some extent, this was achieved opposite the Danes to the west of Irish Town but the defenders had neither the time nor resources to build such extensive works. There was the additional point that Jacobite morale was uncertain during the early stages of the siege and the men may not have remained to defend a trench-line had it come under pressure. The Williamites would have been better advised to concentrate their artillery on breaking down Baal's and Thomond Bridges to isolate both the whole and the two sections of Limerick. William might then have divided his forces by sending a corps to operate in County Clare although this would have been extremely hazardous. After losing the bridging pontoons at Ballyneety, how could these men have been provisioned? What would have happened had the level of the Shannon risen and swamped the already marginal Annaghbeg ford? As the army was trailing back to Caherconlish, a deserter from Limerick reported that the garrison had been running very low on gunpowder and bread towards the end of the siege. 'So it is to be regretted', sighed Württemberg, 'that so little information was available and that we were lacking in the necessary requirements. Thus the Irish war would have been ended at once,' a change of heart for a man who had said at the opening of the campaign that he hoped the war would not end too quickly or he would face unemployment.

Returning to Limerick around 6 September, Tyrconnell appointed Major General William Dorrington governor in place of Boisseleau who travelled to

Galway to rejoin the French Brigade. Tyrconnell then distributed the Jacobite forces into winter quarters, instructing colonels to fill their ranks, and arranged an administration to govern during his coming absence in France. Twelve senators were nominated to manage civil affairs, mostly 'new interest men', a pejorative term for those who had purchased lands formerly held by Cromwellians and Republicans and realized that prompt submission to the English represented the sole route by which their titles might be confirmed. Berwick was selected to command the army but he was young and inexperienced and so an advisory council of officers was appointed comprising Brigadier Thomas Maxwell, Colonel John Hamilton, Colonel Dominic Sheldon and, as an afterthought, Patrick Sarsfield. There was some surprise in Limerick that the army had not been ordered to recapture Leinster and Waterford but Tyrconnell had to reconsider his position and tactics. Although he thought that the defence of Limerick had simply postponed the inevitable he could not ignore the victory and William might respond by offering more munificent terms; the longer the war lasted, his generosity was likely to increase. Therefore, Tyrconnell had publicly to convert himself into an apostle of continuing resistance, alongside Sarsfield and the native Irish, but this new position was inconsistent with the French Brigade sailing away under the premise that the war was irrevocably lost. He could hardly persuade the French Brigade to stay, largely because its officers were determined to leave and its potential military value was low. The fate of the Jacobite cause rested with the native Irish but they could only delay the end of the war if substantial financial and material aid was forthcoming from France. Tyrconnell had to manage the awkward task of advocating the return of the French Brigade while, simultaneously, seeking French economic assistance and advancing a policy of prolonging the fight for as long as possible. Lauzun's position was equally difficult because he had to explain to Louis XIV his decision to withdraw the French Brigade following a major Jacobite success. Tyrconnell suggested a line of argument: the inevitability of Irish defeat was sufficient justification for the withdrawal of the French Brigade and Louis would understand that Lauzun was saving his master's valuable troops rather then leaving them to founder in an ultimately hopeless cause.

On 12 September 1690, Tyrconnell, Lauzun and the French Brigade sailed from Galway aboard a French fleet. In the meantime, distrustful of Tyrconnell and anxious to undermine his credibility in both Ireland and France, Sarsfield and the Irish faction sent their own envoys to St Germain-en-Laye – the Bishop of Cork, Dr Peter Creagh; Colonel Nicholas Purcell; and Colonels Henry and Simon Luttrell – to explain to James why they had opposed Tyrconnell and seek a French general and aid for the 1691 campaign. Although for different reasons, Tyrconnell and Sarsfield were temporarily united in pursuit of the same strategy. Tyrconnell wanted French aid to extend the war into 1691 to force William into offering more generous terms of surrender, preferably showing particular favour to the Old English: Sarsfield required the support of France to enable the native Irish to fight on indefinitely to preserve religion and lands. On the road from Brest to Versailles Tyrconnell and Lauzun came to understand that their agreed stratagem of laying all the blame on the Irish was no longer realistic because the successful defence of Limerick had become a *cause célèbre* and its defenders heroes. Tyrconnell was forced into the unsatisfactory expedient of laying all the blame on Lauzun and the French Brigade. Feigning illness, not difficult for a man with coronary disease, he asked Lauzun to go ahead to Versailles and relate to Louis their original concocted version. When recovered, Tyrconnell would come to court and offer confirmation. Unsuspecting, Lauzun sped on and told Louis and James that Ireland was lost and the great majority of the Irish wished to submit to William, indeed many had done so already. The few who continued to hold out and had defended Limerick owed all their resolution to Tyrconnell who was the life and soul of the Irish cause and James's true supporter.

However, when Tyrconnell arrived he said that matters in Ireland were desperate but something might still be done if the French troops could be persuaded to remain in Galway. Poor, gullible Lauzun was only saved from the deepest dungeon in some nasty frontier fortress by the intervention of his very special friend, Queen Mary. Tyrconnell then set about trying to convince the English at St Germain-en-Laye of his version of events. He explained that he had English interests at heart and wished to see Ireland linked firmly to England and not established as a separate state, as many of the Irish were inclined to favour. Thus he sought little from Louis except arms, provisions, money and a general to command the army instead of Berwick or Sarsfield.[6]

Covered by a rearguard of 5,000 cavalry, on 31 August the Williamite Army withdrew in good order. Because so many wagons and carriages had already been used to convey the sick and wounded there was a shortage of transport and a good deal of ammunition, particularly bombs and hand grenades, was buried beneath what had been the artillery park and a powder trail lit. The resultant explosion rather alarmed the Irish whose inspection of the Williamite siege works and campsite grew more cautious. According to the Reverend Story, who was not present, many Williamite corpses were disinterred in order to strip them of their shirts and shrouds. That night the army camped at Caherconlish, the artillery continuing to Cullen. Realizing that the army would probably pull back into Leinster for the winter, the Protestants in County Limerick prepared to travel in its wake 'with bag and baggage ... and looked something like the Children of Israel, with their cattle, and all their stuff, footing it from Egypt; though most of those poor people had no promised land to retire to, but were driven into the wilderness of confusion; for I saw a great many of both men and women of very good fashion, who had lived plentifully before, yet now knew not which way to steer their course, but went along with the crowd, wither Providence should direct them.' In other words, they joined the tides of refugees moving back and forth across Ireland, ebbing and flooding with the fortunes of the two armies which provided neither food nor medical treatment for camp followers and refugees. The condition of what remained of Jacobite Ireland was even worse. Everywhere, provisions could be obtained only with great difficulty; soldiers billeted in towns pulled down houses to burn the timbers for firewood, thus depriving themselves of shelter; iron was in the shortest supply; and ploughing and agriculture were no longer worthwhile because the military commandeered all the horses, draught animals, foodstuffs and stores offering neither payment nor recompense. The desolation of Connaught, County Clare and the south-western peninsula was 'great and general'. Matters had been exacerbated by the policy of burning and destroying castles and country houses so as to deny their use to the Williamites: the corollary was that Jacobite troops could no longer find staging posts and shelter when on the march. Military discipline had effectively collapsed. Unable to pay the blackmail demanded by junior officers and NCOs, the houses and cabins of the poor were torched, only the wealthier being able to pay the bribes required to avoid *brandschatzen*.[7]

From Caherconlish the army moved first to Cullen then Tipperary on 6 September. Following William's departure the civil government was vested in three Lords Justices – William's old friend and trustee, Henry, First Viscount Sydney; the English Whig, Thomas Coningsby, paymaster-general of the army in Ireland; and, as a counter-balance, Sir Charles Porter, a Tory and lord chancellor of Ireland in 1686 – who visited Solms between 4 and 6 September to deliver money and organize a civil administration in the reoccupied territories.[8] Whilst at Tipperary, the army destroyed the forage to its front to render Jacobite winter operations east of the Shannon as difficult as possible. Around 7 or 8 September, Major General de la Forest, with about 500 cavalry, 400 infantry commanded by Lord Lisburn, and four field guns, was sent to retake Killmallock, an important position on the Limerick–Cork road, which was being used as a base for 100 Jacobite foot and 100 horse and dragoons, under Lieutenant Colonel Francis Boismeral (Carroll's Dragoons), who were interfering with Williamite foragers from Tipperary. Kilmallock's stone walls were badly damaged and Boismeral considered the place untenable in the face of the Williamite cannon. Surrendering at the first summons without firing a shot, the garrison was disarmed and deprived of baggage before being allowed to march to Limerick in semi-disgrace on 9 September.[9] Major General Tettau inspected the fortifications to see whether Kilmallock might serve as a post from which to interrupt Jacobite communications between Limerick and Cork but found the fortifications in such a poor state of repair that demolition was recommended. However, nothing was done and Kilmallock remained unoccupied.

From Whitehall William issued broad guidelines for the conduct of winter operations: Lieutenant General Douglas was to command in the north to protect Ulster and cover Dublin whilst the fleet and the Danes would assist Marlborough against Cork and Kinsale. Accordingly, on 7 September Douglas took five battalions of infantry, three troops of horse guards, a regiment of cavalry and one of dragoons from Tipperary, through Cashel towards the north to establish winter quarters. He soon sent reliable intelligence that the Jacobites intended a three-pronged winter strategy: Ulster was to be 'infested' and destabilized, principally through operations from Sligo; Sarsfield would advance towards Mullingar and destroy the countryside in the direction of Dublin; and the planned Danish winter quarters in eastern Munster would be pressurized. To consider this, Solms held a council of war at Tipperary on 12 September. Having selected Cashel as the army headquarters, it was decided to establish winter quarters along a frontier from Sligo to Youghal with the aim of restricting the availability of forage and provisions to the Jacobites in Connaught and western Munster. In Ulster, where Douglas was the overall commander, ten battalions of infantry, under Colonel Wolseley, and 12 squadrons of cavalry were to be based in counties Donegal, Fermanagh, Monaghan and Cavan. Douglas's detachment left the camp at Tipperary on the morning of 7 September. Further south, in Counties Longford, Westmeath, King's County and Queen's County, were eight battalions under Major General Kirke and ten squadrons of cavalry and dragoons commanded by Sir John Lanier. Further east small forces were quartered in Counties Louth and Meath to protect the country between Ulster and Dublin. Leinster and eastern Munster were occupied by nine battalions, under Ginkel and Scravenmoer, and 13 squadrons commanded by Count Nassau, billeted throughout Counties Tipperary, Kilkenny, Kildare, Carlow and Wicklow. Once Cork and Kinsale had been captured, the Danish Brigade would hold the extreme south of the line, which was expected to be the most active and dangerous sector: under Württemberg's overall command, Major General Tettau's eight battalions and Major General de la Forest's 11 cavalry squadrons were to be billeted in Counties Tipperary, Waterford, Wexford and Cork. Although the location of winter quarters was principally designed to protect the 'frontier', roughly the line of the Shannon, and dominate the no-man's-land between the cantonments of the two armies it was also intended to establish an effective Williamite presence in all conquered areas. A further consideration, which assumed an increasing importance over the winter, was security against raids, harassment and nuisance attacks from raparees, Jacobite deserters and criminal gangs. Sickness amongst the soldiers at Tipperary was increasing to unsustainable levels reviving memories of the Dundalk camp making it imperative for the army to go into winter quarters as quickly as possible. However, before this could be fully achieved, support had to be provided for Marlborough's projected attack on Cork and Kinsale.

General Ginkel, commanding the Dutch and Danish cavalry, was to occupy positions on the River Blackwater whence he could second Marlborough and intercept Jacobite relief expeditions from the Limerick area. Accordingly, Major Generals Scravenmoer and Tettau, commanding 1,200 cavalry and dragoons and two battalions of Danish infantry, marched towards Mallow on the Blackwater on 13 September. Part of the Danish infantry brigade was ordered to establish entrenched blocking positions at Cashel and Clonmel to hold any Jacobite probes aimed at diverting Williamite attention from Cork and Kinsale. If and when Marlborough was successful, the Danes would assume their winter billets.

The fleet carrying Tyrconnell, Lauzun and the French Brigade had barely cleared Galway when Berwick launched an offensive. Douglas's earlier intimations of this movement, namely that Sarsfield was intending to cross the Shannon and attack through either Mullingar or Thurles, subsequently hardened into definite information that a large Jacobite force had already reached Banagher Bridge. Only one detail in this intelligence was incorrect – although Sarsfield, a name which had achieved a degree of moral ascendancy over some of William's less well-motivated generals, accompanied the detachment he was not its commander. On 15 September, Berwick took 14 regiments of horse, dragoons and foot, numbering between 5,000 and 7,500 men, plus three field guns, across the Shannon at Banagher Bridge to besiege Birr Castle, a fortified manor house belonging to an Englishman, Sir Lawrence Parsons, which was garrisoned by 80 men from Colonel Zachariah Tiffin's Enniskillen infantry battalion under Captain John Corry, assisted by armed townsmen. According to Berwick's information, it was a soft target. Solms responded by ordering Kirke, with seven battalions of infantry, and Lanier, leading four regiments of cavalry and one of dragoons, from Tipperary towards Birr on 13 September. Douglas, who had halted near Portlaoise not daring to proceed further north in the face of such danger to his flank and communications, was instructed to lend additional support.

Horsemen appeared on Burkeshill, within 400 m of Birr, on the morning of 16 September sending the outposts scurrying back to the castle. The line gradually thickened as more Irish troops arrived. Captain Corry ordered Ensign Henry Ball to barricade himself into the church with 20 musketeers and man the steeple; Lieutenant Richard Newstead was sent down the lane towards Burkeshill with 20 men to investigate; and Ensign Hamilton remained with Corry in the castle. As the Protestant inhabitants hurried to the safety of the castle, Newstead held a shouted conversation with Captain Richard Oxburgh, commanding the advance troop of Irish horse, who told him that Berwick and Sarsfield were advancing with a train of artillery to capture Birr. Spotting the approach of the main column, Newstead withdrew to the castle. The Irish deployed on Burkeshill and sent cavalry to circle the town, herding all the cattle, whilst some soldiers began to plunder and burn houses that were out of musket range of Corry's infantrymen. When certain that the defenders were confined to the church and the castle, the main body advanced and summoned the garrison to surrender. Even though Corry knew that Birr Castle could not resist a siege, the red flag was hoisted in response.

Whilst Sarsfield attacked the castle with 160 infantry and the three field guns the majority of Berwick's troops stood off ready to counter the expected Williamite reaction. Taking casualties from the musketry of the castle's small garrison, Sarsfield's light cannon could make no impression on the walls and their effectiveness was further reduced when, during the afternoon, one of the barrels burst. News that Kirke and Lanier were approaching with a large force, plus the unexpectedly fierce resistance of the garrison, caused Berwick to order Sarsfield to suspend the attack and withdraw to a campsite 5 km west of Birr, covering the line of retreat to Banagher Bridge (17 September). The relief column, led by Lanier's cavalry, was five or six hours behind an advance guard of 300 horse and dragoons under Colonel John Coy. In the rear came Kirke's infantry. Marching via Thurles, which was then being fortified, and Roscrea, Kirke's infantry caught up with Lanier's cavalry 5 km short of Birr on 16 September where they received information that the castle was under attack and Berwick's detachment very numerous. Kirke and Lanier considered their combined forces too weak and asked Douglas to send reinforcements to Roscrea, Kirke returning thither to provide an escort. On the morning of 17 September, reinforced by some of Douglas's cavalry, Kirke advanced and camped 2 km south of Birr where he was closely observed by Berwick's pickets from adjacent high ground. Kirke drew out all his grenadiers, sent them through a bog and drove the scouts off the hills. Kirke moved through Birr on 18 September and camped 2 km beyond. Lieutenant Henry Kelly (Leveson's Dragoons) was sent to reconnoitre Berwick's position but his patrol was surrounded and captured although Kelly was later exchanged. In a textbook manoeuvre – blind the enemy by forcing away his scouts and patrols before manoeuvring – on the night of 18–19 September Berwick deployed a cavalry screen to drive in Kirke's out-guards and videttes before decamping. Confident that Kirke was not threatening his retreat, Berwick recrossed the Shannon at Banagher Bridge during 19 September. From the Irish point of view, the retreat was the highpoint – Kirke failed to read the signs and remained in temporary ignorance of what was happening – and many senior Jacobite officers were subsequently extremely critical of the feeble outcome and pusillanimous conduct of the majority of the operation. Kirke remained at Birr for 12 days and although his men were busy erecting simple fortifications they still had ample time to rob and plunder the Irish, many of whom had previously received protections. More raparees were thus created.

By 30 September the army had left Tipperary for winter quarters, Solms had returned to England and his fellow Dutchman, Lieutenant General Godard van

Reede, Baron van Ginkel, had taken over command transferring the headquarters to Kilkenny. Raparees were already active along the frontier, unsettling the soldiers, said Solms, by their numbers rather than courage. One of the consequences was that the Jacobites gained the upper hand in the intelligence war, an advantage increased by Williamite brutality in a hostile country. Informants and spies in the guise of merchants, deserters, clergy, travellers, sutlers and refugees wandered between the armies. No native Irish person could be trusted and rumours bounced and magnified between the numerous garrisons with the result that information reaching Ginkel was frequently contradictory. Solms reported to William on 14 September that it was very hard to acquire reliable information and even more difficult to recruit spies. Kirke and Lanier at Birr had been disadvantaged because Berwick had been accurately informed about their movements whilst they had to rely upon physical reconnaissance by their own scouts and patrols. Intelligence from raparees and local people was freely available to Jacobite troops resulting in the surprise and ambush of numerous small Williamite detachments, wagon trains and couriers. A provision and artillery convoy travelling from Clonmel to Carrick was attacked on 12 September and forced to return. From Dublin, the Lords Justices attempted to improve the situation. All Roman Catholics were ordered to remain within their home parishes and were only allowed to travel if going to market. On 26 September, Roman Catholics were forbidden to reside within 16 km of the frontier, although 'frontier' was not defined. All wives, children and dependants of anyone serving in the Jacobite Army, including soldiers who had been killed or taken prisoner, were to migrate west of the Shannon into Connaught and northern Munster by a given date. Many complied, escorted by Williamite troops, the penalty for refusal being prosecution as an enemy or, even worse, a spy. No Irish person who had received a protection from King William was to harbour anyone who had belonged to James's army or engaged in irregular operations. Whilst the Lords Justices sought to contain raparee activity through regulation, the Williamite troops exacerbated it by their behaviour in winter quarters. Although justices of the peace and deputy lieutenants endeavoured to provide markets from which soldiers could purchase locally produced meat, drink and other essentials, the soldiers much preferred to acquire them from the Roman Catholic population by requisition, theft, plunder and violence. It was cheaper and allowed the Protestant troops to indulge themselves against the native Irish. Regimental colonels indirectly connived at their men's indiscipline by encouraging the country people to bring food to pre-arranged places but seizing most for their own personal use. Little or none remained for the soldiers who were left no alternative but theft and plunder in which scant distinction was made between Protestant and Roman Catholic Irish and none between protected and unprotected. Whilst the Williamites plundered by day the raparees, growing desperate for supplies from a diminishing territorial base, robbed equally indiscriminately by night. Raparee activity, apparently co-ordinated by Lord Clancarty, was particularly strong in County Cork. A captain in Leveson's Dragoons, garrisoning Youghal, received intelligence of a large movement of raparees from Cork towards Carrick. With 50 dragoons and some infantry from the garrison, he attacked their rearguard, inflicting 40 casualties. Although much has been written about how the rise of the standing army led to improvements in military discipline and lessened the adverse impact of soldiers upon civilians, it also enabled the deliberate relaxation of that discipline to become a weapon of war. The devastation of the Palatinate by French troops during the winter of 1688–9 was perhaps the most egregious example but the activities of the Williamite Army in Ireland during 1690 and 1691 were similar. The Enniskillen troops, who regarded cattle raiding and humiliating the Roman Catholics as a way of life, advanced from Cavan between 16 and 19 September under the very walls of Athlone where they seized most of the garrison's cattle from pasture. The Jacobite Army also contributed: Berwick conducted a scorched earth policy in northern Munster during September and October 1690 to inhibit Williamite operations towards Limerick and the Shannon estuary.[10]

16

Cork and Kinsale

Major Generals Scravenmoer and Tettau sent Colonel Moritz Melchior von Donop, commander of the second regiment of Danish cavalry, on 16 September to burn the bridge at Mallow and reconnoitre Mallow Castle. Having performed these tasks, Donop returned the next day to report that he had discovered a large body of raparees, perhaps as many as 3,000, close to Mallow. Clearly, they had to be dispersed before the Danes could secure their positions along the Blackwater and so Scravenmoer and Tettau planned an operation in which a Danish major, leading 100 cavalry and 50 dragoons, acted as bait. As expected, the major's party was ambushed but the raparees were then utterly routed by a main body which followed at a discreet distance. The raparees lost, reportedly, about 300 men and it was noted that the plunder included many silver-hilted swords and fine horses.

In pursuance of the Cromwell-Coote-Gorges strategic model for the rapid reduction of Ireland, for some months the English government had been considering the capture of the Munster ports. Descents, or amphibious assaults on enemy coasts, were a long-established feature of English strategy and the Marquis of Carmarthen wrote to William on 23 June 1690 reminding him that such an option should always be considered, especially if the French fleet did not venture that summer into the English Channel. On 7 August 1690, just prior to the siege of Limerick, John Churchill, First Earl of Marlborough, put before the English Privy Council a plan to seize Cork and Kinsale. The timing, if not the content, was audacious because it involved stripping England of most of its regular garrison and committing a substantial portion of the Royal Navy when the French had departed from Torbay only three days previously and the danger of invasion remained. In addition, William was stranded on the far side of the Irish Sea. Carmarthen was firmly against the idea but the Earl of Nottingham and Admiral Russell were in favour. Queen Mary referred it to William and Marlborough wrote separately adumbrating the strategic benefits. William had no love for Marlborough, whom he regarded as a highly competent soldier but a treacherous, slippery, conniving politician who had been instrumental in bringing down one king and, given half an excuse, would repeat the exercise. However, the proposal reached William two days after Sarsfield's raid on Ballyneety, which had substantially reduced the probability of taking Limerick and ending the war in 1690. Anxious to salvage something from the latter stages of the campaign and equally keen to make sure that the war would definitely be brought to a conclusion 1691, William agreed. Marlborough, as he explained, would have to bring his own artillery and ammunition as there was none spare in Ireland although cavalry support could be provided. Marlborough left London for Portsmouth on 26 August, carrying a warrant to embark six battalions of regular infantry (Charles Trelawney, John Churchill, Ferdinando Hastings, John Hales, Sir David Colyear and Edward Fitzpatrick), plus two regiments of marines (Prince George of Denmark and the Earl of Torrington). Marlborough and 5,000 men were aboard 42 warships, ten fire-ships and 17 Dutch transports at Portsmouth by 30 August but adverse winds delayed their departure for a fortnight. By that time, William had returned to England removing one of the hazards of the operation and helping to calm Carmarthen's nerves. Marlborough finally sailed on 17 September carrying instructions from Carmarthen that, should the operation fail, he was to transfer the troops to Solms's command and return to England.[1]

Cork, noted Thomas Phillips in 1686, was the easiest place through which to invade Ireland. Whilst the Great Island in the centre of Cork harbour was the obvious base for an invading force of 10,000 men, there were so many other islands and channels that it was impossible to defend them all. The best that could be done was to position blockhouses and booms at the entrances to Passage West and Passage East. Cork City, surrounded by a stone wall, was a narrow settlement, essentially one long north–south axis, Main Street, occupying the centre of an island between two channels of the River Lee, a stone bridge connecting it to the northern suburb of Shandon. Outside the city, to east and west, Cork's island was a bog. It could never be made into a powerful fortress because it was dominated by high ground to the south whilst Shandon Castle, on the north bank of the River Lee, was also overlooked by hills. The strongest outwork was Catt Fort, situated on a rise to the south occupying the site of the present-day St Bride's Church. The site of the Elizabethan Old Fort, standing on the mainland just to the south-west of the city next to St Fin Barre's Cathedral, was even lower than that of Catt Fort and became untenable should the latter succumb. Berwick considered Cork indefensible and ordered Governor Roger MacElligott to burn the town and retire with his garrison into County Kerry. Instead, MacElligott either delayed in obeying these orders, or ignored them, and was trapped by Marlborough's sudden arrival and rapid advance.[2]

Towards nightfall on 20 September Marlborough's convoy made the coast of Ireland and lay-to until daybreak when it stood in for Crosshaven and the mouth of Cork harbour. Two blockhouses guarded the entrance, each armed with four cannon, which fired at the approaching fleet. Two frigates were detached to bombard the blockhouses causing their garrisons to abandon the guns and run away. At 12:00 on 21 September, the ships came up to Passage West where the narrows were protected by a further blockhouse but Marlborough landed a small vanguard before nightfall and this position was also evacuated. The corps disembarked on 22 September and began to march the 10 km towards Cork, probably rather unsteadily having been cooped up on board for three weeks, camping overnight within 2 km of the city. As soon as he came ashore, Marlborough sent an express to Scravenmoer and Tettau asking them to join him immediately with 1,200 cavalry and dragoons plus two battalions of Danish foot. Dutch and Huguenot infantry would, he hoped, follow. Scravenmoer needed no encouragement having already reported to Solms that supplies along the Blackwater were exhausted; even without Marlborough's order, he would have had to move to another area. Scravenmoer marched on 22 September reaching Cork on the following day (23 September), camping on a hill above the Water Mills on the north bank of the Lee. Tettau remained on the Blackwater to intercept any Jacobite relief attempts from the direction of Limerick. On 23 September, Marlborough formally summoned the governor to surrender but he responded by hanging out the red flag and firing several guns. Marlborough was vulnerable having landed with insufficient infantry and only a handful of horses. So, on 24 September, 600 seamen came ashore to help the two marine regiments tow the artillery into position, 'which they did with great cheerfulness, and the Duke of Grafton at the head of them'. Württemberg then sent Dean Rowland Davies, whose local knowledge later proved invaluable, first to Scravenmoer and then Marlborough to let them know that he was marching from Caher, County Tipperary, for Cork with 4,000 infantry. As rumours were flying that Berwick intended to relieve Cork, Scravenmoer sent Davies back to ask Württemberg, most respectfully, to hurry.[3]

During the afternoon of 23 September, Scravenmoer's adjutant, Reke, returned from Cobh on Great Island with orders from Marlborough to send a party of horse over the water to support his infantry on its march towards Cork. In the evening, the Reverend Davies guided the cavalry detachment over the River Lee at the ford beneath the church of Curragheen – the Cork garrison cheered, thinking them Berwick's relief column – across the Bishop's Brook at Carrigrohane Bridge to Cork Lough where he left them to meet up with Marlborough's approaching infantry, whose drums could be heard in the distance. At about 15:00, Scravenmoer pulled some cannon on to Fair Hill and started to bring the small forts near Shandon Castle under fire as a prelude to an attack. No sooner were his men deployed than the Jacobites deserted both forts, one of which was a substantial work on a hill comprising a gun tower, ravelin and communication trench, and Shandon Castle before setting fire to the 'fine and large' suburb of Shandon and withdrawing over the stone bridge into Cork. All the high ground that overlooked the city from the north was thus abandoned without a fight and the Danes were allowed to encamp close to the North Gate and the stone bridge over the northerly channel of the Lee. From the captured gun-tower redoubt, the streets of Cork could be engaged with long-range musketry.

Württemberg marched his Danes 20 km to Kilworth on 24 September and Marlborough's troops began the construction of a battery overlooking Catt Fort and the Elizabethan Fort, sometimes known as the citadel. The Danes moved through Fermoy to Rathcormack on the next day, joining a party of Scravenmoer's horse that had been sent from Cork to escort them; on Sunday 26 September they reached the still-smoking ruins of Shandon suburb. Although Marlborough was in overall command, he and Württemberg now directed separate camps and corps, one in the south and the other to the north. At 01:00 on 25 September, the garrison launched a sally against Marlborough's positions but it was easily driven back, the Jacobites losing about 20 men. Several deserters came into Marlborough's camp who reported that two regiments had arrived in Cork from Kinsale on 20 September increasing governor Colonel Roger MacElligott's garrison to about 4,000 men. During 26 September, Marlborough brought all his troops into camp 2½ km from Cork. Some minor operations took place in the evening: two small islands, from which a man could wade to Cork at ebb tide, were attacked; whilst a detachment of 1,000 infantry took possession of several advantageous positions on the higher ground within musket-shot of the town. There was no action, the defenders prematurely evacuating all of these posts. Marlborough's battery, mounting six cannon, was finished during the evening and opened fire on Catt Fort and the Elizabethan Fort, whilst Tettau's guns at Shandon Castle bombarded the city.

Catt Fort was vacated on 27 September. Marlborough immediately took possession and used it as a battery from which to fire mortar bombs into the city and solid shot at the Elizabethan Fort. Acting on the advice of the Reverend Davies, Scravenmoer, who had moved his cavalry headquarters to Gill Abbey south-west of the city, caused boards to be laid across the open beams in the steeple of St Fin Barre's Cathedral to create a platform from which snipers could harass the garrison of the Elizabethan Fort. Lieutenant Horatio Townshend (Earl of Torrington's Marines) led some musketeers up the stairs and 'did very good execution'. Davies also took the trouble to ensure that a stream was diverted thus disabling a corn-grinding water mill within the city. Ships arrived at the Red Abbey, on the southern channel of the River Lee, during the morning and unloaded three 36-pounder cannon that were quickly dug into a battery to play upon the eastern city wall. Guns of this weight and calibre soon brought a section of the wall crashing down and, anxious not to waste time, Marlborough arranged for an immediate assault on the defenders' positions before the breach preparatory to a storm: that night (27–28 September) Danish infantry would attack through the East Marsh from the north and his own infantry from the south. However, in the evening the garrison beat a parley releasing the Protestant

Bishop of Cork, Dr Edward Wetenhall, and around 1,300 Protestants as an earnest of good intent. A truce was concluded until the morning of 28 September and the attack was accordingly postponed, which was fortunate because the Jacobites had 400 men on East Marsh, but subsequent negotiations were unable to agree terms for a general surrender.

During the night a captain, one lieutenant and 40 men were posted in the brickyard near Gill Abbey to prevent any of the garrison slipping away through the bog. Around midnight, despite the truce, some made the attempt but Captain Swiney and four men were killed, Captain MacCarthy badly wounded and taken prisoner and the rest forced back. The truce already broken, the bombardment resumed on the morning of 28 September, perceptively widening the breach; when defenders dared to show themselves to either side of the collapsed section the parapet was raked by field guns and musketry from Catt Fort. The double assault on the breach was re-scheduled for 13:00, the next ebb tide. Danes, Dutch and Brandenburgers under Württemberg accompanied by four English battalions commanded by Brigadier Charles Churchill, crossed the Lee and entered the East Marsh, on either side of modern St Patrick's Street. The East Marsh, comprising two islands, was separated from the city wall by a river channel, 6 m wide, whose waters served as a moat and its bank a natural counterscarp. The north island, which was attacked by the Danes, accommodated a number of buildings and gardens, plus the New Customs House, and was really a suburb but one which the garrison had neglected to destroy. Some of the houses were within 40 paces of the wall, backing on to the river channel. The southern island was larger and, except for the civility of a bowling green, contained only a few cottages. The English attack was led by 200 grenadiers under Colonel Richard Savage, First Viscount Colchester, seconded by 300 fusiliers, who waded up to their armpits through the river and then advanced across the deep mud of the East Marsh. The Duke of Grafton; Lord William O'Brien; Colonel Sir Bevil Grenville; Captain Wolfran Cornwall RN, commander of HMS *Swallow*; Captain John Leighton RN, commander of HMS *St Albans*; Captain John Neville RN, commander of HMS *Henrietta*; and Captain Stafford Fairborne RN accompanied the grenadiers as volunteers. Their intention was to drive in the Jacobite outposts on the south island, seize positions opposite the breach and capture the bank of the little river channel. Success, it was hoped, would either induce the garrison to surrender or establish a platform for an assault on the breach. The English vanguard crossed open ground to within 20 m of the breach where they occupied a house close to the wall and lined the bank bordering the river channel. During this approach, the Duke of Grafton was shot on the point of the shoulder, an injury that later proved mortal. HMS *Salamander*, a sixth rate, and another naval vessel, tided up the southern channel of the Lee and anchored by the East Marsh so that their cannon could fire on the breach.

More is known about the Danish attack because Lieutenant Colonel Hans Frederik Munchgaar left a detailed account. Assisted by one lieutenant colonel, two majors and ten captains, Munchgaar led 400 musketeers and 100 grenadiers across the northern branch of the Lee at ebb tide to occupy the northerly island on the East Marsh. Their target was a stone bridge across the river channel leading to a small gate in the city walls. Munchgaar successfully passed the Lee at 13:00 and drove the 200 Jacobite soldiers on the island out of the houses towards the bridge. Twenty or 30 of the retreating Jacobites jumped into the moat and others were left dead on the bridge but the main garrison manned the walls above and to either side of the little gate halting the Danes with musketry. Munchgaar positioned his men under cover amidst the houses and gardens and warded off a sally launched across the bridge. Had they demonstrated more resolution, the Jacobites on the island could have inflicted severe damage on Munchgaar's detachment: even against a weak defence he lost six dead and 22 wounded. A fire fight then ensued between the Danes in the houses and gardens and the defenders on the city walls. Some of Munchgaar's men had only four or five rounds of ammunition left from their standard allocation of 24 and so replenishment had to be sent from the camp, a most unusual event in contemporary warfare. At length, after three hours, the English to the south took their objective but it was difficult to persuade the Danes to cease firing when a truce was arranged because they thought that the cessation applied only to the English front rather than their own.

Several truces were made and broken during the night as the Irish high command debated its options. The Earl of Clancarty advocated burning the town prior to a breakout by the entire garrison but Governor MacElligott countered by emphasising the horrors consequent upon a successful storm and assured these more vigorous spirits that favourable terms were achievable. The Earl of Tyrone and Lieutenant Colonel Philip Ricautt (Clancarty's Foot) came out under a white flag and quickly agreed articles of surrender on behalf of MacElligott: shortage of gunpowder was the official reason for capitulation. The Elizabethan Fort would be handed over within one hour and the city at 08:00 on 29 September. All those in arms in the garrison would become prisoners of war and all remaining Protestants would be released in the evening. When Cork surrendered the Williamites gained the port, harbour and city, much of County Cork, which was as big as any two other Irish counties joined together, and southern County Limerick, substantial, productive and rich tracts of land, as yet relatively untouched by war, ideal for winter quarters. With nearly all the north, east and south coast ports in Williamite hands, the French could only send assistance into either Galway or Limerick, simplifying the Royal Navy's blockading mission. This was achieved for the loss of less than 50 men. In Württemberg's opinion, the capture of Cork compensated for the disappointment before Limerick.

On the morning of 29 September, immediately after the surrender had taken effect, 'loose persons' and several seamen, who arrived by longboat, entered Cork through the breach to plunder houses belonging to Roman Catholics. However, as soon as the stone bridge leading to the South Gate had been repaired, Marlborough, Württemberg and Scravenmoer rode into the city and restored order. During the afternoon all Roman Catholics were ordered, on pain of death, to repair to the East Marsh where all those who had been under arms were stripped of their weapons and equipment and placed under guard. Officers were lodged in the county court house, amongst them the Earls of Tyrone and Clancarty, Colonel MacElligott and Lieutenant Colonel Ricautt. Later, they were shipped to England aboard Marlborough's vessels. Before they sailed, carelessness caused the magazine of HMS *Breda* to catch fire and the ship blew up; some of the Irish officer-prisoners died along with most of the crew. On arrival in England, Tyrone, Clancarty, Baron Cahir and MacElligott were imprisoned in the Tower of London. The common soldiers remained on the East Marsh without provisions for four or five days, subsisting from the carcasses of dead horses. Many succumbed to exposure, starvation and poisoning before they were removed to overcrowded gaols, houses and churches in which there was insufficient room for them all to lie down together on the bare floors. Numbers died daily as they lay in their own excrement amidst animal and human corpses. The Roman Catholic civilian inhabitants, although offered safety and protection under the terms of surrender, were stripped, had their goods and houses seized, and many were evicted from the city. Captain John Lowther (John Hales's Foot) with an ensign and 50 men escorted about 200 of the Cork prisoners to Clonmel in December. Some 16 who collapsed on the march were shot where they lay. Major General Dorrington demanded that Ginkel court-martial Lowther for murder but he retained his commission being promoted major on 31 October 1693.[4]

Kinsale harbour, the estuary of the Bandon River, was not the equal of Cork or, indeed, many other deep water inlets and fjords in south-west Ireland because it was narrow and contained several dangerous shoals. There was not even an advantage in wind direction: a breeze that carried ships clear of Kinsale did the same in the region's other havens. However, it was further south and west than Cork and consequently useful for vessels in need of shelter from Atlantic storms or emergency replenishment of victuals and water. In 1686, Thomas Phillips noted that the old, rotten boom required replacement. The inner harbour was protected by the Old, or James's, Fort on the Castle Park headland, and the Charles, or New, Fort, which dated from the early 1670s, opposite on the east bank of the estuary. Although both positions were regular, pentagonal, modern and star-shaped they were really coastal defence batteries – Charles Fort mounted 94 cannon – dominated by high ground and vulnerable from the land side. Charles Fort's eastern and north-eastern fronts looked impressive but were actually very weak lacking any outworks beyond the rampart, although two streams gave some protection and channelled the axis of attack. Kinsale town was defended on its landward side by a rampart reinforced by towers and bastions but, again, it was commanded by adjacent hills. The town wall was probably in bad condition: in 1674 or early 1675, two sections had fallen down from lack of maintenance.[5] The garrison had been weakened by the dispatch of two regiments to reinforce Cork on 20 September and numbered about 2,000 men.

Anxious not to waste time because the campaigning season was waning rapidly and the weather had turned thoroughly wet, as soon as terms had been agreed at Cork Brigadier Edward Villiers rode to Kinsale with 500 cavalry to summon the garrison to surrender. The governor, Sir Edward Scott, rejected the summons and ordered his garrison to set fire to the town. Scott and the majority of his men then marched into Charles Fort but 450 were sent across the Bandon River to garrison the Old Fort. Seeing what was happening, Villiers's cavalrymen galloped into the town and extinguished the flames before a single house had been wholly destroyed. Leaving Colonel John Hales to govern Cork with a garrison of 200 men and the assistance of the reinstated Protestant magistrates, Marlborough's main force marched on 1 October camping overnight at Fivemilebridge where he received information from cavalry scouts that Scott had abandoned the town and withdrawn into the forts. On 2 October the main body reached Kinsale to join Villiers's cavalry in a camp close to Charles Fort whilst seven warships sailed into the harbour from Cork.

Friction between the super-egos of Marlborough and Württemberg had been present but contained at Cork because they had conducted their own operations against the north and south of the city; even the final attack had been two separate undertakings. On the march to Kinsale, they agreed to share the overall command on alternate days. In the evening they also decided to launch an immediate attack on the Old Fort because, reportedly, the revetment was unfinished and the garrison numbered only 150 men. Major General Tettau and 800 men crossed the Bandon River in boats at 22:00 on 2 October landing, so as not to alert the garrison, about 1,200 m south of the Old Fort near the ruins of Kingroan Castle before edging slowly and quietly into position ready to storm at daybreak on 3 October. However, the suspicions of governor Lieutenant Colonel Cornelius O'Driscoll were sufficiently aroused for him to order a reconnaissance of the southern front but nothing inauspicious was noticed so the men were stood down and drawn back into the main enceinte. At dawn Tettau came marching down the hill directly towards the southern front. Alarmed and surprised, the garrison rushed to man the outworks and managed to engage Tettau's approaching column with some cannon. Tettau was equally surprised to see so many men, 300 more than anticipated. At this point, according to a Danish account, the English infantry began to waver before the cannon fire but Tettau brought through the Danes who continued the advance. They attacked in two columns, headed by grenadiers, who hurled their bombs, rushed through the outworks and came up to the main wall. Scaling ladders were thrown against the ramparts and the leading soldiers began to climb. O'Driscoll and several of his senior officers were killed whilst fighting, pistols in hand, on the 'little bastions', and the leaderless and increasingly demoralized garrison fell back into an old donjon in the centre of the fort, which was armed with 12 iron guns. Unluckily, the fort's gunpowder magazine then blew up, killing 80 men, shattering the donjon's iron gate and throwing the garrison into confusion. Seizing the moment, Tettau urged his men forward, cutting down many of the defenders and taking several prisoners. The 200 survivors in the donjon then hung out the white flag and surrendered as prisoners of war. At a total cost of 60 casualties, Tettau had taken a fort garrisoned by 450 men and armed with 46 guns. Marlborough was in a hurry to complete the capture of Kinsale by taking Charles Fort because the weather was discouraging, sickness had broken out amongst the soldiers and both provisions and ammunition were scarce, especially amongst the Danish Corps. Later on 3 October, he summoned Sir Edward Scott in Charles Fort to surrender but he replied that reapplication might be appropriate in one month's time.

Tettau had been ordered to storm rather than besiege the Old Fort, not just to hasten operations, but also because the heavy, battering cannon were still at Cork. The siege train, consisting of eight 24-ponders, eight 18-pounders, six 12-pounders, eight nine-pounders and 13 mortars, was supposed to have been brought round to Kinsale by sea but the English transport commissary missed the wind and it was decided to haul the guns overland. 'Ten long, Irish miles' were made worse by very wet weather and a shortage of draught animals, the latter problem partially solved after officers had been ordered to lend their wagon horses and personal mounts. Even so, the first heavy cannon did not appear until 11 October. Charles Fort was a tougher proposition than the Old Fort, more heavily fortified and strongly garrisoned: there was no alternative to a formal siege. During the evening of 4 October the garrison launched a sally aimed at levelling some hedges and ditches close to the foot of the glacis but Major General La Forest advanced with the main guard and drove them back, at a cost of some casualties amongst the Danish cavalry led by Lieutenant Colonel Karl Gustav von Gam. Towards evening, ground was broken and the trenches formally opened, the Danes attacking on the left and the English on the right, the few light field guns evenly distributed. To hasten the siege Marlborough and Engineer-General Cambon wanted to put all resources into one axis of attack but Württemberg maintained that this would dishonour the Danes and they should be allowed to mount their own discreet operation. Regardless of martial imperatives and Marlborough's entreaties, with Major General Tettau acting as engineer, Württemberg pressed ahead.

The trenches zigzagged forward on 5 October, as quickly as the heavy rain would allow. As usual, work in the siege excavations was dangerous and a number of English and Danish sappers lost their lives during the day. Third Engineer Claudius Barden, 'a fine mathematician', was shot dead in the English sector on 6 October. From 7 to 10 October the trenches crept closer to the counterscarp, continuous heavy rain hampering progress, until the heads of the saps were about 50 m from the foot of the glacis. Six 24-pounders were finally dragged forward on 11 October to form a breaching battery on the Danish front. They opened fire at daybreak on 12 October but the defenders promptly replied from their own heavy guns, killing some of the Danish gun crews. Württemberg personally commanded on the gun platforms to make sure that his artillerymen maintained a continuous barrage. It was a dangerously exposed position for a corps commander, especially when, because of carelessness, a barrel of gunpowder caught fire and exploded, killing four men, wounding eight and relieving Captain Joachim Tunner of his greatcoat. Two mortars were mounted amidst the English positions, firing all that day and the following night into the interior of the fort. Two more 24-pounders were added to the Danish breaching battery during the night of 12–13 October. Sustained, accurate fire, supervised by Dutch gunners – the Danish battery of eight 24-pounders fired an average of 80 rounds per hour – dismounted the garrison's heavy cannon. Enfiladed from a number of points, the defenders abandoned the counterscarp opposite the Danish attack and fell back to the main enceinte. Officers knowledgeable and competent in the techniques of siege warfare would then have erected traverses across the ramparts but the Irish defenders did nothing. During the night of 13–14 October, Württemberg arranged for a feint attack against the ramparts opposite the Danish sector to test the reactions and spirit of the garrison. They were found to be very alert and, thinking it a general assault, threw hand grenades and bombs and engaged the attackers with musketry. The Danes drew back having lost two men killed and four wounded. During 14 October, the ramparts began to collapse under the weight of cannon fire, the falling masonry destroying the palisades at the foot of the walls. Mortar fire stopped on the English sector when the supply of bombs was exhausted, the tubes standing idle as they waited for artillery wagons to make a third round trip to Cork to collect replenishments. The English formed a battery of three 12-pounders on 15 October but these were not heavy enough to create a breach; indeed, their fire was absorbed by a breastwork, or tenaille, no more than 1 m from the wall. By noon, the breach on the Danish front looked wide enough to storm and highly visible preparations were made for a general assault on the following day. With the walls breached and a storm imminent, at 14:00 on 15 October Scott hung out the white flag and asked for a parley. Hostages were exchanged and Marlborough allowed an honourable capitulation. The garrison of about 1,200 men marched out through the Danish breach on 17 October, headed by the 70-year-old Scott, and was conducted to Limerick by 50 Danish horsemen under Rittmeister Friedrich Bremer. The garrison had lost about 200 men and many of the survivors were in poor health. Considerable stocks of provisions were found in the fort, enough to have supported 1,000 men for a year: 1,000 barrels of wheat; 1,000 barrels of salted beef; 40 tuns of claret and stocks of brandy, sack and strong beer. Brigadier Charles Churchill, Marlborough's brother, was appointed governor. News of the fall of Kinsale took some time to spread. At the beginning of November a French merchantman laden with salt and brandy anchored beneath the guns of Charles Fort unaware of the change of ownership. She was boarded and made a prize. His work done, fame secured, self-advertisement completed, and the grateful thanks of his sovereign due, Marlborough sailed for England on 18 October. Success had mainly derived from the fact that, unusually, Marlborough had commanded both naval and land forces.[6]

During his absence in France, Tyrconnell's position was undermined. A great meeting of the Jacobite nobility, bishops and senior officers, convened at the end of September in Limerick, decided that Tyrconnell's arrangements for the government of Ireland were illegal. The ancient constitution and laws, they concluded, required Ireland to be governed by a king, viceroy or deputy 'now in the kingdom'. Because this was no longer the case, Ireland was at liberty to choose the form of government most appropriate to the present circumstances. Naturally, the assembly took advantage of these arguments to depose Tyrconnell's supporters. Sarsfield, in company with Major General William Dorrington and Colonel Simon Luttrell, attended upon Berwick on 30 September to explain politely that the power vested in him by Tyrconnell lacked legal foundation. Sugar was applied by graciously requesting Berwick to continue as commander-in-chief provided that he accepted absolutely and without question advice tendered by a council of colonels. Two 'able persons' would help with civil administration in every province. Finally, the assembly had decided to send envoys to James to explain its conduct. Berwick's response was predictable and truculent. Although he admitted that the authority vested in him by Tyrconnell might be construed as illegal, he refused to accept any other authority over the nation and army. He would continue to command according to his former commission as lieutenant general. As for the great assembly, in turn he questioned its legitimacy and ordered the members, who had met without his permission, to disperse. The deputies replied that, technically, there was no Irish army because King James, following the Boyne, had ordered them to shift for themselves, which many assumed to be an order to disband after the manner of the notoriously vague and ambiguous instruction to Lord Feversham that had brought about the disbandment of the royal army in England at Uxbridge in 1688. Thus, they had tacit permission from the king either to submit to William or defend themselves. If Berwick would not accept the command of the army on those terms, then other arrangements would have to be made. This was clearly too difficult for Berwick's rather limited intellect and he sought counsel.

On the following morning, 1 October, Sarsfield found Berwick 'more pliant'. In fact, he said that he agreed to all the proposals. Believing the matter settled, Sarsfield departed for Athlone where there seemed some danger that Lieutenant General Douglas was about to make another attempt upon the town. With Sarsfield gone, Berwick slipped back into his former ways. He insisted that the petition to James, which the envoys would convey, included a phrase stating that the assembly was satisfied with Tyrconnell's management of the war and general conduct. He knew that they would never agree to this because they intended to impeach Tyrconnell in order to expose his secret dealings with both James and Louis. Berwick also hoped that the assembly would disband, the officers returning to their commands and the bishops to their dioceses. Winter weather would then, with luck, prevent the envoys from sailing to France and the whole initiative would lose momentum and atrophy. In the meantime, the issue might be clarified by some new instructions from James formally appointing him viceroy.

Berwick's machinations were duplicitous, irritating and obvious. Sarsfield was recalled from Athlone. The assembly passed a second resolution erecting a new government that excluded Berwick, Tyrconnell and all their supporters. However, Berwick found an intelligent ally in the Scot, Brigadier Thomas Maxwell, who realized that the Irish were deadly serious and advised Berwick to play along with them whilst secretly and immediately sending his own envoys to France to inform James and Tyrconnell of the true state of affairs, making sure that they arrived before the assembly's representatives. Thus, when Sarsfield arrived back in Limerick, he found Berwick, once again, amenable and obliging. He signed the credentials for the assembly's envoys, a bishop and three officers, and the petition that they would carry. He agreed to the appointment of two bishops and eight nobles to join with the 12 previously appointed by Tyrconnell to manage provincial affairs. Finally, he consented to admit all general officers to the council of war, a major dispensation because Tyrconnell had only consulted privately with his own supporters amongst the senior officers. Once all this had been achieved, the assembly felt confident that Louis would respond by sending significant assistance. The assembly's envoys – Dr John Molony, the Roman Catholic Bishop of Cork; Colonel Simon Luttrell; Brigadier Henry Luttrell; and Colonel Nicholas Purcell – duly left for France whilst Berwick sent Brigadier Maxwell, with secret instructions, to present his version of events at St Germain-en-Laye and Versailles.

The four assembly envoys boarded ship in Limerick harbour but were delayed by contrary winds for so long that it was well into winter before they came into St Malo. Almost simultaneously, Tyrconnell was embarking at Brest, a royal commission as lord lieutenant of Ireland in his pocket. The envoys had not been long clear of the Shannon when a ship from France docked at Limerick bearing an instruction from James to Berwick, solicited by Tyrconnell, that no envoys were to be allowed to leave Ireland. It also said that the Irish could give no better earnest of their allegiance and loyalty to James than by submitting to Tyrconnell's government. This was a most unwelcome development to the native Irish who thought that James and Tyrconnell still wished to return them to the English yoke whereas James and Tyrconnell feared that, given French assistance, the Old Irish might re-conquer the country and retain it as a separate and independent state, leaning on France for support. The only remaining hope was that the assembly's four envoys would be able to persuade James to adopt a different policy. However, Brigadier Maxwell beat them to St Germain-en-Laye and laid out Berwick's position and version of events. When he finally received the four envoys, James initially treated them as mutineers and threatened imprisonment. Calmer second thoughts prevailed when he realized that such action might well propel the Irish to reach terms with William and then join the Grand Alliance. Instead he lectured them about the inadvisability of impeaching Tyrconnell or saying anything to the French court that might prejudice Tyrconnell's position. Even Queen Mary was heard to say that if James was happy with Tyrconnell she could not see why the Irish should be discontent. The envoys, of course, did not see why their cause should face utter ruin in order to assist James's personal political ends. Therefore, they felt themselves honour-bound to represent their side of the story truthfully. Ireland was prepared to hold out to the last thus preventing William from redeploying all his resources into the Netherlands. James should reconquer Ireland, establish the Roman Catholic faith, and then use Ireland as a base from which to recapture his English throne. They did not waste time criticizing Tyrconnell because they had no wish further to alienate James but begged him to ask Louis to provide material aid plus a French general to command the army. Having thus prepared the ground, James presented the envoys to Louis who was already well acquainted with all the arguments and all the answers. The estrangement of James and Tyrconnell was not in his interest yet he wanted the war in Ireland to continue. Very clearly though, with the Irish falling out amongst themselves, there was every danger that the Irish war effort would implode. There were also doubts about the military competence of the Irish leadership: Sarsfield was a dashing cavalry leader but no army commander; Berwick young, inexperienced and indecisive; whilst Tyrconnell was unwell and heavily compromised. If Louis was to exercise control over developments then he needed Frenchmen in the senior command positions. Accordingly, he agreed to Lieutenant General Charles Chalmont de Saint Ruhe, more usually St Ruth, taking command of the Irish Army with secret instructions to send an accurate assessment of the situation which would inform Louis's decision on whether to send material aid. St Ruth was supported by lieutenant generals Jean de Bonnac, Marquis d'Usson and Philibert-Emmanuel de Froullay, Chevalier de Tessé. Major General Henri de la La Tour Montfort accompanied them as prospective governor of Limerick.[7]

17

A war of posts and ambuscades

By the end of the 1690 campaign the Jacobite Army may have shrunk to 12,000 men but this was probably an over-pessimistic estimate. A French muster of the troops quartered in County Clare in November 1690 listed the four infantry battalions at 422, 458, 524 and 526 rank and file whilst the two cavalry regiments had 328 and 322 troopers. Even in the heady days of summer 1689, said John Stevens, Jacobite foot battalions in the field rarely comprised more than 400 men. Most of the Jacobite forces were contained within northern Munster and Connaught although County Kerry was occupied by three regiments which maintained land communications with Limerick.[1] Over 10,000 cartloads of corn had been sent from County Kerry into Connaught by the end of December. Kerry's climate was vile and mountains and strong castles favoured the defence so the Danish Corps postponed its reduction until the spring. Technically, the remainder of Ireland was occupied by the Williamites though their grip over the frontier region between the two armies was frequently tenuous. In fact, raparees and irregulars could cause mayhem virtually anywhere, even as far east as Kells and County Kildare. Only Ulster was firmly under control.

In the disappointment and demoralization following the failure at Limerick, the army had retreated too far east ceding an excessive amount of territory. Instead of taking winter quarters in towns, villages and castles along the Shannon, where the troops could have been comfortably accommodated, provisioned and supported, Ginkel had to lodge his men in a random assortment of settlements along a front which was open, undefended and mostly undefined by militarily significant features. By holding all the crossings on the middle and lower Shannon, the Jacobites possessed the initiative to operate over the river against Williamite cantonments. To deter raids into their own winter quarters, during October troops from Limerick, County Clare and County Kerry burned many of the towns and villages in Counties Cork and Tipperary 'that had hitherto escaped' to create a *cordon sanitaire*. It was rumoured that Berwick, who was in overall control of these operations, had dined in Charleville House, County Cork, built by the late Earl of Orrery. When he had finished his meal he ordered the house to be torched and remained to see it reduced to ashes. Kilworth and Mallow were similarly treated. Damage was considerable and Berwick was warned that Irish prisoners, including officers, would be burned alive if the destruction continued.

In counties under Williamite occupation the reforming of the Protestant militia began in July 1690 and accelerated throughout the winter. By the summer of 1691 it was reportedly 30,000-strong, although only half were effective, the City of Dublin producing the largest contingent: on parade to mark William's birthday on 4 November 1690, it comprised 2,500 infantry, two troops of cavalry and two of dragoons, all decently uniformed and armed. A general 'regimentation' was introduced during December 1690 and January 1691. An infantry battalion was established at eight 60-man companies, plus one troop of 50 cavalry, a total of 530 men. In May 1691 the Lords Justices appointed regular army officers to supervise the militia. Major Thomas Stroud was assigned to County Cork; Major Thomas Brook to County Wexford; and Captain Thomas Phillips to County Wicklow. Colonel Adam Murray, Lieutenant Colonel Toby Caulfield, Major Benjamin Tichborne and Cornet Joslin Meade were active in Ulster. In May 1691, to compensate for Ginkel's shortage of infantry, two regiments of the Ulster militia and two from County Cork were made available for service with the field army but this was unusual and the militia normally helped the regulars by taking over the tedious chores of garrisoning castles and strongpoints, escorting convoys and prisoners and, a duty loved above all others, hunting raparees. Composed of the wealthier and more industrious English and Scots-Irish Protestants, during Cromwell's war the militia had proved most adept at hunting raparees and tories. Directives from Ginkel in the summer of 1691 made militias specifically responsible for county defence and security when the army marched into the field, tasks which they performed adequately. If, however, they were deployed alongside regular forces in field operations they proved unsteady and unreliable treating both their own and regular army officers with contempt and concentrating on harassing Roman Catholics, cattle raiding and plundering. Colonel Michelburne noted that when there was garrison duty to be done or frontiers to defend he could rarely muster more than 500 Ulster militiamen but mention of a raid and plunder increased numbers dramatically. When chasing raparees and 'preys' of livestock militiamen agreed to serve outside their own counties but were reluctant if asked to perform more mundane duties. The militia and other bounty hunters enjoyed a reputation for being more harsh and cruel in their treatment of raparees and 'those sort of people' than the regular army. Their approach was generalized and unscrupulous especially after the revival of the old practice of offering monetary payment for the heads of certain, nominated offenders.[2]

Major General Kirke's camp at Birr broke up at the beginning of October leaving Lieutenant Colonel Peter Bristow (Lord Drogheda's Foot) to garrison Kilcormac Castle with six companies. Situated to the north of the Slieve Bloom Mountains, Kilcormac commanded an important junction on one of the major roads from Dublin to the west and was centrally located to observe both Birr and

Banagher Bridge. Bristow lodged his men in the open village of Ballyboy, 2 km to the east, because it offered better forage and shelter than the castle. Informed of Bristow's dispositions, detachments of the Irish Army cantoned between Limerick and Athlone slipped across the Shannon and, during the night, took up positions in the adjacent hedges. Suspecting that all was not well, the soldiers asked Bristow to issue ammunition but he was unconvinced. Still uneasy, the garrison remained alert all night sending out a patrol of 20 men commanded by a lieutenant but it failed to discover any Jacobites who were, of course, well concealed. After reveille, assuming that their fears had been unfounded, the men returned to their billets leaving only a regulation guard. Half an hour later, the Irish set fire to houses at both ends of Ballyboy causing Bristow and his soldiers to hurry to a mound in the centre of the village where they formed a perimeter. A fire fight ensued but the Jacobites did not attempt to rush the mound, even though they outnumbered Bristow by four to one, and drew off on the approach of dragoons from Birr. Bristow lost 28 killed and some wounded including Captain Henry Gore who blundered into the Irish as he was making his way to the mound and had his jaw broken and head injured by a clubbed musket.[3] He enjoyed improved fortune around 20 October when a party from the Kilcormac garrison intercepted some raparees marching towards Philipstown (Daingean) in King's County. Most were captured and two officers hanged.

Captain Archer of the County Wicklow militia attacked a party of raparees during mid-November, killing five and taking 23 prisoners, for the loss of five or six of his own men. Raparees from nearby bogs burned Philipstown despite its Williamite garrison and also did 'a great deal of mischief' around Cashel and Clonmel necessitating a joint militia–army operation to destroy forage and corn towards Cullen in the hope that this would restrict their activities. So serious had the security situation become – even Dublin was thought to be in danger – that, on Ginkel's advice, between 19 and 22 November the Lords Justices issued a series of proclamations. Should raparees rob, plunder or burn the house of any of the king's subjects, the losses would be made good by the Roman Catholic inhabitants of the county. No Roman Catholic priest would be allowed to reside in a shire that harboured a band of raparees numbering more than ten. Anyone with a son absent in the enemy's quarters would be ineligible for protection unless he had returned home by 10 December. All Roman Catholics who had not been householders in Dublin during the previous three months were to leave within 48 hours and remain at least 16 km distant, or suffer prosecution as spies. No more than five Roman Catholics were to assemble on any pretext. On 25 December, Roman Catholics were barred from keeping public houses in Dublin to prevent the plotting and caballing that had been conducted in the taverns, wine shops and coffee houses. These measures were totally ineffective and small groups of raparees were still operating within a few kilometres of the capital as late as the third week of March 1691. A scheme whereby individual travellers conveyed small quantities of meat, salt, tobacco and brandy from Dublin to the quarters of the Jacobite Army beyond the Shannon was uncovered to the Lords Justices when some couriers were overtaken on the road in County Kildare but succeeded in making their escape. One was a woman who dropped a petticoat and a roll of tobacco, both of which contained letters confirming a correspondence between the Irish Army and the Dublin Roman Catholics. Accordingly the Dublin militia conducted a general search on the night of 30 November and many suspects were secured for questioning. An immediate result was the discovery of intelligence that the Jacobites had crossed the Shannon at several points. A warning was sent to the frontier garrisons and Colonel Gustavus Hamilton at Birr sent a detachment west towards Portumna, a principal Shannon bridge at the northern end of Lough Derg. It turned back a Jacobite raiding party, killing a few and taking prisoner two officers and 11 infantrymen and dragoons.

West of Castletown, County Cork, on 22 November 60 Williamite cavalry and infantry encountered nearly 500 raparees, led by Colonel O'Driscoll, Captain Teague O'Donovan and Captain John Barry (Carroll's Dragoons). At a significant numerical disadvantage and under pressure, the Williamites fell back towards Castletown. From time to time, they faced about to check their pursuers – killing nine but losing Ensign Brown – until they eventually reached the relative safety of Castletown House, which came under attack on the following day, 23 November. In place of armour, the Irish infantry tied bundles of straw to their chests but heavy, accurate defensive musketry killed 12 and halted the remainder. Captain Cronin drew his sword and tried to rally them but, when he was shot, they scurried from the field leaving about 30 dead, including O'Donovan. Only two Williamite lives were lost.

Long winter nights assisted the raparees. Colonel Robert Byerley moved his cavalry regiment from Dublin to join some infantry from Colonel Thomas Erle's battalion at Mountmellick on 15 November, better to secure the rear of the frontier zone. They responded to frequent alarms as both raparees and raiding parties from the regular Jacobite Army sought to burn the town 'as they had done several others thereabouts'. Helped by his intelligence network, Byerley stayed careful, cautious and alert. On one occasion, learning that the Irish intended to fire the town, he paraded all his cavalry and infantry in readiness so that, when the Irish learned of his preparations, they abandoned the attempt. Byerley received notice on 3 December that a party of raparees was approaching. He sent out Lieutenant Robert Dent with 20 cavalrymen, each carrying a musketeer behind the saddle. On coming close to the raparees but still out of sight, the musketeers jumped off to line some hedges. When the raparees spotted only 20 horsemen, they advanced from the edge of a bog and Dent retired drawing the raparees within range of the concealed infantrymen. The first volley killed several and disordered the remainder allowing Dent's cavalry to turn and charge, supported by the musketeers; 39 raparees were killed and four taken prisoner who were immediately hanged 'without any further ceremony'. The rest escaped into the bog

> and, in a moment, all disappeared; which may seem strange to those that have not seen it, but something of this kind I have seen myself; and those of this party assured me that, after the action was over, some of them looking about amongst the dead found one Dun, a sergeant of the enemy's, who was lying like an otter, all under water in the running brook (except the top of his nose and his mouth). They brought him out and, although he proffered forty shillings in English money to save his life (a great ransom as he believed) yet he was one of the four that was hanged. When the raparees have no mind to show themselves upon the bogs, they commonly slink down between two or three little hills, grown over with long grass, so that you may as soon find a hare as one of them. They conceal their arms thus. They take off the lock and put it in their pockets, or hide it in some dry place. They stop the muzzle with a cork, and the touch-hole with a small quill, and then thrown the piece itself into a running water or pond. You may see an hundred of them without arms, who look like the poorest, humblest slaves in the world, and you may search till you are weary before you find one gun. But yet, when they have a mind to do mischief, they can be ready in an hour's warning, for everyone knows where to go and fetch his own arms, though you do not.[4]

Viewed from his headquarters in Kilkenny, the prospect before Ginkel was bleak but familiar. Winter raids between garrisons occurred throughout the Nine Years' War in all theatres, complicated in Ireland, Savoy-Piedmont and Catalonia by the involvement of irregular forces drawn from the local populations. The rule that the higher the participation ratio of civilians in warfare the greater the levels of brutality and atrocity certainly applied in Ireland. Depopulation was another adverse consequence of the winter war 'of posts and ambuscades'. The inhabitants of small towns and villages along the frontiers and in no-man's-land frequently abandoned their homes and sought temporary shelter within the lines of the two armies.

Early in December, the governor of Clonmel informed Ginkel that his men were in great distress. Out of the two garrison battalions, 250 were sick, 25 had died during the last two days and desertions were increasing.[5] Ginkel responded by sending some troops of the County Wicklow militia cavalry to reinforce the post. In mid-December, Captain Archer, commanding one of these troops, engaged a party of Irish, killing 25 and seizing 30 cattle. Colonel Wolseley sent word from Cavan that provisions and ammunition dispatched into the north had arrived safely. The day before, his men had killed eight Irish and hanged three 'spies'. One MacFinnan, who had escaped from Cork following the siege, marched at the head of about 400 Irish soldiers and raparees towards Enniskean on the Bandon River. However, he found it too well guarded and switched his attention north to Castletown, which was garrisoned by one lieutenant and 30 dragoons. For some time, they defended Castletown bravely, killing ten Irish, but having lost five men and consumed all their ammunition, they surrendered upon quarter but the lieutenant was subsequently murdered. A relief party from Enniskean under Major William Culliford (Royal Dragoons) arrived too late although it managed to attack MacFinnan's detachment, killing 12 and taking five prisoners. Lieutenant Colonel Robert Freke (Colonel Thomas Erle's Foot) led a party of cattle raiders out of Streamstown, County Westmeath, on 12 December but was ambushed by 500 Irish cavalry and infantry, losing about 50 men. Although wounded, Freke cut his way out. Typical of the hazardous security situation was an episode reported by Dr George Clarke, secretary at war in Ireland. Accompanied by some friends and colleagues, he rode eastwards from Clonmel towards Carrick to enjoy a day's shooting. Heading towards a wood on the far bank of the River Suir, which was known to contain game, they were approaching a ford when they noticed a provision boat being towed in their direction. A boatman made signs, which they failed to interpret, so Clarke's party signalled to him to come to the road. This he did and explained that there were about 80 of King James's men lurking in the wood with the obvious intention of seizing the provision boat. Whilst they were talking, three of the Irish left the wood, came down to the riverside and shot at Clarke's party. Fire was returned whereupon the raparees dropped to the ground and remained still. The noise of the gunfire brought another 30 or 40 raparees towards the river and Clarke told the boatman to hurry. Clarke's party remained threatening the raparees until the boat reached a fork in the river, probably the confluence with the Anner, after which it was reasonably safe. Clarke then returned to Clonmel. By not entering the wood he had avoided certain death at the hands of the raparees 'who gave no quarter at that time' and also saved a provision boat.

By this time, the raparees had worked their way to the eastern extremity of the Bog of Allen. From secure bases on the numerous islands, raparees emerged at night to raid and plunder. It was thought that there were 1,000 men, women and children in the bog, although only about 200 were actively involved in military operations. Because the bog allowed the raparees to approach within 20 km of Dublin 'it caused a great noise' and Colonel John Foulkes commanding his own battalion, part of John Cutts's, assisted by Lieutenant Colonel Piper leading some Dublin and County Kildare militia, and supported by three field guns, was ordered to eradicate the plague. Foulkes entered the bog around Carragh during the night and remained stationary until daylight, when he pushed north-westwards along a causeway towards the Island of Allen, in the region of modern Allen and Allenwood. For a while it looked as though the Irish would resist but, as Foulkes advanced – his men having to fill 12 trenches dug across the causeway – they began to give way and made off into the woods.

On the island Foulkes rendezvoused with Piper who had come down from the northern side. Scattered cabins were burned but the majority of raparees escaped. Some troops were left to garrison parts of the bog to encourage 'a better sort of inhabitant' and recruits left Dublin on 26 January to reinforce the principal of these posts at Kilmeage, County Kildare. As well as embarrassing the rear areas of Ginkel's army, such concentrations of raparees were a great nuisance to the local population. Throughout the winter the 'White Sergeant', together with Macabe and Cavanagh, were very troublesome around Kildare. Frequent punitive expeditions by the Kildare and Dublin militias gradually reduced the cohesion and effectiveness of these bands: Cavanagh and his followers eventually found the Bog of Allen too dangerous and redeployed to the Wicklow Mountains where they were intercepted by a Williamite patrol. Fifteen were killed and Cavanagh taken prisoner, the survivors dispersing to join Macabe and the White Sergeant.[6]

Efforts were made to negotiate an end to the war. Ginkel and Portland favoured offering generous terms to Roman Catholic landowners but William was unwilling to concede more than necessary. Central to his policy was the confiscation of sufficient Irish land to reward his supporters, assuage the Westminster parliament and meet army debts. The intermediary in the overtures was John Grady, a Roman Catholic lawyer who had been sent out from Limerick prior to the siege to discover what terms William was willing to offer. Following the conclusion of the siege, Grady travelled to Galway whence he reported that a group led by Judge Denis Daly strongly supported a settlement, provided that Catholics might retain their estates and receive the same treatment they had enjoyed during Charles II's time. Grady returned to Limerick early in December and, in the meantime, William instructed Ginkel to buttress Grady's negotiations by pressurizing the Irish in Sligo and County Kerry.

Against his better judgement – winter operations were hard on the men and often ruinous to the horses – Ginkel accordingly devised operations to secure bridgeheads over the Shannon both to contain the Jacobites within Connaught and County Clare and interrupt their access to the riches of County Kerry. An essential preliminary was to dominate the navigation of the Shannon in order to facilitate river crossings and support subsequent bridgeheads. Early in December, four longboats, 'like men of war's pinnaces', were fitted with 'pattereros'[7] and other small guns, and their bulwarks reinforced and fortified by boards 'and other materials'. They were to be crewed by 100 'choice men' commanded by Captain Hoord (sic) 'who had been provost marshal, but turned out for some irregular things, and was resolved to do some desperate service to be readmitted'. Once equipped, the craft were intended to ply the Shannon between Loughs Derg and Ree where there were numerous islands on which the Irish 'had very considerable riches'. When ready, they were carried on wagons to Mullingar. This done, late in December Ginkel finalized arrangements for five complementary operations which he referred to collectively as 'the expedition'. Under Major Generals Kirke and Sir John Lanier[8] 6,000 men were to concentrate at Mullingar and advance westward to seize a Shannon crossing; Lieutenant General Douglas was ordered to attack Sligo via Jamestown with 8,000 troops from Belturbet and Cavan; and Major General Tettau was to lead an expedition westwards from County Cork into County Kerry to do as much damage as possible to the 'granary of Limerick'. To divert Jacobite attentions away from these three principal operations, Ginkel and Württemberg intended to advance with a substantial force towards Kilmallock. Finally, throughout Williamite-controlled Ireland the militia would take the field to suppress raparee activity. Opposing Ginkel's attempts on the Shannon was Sarsfield, whose headquarters were at Athlone, the *de facto* commander of the Jacobite winter line. He endeavoured to practise forward defence, placing garrisons in Ballymore and Moate, and attempting to secure Birr. Although many of his officers thought these garrisons a waste of precious resources, Sarsfield argued that they protected foraging grounds and dominated the approaches to the Shannon. He inspected the major crossing points at Portumna, Banagher Bridge, Lanesborough and Jamestown and ordered the construction of redoubts and entrenchments.

Ginkel instructed Sir John Lanier to force a passage of the Shannon and establish a bridgehead, leaving him to determine the details. Lanier summoned a council of war to Mullingar on Christmas Day attended by his three senior officers: Major General Kirke, Brigadier Edward Villiers and Lord Lisburn. Rather strangely, Lanier asked them to put their views in writing. Because the four longboats and the available field artillery were already at Mullingar, closer to Lanesborough than any other possible target, Lisburn favoured an attack on Lanesborough Bridge. Lanier strenuously opposed him saying that the operation would split the forces at a time when he was sure that Sarsfield was already on the left bank of the Shannon: any move on Lanesborough would place the attacking troops in a salient that would prove difficult to support or reinforce. No decision was reached except to authorize Lisburn to lead a strong reconnaissance patrol towards Athlone. At 23:00 on 27 December Lisburn took a detachment of 300 infantry and 200 mounted troops from Streamstown and, despite mud and bad roads, came within sight of Athlone at midday on 28 December. Returning to Mullingar on Monday 29 December he reported to Lanier and Kirke that only 20 hostile horsemen had been encountered in a region which, according to Lanier, was firmly in Jacobite possession. Lisburn confirmed that there was a Jacobite presence on the left bank of the Shannon at Lanesborough but the intervening countryside between Mullingar and the Shannon was largely clear of the enemy. Assured that the operation could now proceed safely, approval was given for the movement on Lanesborough Bridge to proceed immediately. Accompanied by Lanier, on Tuesday 30 December Lisburn led out his own and Richard Brewer's battalions, plus some companies from Kirke's – about 1,000 infantry – and 300 cavalry and dragoons. That night they camped at Foxhall, 16 km from Mullingar and, by the evening of 31 December, they had advanced to the foot of the causeway that carried the Mullingar road through two bogs to Lanesborough, 8 km distant. Lisburn drove his men hard, the weather and tracks so bad that the foot often assumed single file and the cavalry had to dismount. Sarsfield's local troops had already broken the causeway in 13 places but Lieutenant Colonel Jacob Richards assured Lisburn that, with 300 men, he could repair it overnight. Although unable to exert much pressure because of the narrow frontage, Brewer's advance guard drove off the light Irish forces sheltering behind flimsy barricades along the causeway but could not prevent them from disengaging and withdrawing through Lanesborough and over the Shannon, herding their cattle, smashing the bridge and demolishing a small fort at its eastern end. Early on 1 January 1691, Lisburn's whole detachment had crossed the causeway and drew up on a hill within 100 m of Lanesborough Bridge. Brewer had occupied Lanesborough and the ruined fort by 12:00 on 1 January 1691. However, although such Jacobite forces as could be seen appeared to be in total confusion, a crossing was out of the question because the boats and artillery were still on the road from Mullingar and there was insufficient infantry. Lanier came to Lanesborough later in the day and took stock of the situation. On 2 January, he rode back to hasten the artillery and boats and sent a courier to order reinforcements from Mullingar. On meeting the train the sight of the gunners and horses struggling through deep mud and snow appears to have undermined his confidence in an operation with which he was not wholly in sympathy. Sensing that nothing would come of the operation apart from blame and the loss of guns, horses and scarce infantry, Lanier instructed the artillery and boats to return to Mullingar. Lanier later explained his decision to Ginkel saying that it would have proved impossible to supply a garrison at Lanesborough and the hand tools for the necessary defensive works were unavailable. A messenger was sent to tell Lisburn and Brewer to abandon Lanesborough and fall back. Whether he distrusted Lanier or because he had personally adumbrated the operation, Lisburn disobeyed and remained focused on crossing the Shannon. Ignoring a repetition of Lanier's instruction he ordered Richards to construct an earthwork at the eastern end of the bridge from which an eventual crossing might be covered; on completion this was occupied by Captain Henry Edgeworth with 100 men and a field gun. Lisburn was now isolated at the tip of a damaged road encased between two bogs, his flanks totally unprotected although frequent patrols had, as yet, detected no Jacobite activity. Compounding his tactical errors and insubordination, Lisburn held his main force 3 km back from Lanesborough leaving Edgeworth unsupported. On 4 January Brigadier Robert Clifford, a man of strange behaviour and questionable judgement, arrived at Lanesborough with three infantry regiments and for 72 hours Irish outposts stood on the west bank trading insults, desultory gunfire, short-lived truces and toasts with Edgeworth's men. Unknown to Lisburn, Clifford's appearance was designed to pin him at Lanesborough whilst Sarsfield crossed the Shannon at Athlone before marching via Ballymore to cut the Mullingar road behind the bogs. However, when preparing the manoeuvre on the night of 4–5 January Sarsfield received information that Douglas was approaching Jamestown with a very large corps. Sarsfield promptly reassessed the situation, decided that Douglas posed the greater threat and marched north. Lisburn was saved. On 8 January, Brigadier Villiers brought a final and peremptory order from Lanier to withdraw. After a week in the cold and wet, his men gnawingly hungry, Lisburn trudged back to Mullingar on the following day.

Meanwhile, Kirke arranged for a detachment of 300 soldiers from Lord Drogheda's, Sir John Hanmer's and Lord George Hamilton's battalions, commanded by Lieutenant Colonels Peter Bristow and Toby Caulfield, to march from Birr to reinforce Lisburn at Lanesborough. Their long, circuitous route lay through Philipstown, Mullingar and Longford, testimony to the absence of direct roads through the midland bogs and the insecurity of the left bank of the Shannon. Between Birr and Philipstown, the column came under a five-hour attack from about 1,500 Irish soldiers and raparees who had been sheltering in the Slieve Bloom. Not only were Bristow and Caulfield at a considerable numerical disadvantage but they had only 30 dragoons whereas the Irish disposed several troops of cavalry. At the cost of one captain, six men, all the baggage and the abandonment of the line of march, the column fought its way to Colonel Robert Byerley's garrison at Mountmellick, which had recently been reinforced.

In fine, cold, frosty weather Tettau marched for County Kerry with a Dutch-Danish detachment of approximately 2,400 infantry and 450 horse and dragoons. He was joined at Macroom on the following day by the infantry battalions of Brigadier Charles Churchill and Colonel Sir David Colyear, Colonel Coy's cavalry regiment and the Royal Dragoons (Colonel Edward Matthews). The combined force, which numbered close to 5,000 men, pressed westwards on 30 December up the valley of the River Sullane towards the Derrynasaggart Mountains, through countryside that had been mostly burned by the Irish to create a zone *non operandi* between their positions in County Kerry and the winter quarters of the Williamites in central and eastern County Cork. The pass over the mountains was blocked by a fort, which had taken 500 Irish two months to build. It delayed Tettau for less than two hours and he hurried on to Brewster's Field where his advance guard of 70 troopers from Eppinger's and Coy's regiments encountered an Irish picket of 160 cavalrymen mounted on small, unshod horses. They refused action and withdrew, as did a larger body of Irish troops, visible in the distance, led by Colonel Nicholas Browne and Colonel Christopher Fleming, Second Viscount Slane, burning the country as they retired. Slane and Browne took fresh horses and galloped towards Limerick. With smoke and flames rising around them, Tettau's force hurried forward to Killarney, which was owned by Browne's father, Lord Kenmare, in an effort to arrive before it was put to the torch. Twenty cabins had been consumed by the time they arrived but the remainder of Killarney, and Brewster's Forge, was saved from destruction. General St Ruth later condemned such conduct: whilst it was regular practice to wreck an enemy's territory or that of a neutral, he was unable to comprehend why the Irish destroyed their own countryside and resources. Tettau then moved south-west to Ross Castle on Lough Leane which he found strong and 'tolerably well fortified', garrisoned by 600 men under Colonel Macarty, 'who wants a thumb'.

Lacking artillery and siege equipment, Ross Castle was beyond Tettau's capabilities[9] and he had to content himself with an attack on a fort situated on a nearby rocky islet in Lough Leane, garrisoned by 77 men. Captain Ludwig von Boyneburg and 50 Danes led the assault assisted by 50 Kinsale militiamen under Captain Carroll. Boyneburg was injured by a grenade, Carroll shot through the leg, six privates were killed and 15 wounded but the attack was successful. Except for five prisoners and 14 Irish who swam to another rock, where they provided target practice for Danish snipers, the garrison was massacred. Tettau decided to waste no more time and headed north for Tralee, garrisoned by Colonel Dominic Sheldon with 21 troops of dragoons and seven of cavalry. Sheldon abandoned the town on Tettau's approach and retired north-east in the direction of Limerick. At this point a thaw set in accompanied by heavy rain. Aware that he could find no sustenance in the devastated countryside and with the unsubdued garrison of Ross Castle threatening his communications, Tettau rounded up all the sheep, cattle and horses he could find and returned to Cork. Throughout, swarms of raparees had hung on the flanks and rear of his column, striking at night to pick off stragglers, couriers, careless patrols, horses and cattle. Several men were lost. Tettau executed the most successful of Ginkel's operations but it was no more than a deep cattle raid. The Irish forces in Kerry were neither driven out nor defeated although large numbers of livestock were taken and the Irish induced to immolate some of their own resources.

Towards the end of December, Württemberg led a detachment towards Kilmallock to attack Kilfinnane Castle, garrisoned by three companies of Irish foot and three troops of dragoons. In support, Ginkel brought a detachment of Dutch and Huguenot troops from Clonmel to make a combined force of about 4,000 men. The Irish burned Kilmallock and retired. Intelligence was received that they had assembled 7,000 men within a few kilometres of Kilfinnane, possibly intending to use the castle as bait to draw the Williamites into an ambush. Ginkel and Württemberg decided to accept the challenge and formed their men into a Swedish-style line of battle, cavalry squadrons positioned in the intervals between the infantry battalions. Rather than face a general action, the Jacobites withdrew, evacuating and burning Kilfinnane Castle, which, in Württemberg's view, could have been defended because it had a deep, wet ditch and thick walls with four corner towers, in addition to a drawbridge covered by a stone ravelin. However, the Jacobite withdrawal was timely because it coincided with the onset of a thaw and the hard, frozen ground reverted to marsh and bog. Determined not to ruin his infantry, Ginkel recalled the advance guard, which had reached Gorteen, and, on 5 January, retraced his steps to Tipperary, the columns continually flanked by raparees who skulked in the hills and woods, attacking foragers and stragglers. Douglas had expressed considerable reluctance to take responsibility for any operation involving a cross-country march by 8,000 men in the depths of winter and set off from Belturbet and Cavan 'with all the ill-will in the world'. As he approached the Shannon, in which the stream was low and fordable in three places, the Jacobites abandoned and burned Jamestown. Although Douglas had made some logistical preparations, his men were fatigued, hungry and cold and unable to force the field fortifications guarding the crossings. A counter-attack by 1,500 men under Colonel Oliver O'Gara drove them back and, having suffered over 100 dead, Douglas hastily retreated, many of his men being captured during the pursuit.[10]

Ginkel's offensives were intended not only to reinforce diplomacy but also take advantage of a conspiracy amongst the pro-Tyrconnell faction within the Irish Army. The conspirators intended to allow the Williamites to cross the Shannon at Jamestown and Lanesborough and then surrender Galway and, possibly, Limerick. Indeed, conditions were so unsuitable for major operations – the weather cold and wet, the roads deep in mud and the ground covered in snow – that there is no other rational explanation for involving so much of the army in mid-winter. Both armies probably contained about 20,000 men but the Irish had more cavalry, the dominant arm in winter manoeuvres. An advance across the Shannon singly by either Lanier's or Douglas's detachments would have been extremely risky and the absence of the intended river flotilla, stuck in Mullingar, would have compounded the danger. Irish geography and meteorology usually favoured the defence.

The Lords Justices observed that the real culprits for the failure of Ginkel's Shannon operations were not conspiracy, geography and meteorology but Lieutenant Generals Lanier and Douglas. If King William wished to see a speedy end to the war, then these gentlemen had to be sacked. They regarded Kirke, a major general, as less malicious although he was clearly unable, or unwilling, to circumvent the obstructionist tactics of Douglas and Lanier and had not tried very hard to expedite operations. Lord Lisburn, himself guilty of gross insubordination however well intentioned, and Brigadier Edward Villiers had both spoken sharply to Lanier about his half-hearted conduct. At this point, the exact story of Douglas's failure even to attempt a Shannon crossing at Jamestown had not been reported but the Lords Justices expected that Colonel Wolseley would soon provide a detailed analysis. During the winter of 1689–90, when Wolseley had been in command on the West Ulster frontier, scarcely a week passed without some operation being undertaken: during Douglas's tenure, nothing had happened. Relations between them were strained because Douglas had formally accused Wolseley's nephew, Captain Richard Wolseley, of cattle stealing and he was under arrest awaiting court-martial. Kirke, Lanier and Douglas, all career soldiers, were in a delicate position. In 1690 there was every prospect that the Grand Alliance might lose the European war and a French-dominated, negotiated settlement would almost certainly require the reinstatement of James II and the expulsion of William III. Whilst there is no extant evidence that they were crypto-Jacobites, all three had committed themselves to the Williamite cause during and immediately after the Glorious Revolution, perhaps, on reflection, over-enthusiastically: it behoved career soldiers always to be ready to tack with any shift in the direction of the political wind. Such attitudes did not lend themselves to the vigorous prosecution of King William's war in Ireland, as Kirke had demonstrated by his shilly-shallying before Derry and Douglas in his spineless expeditions to Athlone and Jamestown. Perhaps also, aware that they would not receive such high positions in the Army of the Grand Alliance in the Netherlands where senior commands were reserved for Dutchmen and Germans, they wished the war in Ireland to continue for as long as possible. Whatever their reasons, until such men were removed Ginkel would be hamstrung.[11]

The failure of the offensives convinced Ginkel that William was overplaying a relatively weak diplomatic hand and wrote to Portland advocating the offer of more generous terms and pointing out that rendering the Irish desperate would only strengthen the party favouring resistance. After all, William's proclamation following the Boyne had been interpreted as a sign of weakness and stiffened Jacobite morale. So discouraging was the military situation in the Netherlands that William agreed to modify his earlier position and Portland was able to inform Ginkel and Grady that he would probably agree to a general pardon provided that certain individuals were exempted. William granted Ginkel full powers to devise moderate terms. Accordingly, he issued a declaration from Dublin on 4 February explaining that the king had no wish to oppress his Irish Roman Catholic subjects in either their religion or properties and was prepared to offer reasonable conditions to all who would submit. In support, on 6 February the Lords Justices published a proclamation aimed at improving the behaviour of the soldiers in their winter quarters. Officers and men were prohibited from plundering, requisitioning and stealing from either Protestants or Roman Catholics; cutting down hedges and fences that defined agricultural enclosures; seizing horses and cattle from the plough; and extorting money. Billeting bills were to be settled from subsistence money, which was ordered to be paid regularly from 1 January. In addition, Ginkel instituted a new policy towards Irish deserters. Instead of interrogation and rough treatment followed by imprisonment or worse, they were to be welcomed and given subsistence money in the hope that this might induce more to follow. The impact of these terms was weakened by the fact that they were issued over Ginkel's signature rather than that of the king but serious rifts in the Jacobite ranks resulted. They held no attraction for gentlemen who had lost lands in the Cromwellian and earlier confiscations but those who had recovered all or part of their ancestral properties under the Restoration Settlement, as well the 'new interest', stood to benefit. Sarsfield was strongly opposed to any negotiations and persuaded Berwick to act against the leading members of the peace party. Thomas Nugent, First Baron Riverston, the secretary of state, and his brother-in-law, Colonel Alexander MacDonnell, governor of Galway, were dismissed and, on 10 January 1691, the day after Lisburn retired from Lanesborough, Judge Daly was arrested on suspicion of correspondence with the enemy although he was released as soon as Tyrconnell reached Limerick. William could not avoid another campaign.[12]

Throughout the winter, the Jacobite position steadily deteriorated because Connaught and County Kerry could not support 20,000 soldiers in addition to camp followers and a civilian population swollen by refugees. Provided that they were located in widely scattered billets and not concentrated into cantonments and temporary field corps, the soldiers could have been fed but only at the cost of starving the civilians. Once assembled, the unpaid troops were expected to forage amongst a friendly population resulting in misery, destitution, starvation and deteriorating civil–military relations. Even in Limerick, the best-provided garrison, by the spring of 1691 half the men had either deserted or been sent off to forage, whilst the situation was much worse up-river. Bread supplies to the garrisons of the Shannon crossings stopped in March and April – reports spoke of soldiers collapsing from hunger – leaving them weakly held and vulnerable. In an effort to prevent a famine within the army, the Jacobites had driven thousands of 'useless mouths' over the Shannon but the Williamites were unresponsive to their plight forcing them to endure the winter in the frontier zone between the two armies in 'a miserable, starving condition'. During the Siege of Ballymore in 1691, 'these wretches' flocked around Ginkel's camp 'devouring all the filth they could meet with. Our dead horses crawling with vermin, as the sun had parched them, were delicious food to them, while their infants sucked those carcasses with as much eagerness as if they were at their mothers' breasts.' Tyrconnell tried to make a financial levy in Connaught but, following the earlier withdrawal of brass money and the exhaustion of the countryside, this produced next to nothing. Instead, the country donated 10,000 head of cattle but there were only six large boats to transport them from Limerick making it impossible to build up magazines along the Shannon: the cargo of one boat had been consumed by the soldiers before the next arrived. The maintenance of the line of the Shannon into the spring and summer depended upon French provision convoys. Fifty-one cargo vessels, escorted by 32 warships, arrived at Limerick on 9 May 1691 bringing Generals St Ruth, d'Usson, Tessé and La Tour Monfort plus sufficient arms, uniforms, corn and meal to sustain the army into the autumn; civilians would have to fend for themselves. However, despite St Ruth commandeering all available draught animals, the Jacobite distribution system remained chaotic and seriously delayed the concentration of the army in the spring. By the time that the troops began to draw benefit from the French provisions, the decisive battle would have been fought and lost. Reports from deserters informed Ginkel of the desperate plight of the Jacobite Army although, as contemporaries pointed out, information from such sources had always to be treated with great caution.[13]

The increasing number of war weary Irish in Connaught and County Clare were almost glad to see Tyrconnell return from France. Accompanied by Sir Richard Nagle, Sir Stephen Rice and a gaggle of Irish lawyers instead of soldiers and significant quantities of arms, provisions and money, he appeared better prepared to make peace than war. However, he came clothed in the authority of a fully fledged lord lieutenant and there could be no questioning his absolute authority over both the army and the civil administration. Whilst waiting for passage at Brest, Tyrconnell heard that the four envoys from the Irish senate had landed at St Malo. Immediately, he wrote to James suggesting that the embassy be suppressed and the envoys punished for their presumption. On arrival at Galway on 15 January 1691, he tried to interrupt communications between the envoys and the anti-Tyrconnell faction. All passengers from France were to be closely examined and searched for letters; any found should be taken to Sir Richard Nagle for perusal. No one was to travel abroad without Tyrconnell's permission and all letters were to be opened and thoroughly inspected. At Brest, letters for Ireland were to be delivered to the chief magistrate who, by prior arrangement, was to put them all into a single bundle addressed to Tyrconnell. His return triggered the departure of Berwick who sailed from Limerick around 24 February. During February, a French officer landed in Galway and gave Sarsfield an intercepted letter from the senate envoys in France which told of Tyrconnell's machinations but also announced the imminent arrival of General St Ruth, who was to command the army without reference or deference to Tyrconnell. Greatly cheered, Sarsfield had the contents widely disseminated but Tyrconnell spread counter-information that it was a sham and St Ruth was subordinate to the Lord Lieutenant. Everywhere, Tyrconnell was greeted with great pomp and ceremony, as befitted his new status, at a time when the majority of the army was starving. This did not greatly concern Tyrconnell who regarded starvation as another means of forcing the war faction to seek terms.

Seventeen transports escorted by two warships sailed from Dublin Bay to Kinsale in January 1691 to embark Marlborough's and Colonel Edward Fitzpatrick's regiments for Flanders together with the prisoners taken in Cork and Kinsale. A party of the Bandon militia advanced into Irish territory in western County Cork, killing some stragglers and seizing a good number of cattle. Before 19 January several thousand raparees and regular soldiers concentrated around Limerick and advanced south towards the Danish frontier in County Cork, burning and devastating the countryside. To deter the Williamites from interfering, Brigadier Francis Carroll led a detachment of about 1,500 towards the crossings of the River Blackwater around Fermoy. The water level being low, they tried to secure a ford close to Fermoy which was protected by a fort manned by Danish infantry. The Irish attacked the fort in a rather half-hearted manner and withdrew after Danish musketry had felled 16 men and a French officer. Carroll then turned his attention to the bridge in Fermoy, which was defended by 80 Danish infantry under Captain Christian Heinrich von Siegler (Prince George of Denmark's battalion). The Irish swarmed around Siegler's entrenchments and summoned him to surrender but he refused. Assisted by two light field guns, which erroneous Irish intelligence indicated had earlier been removed, Siegler beat off the subsequent assault, killing six men. Reinforcements – some troops of Colonel Donop's cavalry regiment – had already reached Castlelyons. Donop's advance guard of 50 horsemen and 30 militia dragoons pressed ahead and encountered a party of Carroll's troops that had by-passed both Fermoy Bridge and ford and was reconnoitring south of the Blackwater. In the subsequent action, the Irish lost 60 men and Donop's troopers pursued the remainder for 3 km until they came to Carroll's main body which disengaged and retired towards Limerick.[14]

Two hundred infantry and 300 dragoons from the Cork garrison marched north on 29 January towards Churchtown and Buttevant, two Irish frontier posts occupied by a detachment of horse and foot. On the approach of the Williamites, both villages were evacuated and fired. Early in February, a mixed party of Williamite regulars and militia left Clonmel and proceeded to within 16 km of Limerick but encountered no organized opposition although 12 straggling raparees were killed, some cabins and shelters burned, and cattle and prisoners gathered. Colonel Richard Brewer, directing 200 infantry from his own battalion, and Major Henry Boad (Royal Horse Guards) commanding 150 cavalrymen, marched west from Mullingar on 8 February to relieve and resupply some small local garrisons. Having done this, Brewer reconnoitred towards the Irish post at Ballymore. Two kilometres short he encountered a small party defending a ford where the main road passed a rivulet. Brewer charged, put the Irish to flight and pursued as far as Ballymore Fort, killing between six and eight men. He then returned to Mullingar, having burned a house at the ford and taken its unfortunate owner prisoner. Tiny, niggling operations and episodes continued almost daily. Around 9 February, one Langston was hanged at Kilkenny for endeavouring to seduce some soldiers of Count Nassau's regiment to desert whilst, in Birr, raparees killed a soldier from Lord George Hamilton's battalion, eviscerating and mutilating his body. A party of Williamites quartered at Ballyhooly on the Blackwater raided north into Irish territory on 10 February and killed 25 raparees. Shortly afterwards, Major James Kirke (Edward Villiers's Horse) killed six raparees and captured an officer. About 400 Irish regulars, commanded by Lieutenant Colonel Thady Connor, rode deep into Williamite territory to Edenberry, east of Philipstown, on 13 February and burned most of the town, killing seven men and one woman. A troop of militia horse in Edenberry counter-attacked and killed 11 Irish but it was heavily outnumbered and forced back into the town where it took up positions in the strongest and most defensible houses. Connor's men then turned south to burn Ballybrittas before marching west into Connaught. Jacobite winter operations lacked the regularity, persistence and single-mindedness of those conducted by the Williamites but they were not ineffective. Every opportunity was taken to surprise Williamite patrols, cut off stragglers and seize horses, often in broad daylight; St Ruth's army would have been hard pressed to put a cavalry force into the field during 1691 had not hundreds of horses been captured over the winter. However, counter-raids aimed at reducing the shelter, forage and provisions available to the Williamites simply added to the destruction of their own country. Also, because they relied for much of their intelligence upon the protected Irish within the Williamite frontiers, gratuitous destruction undermined that co-operation.[15]

Having failed to secure Lanesborough and Jamestown it was generally assumed that the 1691 campaign would open with an attempt to seize a bridge over the Shannon. Athlone was the obvious target: even though the fortifications were relatively strong, the stone bridge could easily be destroyed and it had already resisted Douglas. Having noted Brewer and Boad's reconnaissance on 8 February, the Jacobites occupied Ballymore in strength and improved its fortifications in order to cover the approaches to Athlone and observe the Williamite build-up at Mullingar. Raparees were reported to be swarming everywhere, although the militias were proving useful in controlling their activities. Around 25 February, acting upon intelligence that line infantry and some raparees were operating in the area, Major Luke Lillingston (John Foulkes's Foot) led a party southwest from Roscrea to Moneygall. Lillingston intercepted them, killing 35 and taking five prisoners including their commander, O'Connor. Further north, between 26 and 27 February, Ginkel and Lanier assembled a force of infantry and cavalry at Streamstown, County Westmeath, with a view to reconnoitring towards Ballymore and Athlone. As usual, the Irish knew all about the Williamite movements and, only 7 km out of Streamstown, Ginkel and Lanier encountered

Brigadier Robert Clifford commanding a detachment of horse and foot drawn up to guard the crossing of a small river west of Rosemount. The position was naturally strong and Clifford had further improved it with field fortifications but he proved a weak and irresolute commander. Ginkel ordered Captain John Pepper (Thomas Erle's Foot) to work around Clifford's flank. Seeing his position unhinged, Clifford left the pass, followed closely by Lanier's cavalrymen and dragoons, and dropped back towards his main body of 2,300 men deployed on a hillside adjacent to Moate. However, seeing Clifford's advance guard retiring the main body abandoned its positions and withdrew into the town. Although the entrance was protected by a ditch and a palisaded outwork, the Jacobites did not stand but marched through Moate and out along the road towards Athlone. Colonel Wolseley's advance guard – ten troopers from the Royal Horse Guards and 12 from Lanier's own regiment of cavalry under Cornet Patrick Lisle; 'four choice men' out of each company in Major General Kirke's infantry battalion, mounted on horseback as dragoons and led by Lieutenant Monck;[16] and a section from Colonel Thomas St John's Foot commanded by Captain Worth – attacked before they had fully cleared Moate and then pressed them for 10 km along the Athlone road. Clifford lost about 200 killed plus much baggage and equipment, whilst Ginkel's force suffered one trumpeter dead and four men wounded. Whilst Wolseley drove the Irish west, Ginkel turned north hoping to find Ballymore undermanned and inadequately guarded but he was deterred by heavy musketry and withdrew to Mullingar.

In late February and early March, raparee activity was intense around Mountrath. Lieutenant Colonel Toby Purcell (Charles Herbert's Foot) launched three counter-expeditions, which succeeded in killing about 100. During the march back to their quarters following the final mission, which had accounted for around 52, a large detachment of dragoons, commanded by Lieutenant Colonel Patrick Barnwell, rode into position to ambush Purcell's 140 infantry and 35 dragoons. Quartermaster John Topham (Royal Dragoons), leading the advance guard, was alert and his outriders discovered the presence of the Irish. Sensing that the Jacobite ranks were not completely under control, Topham charged their front. The first rank disintegrated and the rest turned and departed rapidly having lost three dead and five prisoners. During early March a party from Edward Villiers's Horse and some Danish cavalry marched from Tallow into Irish territory, killing two and taking some prisoners. Colonel George Blount, the high sheriff of County Tipperary, led his own troop of militia dragoons, a Danish troop of horse and some others, totalling about 200 men, from Clonmel to Mitchelstown, well within the Irish frontier. They killed 47 raparees, took 13 prisoners, and burned several cabins. Captain Hugh Palliser (Lord Drogheda's Foot) took a party towards Portumna, where he surprised some troopers from Lord Galmoy's Horse and took several prisoners as well as some plunder.[17]

18

Spring, 1691

Reports reached Cork that Sarsfield had concentrated part of the Jacobite Army at Knockainy, south of Limerick, where he had selected ten men from each troop and company to form a detachment with which to attack the frontier post at Fermoy, cross the Blackwater and raid eastward towards Tallow. This alarmed Ginkel who was already worried about a possible French landing through Cork.[1] Accordingly, a detachment was ordered from Youghal to reinforce the line of the Blackwater between Fermoy, Tallow and Tallowbridge but the situation remained quiet. Apparently, Sarsfield had simply mustered and reviewed his troops before choosing the best militiamen for service with the regulars. The advent of slightly improved weather allowed an increase in the regularity and scale of Williamite operations, preparing the ground for the opening of the main campaign. Major Lillingston marched with some of the Roscrea garrison between 20:00 and 21:00 on 14 March. He linked up with additional forces from Birr, forming a combined party of about 300 cavalry, dragoons and infantry before proceeding towards Nenagh Castle, which had been occupied by the Williamites during the siege of Limerick but subsequently abandoned. The Jacobites had put in a garrison and dominated the adjacent countryside. 'Finding the way longer than he expected' and dawn approaching, Lillingston formed an advance group of 18 cavalrymen and 18 infantrymen mounted on garrons and led them ahead, seizing a bridge across the Nenagh River, 1 km to the east of the town. The whole Jacobite garrison, about 100 men under Brigadier Anthony Carroll, plus considerable numbers of local raparees sallied out but, with only 36 men, Lillingston held the bridge until his main body hurried up. Leaving his foot to secure the pass, Lillingston pressed on with the horse and dragoons towards the Jacobites, who responded with a running fire. However, when Lillingston came close, they turned and ran for the castle, losing about 20 men during the chase. Lillingston ordered a detachment to hold a pass on the west side of Nenagh, towards Limerick, whilst the remainder of his command entered the town. Lacking cannon with which to attack the castle, Lillingston burned the town together with considerable stores of malt and meal, and brought off 300 head of black cattle. Two men were killed and one wounded whilst Jacobite casualties amounted to between 40 and 50 dead. No doubt, Lillingston's raid was intended to suggest to the Jacobites that the Shannon bridge at Killaloe was a possible target for the main campaign. Around the same date, a Jacobite party approached the Williamite frontier garrison at Ballyhooly. Reinforcements were sent from Cork but the Jacobites learned of this and withdrew in considerable confusion. Taking advantage of their disorder, the Ballyhooly garrison sallied and killed several as well as taking seven prisoners. On 15 March Major William Culliford (Royal Dragoons) led a detachment of 100 militia cavalry and 130 militia infantry from Cork towards Ballyclogh, north-west of Mallow, where the Jacobites had established an entrenched position, probably to serve as a forward base from which to raid across the Blackwater into the Williamite quarters. When Culliford arrived, the Jacobites fled with such haste that only seven prisoners were taken.

Intelligence indicated that Brigadier Francis Carroll planned to dispatch five companies of foot, together with a supply of ammunition, to reinforce Colonel Daniel O'Donovan's garrison at Bantry. The combined force was then intended to place the countryside around Bantry under contribution. Lieutenant Colonel George Hamilton (Sir David Colyear's Foot) marched from Bandon on 15 March with 200 infantry from Colyear's, 60 cavalry under brevet Lieutenant Colonel Bartholomew Ogleby (Life Guards), and 80 militiamen. They came within sight of Bantry at 14:00 on 16 March but learned that the Jacobites had departed during the morning. Establishing the direction in which they had marched, Hamilton followed as rapidly as possible. When the Jacobites spotted Hamilton's advance guards, they abandoned all their cattle and dispersed into the bogs. The Williamites pursued for around 7 km, killing about 40 and taking 14 prisoners. More important, they seized several thousand cattle, only 1,500 of which could be taken back to Bandon for want of drovers. Hamilton spent the night of 16–17 March in Bantry, burned the town in the morning and set off on the road back to Bandon. About 10 km from Bantry, the Jacobites set an ambush of 600 men but this was discovered by Hamilton's advance guard and put to flight by a single volley.

Having received intelligence that a body of raparees had gathered in some adjoining woods, on 17 and 18 March a party of cavalry from Mountmellick scoured the area, killing 18. In the south, acting on information that about 40 raparees were lodged around Araglin, County Cork, 12 troopers and 30 infantry marched from Cappoquin, County Waterford. The intelligence proved accurate but the raparees were in much greater strength, so much so that the over-confident Williamite cavalry was initially forced back. From a vantage-point on a hill, a very resourceful trumpeter realized what was happening and sounded a march followed by the charge, giving the impression that cavalry reinforcements were approaching. Persuaded that they were facing superior forces, the raparees dispersed into a wood where they were attacked by the Williamite horse and foot: 27 were killed and 13 taken prisoner, 'three of whom were called captains but, being known rogues, they were all hanged'. A patrol from Villiers's Horse beat a party of raparees at Cappagh, County Cork, killing 30 or 40 and taking several prisoners. A 'good detachment' from Cashel advanced to meet an Irish concentration at Emly, in the west of County Tipperary. As the Williamites approached, the Jacobites withdrew, losing 12 men. In the north on 18 March, Colonel Tiffin set out from Ballyshannon with 200 of his own infantry and two troops from Colonel James Wynne's Dragoons. Within 3 km of Sligo he encountered a Jacobite party under Captain MacSherry. In a brisk action, nine of MacSherry's men were killed and the rest dispersed, whilst Tiffin returned to Ballyshannon with a prey of 30 horses, 180 cattle and 50 sheep. Thirty dragoons from the Dublin militia, commanded by Lieutenant Powel, were sent at a date between 21 and 25 March to arrest some raparees who had been involved in the murder of six infantrymen from Colonel John Foulkes's battalion. This was accomplished but, on his return, Powel received notification that a party of raparees was waiting for him not far from Hacketstown, County Carlow, with a view to rescuing the prisoners. Powel ordered 17 of his dragoons to escort the prisoners whilst he took the remaining 13 to tackle the ambush but, first, he had to find the precise location. The parish constable was reluctant to tell him until 'some hard threatening words' changed his mind. With four men, Powel entered a field adjoining the site of the ambush and came upon 28 raparees under a Captain O'Neill. Seeing only Powel and four men, O'Neill's men advanced and fired but failed to do any damage; the reply was more effective, killing two and wounding O'Neill. Powel's nine remaining men then arrived and charged, putting the Irish to flight. Powel lost two horses and three men wounded. At the beginning of April, six soldiers from the garrison at Birr were 'barbarously' murdered by the raparees, 'as were others in several places'.

At 10:00 on 2 April, Rittmeister Melchior Egidius von Schlieben (Colonel Friedrich von Donop's Danish Horse) moved north with 50 troopers from Fermoy into Jacobite territory. Ranging into southern County Limerick, Schlieben fulfilled his orders to reconnoitre by capturing a Jacobite lieutenant before falling into the omnipresent temptation of cattle raiding. Far from home and probably a little disorganized, von Schlieben's party was set upon by Jacobite cavalry. Most Williamite patrol commanders would have launched a furious counter-attack but von Schlieben gave way and retreated towards Fermoy. At some point he lost control of his men, the Jacobite lieutenant escaped, and what should have been an orderly withdrawal under pressure degenerated into rout. Led by a galloping trumpeter sounding the alarm, von Schlieben's scattered and panic-stricken troopers approached Fermoy Bridge at 15:00 on 3 April but the commander of the guard, Captain Christian Ludwig von Boyneburg (Tettau's Zealand Foot), could see no more than 40 or 50 Jacobite horsemen in pursuit. He was furious and refused to allow them to cross, so they took to the water and swam. Von Boyneburg had positioned a corporal and four privates in a trip-wire position 1 km north of the bridge but von Schlieben's broken command galloped past refusing to stop and cover their withdrawal. A lieutenant and 50 musketeers went forward and were able to rescue two of the men but the corporal was captured and two others shot. Von Schlieben, wrote Boyneburg to Tettau, 'cuts a sorry figure and complains that he was unable to keep his men in order'. Tettau passed on Boyneburg's account to Württemberg requesting a thorough investigation and effective action because the episode brought dishonour on the Danish Corps. Von Schlieben was court-martialled and dismissed.

On 4 April, a party from the Longford garrison, where Lieutenant Colonel Tobias Purcell (Charles Herbert's Foot) was governor, met some Jacobite dragoons near the upper reaches of the River Erne in the vicinity of Lough Gowna, and killed six. The remaining Jacobites then tried to recross the Erne at a point where it was not fordable and ten men were drowned. On the following day, 5 April, Brigadier William Stewart, commanding at Belturbet, sent out a detachment of 50 flintlock-armed infantry and 20 dragoons under Captain Alexander Stewart (Wynne's Enniskillen Dragoons) toward Mohill, County Leitrim, to clear the area of raparees. By daybreak on 6 April, Stewart was within 2 km of Mohill when he discovered two troops of Jacobite dragoons and 50 foot guarding a herd of creaghts and cattle. Without hesitation or reconnaissance, Stewart charged. The Jacobites fired one volley before abandoning the livestock and flying for the shelter of the woods and bogs. Stewart pursued, killing 30 and taking five prisoners. Having suffered no casualties, he returned to Belturbet with 100 black cattle and around 70 horses. On 6 April, Quartermaster John Topham of the Royal Dragoons, commanding 18 dragoons and 12 infantrymen mounted on garrons, surprised Jacobite guards near Newcastle, County Tipperary, killing 17 and taking nine prisoners; seven of the latter proved to be raparees and were promptly hanged. On another occasion, Topham, who established a reputation as a raparee hunter, killed six.

Brigadier Stewart's Mohill raid was typical of so many Williamite operations during the winter of 1690–1: brave, audacious and eye-catching but failing fully to achieve its purpose. Aimed at the eradication of raparees, many officers concentrated instead on cattle raiding for their own profit. The Williamite regular army and county militias failed to solve the problems posed by the raparees because their operations were uncoordinated, unsystematic and ill-disciplined. Individual garrison commanders appear to have launched raids on their own initiative without much reference to other units' plans. Central and regional control was entirely absent. No voices were raised in protest because all ranks benefited from the sale of cattle, sheep and horses whilst local acquisition was vital to supplement inadequate supplies from England. Williamite gains, of course, equalled reciprocal Jacobite deprivation. Without sufficient numbers to dominate the countryside, even though helped by the Protestant militias, the

Williamites could never stamp out raparee activity however many patrols, raids and punitive expeditions were launched. To some extent, it was the small size of the Williamite armies in Ireland that prolonged the war.

Yet the Williamites nearly always enjoyed the advantage in these engagements. Small numbers of disciplined and aggressively led troops, Protestant irregulars and militia consistently beat and scattered bands of raparees, many stiffened by regulars, that were four, five and six times larger. In the absence of contrary evidence, much of this has to be accepted but it is unclear whether this was fact or resulted from unbalanced reportage. Within a few months of the Glorious Revolution, political commentary had quickly adjusted to the new orthodoxies and Whig writers rapidly eclipsed their Tory rivals. Almost without exception, accounts of the small war were written by Williamite observers or compiled in London from letters and oral reports provided by sympathetic sources. Many of the open letters, diaries, journals and memoirs published in England were wholly or semi-propagandistic, seeking to justify the Williamite cause through inevitable success on the battlefields of Ireland. Jacobitism, on the other hand, was out of date and its followers retrogressive and could not possibly have defeated modern, progressive Williamitism. Paradoxically, the Irish enjoyed significant advantages: in their own country they dominated the sources of intelligence and were numerically superior. However, without sufficient discipline, training, equipment, arms, money and effective foreign assistance, and recalling defeat in all previous wars against the English, they lacked confidence in their own abilities. In terms of morale, the Jacobites were beaten as soon as the war had started.

General Ginkel returned to Ireland on 18 April and most of the general officers travelled to attend a planning conference in Dublin. In a statement that must have caused Ginkel to wince, Württemberg expressed disappointment that William would not personally command because he thought that only the royal authority could sufficiently galvanize the army to enter the field early: echoing the opinions of both the Lords Justices in Dublin and the Earl of Nottingham in England, Württemberg predicted gloomily that the army would not start the campaign until July. The Dublin conference heard that the Jacobites intended to field 25,000 infantry and 7,000 cavalry in an effort to prolong the war for as long as possible.[2] The fortifications of Athlone and Limerick were being improved and they still held two major posts east of the Shannon – Ballymore and Nenagh – as well as Ross Castle in County Kerry. Ginkel hoped to have available 42 under-strength battalions of infantry, between six and eight of which would be detached for garrison duty; the militia, theoretically numbering 15,000, would be responsible for the majority of security and occupation duties. He intended to open the campaign with the capture of Athlone and so Mullingar was selected as the main base. Provided that the Royal Navy retained control of the Irish Sea and Western Approaches, then victory should be ultimately achievable. However, it remained possible that a French convoy might sneak through and deliver reinforcements into either Galway or Limerick and so, to negate this possibility, Ginkel wished to enter the field as speedily as possible. The army would gather in three concentrations on 18 May, at Belturbet, Mullingar and between Clonmel and Cashel. The only outstanding issue was the point, or points, at which the Shannon would be crossed.[3]

As the generals planned the campaign, the small war continued. On 7 April, Brigadier Francis Carroll brought four regiments, about 1,500 men, before Enniskean, County Cork, 14 km west of Bandon, one of the most remote and exposed of the frontier garrisons. Carroll intended to capture Enniskean and its adjacent supporting outposts preparatory 'to further advancements' along the valley of the Bandon River towards Kinsale. Enniskean was held by 44 men commanded by Ensigns John Lindsay and Robert Dalyell (Colyear's Foot). This Lilliputian party successfully defended the two main streets into the town for two hours until some of the Roman Catholic inhabitants managed to indicate to the Jacobites an alternative approach. Having broken into the town, Carroll's men set fire to the buildings and the two ensigns led their men back into a substantial house that seemed to offer the best cover and shelter. There they defended themselves for a further six hours, spurning an offer of surrender. The Jacobites then gathered firewood and faggots in order to burn down the house but the garrison was saved from immolation by Lieutenant Colonel Ogleby who rode in from Bandon with a relief party of 150 cavalry and infantry: in some disorder, Carroll withdrew followed by Ogleby's horsemen. Williamite reports suggest Jacobite casualties of between 50 and 72, figures that seem ridiculously high when measured against an admitted Williamite loss of just one man: as so often in seventeenth-century war, these casual conflicts were not intense. Frustrated before Enniskean, 500 Irish attacked Clonakilty on 11 April, but were easily beaten off. Again, reported Jacobite casualties of only three men are not indicative of a heavy engagement.

The offensive against the frontier garrisons in west County Cork continued on 19 April, when a Jacobite force approached Macroom on the Sullane River. Major James Kirke (Edward Villiers's Horse) drew out 80 cavalry and 150 dragoons, plus about 200 mounted militiamen, and marched that evening. They came up with the Irish party at daybreak on 20 April and the Jacobites dispersed into the woods and bogs. After a chase of some hours, 20 Jacobite soldiers were killed and four or five taken prisoner and the usual booty of cattle and horses rendered Kirke's expedition doubly worthwhile. Around the same date, a strong party of raparees crossed the Blackwater and surprised four troops of Colonel Donop's Danish horse regiment at Curraglass, west of Tallow, and stole a number of precious cavalry mounts. Donop seized some hostages from around Curraglass and let it be known that they would all be hanged if the horses were not returned. This produced a prompt response and the horses all reappeared at the places from which they had been taken. Deep in territory that the Williamites supposed was their own, 300 raparees placed an ambush near Kinnegad, County Westmeath, and seized 48 sacks of meal from a poorly guarded convoy. The escort escaped to Mullingar and raised the alarm. A party from the Mullingar garrison sallied and retook much of the lost meal, killing several raparees in the process. Also on 19 April, 700 Jacobites appeared before the small round stone tower at Croghan, King's County, where the garrison of six men and a corporal resisted until their powder was consumed and 12 Irish had been shot.

Five days later, on 24 April, the Williamites suffered a rare reverse. Captain Hugh Palliser (Lord Drogheda's Foot) and Lieutenant Charles Armstrong (Tiffin's Enniskillen Foot), acting on information that a body of raparees with some cattle was in the vicinity, marched from their quarters near Birr with 40 flintlock musketeers from the regular army and 20 from the militia. Their guide, Terence Magragh, who had a protection, led them straight into an ambush organized by Brigadier 'Long Anthony' Carroll. Despite being hugely outnumbered – the Irish deployed two regiments – Palliser's men fought their way into an old castle where they defended themselves until they had used all their ammunition and were then smoked out, overpowered and taken to Nenagh. Armstrong purchased his freedom but Palliser remained a prisoner in Limerick until he escaped at the beginning of June whilst the common soldiers remained incarcerated until the end of the war. Around the same date 21 raparees crossed the Shannon but were captured near Belturbet by a Williamite detachment from Fenagh, County Leitrim. In yet another effort to reduce the incidence of robbery and violence, 500 men from the Dublin militia marched to Kildare on 27 April, where they were joined by a regiment of militia horse under Colonel Piper, to sweep the area for raparees.

Lord Meath's and Lord Lisburn's battalions, the first to leave winter quarters, camped outside Mullingar on 27 April where they found large numbers of Irish living in the open fields, having been ordered out of the town by the governor, Colonel Brewer. Families of ten or twelve, young and old, had fashioned shelters by roofing dry ditches with grass or straw spread on a framework of sticks and branches. On 28 April, Brewer and Lieutenant Colonel Frederick Hamilton (Earl of Meath's Foot) took 600 infantry and 20 cavalry into Jacobite territory west of Kilbeggan where over 2,000 raparees were reported sheltering in huts and cabins. On Brewer's appearance, they deployed on some hills in organized bodies of horse and foot and seemed inclined to offer battle but, as the Williamites came closer, they broke up and dispersed. Brewer killed around 50, burned their shelters and returned to Mullingar. As if to emphasize the uncertain hold of the Williamites, around 28 April 15 raparees seized the northern mail from Dublin in the Moyry Pass. Six of the culprits were later apprehended and hanged.

Commanded by Captain Lawrence Clayton, 150 infantry from the Queen's battalion (Colonel Charles Trelawney) were sent from Cork on 29 April to relieve the frontier post at Ballyhooly, where 80 men from Colonel Ferdinando Hastings's battalion were commanded by Captain Edward Thornicroft and Lieutenant Andrew Hayes. Some distance short of Ballyhooly, on 30 April, Clayton's scouts noticed a body of Irish cavalry but neither side sought to engage. Clayton reached Ballyhooly safely and told of his brush with the Irish, providing corroboration for information already received by Thornicroft that the Jacobite garrison at Ballyclogh planned to intercept his march back to Cork. In view of this, Thornicroft decided to travel by night and set off at midnight. Around 03:00 on 1 May, just short of Sixmilewater, the column was attacked by nearly 120 cavalry, 120 dragoons and 250 infantry and raparees, commanded by Brigadier Francis Carroll, Sir James Cotter, Lord Kinsale, Colonel Lesley, Major Slingsby, Captain Henry Coppinger and Captain Combden. Possibly, the Irish reckoned that the column would be carrying little ammunition, having left most of its supplies for the use of the relief garrison. Thornicroft's men faced about and fired an effective volley temporarily breaking the Jacobites' momentum and gaining enough time for them to take cover in a nearby ancient enclosure surrounded by a chest-high mud wall. They had scarcely blocked the single entrance with a hurdle when the advance guard of the Irish cavalry rode up and offered quarter. Thornicroft refused and fired on the horsemen. During the next few hours, the Irish infantry made several 'brisk' attacks but Thornicroft's men resisted stoutly. A relief party was dispatched from Cork but the Irish had withdrawn before it arrived. The Irish left behind Captain Coppinger, two officers and ten men dead, and Major Slingsby wounded. Slingsby admitted that the Irish had carried off a further 50 or 60 injured. Thornicroft lost eight soldiers and two drivers and had five men wounded. On 29 and 30 April, Brigadier William Stewart hanged Captain Duffe, his lieutenant and 21 raparees at Belturbet, as well as a spy in Cavan. A detachment of 500 from the Dublin City and County militias, under Colonel Piper, conducted an unsuccessful anti-raparee sweep into the western fringes of the Bog of Allen. The governor of Clonmel and Colonel George Blount, with a mixed party of regulars and militia, marched west towards Mitchelstown on 3 May. They failed to encounter any Irish and so turned about and set off back to Clonmel but some of the men straggled, including a corporal who was shot at from behind a bush on the edge of a wood by one, Cashean, 'a known rogue'. This encouraged the detachment to surround the wood and 30 Irish were killed during the ensuing manhunt.

Lieutenant Colonel Daniel Hudson (Lord George Hamilton's Foot) and Major Cornelius Wood (Byerley's Horse) left Mountmellick in late April with 250 infantry and a small escort of cavalry and deployed to the south-west of Portarlington. At daybreak, the infantry entered the woods and bogs, scouring the thickets, whilst the horsemen secured the adjacent causeways and escape routes. They netted 18 killed and six prisoners. Very soon after returning to Mountmellick, Wood received information that a considerable body of raparees was gathering around Castlecuffe in the Queen's County on the northern edge of the Slieve Bloom Mountains. He drew 300 of Lord George Hamilton's infantry and 50 troopers from his own regiment and set off on 4 May. Employing similar tactics, nearly 70 raparees were killed during the initial sweep. On 5 May, leaving the majority of the foot to secure the passes and causeways exiting the bogs, Wood pressed on a further 5 km north with 30 horse, commanded by Lieutenant Anthony Ellis, and 110 infantry to seize some cattle. Around 10:00 Ellis and the cavalrymen started to drive the livestock towards Mountmellick whilst Wood and the infantry turned south to rejoin the main body. Wood's scouts then discovered two detachments of Jacobite regulars, each consisting of about 400 men, commanded by Major John Fitzpatrick, marching quietly between the woods and the Slieve Bloom. Wood calculated that Ellis had not yet cleared the woods and would almost certainly encounter these numerically superior forces. Accordingly, he assumed a covering position in a ploughed field but the Jacobites immediately deployed and attacked. The grenadiers came through and over the hedge bounding the field but, seeing Wood's men stand firm, hesitated and halted. Forthwith, Wood wheeled away along the edge of the wood towards Ellis's assumed position, gathering the 80 foot who had been guarding the northern boundary of the bog, but already they could hear brisk firing in the distance. Wood instructed the infantry to advance on either bank of the Clodiagh River and engage the forces attacking Ellis, whilst the horse swept round into their rear. However, so determined was the infantry assault that the Jacobites had dissolved into flight before the flanking cavalry had cut their line of retreat. Wood pursued through the trees to the edge of the bog, killing about 150 and taking over 100 prisoners at a cost of four men killed and one wounded. This extraordinary victory in which 140 men routed 800 regular troops and inflicted casualties 50 times larger than those suffered is not easy to explain, although it was but an exaggeration of what frequently occurred throughout the war. Perhaps, suggested the Reverend Story, it was difficult for the Jacobite officers to persuade their men to stand in open battle when there were convenient bogs and woods from which they could apply their more traditional methods. Take them abroad, though, said Story, 'and they make no contemptible soldiers'.

Also on 1 May, Captain Edward Johnstone (Lord George Hamilton's Foot) marched with 100 infantry from Tyrrellspass, County Westmeath, for Ballynagore where he surprised two troops of Brigadier Robert Clifford's Regiment of Dragoons and three of Lord Merrion's Horse, killing two officers and 15 dragoons. Having burned Ballynagore Johnstone returned to Tyrrellspass with a good booty of arms, horses and cattle. A sergeant and four men straggled from a party from Colonel Richard Brewer's garrison patrolling the road between Mullingar and Kinnegad on 5 May. Always ready to exploit such opportunities, raparees attacked, killing four and putting out the eyes of the fifth with a dagger. Some of the culprits were taken later that day and two were hanged but a third purchased his life by guiding a party of 110 men under Captain Robert Poyntz (Trelawney's Foot) to a spot within 10 km of Mullingar where the raparees had encamped for the night of 5–6 May. Poyntz charged, killing about 40 and seizing a rich booty. Lieutenant Colonel Hudson marched from the ever-active garrison of Mountmellick on 6 May, killing 18 raparees on the following day.[4]

Ginkel held a second planning conference with his senior officers in Dublin on 13 May. Two absentees were Lieutenant Generals Kirke[5] and Sir John Lanier who were removed from Ireland into England on 30 May and thence to commands in the Confederate Army in the Netherlands. Their replacements, Lieutenant General Hugh Mackay and Major General Thomas Talmash (Tollemache), ex-Anglo-Dutch officers who were more overtly committed to the Williamite cause, arrived in Mullingar on 28 May and 2 June respectively. With them came Sir Martin Beckman as chief engineer. Shortly afterwards, the last of the triumvirate of trouble-makers, Lieutenant General Douglas, was also transferred to the Netherlands. It was decided that the army would assemble in three corps by 25 May: the regiments from the north would concentrate at Belturbet; the main force would gather at Mullingar; and the Dutch and Danes would come together at Cashel. The initial plan was for Ginkel at Mullingar to march for Birr to join Württemberg's Dutch-Danish Corps. They would then force a crossing of the Shannon to the north of Lough Derg, probably at Portumna or Banagher Bridge, before advancing north towards Athlone, which was expected to fall easily when threatened from the rear. The combined corps would then move on Galway. A squadron from the Royal Navy would cruise off the west coast of Ireland, paying particular attention to Galway Bay and the estuary of the Shannon. The most recent intelligence reported that the Jacobite Army would now number about 25,000 men, comprising 21,000 infantry and 4,000 well-mounted cavalry; a large French provision convoy had reached Limerick; and 5,000 French reinforcements were expected.

It was essential to finish the war that summer. Despite opposition from those who wished to see the Irish utterly defeated and the House of Commons which was anticipating paying for the war from the sale of confiscated Irish lands, the best route to peace was to extend extremely generous terms for surrender after gaining an early success in the field; the Lords Justices were convinced that the profits from all the forfeited Irish estates did not equal one-tenth of the financial and political costs of another campaign. The revised conditions were 'very large' because the Lords Justices had advised the king that nothing less would overcome Jacobite extremists and the influence of the clergy and, unlike Ginkel's offer in February 1691, the proclamation would carry the full weight of the royal imprimatur. The document sought to exploit the Irish belief that the French intended to subordinate Ireland whilst the Williamites planned to seize Roman Catholics' property and extirpate their religion. Lord Sydney had written from Het Loo on 14 May expressing William's approval of the Lords Justices' political and military strategy; Queen Mary had endorsed the proclamation by 15 June and a copy was forwarded to Ginkel ready for distribution as soon as he had achieved a victory sufficient to justify its publication.[6]

Salutes from the cannon on the ramparts of St John's Castle in Limerick on 9 May marked the arrival of brevet General St Ruth, accompanied by Lieutenant Generals Tessé and d'Usson. Their route from the quay into the city was lined with troops and Tyrconnell walked 100 paces from his 'palace' to escort them to dinner. That night, St Ruth lodged in a specially prepared house. He was a rough, gauche, unattractive man – a wife beater, according to St Simon – who had made his name directing some of the worst of the *dragonnades* against Huguenots in France before and after the Revocation of the Edict of Nantes in 1685. He also lacked operational experience, although he had held commands in the Savoy-Piedmont theatre during 1690, where he was again noted for his barbarity and cruelty, in which he had commanded Mountcashel's Irish Brigade and earned its respect. St Ruth was an insensitive selection. It was pointed out in the London press that the general responsible for massacring Protestants in France was about to do the same in Ireland. Within a few days, he had conducted several reconnaissances, assessed the overall situation and ordered the troops, except for garrisons in Limerick, Galway, Athlone and Sligo, to prepare for entry into the field. Having learned that Athlone was Ginkel's target, St Ruth ordered the army to assemble at Athlone and the first regiments began to arrive during the second week of May. Problems of supply, however, delayed the concentration and an adequate field force had not gathered at Athlone until 20 June. Despite entering the field much later, Ginkel retained the strategic initiative.

Anti-raparee and cattle raiding operations into the Jacobite stronghold of County Kerry, particularly towards Bantry and Castlehaven, occurred during the first two weeks of May whilst the Jacobites continued their offensives into Williamite County Cork. Around 9 May, 150 soldiers from the Irish Army, supported by raparees, crossed the Blackwater to the east of Fermoy and seized a considerable number of cattle and horses from around Castlelyons, which was garrisoned by 20 Danish cavalrymen and 20 militia dragoons commanded by Colonel von Donop, who set off with most of his command in pursuit. The advance guard, consisting of Lieutenant Johan Nicolas Halkus leading eight troopers and six dragoons, was beaten off and Halkus killed when the raiders' rearguard lined some adjacent hedges and opened fire. Donop then came up with 24 men, gathered the advance guard, and pressed forward, putting the Irish into some disorder. Donop followed the Jacobites beyond Kilworth, 3 km north of Fermoy, killing about 50, including four officers, and retaking the lost cattle plus additional livestock, weapons and equipment. On 15 May, the Reverend Story recorded that the Bandon militia had recently captured Captain Hugh O'Donovan and six of his men. More important, a Major O'Neill, who had been sent from Athlone to inspect the fortifications at Ballymore, deserted to the Williamites, no doubt bearing extremely useful information. On the 'common' between Kinnegad and Mullingar, 'a waste country, with woods and bogs in each side', Irish raiders attacked a provision convoy travelling towards Ginkel's main base. The escort, a mere eight infantrymen from Brewer's battalion, beat off the assault although a Williamite sutler was killed by a random shot. The insecurity of the Williamite heartlands, plus the shortage of money, provisions and troops, further delayed Ginkel's entry into the field. Anxious to hasten preparations, he went forward to Mullingar on 18 May but returned to Dublin shortly afterwards. Around the same date, 18 May, a party of 300 Williamite cavalry and dragoons, supported by 200 militia, marched to relieve the garrison at Ballyhooly. When the relief had been successfully accomplished, a detachment marched west to reconnoitre the Jacobite post at Ballyclogh. Initially, the garrison advanced to meet them but then withdrew into Ballyclogh, having lost five dead and five prisoners. On 26 May, Captain William Underhill (Lisburn's Foot) marched with 60 infantry and ten dragoons to Ballinderry, County Tipperary, on the east shore of Lough Derg, where he encountered a detachment of nearly 300 Irish regulars. During the subsequent engagement, Underhill's party killed five officers and 50 privates. Emboldened by this success, on the following day (27 May) Underhill ranged further afield with only 24 men but inflicted an additional 12 casualties. When he finally encountered Colonel Conly Geoghegan leading a significantly larger body of Irish, Underhill skilfully executed a fighting withdrawal, losing one man killed and another wounded.

The train of artillery, comprising 36 cannon and eight mortars, left Dublin on 26 May, reaching Mullingar four days later (30 May). Ginkel departed for Mullingar on Friday 29 May and, on arrival, immediately convened a further planning conference. The previous resolution to form a flying camp to the south, in either County Tipperary or Cork, was abandoned because the Cork militia, provided it was stiffened by two regular battalions under Brigadier Sir John Hanmer, was judged strong enough to protect the south-west. Williamite appreciation of the situation within the Jacobite frontier was unclear because of confused intelligence from Connaught: apparently, Sarsfield had fallen out with St Ruth, who in turn was vigorously opposed by Tyrconnell; St Ruth had ordered the concentration of the Jacobite field army at Loughrea, equidistant from Galway and Athlone; and the Irish would not defend Ballymore. Williamite plans reflected these uncertainties. Crossing the Shannon at Banagher Bridge or Portumna to come at Athlone from the south and west remained an option so Württemberg was ordered to concentrate at Thurles. The final decision to cross at Athlone was taken largely because attempts to storm Banagher Bridge and Portumna during the winter had proved unsuccessful. Crossing at Athlone would be difficult unless portions of the Irish Army were distracted towards Galway by the Royal Navy demonstrating in Galway Bay, although hopes that this might occur were faint. Ginkel was at least confident that he could deploy most of his regular troops into the field army because the militia was proving more than satisfactory in assuming responsibility for internal security. On about 28 May the Protestant gentry of County Meath met at Trim and agreed to scour the adjacent Red Bog, which played host to numerous raparees who had inflicted considerable damage over the winter. The subsequent operation killed 35 raparees and hanged six. The County Waterford militia killed a number of raparees near Kilmallock.[7]

At Mullingar Ginkel found eight battalions of infantry, one regiment of dragoons and six of cavalry, all looking at their best in new uniforms. Still to arrive were the corps of Württemberg and Douglas. When the latter left Belturbet the only regular forces remaining in Ulster were the infantry battalion of Colonel John Michelburne, one company of Colonel Samuel Venner's battalion, one troop of Sir Albert Connyngham's Dragoons and one troop of Colonel Wynne's Dragoons supplemented by a considerable militia under the overall command of Sir Francis Hamilton, Lord Lieutenant of County Donegal. Michelburne, now the senior officer commanding in Ulster, was ordered to post his troops and militia at the various crossing points along the line of the River Erne – Belturbet, Cavan, Enniskillen, Belleek and Ballyshannon – to guard against incursions from the Jacobite garrisons in Jamestown, Boyle and, in particular, Sligo, where Sir Teague O'Regan was governor. Michelburne's task was demanding because the rivers were flowing at a low level following a dry winter and so he organized patrols to ride from post to post every night. About the middle of June, a small party of dragoons that regularly patrolled 7 km of open country between Ballyshannon and Bundoran was surprised whilst fishing for salmon by a Jacobite party under Captain MacSherry, and ten were captured. They were released soon afterwards in exchange for Lieutenant Scott, the brother of Colonel Edward Scott, deputy-governor of Sligo, but their horses and arms were forfeit.[8]

Throughout the winter, the militia had occupied Camgart Castle, 10 km from the regular army post at Birr. Very early on the morning of 1 June, Grace and Galloping Hogan, two raparee leaders, slipped from their lair in the Slieve Bloom with 80 men, surprised and secured the militia garrison and occupied the castle. Ensign Alexander Story (Drogheda's Foot), brother of the Reverend George Story, was close by with some infantry but the information that reached him was confused. Nevertheless, he set off at the head of 30 troops either to prevent the raparees from entering the castle or, if he was already too late, stop them burning it. He posted his main body in an orchard and, accompanied by two soldiers, went forward to within musket-shot of the gate but the raparees remained out of sight. A woman carrying water to a nearby cabin signalled that the castle had already fallen whereupon a volley from the walls killed Story and one of his escorts. Although unable to collect the bodies because of their propinquity to the castle the soldiers in the orchard were allowed to march off without interference. On returning safely to their quarters a drummer was sent to ask for Story's body but the raparees demurred and said that they would bury it honourably themselves, which they did before midday, marking his passing with three volleys.

Württemberg's 7,000 troops decamped from Thurles on 4 June, reaching Roscrea on 5 June where they rested on the following day. From Mullingar, still uncertain about where to attempt to cross the Shannon, Ginkel sent the Reverend Trench 'who has been very forward in their Majesties' service', to Württemberg on 5 June. Trench was to ask Württemberg to reconnoitre Banagher Bridge and Meelick and, if he thought them viable, either to await the arrival of the main army from Mullingar or try to 'bounce' the river. Trench set off with an escort of 30 cavalry but had some difficulty in getting through to the south because the countryside was full of raparees, Irish deserters and other renegades: he eventually met Württemberg at Roscrea on 6 June. In the meantime, realizing that his instructions to Württemberg might result in the opening of a serious gap between the two corps of the army through which the Jacobites could launch an attack on Dublin, Ginkel had changed his mind. Accordingly, Württemberg was told to come north to join Ginkel on the march towards Athlone. Württemberg's corps duly proceeded to Birr on 7 June, where it remained on 8 and 9 June. On 10 June it moved to Streamstown, County Westmeath, but not until 18 June at Ballybornia did it join with Ginkel. Again emphasizing the insecurity of the Midlands, Ginkel ordered the perimeter of the fortifications around the base camp at Mullingar to be shortened so that it could be held by fewer men, thus releasing more troops for the field army. Four cannon were planted on a mound towards the south side of the town.[9]

19

Ballymore and Athlone

South-west of Mullingar a small fort stood on Dysart Island in Lough Ennell, used by the Williamites as a store for goods confiscated from local Roman Catholics. During the winter it had been seized by the Jacobites in a surprise attack who employed it as secure magazine for grain, beef and butter. Lieutenant Colonel Robert Burton, the Jacobite chief engineer, considered Dysart Fort so strong that it could be held by 60 men against any force provided that heavy siege artillery did not come into play. During Sarsfield's absence from his command post in Athlone to confer with Tyrconnell in Limerick, Brigadier Robert Clifford assumed command. Thinking that the Williamites from Mullingar were about to launch a surprise attack on Dysart, he evacuated the stores, burned the fort and pulled the defenders back to Ballymore.

Ginkel was the senior lieutenant general in the Dutch Army. Initially, he had been regarded as a stop-gap until a more prestigious appointment could be made but William was not inclined to look further than his trusted subordinate, despite the reservations expressed by senior politicians. He was not the ideal choice, moaned the Marquis of Carmarthen:

> I despair of any good there [in Ireland] unless the king can find somebody of quality to send thither who is big enough to expect obedience and who may be assisted by some officer experienced in the military part, since his Majesty has no Englishman who hath both these qualifications.[1]

Despite Lieutenant General Hugh Mackay's entreaties, Ginkel did not await Württemberg's arrival and marched from Mullingar on Saturday 6 June. During the morning he was strengthened by Douglas's northern corps of seven battalions of foot, two regiments of dragoons and two of cavalry. The combined army, comprising 15 infantry battalions and 19 squadrons of horse and dragoons, in addition to a train of artillery consisting of nine 24-pounders, one 18-pounder and three mortars, camped that night at Rathconrath. During the hours of darkness, Major General Henri de Massue, Marquis de Ruvigny, went ahead with a strong party of cavalry and dragoons towards Ballymore either to prevent a relief from slipping into the fort or the garrison from escaping. He encountered a patrol from the Ballymore garrison, killing four and taking two prisoners. Although severely injured, one of the prisoners reported that Ballymore was occupied by about 1,000 of the Irish Army's best men. On 7 June Ginkel arrived at the small village, which, within three days, had been totally destroyed. Ballymore Fort, a jumble of old and new structures, stood on a 6-acre peninsula pointing into Lough Sunderlin. At its tip was an ancient Viking fort, which the Jacobites had improved through the addition of a broad, deep ditch and palisade. Close by was 'a pretty strong house', where one Widow White had been in residence in 1690. The double ditch backed by a stone wall that blocked off the landward approach through the neck of the peninsula had been reinforced by a hornwork, two bastions and a retrenchment. Towards the north and north-east, Sunderlin Lough was so wide that breaching cannon could not damage the fortifications, whilst the western and north-western sides were covered by a bog. The only feasible approach was from the south, through Sarsfield's new fortifications across the neck. In 1690 Douglas had thought Ballymore too poor to support a garrison but Sarsfield had appreciated its potential as a post from which to dominate the east bank of the Shannon, disturb Williamite quarters in Leinster and cover Athlone.

Ruvigny's advance guard had driven in the Jacobite outposts by 12:00 on 7 June locking the garrison inside the fort, except for one sergeant and 15 men who occupied a small tower on a low hill, 400 m to the east of the lough. Even when cut off, this sergeant had the audacity to continue firing, causing two casualties. After the position had been stormed by Williamite infantry, he was hanged in sight of the garrison on what became known as 'Sergeant's Hill'. Ginkel summoned the governor, Colonel Ulick Bourke, to surrender but 'he made a shuffling sort of reply in the hopes of getting better terms' so the besiegers set about erecting batteries; four were ready by 22:00 and a fifth, for mortars, was completed during the night of 7–8 June. Fire was opened at daybreak on 8 June: two batteries aimed at the new retrenchment across the neck of the peninsula; another concentrated on the palisades; whilst the fourth and the mortars battered the hornwork. Following a short overture of fire, at 08:00 Ginkel again summoned the fort threatening that if there was no capitulation within two hours the soldiers would suffer the same fate as the corpse dangling on Sergeant's Hill. Again, Bourke played for time. By noon, breaches had been started in the hornwork and the retrenchments before the Viking fort and the palisades had been smashed. A white flag appeared but Ginkel ignored it and the bombardment continued to widen the breaches in readiness for an infantry assault. Ginkel expected the pontoon and bridging train to arrive from Mullingar in the morning and the tin boats could then be used to mount an attack across Sunderlin Lough. However, Captain Hoard's four large longboats were already in camp having wintered in Mullingar. Ginkel ordered them to be packed with infantry and launched on the lough. Ballymore Fort lacked water-side defences and the sight of these amphibious preparations so alarmed the garrison that they hung out the white flag for a second time, waving it more vigorously. Firing ceased at 19:00 and Governor Bourke and several officers emerged from the gate to submit to Ginkel's mercy. Surrender was agreed at 20:00 and Colonel Thomas Erle occupied the fort with 800 men. He found that the garrison had been well provisioned with stocks of oatmeal, 300 cattle, 500 sheep and plentiful powder and shot for the two field guns.

During the night of 8–9 June, the Williamites were alarmed by reports that a relief corps of 5,000 Jacobites was approaching; Ginkel doubled the guards and directed a strong detachment of cavalry along the Athlone road. Within 3 km of the town a camp of 1,000 Irish was encountered but they were allowed to withdraw into Athlone, the horsemen having orders to advance no further. The Ballymore garrison marched for Dublin on 9 June, a total of 780 regular soldiers and 259 raparees, commanded by four field officers, 16 captains, 14 lieutenants, and 12 ensigns and cornets. There were also 645 women and numerous children, for whom Ginkel generously ordered a cartload of ammunition bread. The defenders had lost about 40 men to mortar and cannon fire, whilst Ginkel suffered only eight fatal casualties. Ginkel's soldiers escorted the prisoners to Kilcock whence they handed over to the Dublin militia. The officers remained in Dublin prior to removal to Chester whilst other ranks were interned, under the supervision of militia, on the Island of Lambay, one league off the coast opposite Swords. The Lords Justices were keen to ship the Lambay prisoners to the Netherlands to serve under Protestant officers in the Confederate Army. Because the Jacobites had tried neither to evacuate the fort nor attempt a relief, the equivalent of a full regiment of infantry had been sacrificed.

Ginkel then camped on the west side of the village to await Württemberg's corps. On 10 June, 200 soldiers, mostly from Lord Drogheda's battalion, started to repair the breaches, level the trenches and batteries, and improve the fortifications – a line of communication was dug linking the works across the neck of the peninsula with the entrenchment around the Viking fort and defences were constructed along the shore of the lough – but progress was hampered by bad weather. Whilst waiting outside Ballymore, Ginkel received confirmation that the Jacobite field army was concentrating on Athlone but of immediate concern was the indiscipline of his own troops: stealing was rife within the camp and swearing and profanity abounded. Chaplains were instructed to say prayers daily before their regiments at 10:00 and 19:00. On pain of death sutlers were ordered not to buy weapons, equipment, uniforms or accoutrements from soldiers, who were in the habit of selling possessions for drink and ready cash.[2]

Ginkel was a conventional, methodical, orthodox and systematic soldier. For his first, major, independent command, he had been entrusted with a campaign that would confirm, damage or wreck the new regime in England and Scotland as well as having a major impact on the prospects of the Grand Alliance. Aware of this responsibility, he took no risks, waiting at Ballymore until its defences had been repaired and improved, his communications with Mullingar and Dublin secured, Württemberg's arrival assured, and the pontoons reportedly on the road from Dublin although his information of this point was erroneous and the bridging train was still scattered in Dublin and Waterford.[3] Only when everything was in place did he move on Athlone. Württemberg's march north across the bogs of the Midlands was painfully slow, deliberate and lacking in urgency but there is no record that Ginkel asked him to hurry. Although he could not have known it because intelligence from within Connaught was poor and unreliable, had Ginkel marched the moment that Ballymore surrendered he would have found Athlone occupied by only weak forces – it was still lightly garrisoned as late as 8 June – and uncovered by St Ruth's field army. He might have crossed the Shannon with ease, taken Galway without a fight and obliged St Ruth to fall back on Limerick. In view of Ginkel's earlier interest in Portumna and Banagher, Württemberg's wandering journey north filled St Ruth with doubt about his intentions; Banagher Bridge clearly remained a possible target. Even though Ginkel was at Ballymore, he might well move south and join Württemberg to attack Banagher. The lie of the country did not favour St Ruth. If he concentrated at Athlone and Ginkel crossed at Banagher, he would have to march along two sides of a triangle, via Ballinasloe, to intercept and would probably arrive too late. St Ruth's difficulties in transporting supplies from Limerick – the countryside along and to the west of the Shannon from Limerick to the north of Lough Derg was barren, unpopulated and devastated – also militated against a concentration at Athlone and so he compromised by stringing his men behind the Shannon as far north as Ballinasloe. Not until 19 June, when finally convinced that Athlone was the target, did he shift most of his troops north to achieve a last-minute concentration that could be interpreted as either the epitome of professionalism or damned good luck.[4]

A strong detachment of cavalry reconnoitred from Ballymore towards Athlone on 16 June. Satisfied that no major Jacobite forces were in the field to the east of the Shannon, Ginkel appointed Lieutenant Colonel Tobias Purcell (Herbert's Foot) governor of Ballymore to direct a garrison of four companies from Douglas's infantry battalion. Lieutenant General Douglas himself then departed for the Netherlands. In view of his earlier experience, Colonel Lord Lisburn was sent towards Lanesborough with 2,000 infantry and 500 cavalry to ensure that Jacobite forces were not preparing to descend on Ginkel's open northern flank and communications when he moved on Athlone and became tied down by formal siege operations. Lisburn encountered only a small party of cavalry, which he chased across the Shannon, killing two or three. The Lords Justices were optimistic that the Jacobite Army would collapse as soon as Ginkel crossed the Shannon. Anti-raparee operations continued in the rear areas (17

June), mostly conducted by militia. A strong patrol marching between Cashel and Clonmel diverted on receiving intelligence that 400 raparees were near Tipperary. The Irish, however, dispersed having learned of the Williamite advance, leaving behind 30 men to burn the town. An attempt by raparees to steal cattle from Roscrea failed at a cost of 12 casualties. Captain White led an expedition into the Bog of Allen to tackle McCabe's gang: 12 were killed but McCabe escaped. On 18 June, a detachment from the Williamite garrison of Fermoy raided northwards towards the borders of County Limerick, seizing 120 cattle and killing some raparees.

Finally, on 18 June, Ginkel left Ballymore and camped that night at Ballybornia, where he was joined by Württemberg and Count Nassau with their corps of 7,000 men. This brought Ginkel's strength up to about 18,000 effectives. As his troops filed into camp, Ginkel rode forward, escorted by a detachment of cavalry, to reconnoitre Athlone. He was able to see several small parties of Jacobite horse on some low hills near the town and St Ruth's main army camped on a narrow neck of dry land between two bogs about 3 km beyond the Shannon where it was to remain throughout the coming siege. Very early on the morning of 19 June, Ginkel's advance party marched from Ballybornia and, by 09:00, had beaten the Irish outposts from the hedges, ditches and narrow lanes, which might have been more effectively defended, back under the walls of English Town. In 1690, when Douglas had approached Athlone, the Jacobites had burned English Town and retired across the river into Irish Town but this time they seemed more prepared to offer a defence east of the Shannon. Some commented that Douglas should have demolished the walls of English Town when he left but those who had been with his expedition knew that there had been insufficient time. Anxious to press on, Ginkel ordered three cannon to be placed near a ford on the north side of English Town, which fired all day upon an Irish breastwork. At about 18:00 the siege train arrived and the men laboured throughout the night to raise two batteries.

By obliging Ginkel to consume precious time attacking English Town before attempting to force the Shannon, followed by a siege of Irish Town and, finally, fighting St Ruth's field army camped to the west, Athlone offered the Jacobites the opportunity to mount a long, sustained and staggered defence. The concept, however, was undermined by practical considerations: Irish Town was dominated by high ground on the Leinster side and the Shannon was running at a very low level after a dry spell, only 40 cm deep in places, and was fordable for about 700 m below the bridge. Normally, because of the bogs, Athlone could only be attacked on a very narrow frontage but the dry conditions negated this advantage. Throughout the winter a French engineer had been supervising the refortification of English Town, even though the actual settlement consisted only of charred ruins, in order to create a first line of defence. However, after the fall of

English Town, the defenders would face significant difficulties. The fortifications of Irish Town – which only protected three sides, the bank of the Shannon being almost entirely unfortified – were overlooked by the higher ground in English Town to such an extent that they were effectively untenable. Indeed, the French engineer advocated their total demolition: as soon as the Williamites had crossed the river St Ruth's field army could deliver a heavy counter-attack through an open, unfortified Irish Town before a bridgehead had been established. He also recommended fortifying the narrow neck of land between the two bogs that protected St Ruth's camp in order to create a fortified corridor through which such a counter-attack could develop. However, even that strategy was imperfect because the two bogs were dry and passable enabling the Williamites to cross the Shannon via fords, circle Irish Town and attack the flanks of the advancing Jacobites. The only positive point was that the dry conditions would allow the Jacobites to deploy their numerous and effective cavalry.

Tyrconnell travelled to Athlone on 21 June. St Ruth was under the impression that Tyrconnell was responsible only for civil affairs, James having promised to write to him explaining that the Frenchman was to have sole command of the army. Either James did not send this letter, or its existence was concealed, but Tyrconnell insisted that St Ruth was subordinate in all matters. To assert his complete authority, Tyrconnell presented himself at Athlone. St Ruth pretended not to notice but such a confused command structure could not endure for long. The route from St Ruth's camp to Athlone lay along a causeway and its entry into Irish Town was protected by an entrenchment, excavated in 1690. Tyrconnell, fully endorsing the French engineer's defensive plan, recommended levelling this entrenchment so that the garrison could be easily reinforced and relieved from the camp. In addition, should the Williamites break into Irish Town, the army could advance rapidly through the city to drive them out. However, St Ruth disregarded this advice and the entrenchment remained, seriously hindering the covering army from sustaining the garrison. He reasoned that the garrison of Irish Town was quite sufficient and would not require rapid reinforcement because the Williamites could only attack across the broken bridge; the fact that the low water level activated the fords was ignored. This line of argument was probably disingenuous and it may be that the lord lieutenant's opinion was rejected because St Ruth had been inveigled into Sarsfield's faction, which subsequently sent a message to Tyrconnell via Lieutenant Colonel O'Connor to the effect that the guy ropes on his pavilion would be cut if he did not immediately leave the army, an indignity that would have constituted a direct challenge to the authority of James II and openly riven the army whilst in the face of the enemy. Although Tyrconnell estimated that five cavalry regiments, three or four of dragoons and half of the best infantry would probably side with him, he backed down before the Jacobites imploded. He left the camp quietly and returned to Limerick.[5]

During 20 June, Ginkel's batteries bombarded the bastion to the east of the Dublin Gate, on the north side towards Lanesborough. A breach as wide as the bastion itself had appeared by noon but heavy firing was continued to prevent the garrison, which consisted of only four companies of foot, from digging retrenchments across the neck of the breach. A council of war was held at 15:00 which agreed to assault the breach at 17:00. The storming party consisted of 300 grenadiers, 150 from each of the two wings of the army, commanded by Lieutenant Colonel Francis Gore (Tiffin's Foot), one major, six captains, 12 lieutenants and 12 sergeants. One lieutenant, one sergeant and 30 grenadiers were to enter the breach and then move right to the foot of the Shannon Bridge to intercept reinforcements from Irish Town. Should they discover any retrenchments in front of the bridge, they were to take cover until the arrival of their supports in the form of 50 additional grenadiers, led by a captain, two lieutenants and two sergeants. Both the leading groups wore armour. In turn, the support group would be seconded by Lieutenant Colonel Gore, three captains, five sergeants and 120 grenadiers, who would make their way towards the foot of the bridge. Next, the major, two captains, four lieutenants, four sergeants and 110 grenadiers would turn left out of the breach and clear the rampart. Finally, 25 workmen, carrying hatchets, pick-axes, shovels and hammers would march to the bridge and another 25 proceed to the ramparts. Once these storm troops were on their way, Brigadier William Stewart's battalion of infantry would enter the breach and march towards the bridge, whilst Prince Frederick's Danish battalion, commanded by Colonel Frederik Munchgaar, helped to clear the ramparts. Finally, in the rear of the two supporting battalions, came another 200 workmen carrying fascines and the equipment necessary for the erection of blinds and breastworks. Cavalry stood to the rear. The lieutenant colonel or the major of the storming party, or any other officer who first came to the ford south of the bridge, was to prevent Irish troops crossing at that point. Lieutenant General Hugh Mackay was placed in overall command of the operation, assisted by Brigadiers William Stewart and Otto von Viettinghoff. Officers were enjoined to keep strict control over their men, not to allow them to advance too quickly and get out of hand and to prevent, as far as possible, incidents involving friendly fire.

Commanded by a lieutenant from Cambon's Huguenot regiment, the advance party of 30 grenadiers approached within 150 m of the breach under cover of some low mounds. Upon the starting signal – a volley from all the cannon – they dashed across the open ground, receiving 'brisk' musketry from the defenders, and clambered through the rubble into the breach. The lieutenant threw in his grenade and fired his musket, ordering his men to do the same. He was shot down but his example encouraged the grenadiers who hurled in their grenades, charged across the debris and rushed the breach, the defenders giving way and running for the bridge. Vigorously and closely pursued by the grenadiers, the defenders fled along the bridge until they came to the broken span close to the Connaught side. Despite many of the defenders still being on the wrong side, the planks spanning the broken arch were lifted and several fugitives were thus forced into the river. English Town had fallen in a few minutes. The church bell was rung whilst the grenadiers took up positions at the foot of the bridge and dug in. They had lost about 20 dead, including the unfortunate Lieutenant Colonel James Kirke (Villiers's Horse) mangled by a stray cannon ball as he lay on the side of a hill watching the action, and 40 wounded, amongst whom were Lieutenant Colonel Gore and Brigadier Stewart, shot in the neck and right arm. Apart from those killed or injured whilst negotiating the breach, the majority of Williamite casualties were caused by musketry down the length of the bridge; to provide protection, engineers quickly piled fascines to form blinds. The Irish suffered about 60 fatalities. During the evening, three guns firing on the breastwork by the northern ford were drawn off and a battery of nine 18-pounders was advanced through English Town to the river bank. An adventurous general might have tried to take advantage of shocked, demoralized and disorganized opponents to 'bounce' a crossing of the Shannon along the bridge and over two fords that the Williamites had noticed the English Town defenders using during their withdrawal. Ginkel, however, opted for the orthodox method of softening up Irish Town by artillery bombardment prior to a formal infantry assault. With no defences along the banks of the Shannon, apart from the castle and a half-completed trench facing the fordable reach, Irish Town was fully exposed to Ginkel's guns. Except to shelter as best they could, there was nothing that Governor Sir Nicholas Fitzgerald, assisted by Lieutenant General d'Usson, and his garrison of 1,500 men could do.[6]

During the first three weeks of June, Major Culliford had made several successful cattle raids into Jacobite quarters. On 23 June, hearing that a detachment of about 2,000 Irish cavalry and infantry had been ordered into those parts of Counties Kerry and Cork from which the Irish had drawn supplies during the first siege of Limerick and the winter of 1690–1, Culliford set off with 120 Royal Dragoons and 50 militia infantry. He surprised two troops of Anthony Carroll's regiment of dragoons, killing about 20, seizing 200 cattle and 30 horses, and chasing the remainder as far as Newmarket, north-west of Banteer. Here another 15 Irish soldiers were dispatched and more cattle seized. Culliford then pressed on a further 10 km into the mountains, hoping to find richer spoils, but already too far from base, his command weakened by having to detach 11 dragoons and 24 militiamen to escort the stolen livestock, and the men very tired, he turned back to the south-east straight into an ambush laid by 700 Irish cavalry and dragoons led by Sir James Cotter. Culliford lost 20 killed and 20 taken prisoner but managed to disengage and fell back to the comparative safety of Drumagh Castle, south of Kanturk, where he found the party escorting the stolen livestock plus a reinforcement of 20 men under Captain Bower. Hearing that Culliford was in difficulty, Colonel Ferdinando Hastings, Governor of Cork, and Lieutenant Colonel Ogleby took 200 regulars and 500 militia from Ballyhooly and marched beyond Ballyclogh to his relief. The Irish tried to obstruct their passage by lining hedges and ditches with musketeers but Hastings and Ogleby forced their way through, killing about 50 Irish. On the next morning they relieved Culliford in Drumagh Castle, killing another 13 Irish and burning the adjacent countryside. Culliford's misfortunes were in the context of wider operations aimed at extending the Williamite frontiers to restrict Jacobite access to the resources of County Kerry. On 17 June, Richard Cox, the Governor of County Cork, travelled to Enniskean with an engineer on whose advice he ordered the fortification of part of the town and placed a garrison of militia in the castle. Cox then went further west to Dunmanway 'which he found totally demolished'. From here he dispatched 250 militia, commanded by Colonel Townshend, to Bantry, where, on 20 June, they took a considerable prey of cattle and killed over 100 raparees at a cost of just four horses. Reinforcements were also sent to the garrison at Mallow in order to keep a close eye on the advanced Jacobite post at Ballyclogh, whence many of the raids into Williamite territory had been launched.

In the bogs of the Midlands, a combination of relentless pressure and the final retreat of the Irish Army behind the line of the Shannon gradually reduced the efficacy of the raparee bands. Denied reinforcements and material support and hounded by enthusiastic Protestant militias, they declined in number, cohesion and motivation. Anti-raparee sweeps resembled field sports rather than martial operations. The Dean of St Patrick's, Dublin, Dr Samuel Synge, marched from Kildare on 23 June at the head of Captain Baggott's militia dragoons and joined Captains White and Chabenor at Edenberry to search for a reported party of raparees. At daybreak, the militia entered a bog from the north and south. Raparees, to the number of about 60, were first encountered by the County Wicklow militia, directed by Lieutenant Hamilton and Ensign Hawkshead, but promptly dispersed into several small groups, so Hamilton split his men into three parties, each of which fell in with some of the raparees killing 13. Hamilton's men then pushed the bulk of the trapped raparees towards Captain Chabenor's cavalry, which beat them back into the bog directly into the fire of Hamilton's musketeers: a further eight raparees lost their lives. Hamilton and Chabenor next scoured the bog towards Dean Synge and Captain Baggott's dismounted dragoons. Rather than face Baggott and the church militant, the raparees fled back into the bog into the sights of Corporal Howard leading 20 of Hamilton's men, and a further eight fell. Howard pushed the survivors towards Clonbulloge, south of Edenberry, where James Purefoy stood with six horsemen, whose fire dispatched another three. Those still alive escaped into thick woods where, despite vigorous efforts, they could not be found.[7]

On 21 June, several detachments of cavalry patrolled the area around Athlone. One, under Colonel Wolseley, went back towards Ballymore to escort 11 cannon and three mortars 'and also to hasten the pontoons'. Escorted by elements of Robert Byerley's cavalry regiment and the Royal Horse Guards, the bridging train finally arrived early in the afternoon of 23 June. Two batteries, one of six 24-pounders and the other comprising eight 18-pounders, were ready by 20:00 on 21 June whilst a mortar battery, situated to the north of English Town, was completed by 05:00 on 22 June. Bombs rained down on the north-east side of the castle, its weakest sector, and a large breach was opened within two hours. During the afternoon of 22 June, a French lieutenant colonel who had lain beneath the bridge, wounded, since 20 June was carried to the Williamite camp. Despite suffering from a severe back injury and heavy bruising, he was concerned less for himself than the pusillanimous Irish who were likely to prove but 'very indifferent defenders of his master, the French king's, interest in that kingdom'. Another deserter reported that a number of Jacobite infantry had been burned to death when Williamite grenades had set fire to a mill upon the bridge during the attack on 20 June. The mortars roared throughout the night of 22–23 June and one side of the castle had been demolished by 05:00 on 23 June; within a further 48 hours, it had become untenable.

Two additional batteries were constructed on the river bank above and below the bridge during 24 June. In the evening one of Lord Lisburn's grenadiers ventured underneath the bridge searching for plunder amongst Jacobite corpses and found two standards belonging to Lord Clanricard's infantry regiment lying on the beach. Despite heavy musketry, he carried them to Ginkel who rewarded him with five guineas. Acting on a report that a ford towards Lanesborough was tenable, a lieutenant of cavalry was ordered to reconnoitre. Arriving at the site, despite clear orders to return as soon as he had tested the ford, he spotted some black cattle in the distance and galloped after them thus revealing his presence to the Irish who promptly began building strong earthworks to protect the crossing. He was later court-martialled and 'suffered for it'. Because of the lieutenant's indiscipline, Ginkel now had no alternative but to force a crossing at Athlone. The defenders raised two small batteries north of the castle during the night of 24–25 June, one of three six-pounders close to the Shannon and another comprising four six-pounders set back on some rising ground. Both opened fire on 25 June, the smaller shooting at Williamite positions in English Town whilst the larger engaged Ginkel's main camp on the river bank, forcing it to be shifted to safer ground.

The attackers completed a second Williamite battery below the bridge, consisting of six 24-pounders, on 25 June and bombarded the entrenchment covering the fordable reach from 06:00; it was soon levelled and the few remaining standing houses in the east part of Irish Town flattened. The entrenchments within the eastern sector of Irish Town were now so exposed that they had to be abandoned and three retrenchments were dug close to the fortifications lining the western side. By 26 June, seven batteries were blasting Irish Town, making it difficult for the Irish to repair their retrenchments without suffering heavy casualties. Seven powder wagons arrived in Ginkel's camp to replenish the artillery and repairs to the tin boats were completed. The bombardment continued throughout the night of 26–27 June and some of Ginkel's infantry quietly occupied the bridge up to the broken arch, mending a second damaged span as they advanced. The next day, 27 June, was occupied with preparations for a major assault. Seven raparees were captured at Ballynahown, south-east of Athlone, and Ginkel ordered the village to be garrisoned by a lieutenant and 20 men as a sounding post on the vulnerable southern flank. During the afternoon 100 ammunition carts arrived from Dublin and a new battery of five cannon was constructed in a meadow to the south to enfilade the corridor between Irish Town and St Ruth's camp. During the evening, Williamite grenades set fire to the fascine breastworks that had been raised on the bridge behind the broken arch and they blazed fiercely in the hot, dry weather. Their destruction forced the Irish to abandon their positions on the bridge and occupy retrenchments at its foot.

Working from behind their own fascine and timber breastworks during the night of 27–28 June Ginkel's soldiers laid beams and planks across the broken arch to form a walkway. The jury bridge was almost complete when, early on the morning of 28 June, a sergeant and ten men from Brigadier Thomas Maxwell's regiment, all clad in armour, sallied from their retrenchments with the aim of destroying the breastworks and temporary repairs. They were all killed but more and more parties sallied and eventually succeeded in throwing the beams and planks into the river, despite heavy casualties. Around midday, Williamite grenades ignited Jacobite fascines and barricades on the bridge and the resultant fire spread to some neighbouring houses. To discourage firefighters, 30 Williamite guns concentrated on the foot of the bridge the mortars firing stones which shattered against the walls of the castle showering the area with splinters. It was said John Stevens, 'a mere hell on earth', the hottest spot of his military career. The conflagration was only extinguished by blowing up one of the houses to form a firebreak. Ginkel's engineers then decided that a 'close gallery', a timber tunnel, would have to be erected on the bridge to protect the infantry charged with making a second attempt to repair the arch. This was duly accomplished although the arch was spanned with fascines rather than solid timber.

Ginkel, 'wavering irresolute' and prone to reflecting the last opinion he had received, according to Hugh Mackay, summoned a council of war on the afternoon of 28 June. There were three options for consideration: erect a pontoon crossing above the stone bridge; force the stone bridge; or attack via the ford below the stone bridge. Mackay, stern and orthodox, disapproved of them all because they were both hazardous and impractical and argued instead for an outflanking manoeuvre via Lanesborough or Meelick but he was over-ruled by a large majority, which included Ginkel.[8] It was decided to force the Shannon on the following morning (29 June). There would be three attacks: the main assault across the stone bridge plus secondary crossings via a pontoon bridge and through the ford south of the bridge. The cavalry would follow the infantry over the ford, a large breach having been made in the opposite retrenchment for this purpose. Orders were issued that evening. Forty-three grenadiers, 83 privates, three captains, five lieutenants, two ensigns and seven sergeants were to be drawn from every battalion of infantry. Each was to be given 15 rounds of ammunition, wear a green bough in his hat band and be ready at 06:00. Lieutenant General Hugh Mackay was in overall command. Silence and secrecy were essential and the password was 'Kilkenny'. It was not the most subtle plan; there were no feints, no diversions, just three frontal assaults at obvious locations.

Ready, nervous and probably terrified, the selected infantry marched to the west wall of English Town and stood to arms. However, it was 10:00 before the boats, pontoons and floats had been towed to the river bank and, all morning, Ginkel watched as reinforcements marched along the corridor from St Ruth's camp into Irish Town, braving enfilading fire from the southerly battery. Obviously, through deserters or simply by observation – crowds of local people had gathered on the surrounding hills to watch the fun – the Irish had anticipated the storm. Throughout the morning, the Williamite grenadiers on the bridge and the Jacobite defenders at its foot hurled grenades. The Williamite breastwork was burned down but another was rapidly thrown up to the rear. At midday Ginkel realized that an assault via the bridge would prove impossibly costly and the operation was cancelled. This was providential because, had the Williamites broken in via the bridge, there would have been no viable line either for retreat or rapid reinforcement whilst Irish Town was steadily filling with fresh defenders. Ginkel, though, was in a difficult position. Remaining longer at Athlone was impossible because most of the available forage had been consumed, so either a radical solution had to be discovered immediately or the siege abandoned. Banagher Bridge remained an option but it was an obvious manoeuvre and would have allowed the strong Jacobite cavalry to rampage across the Midlands intercepting communications with Dublin.

The ford to the south of the bridge had to be forced. To test its feasibility a Danish quartermaster and two privates, under sentence of death for cowardice in the face of the enemy, went forward at 10:00 on 29 June. As they waded through the water, musketeers fired over their heads to give the impression that they were deserters. They discovered the water not to be above knee-depth in most places and 20 men might cross abreast, the quartermaster venturing as far as the west bank where he tried to pull down some palisades; all three returned safely, the two privates suffering slight injuries. The corollary was a council of war on the afternoon of 30 June at which Talmash, a 'thruster', strongly supported by Württemberg, Tettau and Ruvigny, loudly advocated attacking across the ford; it was, he argued, time to gamble. Although Mackay demurred, Ginkel agreed and ordered the original storming parties to reform for 18:00 that evening: this was the usual hour for changing the guards and so the Jacobites would not suspect any abnormal activity. The risks were, indeed, considerable. Not only would the attack be made without diversions on a very narrow, predictable front but Ginkel fully anticipated that the western fortifications of Irish Town would have been demolished so that he would face the whole Irish field army amidst the rubble. The odds of success were slightly increased by posting sentries on the neighbouring hills to keep away spectators.

Prospects brightened slightly when information from two Jacobite deserters suggested that an immediate attack might be propitious because the defenders had relaxed following the destruction of the Williamite works on the bridge. They also believed, apparently, that Ginkel would not attempt the ford because of the strong garrison in Irish Town seconded by the propinquity of St Ruth. This advantage, however, was immediately forfeit when a Williamite deserter revealed all to the Irish, including time and place, but the intelligence did not mesh with preconceptions and was ignored. Even more unfortunate, as part of a regular cycle of reliefs, the troops that had defended the bridge so effectively on 28 and 29 June were replaced during the night of 29–30 June by three regiments of foot, two of which, Oliver O'Gara's and Anthony MacMahon's, had been raised during the winter and seen no action. With them came Major General Thomas Maxwell 'for better managing the defence' thus adding an additional, unnecessary layer to the command structure. With the exception of the precipitate fall of English Town, the defence of Athlone had been proceeding according to plan and morale was high. St Ruth was largely responsible, rewarding his soldiers with money and believing in instant promotion and preferment for those who performed exceptional service.

Before his 2,000 infantry advanced, aware of the dangers and risks, Ginkel made a judicious distribution of brandy and a guinea to each grenadier of the advance guard. Mackay again commanded, assisted by Tettau, the Prince of Hesse and Melonière, whilst Talmash went as a volunteer, carried over the water on the shoulders of one of Colonel Gustavus Hamilton's grenadiers. Mackay addressed the men stressing the need to maintain tight formation so that they enjoyed mass and weight when they exited the water. At 18:00, on the tolling of the church bell, Captain Adam Sandys (First Foot Guards) and two lieutenants led 60 grenadiers into the swiftly flowing stream, all wearing armour borrowed from the cavalry, in three ranks of 20, supported by another party of grenadiers in column. Cannon and muskets in all the English riverside positions provided covering fire, which not only kept the Jacobites beneath the parapets of their trenches but produced a dense smokescreen. Sandys reached the far bank. Under cover of the noise, confusion and reduced visibility, more grenadiers laid beams and planks across the broken arch of the bridge whilst, well to the south of the ford, engineers began to erect a pontoon bridge. The complacent Irish were surprised. Safely across, the grenadiers split into three parties: one dashed for the western side of the town in order to pull up the drawbridge across the ditch to prevent St Ruth sending reinforcements; a second made for the foot of the bridge to help mend the broken arch; whilst a third turned left to assist with the building of the pontoon bridge. Ginkel was master of Athlone within 30 minutes, only the entrenchment beyond Irish Town across the causeway leading to St Ruth's camp remaining in Jacobite possession. Some defenders were killed but the majority fled back to the main camp, their retreat assisted by the mounds of rubble from ruined buildings that prevented Ginkel's infantry from advancing rapidly through the town. Frustrated, the Williamite infantry cursed, earning the wrath of the sanctimonious Mackay who suggested that they had more reason to fall on their knees and thank God for victory instead of swearing.

When Captain Sandys led the grenadiers into the Shannon, an express was sent from Irish Town to St Ruth. Some said he was busy honing rude remarks about Tyrconnell, others that he was hunting. Wherever he was and whatever he was doing, he dismissed the initial reports commenting that it was impossible to attack a town when a relieving army was so close. When informed, very shortly afterwards, of the fall of Irish Town he ordered several detachments to counter-attack. The consequences of his failure to heed in time Tyrconnell's earlier advice either to level the entrenchment before the western gate into Irish Town or, preferably, demolish the entire enceinte, were dire. Belatedly, on 29 June Lieutenant General d'Usson had been ordered to demolish the fortifications but execution had been postponed until daylight on 30 June. Although St Ruth took responsibility for failing to ensure that his instruction had been carried out the real cause was embedded within contemporary military practice. Matters pertaining to fortifications were the responsibility of the garrison governor, d'Usson, who vigorously disputed St Ruth's authority to interfere. Ginkel's men now held the works and prevented St Ruth's counter-attack from coming close to the town; all that could be done was to support the retreating garrison and gather stragglers. Observing this, Colonel Gustavus Hamilton advanced beyond the fortifications with a party of grenadiers and, following a sharp engagement during which Maxwell was captured, St Ruth's reinforcements fell back on their camp. At about 22:00, St Ruth's cavalry stood across the neck of the causeway to impede further Williamite progress, whilst his infantry marched towards Ballinasloe. Some said that the French general consequently became a changed man. Tyrconnell had been proved right about the fortifications of Irish Town whereas St Ruth's judgement of people, operations and intelligence had been at fault. Having lost Athlone and the line of the Shannon, he realized that his own reputation was synonymous with the fate of the Irish and he grew more approachable, friendly and respectful towards the Jacobite officers and soldiers, siding more firmly with Sarsfield's faction. He also appreciated that he would have to fight a major battle to restore his damaged credibility for which he would need the full support of the army. D'Usson, on the other hand, thoroughly disenchanted with St Ruth, moved closer to Tyrconnell who made him governor of Galway in order to forestall the appointment of the hated Balldearg O'Donnell.

The immediate scapegoat was Maxwell, the effective governor on 30 June. One of Maxwell's men swam the Shannon on the afternoon of 30 June and, allegedly, delivered a private message to Ginkel: very soon after this, the assault was launched. When the soldiers asked Maxwell for ammunition he refused, asking them 'whether they would shoot against the birds of the air?' He also ordered his men to lie down and rest, saying that there would be no attack until nightfall; when the storm began, many men were thus asleep and very few at their posts. Finally, when the first Williamite grenadier mounted the breach, Maxwell asked him, 'Do you know me?', whereupon he was granted quarter although other prisoners were put to the sword. Maxwell was a Scotsman, of humble origins, and a Roman Catholic by convenience. More important, he was a follower of Tyrconnell and Sarsfield had publicly questioned his commitment to the Jacobite cause only a few days before the fall of Athlone. Whatever the rights and wrongs of Maxwell's supposed treachery, it was very unwise for St Ruth to entrust a man under suspicion with such an important command but, apparently, Tyrconnell had insisted and St Ruth had not wished to foment further disagreements at a critical time.

Ginkel's soldiers found numerous corpses among the ruins of the castle but little useful plunder; anticipating attack, most of the substantial inhabitants had long since evacuated the city taking with them their belongings and valuables. The army gathered six brass guns, two mortars, 20 barrels of powder, as well as meal, wheat and other provisions. In taking Irish Town, Ginkel lost only 12 men killed and 35 wounded – a later, official reckoning listed total casualties at Athlone of 60 fatalities and 120 injured – whereas the Jacobites admitted to 500 slain in the assault plus a further 500 during the siege. After the town had been secured, Ginkel ordered the dead to be buried. Later in the evening, the whole army was drawn up and each of the 41 cannon fired three rounds, followed by a celebratory bonfire. The siege of Athlone had consumed 12,000 cannon balls, 600 bombs, nearly 50 tonnes of gunpowder and many tonnes of stone. During the ten-day bombardment, 32 battering cannon and mortars had sent over one shot every minute, the heaviest bombardment suffered by any British city up to that time. Irish Town was wrecked. In the immediate aftermath, the Williamite soldiers committed many outrages – they were alleged to have murdered, in cold blood,

100 men inside the ruins of the castle – and, that night, orders were given that no soldier should go into Irish Town, or cross the Shannon, on pain of death. Sutlers returning to Dublin to replenish their stocks were instructed to travel via the field hospital in order to transport the sick and wounded back to Dublin.

St Ruth decamped on the night of 30 June–1 July and fell back 16 km to Ballinasloe, behind the line of the River Suck. Here, he gathered in the garrisons of Lanesborough and Jamestown to maximize his field army ready for the anticipated battle. Again, there was a major disagreement over strategy. While St Ruth favoured risking an engagement both to save Galway and Limerick and resurrect his reputation, Tyrconnell wanted to fight a delaying campaign of manoeuvre for the remainder of 1691, hoping for relief from France and an improvement in the Jacobite position for 1692. St Ruth still commanded a strong field army and thus felt that his decision was justified. To fight a single, major battle, said Tyrconnell, and lose, would mean the end of the Jacobite cause within the campaigning season of 1691. His preferred strategy was to concentrate the infantry at Limerick whilst dispatching the cavalry through Banagher Bridge into Leinster to gather provisions and recruits from amongst the Roman Catholic population. This would oblige Ginkel to send his own cavalry after them in order to secure Leinster, from which he drew most of his supplies, and his communications with Dublin. In the absence of the cavalry, the infantry would be unable to operate in isolation and so Ginkel would make little progress in the invasion of Connaught. The Irish cavalry, he reasoned, would always have the advantage over the Williamite horsemen because it was lighter and, if the worse did come to the worse, could always retire into Connaught via Banagher Bridge or Limerick. Tyrconnell's advice was not followed and he returned to Limerick and sent his secretary to France, armed with a long list of complaints against French generals, Sarsfield and 'fractious colonels'.

Although the capture of Athlone presented Ginkel with a gateway into central Connaught, it did not untie every strategic knot. Using the advantage of interior lines, St Ruth was potentially able to create all manner of difficulties by switching forces north and south, between Sligo and Limerick. Ginkel was thus obliged to retain substantial garrisons to hold the key posts and areas: Coy's Horse, Matthews's Dragoons, the infantry battalions of Hastings, Hanmer, Princess Anne, Trelawney and Hales, plus the Brandenburgers and a Danish battalion, assisted by the militia. Samuel Venner's and John Michelburne's battalions defended Ulster whilst Drogheda's battalion occupied County Westmeath to protect Leinster and communications with Dublin. Two solutions presented themselves: Michelburne might capture Sligo to block Jacobite activity in the north and occupy O'Donnell and, by maintaining a continuous offensive into Connaught, Ginkel could keep St Ruth under so much pressure that he would be unable to switch forces.[9]

20

Aughrim and Galway

St Ruth held a council of war at Ballinasloe. Some wanted to remain and defend the line of the River Suck, on the grounds that Ginkel would have to cross on the way to either Galway or Limerick. St Ruth strongly supported this option because, almost certainly, it would induce a major battle. However, Sarsfield and most regimental colonels argued that Ginkel's army was larger, better-disciplined and more experienced. To hazard action with a numerically weaker, ill-clad, half-starved, under-paid and badly equipped force, demoralized by the loss of Athlone, would endanger the whole of Ireland. They adumbrated a version of Tyrconnell's strategy of releasing the cavalry into Leinster and Munster whilst the infantry retired into the strong fortress of Galway. Even if Ginkel ignored the Jacobite horsemen and attacked Galway, it could hold out for a long time, allowing the cavalry to raid as far as Dublin. If, on the other hand, Ginkel followed the cavalry into Leinster, the infantry could cross the Shannon via Limerick and reoccupy Munster. This would buy time and might even consume the remainder of the campaigning season. When additional aid arrived from France, a new strategy could be planned for 1692. It was difficult to counter this rational, majority opinion, so St Ruth made no decision, waited and hoped that Ginkel's movements would draw him into battle. Remaining encamped behind the River Suck, he reconnoitred to the west searching for favourable ground on which to fight.

At Aughrim, 8 km west-south-west of Ballinasloe, he found a promising location where Kilcommodon Hill commanded the Athlone–Galway road. Whether intent on Galway or Limerick, the Williamites would have to fight. The position, about 3 km in length, faced east on to a morass, which was just passable to infantry but not cavalry. At both ends were narrow corridors or 'passes' along which horsemen might attack; on the right the Laurencetown road ran along an esker, Urraghy Hill, before crossing the Tristaun stream, which drained from the morass, via a small bridge; and on the left the Athlone–Galway road ran on 'an old, broken causeway', 70 m long and wide enough for only two horsemen to ride abreast, beyond which stood the ancient, semi-ruined Castle of Aughrim. On the other side of the causeway lay another bog. The ground between the clear upper slopes of Kilcommodon Hill and the edge of the morass was heavily enclosed by thick hedges. St Ruth subsequently set his men to work to prepare the battlefield and create a defensive zone by cutting communication gaps in these hedges. The site was an astute choice: the combat performance of Irish, and French, infantry was normally enhanced by field fortifications. Provided that Urraghy Pass and the Tristaun Bridge, the only axis along which Ginkel could develop a balanced attack, and the Aughrim causeway held, there was some cause for optimism.

As the main campaign was prosecuted in Connaught, the small war continued, some of its activities directly contributing to the operations of the field armies. Towards the end of June Lord Blaney and elements of the Ulster militia conducted sweeps in Counties Monaghan and Armagh, diverting raparees and irregulars from the coming operations against Sligo. Harrying operations were conducted across the Midlands and south-west. Lieutenant Colonel Dawson marched a party of the County Waterford militia into the Comeragh Mountains, where three raparees were killed. Early in July, Major Stroud, leading the County Cork militia, took a detachment towards the Jacobite garrison at Ballyclogh and killed ten. By 11 July, 60 raparees had been accounted for around Bandon by militia under Lieutenant Colonel More. Colonel Blount killed another five near Cashel. Around 8 July, 25 raparees died near Mountmellick whilst a party of militia from Roscrea conducted a cattle raid towards Nenagh, killing ten raparees. Captain Warren dispatched nine in County Kilkenny. John Weaver, the high sheriff of County Westmeath, discovered 'a knot of rogues'. His militia killed 23 and discovered three gunsmiths working a forge in the middle of a wood. The majority of these petty actions went massively in the Williamites' favour but occasional reverses were suffered. Before 20 July, Colonel James Barrow, commanding a party of County Waterford militia, killed 35 raparees near Tallow but was ambushed on the return march and most of his men were killed or taken prisoner; Barrow spent the remainder of the war in Limerick gaol. Colonel Beecher marched with 500 of the County Cork militia around 23 July and encountered about 400 regulars and raparees west of Skibbereen. After a short fight the Irish were routed but Beecher's victorious men grew careless and were almost surprised by the arrival of Irish reinforcements under Colonel Charles Macarthy More and Colonel Daniel O'Donovan.[1]

Ginkel's soldiers hoped that the war would soon be over. A flood of country people streaming into Ginkel's camp to request protections encouraged speculation that the Jacobite cause was nearing collapse. Some of the Danes, in particular, were keen to leave the Irish backwater. Reports from cavalry patrols and deserters located St Ruth just west of Ballinasloe and confirmed that he intended to offer battle. Captain John Auchmuty (Wolseley's Horse) reported that the Jacobites had evacuated Lanesborough, clearing any threat to the northern flank. Ginkel proceeded methodically and slowly. The first task was to create a forward base at Athlone by levelling the siege trenches and batteries and repairing the fortifications, a considerable undertaking because the damage was severe and not a single building in Irish Town was intact. First, some houses were mended to store the supplies arriving daily from Dublin and Mullingar, to establish a magazine before the advance was resumed. Progress was hampered by wet weather. In the evening of 4 July, a patrol of ten mounted grenadiers from Kirke's infantry battalion and 20 cavalry reconnoitred the Jacobite positions, guided by a converted priest named Higgins. Whilst passing through some woods they were ambushed by 400 Irish cavalry. The Williamites fell back to a bridge which they defended stoutly for some time, losing 15 killed and four prisoners, but were eventually obliged to retire, along with Higgins who was wounded.[2]

Leaving Colonel Edward Lloyd to occupy Athlone with a garrison of two infantry battalions, on 6 July Ginkel ordered the army to advance at 05:00 the following morning, the left wing crossing the Shannon via the pontoons and the right wing over the stone bridge, to encamp on the west bank. Each musketeer was to carry 15 rounds of ammunition. The heavy baggage crossed a day later (8 July) and the militia moved to occupy other bridging and fording points to the north and south. Athlone was deemed a victory of sufficient importance to justify the publication of the Lords Justices' proclamation. All private soldiers who surrendered by 28 July would receive a free pardon and a reasonable price for their arms, horses and equipment. Officers commanding forts, towns and garrisons who agreed to surrender both their persons and governments by the same date would receive free pardons, the restoration of forfeited estates and assurances that they would not face prosecution for treason or other crimes. Any citizen of Limerick and Galway who assisted in the surrender of those towns would be rewarded by a free pardon and receive back any confiscated lands. Officers or soldiers who had not previously forfeited estates for treason or other crimes would be well rewarded *pro rata* for any helpful services provided. Military men who wished to join the Williamite forces would be welcomed and given similar, or higher, rank and pay.

As soon as Ireland was pacified, William and Mary would seek security for Roman Catholic worship through an Irish parliament. In addition, in order to encourage desertion, Ginkel allowed subsistence pay to all those who came over, a colonel of horse or dragoons receiving £11 10s. per month, colonels of foot £10, and so on according to rank. The Williamites were so confident of a favourable reception that on 14 July Carmarthen asked William to consider which troops he wished to withdraw from Ireland because 10,000 would soon be sufficient for that theatre. Three days later Carmarthen suggested that the released soldiers might best be employed on a descent against the French coast, possibly around Bordeaux and the Gironde, or in Normandy. Either option might draw the French fleet into a decisive encounter and prove more acceptable to Parliament than simply committing troops to the Confederate Army in the Netherlands.

Ginkel remained concerned about the condition of his army. Theft from tents within the camp, plundering, indiscipline, drunkenness and gambling remained widespread and officers were instructed to conduct frequent tours of inspection and send all men found drinking or gaming after tattoo to the provost marshal. It was very hot and humid on 9 July and a violent thunder storm burst at about 17:00 which lasted for a couple of hours; two men and a boy were killed by lightning and some soldiers of the Prince of Hesse's regiment injured. Finally, on 10 July, satisfied that the ammunition had been replenished, Ginkel watched the troops move out along the Galway road to encamp at Kilcashel before he reconnoitred the passage of the River Suck in front of Ballinasloe. The crossing was covered by a strong defensive position whence the Irish might have created difficulties but St Ruth, who reportedly commanded 36 battalions of infantry and 8,000 horse and dragoons, had withdrawn 8 km further west to Aughrim. Ginkel was acutely aware of his assumed numerical inferiority; already, the need to occupy Mullingar and Athlone had consumed another three battalions of scarce infantry. As the army filed into camp along the east bank of the River Suck on 11 July, Ginkel and his senior officers rode on to the hills from where they could see Irish outposts around Garbally. Observing Ginkel's party, the videttes retired westwards and Ginkel followed far enough to gain a distant sight of St Ruth's position on Kilcommodon Hill. On consulting a map, Ginkel fully appreciated St Ruth's excellent choice of ground but Württemberg said that the Williamites were prepared to attack, however strong and narrow the position, because they now held the Jacobites in contempt. Orders were given that night for the army to advance on 12 July. Rittmeister Franz Joachim von Dewitz (Donop's Danish Horse) led the advance guard, charged with beating in the Jacobite outposts. All non-combatants – clerks, sutlers, women and children – were to remain in the camp along the Suck with two battalions detailed to guard the baggage. The remainder of the army, about 14,000 infantry, 4,000 cavalry and 2,000 dragoons, was to go into the battle. St Ruth also had nearly 20,000 men: about 14,000 infantry in 35 weak battalions, 2,500 cavalry and 3,500 dragoons.

St Ruth placed Colonel Walter Burke inside Aughrim Castle with 200 musketeers and positioned two infantry battalions around the head of the Aughrim causeway. Four regiments of horse (Sarsfield, Henry Luttrell, John Parker and Nicholas Purcell), four of dragoons – one of which was deployed, dismounted around Aughrim Castle – seconded by two infantry regiments, stood in the rear of Aughrim village and castle. Major General Dominic Sheldon was in overall command of the left, charged with holding the causeway and securing the left flank, and Brigadier Henry Luttrell directed the first line of cavalry. Four horse regiments (Sutherland, Abercorn, Edmund Prendergast and Tyrconnell), one troop of the Life Guards, plus the remainder of the dragoons, were on the right between Kilcommodon church and the Tristaun Bridge. Dragoons occupied a bridgehead over the Tristaun stream and held advanced positions along the Laurencetown road. Lieutenants General Tessé and Sarsfield led the right with instructions to prevent Ginkel's cavalry from crossing the Tristaun stream and advancing between the great and little morass into the right flank of St Ruth's centre. The bulk of the infantry stood in two lines across the centre, musketeers occupying the enclosures – 'old garden ditches' – in strength. Lord Galmoy's regiment of horse was drawn up in the left rear of the second line of infantry both to act as a reserve and discourage the foot soldiers from running away. Major Generals William Dorrington and John Hamilton commanded the infantry of the centre. St Ruth had nine brass field guns, three of which were deployed around the castle, the other six distributed separately rather than grouped in batteries. Despite having chosen and prepared the battlefield, St Ruth lacked sufficient troops to defend it in strength and he anticipated significant troop movements within his lines in reponse to Ginkel's axes of attack.

Slowly and cautiously, at 06:00 on 12 July in early morning mist, Ginkel moved forward. St Ruth's clever choice of ground made it impossible for Ginkel to deploy his full strength until he had secured the defiles on either wing and advanced the army beyond the central morass on to the lower slope of Kilcommodon Hill. Only then could the main battle commence; a development that St Ruth sought to forestall by defeating Ginkel in detail as he attempted to clear the flank defiles and the bog. Given the seeming impossibility of forcing the central morass and Aughrim causeway, Ginkel initially decided to probe along Urraghry Hill towards Tristaun Bridge both in an effort to find space for the deployment of the infantry of the left wing and because several tracks reached from Tristaun Bridge into the centre of the Jacobite position. As a preliminary, he needed to drive the Jacobite dragoons from their bridgehead across the Tristaun stream. A long-distance artillery exchange opened the action and, around 11:00, Ginkel ordered a troop from Donop's Danish cavalry regiment to expel the advance guards of dismounted Jacobite dragoons from some houses flanking the approach to Tristaun Bridge. Coming under pressure, the Danes fell back on to their supports comprising 200 of Sir Albert Conyngham's Dragoons who went forward, dismounted and lined some ditches near the bridge to prevent the Jacobites from sending over reinforcements.

Ginkel, who was personally directing this opening encounter, ordered Conygham's Dragoons to advance across the Tristaun stream but the Jacobites thickened their outposts and Conygham's men were obliged to retire. Ginkel then instructed Eppinger's Dragoons to flank the Irish dragoons and cut off their retreat to Tristaun Bridge by getting between them and the main Jacobite positions. Observing this manoeuvre, the Irish threw in reinforcements and the whole of Ginkel's dragoon detachment was in danger of being overwhelmed until the supporting cavalry regiments of Portland and La Forest came up and halted the Irish, although at some cost in men and horses. What had started as a skirmish had now drawn in considerable numbers of men. After an hour's fighting the Irish withdrew over the stream and Ginkel's horsemen paused close to the bank, further progress prevented by sizeable bodies of Irish cavalry and the lack of space for deployment between the great and little morasses. Gradually, Danish infantry and cavalry filed into position, extending and thickening the line to the south, separated from the Jacobites by the Tristaun stream, ensuring that St Ruth would not be able to outflank Ginkel's line of battle from that direction. More importantly, Ginkel had noticed that St Ruth had already moved infantry and cavalry from his centre, and probably also from his left, to reinforce the right. It probably seemed fairly clear to Ginkel that he had persuaded St Ruth that the main attack would eventually develop across the Tristaun stream.

Quiet descended on the battlefield whilst, at about 14:00, Ginkel consulted with his generals about whether to press on or wait until morning. Given the difficulties presented, the majority opinion, with which Ginkel concurred, was to postpone the attack until 13 July to give time for the army to be fully organized and deployed and the battlefield reconnoitred, so the tents were ordered up from Ballinasloe. At this point, it was noticed that the action around Urraghry Pass had left the Jacobites in some confusion and so the decision to delay was countermanded in order to take immediate advantage of this opportunity, even though much of the army was still marching into position.

On the advice of Mackay, 'a man of great judgement and long experience', Ginkel decided to renew the earlier pressure on the Irish right to oblige St Ruth to draw down more troops from his centre and Aughrim Castle. Hopefully, this would enable attacks across both the causeway and the central morass to achieve bridgeheads from which the army might deploy prior to assaulting the main Irish position on Kilcommodon Hill, probably on the following day.

As the infantry came into line along the edge of the morass, at about 16:30 the Danes restarted the action at Urraghry Pass in order to pin St Ruth's troops to that sector. The fighting was close, characterized by numerous small Irish counter-attacks, and the engagement of pikemen. Indeed, it was one of the few occasions during the war that old-fashioned 'push of pike' was employed. Because the modern Danish infantry battalions lacked pikes, they appear to have fought from behind 'chevaux-de-frise', a clear indication that their stance was defensive rather than offensive. Supported by cavalry ready to deliver local counter-attacks, the infantry advanced up to the hedges and ditches, lined with Jacobite musketeers also closely seconded by horsemen, and engaged in a series of fire fights. The Irish usually waited until the Williamites had put their muskets over a hedge before, via the pre-cut communication gaps, repositioning themselves to flank the attackers. In this manner the fighting continued on the Irish right for over 90 minutes until gradually, assisted by field guns, the Williamite infantry gained the far bank of the Tristaun stream, wheeled right, and moved forward as far as Bloody Hollow where the advance lost momentum.

In the meantime, the majority of Ginkel's infantry struggled over the rough terrain to form two approximate lines opposite the Jacobite centre and Aughrim causeway. Mackay noticed St Ruth respond to the renewed pressure on his right by diverting some forces from around Aughrim Castle towards Tristaun Bridge and decided that the moment was propitious to attack in the centre. Both lines of infantry pressed forward but were halted along the edge of the morass by heavy Jacobite musketry. Only where Colonel Thomas Erle led his men into the bog was any progress made. Flanked by the battalions of Charles Herbert, Gustavus Hamilton (commanded by Lieutenant Colonel Abraham Creighton) and Richard Brewer, seconded by those of John Foulkes and William Stewart, Erle attacked at the point where the morass was narrowest and the hedges on the Irish side ran furthest into the bog. These four battalions advanced in column, one behind the other, and were ordered to take and hold the lowest of the ditches and then wait until the Williamite horse on the right had mastered the causeway and reached Aughrim Castle. They were then to support the cavalry whilst additional infantry battalions made their way through the wider sections of the morass on their left.

With Erle's in the van, the four battalions waded up to their waists through the marsh and the central rivulet. As they neared the far side, the Irish musketeers fired but Erle pressed on and drove them from the lowest hedges. Thereupon, the Irish retired through their communication gaps to the next hedge line, a sequence of advance and retreat repeated until Erle was close to the main battle line. Erle, though, had attacked on a very narrow front and created a deep, thin salient lacking support to its flanks. Moving through the specially prepared passages between the hedges, Irish cavalry joined their infantry in a counter-attack. Erle rode to the head of his men, rallied them and shouted that, 'there was no way to come off but to be brave'. However, fronted and flanked, his men retired along the route by which they had advanced, suffering considerable casualties. Colonels Erle and Herbert were captured during the withdrawal. Despite being wounded Erle escaped, was retaken, but escaped again.

Although too late to sustain Erle's advance, the battalions of St John, Tiffin, Belcastel, Du Cambon and Melonière waded into the bog on his left. Under cover of the hedges and ditches the Irish waited until the leading ranks were within 20 m before giving a volley. The Williamites halted and replied – although no one could see very much through the dense, grey-white smoke settling in the damp, still airs above the bog – before pressing forward once more straight into a counter-attack mounted by infantry wielding clubbed muskets. Seriously unsettled, they gave ground. At this stage the battle was balanced and a neutral observer might have awarded a slight advantage to St Ruth. Under pressure, Major General William

Dorrington, commanding the Irish centre, asked for two fresh infantry regiments to be sent from their position covering the Aughrim causeway. In the Williamite centre, Talmash took charge. He rallied Erle's retreating troops, turned them round and led them back into the assault. They fell on the Irish, many of whom had left the shelter of their hedges and ditches and advanced into the centre of the morass in pursuit. Although no more than 200 m from the lowest of the ditches, the Irish could not regain cover fast enough through the mud and water and lost over 300 dead. Thereafter, the fighting in the centre continued but was indecisive, the Irish infantry more than holding their own.

Thwarted in the centre and left, Ginkel turned to the Aughrim causeway. Against the two infantry battalions and a regiment of dragoons defending the head of the causeway, Ginkel committed four battalions, led by those of Percy Kirke and Lord George Hamilton. Following hand-to-hand fighting, they secured a lodgement along a ditch at the foot of the castle. Covered by these four battalions, although taking fire from Burke's garrison in the castle, Colonel Sir Francis Compton led out the Royal Horse Guards. Twice they faltered but, on the third attempt, got across, followed by the cavalry regiments of Ruvigny, Lanier, Langston and Byerley, as well as Leveson's Dragoons. Watching them riding over the causeway in a narrow, two-man column, St Ruth was unperturbed. It would be a while until they had all completed the passage of the causeway and deployed, if indeed there was sufficient space to enable them to do so. Long before that Brigadier Henry Luttrell would bring his cavalry around from the rear of Aughrim village and attack. St Ruth felt sufficiently confident to declare that he would beat Ginkel back to the gates of Dublin.

As the sun was setting, very shortly after Ginkel's cavalry had traversed the causeway, whilst riding down Kilcommodon Hill St Ruth was decapitated by a cannon ball. Covered by a cloak, his body was hurried from the field and carried on horseback to burial in Loughrea. He was the only general who managed to make the Jacobite Army fight as a unit and with spirit during a major engagement. St Ruth had formed a bond with his soldiers founded on admiration for the manner in which they continued to fight despite the ultimate hopelessness of their cause. After his death, the Jacobites did nothing 'that was great and glorious' and they never again thrived. St Ruth's death was bad enough – he was an iconic figure during the fighting, riding back and forth, visible to most of his troops – but his deputy, Tessé, lacked his superior's charisma and rapport with the soldiers and was injured soon after assuming command. Leaderless, the Jacobite Army began to fragment as individual sector, line and regimental commanders made individual decisions or, far more serious, none at all.

Having more to lose than the infantry, many of the Irish cavalry were keen to reach terms with William and their morale was already low. Rather than organized treachery, this factor probably explained Henry Luttrell's conduct. Instead of attacking the Williamite cavalry as it tried to deploy in front of Aughrim Castle, as St Ruth had expected, he offered only token resistance before wheeling his men and riding off the field towards Loughrea and Limerick, closely followed by Major General Dominic Sheldon. Williamite infantry then pressed forward, past Aughrim Castle, only slightly incommoded by a feeble fire from Colonel Burke's garrison, which had been equipped with French muskets but English ammunition. Seeing the Jacobite position around Aughrim disintegrate, the Williamite infantry in the centre advanced once more and pressed the Irish foot from hedge to hedge to the top of hill, through the now-levelled Irish camp, before the majority broke and ran, heading for the great bog behind Aughrim Castle. Unlike their colleagues around Aughrim, the Irish cavalry on the right opposite Tristaun Bridge held firm. Seeing Mackay's battalions return to the attack in the centre and advance strongly, the Irish right wing finally disengaged and joined the remainder in flight; Sarsfield and Lord Galmoy, with some troops of horse, tried to provide a measure of rearguard cover. Ginkel's mounted troops pursued through the bogs and low hills for 5 km until halted by darkness and the onset of a thick drizzle, which discouraged an attempt to cut off the Irish at Loughrea pass.

The booty was considerable: nine cannon; all the ammunition, tents, baggage and equipment; 11 standards; and 30 pairs of colours. The Reverend Story inspected the battlefield and found most of the Irish dead clustered in ditches and behind hedges; in one single enclosure he discovered between 120 and 150 bodies. However, most of the 7,000 dead fell during the withdrawal and flight: viewed from the site of the Irish camp on the ridge of Kilcommodon Hill the naked corpses resembled 'a great flock of sheep, scattered up and down the country, for almost four miles around'. Soldiers received 6d. for every Jacobite musket brought to the artillery train but there were so many that the price rapidly dropped to 2d. Ginkel's casualties, especially amongst the infantry battalions engaged in the centre, were not negligible. The casualty return compiled two days after the battle listed 73 officers dead and 111 injured, whilst 600 other ranks lost their lives and a further 960 were wounded, although the number of dead was probably over-stated because all the infantry battalions were under-strength before the battle. Ginkel's wounded were carried in empty bread wagons to the field hospital at either Garbally or Athlone. Ginkel had achieved a military rarity: victory in an offensive battle when numerically equal to the defence. Even more remarkably, casualties numbered less than 10 per cent of his initial strength. It was a great victory coming at a time when the forces of the Grand Alliance had achieved little. Even in the Essex town of Coggleshall the news of Aughrim was celebrated by great bonfires.[3]

Very soon after the battle, there were well-founded accusations and counter-accusations that atrocities had been committed. After the Williamites had become 'absolute masters of the field', over 2,000 Irish who had thrown down their weapons and asked for quarter were supposedly murdered in cold blood. Several more, who had been granted quarter, were later massacred, including Lord Galway and Colonel Charles Moore, a fact later verified by the major of Eppinger's Dragoons. When the Irish had held the advantage in the hedges and ditches of the centre, they had taken some prisoners. Unable to carry them off and faced with Williamite counter-attacks, they had been murdered, amongst them Colonel Charles Herbert. Similarly, when Aughrim Castle had fallen, Colonel Walter Burke and many of his garrison were put to the sword, although 51 were also taken prisoner. At the time, such practices were not overtly condemned – regrettable and unfortunate incidents always occurred in the heat and immediate aftermath of battle – and there was always the precedent of Agincourt. The stories about the Aughrim atrocities were amplified by the treatment of the Jacobite prisoners. Apparently, Ginkel gave his word to his prisoner, Major General William Dorrington, witnessed by Württemberg and Major General de la Forest, that all the captured soldiers, numbering around 450, would be regarded as prisoners of war and receive treatment similar to that given to the Williamite captives following the first siege of Limerick. The reality was slightly different. General officers were taken to the Tower of London, instantly translating them from prisoners of war into prisoners of state, and most of the common soldiers were incarcerated on Lambay Island, 'a waste desert in the sea near Dublin', where many died from disease and starvation.[4]

Ginkel devoted 13 July to a public thanksgiving throughout the army. He ordered the burial of all the Williamite dead and those Irish that lay on the ground where he wanted to pitch his own tents. The rest were left scattered across several kilometres of countryside because there were insufficient local people remaining in the vicinity to dig grave pits and gather corpses: the white bones remained visible for years afterwards. Tyrconnell heard the ill tidings in Limerick on the morning of 13 July and immediately sent three expresses to James – only one of which got through – requesting reinforcements from France, to arrive no later than the spring of 1692, as well as interim supplies of provisions and ammunition. Plenty of infantry was making for Limerick 'rather like people going to a fair', although it was disorganized, confused and demoralized, so Tyrconnell hoped to be able to defend the city until the end of the campaigning season and into the spring of 1692. On 17 July, he travelled north to meet the cavalry coming from Aughrim and arranged cantons for them in County Clare, within 10 km of Limerick. In his gloomy court in the gloomy castle at St Germain-en-Laye, James heard the news and approved Tyrconnell's proposed policy of trying to fight a delaying campaign whilst seeking assistance from France. When he explained the situation to Louis, James was told that there were no troops to spare although some might possibly become available in 1692. However, he ordered a convoy of arms, provisions, ammunition and supplies to be sent from Brest to Limerick.

Ginkel was anxious to exploit Aughrim as quickly as possible because, at the most, only three months of the campaigning season remained. Loughrea and Meelick were found to have been abandoned. Brigadier Eppinger, with 1,200 cavalry and dragoons, was ordered to Portumna and Banagher, where the Jacobites still retained garrisons. Both surrendered on 14 July giving Ginkel control of the line of the Shannon as far as Killaloe. Galway, the first port and city of Connaught, even though access roads through 'wild and desolate' country severely inhibited its commercial value, was the next target. Standing on a peninsula jutting into the River Corrib, Galway's northern and north-eastern sides were covered by a deep channel and an extensive bog and approaches could only be made via a narrow ridge running from the east, between the morass and Galway Bay. Naturally, the most extensive fortifications covered this sector, the ridge additionally defended by an entrenchment that had fallen into disrepair. Under French supervision the Irish were excavating a new entrenchment but it was incomplete. The suburbs before the east gate had been levelled, along with all the hedges. The old enceinte, based around a wall and three small bastions, had been protected by an outer envelope incorporating a ravelin, counter-guard and counterscarp but the ground plan was too irregular to accommodate a set of effective, modern fortifications and Galway was overlooked by high ground. Inside the walls, immediately to the rear of the east front, stood the round Upper Citadel, mounting eight cannon, and the Lower Citadel was situated within the north-west front covering the bridge on to the Great Island and the route to the west. In addition, because many of the large stone houses, 'like castles for strength', had castellated roofs, considerable resistance might be offered to any force that broke into the town. Forty-six cannon were available to the defenders.

Having abandoned earlier plans to secure the fall of Galway through naval pressure alone, on 15 July Ginkel received reliable intelligence from the mayor of Galway, Arthur Ffrench, via one of his municipal officials, an English Protestant, who managed to slip out of the town. He reported that the garrison comprised only seven weak regiments, totalling no more than 700 men, poorly armed, and internally divided about whether to defend the town. Henry, Eighth Viscount Dillon, was governor, assisted by Lieutenant General d'Usson, both associates of Tyrconnell and more disposed towards ending the war by treaty than prolonged resistance; James later wrote to d'Usson thanking him for the early surrender of Galway before the town and its inhabitants had suffered serious hardships. Ffrench also said that the garrison's hopes rested upon the anticipated arrival of Hugh O'Donnell out of north Connaught with his rag-tag army. In addition, the works on the ridge were unfinished and most of the townspeople were weary of the Jacobite government and yearned for the jurisdiction of King William. If Galway could be surrounded before O'Donnell's arrival, he added, then the garrison could not resist for long without the active participation of the townspeople, which would not be forthcoming. Ginkel appears to have based his initial strategy towards Galway on this intelligence, which was corroborated on 18 July when a Mr Shaw and some other townsmen came into the camp at Athenry and presented a similar appreciation. Without an intervention from O'Donnell, Shaw and his associates were of the opinion that Galway could not resist a 'brisk attack'.

Having allowed his soldiers a brief rest on the Aughrim battlefield, the army marched for Galway on 16 July. Again, reflecting his belief in the intelligence reports, Ginkel took only field guns, the siege train returning to Athlone from where it would later travel by water to Limerick. That night, Ginkel reached Loughrea. This 'small town seated in an indifferent good country' had been thoroughly stripped and plundered by the retreating Jacobites, Protestants and Roman Catholics suffering equally. Athenry was reached on the following day (17 July), a 'town' that consisted of no more than 30 Irish cabins, mostly deserted, the inhabitants having taken refuge in the Slieve Aught. The army rested on the plains near Athenry on 18 July whilst Ginkel went forward to Oranmore, at the eastern end of Galway Bay, which the Irish had burned some days before. He rode to within 1 km of Galway, searching out the best routes for the wagons, carriages and artillery. On his return to camp, Ginkel read some intelligence from Judge Denis Daly and other gentlemen from County Galway contradicting the reports of Ffrench and Shaw. Whether Daly and his friends were actually double-agents – some of Ginkel's unsuccessful winter operations towards the Shannon had been based upon their intelligence – or simply ill-informed, remains unclear but they told Ginkel that Galway was almost impregnable, adequately provisioned and garrisoned by 5,000 well-armed men. They added that O'Donnell was in the vicinity with 6,000 troops. Thrown into two minds, the naturally cautious Ginkel pondered whether to proceed with an immediate siege or await the arrival of his siege train from Athlone. He was strongly advised that the new intelligence was erroneous and no more than an Irish ruse designed to gain time. Persuaded to follow his previously determined scheme of operations, he gave orders for the army to march on 19 July in two columns. Because the countryside around Galway was barren and rocky and did not offer sufficient forage, Scravenmoer and Ruvigny remained at Athenry with 3,000 cavalry and dragoons. They were charged with covering the rear and communications of the main army which would be relatively isolated before Galway and, if necessary, escorting the siege train from Athlone.

As Ginkel approached Galway, no resistance was offered although a small Irish party burned a country house, close to the shore, lingering in the orchard until driven out by a party of horse. The suburbs to the north also went up in flames and, for a while, it looked as though serious resistance might be encountered. Ginkel sent a trumpet offering the terms of the Lords Justices' proclamation if the garrison would surrender immediately. Whilst the trumpeter was in the town awaiting an answer, the defenders fired three or four cannon which, although not unusual in such cases, was later excused on the grounds that the gunners did not know of the trumpeter's presence. Eventually, Dillon replied that Galway would be defended to the last man. The afternoon was spent in positioning the attacking forces, to which the garrison responded by firing cannon but doing little damage to Ginkel's well-located camp. During the evening Captain Burke deserted and reported that the entrenchment being built across the ridge to the east was nearly complete and the sooner it was attacked the better because it commanded virtually all the fortifications to the east and south-east. As soon as it was dark, Mackay, Tiffin, Cambon, St John, Lord George Hamilton, six battalions, plus four squadrons of horse and dragoons, embarked in the pontoons of the bridging train and crossed the River Corrib 3 km above Galway. By daybreak on 20 July, this detachment was safely on the west bank having met virtually no opposition: a party of 60 Irish dragoons had fired from a house when they first came ashore but had quickly retired. Mackay moved south and took position covering the head of the bridge leading into Galway from the west and north-west, blocking O'Donnell's only possible approach.

Hugh O'Donnell had been staying at the house of a Mr Miller, 10 km north of Tuam, County Galway. He commanded a maximum of 1,000 men, billeted throughout Counties Mayo and Galway with concentrations at Headford and Ballinrobe. Upon hearing of Aughrim, most of O'Donnell's men favoured marching post haste for the mountains of County Mayo but Ginkel did not move towards Galway quite as quickly as had been anticipated and, on the suggestion of the Reverend Lynch, the self-styled Dean of Tuam, O'Donnell sent a reconnaissance party into Tuam. Allegedly, it found the townspeople making ready to accept the inevitable by gathering the harvest before seeking protections from Ginkel; the O'Donnellites rewarded such treachery by burning the town and plundering the inhabitants. O'Donnell then withdrew to Cong, on the northern shore of Lough Corrib, ready to retire into the mountains should he come under pressure. By this time, his army had dwindled to about 600 men and he had resolved to seek the best possible personal terms from Ginkel. However, he received orders from the Jacobite high command to relieve Galway. Discovering that Ginkel was already advancing towards the east of the town, O'Donnell ascertained that the sole feasible approach lay around Lough Corrib, through the Maumturk Mountains to come in from the west. He struggled across extremely difficult, rugged country and was within 16 km of Galway when he discovered that Mackay had crossed the River Corrib and held the head of the bridge into Galway.

Early on the morning of 20 July, Major General Count Nassau led a detachment of 200 grenadiers and 800 fusiliers, supported by two infantry battalions – the firebrand Talmash accompanied as a volunteer – to storm the new fortifications, guided along the safest approach by the deserter, Captain Burke; it was done so well that the grenadiers had almost reached the foot of the fortifications before they were discovered. The garrison of 200 men, supported by another 300 in the covered way, made 'some faint firings' but the grenadiers rushed forward, hurled their grenades and forced them back into a line of communication that led to the town. Nassau lost only one lieutenant and five men killed and two lieutenants and eight soldiers wounded. Cannon from the main ramparts then bombarded the captured position, wounding several and killing Monsieur Madronet, a engineer who was supervising the reorientation of the earthworks to face towards the town. At 05:00, five troopers who had deserted from O'Donnell came into Ginkel's camp to report on his present position and probable intentions. Although d'Usson had urged both the garrison and townspeople to defend Galway, following the feeble performance in the entrenchment and the successful crossing of the Corrib Judge Daly summoned the town council, which decided that capitulation was the best option. D'Usson dismissed their recommendation and arrested Mayor Ffrench for corresponding with the enemy but, despite the presence of an armed guard, the council secured his immediate release. The bishop, dean and nearly everyone else in civil authority then called on d'Usson to surrender, a course of events strongly suggesting that Ginkel had agents working on his behalf in Galway. When the garrison observed Mackay's corps ensconced on the far bank of the Corrib, they set fire to the extensive suburbs on the west side of the town, a task which they probably enjoyed because most of the buildings belonged to Englishmen. At 10:00, whilst the suburbs were still burning, Dillon beat a parley, sending a drummer with a letter asking for safe conduct to enable envoys to leave the town to negotiate a capitulation. Ginkel was only too happy to accept and a truce was agreed. At this, the garrison crowded on to the ramparts and Ginkel's soldiers walked up to the fortifications, gossiping and seeking news of friends and acquaintances in each other's armies. Hostages were exchanged during the afternoon and, although terms were not agreed that day, Ginkel extended the truce until 10:00 on 21 July.

Negotiations continued throughout the night, with a good deal of coming and going between the negotiators and Dillon and d'Usson in the town. Ginkel was growing impatient and, encouraged by Talmash, as the deadline of 10:00 on 21 July approached, ordered eight cannon and four mortars into the captured entrenchments and sent a drummer to escort his hostages out of Galway. The problem was not the decision to capitulate but the terms. At length they agreed that whoever wished might either take advantage of the Lords Justices' proclamation and go home or join Ginkel's army; the remainder, including a few French officers, would be escorted along the quickest route to Limerick with arms and baggage. Galway was to be allowed free practice of Roman

Catholicism, complete with a clerical hierarchy, and civilians might stay or leave to go into other parts of Connaught. Finally, and most important, the defenders were permitted, encouraged indeed, to inform Tyrconnell of the agreement in an attempt to persuade him to accept similar conditions for the concomitant capitulation of Limerick.[5] Time was required for a letter to be sent and a reply received and so the ceasefire was continued until Sunday 26 July, when the garrison would leave during the morning. Tyrconnell forfeited his small reservoir of political credit in trying unsuccessfully to persuade the Irish faction to submit, leaving him with no alternative but to adopt Sarsfield's delaying strategy. He had expected Dillon and d'Usson to resist for much longer – Galway had held out against Sir Charles Coote for nine months in 1652 – taking the campaign deep into the autumn thus denying Ginkel the opportunity to besiege Limerick in 1691. Yet, there was still hope. The resistance of the Irish infantry at Aughrim had surprised the Williamites and Ginkel had lost a number of men. He would also need to find garrisons for Galway, Athlone and, later, Sligo. In an effort to boost morale Tyrconnell moved the reassembling Jacobite Army over Thomond Bridge and through Limerick to encamp on the mythically important Singland Hill. More practically, he ordered all men between 16 and 60 in the territories remaining under Jacobite control to report for duty.

When 26 July arrived, d'Usson slipped into Ginkel's camp at 07:00 and was conducted, incognito, towards Limerick. At 09:00, Sir Henry Bellasise, the newly appointed governor, entered Galway and took over all the guard posts. Assembling in the street ready to march out, Irish soldiers were fooling about with some gunpowder when it exploded. Some lost their eyes, others their hair and clothes, and over 20 were disfigured. As there were already three English battalions within the town, the Irish feared that the explosion was the prelude to a massacre but the tension quickly diminished and the injured received treatment. At 10:00, Lord Dillon led out 2,300 men, half-starved and clad in rags, accompanied by six cannon: the majority were escorted to Limerick; some went home; but very few entered Ginkel's army. During 27 July, Mackay led the detachment that had occupied the western bank of the River Corrib back through Galway. The soldiers were then set to work levelling the batteries and siege works and repairing the fortifications, particularly the new entrenchments to the south-east of the town. Sick and wounded soldiers unable to march were left in the care of the new governor. As the army was preparing to move back to Athenry on 28 July, Captain Cole RN sailed belatedly into Galway Bay with nine warships and 18 other vessels. Ginkel sent him orders to sail for the Shannon. The siege train in Athlone was instructed to join the main army at Portumna.

When O'Donnell learned that a treaty of surrender had been concluded and terms for a general Jacobite submission had been forwarded to Tyrconnell, he realized that he was supporting the wrong cause. After all, he had entered the war to pursue an entirely personal agenda that could only be advanced by ending on the winning side. Ginkel received intimations that this might be the case and used Jacob Richards, an acquaintance of O'Donnell's in the Williamite camp, as an intermediary to convey to O'Donnell a letter, replete with flattery and flowery language, hinting that there might be an opportunity for him to gain revenge for the ill treatment he had received from Tyrconnell. O'Donnell circulated the contents amongst his principal officers. Because O'Donnell's army was badly armed and equipped and far less numerous than Ginkel supposed, they advised putting as much distance as possible between themselves and the Williamites before considering what to do. Anxious not to lose the contact, O'Donnell sent an Englishman, who had accompanied him to Ireland from Spain, to visit Richards in Ginkel's camp. In the meantime, as O'Donnell led his men back into the mountains of Connemara, he received letters from Limerick accusing him of responsibility for the loss of Galway because he had not responded more speedily. When added to previous affronts from Tyrconnell and the weak defence of Galway, this gratuitous insult persuaded O'Donnell that there was no future with the Jacobites and he began to pursue more energetically a possible agreement with Ginkel. Before finally making up his mind whether to change sides, the developing situation around Sligo offered excellent occasions for extracting maximum advantage.

On 29 July Ginkel marched from Athenry to Loughrea where extremely wet weather caused the soldiers to rest on the next day. The march was resumed towards Eyrecourt, west of Banagher, on 31 July. That night, either because the heavy rain of the previous day had swollen many streams and rivers or through bad staff work, the army camped in three separate places but the Irish were too distant and disorganized to take advantage. Expecting that a re-concentrated Irish army would defend Limerick desperately and realizing that his own men were reduced in number, tired, and short of bread and other essentials, Ginkel summoned all regular units in Munster and Leinster to join him on the march. Only Colonel Ferdinando Hastings's battalion in Cork, Michelburne's two battalions in Ulster, the Galway garrison and Colonel Edward Lloyd's troops in Athlone remained on station, principally to observe and isolate O'Donnell. Ginkel reached Banagher Bridge on 1 August, where the Royal Dragoons (Colonel Edward Matthews) linked up, and halted for two nights. Four men were detached from each troop of horse and, together with a party of dragoons, made up a detachment of 500 men under Brigadier Richard Leveson which set off to scour the country along the intended route to Limerick. On 4 August, Leveson arrived at Nenagh. The roof of the old Norman castle had been burned when the Williamites had evacuated Nenagh in 1690 but the walls remained intact. All winter it had been occupied by Brigadier Anthony Carroll commanding a garrison of about 500 men. Hearing of Leveson's approach, Carroll sent a party north out of the town towards the bridge over the Nenagh River, 1 km distant, hoping to hold the pass long enough for the majority of his men to escape down the Limerick road. However, on approaching the bridge he saw Leveson's men already manoeuvring left and right to outflank him and, after exchanging a few shots, fell back into Nenagh, setting fire to the small fraction of the town still intact: some English prisoners, released on Carroll's departure, extinguished the flames. Major Wood chased Carroll almost as far as Caherconlish, seizing his baggage and about 400 large cattle.

Ginkel marched from Banagher Bridge to Birr on 3 August. Banagher Bridge proved troublesome because two arches had been broken down and it was very late in the evening before all the artillery and carriages reached the campsite. On 5 August, Ginkel moved to Borrisokane, a crossing point of the River Ballyfinboy, where the Williamite garrison of Birr had burned down 'a pretty English plantation' during the winter to deny the raparees a base so close to their own position. The march continued to Nenagh on 6 August where the army rested for four days, awaiting a supply of bread. A party left the camp in the direction of Killaloe and killed two raparees, took nine prisoners and returned in the evening with a great prey of cattle. During the morning of 8 August, escorted by a strong detachment of cavalry, pioneers moved out from Nenagh to repair the roads south towards the Slieve Bloom: throughout the march from Galway, Ginkel's route had been determined solely by the need to select roads which could be negotiated by the artillery. On the morning of 11 August, Ginkel left Nenagh and marched to Shallee, about 3 km from the Silver Mine Mountains, 'a very wild part of the country', where Colonel Charles Trelawney's battalion joined. Ginkel issued a proclamation extending the deadline of the Lords Justices' proclamation, hoping to induce more Jacobites to surrender and avoid further bloodshed. On 12 August, the army advanced from Shallee to Cullen, where the soldiers rested on 13 August. Prisoners reported that Tyrconnell was ill and the Irish infantry had concentrated at Limerick and was camped on the County Clare side of the Shannon. On 14 August, Ginkel moved forward to Caherconlish. As his troops filed in, Ginkel rode at the head of 1,500 horse and dragoons to within sight of Limerick, viewing the Jacobite outworks from the hill where the Williamite artillery had camped in 1690. In the evening he returned to Caherconlish.[6]

21

The curious affair at Sligo,
or the banalities of the small war

The capture of Sligo promised control over northern Connaught, prevention of Jacobite raids into Ulster and observation of the wavering O'Donnell. On 4 July John Davis, secretary to the Lords Justices, wrote to Colonel Michelburne, commanding the regular forces in Ulster, informing him of recent intelligence indicating that the Jacobites had evacuated Sligo and Jamestown. He was asked to verify this and, should it prove correct and a feasible operation, occupy both places. When this request was reinforced by a direct order from Ginkel, Michelburne sent a drummer to Sligo on 10 July carrying letters from Jacobite prisoners in Derry wrapped in some vague compliments to Governor Sir Teague O'Regan and his deputy, Colonel Edward Scott. The messenger was urged to hurry and return that night or the next day. Seventy-two hours later, fearing that the drummer had been either attacked by raparees or detained because O'Regan was evacuating Sligo and did not want the knowledge spread abroad, Michelburne summoned a council of war (13 July), which decided to dispatch a strong reconnaissance expedition at 21:00 that evening.

Michelburne led out of Ballyshannon 80 regular dragoons, 200 infantry from his own battalion[1] plus 100 from Colonel Samuel Venner's, and 200 militia; travelling via the winding coast road, they came to Mullaghmore at daybreak. Here Captain Henry Hart made Michelburne aware of some dissatisfaction amongst the militia, fomented by Captain John Forward's remarks that, should they be defeated, the consequences would be dire because most of Ulster would be open to Jacobite incursions. At 05:00 they reached Grange and the murmurings had grown considerably louder. Michelburne, who was not a charismatic leader, summoned his officers and explained that he had no intention of fighting but was simply conducting a reconnaissance to see whether Sligo was still occupied. It would be a pity, he said, to turn back because they were over halfway and, besides, why had nothing been said at the earlier council of war? Unable to assert his authority over the surly, unpersuaded militia, Michelburne decided to press on with the regular soldiers and the more co-operative militia, allowing the recalcitrant to return to Ballyshannon. At Grange, he positioned the remaining militia foot and most of the regular infantry under Lieutenant Colonel Staughton in an ambush behind the stone walls of the grange itself. Reinforcing his regular dragoons by mounting 40 grenadiers on the officers' horses, he rode the 16 km to Sligo.

Leaving a mounted scout on every hill-top to establish a chain of communication to Grange, Michelburne hurried to make it difficult for the Jacobites to mount ambushes or other unpleasant surprises. Within 1½ km of Sligo, seeing no Jacobite cavalry, he moved closer and observed between 300 and 400 infantry drawn up. Sligo had clearly not been evacuated. Having acquired his information, and aware of the disquiet in his ranks, Michelburne sent a girl to O'Regan to ask for the return of the drummer and hovered for an hour or so before drawing back to the beach at Drumcliff. Some Jacobite horse then emerged from the town and a few shots were exchanged but as soon as O'Regan had sent a reply explaining that he had arrested the drummer as a spy because he had appeared uncommonly nosey, Michelburne returned to Grange where he collected the infantry and arrived back in Ballyshannon at 20:00 on 14 July. Michelburne's initial visit had given him a view of Sligo and he decided to return within two or three days to conduct a more detailed reconnaissance to assess how it might be captured. O'Regan immediately set his men to repairing the fortifications.

Michelburne was short of mounted troops. He explained to the Lords Justices that he had only six troops of County Donegal militia dragoons and a section of Captain Patrick Hamilton's troop from County Derry, insufficient to mount a successful attack on Sligo even though O'Regan's garrison was nothing but a rabble 'all ragged and have no allowance but one pound of bread a day'. However, as the next expedition was another reconnaissance he was prepared to manage with existing resources. Having sent a letter asking Lieutenant Colonel Alexander Ramsay (Venner's Foot), commanding at Enniskillen, to join him at Manorhamilton with 100 regular infantry, Michelburne set off from Ballyshannon on 15 July but, *en route*, received an express from Ramsay explaining that he could not comply having been ordered by Ginkel to move to Drogheda. The situation then deteriorated rapidly. Although Ramsay could not bring his regulars to Manorhamilton, he dispatched a substantial party of militia which ignored the Manorhamilton rendezvous and dashed off on a cattle raid towards Killerry Mountain, on the southern shore of Lough Gill. The alarm reached the Sligo garrison and O'Regan personally laid an ambush with 500 infantry to catch the raiders as they journeyed north driving a considerable booty of cattle, sheep and horses. Sensing such a development, Michelburne ordered Sir Francis Hamilton with a detachment of 200 horse and dragoons south from Manorhamilton, who came up to the raiding party just as it was being engaged by O'Regan. Almost simultaneously, Colonel Edward Scott arrived with his regiment to reinforce O'Regan. Both sides stood off until Hamilton began to advance and the Irish broke and ran for Sligo, a race that was won, according to the rather unsporting Protestant accounts, by Sir Teague himself. Another account said that O'Regan, who clearly had not visited a tailor since the blockade of Charlemont, narrowly evaded capture because his scruffy appearance led the

Ulstermen to think he was a person of no importance. Lieutenant Patrick Moore, formerly a lieutenant in Derry during the siege, rode into the centre of Sligo and, mistakenly assuming that he was supported by his own men, cried out for King William. He was knocked down and taken before the governor who pumped him for information about Michelburne and the Ulster forces. Had Sir Francis Hamilton exploited his victory, Sligo could easily have been taken and a great deal of subsequent fuss and bother avoided. Instead, abiding by instructions, he recalled his troops and returned north.

Michelburne was back in Ballyshannon on 16 July to find orders to provide 25 regular infantry to protect two biscuit ships on their voyage to Galway. Despite the shortage of good troops, he complied. A muddle of contradictory orders then followed. First, on 14 July (received 17 July) Ginkel asked Michelburne to proceed to Athlone but this was countermanded two days later (16 July). Colonel Adam Murray, of Derry fame, was supposed to arrive at Ballyshannon on 17 July with the northern militia to take over seven frontier garrisons along the line of the Erne releasing enough forces to allow Michelburne to mount another expedition to Sligo. There being no sign of Murray, Michelburne held a council of war. To take advantage of the victory at Aughrim and assuage the militia, it was decided to assemble troops on 21 July to raid into County Sligo and northern Connaught. Although the council was sworn to secrecy, its resolution was public knowledge within two hours.

Although the proposed assembly on 21 July failed to occur, Michelburne was determined to return to Sligo for a third, deeper reconnaissance despite the fact that, since the departure of Venner's battalion for Drogheda, he was very short of regular troops and had seven garrisons to maintain. In the meantime, Michelburne wrote to O'Regan on 17 July enquiring whether, following the defeat at Aughrim, he might wish to consider accepting the Lords Justices' proclamation, which he had great pleasure in enclosing along with a gift of snuff and two bottles of whiskey. O'Regan replied in the negative on 28 July. On 30 July, Michelburne set out again from Ballyshannon, arriving at Belleek at 15:00. Here he reviewed all his men – 300 regular infantry from his own battalion; two troops of regular dragoons, one from Colonel Wynne's regiment and one from Sir Albert Conyngham's; 12 troops of militia horse; and two companies of militia infantry – and set off for Manorhamilton at 17:00 over 17 km of bad roads. Sir Francis Hamilton commanded the vanguard and Captain Hugh Caldwell the rearguard. They arrived in Manorhamilton at 02:00 on 31 July and rested for four hours. Before leaving, Michelburne sent an express to Major John Hamilton (Michelburne's Foot) ordering him to detach 100 flintlock musketeers from Michelburne's companies in garrison at Belturbet, Enniskillen and Cavan and bring them to a rendezvous at Collooney. Michelburne marched at 06:00 for Collooney and Sligo. On the road he encountered about 60 cattle and horses and several of the militia broke ranks to seize them but Michelburne managed to force them back to their stations. This was the beginning of a long series of trying incidents in which the militia showed itself far more interested in cattle raiding than adhering to military discipline. Possibly, they regarded Michelburne as a *parvenu* who had only recently been fortunate enough to acquire high rank in the regular army; Colonel Wolseley did not suffer such indignities and frustrations when leading Ulster forces.

At midday they reached Dromahair, 15 km from Manorhamilton, where Michelburne brought his men into column of companies and marched throughout the afternoon until, at 17:00, they observed Jacobite outposts which retired steadily avoiding contact. During the evening of 31 July, they reached Collooney and camped in a well-protected position on a peninsula, a river and Collooney Castle on the left and a bog to the right. Michelburne rode forward 3 km to Ballysadare Bridge over the River Owenbeg to find it covered by about 100 Jacobite cavalry. Sentries and guards were placed all round the camp and the men tucked into a supper of boiled mutton. At 06:00 on 1 August, with Captain Caldwell leading the vanguard and the rearguard under the command of Captain Andrew Nesbitt (Conyngham's Dragoons), an old and highly experienced soldier, Michelburne marched the 12 km to Sligo: either he took the road through Ballygawley and the Castledargan Forest in order to by-pass Ballysadare Bridge, or the Jacobite cavalry at Ballysadare had withdrawn during the night. Caldwell drove in the Jacobite out-guards at 10:00 and the whole force drew up within cannon-shot of Sligo one hour later. The garrison fired 15 cannon but Michelburne beat for a parley at 13:00 and sent forward a drummer with a letter for O'Regan. Subsequently a meeting was arranged between Colonel Edward Scott, Colonel Ternon O'Rourke and Lieutenant O'Rourke on the Jacobite side, and Michelburne, Captain Hugh Caldwell and Sir Francis Hamilton. Discussions lasted all afternoon into early evening. It was eventually agreed that O'Regan would send a messenger to Ginkel, escorted by one of Michelburne's officers, to seek permission to consult with Tyrconnell about terms for a possible surrender. In the noble art of playing for time, Michelburne had much to learn.

He also had much to learn about organizing military expeditions, having departed from Ballyshannon without any provisions, trusting to the seizure of cattle and sheep *en route*. Such obvious inadequacies further reduced Michelburne in the eyes of the militia and encouraged cattle raiding. At 19:00 on 1 August, he pulled back from Sligo after being informed that the militia troops of Captains Henderson and John Forward, including their commanders, had deserted their posts to go plundering. Michelburne sent eight men from every troop under the overall command of Captain Anthony Shamberg (Michelburne's Foot, Captain of Grenadiers) to follow the errant militia but also to find some cattle with which to feed the rest of the men. Instead of just eight men from every troop accompanying Shamberg, many militiamen took the opportunity to sneak away and abandon the expedition. When the remains of the force straggled into the Collooney camp that evening, it was as much as the two troops of regular dragoons could do to prevent the rest of the militia from deserting. Further haemorrhages amongst the militia on the morning of 2 August demonstrated to Michelburne that the only reliable troops were the 300 infantry from his own battalion and the two troops of regular dragoons. Fortunately, Major John Hamilton reached Collooney at 15:00 with 100 musketeers from Michelburne's battalion, sufficient to encourage Michelburne to renew the pressure on Sligo. Two hours later (17:00), Michelburne received a report that the militia troops of Captains Henderson and William Vaughan, having stolen 100 cattle and between 200 and 300 sheep, were marching for home rather than the camp at Collooney. Thirty men went on a mission of dissuasion but, although they intercepted them within 5 km of Collooney, they refused to reconsider. Michelburne then dispatched a stronger party that was successful in diverting the cattle and sheep to Collooney although the militia continued to travel north. Later on Sunday 2 August, Captain Shamberg herded between 700 and 800 cattle into the camp, enough to influence two militia troops, on the point of deserting, to remain. Michelburne awarded one fat sheep to every four men.

On the morning of 3 August, reinforced by Hamilton's detachment and with Captain Shamberg's grenadiers transformed into temporary dragoons on captured mounts, Michelburne marched back towards Sligo, driving along all the cattle. It was one way to make the militia stick to their duty: 'no prey, no militia!' Reaching Sligo at 12:00, Michelburne divided his men into two parties of 200 men each. Sir Francis Hamilton and Major John Hamilton led one along the west side of the River Garvoge to block off Sligo from that side whilst, at low tide, Michelburne took the other on to the far bank. Each rider carried an infantryman behind him and Michelburne forded without opposition, except for a few shots from the Earth Fort. Once across, noticing the Jacobites forming up on the east side of the town, he deployed into line of battle and advanced to within cannon-shot of Sligo, to the right of the Earth Fort, where he camped for the night, the Jacobites having retired into the fort and town. Although Michelburne was heavily outnumbered by O'Regan's garrison, Sligo was technically surrounded and thus, according to the Laws of War, blockaded. Short of men and provisions, Michelburne had also nearly run out of ammunition – six rounds per man remained – so one officer and six dragoons rode back to Ballyshannon, a distance of 32 km, to fetch replenishments. In the interim, to conserve ammunition, orders were given that there should be as little firing as possible during the night of 3–4 August. Michelburne remained in his exposed and vulnerable position on 4 August, distributing sheep and cows and ordering the soldiers to build huts as shelter against the very wet weather.

On 5 August, Michelburne was undermined by an express from John Davis on behalf of the Lords Justices ordering him take no further measures against Sligo because Ginkel was pursuing other methods of securing its capitulation, a reference, no doubt, to contacts with O'Donnell. Between 11:00 and 12:00, O'Regan beat for a parley. At this point, the Ulster militia proved itself not just militarily useless but a hazard to the whole Williamite cause. The soldiers were unruly, ignored their officers and refused to obey orders. If placed on guard, within an hour they had drifted away. They had ridden with Michelburne not to capture Sligo but to plunder and steal cattle, sheep and horses to restock their own farms. Captain John Forward, 'a leading card to the rest of the militia', quit his post at midday on 6 August and led away his entire troop, forcing aside the out-guards, crossing the river at Ballysadare, before plundering the countryside south-east towards Boyle for a distance of 90 km. He then rode home. As Michelburne, Sir Francis Hamilton and Major John Hamilton negotiated with O'Regan about protections, the application of the Lords Justices' proclamation and the surrender of Sligo, the Ulster militia was ransacking the adjacent countryside. Davis's letter had made Michelburne's position difficult; the militia's behaviour rendered it untenable. On the Connaught side of Sligo, nearly all the militia left their positions and conducted cattle raids. Droves of 'idle people, especially the Lagganneers', had travelled to the camp with and in the wake of Michelburne's expedition and every militiaman seems to have been helped to run off cattle, horses and sheep by two or three 'attenders'. In Michelburne's opinion, there was but one honest man for every 20 thieves. The regulars were not blameless. As soon as Michelburne's back was turned, despite the fact that the Williamite and Jacobite out-guards were within musket-shot of one another, soldiers went 'rogueing' with the militia. The sole ambition of the militia was to depart for home as soon as possible taking all the livestock with them and they pressed Michelburne to release the cattle and sheep from central control and make a fair division. Michelburne refused knowing that retention of the livestock was his only means of keeping the remaining militia at Sligo. In an effort to improve the atmosphere in which the negotiations with Sligo were taking place, Michelburne suggested returning some of the stolen cattle to the local people, provided that they could show their protections, but this further enraged the militia.

At 15:00 on 6 August, the senior officers agreed the articles of surrender. The garrison would march out with the full honours of war, complete with carts, horses and two field guns, and take the shortest route to Limerick. Sick and wounded officers, soldiers and civilians would remain in Sligo until fit when they would be given safe conduct to destinations of their choice. Michelburne would take possession of Sligo's two forts at 08:00 on 15 August, provided that, in the interim, Galway had surrendered – in which case any additional benefits granted to the garrison and citizens of Galway at its capitulation would be added to the Sligo treaty of surrender – and no relief had reached Sligo. The document of surrender was entrusted to Major John Hamilton and the brother of Colonel Edward Scott who carried it to Ginkel for approval. Ginkel, who would have signed a Faustian pact with the Devil at this stage of the campaign, nodded assent on 10 August whilst camped at Nenagh. Michelburne had achieved something but O'Regan had gained at least nine precious days during which the situation at Galway would clarify and O'Donnell might come to his relief.

Arguing that the campaign was now over because the articles of surrender had been signed, the remaining militia pressed Michelburne to divide up the livestock and allow them to go home. Trying to strike a bargain, Michelburne asked them to remain for another eight days at the end of which the surrender would be guaranteed and secured. The camp was 'now like a fair, buying and selling, robbing and stealing the sheep in the night and killing them for their skins'. Michelburne was strongly advised to share the remaining prey between the militia and the regulars immediately or there would be nothing left; the very officers and soldiers supposedly guarding the animals were actually selling them. So, on the evening of 6 August, Captain William Stewart (St John's Foot) was ordered to distribute the prey equally between the regular soldiers and the militia. Despite this, during the night of 6–7 August, 200 militia led by Captain Vaughan, who had induced the men to desert by promising them a barrel of beer at his house at Buncrana, County Donegal, overpowered the guard of 20 regulars under Captains Michael Conyngham and John Bickerstaffe (Michelburne's Foot) and drove off all the livestock. Once clear of the camp, the cattle drive was accompanied by pillaging, regardless of whether the country people had received protections from Michelburne. Thinking the noise and confusion presaged an attack Michelburne doubled the guards and ordered his men stand to arms until dawn. First light revealed that the only militia remaining were the troops and companies of Sir Francis Hamilton, Charles Hamilton, William Stewart and John Hamilton: a total of ten troops and companies had deserted. Michelburne and Sir Francis Hamilton were left badly exposed, their weak and unsupported detachments separated by the River Garvoge, and reports had been received that O'Donnell was advancing from northern Connaught via Collooney and Ballysadare Bridge with a view to relieving Sligo. As soon as the garrison appreciated their predicament, they would be in peril of defeat in detail. Fortunately, either O'Regan had no wish to endanger the advantageous agreement of the previous afternoon or he had failed to spot the opportunity. Early on the morning of 7 August, Sir Francis Hamilton and Captain Shamberg recrossed the river and were reunited with Michelburne on the north bank.

O'Donnell had left his lair in the mountains of Mayo, into which he had disappeared following his failure to relieve Galway, and reached Collooney on 7 August. Michelburne's weak, demoralized, outnumbered and internally divided command was sandwiched between O'Donnell's men at Collooney, which Michelburne mistakenly understood to number 3,000, and the two regiments of the Sligo garrison. Having gathered his men on the north bank of the Garvoge, Michelburne called a council of war at which he was strongly advised to retire to Ballyshannon as quickly as possible. Michelburne broke camp on the morning of Saturday 8 August and ordered most of his remaining troops to march. Together with Sir Francis Hamilton, Captain Charles Hamilton, Captain William Stewart, some of the few remaining militia officers and the two troops of regular dragoons, Michelburne stayed before Sligo to observe O'Regan's reactions before forming the rearguard. The garrison showed no inclination to sally and attack the retreating Williamites and so Michelburne drew off the dragoons at 09:00 and set out along the coast road. Michelburne had been duped and outmanoeuvred by O'Regan and O'Donnell. He had released all pressure on Sligo, had taken no hostages, left no troops in the vicinity and appeared to trust O'Regan to execute the terms of the agreement like a gentleman. O'Regan, no doubt, had taken cognizance of the indiscipline of the Ulster and Donegal militia and formed a view about the effectiveness of any martial pressure that Michelburne might be able to exert in the future. Michelburne reached Ballyshannon on the evening of 9 August only to hear that O'Donnell had marched to Sligo directly his back had been turned enabling O'Regan to demonstrate that a relief had been completed and the treaty of 6 August thus null and void. If he was not to look a complete fool, Michelburne had to return immediately. He issued orders for 300 from his own infantry battalion to join him at Ballyshannon on 14 August and wrote to Major Richard Tichborne and Cornet Mead, the supervisors of the Ulster militia, asking them to bring to the same rendezvous as many mounted and foot militia as they could gather, each man carrying provisions for six days.

Through the agency of an acquaintance in Ginkel's camp, James Richards, brother of Lieutenant Colonel Jacob, on 6 August O'Donnell forwarded some conditions upon which his followers might be prepared to lay down their arms: the soldiers would join the Williamite Army for service in Flanders, under his command, whilst he was created Earl of Tyrconnell and received £2,000 to cover expenses. In other words, he was offering to sell his own supporters to Ginkel in return for title and money. Until matters were settled he undertook not to act against the Williamites and asked Ginkel for a cease-fire – his 'relief' of Sligo had not involved violence and thus had not compromised this request – and to nominate a place where his men might remain, unmolested. Ginkel could not agree to all the proposals but forwarded them to Lord Portland for consideration. He suggested that O'Donnell be asked to stay in the Sligo area. Peace with O'Donnell would have been welcome, especially as it offered the joyous prospect of Roman Catholic factions fighting one another. Although now universally distrusted, O'Donnell remained potentially useful to both sides; the more untrustworthy he became the more his political utility increased. Fearing that his own men might seize him *à la* Wallenstein at Eger, O'Donnell slipped away from Sligo on the night of 8 August and opened full negotiations with the Williamites. Ginkel concluded a partial agreement and published the text in both the *Dublin Intelligence* and *London Gazette* on 13 August. Although publication was premature and pre-empted detailed negotiations, the likelihood that O'Donnell would renege was thereby much reduced and his propensity for double-dealing constrained. O'Donnell complained that this advance publicity prejudiced the chances of bringing over large numbers of men but, privately, his only regret was the limitation placed upon his opportunities to play off one side against the other.

Michelburne, though, was not yet privy to these developments and needed to know O'Donnell's status and situation before plunging south on his fourth visit to Sligo. On 11 August, he sent a drummer with a packet of communications from Jacobite prisoners in Derry and a letter for Colonel Edward Scott in which he explained that when Captain John Forward returned from his pillaging expedition – and he was still abroad – Michelburne would endeavour to compensate all who had suffered. Michelburne also accused Scott and O'Regan of having enticed O'Donnell to come to the relief of Sligo. Lieutenant Colonel Ternon McDonagh replied on the same day, rather disingenuously, stating that the garrison had not invited O'Donnell. Indeed they had wanted neither him nor his men as they were devouring the local provisions but, as a brigadier in the Jacobite Army, O'Donnell outranked both Scott and O'Regan so they had to follow his orders. The drummer returned with McDonagh's letter on 12 August and the useful intelligence that O'Donnell's men were encamped within 5 km of Sligo. Michelburne also received a report from one of his spies that O'Donnell's command comprised six infantry regiments, one troop of cavalry and two of dragoons, all numerically weak and poorly armed. More intelligence arrived on 19 August when Michelburne received via Ginkel an intercepted letter from Colonel Edward Scott to Sarsfield, recently elevated to the Earldom of Lucan, written on 13 August. Scott explained that Michelburne had come to Sligo 12 days previously with his own battalion of infantry, two troops of army dragoons and about 2,000 militiamen. Michelburne had then sent them a letter from Ginkel offering terms and money in return for agreeing to surrender the town, which Scott and O'Regan had refused. However, after three or four days they agreed to surrender if not relieved within ten days, 'which was only a project to save about 5,000 cows we had about the fort, and thereby got an opportunity to send to O'Donnell in County Mayo'. Scott then personally travelled to meet O'Donnell who duly marched to effect the relief. Scott added that O'Donnell's force was presently camped around Boyle where they would remain until Sligo had been resupplied. Ginkel wrote a covering note to this useful enclosure warning Michelburne to be on his guard against incursions into Ulster and use the militia to cover the frontier. If he had not already paid the treacherous O'Donnell 200 guineas, then he was not to do so.

On 13 and 14 August several detachments of Michelburne's infantry battalion from Belturbet, Cavan, Enniskillen and Killybegs assembled at Ballyshannon, making a force of 600 regular infantry plus two troops of army dragoons. Despite the entreaties of Sir Francis Hamilton, most of the Ulster and Donegal militia could not be persuaded to leave their homes despite the offer of one shilling per day. Only four troops of militia cavalry – Captain Charles Hamilton, Captain William Stewart, Captain Hamilton of Murvough (sic) and Captain Irwin of Fermanagh – turned up at the rendezvous. Michelburne marched on 14 August via the coast road to keep well clear of O'Donnell and camped overnight at Bundoran. He set off again at daybreak on 15 August, stopping at Grange from where he sent Captain Shamberg ahead with a letter for O'Regan. It was a rather optimistic epistle, hoping that Lieutenant Scott and Major John Hamilton had by now returned from Ginkel with the terms of the surrender ratified. O'Regan replied that Scott and Hamilton had indeed returned but that Ginkel had 'not altogether confirmed' the articles. However, although O'Regan was willing to sign the articles, O'Donnell stood close by with a 'strong brigade ... who, if he stands by us, alters all affairs, for 'tis a relief if he makes it so'. He suggested a meeting. At 15:00, Scott and Hamilton rode back to Michelburne's camp, which had now been established close to Sligo. They explained that O'Regan and the garrison had been keen to sign the articles and would have done so had not O'Donnell intervened. Scott and Hamilton had been thoroughly deceived by O'Regan who, as we have seen, had himself approached O'Donnell seeking his intervention and had then declared the articles void because a relief had taken place. O'Regan had also misrepresented Ginkel's position. On 10 August, Ginkel had written to Michelburne from Nenagh confirming all the articles of surrender urging Michelburne to treat the garrison leniently, act civilly, return stolen horses and give them protections, if requested. O'Donnell, said Ginkel, had submitted but not before Ginkel had bribed him with a promise of 200 guineas, which Michelburne was to pay over to him, if he had sufficient cash available, and seek reimbursement from the army paymaster. Should other Jacobite garrisons wish to surrender, Michelburne was instructed to take their weapons and invite the officers and soldiers to enlist in the Williamite forces, paying each captain five pounds, a lieutenant three pounds and an ensign two pounds. They would then be placed upon the half-pay list until put into service.

Also on 15 August, O'Donnell contacted Michelburne asking for a meeting to be held between Sligo and the Williamite camp. Shortly after receiving Michelburne's positive reply, O'Donnell appeared with ten horsemen and Michelburne advanced to meet him, escorted by a similar number, including

Sir Francis Hamilton, Cornet Mead and Captain Charles Hamilton. O'Donnell explained that, although there was an arrangement between him and Ginkel, it was rather vague and he had not yet decided what to do although, ultimately, he expected very favourable terms. He offered his services as a third party in the dispute between Michelburne and the Sligo garrison. When, he mused, Michelburne and O'Regan concluded terms of surrender, he could occupy Sligo fort whilst Michelburne escorted O'Regan's troops to Limerick. Then, after ten days or a fortnight, O'Donnell might deliver up the fort to Michelburne, or any other officer appointed by Ginkel. Realizing that O'Donnell and O'Regan were not in agreement, Michelburne, riding alongside O'Donnell, replied that this was not quite his understanding of the situation. He showed him a letter from Ginkel written on 10 August at Nenagh in which he suggested that O'Donnell should assist in the surrender of Sligo, not take possession himself. He also mentioned the payment of 200 guineas. O'Donnell replied that he would give his response on the following morning after he had consulted with O'Regan. After some glasses of sherry and whiskey, they parted.

As arranged, they reconvened on the morning of 16 August. After exchanging a few polite words, they rode off together leaving their escorts at a distance. Michelburne began by giving O'Donnell 100 guineas, promising the balance within a day or two, and asking him what he intended to do because O'Regan was willing to surrender the fort. O'Donnell explained that he could not agree to a capitulation until he and his followers had received acceptable terms. Michelburne responded that O'Donnell was the only man obstructing the surrender and requested that he withdraw his men and allow it to take place. Unfortunately, said O'Donnell, such a course of action would not be permitted by his followers but, as soon as he had concluded a deal with James Richards, Ginkel's envoy in this matter, he would return and assist in the surrender. Having achieved nothing, Michelburne decided to exploit the fissure between O'Donnell and O'Regan by talking to the latter. He explained that O'Donnell had not been mentioned in the articles of surrender of 6 August, approved by Ginkel, yet O'Donnell was now in the Williamite service, having accepted 100 guineas from Michelburne. It was now impossible to argue that O'Donnell had legally relieved Sligo so the original articles must stand. Michelburne also asked for 20 cattle to provision his men, for which he would pay. O'Regan replied with the old argument that Brigadier O'Donnell outranked him. Also, the surrender could not occur until Michelburne had provided horses to pull the wagons and artillery, as stipulated in the articles, because horses stolen from Colonel Scott and others had not been returned. Further, the prisoners had not yet been released, another stipulation of the treaty. Finally, O'Regan said that he had no cattle to give but Michelburne was welcome to send a man into Sligo to buy some.

Somehow, Michelburne misinterpreted this as a helpful reply and dispatched

Major John Hamilton into Sligo to inform the garrison that everything was ready for the surrender. Hamilton promised compensation for the missing horses and freedom for all prisoners once the treaty had been signed. Michelburne must have felt close to securing agreement when O'Donnell rode into Sligo on 18 August waving a 'certificate' which stated that, on his honour, his sole intention in marching to Sligo had been to relieve the garrison regardless of any existing agreement between himself and Ginkel. In the interest of King James, he wished now to defer the surrender of Sligo, and promised to support O'Regan against any force that Ginkel might send. Major John Hamilton, then in Sligo negotiating about the horses and the precise arrangements for capitulation, promptly withdrew bringing Michelburne a copy of O'Donnell's 'certificate'. Disappointed and probably furious, Michelburne broke off negotiations. Further insult followed when O'Regan sent a message asking Michelburne to withdraw from before Sligo or the garrison, reinforced by O'Donnell, would sally and beat him back. Outnumbered by about ten to one, Michelburne had no option but to comply although he departed with the defiant words that he would march where he pleased and would return within a few days to drive them from the fort. Michelburne broke camp at 13:00 on 18 August, marching via the coast road to keep clear of O'Donnell, with the baggage at the head of the column, followed by the infantry. One hour later, Michelburne led off with the rearguard of four troops of militia cavalry and two of regular dragoons; he camped overnight at Mullaghmore and arrived in Ballyshannon on 19 August. Michelburne then sat down and wrote a detailed description of events and O'Donnell's double-dealing for the benefit of the Lords Justices. Assuming that the Ulster frontier was now vulnerable to attack from the combined forces of O'Regan and O'Donnell, he added that he had only two troops of regular dragoons with which to cover 65 km of frontier, the militia cavalry having gone home the moment that the expedition had returned to Ballyshannon. In London, when he heard the full story, the Marquis of Carmarthen was highly critical of Michelburne's 'foolish conduct' which had encouraged Sligo to defend itself and allowed O'Donnell and O'Regan to 'play one of [their] Irish tricks'.

The Lords Justices replied on 22 August stating their intention to reinforce Michelburne with the whole northern militia from Counties Derry, Donegal, Tyrone, Cavan, Monaghan, Fermanagh, Down and Antrim, all of which had been ordered to report to Ballyshannon. Also, Arthur Forbes, First Earl of Granard, a man with some military experience having served as Marshal of the Irish Army under Charles II and commanded an infantry regiment until removed by Tyrconnell in 1686, had been ordered to rendezvous with the County Athlone militia. The aim of the expedition was the reduction of Sligo and its forts and the suppression of O'Donnell and his brigade. Granard was appointed commander-in-chief of the expedition, with Michelburne – offended, relieved, or both

– reduced to a subordinate rôle. Probably, the Lords Justices felt that a senior Protestant aristocrat was required to bring authority to both the operations and any subsequent negotiations. On receipt of this letter, Michelburne immediately sent for Sir Francis Hamilton to join him at Ballyshannon with all possible speed and to Major Tichborne and Cornet Mead to rouse the militias of Counties Cavan and Fermanagh. Unknown to Michelburne, on 19 August James Richards had written to him explaining that O'Donnell had now turned another somersault and agreed to throw in his lot with the Williamites and assist Ginkel. Richards hoped that Michelburne would be able to supply O'Donnell from Ballyshannon. Following the fall of Sligo, Richards mused that O'Donnell would march to join Ginkel's army before Limerick and supplies for his men could be drawn from Galway. Sir Albert Conyngham, with his regiment of dragoons, had been ordered to march from the main army camp at Limerick to the borders between Counties Clare and Galway, and would thus be available to operate against Sligo from the south. This 'express' should have reached Michelburne on 21 or 22 August but was not delivered until 14 September.

Granard suggested to Michelburne on 21 August that, should there be an operational need to unite their forces, they might rendezvous at Boyle. He added that recent information concerning O'Donnell was confused: some reports said that he had reached an accommodation with Ginkel; others that his officers refused to accept the terms. Michelburne replied that Sir Francis Hamilton would concentrate the County Donegal militia at Ballybofey on Sunday 30 August and reach Ballyshannon between 31 August and 2 September, by which time Michelburne would have assembled his own battalion and the militia from other counties. He would then proceed directly to Sligo. The Lords Justices informed Granard at Athlone on 22 August that, because of O'Donnell's treachery, he would soon receive militia reinforcements from Dublin: 1,000 infantry, 500 cavalry and dragoons, and three field guns, marched on 25 August. When all 5,000 troops had gathered, Granard would destroy O'Donnell and his followers before attacking Sligo. Ammunition and supplies could be drawn from the storekeeper in Athlone but, with the country still insecure from raparees, Granard was to ensure that Ballymore remained garrisoned. Above all, Granard was to liaise closely with Michelburne. The Lords Justices also wrote to Ginkel to enquire, unsuccessfully, whether any regular troops in County Galway could be spared to reinforce Granard.

On either 22 or 23 August, Michelburne received a useful report from a spy who had been present in Ballinrobe on Friday 21 August when O'Donnell had signed an agreement with James Richards. Soon afterwards O'Donnell received an express from one of his colonels advising him to remain at Ballinrobe rather than come to the camp because there was a plot to murder him for having agreed articles with Ginkel. Reaching Boyle the spy heard that only three of O'Donnell's regiments, including his own and his brother's, were resolved to join Michelburne. Further information was received from Edward Wade and a friar, Father Petton, who told Michelburne that O'Donnell was encamped at Collooney close to Sir Albert Conyngham's regiment of dragoons. Michelburne was highly suspicious of this pair until their intelligence was partially confirmed by a Jacobite gunner who had deserted from Sligo and one of Conyngham's dragoons. Whilst lying sick at Collooney this unlikely pair heard a great commotion and the word circulated that O'Donnell had defeated Conyngham's Dragoons; routed them according to the Jacobite gunner. They rushed from the house, raising questions about the gravity of their ill-health, and hid in a ditch within the garden. Hearing shouting in the distance, they saw some of the women who were known to have been accompanying Conyngham's regiment running into the town stripped. They also heard that Sir Albert Conyngham himself had been killed. Having procured horses they took the road to Ballyshannon through Manorhamilton. This news proved the usual mixture of truth, half-truth and fiction. Conyngham's main body, except for the troop serving with Michelburne, had left the Limerick camp commanded by Sir Albert and Lieutenant Colonel Robert Echlin and marched north to reinforce Granard before Sligo. *En route*, they were joined by O'Donnell's men and the joint party reached Colloony on 4 September. During the night of 4–5 September, Colonel Edward Scott led 700 men out of Sligo to launch a surprise attack on the foggy morning of 5 September. Sir Albert and eight dragoons lost their lives, O'Donnell narrowly escaped capture and instant lynching and both the dragoons and O'Donnell's troops fell back in confusion to Boyle. Scott then returned to Sligo enabling the force to return to Colloony.[2]

Whilst waiting for the troops to assemble, Michelburne gave instructions for some of the brass cannon captured at Newtownbutler, subsequently stored in Enniskillen, to be forwarded to Ballyshannon and mounted on field carriages. He also sent to Belturbet for bread and Killybegs for shipping to convey ammunition, engineering equipment, provisions and the brass cannon to Sligo, essential because the small local horses were incapable of towing artillery. The concentration of the militia was delayed. Sir Francis Hamilton wrote from Cavan on 27 August that he would not arrive at Ballyshannon until Monday 31 August, at the earliest; units from remoter regions would take even longer to assemble. Hamilton had also heard via the Lords Justices that O'Donnell's men were busy ravaging and plundering in northern Connaught and Granard had been ordered to intercept him. By 8 September, Michelburne had gathered at Ballyshannon four troops of militia dragoons from County Donegal, 175 men; two companies of infantry from the County Derry militia, 100 men; one troop of cavalry and one company of infantry from the County Monaghan militia, 100 men; one troop of cavalry from the County Fermanagh militia, 50 men; one company of infantry from the County Antrim militia, 60 men; two companies of infantry from the

County Tyrone militia, 120 men; 650 regular infantry from his own battalion; one troop of Sir Albert Conyngham's regular dragoons, 50 men; and one troop from Wynne's regular dragoons, 50 men. Michelburne thus led a force of 830 infantry and 575 horse and dragoons, totalling 1,405 men. Granard had already left Athlone by 8 September and was marching north. Whilst Michelburne was readying his expedition, O'Donnell finally made peace with Ginkel and joined his 1,200 men[3] to those of Lord Granard at Boyle Abbey on 9 September. The road for the combined force lay over the Curlew Mountains which proved a hard and difficult route because Granard's draught horses were of poor quality and the guns had to be man-hauled. As a test of O'Donnell's real intentions, Granard asked him to attack Ballymote, a Jacobite garrison controlling the road to Collooney and Sligo. He moved forward obediently but, catching sight of artillery, Governor O'Connor surrendered on terms and marched to Sligo allowing a relieved O'Donnell to avoid sitting the examination.

Michelburne left Ballyshannon on 9 September and, marching via the coast road, reached Drumcliff that night. Captain Vaughan, with 60 militia horse, was sent ahead from Drumcliff to contact Granard and inform him of Michelburne's movements. At 07:00 on 10 September, Michelburne advanced to within 1 km of Sligo and took possession of the Rabaccan, a small Cromwellian fort north-west of the town on the north bank of the Garvoge. Rain poured down on 11 September and the day was spent repairing the Rabaccan and cutting brushwood to bind into fascines. A drummer walked into Sligo to summon O'Regan to surrender but, later that day, the offer was politely declined. Early on the following day, 12 September, Michelburne rode out to inspect every inch of Sligo's fortifications. He observed 200 of the garrison filling an old ditch some distance from the Earth Fort and was informed by some local people that the garrison had recently been reinforced by two companies of infantry. He watched numbers of soldiers walking between the Earth Fort and the town but detected only one company of grenadiers actually guarding the fort: O'Regan evidently did not expect Michelburne to make any major movement until he had linked up with Granard. However, with the militia behaving uncommonly well, Michelburne felt strong enough to take the offensive, an option he had been denied on previous excursions because of numerical weakness. At 08:00 he ordered the company of grenadiers from his own infantry battalion, plus one troop of dragoons and 200 foot to draw up under cover of the Rabaccan. The cavalrymen, deployed on a nearby hill, were instructed to stand at their horses' heads, ready to mount.

Michelburne advanced intending to secure the ditches and beat the Jacobites out of the Earth Fort. At the first volley, the Jacobites abandoned advanced positions and scurried back to their trenches. Michelburne pursued. In the meantime, the Jacobite artillery played upon the Williamite cavalry but did little damage. Michelburne's infantry drove the Jacobites from ditch to ditch, the militia in the van led by Sir Francis Hamilton, Major Tichborne and Cornet Mead. Once within the complex of trenches Jacobite resistance stiffened so Michelburne ordered up three troops of horse which increased the pressure to such an extent that the Jacobites retreated back into the Earth Fort. Giving the Jacobites no time to rally and reorganize, Michelburne advanced on horseback at the head of the grenadiers and about 100 foot soldiers and broke into the fort, the Jacobites escaping by jumping over the parapets and running back to the Stone Fort. Within 60 minutes, all the outworks and the town of Sligo itself had fallen and the Stone Fort was isolated. Michelburne's casualties amounted to one ensign killed by a cannon ball, and nine men wounded. A lieutenant and 30 men were sent to guard the bridges over the Garvoge, to prevent the militia and other riff-raff from entering the town to plunder, and a gallows was erected in the market place ready to make an example of the first offender. This was a great relief to the garrison in the fort who had expected to witness the massacre of their wives and children in Sligo town. Seizing the moment, Michelburne sent a second summons to the fort, adding that if they did not surrender he would have seized the fort's counterscarp by the following morning. O'Regan asked for two hours' grace to consult his officers and for work on the approach trenches to halt during that period, to which Michelburne misguidedly agreed. At the end of the second hour, O'Regan sent three commissioners – Colonel Ternon O'Rourke, Major Conner and Lieutenant Colonel MacDonagh – who stated that O'Regan was agreeable to a restitution of the terms agreed on 6 August provided that the additional forces which had entered the garrison were included. They would accordingly surrender in nine days. Michelburne, at last realizing that the way to conduct military operations was to maintain continuous pressure, replied that surrender must occur within 24 hours. The commissioners returned with a compromise of four days but Michelburne refused and sent them back to reconsider until morning. All night, his artillery fired on the Stone Fort and his men stood to arms in full view of the garrison.

At 22:00 on 12 September, scouts commanded by Captain Harrison gave an account of a considerable unidentified camp between Sligo and Ballysadare. It was unlikely to be Granard, who was not yet expected; perhaps it was a relief detachment under Sarsfield which had been rumoured marching from Limerick? Harrison was ordered to push forward 20 men until they were challenged to discover the nature of the mysterious visitors. This they did and discovered the camp to be Granard's advance guard and thus contact between the two forces was established. On the morning of 13 September, Michelburne wrote to O'Regan that if the garrison did not immediately reach a decision, all Roman Catholic civilians must leave the fort but this was not a dire threat because only three women were involved, Mrs Conner, Mrs Riley and O'Regan's maid. O'Regan responded by asking that the same three commissioners be allowed to continue negotiations. Michelburne had in his hand a letter from Ginkel at Limerick, dated 7 September, informing him that O'Donnell was now definitely committed to the Williamite cause, having signed a treaty with James Richards, and would actively assist against Sligo. Ginkel hoped that Michelburne would be able to exclude O'Regan and Edward Scott from the terms of surrender so that they might be punished for their treachery but Michelburne was not to insist on this point to the extent that it might prejudice negotiations. The principal objective was to secure Sligo.

On 13 September, Granard moved his troops within sight of Michelburne and asked him to ride over, attended by some of his officers. No doubt with some satisfaction, Michelburne reported that the garrison of 28 companies of foot was bottled up in the Stone Fort and a satisfactory resolution fast approaching. Michelburne and his officers then accompanied Granard into Sligo town and entered the house of Sir Arthur Gore. Here Sir Francis Hamilton, Major John Hamilton and Major Tichborne gave Granard a detailed account of the situation. Granard gave full permission to conclude a settlement based almost entirely on the articles previously agreed on 6 August. This was promptly achieved, O'Regan realizing that Granard's arrival and the final and absolute desertion of O'Donnell ended all hope of relief. Even more persuasive were Granard's cannon and mortars. The only substantial alteration to the 6 August articles was the date of surrender: O'Regan had wished to surrender at 12:00 on Sunday 13 September but this was altered to 07:00 on Monday 14 September. Using Michelburne's horses to tow his field guns and wagons, O'Regan duly left the fort and handed the keys to Michelburne who immediately marched in at the head of his own battalion. Granard followed, accompanied by a number of local gentry. With due ceremony, he appointed Michelburne governor of Sligo.

The Dublin militia began their march home on 15 September but, for Michelburne, another campaign was beginning. Towards the end of August, anxious to make an example before the Ulster and County Donegal militias, Michelburne had arrested Captain John Forward at Ballyshannon and charged him with deserting his post in the face of the enemy, indiscipline and conducting an unauthorized pillage towards Boyle. Michelburne sent him to Ginkel, giving a strong hint to the general that Forward might be granted bail before having to answer the allegations. He used the next two months to very good effect, refining his version of events. As soon as Sligo had surrendered, Forward launched a tirade of counter-allegations against Michelburne. Accordingly, Michelburne was summoned to appear before the Lords Justices in Dublin on 19 November 1691 to account for his actions. Before he left Ballyshannon, Michelburne secured favourable affidavits from Sir Francis Hamilton and many other officers, gentlemen and militia commanders who had been with him on the expeditions to Sligo. Here, Michelburne was cashing in his cheques of obligation because he had previously issued many of these gentlemen with certificates attesting to their good conduct during the Sligo expeditions, despite the fact that many had behaved badly.

Not until he was in the presence of the Lords Justices in Dublin was Michelburne allowed to read the accusations made against him. Captain Forward and his men had deserted because Michelburne had failed to provide subsistence from amongst the cattle and sheep seized by Captain Shamberg. Some of the affidavits asserted that 6,000 contraband cattle were in the camp; some said 1,500; others only 800. The highest figure came from one Robb, a tobacco seller in the Collooney camp, but he refused to make a statement on oath. The case was heard before the Lords Justices and Ginkel at 09:00 on Thursday 19 November. Michelburne was represented by the Principal Serjeant at Law, Osborne, and Counsellors Wright and Wingfield. Forward's legal team was led by Sir John Meade. In good seventeenth-century fashion, the hearing was adjourned until 30 November but Michelburne was granted some money so that he could retain his main witnesses in Dublin. On 30 November, the hearing was postponed until 17 December, Michelburne being allowed a further ten guineas to keep his witnesses in town. Finally, on 17 December Captain Forward produced Captain Vaughan; Captain Patrick Hamilton, who had to be released from debtor's prison for a sum of £36; two of Forward's troopers; Forward's boy and Vaughan's boy. Michelburne brought Major John Hamilton, Captains Hugh Colwell, Andrew Nesbitt, James Manson, Anthony Shamberg, Michael Cunningham, Stephen Miller, Lieutenants Ferguson and Thomas Bennet, and Dr Magee. In addition there was an affidavit from Sir Francis Hamilton. The substance of Forward's case was that he and his men were short of provisions and this was the only reason that they withdrew from the siege and set off plundering. However, Michelburne managed to demonstrate that the cattle brought in by Shamberg was sufficient for the army but that Forward's men had killed the sheep and left the carcasses to rot whilst they sold the hides for 2d. apiece. The hearing was halfway through when Lord Justice Thomas Coningsby took his pen from behind his ear and threw it on the table declaring: 'Here the militia complains that they were starved and that Colonel Michelburne converted the prey to his own use, when we find plainly that the militia plundered and took all away.' With that, the court rose, the hearing ended and Michelburne was exonerated.[4]

22

The second siege of Limerick

During the first week of August, another raid was launched beyond Bantry to restrict Jacobite access to supplies from County Kerry. Led by Colonel Thomas Becher and Lieutenant Colonel Moore, a detachment of the County Cork militia marched to link up with a second body under Lieutenant Colonel Roberts and Majors Wade and Morris. *En route* to the junction Becher's party encountered and defeated 400 Jacobites at Skibbereen, killing 60 and taking several prisoners. The combined force, numbering 500 men commanded by the regular Lieutenant Colonel Robert Freake (Erle's Foot), then marched towards the last-reported location of the regiments of Colonels MacCarthy More and O'Donovan. The approach was via a difficult pass, which might have been effectively defended, but once this had been successfully traversed the Jacobites lost heart and dispersed abandoning 1,000 black cattle, 500 garrons, 500 goats, 2,000 sheep and much additional booty. Before 16 August some Irish military fugitives from Aughrim seized a number of cattle near Kinsale and drove them for 24 km but were chased by a party of militia which killed four and retook the livestock. The militia was also active at sea. A Dutch vessel, laden with wine and salt – a precious commodity in Ireland, always in short supply – came into Bantry Bay and was surprised by Colonel O'Donovan's men as she lay at anchor. Colonel Becher embarked some of the County Cork militia in four boats and sailed to the rescue. Around 12 August, John McCabe, a raparee leader operating in the Bog of Allen, was captured by two militia lieutenants, Shields and Courtney, brought to Dublin along with four companions and hanged in chains on 19 August. McCabe and the White Sergeant, who was killed in the Bog of Allen at about this time, had both served in the Irish Army but had been cashiered for 'some rogueries'. Although there was some improvement the internal security situation remained uncertain, especially in the south. Around the beginning of August, raparees killed one militiaman and wounded several more near Cappoquin, County Waterford. In retaliation, the militia killed five raparees.

Upon receiving the news of Aughrim, Tyrconnell told James that prompt submission was the only way to save what remained; D'Usson, who had experienced more than enough of Ireland, concurred. They dined together on 11 August and Tyrconnell seemed 'very merry and jocose' but, after retiring to his chamber, suffered a stroke at about 14:00 that deprived him of speech and sensation. He lingered for three days but died early in the afternoon of 14 August and was buried privately in Limerick at 22:00 the next day. Some blamed an excess of ratafia, others poison administered by the Irish faction, but the real culprits were obesity and coronary-vascular disease. Supported by D'Usson, Tessé, Dominic Sheldon and Lord Galmoy, the lawyers who had come from France actively pressed for the continuation of Tyrconnell's peace policy and its survival was assured when overall command of the Jacobite forces passed to D'Usson, whose devotion to the Roman Catholic cause was suspect on account of his recent conversion from Protestantism. Amongst the general officers only Major General John Wauchope supported Sarsfield's strategy, predicated on the hope of major resupply from France. The civil government, according to a sealed commission previously issued by James, passed to three Lords Justices: Alexander Fitton, Baron Gawsworth, the Lord Chancellor; Sir Richard Nagle, the Attorney-General; and the Englishman Francis Plowden, a revenue commissioner.

Ginkel's siege train of nine 24-pounders, nine 18-pounders and three mortars left Athlone on 12 August, escorted by militia and Lord George Hamilton's infantry battalion. The original plan had been to transport the artillery by water but there were not enough large boats and the Shannon was too low. Mindful of Ballyneety Ginkel took no chances: Samuel Venner's and the Earl of Drogheda's battalions plus a small party of cavalry met the train on the road and, on 16 August, were reinforced by a sizeable detachment of horse and dragoons under Major General de la Forest. Early on the morning of 15 August Ginkel and all the general officers marched from Caherconlish towards Limerick escorted by Ruvigny leading 1,500 mounted troops and six field guns supported by the Prince of Hesse with a reserve of 1,000 infantry. In several places Irish musketeers lined the hedges but their fire did little damage while two squadrons of cavalry and a party of dragoons appeared within 1½ km of the city and observed Ruvigny for some time until, sensing that he intended to press on, drew back closer to the walls. The advance guard stood for several hours on the site of the 1690 camp whilst Ginkel conducted a thorough reconnaissance. Ireton's Fort had been repaired and mounted two field guns, although they were withdrawn into the city on 16 August. A new position had been erected towards the right, on the site of an old church, and a third fort was under construction, all three positions connected by an entrenchment. A drummer and Captain Hagan then deserted, reporting Tyrconnell's death and the fact that Sarsfield had taken the Jacobite cavalry to a camp about 7 km into County Clare. On returning to Caherconlish, Ginkel found that a considerable number of bread wagons had arrived from Tipperary under militia escort. During the afternoon of 16 August, the infantry battalions of Sir John Hanmer and John Hales, together with a Danish battalion, the Brandenburg regiment and John Coy's regiment of cavalry entered the camp, having marched from Cork. Including the units conducting the train from Athlone, the field army was stronger than at any previous time during the campaign.

Anxious to avoid unnecessary expense, Louvois had ordered engineers Robert, Lacombe, Savin and engineer-in-chief Noblesse – De la Vigne having returned to France in September 1690 – to give priority to fortifying Limerick, Athlone and Galway. However, progress at Limerick had been hampered by arguments amongst the engineers and a lack of food and money. Work had stopped altogether in mid-April but there was a dramatic improvement following the arrival of the French resupply convoy on 19 May and, within a week, 1,500 men were labouring on the defences. Work was then continuous, ending only on 23 September, two days after the signature of the Treaty of Limerick. At the height of the siege the labourers were bribed with brandy and silver to repair the breaches earning praise from the stony-hearted French. First, the damage from the previous year was repaired before the defences were thickened and strengthened. The new Irish Town fortifications were between 25 and 200 m deep and included five large bastions, their salient angles protected by counterguards, whilst the old hornwork outside the Mungret Street Gate was incorporated into a demilune, again covered by a counterguard. Work was also carried out to protect the vital Baal's Bridge from artillery fire. To a large extent, the new fortifications refused the most attractive avenues of attack but two vulnerable points remained: the uninhabited sections to the east and north of King's Island and the high ground on the Clare side of Thomond Bridge. French engineers had suggested tackling the former by digging a moat around the fortifications of English Town between the Shannon and Abbey River but no action was taken. The weakness to the north end of Thomond Bridge was more serious because the seizure of this higher ground would cut off Limerick from County Clare leaving the Shannon as the sole line of communication. The French had recommended building a heavily fortified bridgehead on these heights but, again, nothing was done. All that was achieved was the enlargement of the old Cromwellian star sconce at the northern extremity of King's Island and the excavation of some entrenchments at the northern exit from Thomond Bridge.[1]

The rain and storms of 17 August improved slightly on 18 August and Colonel Henry Lumley took a party of 400 cavalry south towards Charleville, acting on information that some Irish were assembling but on his approach they retired except for Captain Massey and a cornet who stayed behind and fired their pistols at the advance guard; both were seized and, because protections were found in their pockets, hanged as deserters. Lumley returned to camp on 21 August with a prey of 250 black cattle, 300 sheep and some horses. Heavy rain returned on 19 August delaying the progress of the artillery but it also hindered the Irish, inundating the low-lying entrenchments and fortifications. A spy was infiltrated into Limerick to disseminate copies of the Lords Justices' Proclamation and brought back a useful account of affairs in the city: the Irish cavalry and dragoons, about 5,000 strong, were stationed in County Clare amidst considerable numbers of refugees and their livestock whilst most of the infantry was in Limerick. By 20 August, the weather had become so foul that major movements were impaired and the siege train was mired in mud, struggling into Birr on the following day. Several regiments were obliged to move their tents to drier ground and the men were kept occupied gathering and binding 2,000 fascines and faggots. A steady trickle of desertions, particularly officers, confirmed the defenders' low morale and provided Ginkel with up-to-date information. One group suggested that, should he seize the Shannon crossings at Killaloe and O'Briensbridge, many of the Irish cavalry and dragoons would desert. The bridging train entered the camp during the evening of 21 August, having travelled by water from Athlone to Killaloe and then overland because the Jacobites controlled the north bank of the Shannon below Lough Derg. The weather improved on 22 August and Francis Burton was sent to Captain Cole to ask him to bring his warships further up the Shannon, closer to Limerick.

Ginkel summoned a council of war at Caherconlish on either 22 or 23 August to consider how best to proceed: by siege or blockade? The Lords Justices had already advised Ginkel to undertake a siege: a blockade would indicate to the Jacobites Ginkel's numerical weakness and encourage them to hold out and await resupply from France. More important, a blockade would not end the campaign in 1691 rendering the Irish Army unavailable for redeployment into Flanders. To reinforce the point, they told Ginkel that he could not expect reinforcements from England should the war continue into 1692.[2] Together with Scravenmoer, Talmash, Ruvigny and Württemberg, Ginkel accordingly argued in favour of a siege arguing that there was insufficient infantry to make a blockade effective: nothing would be achieved, the soldiers would fall sick, the war would be prolonged and Limerick would be just as hard to capture in 1692. On the other hand, by attacking their women and children the bombardment associated with a siege could exploit the divisions and demonstrably poor morale amongst the Jacobites. Tettau, Mackay, Nassau and de la Forest favoured a blockade contending that not enough of the campaigning season remained during which to conclude a siege – the army's arrival before Limerick on 15 August was even later than William's in 1690 – and the artillery train was still awaited. Second, a siege would prove difficult because the attackers were outnumbered by the defenders; the weak trench garrisons would be unable to resist sallies and there would be insufficient mass to launch an effective final storm. Crossing the Shannon to attack from the Clare side would leave the forces remaining before Irish Town dangerously outnumbered and the army split into two detachments linked by a vulnerable pontoon bridge. They were out-voted by two to one and the decision was made in favour of a siege. Ginkel hoped to take Limerick in 1691 but, should he fail, then the army might winter in Ireland and return to the attack in the spring although this was both politically and militarily undesirable because French resupply convoys might reach the Jacobites in the interim; his army would not be reinforced; and he was under pressure to close the war in 1691, his troops already earmarked for operations on mainland Europe. Ginkel's circumstances were little improved over those of William in 1690 except that the garrison was expected to be supine, the supply line to Dublin was reasonably secure and a Royal Naval squadron, under Captain Cole, which had sailed from Galway, blocked the mouth of the Shannon and later provided heavy guns, ammunition and naval gunners. The Jacobites, whose own food supplies from County Clare were adequate if not abundant, had some difficulty in deciphering Ginkel's initial intentions. The new fortifications had made Irish Town virtually inviolate whilst a major assault on English Town was unlikely. Perhaps he intended to pound Limerick into rubble to encourage the peace party to persuade their more headstrong comrades to come to terms?

Ginkel had 32 battalions of infantry, around 14,000 effective men, plus about 6,000 cavalry and dragoons. In Limerick were 15,000 Jacobite infantry armed with muskets and many more equipped with pikes and scythes, and 5,000 cavalry in County Clare. On the morning of 23 August, Major Johan Sigmund Schlundt, chief fire-master of the artillery, dispatched 250 fresh draught horses to hasten the siege train. Satisfied that the siege train was close, Ginkel commenced operations. Fearing that the Irish would learn from 1690 and defend the enclosed country between Caherconlish and Limerick, Ginkel ordered the army to march at daybreak on 24 August 'without beat of drum'. The advance guards of the two wings of the army, each comprising 600 cavalry, 300 dragoons and 200 grenadiers, drawn up in two lines, supported by 25 pioneers and four field guns, would initially march separately along different lanes: the remainder of the army following the advance guard of the right. The advance guard of the left would rendezvous with the right at the Quaker's House where the whole army would form line of battle and proceed towards Limerick, halting periodically to dress ranks and respond to Irish movements. The advance guards encountered only sporadic, weak resistance amongst the hedges and ditches and the army reached its camping grounds before Limerick unhindered, a further indication of the poor spirit amongst the defenders. They inclined more to the south than in 1690 and encamped slightly farther from the city. The extreme left wing regiments reached to the banks of the Shannon but had to move a little inland after they came under fire from two field guns positioned on the Clare bank. When the majority of the army had come up, by about 15:00, Lieutenant General Mackay was ordered to take the 400 detached grenadiers of the two advance guards and attack Ireton's Fort and the new fort built on the site of the old church, rather unimaginatively known as Old Church Fort. The grenadiers formed a line across the fields, supported by several complete infantry battalions and a body of cavalry. Mackay advanced towards both forts simultaneously. Old Church Fort was deserted and, when the grenadiers were within musket-shot of Ireton's Fort, the garrison withdrew to a little stone redoubt closer to the Irish Town outworks. In the early evening, Count Nassau attacked Cromwell's Fort, which the Irish had improved since 1690, and garrisoned with 500 men. The grenadiers approached in line, received a volley from the defenders, and then dashed forward to hurl in their grenades, supported by the main body of infantry. Within 30 minutes the fort had been evacuated, the garrison losing ten men. Nassau's casualties amounted to three killed. Thereafter Ireton's Fort became Mackay's and Cromwell's Fort, Nassau's. Ginkel thought that the garrison might sally during the night because his men had not had time to dig defensive positions and ordered the cavalry not to unsaddle and to lie by the horses' heads but all remained quiet.

At 14:00 on 26 August the siege train finally reached Limerick but Colonel Johan Wynant Goor, the artillery commander, informed Ginkel that it carried only 1,200 18-pounder shot and few musket balls; Ginkel wrote to the Lords Justices for additional stocks. In the evening, two 12-pounders were dragged to the left wing to counter the pair of annoying Jacobite field guns across the river. The trenches were opened on the night of 26–27 August and some earthworks thrown up to protect the Danish camp on the extreme left of Ginkel's line towards the Shannon. The Jacobites manoeuvred light field guns to enfilade the Williamite camp and trenches but accomplished little execution. On the morning of 27 August, the Prince of Hesse-Darmstadt, commanding his own battalion, Tiffin's and St John's, with three 12-pounder field guns and about 700 cavalry and dragoons, marched to Castleconnell, which the Williamites had not completely destroyed in 1690 and was now garrisoned by 250 Irish. Hesse had orders to take the castle, hang all the officers and massacre the other ranks. The garrison rejected the initial summons and, at 17:00, Hesse informed Ginkel that Castleconnell was too strong to be stormed and so Colonel Jacob Richards, the chief engineer, was sent to advise. Thinking ahead, Richards took additional ammunition, plus a petard and petardier. Arriving during the night, Richards rapidly assessed the situation and ordered the 12-pounders to bombard the outer wall, or envelope, which included a stone house close to the principal entrance. Not only did this building control the garrison's water supply but its occupation would bring the attackers close enough 'to petard' the main gate. Under cover of darkness, Richards asked Hesse to position a captain, two lieutenants commanding fifty grenadiers, plus a captain, lieutenant, ensign and 50 fusiliers, behind a hedge close to the castle. On an agreed signal in the morning, they were to capture the stone house and petard the gate. When all was ready, Richards sent an express to Colonel Goor requesting engineering equipment and additional artillery.

The cannon began to batter the envelope at 06:00 on Friday 28 August but one barrel split. However, two extra guns arrived from Goor at 08:00 together with the requested equipment. A rider then galloped in from Annaghbeg ford to report that Jacobite mounted troops had driven off the weak guard left by Hesse and were advancing along the south bank of the Shannon to relieve Castleconnell. Shortly afterwards, between 400 and 500 horsemen appeared on a distant ridge and signalled to the garrison that they would be relieved. Richards ordered the broken cannon to be towed to the top of an adjacent hill, a threat that proved sufficient to persuade the cavalry to retire temporarily, giving Richards and Hesse time to make defensive preparations. The envelope was now sufficiently damaged to risk an infantry assault. On the signal – three huzzahs and the discharge of the four serviceable cannon – Captain Charles Johnson (Trelawney's Foot), commanding the grenadiers, and another captain leading the fusiliers, advanced towards the house. The defenders flung hand grenades and stones, killing five and wounding seven, before falling back into the castle. Two grenadiers hurried forward, fastened the petard to the gate, lit the fuse and, when the smoke had cleared, saw that the entry into the castle had been cleared. The defenders immediately beat for a parley but the initially extravagant terms were ignored until a report that the Jacobite relief party was advancing again changed Hesse's mind and they were allowed to leave for Clonmel that night, without arms, to be provided for by the Williamites pending dispatch to fight the Turks in Hungary. Hesse discovered 50 barrels of barley and meal, a hay stack, 30 cows, two casks of brandy, one of claret, several barrels of powdered beef but little gunpowder. Major William Ogle (Langston's Horse) rode in from Limerick to say that the Jacobite relief party had been intercepted and turned back by a detachment from the main camp. Even so, Hesse kept his men under arms all night.

Scravenmoer led a detachment, including two 12-pounder field guns, from Limerick camp on 27 August to destroy the line of communication along which the Jacobites continued to draw some supplies from County Kerry. He reduced Carrigogunnel Castle, 5 km west of Limerick, occupied by 150 men under Captain Archbold, on the same day and two other small garrisons along the Shannon on 28 August, mopping up over 400 prisoners. Having squandered so many irreplaceable infantry in unsupported, isolated garrisons, the Jacobites evacuated Kilmallock. During 27 August, Captain Cole's squadron of 18 warships sailed up the Shannon and anchored 5 km below the city. Passing the Jacobite cavalry camp at Cratloe, they opened fire forcing many to disperse into the woods lining Woodcock Hill. The presence in the river of a strong Royal Naval squadron further demoralized the Irish, rendering the successful passage of a possible French resupply convoy very uncertain. The soldiers laboured on the trenches and a line of contravallation along the south-west side of Irish Town, which would house the principal batteries. Württemberg mentioned in a letter to King Christian V of Denmark that plans were being drawn up to advance all the cavalry, supported by two battalions of infantry, across the Shannon to attack Limerick from all sides. Carmarthen, writing from Whitehall to William in Flanders, expressed disappointment at the slow progress. He had hoped, without benefit of any first-hand knowledge, that the generous terms granted to Galway would have induced the defenders of Limerick to surrender. He blamed the unfortunate Michelburne whose peregrinations about Sligo encouraged the defenders of Limerick to postpone the inevitable.

Several mortars and heavy naval guns were brought ashore on 29 August. The line of contravallation was completed during the evening and, in the hours of darkness, labourers prepared batteries for ten cannon and seven mortars. Mortar bombs began to fly – 101 had been thrown by midnight on 30 August – towards Thomond Bridge and the houses on the west side of English Town. Mortars were the terror weapon of seventeenth-century siege warfare, firing explosive and incendiary shells to destroy buildings and demoralize soldiers and civilians. Shooting in a straight line, north-south, through Irish and English Towns, Ginkel's mortars were sure of causing damage with virtually every shot. Major Joseph Stroud (Theodore Russell's Horse), commanding elements of the County Cork militia at Limerick, was supervising the relief of his out-guards on 30 August when a Jacobite captain-lieutenant, a cornet and a trooper deserted and reported that 200 Protestant inhabitants had been interned on St Thomas's Island in the Shannon 1½ km above the city. Half-starved and with only a ruined chapel, two or three small houses, a few huts and hedges for shelter and hay for bedding, they were in poor condition. During the night Stroud took 16 dragoons in four boats and rescued the Protestants but the militia stole their few remaining possessions. Even in camp, these unfortunates were offered nothing and were left to fend for themselves, sheltering in little caves burrowed out of the piles of fascines. After a few days, some wagons took them away into the country.

Acting on reliable intelligence that some Jacobite cavalry regiments, together with raparees, were assembling within 26 km of Limerick, Ginkel ordered Brigadier Richard Leveson to deal with the threat. Commanding 400 horse and dragoons, he left at 02:00 on 31 August and found southern and western County Cork swarming with raparees and irregulars, supported by the cavalry regiments of Lords Merrion, Brittas and Fitzwilliam. Acting on information, Leveson marched southwards quietly and at 01:00 on 1 September fell on Brittas and Fitzwilliam's regiments near Newmarket. Several were killed and the rest dispersed into two parties. Leveson tried to pursue but the Jacobites knew the country and escaped. Major Wood broke his leg during the chase. Ginkel sent 300 reinforcements on 4 September enabling Leveson to break up Jacobite concentrations and reduce many of the small garrisons between Limerick and Cork that were interrupting the flow of provisions from the countryside into the Limerick camp. Subsequently he pressed on into County Kerry as far as Tralee, which the Irish had burned. On 6 September Ginkel ordered him to remain in the west and sent a further reinforcement in the form of the Princess Anne of Denmark's infantry battalion (John Beaumont) and six field guns.

Ginkel's order of 6 September was carried to Leveson by Captain William Fitzmaurice (Drogheda's Foot), the son of Baron Kerry. He left the Limerick camp on the morning of 7 September in the company of between 20 and 30 Kerry gentlemen, collecting an escort of cavalry and dragoons from Askeaton garrison. They came to Listowel on 8 September, within 8 km of Leveson's camp at Lixnaw, where they were approached by an Irish dragoon who mistook them for his own side and reported that the cavalry regiments of Lords Merrion and Brittas, plus the dragoon regiments of Sir Eustace Maurice and Sir James Cotter, between 3,000 and 4,000 men, were drawn up behind a nearby hill. Fitzmaurice had the confused dragoon shot and dispatched a messenger to warn Leveson. However, the Irish had already learned of the presence of Fitzmaurice's small party and moved to destroy it, sending out several interception patrols. Having avoided most of these, Fitzmaurice was negotiating a pass when, at much the same time, the main Irish force approached from one direction and Leveson from another. Leveson, who had not received Fitzmaurice's warning, had heard of the Irish concentration and decided to investigate; sheer good fortune had brought him to Fitzmaurice. On spotting Leveson, Fitzmaurice's men gave a loud huzzah whilst the Irish drew back in some confusion. Leveson charged, killing 30 and taking 30 prisoners including Lieutenant Colonel O'Bryan, the rest escaping, before raiding the Jacobites' camp, recovering much plunder and two barrels of gunpowder. Leveson remained in County Kerry until the termination of hostilities and his operations, including a significant defeat inflicted on the regiments of Merrion, Fitzwilliam and Dunboyne around 20 September, were so effective that the Jacobite forces in Limerick and Connaught were unable to draw further supplies from the region. Indeed, the fearsome Leveson appears to have induced many of the inhabitants to take Williamite protections. On 1 September, Colonel Wolseley, commanding 500 horse and dragoons, marched towards Killaloe in response to a report that Sarsfield was moving that way: memories of Ballyneety remained vivid.

Captain Maurice, a lieutenant and 11 dragoon troopers deserted on 31 August, relaying the useful information that D'Usson feared a Shannon crossing and intended to deploy the Irish cavalry to interrupt such a movement. The cannon and mortars fired all day starting many fires. At night, four men from each troop of cavalry and dragoons, a total of about 600, were detailed to build a new battery to the right of the main artillery position. It was most unusual for mounted soldiers to be asked to dig but Ginkel was very short of infantry: already his foot were garrisoning the siege works every second night in addition to providing detachments and work details. Colonel Henry Withers, the adjutant general, forbade battalions from displaying their colours when in the trenches lest the defenders discovered how frequently their units were on duty. Progress on battery construction was then delayed by a scarcity of timber caused when the *Maid of Dort*, a merchantman laden with planks, was captured in Kinsale harbour by a French privateer. Horses were sent on 31 August to bring up five wagons loaded with wood which had been left in Nenagh. When these arrived, incompetence imposed a more serious setback: the two large batteries were found to be too far from Thomond Bridge and English Town to inflict serious damage. Many anticipated that Ginkel would now abandon the siege and go into winter quarters, returning to Limerick in the spring, but he had information, either from deserters or local Protestants, that a section of the wall on the east side of English Town on King's Island was particularly vulnerable. Having already realized that Irish Town was prohibitively strong he took the opportunity presented by the ill-positioning of the batteries to re-direct his attack. On 1 September, Ginkel ordered Colonel Goor to re-embark the naval artillery, a task that would take three days on account of the marshy ground, leaving ashore six mortars and nine 24-pounders.

Shortly before the guards were due to be relieved during the night of 1–2 September, a considerable body of Irish was observed advancing towards the Earl of Drogheda's infantry battalion defending the 300-m sector of the trenches between Nassau's Fort and the Great Battery in the Lines of Contravallation. Appreciating that his unit was over-stretched, Drogheda ordered his men to hold their fire until the Irish were within pistol-shot, under 50 m, before delivering a volley but the nervous, poorly disciplined musketeers 'popped off' prematurely and individually. However, even this weak musketry was sufficient to turn back an irresolute sally. Drogheda was then reinforced by Venner's battalion and a party of cavalry.

Württemberg predicted that the repositioning of the batteries to fire on the east side of English Town would lead to the establishment of a bridgehead on King's Island as a prelude to a general assault on a subsequent breach but this would have been extremely hazardous. Abbey River was not fordable necessitating the building of a pontoon bridge in the face of heavy fire from the ramparts. Had this proved possible, a storming party would then have to traverse about 150 m of open, boggy ground before reaching the breach; contemporary orthodoxy suggested that infantry assaults on breaches were ideally launched from trenches at the foot of the glacis. In addition, the storming column would be enfiladed from the star-shaped fort at the northern apex of King's Island and the double communication entrenchment linking it to the town. Despite the knowledge that Henry Ireton had unsuccessfully attempted a similar operation in 1651, following a council of war Ginkel decided to take the risk. The Jacobites noticed the dismantling of the batteries and D'Usson concluded that Ginkel was about to cross the Shannon. Accordingly, the Jacobite cavalry camp was moved north-east to cover Annaghbeg ford, which was closely defended by three infantry battalions supported by four regiments of dragoons. Unknown to Ginkel the bombardment had already proved very destructive causing the majority of the civilian inhabitants to evacuate the city and huddle beneath sheets and blankets near the cavalry camp giving the impression, from a distance, that the horse was more numerous than was the case. On 2 September, Ginkel reconnoitred the ground close to where Henry Ireton had bridged the Abbey River in 1651 and countermanded earlier orders to re-embark the naval cannon.

Württemberg and Tettau inspected the same ground on 3 September. The bridging train was alerted for action that night and Colonel Richards reconnoitred the Shannon to locate positions from which ships and land-based artillery might best interdict the passage of water-borne supplies and reinforcements *en route* to Limerick. On 4 September, Colonel Goor, Major Schlundt and Engineer Adrian Cock examined the site selected for the repositioned batteries. They had to be located on the east bank of Abbey River, about 300 m distant from the wall; it was impossible to bring the guns any closer because of the boggy river banks. Work on the new emplacements for 22 cannon and 11 mortars was commenced by 700 workmen during the night of 4–5 September and several battalions were moved into covering positions. During Saturday 5 September, 150 dragoons built a road from the lines of contravallation to the new batteries. Forty naval gunners came ashore from the English and Dutch warships on Sunday 6 September and the Danish regiments provided fireworkers. Wet and unpleasant weather hindered progress but the mortar battery was ready and the two cannon batteries almost completed by evening. Deserters reported that, although still determined to defend Limerick, most of the garrison had abandoned the houses and was sheltering under the walls so that bombardment was not inflicting many casualties. However, they also reported that the raparees and militia who had come into Limerick after Aughrim were close to mutiny, D'Usson only able to assuage them with a promise that they would be allowed to go home if relief from France had not arrived within 12 days.

Despite the attentions of eight Jacobite cannon on King's Island, all the batteries were completed on 7 September but Ginkel postponed the re-commencement of the bombardment until the following day. In the meantime, another battery was erected from which ten 3-pounder field guns would ply red-hot shot. Twenty-five 18- and 24-pounder cannon, eight mortars, eight 12-pounders at Mackay's Fort plus some guns in the south-west protecting the Danish camp finally opened fire on 8 September. One day's bombardment produced a wide breach between the abbey and Baal's Bridge, extended to a width of 30 m on the following day, and set fire to numerous buildings. During the afternoon, a sally attempted to secure a ditch between Irish Town and the great battery in the lines of contravallation to the south-west but was easily beaten back. English Town appeared ripe for storm but the distance was too great and the ground unsuitable: the batteries stood 150 m back from the Abbey River and the intervening marsh flooded after high tides and periods of heavy rain – an earthwork excavated close to the Abbey River to cover the crossing was inundated by a spring tide on 10 September – whilst the breach lay 150 m from the west bank. Nevertheless, preparations for a storm across the bog and river continued. Empty casks were ordered to be delivered to the engineers in order to make floats and woolsacks were gathered near the intended crossing point. During the night they were left under the guard of a single sentry enabling some Irish to cross the Abbey River in boats and cause significant damage.

On 10 September a pinnace was ordered to attend Mr Francis Burton who had already made several trips across the Shannon trying to arrange the surrender of Clarecastle but Ginkel did not press this initiative which would only have created an isolated and unsupported garrison on the north bank. The bombardment hammered all day, doing great damage and causing many casualties; in the evening a mortar shell ignited a large magazine of wine, brandy, oats and biscuit. Two mortars were brought from the ships and positioned at Mackay's Fort under the command of Lieutenant Thomas Brown (Captain John Pitt's Company of Miners). They did more damage than all the other mortars together and achieved triple the rate of fire because he dropped the bombs into the tubes and used the flash of the propellant to ignite the fuse. This proved safer for the gunners, ensured that the fuse remained alight and permitted more bombs to be fired. The breach had been stretched to 40 m by 11 September and Ginkel had to decide whether to storm. Informed opinion had consistently regarded a storm as impractical and the bombardment and breaching of English Town had always been intended to attack the defenders' morale. The distance to be covered, the river, the bogs, the fort on King's Island and the fact that the defenders outnumbered the attackers all rendered an assault impossibly hazardous and likely to result in disaster and the termination of the siege.

Deserters reported that, amidst the fires, rubble and destruction – half of English Town was ruined – D'Usson and his officers tried to maintain morale by assuring the soldiers that a French relief fleet was already at sea: Captain Cole's ships were living evidence having been driven into the river by the approaching French. Similar rumours also reached Ginkel who dispatched Adjutant General Withers by sea and Mr Robert Powley overland to ask the naval squadron at Cork to block the mouth of the Shannon, unaware that these ships had suffered considerable damage in a recent storm. In Whitehall the lack of encouraging news and the definite knowledge that a relief expedition was preparing at Brest produced disquiet and unease. Ginkel sent Colonel Thomas Erle to the queen on 13 September to stress that it was essential to post more frigates to block the Shannon if Limerick was to be captured, Captain Cole having estimated that he would need 20 frigates, well positioned and hidden behind islands, to defend the estuary throughout the winter. Erle was also to tell the queen that Limerick would fall if it was fully blockaded; in other words, aware that time was fast eroding, Ginkel had decided to cross the Shannon leaving just a weak trench guard before Irish Town.

Although the 14-day bombardment had not caused many physical casualties amongst the garrison, psychological damage was much heavier whilst the unremitting work of repairing fortifications under constant fire had sapped morale and energy. Only the possession of Thomond Bridge and County Clare enabled the Jacobites to continue resistance. Ginkel planned a series of deception operations to confuse the defenders about what was planned for the night of 15–16 September. First, the guns were relocated towards the south to give the impression that the siege of Irish Town was to be resumed. However, the artillery was carefully positioned so that it could attack all of Limerick in a straight north-south line, even inaccurate shots finding a target. Engineers were ordered to blow up Castleconnell, Castle Carrick and the other small fortifications recently captured along the banks of the Shannon to deprive the raparees of bases and hiding places. Finally, two battalions, including the Danish Funen Regiment, were ordered to Clonmel and Waterford on 15 September, purportedly to reinforce the local militias because raparee activity was again increasing. Actually, both the latter operations were intended to persuade the Jacobites that Ginkel was about to abandon Limerick and go into winter quarters. Ginkel was able to confuse the garrison further when, late on the evening of 14 September, the siege works were double-manned and, beginning from the right, all the cannon made three running fires along the whole line, seconded by pistol and musket fire from the cavalry and infantry drawn up at the head of their camps to mark the victory of the Imperial army under Ludwig Wilhelm von Baden over the Turks at Slankamen in the Banat (9 August 1691). The Jacobites did not know what to make of it and stood to arms throughout the night.

Colonel Goor accompanied by the bridge-master, Captain Govert van Erp, had ridden along the banks of the Shannon on 11 September searching for a suitable crossing site. Because there were not enough pontoons to span the full width of the river, on the following day, Saturday 12 September, Goor measured a selected bridging point by sending over a swimmer towing a line: on reaching the far bank, he found the bottom so rocky and the current so swift that he was unable to haul over the rope. Clearly, anchors would not hold in such conditions. On Sunday 13 September he rode as far as O'Briensbridge but all the likely crossings either had marshy banks or were covered by entrenchments on the far bank. Castleconnell was reviewed on 14 September but it was too far from Limerick and would have resulted in over-extended lines of communication. Eventually a compromise site was found in the great bend of the Shannon, opposite the battery that had been pounding English Town, where a cluster of four islands divided the river: the streams adjacent to the banks were fordable, whilst the central channel might be spanned with 25 pontoons. The far bank appeared dry and sound whilst the latest intelligence indicated that the Jacobite cavalry was sufficiently distant, about 6 km above the proposed crossing point on the road between O'Briensbridge and Limerick, to prevent interference until a bridgehead had been established. Six 12-pounders and six 3-pounders were positioned on rising ground to the left of the crossing point to enfilade any horse advancing from O'Briensbridge, whilst four 3-pounders were placed to defend the foot of the crossing against infantry spoiling attacks. Quietly and unobtrusively, the bridging equipment was redeployed eastwards from the Abbey River. Preparations were effectively masked by the redeployment of the bombarding artillery which was not completed until 01:00 on 16 September.

As soon as darkness fell on 15 September, 400 grenadiers paraded at the head of Kirke's battalion where they were joined by 600 workmen, the bridging train, five supporting battalions under Talmash, Scravenmoer with a detachment of cavalry and dragoons, plus six field guns. They trudged east for the crossing point at 21:00 and, around midnight, the workmen began to lay the pontoons over the main channel between two of the islands. Simultaneously, 400 grenadiers under Sir David Colyear, assisted by Captain William Catchmey (Hanmer's Foot), Captain Thomas Allnutte (Drogheda's Foot), Captain Vernon Parker (Gustavus Hamilton's Foot), another captain and eight more officers, were 'wafted over' on some of the tin boats to the island where the bridge would terminate. From here, the Shannon was fordable to the right bank. A few Irish pickets let off one or two shots at the workmen before they were beaten off but no alarm was sounded and the Irish appeared inattentive, confident in the expectation that Ginkel was in the process of lifting the siege. It was also a very dark night and the bridge was almost finished before the defenders began slowly to react. Colyear's 400 grenadiers were waiting under cover on the second island ready to charge through the ford to the right bank. Behind them, the bridge was completed by 07:00 and the Royal Dragoons (Edward Matthews) were preparing to cross, followed by the covering grenadiers and fusiliers, four battalions of infantry and the remaining cavalry. All this while, Brigadier Robert Clifford lay at Partine with four regiments of dragoons within easy reach of the crossing, supporting a small infantry detachment opposite the ford itself. A dragoon sentry had spotted Colyear's grenadiers hiding on the island and reported to Clifford but he dismissed this as fantasy, refusing to believe that Ginkel would hazard such a dangerous operation. However, the alarm began to spread throughout Clifford's camp and Lieutenant Colonel Dudley Colclough, commanding one of the dragoon regiments, led his dismounted men to Clifford's tent demanding ammunition and orders to oppose the crossing. Clifford blustered, during which interval the bridge was finished, before instructing his dragoons to advance on foot – their horses were grazing and could not be collected in time – towards the head of the crossing supported by four or five very weak infantry battalions.

Informed of developments, Talmash ordered the 400 grenadiers to wade ashore from the island. Moving rapidly, they were able to occupy an old house and some hedges, about 100 m in front of Clifford's approaching dragoons. Talmash told his men to be sparing with their fire, presumably because ammunition resupply was not locally available, and receive rather than return Irish musketry. Colonel Mathews led the Royal Dragoons over the bridge and through the ford, coming up on the right of Colyear's grenadiers to counter an Irish flanking attack. Already enough Williamite troops were on the right bank for Talmash to order the grenadiers to leave their cover and advance, supported by the infantry battalions of Lord Drogheda, commanded by Lieutenant Colonel Peter Bristow, and Colonel Tiffin, some of the Royal Dragoons and a squadron of Colonel John Coy's regiment of cavalry. Demoralized, unprepared, surprised and dismounted, Clifford's dragoons ran towards a large bog and wood, flinging away their weapons and leaving behind two field guns, the standard of Major General Thomas Maxwell's dragoon regiment, tents, baggage and horse furniture. Talmash's men pursued for a short distance but then returned to establish a firm bridgehead.

The news quickly reached the Jacobite cavalry camp, about 2 km distant towards Killaloe, and Major General Dominic Sheldon promptly led his 4,000 horsemen towards the bridgehead. They were advantageously placed, outnumbering the Williamites on the right bank who could not be quickly reinforced via the narrow bridge. This was the defining moment for the Jacobite horsemen. Had they driven the Williamites into the river or contained them within a small bridgehead, Ginkel would probably have lifted the siege and trailed away into winter quarters. One bold 'huzzah' and the war might have been extended into 1692. However, the initial show of defiance was apparently only designed to gain time for their camp to be dismantled and the baggage secured. As soon as the Williamite cavalry trotted forward across one of two intervening lanes to meet the anticipated charge, the Irish wheeled away, not regrouping until they were 25 km from the Shannon in the vicinity of Ennis. The several refugee camps on the County Clare side broke up, their inmates hurrying for Thomond Bridge and the safety of Limerick. In a small white house, about 1 km from Thomond Bridge, were the Jacobite Lords Justices, their wives, archive, treasury and officials, protected by one regiment of cavalry and a single battalion of infantry. Had Ginkel known of this the war might have been won that afternoon but, ignorant of the country and fearful of ambushes amidst the mass of bogs, tall grass, thickets and water rushes, he restrained his troopers and concentrated on consolidating the bridgehead. The most important task was to reduce the length of the crossing by moving the bridge to a narrower reach which could be spanned solely by the pontoons and floats. During the day the equipment was transferred upstream to the Annaghbeg ford but the bottom proved too rocky so, on 18 September, it was shifted again to within a short musket-shot above the original location. A small earthwork fort was constructed to defend the bridgehead but the engineers were not finished until 20 September. The minuscule Jacobite garrison on St Thomas's Island duly surrendered, gifting Ginkel two brass field guns. An ensign and 20 men in Weir Castle, standing in the centre of the Shannon guarding the salmon weir, also capitulated. Ginkel's total casualties amounted to one dead sergeant and 20 wounded men. The Irish lost no more than 20 soldiers.

On the morning of 16 September, D'Usson and Tessé ordered Sheldon to bring the cavalry back to Limerick, immediately. Sheldon, an over-promoted client of James and Tyrconnell, duly marched the horse into a secure camp close to the city where they remained for three days until obliged to journey back into County Clare in search of forage. Although the strongest branch of the army, the cavalry had made no contribution to the defence. From Limerick, or even Ennis, they could have raided Ginkel's communications with Dublin or supported raparee operations in Leinster – Limerick contained two months' supply of horse feed – but it remained supine. Clifford was another of Tyrconnell's creatures, 'vain and very airy, of shallow parts … malcontent and very unfortunate in all his undertakings'. Sarsfield had been ill-advised to entrust the right bank command to this poor and ill-motivated soldier, even though he was an old personal friend, instead of the more capable and resolute Brigadier John Wauchope. During the period from 16 to 20 September, when the cavalry was camped close to Limerick, a council of war examined Clifford's conduct. It was demonstrated that, whilst on their regular rounds, his officers had informed him on several occasions that the Williamites were working on a bridge but he insisted that they were mistaken. When the Royal Dragoons had clattered across, Clifford's dragoons, charged with supporting the small infantry guard, were surprised and did not have time to collect their horses or baggage. Clifford admitted 'unpardonable conduct' but denied outright treachery. He was committed to St John's Castle to await formal court-martial.

Because Ginkel did not have enough troops, the establishment of the Shannon crossing complicated rather than solved his tactical dilemma. He was unsure whether to press into County Clare or prosecute the siege and tried initially to do both whilst simultaneously continuing preparations to abandon the entire operation. With a view to further restricting Ginkel's options, Sarsfield brought 1,500 of the cavalry into Limerick ready to erupt into the Williamite rear should a substantial force be committed over the river but it was an empty threat because the whole mounted arm, still commanded by Sheldon, had been thoroughly demoralized by the débâcle on the night of 15–16 September and was no longer operationally effective. It decamped for Sixmilebridge, about 10 km north-west, on 20 September. A deserter, Captain Taafe of the Royal Irish Regiment, reported that the garrison had bread for ten more days, gunfire having destroyed 3,000 barrels of biscuit, gallons of brandy, and most of the ammunition reserve; a show of clemency might just be sufficient to bring matters to a head. Urgently seeking an alternative approach, Ginkel declared that the terms of the Lords Justices' proclamation of 7 July would apply should Limerick surrender within eight days. Meanwhile the bombardment continued from the great battery in the lines of contravallation but, still with a view to lifting the siege, some of the heavy cannon and mortars were embarked on the artillery ships under the supervision of Colonels Goor and Richards. An ammunition convoy of 300 wagons arrived from Dublin. Captain Cole was asked to land some men to destroy the forage and harvest along the north bank of the Shannon: if the siege could not be concluded then Ginkel intended to leave the area stripped bare. Three days of rain finally cleared on the afternoon of 20 September and it was evident that the campaigning season was drawing to a close. More deserters and escaped prisoners reported that Limerick would continue to resist provided that access to County Clare remained open. If the war was to end in 1691, Ginkel had no alterative but to commit a major expeditionary force across the Shannon, a decision reached on 21 September. He probably understood enough about the internal divisions amongst the garrison to realize that the risks were not actually as great as they may have appeared.

Ginkel recognized that the defenders might sally against the siege works around Irish Town as soon as he was over the river. The alarm would then be raised by placing a lighted torch on a pike within Mackay's Fort, a duty entrusted to the officer of the quarter-guard who was to remain 'very vigilant'. Mackay and Talmash would then hurry the remaining infantry battalions into the lines of contravallation and the trenches and do their best. On the morning of 22 September, Ginkel, Württemberg, Ruvigny and Scravenmoer led all the cavalry and dragoons – except Coy's regiment of horse and 50 troopers from each dragoon regiment – ten battalions of infantry and 14 field guns towards the bridge. The wagon train carried provisions for ten days. All morning they filed away in open view of the defenders who fired from several batteries but did little damage; by 12:00 the whole force was in County Clare. At about 14:00, when attacked by 200 Irish under deputy-governor Colonel Stapleton, the advance guard of 18 Royal Dragoons fell back on their supports. Stapleton was reinforced and a stand-off ensued, occasionally interrupted by some desultory firing, whilst the Williamite infantry deployed. The advance was resumed at 16:00 and the Jacobites retired under the cover of the cannon of English Town. Ginkel halted again and organized all the available grenadiers into a task force under the command of Colonel Tiffin, Lieutenant Colonel Hudson and Major John Noble (Thomas St John's Foot), sustained by the infantry battalions of Kirke, Tiffin, St John and Lord George Hamilton. Tiffin was ordered to attack the fort covering the head of Thomond Bridge, garrisoned by 800 musketeers, and several outposts in adjacent stone pits and gravel quarries. The grenadiers and supporting infantry moved forward into steady musketry, seconded by cannon fire from King John's Castle. For two hours, Ginkel's field guns pounded the fort. Rather than face the anticipated infantry assault, the Irish abandoned the position and made for Thomond Bridge. Tiffin's grenadiers rushed through the ruins of the fort and chased the retreating Irish towards the head of the bridge causing the retreat to disintegrate into flight. Built in the fifteenth century on 14 arches, Thomond Bridge was 150 m long but not wide enough to permit wheeled traffic; halfway along stood a castellated gateway and drawbridge. Fearing that the Williamites might rush the bridge and enter English Town, the town major, a Frenchman, panicked and ordered the drawbridge to be raised, leaving most of the Irish infantry on the wrong side. Despite vigorous waving of white scarves and handkerchiefs, the Williamite infantry fired into the crowd. When the killing finally stopped there were piles of dead and wounded along the bridge and many corpses floating in the river. Only 120 succeeded in re-entering the town, 600 were shot, hacked down or drowned, and the remainder captured. Ginkel's losses amounted to one officer and 25 men killed and about 60 wounded.

Although the grenadiers lodged themselves within 10 m of the head of Thomond Bridge cutting off Limerick from County Clare, Ginkel's position remained hazardous, his army in danger of defeat in detail. This was the point at which the Jacobite cavalry might have attacked the pontoon bridge whilst the garrison, still numbering about 14,000 men, sallied against the siege works. Instead, lacking a universally acknowledged leader, the cavalry remained near Ennis whilst the garrison began to think of surrender. Laying aside morale, spirit, hope, war-weariness and the non-appearance of the promised French relief convoy, there was no obvious reason for Limerick to submit; Thomond Bridge could easily have been defended by a few musketeers and the Shannon was not fordable. Even the loss of communication between the garrison and the cavalry was not significant: this had happened in 1690 but had not resulted in the loss of Limerick. There was no acute shortage of supplies in the town and the French relief convoy was on its way, arriving at the mouth of the Shannon 16 days after the surrender. However, exacerbated by internal squabbles and divisions – there was probably a conspiracy amongst Tyrconnell's followers, including Clifford, to allow Ginkel to cross the Shannon in order to create a credible reason for surrender – morale, spirit, hope and war-weariness outweighed all other factors. With D'Usson, Tessé and all Frenchmen utterly discredited, Sarsfield was elevated to the supreme command. Rather than try to take advantage of

Ginkel's unbalanced deployment, he decided to sue for peace. George Clarke rather cynically commented that Limerick surrendered because Sarsfield thought he could cut a more impressive figure in France than Ireland whilst the French officers were impatient to go home.

On 23 September, 700 cattle arrived from Brigadier Leveson in County Kerry and, despite the wet weather, the cannon and mortars continued to fire. In the morning there was a meeting on the river bank between Scravenmoer, Ruvigny and Sarsfield. The latter admitted that the raising of the drawbridge had caused a near-mutiny, the soldiers having to be restrained from throwing all Frenchmen over the walls. Without committing himself, Sarsfield asked for blank passports to be sent to Dominic Sheldon in the cavalry camp because there could be no settlement without the agreement of the horse officers. The rain ceased towards evening and, at about 18:00, the Limerick garrison beat a parley 'on both sides of the town'. Following a short conference, a three-day ceasefire was agreed. Overnight, Sheldon was informed of the truce and Ginkel sent blank passports to enable him to send representatives to subsequent meetings. Sheldon filled in his own the name and those of Lords Galmoy, Westmeath, Dillon and Trimleston, Archbishop Maguire of Armagh, the Archbishop of Cashel and Sir Theobald Butler. They travelled to Limerick on 25 September.

Swollen by the heavy rains, the Shannon rose over a metre on 24 September and the pontoon bridge became detached at one end, although it was repaired within one hour. Ginkel promptly improved his insecure communications by organizing a ferry just below Limerick. Near Cullen on 24 September over 100 raparees, led by Galloping Hogan, ambushed a bread convoy comprising 44 wagons, killed most of the escort of 20 cavalry troopers and stole 71 draught horses. During the afternoon, Sarsfield returned the 210 Williamite prisoners held in Limerick: a further 30 prisoners had been killed during the bombardment. They were in poor condition. Those unable to walk were carried out on 'poor, lean garrons', some expiring where they were dumped on the ground. The wounds of many had not been dressed and a Royal Dragoon, whose shattered hand had been left unattended, died within an hour of release. In return, Ginkel invited Sarsfield to submit a list of an equivalent number in Williamite captivity he wished to see exchanged and work details were allowed out of the city to bury the dead suffered in the action of 22 September. On 25 September, Sheldon and the officers and clerics from the cavalry camp dined in Ginkel's tent before proceeding into Limerick. To keep up the pressure, Ginkel ordered Colonel Goor to send for the ammunition stored at Carrick and to have the artillery and mortars ready to renew the bombardment should the ceasefire break down.

Having held discussions in Limerick on 25 September, the senior officers, Lords Justices and clergy sent Sarsfield, Brigadier Wauchope and two more brigadiers to the English camp to lay out the Irish proposals. There seemed to be enough common ground for hostages to be exchanged. Lords Westmeath, Iveagh, Lowth and Trimleston surrendered themselves to Ginkel, whilst Lord Cutts, Sir David Colyear, Colonel Tiffin and Colonel Piper agreed to accept temporary Jacobite custody. When the two teams of negotiators first met Ginkel was impatient fearing the imminent arrival of the French relief convoy: Captain Cole commanded only seven light warships, not having received the requested reinforcement of 20 frigates. Châteaurenault's approaching fleet was potentially strong enough to force the river, sink Cole's vessels and reach Limerick. Ginkel was ready to offer very generous terms.[3]

23

Dispersal

Negotiations began on 26 September and concluded on 3 October. Sarsfield was the principal facilitator having rapidly mutated from chief of the resistance party to leading advocate of peace. He justified his stance by explaining that provisions in Limerick were almost consumed, no resupply could be expected from France until the spring of 1692 and, if the proffered terms were rejected, none better would be forthcoming. Still regarded as the heart and soul of the Jacobite cause, Sarsfield was very influential and persuaded many doubters. Knowing, as they must, of Ginkel's desperation to end the war in 1691, the Jacobite negotiators failed to exploit their advantage to achieve effective safeguards for the future of the Roman Catholic religion and clergy. Other categories ignored by the Jacobite negotiators were the orphans of those killed in James's service and prisoners of war. As news began to spread around Ireland that Limerick had surrendered and the war was ending, the security situation slowly began to improve as raparees, tories, deserters, renegades and bandits realized that it was time to make the best settlements that they could with the authorities. Callaghan, together with some of his gang, took protection at Edenberry but it was, generally, a slow process. Galloping Hogan continued to terrorize the highways of County Tipperary and raparees operated around Mountmellick. Around the beginning of October, militia killed raparees in Counties Waterford and Cork whilst five Protestants were murdered on the road in the Queen's County.

The initial Jacobite proposals, seeking to restore the situation of 1686–7, were formally delivered to Ginkel on 27 September. They wished for a general indemnity for all past crimes and offences and the return of confiscated Roman Catholic estates. Roman Catholics might be entitled to hold military, legal and civil employments and pursue trades, professions and vocations. They would be allowed to live in corporate towns and enjoy full membership of corporations and guilds, equal in status to Protestants. The Jacobite Army was to be retained, paid and supplied in case it decided to fight for William and the Grand Alliance. Finally, they requested that the peace settlement be embodied in a statute of the Irish Parliament. Ginkel read them through, thought them thoroughly unreasonable, returned a negative answer and ordered the building of a new battery next to Mackay's Fort. The Irish then asked Ginkel what terms he was prepared to admit and so he returned 12 articles: these and no others was he prepared to accept.

However, as an earnest of goodwill, the Irish prisoners were sent into Limerick.

Face-to-face negotiations began in Ginkel's camp on 28 September. The Jacobites were represented by Sarsfield, Lord Galmoy, Colonel Nicholas Purcell, Colonel Nicholas Cusack, Sir Toby Butler, Colonel Garret Dillon and Colonel John Brown. Ginkel appointed all his general officers as commissioners granting them freedom to participate in the discussions. Following a long session, all issues were settled save a few matters that had to await the arrival of the Lords Justices from Dublin. A strange hiatus ensued, midway between a temporary truce and unratified peace. During the afternoon Ginkel ordered some transport ships from Cork to the Shannon to take on board some of the Irish soldiers. He also wrote to Vice Admiral Sir Ralph Delavall, commanding an English squadron off the Irish coast, informing him of the imminent treaty – it applied at sea as well as on land – and asking him to allow French ships into Dingle Bay to help transport Irish soldiers to France. All Ginkel's cavalry and dragoons, commanded by Ruvigny, rode into County Clare on 29 September but had to camp north of Sixmilebridge in order to find sufficient forage. Soldiers wandered between Limerick and the Williamite camp establishing a shallow, temporary camaraderie but it soon evaporated and, by 1 October, Ginkel was receiving complaints from Sarsfield that his men were plundering and stripping the Irish 'as they found opportunities'. Ginkel confined his troops within the siege works but Irish safety could only be guaranteed by locking the gates of English Town transforming King's Island into a prison camp. Increasingly, the Jacobite soldiers left the stinking, insanitary ruins of English Town to build huts and primitive shelters on the marshes of King's Island. Although initially intended as a measure of protection, when rumours gathered pace that the Jacobite Army was to serve Louis XIV it became clear that the Irish had effectively incarcerated themselves in a homemade gaol and could not escape.

Lords Justices Sir Charles Porter and Thomas Coningsby arrived on the evening of 1 October and Lords Merrion and Brittas came from County Kerry on the following day so that they could be included in the provisions of the surrender. Coningsby and Porter met the Jacobite and Williamite commissioners at 15:00 on 2 October and concluded the treaty at midnight. Demonstrating a rare sensitivity, the French officers did not attend, pleading indisposition. Most of the Irish officers returned again to the Williamite camp on 3 October where they dined with Württemberg before repairing to Ginkel's tent to sign the document; the French officers also appending their signatures. The treaty, ratified at Westminster on 24 February 1692, combined two elements: a general peace settlement and specific military arrangements to terminate the siege of Limerick and receive the surrender of other small Jacobite garrisons. The former was agreed between Sir Charles Porter, Thomas Coningsby and Ginkel on behalf of William and Mary, and Sarsfield, Lord Galmoy, Colonel Nicholas Purcell, Colonel Nicholas Cusack,

Sir Toby Butler, Colonel Garrett Dillon and Colonel John Brown for the Jacobites. Roman Catholics, including soldiers and civilians who had been in arms but had submitted already or would do so, were permitted to enjoy the estates, rights and privileges that they had lawfully possessed under Charles II. William and Mary were committed to summoning an Irish Parliament to secure these liberties. However, these benefits were conditional upon swearing a specially prescribed oath of loyalty to William and Mary. By forbidding prosecution and molestation for any acts committed during the war, it was hoped that peace could be quickly restored. The military articles were agreed between Ginkel, D'Usson and Tessé. Any soldier or civilian in a garrison or post still in Irish possession would be allowed go anywhere overseas, except England and Scotland, with their families and possessions. Those willing to serve in France were required to declare their intentions. All French officers and soldiers would be provided with passports and allowed to return home. To convey the Irish and French soldiers to Brest Ginkel would provide, gratis, 50 200-ton ships fully equipped and provisioned. During the march to Cork, the designated port of embarkation, they would be granted the full honours of war. If any French or Irish soldier was plundered of his property, Ginkel undertook either to restore it or pay full compensation. All prisoners of war in Ireland would be released on 28 September. Any remaining Irish garrisons were to be informed of the treaty and allowed to travel to English Town with the full honours of war.[1]

Dusk had fallen before everyone had signed all the articles and Talmash thought it too late in the day to take formal possession of Irish Town so he ordered the battalions of Nassau and Gustavus Hamilton to occupy the stone fort and the outworks; English Town was reserved for the Irish Army until it could be transferred to France. Next morning (4 October) peace was officially proclaimed in all the camps and Talmash, leading five battalions, made a ceremonial entry into Irish Town. Pomp was rapidly replaced by squalor. Irish Town consisted of rubbish, rubble and unburied corpses; there was practically no shelter and in the interests of sanitation and human tolerance, infantry garrisons had to be relieved daily. At Baal's Bridge, the Williamites stood at the southern exit whilst the Jacobites guarded the gate at the north end. On 5 October 100 men from each Williamite regiment began to level the siege works and the Jacobite cavalry rode down to Limerick. The Jacobite soldiery was informed that the treaty offered them three options: to go home and live peaceably and quietly; continue their military service in an Irish corps within the army of King Louis XIV; or transfer into William's army. Nearly all the Jacobite officers who possessed estates decided to relinquish the martial life and remain in Ireland, except for Galmoy, Sarsfield, Garret Dillon, Sir Maurice Eustace, Gordon O'Neill, John Barrett and Lieutenant Colonel Walter Nugent of Davidstown, who determined to seek their fortunes in France. They were joined across the English Channel by Jacobite officers who had been imprisoned in England: the Earl of Tyrone, Baron Cahir, the Earl of Clancarty and Baron Slane. There were, of course, some Jacobite officers already in France, principally Justin Macarty, now Earl of Limerick, Colonel Dudley Bagnal and Colonel Simon Luttrell.

Already the detail of the treaty was coming under examination. At 10:00 on 5 October Ginkel received a letter from an Irish lieutenant colonel complaining that he had been imprisoned by fellow Jacobites for refusing to volunteer to go to France. Ginkel was furious and swore 'with some heat, that he would teach them to play tricks with him', and ordered four cannon to be towed to the foot of Baal's Bridge. Sarsfield rode to Ginkel's camp to exchange a few sharp words. He explained that the lieutenant colonel was a recently released prisoner of war who had employed his freedom to abuse Irish officers. Ginkel was unpersuaded and suspected that the pro-treaty Jacobites were pressurising those who had not chosen the French option. Obviously, it was in the interests of the Grand Alliance to ensure that the smallest possible number of Jacobites joined the French Army. Accordingly, Ginkel moved ten heavy cannon and two more field guns into Irish Town and, during the afternoon, issued a declaration which both explained and glossed the terms of the treaty. Whether Jacobite officers and soldiers either remained in Ireland or served William and Mary overseas, they would be expected to promote British interests. All who wished would be allowed to go home with their goods and families and enjoy government protection. Cavalry troopers and dragoons could sell their mounts but all who elected to return home had to leave their arms with the Williamite train of artillery. To counter rapidly spreading rumours, Ginkel stressed that those who decided to serve William and Mary would not be sent into Hungary 'and other remote parts' to fight in the Imperial armies against the Turk. Indeed, they would be not be obliged to serve anywhere against their will. In the meantime, they would be assigned billets and receive subsistence pay. However, those who elected for France would be forbidden to return: exile was permanent.

Later in the afternoon, Sarsfield and John Wauchope addressed a mass meeting of the Irish soldiers in English Town. In an effort, no doubt, to suppress increasing agitation they grossly misrepresented the facts saying that, although the soldiers' current situation left much to be desired, by the spring of 1692, whether in France or England, they would receive English rates of pay. They perjured themselves further by stating that those who took service with William and Mary would probably find themselves back in their homeland by the spring in a new Williamite army of Ireland. These blatant lies were reinforced on 6 October when regimental chaplains preached a common sermon on the text that salvation would only be found through volunteering to serve in France whilst damnation awaited those who joined the heretics. Much holy brandy and an episcopal blessing helped inculcate the message.

Probably less than sober, 14,000 Jacobite infantry then crossed Thomond Bridge into County Clare where they formed up for review by Ginkel and the Lords Justices. First they were addressed by Adjutant General Withers who tried to counter the Roman Catholic propaganda by stressing the advantages of joining King William rather than journeying to face an uncertain future in France. It was unnatural, said Withers, to serve a foreign country against the interests of one's own. He concluded by distributing numerous copies of Ginkel's declaration of the previous day (5 October). The moment of decision had arrived: those for France remained on parade, whilst those wishing to join the Williamite service filed off. The influential Irish Foot Guards set the tone; all but seven stayed stationary in their ranks. Lord Iveagh's regiment of Ulster Irish filed off as did the battalions of Colonel Wilson and half of Lord Louth's plus 'a great many out of most other regiments'. Brigadier Robert Clifford's, Colonel Henry Luttrell's and Colonel Nicholas Purcell's 'all appeared averse to the going to France'. However, probably because of peer pressure, the majority remained on parade even though many were very uncertain about entering French service.

Whilst Ginkel began to send his regiments into winter quarters – Colonel Thomas Erle's battalion marched for Cork on 7 October – the Jacobite high command exerted considerable pressure on the common soldiers to convince them to go to France. One highly effective method was the distribution of the remaining bread, brandy and claret only amongst those who made the right decision. The gates of English Town were kept firmly locked and guarded to prevent men from slipping away. Determined to do everything possible to dissuade the Irish from engorging the armies of Louis XIV, Ginkel issued a second declaration on 6 October. Everyone, of whatever rank or quality, had complete freedom to leave for home with their goods, livestock and families and live quietly under the protection of the government. All 'straggling people' – raparees, volunteers, renegades, deserters and creaghts – still under arms would receive quarter provided that they returned to their home parishes, surrendered their weapons and registered with the local justices of the peace within the time allowed in the Lords Justices' declaration. No one, on either side, was to commit acts of violence. Colonels Edward Matthews and Henry Lumley rode to the Jacobite cavalry camp on 7 October to continue the mission of persuasion and Withers issued bread, cheese, brandy, tobacco and a fortnight's subsistence pay to the men who had elected either to serve William or quit the military calling. The results, however, were meagre. By 8 October only 1,046 Jacobite soldiers had elected to join William's forces whilst about 2,000 had been given passes for home: the overwhelming majority, around 11,000 men, looked set for France.

Brigadier Leveson's detachment returned to County Kerry on 8 October to advertise the treaty and supervise pacification. Two cavalry regiments were ordered to march into County Tipperary to secure the roads towards Dublin from Galloping Hogan who continued to be a nuisance. Many of Ginkel's infantry battalions were very weak so their ranks were filled by drafting a number of the Irish soldiers who had chosen to join the service. During the morning of 8 October, numerous Irish gentlemen and their families who had not been concerned with the Jacobite Army but had taken refuge in camps near Limerick departed for their homes. Likewise, the officers and soldiers who had opted to return to civilian life began to drift away having first delivered their weapons to the train of artillery in return for money and passes. The first instalment for France commenced its march to Cork, a process that continued piecemeal until the final detachment left on 1 November. Three Danish regiments marched towards their winter quarters on 9 October. Most of Ginkel's army had returned from County Clare by 10 October and the 1,000 Irish horse and dragoons that had come over to Ginkel were mustered by Commissary Allen. The cavalry intending for France, also numbering around 1,000, marched through English Town and out of the Water Gate towards Cork. The remainder of the Jacobite cavalry, about 2,000 men, had decided to give up the military life. On 13 October, Ginkel led the majority of the army into winter quarters. Colonel Sir David Colyear was appointed governor of Limerick to command a garrison of five infantry battalions: his own, Samuel Venner's, Thomas St John's and Abraham Creighton's in Irish Town, and Lord Drogheda's in English Town. Lord Lisburn's battalion was to remain in camp outside the city until all the Irish had evacuated English Town. Talmash remained at Limerick to ensure that order was maintained and the treaty observed. As soon as Ginkel marched away the Irish Foot Guards left English Town for Cork but, as they marched past, Lord Drogheda counted no more than 482 and this number had diminished further by the time they had reached their destination. The Prince of Hesse accompanied some of the Irish detachments towards Cork to prevent plundering and resolve any little quarrels and misunderstandings that might arise. Appointed to supervise the embarkations at Cork, Sarsfield left Limerick on 16 October with six Jacobite regiments which, as they marched through Irish Town, numbered only 618 men, the soldiers running away 'in dozens'. Some escaped by swimming the Shannon. At Cork, Count Nassau raised a number of difficulties concerning the enshipment of wives and children which were referred to Ginkel for adjudication.

Raparees continued to submit, especially towards Dublin and eastern extremities of the Bog of Allen where the militia had made their activities increasingly untenable. Colonel Burk, 'a popular man amongst the raparees', along with many of his followers, surrendered on 14 October at Loughrea, County Galway. On the same day, in a further effort to restore law, order and peace, the Lords Justices issued two proclamations. The first was a reissue of that originally published on 18 September promising pardon and protection to all robbers, thieves and raparees who surrendered their arms to justices of the peace before the end of

September and took the oaths of fidelity to William and Mary. Anyone knowingly sheltering raparees after that date would forfeit their own protections and face prosecution. These provisions were extended to 5 November. The second proclamation forbade anyone from harming or injuring an Irish person or making 'any distinction of nations'. Everyone who submitted and took the oaths of fidelity was to be regarded as a full subject entitled to civil and legal rights 'by which means all things became so calm on a sudden, as if there had been no storm at all in that kingdom'. Galloping Hogan and his gang capitulated at Roscrea on 14 October. Ever the pragmatist, Ginkel then turned the poacher into a gamekeeper by allowing him 24 men to round up and suppress other raparees remaining at large. This was rather too much for all concerned and Hogan was murdered shortly afterwards. In the last week of October, in County Kerry alone, Danish sources said that 10,000 raparees had 'come in'.

Châteaurenault's resupply convoy comprising 18 warships, four fire-ships, and 20 merchantmen laden with victuals, ammunition, money and miscellaneous supplies arrived off Scattery Island in the mouth of the Shannon on 20 October. Aboard was Colonel Simon Luttrell, who had been instrumental in securing its speedy preparation and sailing. Three frigates, HMS *Plymouth*, *Adventure* and *Centurion*, sailed into Kinsale harbour escorting two pinks carrying ammunition for Fort Charles. They reported that they had left Sir Ralph Delavall with 30 warships about 25 leagues from Kinsale. Receiving notice of this in his new headquarters at Kilkenny, Ginkel wrote to Delavall on 25 October informing him of the arrival of the French fleet in the mouth of the Shannon and asking him to sail in that direction. On the same day, Ginkel received a letter from Talmash in Limerick saying how impossible and arrogant the French officers had become now that their fleet had seen sighted. Ginkel penned a second message to Delavall on 26 October pressing him urgently to hurry to the Shannon to join Captain Cole's squadron. Because Ginkel had retained only seven under-strength and poorly supplied battalions in the vicinity of Limerick, Delavall's presence was essential to re-impose Williamite authority and eradicate any suggestion of an Irish revival.

There was, indeed, cause to fear that the Irish and French might reject the treaty and use the arrival of the French fleet as a reason to renew the struggle. At the time English Town was still occupied by a sizeable body of Jacobite troops who could have broken the peace, driven out Talmash and Colyear's seven battalions, secured the town and summoned the French fleet to sail up river. That they did not was due to the presence of Captain Cole's squadron and the decency and honour of Châteaurenault and the Irish officers. More important, had they broken the treaty and then suffered defeat in 1692, the Jacobites would have received appallingly bad terms and forfeited all the advantages made available to them by the Treaty of Limerick. On 18 October, still puzzled at the sudden Jacobite collapse, Dr George Clarke had written to Sarsfield asking him why Limerick had surrendered. Major General John Wauchope replied on Sarsfield's behalf. In the first place, Clifford was blamed for allowing Ginkel to cross the Shannon resulting in the fatal separation of the mounted troops from the infantry garrison. The crossing also completed the blockade of the city on all sides so that supplies could no longer be drawn from County Clare, which had provided over half Limerick's requirements. At the time of the surrender, bread supplies would only have lasted until 15 October but the French convoy would have taken until the end of October to fight their vessels through Cole's screen and negotiate all the batteries along the river bank. Had Limerick resisted until the end of October and then been forced to surrender through starvation, the Jacobite Army would have become prisoners of war. By agreeing to an earlier settlement which allowed the army to go to France, the Jacobite flame was kept alight. When Louis XIV learned of the surrender, he was furious with D'Usson, Tessé and La Tour for signing the treaty: he may have acquired some Irish soldiers but the Grand Alliance had regained an entire army.

The last of the Irish troops left English Town on 1 November and Colyear's garrison took full possession, by which time it was estimated that only 5,650 Irish soldiers had actually embarked for France many having deserted *en route* to Cork. Most of the French, including D'Usson, Tessé and La Tour, plus 6,659 Irishmen, women and children were shipped aboard Châteaurenault's vessels in the Shannon. A merchantman, the *Rose of Chester*, acting as a tender to the French fleet hit rocks whilst running down the Shannon and sank: the majority of the English crew was saved but 120 Irish soldiers lost their lives. The French immediately accused the master of deliberately sinking his vessel to reduce the numbers going to France, until persuaded that it was an accident. Châteaurenault sailed on 16 November, putting into Brest on 3 December. Ginkel, meanwhile, reached Dublin on 3 November where he was received with great ceremony, leaving for England on 6 December. Now that the Irish soldiers had all departed from Limerick towards Cork, Talmash's duties were over and he too came up to Dublin from where, along with Lieutenant General Hugh Mackay, he sailed for England.

On 6 December, the transport ships that had taken the first tranche of Irish to Brest returned to Cork and another 20 entered Dublin a week later. Their masters reported that the arrangements had worked well, the French observing all the stipulations of the Treaty of Limerick although the reception of the Irish soldiers had not met expectations. They had not been permitted to enter the town of Brest but had to shelter in the hedges and ditches alongside nearby roads and lanes for two or three days before being allocated billets in the countryside. Instructions then arrived from Versailles to reorganize the Irish troops to conform to French practice. Major generals were reduced to colonels; colonels to captains; captains to lieutenants; and ensigns to sergeants. This, perhaps, should not have been surprising because many of the senior Irish officers had been over-promoted during the war and their professional expertise was substantially inferior to that encountered in the French Army. Understandably angry at this treatment, some tried to offer ships' masters considerable sums of money for passages back to Ireland but they were placed under close guard. The French *intendant* treated the Irish with a mixture of contempt and rudeness, keeping them short of food, clothing and money.

News of this ill reception naturally leaked back into Ireland infecting those troops awaiting passage. Two whole regiments, those of Colonels MacDermot and Brian O'Neill, changed their minds and marched back into County Clare, followed a day or two later by the soldiers of Colonel Felix O'Neill. Unsure of what to do, some of these soldiers surrendered their arms to Colonel Tiffin's battalion and went home. There had also been serious problems about transporting all of the women and children who wished to accompany the soldiers and a considerable number of these poor, homeless and starving dependants had been left behind. Many soldiers waiting at Cork accordingly deserted rather than abandon their families. To quell the disquiet, Sarsfield and Wauchope issued another dishonest declaration stating that all who wished to take their wives and families to France would be able do so. No doubt not all of the soldiers' companions were *bona fide* wives but the terms of the declaration were not honoured and the problem was circumvented in the cruellest manner possible: first the soldiers were embarked and then the ships pushed off leaving the wives and children standing on the quayside. On 8 December, all the embarkations had been achieved and Sarsfield wrote to Ginkel releasing him from his obligations under the Treaty of Limerick. Finally, on 22 December, Sarsfield and the remainder of the senior Irish officers boarded transport vessels at Cork, leaving behind hostages against the safe return of the ships. The arrival of the last instalment of Irish troops in Brest induced a reaction from the pathetic creature in whose name the war had been fought: James II sent Sir Andrew Lee into Brittany to inspect the new arrivals.

Abraham Yarner, the commissary-general of the musters in Ireland, was ordered on 24 December to take a full account of all the Williamite and ex-Jacobite forces remaining in Ireland in order to make up pay lists to meet arrears due and allocate quarters. Once this had been completed, the majority of the Williamite Army in Ireland was ready to be disposed into other theatres. Yarner's final reckonings suggested that the greater part of the Jacobite infantry, about 14,000 men, went to France, accompanied by around 6,000 women and children. The remainder, particularly the cavalry and dragoons, left the army and stayed in Ireland. Somewhere between 2,000 and 2,500 men volunteered for the Willimate Army in Ireland but most were poorly behaved and ill-disciplined; disbandment was recommended. On 11 and 12 February 1692, Colonels Foulkes and St John and Brigadier Villiers were instructed to disband all the Irish forces that had decided to join William, except for 1,400 'choice men' who were to be regrouped into two battalions commanded by Colonel Wilson and Hugh Balldearg O'Donnell, no doubt with a view to them being sent into either the Spanish or Imperial service. Officers and soldiers in 15 regiments of infantry, two regiments and two troops of cavalry, and two regiments of dragoons were paraded, disbanded and sent home. The remnant of O'Donnell's army was disbanded in County Donegal by Sir Francis Hamilton. Soldiers with weapons received nine shillings, and those without six shillings. Many of the regiments contained scarcely 100 men.

Throughout Connaught and Munster, which had been the seat of the final two years of the war, food supplies during the winter of 1691-2 were extremely short and many died from cold and starvation during the severe frosts in January. On 19 January 1692, the Danish Corps sailed home in 46 transports, escorted by two warships. Following the ratification of the Treaty of Limerick, on 3 March William and Mary published a proclamation in Dublin stating that the war was over, Ireland having been reduced to obedience.[2]

James's attempts to regain his thrones by victory in Ireland had been defeated. Despite schemes to invade England from France in 1692 and 1696, which were just the nervous spasms of an expiring corpse, the Jacobite cause was dead and the new English regime established by the Glorious Revolution had overcome its first major obstacle. However, its future was still not assured. The armies of the Grand Alliance suffered major defeats at Namur and Steenkirk in 1692 and Neerwiden/Landen and Marsaglia in 1693. Not until the capture of Huy in 1694 and Namur in 1695 did the military tide turn against France. At the Peace of Rijswijk in 1697, Louis XIV, with very bad grace, recognized William as the legitimate king of England and promised to cease promoting the exiled James. For the third time within 100 years, Ireland had been reconquered by the English and the Protestant Ascendancy reasserted but this time it was to endure until the nineteenth century.

Notes

Notes to Chapter 1: Preliminaries, 1688

1   *HMC, Stuart MSS.*, vi., pp. 27–8, 'Sheridan's Account'.

2   Charles Leslie, *An Answer to a Book, Inituled, The State of the Protestants in Ireland under the Late King James's Government* (London, 1692), pp. 77–85; *A Faithful History of the Northern Affairs of Ireland from the Late K. James Accession to the Crown, to the Siege of Derry ... By a Person who bore a great Share in those Transactions* (London, 1690), p. 7.

3   J. P. Kenyon, *Robert Spencer, Earl of Sunderland, 1641–1702* (London, 1958), pp. 101–3, 107–8.

4   Robert Parker, *Memoirs of the Most Remarkable Military Transactions from the Year 1683, to 1718* (London, 1747), pp. 12–13. Forbes's zeal did not endure and he joined the Jacobites in 1689.

5   An Irish, or Scottish, dagger.

6   John Mackenzie, *A Narrative of the Siege of London-Derry: or, the late Memorable Transactions of that City. Faithfully Represented to Rectifie the Mistakes and supply the Omissions of Mr. Walker's Account* (London, 1690), pp. 1–2; *HMC, Ormonde MSS.*, n.s. viii., pp. 355–7, Diary of Mr. Colles, 6 December 1688.

7   Mackenzie, pp. 3–4.

8   See petitions for relief from departed Irish Protestants addressed to the Treasury (*CTP*, pp. 47–51).

9   *HMC, Ormonde MSS.*, n.s. viii., pp. 355–7, 387–9. Rumours gave rise to a flood of propaganda, e.g. *An Account of a Late, Horrid and Bloody Massacre in Ireland of several thousands of Protestants, procured and carry'd on by the L. Tyrconnel and his Adherents* (London, 1689); *The Siege and History of Londonderry*, ed. John Hempton (Londonderry, 1861), p. 280.

10 *A True and Impartial Account of the most Material Passages in Ireland since December 1688, with a Particular Relation of the Forces of Derry* (London, 1689), pp. 5–6; *The History of the Wars in Ireland, betwixt Their Majesties Army and the Forces of the late King James, by an Officer in the Royal Army* (2nd edn, London, 1691), pp. 4–5; John Young, 'Invasions: Scotland and Ireland, 1641–1691', in *Conquest and Resistance: War in Seventeenth-Century Ireland*, ed. Pádraig Lenihan (Leiden, 2001), p. 79.

11 Dr Hopkins (1633–90), a Devonian, was subsequently elected preacher to the parish of St Mary Aldermanbury, London, in September 1689. He died on 22 June 1690. Adhering to the Anglican doctrine of 'passive obedience' to the will of the king, Hopkins declared the closing of Derry's gates sinful.

12 George Walker, *A True Account of the Siege of London-Derry* (2nd edn, London, 1689), ed. P. Dwyer (Wakefield, 1971), pp. 11–12; Mackenzie, pp. 4–10, 50–1; *Particular Relation of the Forces of Derry*, pp. 4–6; *The History of the Wars in Ireland*, pp. 4–5.

13 William McCarmick, *A Farther Impartial Account of the Actions of the Inniskilling-men containing the Reasons of their First Rising* (London, 1691), pp. 1–3; Andrew Hamilton, *A True Relation of the Actions of the Inniskilling-Men, from their first taking up of Arms in December 1688* (London, 1690), pp. 1–2.

14 McCarmick, pp. 4–6; Hamilton, p. 3.

15 Mackenzie, pp. 4–5.

16 Leslie, pp. 141–2; McCarmick, pp. 6–17; Hamilton, pp. 3–6; *History of the Wars in Ireland*, pp. 5–8; *HMC, Ormonde MSS.*, n.s. viii., pp. 357–8.

Notes to Chapter 2: Practical matters

1 Pádraig Lenihan, 'Strategic Geography, 1641–1691', in *Conquest and Resistance: War in Seventeenth-Century Ireland*, ed. Pádraig Lenihan (Leiden, 2001), pp. 121–3.

2 J. C. O'Callaghan, *History of the Irish Brigades in the Service of France* (Shannon, 1969), p. 6; L. M. Cullen, 'Population Trends in Seventeenth Century Ireland', *Economic and Social Review*, vi. (1974–5); J. G. Simms, *Jacobite Ireland, 1685–91* (London, 1969), p. 12; L. A. Clarkson, 'Irish Population Revisited, 1687–1821', *Irish Population, Economy, and Society*, ed. J. M. Goldstrom and L. A. Clarkson (Oxford, 1981), pp. 25–7; Gregory King, *Natural and Political Observations and Conclusions upon the State and Condition of England, 1696* (London, 1804), p. 48; D. Coleman and J. Salt, *The British Population: Patterns, Trends and Processes* (Oxford, 1992), pp. 1–35.

3 John R. Young, 'The Scottish Response to the Siege of Derry, 1689–90', in *The Sieges of Derry*, ed. William Kelly (Dublin, 2001), pp. 53–74; John R. Young, 'Invasions: Scotland and Ireland, 1641–1691', in Lenihan, *Conquest*, pp. 54–5.

4 John Childs, *The Nine Years' War and the British Army, 1688–97* (Manchester, 1991), pp. 46–58.

5 BL Egerton MSS. 3340, f. 86.

6 Sir John Dalrymple, *Memoirs of Great Britain and Ireland; from the Dissolution of the last Parliament of Charles II till the Capture of the French and Spanish Fleets at Vigo* (London and Edinburgh, 1790), ii. Part 2, pp. 167–8.

7 *Correspondentie van Willem III en van Hans Willem Bentinck*, ed. N. Japikse (The Hague, 1927–8), ii. pp. 27–8.

8 *Journals of the House of Commons*, x. pp. 295–6, Nottingham to Schomberg, 6 November 1689; *CSPD 1690–1*, p. 10; *CTB*, pp. 348–9.

9 Anchitell Grey, *Debates of the House of Commons, from the Year 1667 to 1694* (London, 1763), ix. pp. 451–3, 26 November 1689; *The House of Commons, 1660–1690*, ed. B. D. Henning (London, 1983), ii. pp. 482–8; Dalrymple, ii. Part 2, pp. 179–80.

10 DCRO Ilchester Papers D. 124; *CSPD 1690–1*, pp. 7, 234, 251, 278–9; *Journal of the Very Rev. Rowland Davies, LL.D.*, ed. Richard Caulfield (Camden Society, London, 1857), p. 146; *The Danish Force in Ireland, 1690–1691*, ed. K. Danaher and J. G. Simms (Dublin, 1962), pp. 128–9; *CTB*, pp. 639–41, 1095, 1424.

11 Leopold von Ranke, *A History of England, principally in the Seventeenth Century* (Oxford, 1875), vi. pp. 138–9, 'Extracts from the Diary of a Jacobite relating to the War in Ireland, 1689 and 1690'; *The Journal of John Stevens, containing a Brief Account of the War in Ireland, 1689–1691*, ed. Robert H. Murray (Oxford, 1912), pp. 83–4; *An Order Published by the Command of the Duke of Schonberg, in the Camp at Dundalk, for Establishing the Rates and Prizes of Provisions in the Army* (London, 1689), 3 October 1689; George Story, *A True and Impartial History of the Most Material Occurrences in the Kingdom of Ireland during the Last Two Years* (London, 1691), p. 48; George Story, *A Continuation of the Impartial History of the*

Wars of Ireland, From the Time that the Duke Schonberg Landed with an Army in that Kingdom, to the 23rd of March 1691/2 when Their Majesties' Proclamation was published, declaring the War to be ended (London, 1693), pp. 185–6; *HMC, Ormonde MSS.*, o.s. ii. p. 415.

12 Robert Steele, *A Bibliography of Royal Proclamations of the Tudor and Stuart Sovereigns … 1485–1714* (Oxford, 1910), ii. p. 149.

13 Steele, ii. p. 133.

14 *HMC, Ormonde MSS.*, o.s. ii. pp. 436–7.

15 *HMC, Stuart MSS.*, i. pp. 44, 94; *FIC*, nos. 628, 633, 645, 677.

16 *HMC, Ormonde MSS.*, o.s. ii. pp. 399, 413, 437; n.s. viii. p. 384; 'The Longford Papers', ed. Edward MacLysaght, *Analecta Hibernica*, xv. (1944), pp. 58–9, 61–2.

17 John Ehrman, *The Navy in the War of William IIII, 1689–97* (Cambridge, 1953), pp. 623–32; James Scott Wheeler, 'The Logistics of Conquest', in Lenihan, *Conquest*, pp. 177–209; *FIC*, i. pp. xlii–xliii.

18 LBRT, pp. 102–3, 137–8; *HMC, Ormonde MSS.*, o.s. ii. pp. 413–15.

19 Charles O'Kelly, *Macariae Excidium, or the Destruction of Cyprus*, ed. G. N. Plunkett and E. Hogan (Dublin, 1896), pp. 60–1.

20 *HMC, Stuart MSS.*, i. p. 44; 'Letters from Lord Longford and others on Irish Affairs, 1687–1702: Ellis Papers BL. MS., ed. Patrick Melvin, *Analecta Hibernia*, xxxii. (1985), pp. 58–9; *HMC, Ormonde MSS.*, o.s. ii. pp. 413, 436–7; n.s. viii. p. 384; O'Kelly, pp. 60–1.

21 *HMC, Ormonde MSS.*, o.s. ii. pp. 366, 401, 413–14; LBRT, pp. 114–15; Story, *Continuation*, pp. 85–6, 181; *A True and Impartial Account of Their Majesties Army in Ireland* (London, 1690), p. 11; *The Inchiquin Manuscripts*, ed. J. Ainsworth (Dublin, 1961), pp. 254–5.

22 *HMC, Ormonde MSS.*, o.s. ii. pp. 416, 419–20, 437; *CSPD 1689–90*, p. 506; Steele, ii. p. 140; 'The Nugent Papers', ed. J. F. Ainsworth and Edward MacLysaght, *Analecta Hibernica*, xx. (1958), p. 162.

23 *CSPD 1689–90*, p. 509.

24 *HMC, Ormonde MSS.*, o.s. ii. p. 409.

25 Danaher and Simms, pp. 47, 50–2.

26 Lawrence was appointed on 6 March 1689.

27 *CSPD 1690–1*, pp. 233, 256–7; Story, *Continuation*, p. 115; Eric Gruber von Arni, *Hospital Care and the British Standing Army, 1660–1714* (Aldershot, 2006), pp. 53–75.

28 *CSPD 1690–1*, p. 233, Lords Justices to Lord Sydney, 24 January 1691.

29 *A Jacobite Narrative of the War in Ireland, 1688–1691*, ed. John T. Gilbert (Shannon, 1971), p. 38.

30 'Franco-Irish Correspondence, December 1688–August 1691', ed. Lilian Tate, *Analecta Hibernica*, xxi. (1959), pp. 135–8; Gilbert, pp. 201–41; *FIC*, nos. 1874, 1899; Diarmuid and Harman Murtagh, 'The Irish Jacobite Army, 1689–91', *Irish Sword*, xiii. (1990), pp. 33, 45–8; Story, pp. 97–8; *Négociations de M. Le Comte D'Avaux en Irlande, 1689–90: Supplementary Volume*, ed. James Hogan (Dublin, 1958), pp. 8–24.

31 O'Callaghan, p. 8; Gilbert, pp. 89, 92; Danaher and Simms, p. 61; *A Full and Impartial Account of the Late Besieging and Taking of the Famous Castle of Killishandrea, in the Province of Ulster in Ireland, by the Brave Inniskilling Forces* (London, 1690), p. 2; *Great News from Ireland: Being a full and true Relation of the several Great and Successful Defeats, which the Danish and Inniskilling Forces hath lately obtained over a Party of the Irish Rebels at Cliff and Emismack* (London, 1690), pp. 1–2; *HMC, Ormonde MSS.*, o.s. ii. pp. 426–7; n.s. viii. pp. 364, 380–5; *An Account of the Transactions of the Late King James in Ireland, wherein is contain'd The Act of Attainder past at Dublin in May, 1689* (London, 1690), pp. 19–21, 58–9; *History of the Wars in Ireland*, pp. 73–4.

32 O'Kelly, pp. 81–3; Gilbert, p. 151; *A True and Impartial Account of Their Majesties Army in Ireland*, p. 25; Simms, *Jacobite Ireland*, p. 165; 'Irish Jacobite army', p. 34; Richard Doherty, *The Williamite War in Ireland, 1688–1691* (Dublin, 1998), pp. 185–6; *HMC, Finch MSS.*, iii. p. 452.

33 'Longford Papers', pp. 75–6.

34 Charles Leslie MA (1650–1722) was a Protestant minister in the Episcopalian Church of Ireland until dismissed in 1689 for refusing to take the oaths to William and Mary.

35 Story, p. 6; Story, *Continuation*, pp. 78–9; Ranke, vi. p. 113; Leslie, pp. 154–5; *HMC, Ormonde MSS.*, o.s. ii. pp. 409–10; Bod. Lib. Rawlinson MSS. C. 984, f. 85, Archbishop Boyle to Viscount Blessington, 15 November 1690.

36 *HMC, Ormonde MSS.*, o.s. ii. p. 412. On raparees see, Éamonn Ó Ciardha, *Ireland the Jacobite Cause, 1685–1766* (Dublin, 2002), pp. 68–86.

37 John Childs, *The Army of Charles II* (London, 1976), p. 64; J. A. Houlding, *Fit for Service: The Training of the British Army, 1715–1795* (Oxford, 1981), p. 173n.

38 Lenihan, 'Strategic Geography', in Lenihan, *Conquest*, pp. 121–48.

39 John Childs, *The British Army of William III, 1689–1702* (Manchester, 1987), p. 127, n. 2. William Blathwayt, the secretary at war in England, reckoned the average field strength of a foot battalion at 600 men and a cavalry squadron, 130.

Notes to Chapter 3: Towards war, 1689

1 Childs, *Army of William III*, pp. 9–11; John Childs, *The Army, James II and the Glorious Revolution* (Manchester, 1980), pp. 194–7; *HMC, Finch MSS.*, ii. p. 223.

2 Childs, *Army of William III*, pp. 4–33; Childs, *Nine Years' War*, pp. 100–1.

3 Mackenzie, pp. 10–11; 'Longford Letters', p. 51.

4 Gustavus Hamilton (1642–1723), Viscount Boyne after 1717. Not to be confused with the governor of Enniskillen.

5 Hillsborough Fort was an artillery fortification begun around 1630 and finished in 1650 by Colonel Arthur Hill, the town's proprietor. Hillsborough Castle, presently the residence of the British secretary of state for Northern Ireland, dates from 1760.

6 Leslie, pp. 91–2; *HMC, Ormonde MSS.*, n.s. viii. p. 359.

7 McCarmick, pp. 19–24; Mackenzie, pp. 10–11; Leslie, pp. 160–1; *Particular Relation of the Forces of Derry*, pp. 7–8.

8 *HMC, Ormonde MSS.*, n.s. viii. pp. 358–9; Mackenzie, p. 8; Simms, *Jacobite Ireland*, pp. 52–3; 'Longford Letters', p. 52, Herbert Aubrey to John Ellis, 20 January 1689, Dublin; 'Longford Letters', pp. 54–5, Lord Longford to Duke of Ormond, 22 January 1689, Dublin.

9 Ulysses S. Grant, *Personal Memoirs of U. S. Grant* (London, 1999), pp. 131–2.

10 *Particular Relation of the Forces of Derry*, pp. 8–11; 'Longford Letters', p. 51.

11 Mackenzie, pp. 9–10.

12 McCarmick, pp. 15–16.

13 A 'sod' fort: an earthwork fortification lacking stone or brick revetment.

14 Mackenzie, pp. 15–17.

15 'Longford Letters', p. 51, unsigned letter to Captain Oliver Long, 18 January 1689, Hillsborough.

16 McCarmick, pp. 19, 37, 57.

17 McCarmick, pp. 14–19; Hamilton, pp. 6–7.

18 'Longford Letters', pp. 57–8; *HMC, Ormonde MSS.*, o.s. ii. pp. 390–1; *FIC*, no. 2040.

19 Walker, *True Account*, p. 13; Mackenzie, p. 14.

20 McCarmick, p. 25.

21 John Michelburne had been appointed major of Skeffington's regiment on 5 February 1689 but his commission had yet to reach Ireland (*CTP*, p. 171).

22 Leslie, pp. 86–8; Mackenzie, p. 14.

23 *HMC, Ormonde MSS.*, n.s. viii. p. 319; Story, p. 10.

24 D'Alton, pp. 49–50; Mackenzie, pp. 11–13; Leslie, pp. 88–9; *A Faithful History of the Northern Affairs*, pp. 27–32.

25 See, James Lucas, *War on the Eastern Front: The German Soldier in Russia, 1942–1945* (London, 1991), pp. 119–54.

26 Kenneth Ferguson, 'The Organisation of King William's Army in Ireland, 1689–92', *Irish Sword*, xviii. (1990), p. 63.

27 *HMC, Ormonde MSS.*, n.s. viii. pp. 359–60; o.s. ii. 392–3.

28 *HMC, Ormonde MSS.*, o.s. ii. 395–6.

Notes to Chapter 4: The Break of Dromore and the retreat to Coleraine

1 *Particular Relation of the Forces of Derry*, pp. 11–12; Mackenzie, p. 13. If the Council of Five actually believed that 15,000 troops were indeed on their way from England, some of the decisions taken during the coming campaign appear more comprehensible.

2 Walker, *True Account*, pp. 51–2; Mackenzie, p. 13; McCarmick, pp. 25–8.

3 Mackenzie, p. 13.

4 O'Callaghan, pp. 10–11; Leslie, pp. 141–2; Gilbert, pp. 42–3.

5 Simms, *Jacobite Ireland*, pp. 62–3; O'Kelly, pp. 3–4; Gilbert, pp. 42–6; *HMC, Ormonde MSS.*, n.s. viii. p. 362; 'Longford Letters', p. 63; Sheila Mulloy, 'The French Navy and the Jacobite War in Ireland, 1689–91', *Irish Sword*, xviii. (1990), p. 23; *HMC, 7th Report*, pp. 158–9; *HMC, Buccleuch MSS.*, ii.(i). pp. 36–7; *HMC, 8th Report, Appendix*, p. 493; *The Life of James the Second*, ed. J. S. Clarke (London, 1816), ii. p. 327; James Fitzjames, Duke of Berwick, *Memoirs of the Marshal Duke of Berwick. Written by himself. With a summary continuation from the year 1716, to his death in 1734* (London, 1779), i. pp. 43–4. A list of those who came to Ireland with James is given in, *HMC, Finch MSS.*, iii. pp. 424–5.

6 *Aphorisms relating to the Kingdom of Ireland humbly submitted to the most noble assembly of Lords & Commons at the great convention at Westminster* (London, 1689).

7 S. B. Baxter, *William III* (London, 1966), pp. 253–4; Simms, *Jacobite Ireland*, pp. 51–2; Andrew Browning, *Thomas Osborne, Earl of Danby and Duke of Leeds, 1632–1712* (Glasgow, 1951), i. pp. 423–4; E. B. Powley, *The Naval Side of King William's War* (London, 1972), pp. 53–7; Ferguson, p. 62.

8 BL Egerton MSS. 3340, ff. 94–7.

9 *HMC, House of Lords MSS.*, ii. p. 166.

10 BL Add. MSS. 15, 897, ff. 88–90.

11 BL Egerton MSS. 3340, f. 84.

12 Walker, *True Account*, pp. 48–50, William's orders to John Cunningham, 12 March 1689.

13 Hamilton was knighted in 1690.

14 Hamilton, p. 35; *Particular Relation of the Forces of Derry*, p. 15; Mackenzie, pp. 14–15.

15 *The Montgomery Manuscripts*, ed. G. Hill (Belfast, 1869), pp. 278–81; *HMC, House of Lords MSS.*, ii. p. 160; Clarke, ii. p. 327; *D'Avaux: Supplementary*, pp. 6–8; *Particular Relation of the Forces of Derry*, pp. 12–16; Mackenzie, pp. 13–15; McCarmick, p. 33.

16 Walker, *True Account*, pp. 46–7.

17 Walker, *True Account*, pp. 13–14.

18   Hamilton, pp. 8–9; McCarmick, pp. 29–31.

19   *Particular Relation of the Forces of Derry*, pp. 15–16; Mackenzie, p. 15.

20   *History of the Wars in Ireland*, pp. 12–13; Hamilton, pp. 9–12; McCarmick, pp. 29–31. There has been some suggestion that Galmoy's two cannon were actually light field guns after the manner of the 'leather guns' favoured in the Swedish Army under Gustav II Adolf. The fact that Galmoy fired one of his cannon suggests that they were real guns, just poorly made, rather than imitations. Also, Hamilton's statement that the cannon were captured and one taken to Enniskillen and one left at Crom again indicates that they were effective weapons. McCarmick notes that these cannon were fired at Crom Castle making much noise but doing little damage. McCarmick examined these curiosities: 'their two great guns which proved to be boxes of tin about two foot and a half long, five inches diameter, well bound about with pitched canvas and small cording. They had fired one of them with a wooden bullet and burst out her britch [*sic*]' (McCarmick, pp. 31–2).

21   Hamilton, pp. 12–13.

22   Mackenzie, p. 19; Walker, *True Account*, p. 14; *History of the Wars in Ireland*, pp. 9–10; *Particular Relation of the Forces of Derry*, p. 16; HMC, *House of Lords MSS.*, ii. pp. 162–4, 20 February 1689.

23   Mackenzie, p. 17.

24   HMC, *Ormonde MSS.*, o.s. ii. pp. 396–8; n.s. viii. p. 362.

25   Hamilton, pp. 13–14; *History of the Wars in Ireland*, p. 13; McCarmick, p. 33.

26   *Particular Relation of the Forces of Derry*, p. 14.

27   The original Limavady was 3 km further upstream, centred on the thirteenth-century Castle O'Cahan. It was refounded as Newtown Limavady early in the seventeenth century by Sir Thomas Phillips, chief agent of the City of London in Ulster.

28   Mackenzie, p. 18.

29   Mackenzie, p. 19; Walker, *True Account*, pp. 14, 148–50.

30   Mackenzie, pp. 19–20; *Particular Relation of the Forces of Derry*, pp. 16–17; *An Account of the Present Miserable State of Affairs in Ireland* (London, 1689); 'Longford Letters', pp. 64–6; McCarmick, pp. 33–4; *Davies*, pp. 6–7. The Duke of Berwick, who was present at Coleraine, says nothing about the action (Berwick, i. p. 44).

31   Mackenzie, p. 20.

32   Gilbert, p. 45; Clarke, ii. pp. 330–1.

33   HMC, *8th Report, Appendix*, p. 493.

Notes to Chapter 5: *Clady and the Ards Peninsula*

1   'Longford Letters', p. 64, Arthur Bushe to John Ellis, 7 April 1689, Whitehaven.

2   Mackenzie, pp. 21–2; Hempton, pp. 280–1; Clarke, ii. p. 331; *Négociations de M. Le Comte D'Avaux en Irlande, 1689–90*, ed. James Hogan (Dublin, 1934), pp. 96–9.

3   Walker, *True Account*, pp. 44–5; McCarmick, pp. 33–4; Mackenzie, pp. 22–3.

4   C. H. Firth and Godfrey Davies, *A Regimental History of Cromwell's Army* (Oxford, 1940), pp. 384–6; Dalton, i. p. 318; ii. p. 22; iii. p. 100 n. 14; Walker, *True Account*, p.146; David Francis, *The First Peninsula War, 1702–1713* (London, 1975), p. 136; Piers Wauchope, 'Lundy, Robert', *DNB*; HMC, *Finch MSS.*, ii. pp. 250–3; HMC, *House of Lords MSS.*, n.s. ix. p. 72.

5   Believed to have been near Porthall.

6   Mackenzie, pp. 15–18; McCarmick, pp. 34–5. Walker, *True Account*, p. 62, rearranges the evidence, presumably to portray Lundy in the worst possible light, whilst the *Particular Relation of the Forces of Derry*, p. 22, appears unreliable on this point.

7   *HMC, Downshire MSS.*, iii. pp. 308–9.

8   *FIC*, iii. pp. 11–12; Mackenzie, pp. 23–4; Gilbert, pp. 45–6; 'Franco-Irish Correspondence', pp. 87–9; *Particular Relation of the Forces of Derry*, pp. 18–20; *History of the Wars in Ireland*, pp. 10–11; Hempton, p. 281; Clarke, ii. pp. 331–2; Berwick, i. pp. 44–7; *D'Avaux*, pp. 158–60.

9   Walker, *True Account*, pp. 15, 47–8; Mackenzie, p. 23.

10   Mackenzie, pp. 24–5.

11   Walker, *True Account*, pp. 15–16; *HMC, Finch MSS.*, iii. pp. 434–6.

12   It is possible that Cunningham was a Roman Catholic, one of the few to survive the Glorious Revolution (Dalton, ii. pp. 7, 89, 123). This may explain his readiness to accept Lundy's appreciation of the military situation.

13   Mackenzie, pp. 25–7.

14   *History of the Wars in Ireland*, p. 11; *Particular Relation of the Forces of Derry*, pp. 20–1; Mackenzie, pp. 27–30; Walker, *True Account*, pp. 16–17.

15   Hamilton, pp. 14–15; *History of the Wars in Ireland*, pp. 13–14.

16   Hamilton, pp. 15–17; *Particular Relation of the Forces of Derry*, p. 26.

17   Bryan Magennis, Fifth Viscount Magennis of Iveagh, a Roman Catholic and colonel of a regiment of infantry in the Irish Army. Captain Conn Magennis was a relative and company commander in the same unit (D'Alton, pp. 908–11).

18   *Particular Relation of the Forces of Derry*, pp. 28–9.

19   This did not happen. Iveagh continued to command an infantry battalion until the end of the war ('Irish Jacobite Army', p. 46).

20   Paul Hopkins, *Glencoe and the End of the Highland War* (Edinburgh, 1986), p. 140; Dalton, *Scots Army*, pp. 115–18.

21   Leslie, pp. 154–8.

22   'Placing under contribution' was a method of supplying armies in the field, usually associated with the Thirty Years' War although it continued throughout the seventeenth century. When an army occupied a region, in return for protection of life and property, the inhabitants were ordered to supply quotas of money, provisions and lodging. Failure to comply resulted in the burning of property, plundering and the killing of hostages.

23   *Particular Relation of the Forces of Derry*, pp. 28–30.

Notes to Chapter 6: The defence of Derry and Enniskillen

1   *HMC, Egmont MSS.*, ii. p. 190, 24 April 1689, William Taylor to Edward Lloyd.

2   'Longford Letters', p. 66; *HMC, Portland MSS.*, iii. p. 437.

3   Mackenzie, pp. 31–4; Walker, *True Account*, pp. 18–22; *Particular Relation of the Forces of Derry*, pp. 21–4; Hempton, p. 281.

4   *Particular Relation of the Forces of Derry*, pp. 24–5; Kelly, *Sieges of Derry*, pp. 19–20; Gilbert, pp. 86–7; *Kings in Conflict: Ireland in the 1690s*, ed. Eileen Black (Antrim, 1690), pp. 92–6; Berwick, i. pp. 48–50.

5   *Particular Relation of the Forces of Derry*, pp. 22–3; Mackenzie, p. 32; Walker, *True Account*, p. 22; *History of the Wars in Ireland*, p. 18.

6   Berwick, i. pp. 50–1.

7   Governor Baker's regiment (26 companies); Michelburne (17); Dr George Walker (14); Monro (12); Lance (13); Hamill (15); Crofton (12); Murray's cavalry (8 troops) (Mackenzie, p. 33).

8   *Particular Relation of the Forces of Derry*, pp. 25–7; Walker, *True Account*, p. 22.

9   Mackenzie, p. 32; Walker, *True Account*, p. 22; *History of the Wars in Ireland*, p. 18.

10   Mackenzie, pp. 32–4. Colonel Murray; Majors Alexander Stuart, John Dobbins; Captains Noble, Dunbar, Andrew Adams (later major), Wilson, Archibald Hamilton, Beatty, Alexander Sanderson junior, Alexander Sanderson senior, Samuel Wright, James MacCormick, Bashford, Cunningham; Lieutenants Dunlop and Maghlin, all performed valuable service during this period.

11   Hamilton, pp. 17–18.

12   McCarmick, pp. 37–8, 42.

13   *History of the Wars in Ireland*, p. 14; Hamilton, pp. 17–18; McCarmick, pp. 39–40.

14   Ranke, vi. p. 130.

15   Simms, *Jacobite Ireland*, pp. 66–9; E. H. Jenkins, *A History of the French Navy* (London, 1973), pp. 69–72; HMC, *Ormonde MSS.*, n.s. viii. pp. 363–4; Ehrman, *Navy in the War of William III*, p. 246; HMC, *Finch MSS.*, ii. pp. 205–7, 209–10; *Stevens*, p. 45; *FIC*, i. p. xlii.

16   Hamilton, pp. 18–19.

17   Doherty, *Williamite War*, pp. 75–8; McCarmick, pp. 40–4; Hamilton, pp. 19–21; *History of the Wars in Ireland*, pp. 14–15; Piers Wauchope, *Patrick Sarsfield and the Williamite War* (Dublin, 1992), pp. 60–2.

18   *History of the Wars in Ireland*, pp. 15–16, 87–9; McCarmick, p. 42; Hamilton, pp. 21–2; Hempton, pp. 282–3.

19   Walker, *True Account*, p. 23; Mackenzie, p. 34; *History of the Wars in Ireland*, p. 18; Berwick, i. pp. 51–2.

20   *The Bishopric of Derry and the Irish Society of London, 1602–1705*, ed. T. W. Moody and J. G. Simms (Dublin, 1968–83), ii. pp. 115–16. This tale would appear to be a wild conflation of the revolt in the Ards Peninsula and the action on Windmill Hill.

21   Walker, *True Account*, p. 25.

22   Hempton, pp. 283–4.

23   Mackenzie, pp. 34–7.

Notes to Chapter 7: General Kirke

1   *HMC, 8th Report, Appendix*, p. 494.

2   McCarmick, pp. 44–5, 51–2; Hamilton, pp. 22–3; *History of the Wars in Ireland*, pp. 23–4; Berwick, i. p. 53.

3   Walker, *True Account*, pp. 25–6; Mackenzie, pp. 35–8; *History of the Wars in Ireland*, pp. 18–19; Hempton, p. 286.

4   Hamilton, pp. 23–8; *History of the Wars in Ireland*, pp. 25–6, 34–5; McCarmick, pp. 45–50.

5   Mackenzie, p. 38; Walker, *True Account*, pp. 28–9.

6   J. R. Western, *Monarchy and Revolution: The English State in the 1680s* (London, 1972), p. 382; F. C. Foxcroft, *The Life and Letters of Sir George Savile, First Marquis of Halifax* (London, 1898), ii. pp. 219–20, 228.

7   *Letters and Second Diary of Samuel Pepys*, ed. R. G. Howarth (London, 1933), pp. 395–6; *Pepys's Later Diaries*, ed. C. S. Knighton (Stroud, 2004), pp. 127–78.

8   *The Diary of Abraham de la Pryme*, ed. Charles Jackson (Surtees Society, 1870), p. 30, 3 September 1693.

9   Henning, iii. pp. 690–1; John Childs, *Nobles, Gentlemen and the Profession of Arms in Restoration England, 1660–1688* (Society for Army Historical Research, Special Publication No.13: London, 1987), p. 48; Gilbert Burnet, *History of His Own Time* (London, 1857), p. 415; *DNB*.

10 Messrs Dompierre, de la Barte, Mainvilliers and Sundini (Jacob Richards, 'The Diary of the Fleet, 1689', in *Two Diaries of Derry in 1689*, ed. Thomas Witherow (Londonderry, 1888), p. 1.

11 Captain Thomas Ash noted that four ships were observed below Culmore Fort on 3 June (Hempton, p. 285).

12 Jacobs, 'Diary', pp. 1–12; Powley, pp. 218–24; *Particular Relation of the Forces of Derry*, p. 31; Walker, *True Account*, p. 26; Mackenzie, p. 38.

13 *CSPD 1689–90*, p. 81; *An Exact Relation of the Glorious Victory Obtain'd upon the French and Irish Army before London-Derry on Sunday, June the 2nd, 1689* (London, 1689), pp. 1–2.

14 Walker, *True Account*, pp. 26–8; Mackenzie, pp. 38–40; Hempton, p. 287.

15 George Walker, *A Vindication of the True Account of the Siege of Derry in Ireland* (London, 1689), ed. P. Dwyer (Wakefield, 1971), pp. 88–93.

16 *A True and Impartial Account of the Present State of Affairs in London-Derry in Ireland, being a Relation of the late Great Fight betwixt the Protestants and the French and Irish Papists: A Letter from Captain Woosley [Wolseley] from on board the fleet with Major General Kirk lying at anchor in the mouth of London-Derry Harbour, 13 July 1689* (London, 1689), p. 1; Powley, pp. 226–8; Richards, 'Diary', pp. 15–16.

17 Hempton, pp. 287–8.

Notes to Chapter 8: Endurance

1 *HMC, Frankland-Russell-Astley MSS.*, pp. 72–3; Kelly, *Sieges of Derry*, pp. 43–4; *Kirck, and London-Derry*, p. 1; Kirke, *True Account*, p. 28.

2 Mackenzie, pp. 39–40; Walker, *True Account*, pp. 28–9; *HMC, 8th Report, Appendix*, p. 494.

3 Usually cannon firing a ball above 24 pounds (11 kg) in weight.

4 Flesh scraped from hides prior to tanning.

5 Walker, *True Account*, pp. 29–31; Mackenzie, pp. 40–1; Hempton, pp. 288–9.

6 Dalton, ii. p. 269; iii. p. 83; Dalton, *Irish Army*, pp. 151, 154–5; Childs, *Army of James II*, p. 42; Kelly, *Sieges of Derry*, p. 14; Michelburne, p. 4; *DNB*.

7 Mackenzie, pp. 41–2; Walker, *True Account*, pp. 31–2, 52–4; *FIC*, no. 1825; *D'Avaux: Supplementary*, pp. 36–7; *D'Avaux*, pp. 259–60.

8 Walker, *True Account*, pp. 31–5, 54–5; Mackenzie, pp. 42–3; *History of the Wars in Ireland*, p. 20; Bod. Lib. Rawlinson MSS. D. 21, f. 16, *An Account of the Life of James II*; Hempton, pp. 291–2; *HMC, Hamilton MSS.*, pp. 185–6; *Stevens*, pp. 70–2.

9 Hamilton, pp. 28–32; McCarmick, pp. 50–1; *History of the Wars in Ireland*, pp. 26–9.

10 Walker, *True Account*, p. 35; Mackenzie, p. 43.

11 Hopkins, p. 154; *A Full and True Relation of the Remarkable Fight betwixt Capt. Hamilton and Capt. Brown, Commanders of the Two Scotch Frigats, and Three French Men of War* (London, 1689), pp. 1–2; *The Old Scots Navy, 1689–1710*, ed. James Grant (Navy Records Society, 1912), pp. 26–9; Powley, pp. 240–2; Jenkins, *French Navy*, p. 72; *A Letter from on board Major General Kirke giving a Full Account of the Posture of Affairs of London-Derry* (London, 1689), p. 2.

12 Captain Ash was led to believe that 12,000 infantry and 2,000 cavalry had been disembarked at Inch (Hempton, p. 294).

13 Mackenzie, pp. 43–4; Hempton, p. 294.

14 Hamilton, pp. 32–3; Powley, pp. 239–48; *A Particular Account from Collonel Kirke of the State of London-Derry and Iniskilling* (London, 1689), pp. 1–2; *Full Account of the Posture of Affairs of London-Derry*, pp. 1–2. On Rathmullan, see James Shirley, *A True Impartial*

History and Wars of the Kingdom of Ireland (London, 1692), pp. 44–5; Jacobs, 'Diary', pp. 27–34.

15   Hamilton, pp. 29–31; Berwick, i. pp. 53–4; McCarmick, pp. 52–7. McCarmick's account has been more heavily used than that of Hamilton because McCarmick was in the heart of this action whereas Hamilton was with Thomas Lloyd at Ballyshannon *en route* to meet Kirke. There is also a problem with the dating. Hamilton says that this action occurred on either 6 or 7 July whereas McCarmick gives 13 July. Because McCarmick both fought and was captured, it is most unlikely that an incorrect date was imprinted upon his memory so his date has been accepted.

16   McCarmick, p. 58.

17   Mackenzie, pp. 44–5. Captain Ash dates this action on 17 July (Hempton, p. 295). *HMC, Hamilton MSS.*, p. 185.

18   *HMC, House of Lords MSS.*, ii. p. 180.

19   *A Letter from Chester of the Twenty Second Instant, Giving an Account of Some Affairs in Ireland, and of the Arrival and Reception of the General the Duke of Schomberg, and of the Forces there* (London, 1689), p. 1; *A Further Account of the State of Ireland and the Proceedings of the Late King James in that Kingdom* (London, 1689), p. 1; *The Diary of Thomas Bellingham, an Officer under William III*, ed. Anthony Hewitson (Preston, 1908), pp. 75–80.

20   Walker, *True Account*, pp. 35–6; Mackenzie, p. 45; *History of the Wars in Ireland*, p. 20; Hempton, pp. 298–9.

Notes to Chapter 9: The relief of Derry and Newtownbutler

1   Captain Ash says 17:00 (Hempton, p. 301).

2   Mackenzie, pp. 45–6; Walker, *True Account*, p. 36; *History of the Wars in Ireland*, p. 20; Hempton, pp. 301–2; Powley, pp. 245–6; *An Account of Major General Kirck's Safe Arrival at London-Derry* (London, 1689), p. 1; *HMC, Hamilton MSS.*, pp. 185–6. William III rewarded Browning's widow with a diamond necklace and a pension.

3   *Account from Colonel Kirk of the Relieving of London-Derry* (London, 1689), p. 1; Gilbert, pp. 83–6; Walker, *True Account*, pp. 37–8; Mackenzie, p. 46; Powley, pp. 247–9; *Stevens*, pp. 70–2.

4   Walker, *True Account*, pp. 55–60; Mackenzie, pp. 63–4; Maarten Prak, *The Dutch Republic in the Seventeenth Century* (Cambridge, 2005), p. 68; Childs, *Nine Years' War*, p. 190.

5   *Major General Kirk's Letter to his Grace the Duke of Hamilton, Dated from the Isle of Inch, August the 5. 1689* (Edinburgh, 1689), p. 2.

6   Story, p. 24.

7   Mackenzie, pp. 46–7; Walker, *True Account*, pp. 38–9; *History of the Wars in Ireland*, pp. 20–1; Hempton, pp. 303–5; Walker, *Vindication*, pp. 80–2.

8   Dalton, i. pp. 81, 136, 259; ii. pp. 32, 37, 141; iii. pp. 27, 344; *CSPD 1687–9*, p. 268; Henning, iii. p. 754; Sir George Duckett, *Penal Laws and Test Act* (London, 1882–3), i. p. 451; Hamilton, pp. 33–4.

9   Hamilton, pp. 34–6.

10   Berry had previously been captain-lieutenant of Kirke's infantry battalion.

11   Both Brigadier Anthony Hamilton and Captain Lavallin were court-martialled in Dublin two weeks later, General Conrad Rosen presiding. Hamilton was acquitted but Lavallin was sentenced to a 'military death' although he protested repeatedly that he had obeyed Hamilton's order as it had been relayed to him. Although his version was widely believed,

he was shot at the army camp at Finglas on 19 August (Gilbert, p. 82; *HMC, Ormonde MSS.*, n.s. viii. p. 369). For the possible location of this action, and of the subsequent Battle of Newtownbutler, see, Darren P. Graham, 'Enniskillen and the Newtownbutler Campaign, 1689' (MA Thesis, University of Leeds, 1999).

12 Hamilton, pp. 36–9; *Inchiquin MSS.*, pp. 17–18; O'Callaghan, pp. 13–17; McCarmick, pp. 59–65; *History of the Wars in Ireland*, pp. 29–38; Gilbert, pp. 81–2; *Major-General Kirk's Letter*, p. 1.

13 Tiffin was another officer who had come with Wolseley from Kirke. He had considerable experience of active service in the French Army during the Franco-Dutch war and against the Moors in Tangier. Before elevation to the command of the Enniskillen Foot, Tiffin had been lieutenant colonel of Charles Trelawney's infantry battalion.

14 Hamilton, pp. 39–46; McCarmick, pp. 59–65; Gilbert, pp. 81–2; O'Callaghan, pp. 21–2; *Major-General Kirk's Letter*, pp. 1–2; *History of the Wars in Ireland*, pp. 29–38; *Great and Good News from His Grace the Duke of Schomberg's Camp at Dundalk* (London, 1689), p. 2; *A Full Account of the Great Victory obtained by the Protestants in Ireland since the Arrival of his Grace the Duke of Shcomberg* [sic] *as it was communicated by the Reverend and Valliant Gouvernour Walker at Chester* (London, 1689), pp. 1–2; Charles Petrie, *The Great Tyrconnel: a Chapter in Anglo-Irish Relations* (Cork and Dublin, 1972), pp. 221–2;

15 O'Kelly, p. 10; *Great Victory*, p. 2; Hamilton, pp. 46–7; McCarmick, p. 66.

Notes to Chapter 10: A tired old man

1 *HMC, Finch MSS.*, ii. pp. 216–19, Dr Gorges's Considerations concerning the Government of Ireland, 13–15 June 1689.

2 *Correspondence of the Family of Hatton*, ed. E. M. Thompson (Camden Society, London, 1878), ii. p. 137.

3 *A Letter from an Officer belonging to the Ordnance on Board the Fleet lying in the Bay before the Isle of Man, giving an Account of the Duke of Schomberg's Arrival and Landing of the Forces under his Command at Carrick Fergus* (London, 1689), pp. 1–2; Story, pp. 6–7; *History of the Wars in Ireland*, p. 40; *An Exact Account of the Duke of Schombergs Happy Voyage from Highlake to his Safe Arrival at Carrick-Fergus, with the Particulars of the Engagement with Three French Men of War in that Bay* (London, 1689), pp. 1–2; James Nihell, *A Journal of the Most Remarkable Occurrences that happened between his Majesty's Army; and the Forces under the Command of Mareschal de Schomberg, in Ireland, from the 12th of August to the 23rd of October 1689* (Dublin, 1689), p. 3; Bellingham, pp. 80–1.

4 Hamilton, pp. 47–8; McCarmick, p. 66; *History of the Wars in Ireland*, pp. 38–9.

5 Hamilton, pp. 48–51; McCarmick, pp. 66–7; *A True and Particular Account of the Total Defeat of Coll. Sarsfield and his Party not far from Bellishannon* (London, 1689), pp. 1–2.

6 *HMC, Ormonde MSS.*, o.s. ii. pp. 407–8; n.s. viii. pp. 368–9; D'Avaux, pp. 450–4.

7 *A Relation of what most Remarkably happened during the Last Campaign in Ireland betwixt His Majesties Army Royal, and the Forces of the Prince of Orange, sent to Joyn the Rebels, under the Command of the Count de Schomberg* (Dublin, 1689), p. 3.

8 Paul M. Kerrigan, 'Seventeenth-century fortifications, forts and garrisons in Ireland: a preliminary list', *Irish Sword*, xiv. (1980), p. 7. There is some uncertainty on this point. Belfast had been fortified in 1642 and maps of these earthworks were printed in 1660 and 1685. The Rev. Story's map of Belfast Lough, published in 1693, clearly shows the city protected by simple fortifications on three sides (Gerald Müller and Gavin Williamson, 'Fortification of Belfast', *Irish Sword*, xix. (1995), pp. 306–23; Story, *Continuation*, p. 8).

9   Story, pp. 8–10; *History of the Wars in Ireland*, pp. 43–5; Leslie, p. 161; *A Relation of what most Remarkably happened*, p. 4; *A True and Impartial Account of Their Majesties Army in Ireland*, pp. 1–2; *An Account of the Joyning of Major-General Kirk's Forces with Duke Schomberg's and the taking the Town and Castle of Carrickfergus: As also an Account of the Irish Army under K. James* (London, 1689), pp. 1–2; *An Account of the Great Defeat that Major General Kirk gave the Irish Forces near Charlemont, under the Command of Lord Strabane and Colonel Gordon O-Neal* (London, 1689), p.1; Gilbert, p. 87; Nihell, pp. 3–4; D'Avaux, pp. 462, 467.

10 Ingoldsby's battalion had not performed well during the siege and the commander of its grenadier company, Captain Lewis, was cashiered for cowardice (*Bellingham*, p. 81).

11 Story, p. 11.

12 Dalrymple, ii. Part 2, p. 168; Berwick, i. pp. 56–7.

13 *HMC, Ormonde MSS.*, o.s. ii. p. 412; Ranke, vi. pp. 136–7; Clarke, ii. p. 373; *A Relation of what most Remarkably happened*, pp. 4–5; *A Full and True Account of His Grace Duke Schomberg's marching towards Dublin, and of the Preparations the late King James is making to oppose him* (London, 1689), pp. 1–2; *Stevens*, pp. 78–9.

14 Pádraig Lenihan and Geraldine Sheridan, 'A Swiss Soldier in Ireland, 1689–90', *Irish Studies Review*, xiii. (2005), pp. 483–4; J. F. A. Kazner, *Leben Friedrichs von Schomberg oder Schoenberg* (Mannheim, 1789), ii. pp. 305–6.

15 *A Relation of what most Remarkably happened*, pp. 5–6; Nihell, p. 4; Berwick, i. p. 57.

16 *HMC, 5th Report*, p. 198.

17 Richard Kane, *Campaigns of King William and Queen Anne, from 1689 to 1712* (Dublin, 1748), p. 4; Parker, p. 16.

18 Story, pp. 13–15; *History of the Wars in Ireland*, pp. 46–8; Gilbert, p. 87; Parker, pp. 17–18; Lenihan and Sheridan, p. 484; *Bellingham*, p. 83.

19 Clarke, ii. p. 379.

20 Parker, pp. 16, 18.

21 *An Exact Account of the Royal Army under the Command of His Grace Duke Schomberg with the Particulars of a Great Defeat given to the Irish Army near Boyle* (London, 1689), p. 2; *HMC, Downshire MSS.*, 1.i. pp. 316–17; Ranke, vi. p. 138; Story, pp. 25–6. Wildly inaccurate accounts of the Battle of Boyle occur in *History of the Wars in Ireland*, pp. 48–9 and *An Account of the Great Success and Victory that the Garrison in Sligo has obtained over the Irish Army* (London, 1689), pp. 1–2.

22 *History of the Wars in Ireland*, pp. 51–2; McCarmick, pp. 27–8.

23 Ranke, vi. p. 137; Gilbert, pp. 87–8; Clarke, ii. p. 379; Nihell, pp. 4–5; *Stevens*, pp. 80–1.

24 McCarmick, p. 67.

25 *Bellingham*, p. 85; *HMC, Frankland-Russell-Astley MSS.*, p. 73.

26 The detachment comprised Henry Luttrell's Regiment of Horse, Sir Neill O'Neill's Dragoons and the infantry battalions of Oliver O'Gara and Charles Moore (Clarke, ii. pp. 381–2).

27 *Bellingham*, p. 85; *A Relation of what most Remarkably happened*, pp. 8ff; BL Add. MSS. 38,145, f. 1; Clarke, ii. pp. 379–80.

28 Story, pp. 22–3; *Their Majesties Army in Ireland*, 21 September 1689; *A Relation of what most Remarkably happened*, pp. 8–9; Gilbert, pp. 88–9; *A Letter from Duke Schomberge's Camp, giving an Account of the Condition of the English and Irish Army* (London, 1689), pp. 1–2; Ranke, vi. pp. 137–8; Nihell, pp. 5–6; Parker, p. 18; *Stevens*, p. 82; *Bellingham*, p. 85.

29 Luttrell, *Historical Relation*, ii. p. 508; *A Relation of what most Remarkably happened*, p. 10; Story, p. 24.

30 *London Gazette*, No. 2,496, 9/19 Oct. 1689. Richard Kane, who was at Dundalk, says that

many of these Roman Catholics had deserted from the French Brigade in the Jacobite Army in order to infiltrate the Huguenot regiments (*Campaigns*, p. 5). A Swiss volunteer in Caillemotte's Huguenot regiment does not mention this incident ('Journal de Jean-Francois De Morsier', *Soldats Suisses au service étranger*, ed. A. Jullien (Geneva, 1908–19), pp. 87–105).

31   *The History of the Wars in Ireland*, pp. 49–50; *Great and Good News*, p. 1; Dalton, iii. pp. 118–20; *D'Avaux*, p. 495; Nihell, pp. 6–7; Parker, pp. 18–19.

32   Story, p. 72.

33   BL Add. MSS. 9,731, ff. 31, 51.

34   *HMC, Ormonde MSS.*, n.s. viii. p. 371; *A Relation of what most Remarkably happened*, p. 11.

35   Nihell, p. 6.

36   *Stevens*, p. 83; *Bellingham*, p. 87.

Notes to Chapter 11: *Sligo and Dundalk*

1   Dalton, *Irish Army*, pp. 91–2; John Childs, *The Army of Charles II* (London, 1976), p. 237.

2   It is unclear who was in overall command: seniority by date of commission would have determined the issue. Russell succeeded Lord Delamere as colonel of horse in 1689 but the precise date of his commission has not been found; Lloyd's commission as colonel of horse was dated 20 June 1689.

3   *A Relation of what passed in Connaught between His Majesties Forces under the Command of Brigadier Sarsfield, and the Rebels led by the Lord Weyer, the Colonels Floyd, Russel, &c. upon the Army Decamping from Allardstwon* (1689), pp. 1–3; McCarmick, p. 68; Story, pp. 33–5; *History of the Wars in Ireland*, pp. 53–5; *A Relation of what most Remarkably happened*, p. 12; *A Full and True Account of all the Remarkable Actions and Things that have happened in the North of Ireland since 15th of November to the 17th Instant. And particularly of the Actions at Sligo, the Newry and Charlemont* (London, 1689), pp. 1–2; Simms, *War and Politics*, pp. 172–4. Neither did Russell's career prosper. His regiment of horse was disbanded on 20 March 1691and he was not re-employed. He died in 1700.

4   Charlemont Fort was burned down in 1922, although it is still possible to trace the outline on the ground.

5   *A Relation of what most Remarkably happened*, p. 12; *An Account of the Town and Castle of Charlemont in Ireland, Besieged by a Detached Body of the Duke of Schombergs Army under the Command of Lieutenant General Douglas* (London, 1689), p. 1; *D'Avaux*, pp. 92–3, 631.

6   BL Egerton MSS. 3340, f. 89.

7   Dalrymple, ii. Part 2, pp. 169–70.

8   Nihell, p. 7; *Stevens*, p. 83.

9   BL Add. MSS. 38,145, ff. 2–3; Nihell, pp. 7–8; *Stevens*, pp. 84–5.

10   Ranke, vi. pp. 138–9; *Stevens*, p. 85; *Their Majesties Army in Ireland*, 6 October 1689; Dalrymple, ii. Part 2, pp. 172–3; *An Exact Account of the Royal Army*, p. 1.

11   Hastings's battalion had been badly mauled at Killiecrankie, 27 July 1689 (Hopkins, *Glencoe*, pp. 156–60); 'Longford Papers', pp. 68–9, William Smith to John Ellis, 25 October 1689, Belfast.

12   Dalrymple, ii. Part 2, pp. 173–5, Schomberg to William, 12 October 1689.

13   *A Relation of what most Remarkably happened*, pp. 13–14.

14   BL Egerton MSS. 3340, f. 91.

15   *HMC, Downshire MSS.*, l.i., p. 319; *Bellingham*, p. 92; *Stevens*, pp. 87–8.

16 Story, pp. 32–5; *Stevens*, p. 89; *Bellingham*, p. 93.

17 Lenihan and Sheridan, pp. 484–5; *Bellingham*, pp. 93–5.

18 'Longford Papers', pp. 69–70; Story, p. 38.

19 Story, pp. 47–8; Gilbert, pp. 90–1; *History of the Wars in Ireland*, pp. 55–6; *Full and True Account*, p. 2; *Their Majesties Army in Ireland*, 8–9 December 1689; *HMC, Downshire MSS.*, 1. i. p. 325; *FIC*, no. 655.

20 Story, p. 48; *History of the Wars in Ireland*, pp. 56–9.

21 BL Add. MSS. 38,145, ff. 3–4; *Full and True Account*, p. 2; *HMC, Ormonde MSS.*, n.s. viii. p. 376; Story, pp. 48–51; *Stevens*, p. 92.

22 Gilbert, p. 88.

23 Dalrymple, ii. Part 2, pp. 178–9.

24 Story, pp. 41–6; Parker, pp. 20–1.

25 Story, pp. 38–40.

26 Gilbert, pp. 88–9; O'Kelly, pp. 11–12; *D'Avaux*, pp. 598–609.

Notes to Chapter 12: Winter operations, 1689–90

1   *CSPD 1689–90*, p. 440.

2   Tadhg Ó hAnnracháin, 'The Strategic Involvement of Continental Powers in Ireland, 1596–1691', in Lenihan, *Conquest*, pp. 44ff.; *CSPD 1689–90*, pp. 444–5, 455; NA SP 8/6, f. 111; Gilbert, p. 90.

3   LBRT, pp. 108–9, 120–1; O'Kelly, pp. 11–12.

4   Ó hAnnracháin, 'Strategic Involvement', pp. 45–8; O'Kelly, pp. ix–x; *FIC*, i. pp. xlii–xliii.

5   *Transactions*, pp. 58–9.

6   O'Kelly, pp. 12–19; Gilbert, pp. 89–94; *Stevens*, pp. 91–2.

7   BL Egerton MSS. 3340, ff. 98–9; Story, pp. 51–2; *An Exact Account of the Late Action at the Town of Dundalk against the Irish by Their Majesties Forces commanded by Sir John Lanier* (London, 1690), p. 2; Gilbert, pp. 91–2.

8   Story, pp. 52–3.

9   *CSPD 1689–90*, p. 485.

10 Story, pp. 53–4; Gilbert, pp. 92–3; *Dundalk*, pp. 1–2; *CSPD 1689–90*, pp. 452–3, 534; *A Full and True Account of the Late Brave Action Performed by the Inniskilling-Men and some English and Dutch Forces under the Command of Coll. Woseley against a Great Body of the Irish, under the Command of the Duke of Berwick, at the Town of Cavan* (London, 1690), pp. 1–2; *History of the Wars in Ireland*, pp. 65–9, Wolseley to Schomberg, 12 and 14 February 1690, Belturbet; *The Anglo-Celt Cavan*, 1 Sept. 1848; *HMC, Ormonde MSS.*, n.s. viii. p. 376; *Their Majesties Army in Ireland*, 12 March 1690; *FIC*, nos. 675–8; *Stevens*, pp. 99–100; Berwick, i. pp. 61–2.

11 *CSPD 1689–90*, pp. 462, 490–1, 498; *Dundalk*, pp. 1–2; Story, pp. 55–6; *History of the Wars in Ireland*, p. 70.

12 *Great and Good News both from Scotland and Ireland, being a Faithful and Particular Account of a late Terrible Engagement betwixt Major-General Kirk and the Duke of Berwick and Collonel Sarsfield* (London, 1690), pp. 1–2. There is no corroboration of this story but it does not appear to be either a conflation of other events or a garbled account of a known incident.

13 The very high ratio of officers reflects the large number of reformadoes in the Huguenot regiments, all anxious to make an impression. Relief of winter boredom may also have been a factor.

14 Story, pp. 56–7; *History of the Wars in Ireland*, pp. 72–3.

15 Danaher and Simms, pp. 1–14; *HMC, Downshire MSS.*, 1. i. pp. 319–20; *CSPD 1689–90*, p. 442; *CTP*, pp. 76–100; *HMC, Finch MSS.*, ii. p. 223; *HMC, Finch MSS.*, iii. p. 428.

16 *An Abstract of Three Letters from Belfast to a Person in London* (London, 1690), p. 1–2.

17 The surviving soldiers from Drogheda's, a Welsh battalion raised in Brecknock and Abergavenny, were drafted into the battalion of the late Sir Thomas Gower. Drogheda was then appointed to command this battalion (Dalton, iii. p. 73).

18 Danaher and Simms, pp. 31–2.

19 *CSPD 1689–90*, pp. 441, 558, 568; *CSPD 1690–1*, p. 26; NA SP 8/8, ff. 333–8.

20 Ferguson, pp. 69–70.

21 O'Callaghan, p. 8; Danaher and Simms, p. 61; *Cliff and Emismack*, pp. 1–2; *HMC, Ormonde MSS.*, n.s. viii. pp. 384–5; Armstrong Starkey, *War in the Age of Enlightenment, 1700–1789* (Westport, CT, 2003), pp. 21–2; Story, pp. 24–5.

22 *CSPD 1689–90*, pp. 509–10; O'Callaghan, p. 8; Gilbert, pp. 89, 92; *Transactions*, pp. 19–21, 58–9; *Killishandrea*, p. 2.

23 *CSPD 1689–90*, pp. 571–2; *HMC, Ormonde MSS.*, o.s. ii. pp. 426–7; n.s. viii. pp. 364, 379, 380–5; Story, p. 57; *History of the Wars in Ireland*, pp. 73–5; *Cliff and Emismack*, pp. 1–2; Danaher and Simms, pp. 33–4.

24 *History of the Wars in Ireland*, pp. 75–7; Danaher and Simms, pp. 35–6; *Killishandrea*, p. 2; Story, pp. 57–8; *CSPD 1689–90*, pp. 556–7.

25 A coarse, woollen cloth.

26 *Transactions*, pp. 56–7; Story, pp. 58–9; *HMC, Ormonde MSS.*, n.s. viii. pp. 380–1; *History of the Wars in Ireland*, pp. 78–81.

27 *CSPD 1689–90*, pp. 566–7; D'Alton, p. 821.

28 *CSPD 1689–90*, pp. 561, 563, 566–67; *CSPD 1690–1*, pp. 5, 8–9, 15; *Great News from Scotland and Ireland giving an Account of the Death of the Chief of the Rebels Clans in Scotland, of the State of King James in Ireland, and of the Divisions betwixt the Irish and French Generals, in a Letter from Edenborough* (London, 1690), p. 2; LBRT, pp. 119–20, 122–3, 128; Gilbert, pp. 93–4; *HMC, Ormonde MSS.*, n.s. viii. p. 381; *History of the Wars in Ireland*, pp. 81–4; Story, pp. 59–64; *The most acceptable and faithful Account of the Capitulation the Irish Governor of Charlemont made to D. Schonbergh's Forces* (London, 1690), p. 1; *Articles of War agreed upon between his Grace the Duke of Schonberg and Teige O Regan, for the Surrender of Charlemont, the Twelfth of May, 1690* (London, 1690), p. 1; *FIC*, no. 837.

29 *History of the Wars in Ireland*, pp. 87–9; Story, p. 64; McCarmick, p. 43; Davies, p. 114; *CSPD 1690–1*, p. 13; *FIC*, nos. 836, 839.

30 Danaher and Simms, p. 40.

Notes to Chapter 13: The Battle of the Boyne

1 *History of the Wars in Ireland*, pp. 109–12.

2 Story, p. 66; *A True Relation of the Battle of the Boyne in Ireland fought by his Majesty King William in the Year 1690, without Observation or Reflection* (London, 1700), p. 1; *HMC, Leyborne-Popham MSS.*, pp. 271–2; Danaher and Simms, p. 40.

3 LBRT, pp. 126–8, Tyrconnell to Queen Mary, 20 May 1690, Dublin Castle.

4 Gilbert, pp. 95–7.

5 *A True and Perfect Journal of the Affairs in Ireland since His Majesties Arrival in that Kingdom* (London, 1690), pp. 1–2; *HMC, Ormonde MSS.*, n.s. viii. pp. 384–5; *HMC, Finch MSS.*, ii. p. 298.

6 Gilbert, pp. 94–5.

7   *True and Perfect Journal*, pp. 1–2; *A Journal of The Three Months Royal Campaign of His Majesty in Ireland, together with a True and Perfect Diary of the Siege of Lymerick* (London, 1690), p. 11; *HMC, Finch MSS.*, ii. pp. 320–1; *Stevens*, pp. 115–16.

8   Gilbert, pp. 96–7; *Royal Campaign*, p. 8; Story, p. 68; *HMC, Ormonde MSS.*, n.s. viii. pp. 385–6; *HMC, Finch MSS.*, ii. pp. 310–12; *FIC*, no. 866; *Stevens*, p. 118; D'Alton, pp. 108–9; *Bellingham*, p. 128.

9   Story, pp. 69–70; *Royal Campaign*, p. 8; *History of the Wars in Ireland*, pp. 115–16; *Davies*, pp. 123–4; Ranke, vi. p. 140; *Bellingham*, p. 125; *Stevens*, p. 119.

10 LBRT, pp. 129–33; *HMC, Finch MSS.*, ii. pp. 310–12; Pádraig Lenihan, *1690: The Battle of the Boyne* (Stroud, 2003), p. 129; *Stevens*, p. 119.

11 *Davies*, pp. 122–3; Story, pp. 70–1; *Royal Campaign*, p. 8; *History of the Wars in Ireland*, p. 116; *HMC, Finch MSS.*, ii. pp. 320–1; Ranke, vi. pp. 140–1; Danaher and Simms, p. 41; *Stevens*, p. 119; *Bellingham*, p. 128.

12 Ranke, vi. p. 141; *Royal Campaign*, p. 12; Gilbert, pp. 97–8; *HMC, Ormonde MSS.*, n.s. viii. p. 386; *Stevens*, p. 120.

13 'The Battle of the Boyne: Jean Payan de La Fouleresse to Christian V of Denmark, 2 July 1690', ed. L. Barbé, *Notes and Queries*, 5th series, viii. (1877) p. 21; *HMC, Finch MSS.*, ii. p. 326, Sir Robert Southwell to Earl of Nottingham, 1 July 1690, camp near Drogheda.

14 *HMC, Finch MSS.*, ii. p. 327; Parker, pp. 21–2; Lenihan and Sheridan, p. 486; *Stevens*, p. 120; *Bellingham*, p. 130.

15 *History of the Wars in Ireland*, pp. 116–18; *HMC, Leyborne-Popham MSS.*, p. 272; *Royal Campaign*, pp. 8–9; Story, pp. 73–7; Fouleresse to Christian V, 2 July 1690, p. 22.

16 Clarke, ii. p. 394.

17 Captain Robert Parker was one of the few contemporaries to have remarked upon the contrast between James's martial reputation and his conduct at the Boyne (Parker, p. 24).

18 Story, pp. 77–8; Gilbert, pp. 98–103; Ranke, vi. pp. 141–3. In his memoirs, James says that he instructed the left to shadow Portland and Schomberg prior to ordering the baggage to Dublin (Clarke, ii. p. 396).

19 Story, p. 78.

20 Or 09:30 (Fouleresse to Christian V, 2 July 1690, p. 22).

21 About 200 m.

22 Mark Napier, *Memorials and Letters illustrative of the Life and Times of John Graham of Claverhouse, Viscount Dundee* (Edinburgh, 1859–62), iii. pp. 715–18; Douglas to Queensberry, 7 July 1690.

23 Story, pp. 78–85; Gilbert, pp. 98–103; Danaher and Simms, pp. 42–6, 60–6; *HMC, Leyborne-Popham MSS.*, pp. 273–4; *An Exact Account of the King's March to Ardee and of his forcing the Irish to abandon the Pass of the River Boyne* (London, 1690), p. 1; *Royal Campaign*, pp. 9–10; *History of the Wars in Ireland*, pp. 118–23; *A Relation of the Victory obtained by the King in Ireland at the Passage of the Boyne on the First Day of this Instant July 1690 and of the Surrender of Drogheda* (London, 1690), pp. 1–2; *True and Perfect Journal*, pp. 5–7; *Stevens*, pp. 120–30; Fouleresse to Christian V, 2 July 1690, pp. 21–3; Napier, *Claverhouse*, iii. pp. 715–18; *HMC, Finch MSS.*, ii. pp. 328–31; Clarke, ii. pp. 394–404; Abel Boyer, *The History of King William the Third* (London, 1702–3), ii. pp. 184–92; Parker, pp. 21–4; Lenihan and Sheridan, pp. 486–7; *Bellingham*, pp. 130–1; *FIC*, nos. 187, 629, 872–7, 1035, 1874, 1878, 1931, 1952, 1961, 1966, 1967; Berwick, i. pp. 63–6, 68. Generally see, Pádraig Lenihan, *1690, Battle of the Boyne* (Stroud, 2003).

24 O'Kelly, pp. 19–21, 114–15; Bod. Lib. Rawlinson MSS. D.21, f. 11; *Royal Campaign*, p. 15; *HMC, Finch MSS.*, ii. pp. 328, 336–7; *Stevens*, pp. 122–3.

25 *A Letter from Major-General Kirk in Ireland to his Friend here in London* (London, 1690), p. 1.

26 Story, p. 87.

Notes to Chapter 14: From Dublin to Limerick

1 *HMC, Ormonde MSS.*, n.s. viii. p. 386; Bod. Lib. Rawlinson MSS. D.21, f. 16; *HMC, Finch MSS.*, ii. pp. 336–7, 352, 366, 371–3; *FIC*, no. 874.

2 *HMC, Leyborne-Popham MSS.*, p. 274; *True and Perfect Journal*, pp. 7–8; *Royal Campaign*, p. 12; Gilbert, pp. 102–8; O'Kelly, pp. 23–5.

3 Story, pp. 92–4, 111–12; *Royal Campaign*, pp. 15–19; Gilbert, pp. 105–6.

4 Story, pp. 89–90; *History of the Wars in Ireland*, pp. 123–5; Gilbert, p. 105; *Royal Campaign*, pp. 10–11; *Relation of the Boyne*, p. 2; Leslie, p. 161; *Davies*, p. 125; Danaher and Simms, p. 43; *Great News from Ireland, being an Account of the Late King James's Quitting that Kingdom and going for France* (London, 1690), pp. 1–2; *HMC, Finch MSS.*, ii. pp. 337–8.

5 *True and Perfect Journal*, pp. 8–11; Story, p. 91; *History of the Wars in Ireland*, pp. 125–8; *Royal Campaign*, pp. 13–14; *HMC, Ormonde MSS.*, n.s. viii. pp. 386–8; Davies, p. 125.

6 *History of the Wars in Ireland*, pp. 128–30; *HMC, Leyborne-Popham MSS.*, p. 274; *Royal Campaign*, pp. 14–15; Story, p. 91; *HMC, Finch MSS.*, ii. pp. 345–6; *D'Avaux*, pp. 620–3.

7 Davies, pp. 125–6; *HMC, Finch MSS.*, ii. pp. 339–40, 343.

8 Dalton, *Scots Army*, pp. 78–87; Childs, *Nobles, Gentlemen*, p. 27; *CSPD 1689–90*, pp. 557–8, 567; *CSPD 1690–1*, p. 8; Gilbert, p. 131; P. W. J. Riley, *King William and the Scottish Politicians* (Manchester, 1979), p. 58; Napier, *Claverhouse*, iii. pp. 431–2, 472–7, 480–2; John Lauder of Fountainhall, *Historical Notices of Scottish Affairs* (Edinburgh, 1848), ii., 13 October 1684.

9 *An Account of the Nature, Situation, Natural Strength and Ancient and Modern Fortifications of the Several Cities and Garrison-Towns in Ireland that are still possessed by the Forces of the Late King James* (London, 1690), p. 5; *HMC, Ormonde MSS.*, n.s. viii. p. 317; Story, p. 101.

10 *Stevens*, pp. 151–63.

11 Gilbert, pp. 106–7; *FIC*, no. 1032; O'Kelly, p. 27; Story, pp. 99–106. The Reverend Story, chaplain to the Earl of Drogheda's infantry battalion, was present throughout Douglas's excursion to Athlone.

12 The Reverend Rowland Davies, chaplain of Meinhard, Count Schomberg's regiment of horse, accompanied the cavalry.

13 Wheeler, 'Logistics', pp. 177–207.

14 *Stevens*, pp. 131–44.

15 Danaher and Simms, pp. 47–50; *Royal Campaign*, pp. 16–17; *History of the Wars in Ireland*, pp. 111–13; *Davies*, pp. 127–9; Story, pp. 107–9; *HMC, Ormonde MSS.*, n.s. viii. p. 314; *HMC, Finch MSS.*, ii. pp. 379–80, 383, 387–8; *HMC, Lonsdale MSS.*, p. 102.

16 Davies, pp. 120–31; *A Letter from an English Officer in his Majesty's Army in Ireland giving a True Account of the Progress of Affairs in that Kingdom: Together with what past at the Surrender of Waterford and Duncannon: And of his Majesty's March towards Limmerick* (London, 1690), pp. 1–2; Story, pp. 109–11; Danaher and Simms, pp. 48–9; *Royal Campaign*, pp. 17–21.

17 *HMC, Finch MSS.*, ii. p. 397.

18 *Stevens*, pp. 163–4.

19 *Royal Campaign*, pp. 21–2; *Davies*, pp. 131–5; *Great News From Lymerick in Ireland: A Full and True Account of the State and Siege of that City, by His Majesties Forces, commanded by*

Count Solms, and Lieutenant General Douglas. With a particular Relation of the Surrendering of Cork and Yaughall, by the Irish (London, 1690); Story, p. 112; *History of the Wars in Ireland*, pp. 117–19; O'Kelly, p. 28; Danaher and Simms, p. 51; *HMC, Finch MSS.*, ii. pp. 387, 406–9; *Stevens*, p. 165.

20 *Royal Campaign*, p. 22; Story, p. 112; *Davies*, p. 135; *The Approach and Signal Victory of K. Williams Forces over the Irish Army encamped round Limmrick* (London, 1690), pp. 1–2.

21 *HMC, Ormonde MSS.*, n.s. viii. pp. 316–17; *An Account of the Nature*, p. 3; Story, pp. 116–18; Gilbert, p. 109; James Burke, 'Siege Warfare in Seventeenth-Century Ireland', in Lenihan, *Conquest*, pp. 277–8; *Stevens*, pp. 147–51.

22 Gilbert, p. 112; *FIC*, nos. 925, 1058, 1059.

23 'Siege of Limerick: Jean Payen de la Fouleresse to Christian V of Denmark, 24 August 1690', ed. L. Barbé, *Notes and Queries*, 5th series, viii. (1877) p. 121; *HMC, Finch MSS.*, ii. pp. 406–7, 409; *Stevens*, pp. 166–8.

24 Story, pp. 112–16; *Royal Campaign*, pp. 22–3; *History of the Wars in Ireland*, pp. 120–1; *Davies*, p. 135; *Limmrick*, pp. 1–2; Danaher and Simms, pp. 52–7; *A Full and True Account of the Two Great Victories lately obtained before Lymerick by K. William's Forces over the French and Irish Rebels which were commanded by D. Tyrconnel and General Lauson* (London, 1690), p. 2.

Notes to Chapter 15: The first siege of Limerick

1 Gilbert, pp. 112–13; O'Kelly, pp. 29–30; *Davies*, p. 136; *Great News from Ireland: An Account of the King's Royal Camp before the City of Limmerick, and of a Late Defeat of the Enemy There* (London, 1690), p. 2; *HMC, Finch MSS.*, ii. p. 407.

2 Kane, *Campaigns*, p. 8; Parker, pp. 26–7.

3 Fouleresse to Christian V, p. 121; *HMC, Finch MSS.*, ii. pp. 414–15.

4 Wauchope, *Sarsfield*, pp. 16–44; Gilbert, p. 114; Shirley, p. 87; O'Kelly, pp. 30–3; *Davies*, pp. 136–8; *Royal Campaign*, pp. 23–4; *History of the Wars in Ireland*, pp. 122–3; Story, p. 116–22; *HMC, Finch MSS.*, ii. pp. 412–13.

5 *Royal Campaign*, pp. 25–6; *History of the Wars in Ireland*, p. 123; *Davies*, pp. 139–41; Story, pp. 124–32; Danaher and Simms, pp. 58–9, 66–75; *CSPD 1690–1*, p. 106; Gilbert, pp. 115–16, 260–7; O'Kelly, p. 115; Fouleresse to Christian V, 24 August 1690, pp. 121–2; 'Siege of Limerick: Jean Payan de Fouleresse to Christian V of Denmark, 29 August 1690', ed. L. Barbé, *Notes and Queries*, 5th series, viii. (1877), pp. 122–3; *HMC, Finch MSS.*, ii. pp. 416–35; Lenihan and Sheridan, p. 488; *Stevens*, pp. 177–81; Berwick, i. pp. 69–71. Robert Parker, who was present in the Earl of Meath's infantry regiment, one of the supporting battalions on the right, had a markedly different recollection. He says that Cutts's grenadiers did not attack into the breach but veered off towards St John's Gate which they found shut and barred. However, this view is uncorroborated (Parker, p. 27).

6 O'Kelly, pp. 34–43; Gilbert, pp. 117–18; *HMC, Finch MSS.*, ii. pp. 434–5, 471–5.

7 Story, p. 133; *HMC, Finch MSS.*, ii. pp. 474–5, 478–80.

8 Sydney was appointed secretary of state in England in December 1690. Thereafter the weight of Irish administration was carried by Coningsby and Porter.

9 *Stevens*, pp. 184–5.

10 Story, pp. 132–40; Gilbert, pp. 116–18; *Davies*, pp. 141–6; *A True and Faithful Account of the Present State and Condition of the Kingdom of Ireland* (London, 1690), p. 1; *CSPD 1690–1*, pp. 111–12, 114–15, 118–19, 120–1; *History of the Wars in Ireland*, pp. 125–6; *A Full and True Account of Two Famous and Signal Victories Obtained by Their Majesties Forces over the Irish Rebels: The First over General Sarsfield, near the Shannon, Raising the Siege of Bir*

... *The Second over Four Thousand Raparees* (London, 1691), p. 2; Danaher and Simms, pp. 58–9, 66–77; *Royal Campaign*, pp. 26–7; O'Kelly, pp. 34–6, 39–43, 102, 260–7; Burke, 'Siege Warfare', pp. 278–80; Wauchope, *Sarsfield*, pp. 154–63; *HMC, Finch MSS.*, ii. p. 450; *FIC*, no. 1062; Berwick, i. p. 77.

Notes to Chapter 16: Cork and Kinsale

1   Simms, *Jacobite Ireland*, pp. 174–5; *CSPD 1690–1*, pp. 38–9, 106, 108–9; *HMC, Finch MSS.*, ii. pp. 414–15, 438, 440, 457. In general see, G. S. Cox, 'Marlborough in Ireland – Last Sieges of Cork and Kinsale', *An Cosantóir*, viii. (1948); J. Jordan, 'The Siege of Kinsale, 1690', *An Cosantóir*, xv. (1954–5); J. G. Simms, 'Marlborough's Siege of Cork, 1690', *Irish Sword*, 9 (1969–70) and *War and Politics in Ireland, 1649–1720* (London, 1986), pp. 117–27; *HMC, Finch MSS.*, ii. p. 457.

2   *HMC, Ormonde MSS.*, n.s. viii. pp. 314–15; *An Account of the Nature*, p. 6; D'Alton, pp. 915–16.

3   Danaher and Simms, pp. 78–80; *CSPD 1690–1*, pp. 106, 108–9, 127; *The Glorious Conquest: or the Repeated Victory of the Right Honourable the Earl of Marlborough: First in taking the City of Cork; Secondly, Kings-Sale; and the strong adjacent Forts* (London, 1690); Davies, p. 148; *History of the Wars in Ireland*, p. 127; Story, pp. 140–1; Gilbert, p. 119.

4   *History of the Wars in Ireland*, pp. 127–8; Davies, pp. 148–56; Story, pp. 141–3; *CSPD 1690–1*, pp. 130–2; Gilbert, pp. 119–29; Danaher and Simms, pp. 83–4, 151–2; *A Full and True Relation of the Taking Cork, by the Right Honorable the Earl of Marlborough, Lieut: Gen. of their Majesties Forces: Together with the Articles of their Surrender* (London, 1690); Leslie, p. 162; Dalton, iii. p. 321; *HMC, Finch MSS.*, ii. pp. 470–1, 475–6; *FIC*, nos. 1242, 1322, 1323, 2116, 2117.

5   *HMC, Ormonde MSS.*, n.s. viii. pp. 315–16; *An Account of the Nature*, p. 5; 'Manuscripts of the Old Corporation of Kinsale', ed. Edward MacLysaght, *Analecta Hibernica*, xv. (1944), p. 179.

6   *History of the Wars in Ireland*, pp. 129–30; Gilbert, pp. 120–1; Story, pp. 144–7; *CSPD 1690–1*, pp. 140, 146; Danaher and Simms, pp. 84–9; *An Account of the Taking of the New Fort in Kinsale by the Forces of the Earl of Marlborough* (London, 1690); *HMC, Finch MSS.*, ii. pp. 471–2, 475–7; *FIC*, nos. 1062, 1063.

7   O'Kelly, pp. 46–55; Gilbert, pp. 126–7; *FIC*, pp. xxxviii–xl; Berwick, i. pp. 78–83.

Notes to Chapter 17: A war of posts and ambuscades

1   *FIC*, nos. 1988, 2092; Stevens, p. 62.

2   *CSPD 1690–1*, pp. 399–402, 418; Story, pp. 75, 82, 83, 148, 177; O'Callaghan, pp. 6–7; Michelburne, pp. 19–20; Davies, p. 160; Story, *Continuation*, pp. 58, 177; Roger B. Manning, *An Apprenticeship in Arms: the Origins of the British Army, 1585–1702* (Oxford, 2006), pp. 12–14.

3   Bristow's sub-standard performance did not adversely affect his career. He retained his commission until disbandment in 1698, when he was placed on the half-pay list. In June 1701 he was appointed lieutenant colonel of the Earl of Donegal's Foot and died two years later on active service in the West Indies.

4   Story, pp. 148–53; Bod. Lib. Rawlinson MSS. C. 984, f. 85; 'Longford Letters', p. 74; *CSPD 1690–1*, p. 182.

5   *HMC, 4th Report, Appendix, MSS. of Lord de Ros*, p. 317.

6   *HMC, Rutland MSS.*, ii. p. 132.

7 Probably 'petraras', light, swivel-mounted, breech-loading cannon designed for anti-personnel work on board ship, forerunners of the Carronade (John Childs, *Warfare in the Seventeenth Century* (London, 2001), p. 104).

8 Kirke appears to have taken no part in the operation, Lanier acting as field commander.

9 And so it remained. It was still occupied by the Jacobites at the end of the war (*FIC*, no. 1513).

10 Story, pp. 153–8; Danaher and Simms, pp. 93–4; *CSPD 1690*, pp. 191–2, 409–10; *A Relation of Several Signal Victories and Other Considerable Enterprizes lately obtained by Their Majesties' Forces over the Rebels in Ireland* (London, 1691), p. 1; HMC, *Leyborne-Popham MSS.*, pp. 277–8; *Signal Victories*, p. 1; Wauchope, *Sarsfield*, pp. 177–87; HMC, *4th Report, Appendix, MSS. of Lord de Ros*, p. 318; *FIC*, nos. 1238, 1254.

11 HMC, *4th Report, Appendix, MSS. of Lord de Ros*, pp. 317–18; *CSPD 1690–1*, pp. 226–7.

12 *CSPD 1690–1*, p. 152; Danaher and Simms, pp. 90–1; Dalton, iii. p. 119; iv. p. 257; Story, pp. 145–7; O'Kelly, pp. 62–4; Simms, *Jacobite Ireland*, pp. 189–93.

13 Lenihan, 'Strategic Geography', pp. 141–4; Story, pp. 157–8, 162; Story, *Continuation*, p. 51; Danaher and Simms, pp. 94–7; Parker, p. 29; *FIC*, i. p. xliii.

14 Danaher and Simms, p. 97.

15 Story, pp. 157–8, 162; O'Kelly, pp. 64–71; Gilbert, pp. 121, 128–9; Story, *Continuation*, pp. 33–4, 51–6; *Signal Victories*, p. 1; *Siege of Bir*, pp. 1–2; Danaher and Simms, pp. 94–7.

16 Lieutenant Monck's men served as *ad hoc* dragoons throughout 1690 and 1691.

17 Danaher and Simms, p. 99; *CSPD 1690–1*, pp. 264–6, 280–1; Gilbert, p. 129; Story, *Continuation*, pp. 57–60; HMC, *4th Report, Appendix, MSS. of Lord de Ros*, pp. 318–19.

Notes to Chapter 18: Spring, 1691

1 HMC, *4th Report, Appendix, MSS. of Lord de Ros*, p. 319.

2 A French list of March 1691 numbered the Jacobite field army at 25,000 infantry, 2,500 dragoons and 3,000 cavalry. A further 14 weak battalions (9,100 men) and two regiments of horse and dragoons were in garrison (*FIC*, nos. 1461, 1462, 2096).

3 HMC, *4th Report, Appendix, MSS. of Lord de Ros*, pp. 319–20. HMC, *Finch MSS.*, iii. pp. 42–3, 52–4.

4 *An Exact Journal of the Victorious Progress of their Majesties Forces under the Command of Gen. Ginckle, this Summer in Ireland* (London), pp. 2–13; Story, *Continuation*, pp. 59–75; Gilbert, pp.129–30; Danaher and Simms, pp. 101–2, 107–11.

5 Kirke had been promoted on 24 December 1690.

6 *CSPD 1690–1*, pp. 365–6, 373, 393–5, 412, 446, 450–1; Danaher and Simms, pp. 110–13.

7 O'Kelly, pp. 72–4; Story, *Continuation*, pp. 75–81; *Ginckle*, pp. 13–14; *CSPD 1690–1*, pp. 373, 378, 385–7, 389–95; Danaher and Simms, pp. 112–13.

8 Michelburne, pp. 1–2.

9 Story, *Continuation*, pp. 81–5; *Ginckle*, p. 1.

Notes to Chapter 19: Ballymore and Athlone

1 HMC, *Finch MSS.*, iii. p. 10; John Mackay, *The Life of Lieutenant-General Hugh Mackay of Scoury* (London, 1842), pp. 141–2.

2 Wauchope, *Sarsfield*, pp. 195–6; *CSPD 1690–1*, pp. 412–13, 418; *An Account of the Taking of the Fort of Ballymore, within ten miles of Athlone, on Monday the eight of June, 1691* (Edinburgh, 1691), p. 1; Story, *Continuation*, pp. 86–93; *Ginckle*, pp. 15–16; Gilbert,

pp. 130–1, 272–3; O'Kelly, p. 74; Danaher and Simms, p. 114; Boyer, ii. p. 256; Kane, *Campaigns*, p. 8; *HMC, 4th Report, Appendix, MSS. of Lord de Ros*, p. 320; *FIC*, nos. 1254, 1297, 1486, 1498.

3   Because no replacements had been received, the pontoons damaged at Ballyneety were hurriedly repaired.

4   *Stevens*, pp. 151–62, 199–205; Lenihan, 'Strategic Geography', pp. 141–9.

5   *An Account of the Nature*, p. 5; *FIC*, no. 1484; Story, p. 101; *HMC, Ormonde MSS.*, n.s. viii. p. 317.

6   Story, *Continuation*, pp. 93–8, 111–12; *CSPD 1690–1*, pp. 417–19, 441–2; *An Exact and Particular Account of the Defeat given to the Rebels in the County of Cork by Lord Justice Cox and Coll. Hastings, with 2000 of the Army and Militia of the Lord Lisburn's cutting off a Party of the French and Irish Horse near Lanesborough Pass … in a Letter from Dublin, June the 25th 1691* (London, 1691), p. 1; *Ginckle*, pp. 17–18; Gilbert, pp. 131–4; *An Exact Account of the taking by Storm the English Town of Athlone, June the 21st, in a Letter from Dublin June the 23rd* (London, 1691), pp. 1–2; O'Kelly, pp. 74–6; Danaher and Simms, pp. 114–15; Boyer, ii. pp. 257–9; Kane, *Campaigns*, pp. 8–12; *Mackay*, pp. 143–4.

7   Story, *Continuation*, pp. 110–11; *Defeat given to the Rebels in the County of Cork*, p. 1; *A Diary of the Siege of Athlone … by an Engineer of the Army* (London, 1691), pp. 1–2.

8   Mackay appears to have been in a minority of one in nearly all the councils of war that he attended. Not only was he regarded as old-fashioned but his defeat by Dundee's Highlanders at Killiecrankie in 1689 may have prejudiced opinion of his military judgement.

9   Lenihan, 'Strategic Geography', pp. 144–9; Story, *Continuation*, pp. 99–110, 114–15; *Defeat given to the Rebels in the County of Cork*, p. 1; *Ginckle*, pp. 18–20; *A Faithful Account of the Taking the Bridge, and beating down, the Irish Town of Athlone* (London, 1691), pp. 1–2; Gilbert, pp. 134–7, 139; Danaher and Simms, pp. 115–16; *CSPD 1690–1*, p. 429; *Inchiquin MSS.*, pp. 29–30; *HMC, Leyborne-Popham MSS.*, pp. 278–9; O'Kelly, pp. 76–81; Shirley, p. 137; Leslie, p. 162; Danaher and Simms, pp. 116–18; Boyer, ii. pp. 257–9; *Stevens*, pp. 206–11; *FIC*, nos. 1242, 1484; *Diary of the Siege of Athlone*, pp. 1–8; Kane, *Campaigns*, pp. 10–12; *Mackay*, pp.145–9; *HMC, 4th Report, Appendix, MSS. of Lord de Ros*, pp. 320–1. Captain Robert Parker's account (Parker, pp. 29–34) is garbled. He had received a minor head wound early in the action and the resulting concussion may have affected his subsequent recollection.

Notes to Chapter 20: Aughrim and Galway

1   Story, *Continuation*, pp. 113, 174–7; O'Kelly, pp. 83–5; Gilbert, pp. 136–7.

2   *Stevens*, p. 212.

3   *HMC, MSS. in Various Collections*, viii. p. 571.

4   Danaher and Simms, pp. 116, 118–24; Story, *Continuation*, pp. 115–41, 146–7; *Inchiquin MSS.*, p. 30; *CSPD 1690–1*, pp. 440–2, 444–5; *Ginckle*, pp. 20–2; O'Kelly, pp. 86–90; Gilbert, pp. 136–7; Leslie, pp. 162–4; Donal O'Carroll, 'Change and Continuity in Weapons and Tactics, 1594–1691', in Lenihan, *Conquest*, pp. 249–52; Michelburne, pp. 11–12; 'The Seagrave Papers', ed. Edward MacLysaght, *Analecta Hibernica*, xv. (1944), pp. 358–68; Bod. Lib. Rawlinson MSS. C.439, ff. 232–4; Boyer, ii. pp. 262–7; G. A. Hayes-McCoy, *Irish Battles: a Military History of Ireland* (Belfast, 1990), pp. 254–70; *FIC*, nos. 1502, 1516, 1517; *Stevens*, pp. 212–14; Kane, *Campaigns*, pp. 12–14; Parker, pp. 34–6; *Mackay*, pp. 150–5; Robert Ashton, *The Battle of Aughrim: or the Fall of Monsieur St Ruth. A Tragedy* (Dublin, 1777), pp. v–x; *HMC, 4th Report, Appendix, MSS. of Lord de Ros*, pp. 321–2.

5   *HMC, 3rd Report, MSS. of the Duke of Northumberland*, p. 101.
6   Gilbert, pp. 148–54; Story, *Continuation*, pp. 147–52, 159–74, 179–97; *Ginckle*, pp. 20–3, 25–6; O'Kelly, pp. 90–4; Danaher and Simms, pp. 124–6; *CSPD 1690–1*, pp. 455, 480–1; *A Diary of the Siege and Surrender of Lymerick with the Articles at Large, Both Civil and Military* (London, 1692), pp. 1–3; *HMC, 4th Report, Appendix, MSS. of Lord de Ros*, pp. 322–3.

Notes to Chapter 21: *The curious affair at Sligo, or the banalities of the small war*

1   Michelburne's battalion was very well presented. The officers sported orange sashes, scarlet cloaks, gloves trimmed with gold and silver lace, laced-edged hats, and gold and silver gilt gorgettes. They camped in lined tents complete with fans (*CTB*, pp. 1135–6).
2   Simms, *War and Politics*, pp. 177–8.
3   Estimates of the numerical strength of O'Donnell's Brigade vary. Because of desertions, the incorporation of some regiments (e.g. Merrion's Horse) into the main Jacobite Army, uncertainty about how many of his men remained loyal and the fact that it was always in his interest to exaggerate the size of the brigade, precision is impossible. Sources suggest a maximum of 1,200 and a minimum of 600 in August–September 1691.
4   O'Kelly, pp. 94–6; Michelburne, pp. 3–102; Story, *Continuation*, pp. 151–2, 176–7, 190–1, 202, 213, 222, 234–5; *Ginckle*, pp. 25–6, 30–1; *CSPD 1690–1*, pp. 501, 528; *Diary of the Siege of Lymerick*, pp. 10–11, 14–15; Gilbert, pp. 164–5; *FIC*, nos. 1722, 1725, 1732.

Notes to Chapter 22: *The second siege of Limerick*

1   *Stevens*, pp. 195–6; Burke, 'Siege Warfare', pp. 280–1. After 1691, the English considered erecting a major work beyond Thomond Bridge which would have occupied more space than the acreage of English and Irish Towns combined but estimates proved too expensive.
2   *HMC, 4th Report, Appendix, MSS. of Lord de Ros*, p. 323.
3   *CSPD 1690–1*, pp. 493, 501–2, 515, 516–17, 528; Burke, 'Siege Warfare', pp. 276–89; *Diary of the Siege of Lymerick*, pp. 3–16; Story, *Continuation*, pp. 185–230, 234, 236; Danaher and Simms, pp. 126–35; *Ginckle*, pp. 26–32; O'Kelly, pp. 96–105; Gilbert, pp. 157–78, 282–98; *FIC*, nos. 1599, 1600, 1601, 1608, 1609, 1613, 1614, 1615, 1617, 1618, 1619, 1622, 1623, 1659, 1660, 1696, 1698, 1699, 1701, 1702, 1703, 1704, 1705, 1709–10, 1714, 1715, 1716, 1722, 1723, 1724, 1725, 1726, 1748, 1749; *An Exact Relation of Routing the Irish Army under Sarsfield, and of the Hostages agreed on, in order to a Capitulation for Surrender of Limerick into Their Majesties Hands* (London, 1691), p. 1; *HMC, Leyborne-Popham MSS.*, pp. 279–81; Parker, pp. 37–8; *HMC, 4th Report, Appendix, MSS of Lord de Ros*, pp. 323–4; Simms, *War and Government*, pp. 203–24.

Notes to Chapter 23: *Dispersal*

1   *HMC, 3rd Report, MSS. of the Duke of Northumberland*, p. 101.
2   O'Kelly, pp. 106–11; *Diary of the Siege of Lymerick*, pp. 16–18, 31; Gilbert, pp. 188–92, 298–302, 308–11, 314; Danaher and Simms, pp. 135–8; Story, *Continuation*, pp. 230–3, 236–73, 281–98, 302; *HMC, Stuart MSS.*, i. p. 66.

Select bibliography

MANUSCRIPTS

BRITISH LIBRARY

Additional MSS.
Egerton MSS.
Stowe MSS.

CHURCHILL COLLEGE, CAMBRIDGE

Erle-Drax MSS.

DORSET COUNTY RECORD OFFICE (DCRO)

Ilchester MSS.

PUBLIC RECORD OFFICE

War Office Papers (WO)

PRINTED SOURCES

An Abstract of Three Letters from Belfast to a Person in London (London, 1690).
Account from Colonel Kirk of the Relieving of London-Derry (London, 1689).
An Account of a Fight between the French and Irish, for refusing to admit the French to be Governors of Cork and Waterford in Ireland (London, 1689).
An Account of Major General Kirck, and London-Derry, with a Geographical Account of the River he Sail'd down, and the Various Forts on it, perticularly that of Kulmore (London, 1689).
An Account of Major General Kirck's Safe Arrival at London-Derry (London, 1689).
An Account of the Great Defeat that Major General Kirk gave the Irish Forces near Charlemont, under the Command of Lord Strabane and Colonel Gordon O-Neal (London, 1689).
An Account of the Great Success and Victory that the Garrison in Sligo has obtained over the Irish Army (London, 1689).
An Account of the Joyning of Major-General Kirk's Forces with Duke Schomberg's and the taking the Town and Castle of Carrickfergus: As also an Account of the Irish Army under K. James (London, 1689).
An Account of the late Barbarous Proceedings of the Earl of Tyrconnel and his Soldiers, against the poor Protestants in Ireland (London, 1689)

An Account of the Nature, Situation, Natural Strength and Ancient and Modern Fortifications of the Several Cities and Garrison-Towns in Ireland that are still possessed by the Forces of the Late King James (London, 1690).

An Account of the Present Miserable State of Affairs in Ireland (London, 1689).

An Account of the Taking of the Fort of Ballymore, within ten miles of Athlone, on Monday the eight of June, 1691 (Edinburgh, 1691).

An Account of the Taking of the New Fort in Kinsale by the Forces of the Earl of Marlborough (London, 1690).

An Account of the Town and Castle of Charlemont in Ireland, Besieged by a Detached Body of the Duke of Schomberg's Army under the Command of Lieutenant General Douglas (London, 1689).

An Account of the Transactions of the Late King James in Ireland, wherein is contain'd The Act of Attainder past at Dublin in May, 1689 (London, 1690).

Ainsworth, J. (ed.) (1961) *The Inchiquin Manuscripts*, Dublin: Irish Manuscripts Commission.

Ainsworth, J. F. and MacLysaght, E. (eds) (1958) 'The Nugent Papers', *Analecta Hibernica*, xx.

The Approach and Signal Victory of K. Williams Forces over the Irish Army encamped round Limmrick (London, 1690).

Articles of War agreed upon between his Grace the Duke of Schonberg and Teige O Regan, for the Surrender of Charlemont, the Twelfth of May, 1690 (London, 1690).

Ash, T. (1888) 'A Circumstantial Journal of the Siege of Londonderry', in T. Witherow, *Two Diaries of Derry in 1689*, Derry: William Gailey, pp. 57–104.

Barbé, L. (ed.) (1877) 'Siege of Limerick: Letters from Jean Payan de La Fouleresse to Christian V of Denmark', *Notes and Queries*, 5th series, viii, pp. 121–3.

Berwick, see Fitzjames.

Berwick, E. (ed.) (1819) *The Rawdon Papers* (London).

Boyer, A. (1702–3) *The History of King William III. In III Parts*, London, 3 vols.

Calendar of State Papers Domestic, William III and Mary, 1689–90 (London: HMSO, 1895–1937).

Calendar of State Papers Domestic, William III and Mary, 1690–91 (London: HMSO, 1895–1937).

Calendar of State Papers Domestic, William III and Mary, 1691–92 (London: HMSO, 1895–1937).

Calendar of Treasury Papers, 1557–1696, London: HMSO (1868).

Caulfield, R. (1857) *Journal of the Very Rev. Rowland Davies, LL.D.*, London: Camden Society.

Clarke, J. S. (1816) *The Life of James the Second*, 2 vols (London).

Dalrymple, Sir John (1790) *Memoirs of Great Britain and Ireland; from the Dissolution of the last Parliament of Charles II till the Capture of the French and Spanish Fleets at Vigo*, 3 vols (London and Edinburgh).

Danaher, K. and Simms, J. G. (1962) *The Danish Force in Ireland, 1690–1691*, Dublin: Irish Manuscripts Commission.

De Beer, E. S. (ed.) (1976–89) *The Correspondence of John Locke* (8 vols), Oxford: Clarendon Press.

A Description of Tredagh in Ireland, with the Antiquity, Scituation, Natural Strength, and Fortifications of the said Place (London, 1689).

A Diary of the Siege and Surrender of Lymerick with the Articles at Large, Both Civil and Military (London, 1692).

A Diary of the Siege of Athlone, Giving a Perfect Account of the Taking of the Castle, Forts and Irish-Town by Storme ... By an Engineer of the Army (London, 1691).

Dumont de Bostaque, I. (1968) *Mémoires d'Isaac Dumont de Bostaque* (2nd ed.) (Paris).

An Exact Account of the Duke of Schombergs Happy Voyage from Highlake to his Safe Arrival at Carrick-Fergus, with the Particulars of the Engagement with Three French Men of War in that Bay (London, 1689).

An Exact Account of the King's March to Ardee and of his forcing the Irish to abandon the Pass of the River Boyne (London, 1690).

An Exact Account of the Late Action at the Town of Dundalk against the Irish by Their Majesties Forces commanded by Sir John Lanier (London, 1690).

An Exact Account of the Royal Army under the Command of His Grace Duke Schomberg with the Particulars of a Great Defeat given to the Irish Army near Boyle (London, 1689).

An Exact Account of the taking by Storm the English Town of Athlone, June the 21st, in a Letter from Dublin June the 23rd (London, 1691).

An Exact and Particular Account of the Defeat given to the Rebels in the County of Cork by Lord Justice Cox and Coll. Hastings, with 2000 of the Army and Militia and of the Lord Lisburn's cutting off a Party of the French and Irish Horse near Lanesborough Pass … in a Letter from Dublin, June the 25th 1691 (London, 1691).

An Exact Journal of the Victorious Progress of their Majesties Forces under the Command of Gen. Ginckle, this Summer in Ireland (London, 1691).

An Exact Relation of Routing the Irish Army under Sarsfield, and of the Hostages agreed on, in order to a Capitulation for Surrender of Limerick into Their Majesties Hands (London, 1691).

An Exact Relation of the Glorious Victory Obtain'd upon the French and Irish Army before London-Derry on Sunday, June the 2nd, 1689 (London, 1689).

A Faithful Account of the Taking the Bridge, and beating down, the Irish Town of Athlone (London, 1691).

Fitzjames, J., Duke of Berwick (1779) *Memoirs of the Marshal Duke of Berwick. Written by himself. With a summary continuation from the year 1716, to his death in 1734*, 2 vols (London).

Fountainhall, J. L. (1848) *Historical Notices of Scottish Affairs*, 2 vols, Edinburgh: Bannatyne Club.

A Full Account of the Great Victory obtained by the Protestants in Ireland since the Arrival of his Grace the Duke of Shcomberg [sic] as it was communicated by the Reverend and Valliant Gouvernour Walker at Chester (London, 1689).

A Full and Impartial Account of all the Secret Consults, Negotiations, Strategems, and Intrigues of the Romish Party in Ireland, from 1660 to this Present Year 1689 (London, 1689).

A Full and Impartial Account of the Late Besieging and Taking of the Famous Castle of Killishandrea, in the Province of Ulster in Ireland, by the Brave Inniskilling Forces (London, 1690).

A Full and Particular Relation of the Taking the Town and Forts of Kinsale, and how they were Besieged by both Sea and Land (London, 1690).

A Full and True Account of all the Remarkable Actions and Things that have happened in the North of Ireland since 15th of November to the 17th Instant. And particularly of the Actions at Sligo, Newry and Charlemont (London, 1689).

A Full and True Account of His Grace Duke Schomberg's marching towards Dublin, and of the Preparations the late King James is making to oppose him (London, 1689).

A Full and True Account of the Besieging and Taking of Carrickfergus by the Duke of Schomberg (London, 1689).

A Full and True Account of the Late Brave Action Performed by the Inniskilling-Men and some English and Dutch Forces under the Command of Coll. Woseley against a Great Body of the Irish, under the Command of the Duke of Berwick, at the Town of Cavan (London, 1690).

A Full and True Account of the Two Great Victories lately obtained before Lymerick by K. William's Forces over the French and Irish Rebels which were commanded by D. Tyrconnel and General Lauson (London, 1690).

A Full and True Account of Two Famous and Signal Victories Obtained by Their Majesties Forces over the Irish Rebels: The First over General Sarsfield, near the Shannon, Raising the Siege of Bir … The Second over Four Thousand Raparees (London, 1691).

A Full and True Relation of the Taking of Cork, by the Right Honorable the Earl of Marlborough, Lieut: Gen. of their Majesties Forces: Together with the Articles of their Surrender (London, 1690).

A Further Account of the State of Ireland and the Proceedings of the Late King James in that Kingdom (London, 1689).

Gilbert, J. T. (ed.) (1971) *A Jacobite Narrative of the War in Ireland, 1688–1691*, Shannon: Irish University Press.

The Glorious Conquest: or the Repeated Victory of the Right Honourable the Earl of Marlborough: First in taking the City of Cork; Secondly, Kings-Sale; and the strong adjacent Forts (London, 1690).

Great and Good News from His Grace the Duke of Schomberg's Camp at Dundalk (London, 1689).

Great News from Dundalk giving a Full and Particular Account of the late Great and Famous Action between His Majesties Forces under the Command of Brigadier Stuart and a Party of the late King James's, near the Town of Dundalk (London, 1690).

Great News from Ireland: Being a full and true Relation of the several Great and Successful Defeats, which the Danish and Inniskilling Forces hath lately obtained over a Party of the Irish Rebels at Cliff and Emismack (London, 1690).

Great News From Lymerick in Ireland: A Full and True Account of the State and Siege of that City, by His Majesties Forces, commanded by Count Solms, and Lieutenant General Douglas. With a particular Relation of the Surrendering of Cork and Yaughall, by the Irish (London, 1690).

Great News from Scotland and Ireland giving an Account of the Death of the Chief of the Rebels Clans in Scotland, of the State of King James in Ireland, and of the Divisions betwixt the Irish and French Generals, in a Letter from Edenborough (London, 1690).

Grey, A. (1763) *Debates of the House of Commons, from the Year 1667 to 1694*, 10 vols (London).

Hainsworth, D. R. (ed.) (1983) *The Correspondence of Sir John Lowther of Whitehaven, 1693–1698*, London: British Academy.

Hamilton, A. (1690) *A True Relation of the Actions of the Inniskilling-Men, from their first taking up of Arms in December 1688* (London).

Hewitson, A. (ed.) (1908) *The Diary of Thomas Bellingham, an Officer under William III* (Preston).

Hill, G. (ed.) (1869) *The Montgomery Manuscripts* (Belfast).

His Grace the Duke of Schomberge's Character, according to the Ignorant Notions that the Irish Papists in Ireland have formed of Him: Together with some Old Prophecies foretelling the Conquest of that Kingdom by the Protestant Army under his Grace's Command (London, 1689).

Historical Manuscripts Commission (HMC), Reports of the Royal Commission on Historical Manuscripts:

> 1st Report
> 3rd Report
> 4th Report, Appendix, MSS. of Lord de Ros
> 5th Report

7th Report

8th Report, Appendix, MSS. of Lord Talbot de Malahide

10th Report, Appendix, Part 4, MSS. of the Earl of Fingall, pp. 107–200, 'A Light to the Blind' (1711)

Athole and Home MSS.

Bath MSS.

Buccleuch (Montagu House and Whitehall) MSS.

Cowper MSS.

Downshire MSS.

Egmont MSS.

Finch MSS.

Frankland-Russell-Astley MSS.

Hamilton MSS.

House of Lords MSS.

Kenyon MSS.

Le Fleming MSS.

Leyborne-Popham MSS.

Lonsdale MSS.

Ormonde MSS.

Portland MSS.

Rutland MSS.

Stuart MSS.

MSS. in various collections

The History of the Wars in Ireland, betwixt Their Majesties Army and the Forces of the late King James, by an Officer in the Royal Army (2nd edn, London, 1691).

Hogan, J. (ed.) (1934) Négociations de M. Le Comte D'Avaux en Irlande, 1689–90, Dublin: Irish Manuscripts Commission.

Hogan, J. (ed.) (1958) Négociations de M. Le Comte D'Avaux en Irlande, 1689–90: Supplementary Volume, Dublin: Irish Manuscripts Commission.

Japikse, N. (ed.) (1927–8) Correspondentie van Willem III en van Hans Willem Bentinck, 2 vols (The Hague: Nijhoff).

Japikse, N. (ed.) (1932–72) Correspondentie van Willem III en van Hans Willem Bentinck, 3 vols (The Hague: Nijhoff).

A Journal of The Three Months Royal Campaign of His Majesty in Ireland, together with a True and Perfect Diary of the Siege of Lymerick (London, 1690).

Journals of the House of Commons

Journals of the House of Lords

Kane, R. (1748) Campaigns of King William and Queen Anne, from 1689 to 1712 (Dublin).

King, W. (1691) The State of the Protestants of Ireland under the late King James's Government (London).

Lenihan, P. and Sheridan, G. (2005) 'A Swiss soldier in Ireland, 1690–90', Irish Studies Review, xiii., 479–97.

A Letter from an English Officer in his Majesty's Army in Ireland giving a True Account of the Progress of Affairs in that Kingdom: Together with what past at the Surrender of Waterford and Duncannon: And of his Majesty's March towards Limmerick (London, 1690).

A Letter from an Officer belonging to the Ordnance on Board the Fleet lying in the Bay before the Isle of Man, giving an Account of the Duke of Schomberg's Arrival and Landing of the Forces under his Command at Carrick Fergus (London,1689).

A Letter from Chester of the Twenty Second Instant, Giving an Account of Some Affairs in Ireland, and of the Arrival and Reception of the General the Duke of Schomberg, and of the Forces there (London, 1689).

A Letter from Duke Schomberge's Camp, giving an Account of the Condition of the English and Irish Army (London, 1689).

A Letter from Major-General Kirk in Ireland to his Friend here in London (London, 1690).

A Letter from on board Major General Kirke giving a Full Account of the Posture of Affairs of London-Derry (London, 1689).

London Gazette

Luttrell, N. (1857) *A Brief Historical Relation of State Affairs, from September 1678 to April 1714*, 6 vols (Oxford).

McCarmick, Captain W. (1691) *A Farther Impartial Account of the Actions of the Inniskilling-men containing the Reasons of their First Rising* (London).

Mackay, H. (1833) *Memoirs of the War carried on in Scotland and Ireland, 1689–1691*, Edinburgh: Bannatyne Club.

Mackenzie, J. (1690) *A Narrative of the Siege of London-Derry: or, the late Memorable Transactions of that City. Faithfully Represented to Rectifie the Mistakes and supply the Omissions of Mr Walker's Account* (London).

MacLysaght, E. (ed.) (1944) 'The Longford Papers', *Analecta Hibernica*, xv.

MacLysaght, E. (ed.) (1944) 'Manuscripts of the Old Corporation of Kinsale', *Analecta Hibernica*, xv.

MacLysaght, E. (ed.) (1944) 'The Seagrave Papers', *Analecta Hibernica*, xv.

McNeill, C. (ed.) (1943) *The Tanner Letters*, Dublin: Irish Manuscripts Commission.

Major General Kirk's Letter to his Grace the Duke of Hamilton (Edinburgh, 1689).

Melvin, P. (1985) 'Letters from Lord Longford and Others on Irish Affairs, 1687–1702: Ellis Papers BL. MS.', *Analecta Hibernica*, xxxii., pp. 35–111.

Mitchelburne, J. (1692) *An Account of the Transactions in the North of Ireland, Anno Domini, 1691* (London).

Mitchelburne, J. (1705) *Ireland Preserv'd: or the Siege of London-Derry* (London).

Moody, T. W and Simms, J. G. (eds) (1969–83) *The Bishopric of Derry and the Irish Society of London, 1602–1705*, 2 vols, Dublin: Irish Manuscripts Commission.

Morsier, J.-F. de (1908–19) 'Journal de Jean-Francois De Morsier', in *Soldats Suisses au service étranger*, A. Jullien (ed.) 8 vols. (Geneva), pp. 87–105.

The most acceptable and faithful Account of the Capitulation the Irish Governor of Charlemont made to D. Schonbergh's Forces (London, 1690).

Mulleneaux, S., see *A Journal of The Three Months Royal Campaign.*

Mulloy, S. (ed.) (1983)*Franco-Irish Correspondence, December 1688–February 1692*, 3 vols, Dublin: Irish Manuscripts Commission.

Murray, R. H. (1912) *The Journal of John Stevens, containing a Brief Account of the War in Ireland, 1689–1691*, Oxford: Clarendon Press.

Nihell, J. (1689) *A Journal of the Most Remarkable Occurrences that happened between His Majesty's Army; and the Forces under the command of Mareschal de Schomberg, in Ireland, from the 12th of August to the 23rd of October 1689* (Dublin).

O'Kelly, C. (1896) *Macariae Excidium, or the Destruction of Cyprus*, G. N. Plunkett and E. Hogan (eds), Dublin: Sealy, Bryers and Walker.

An Order Published by the Command of the Duke of Schonberg, in the Camp at Dundalk, for Establishing the Rates and Prizes of Provisions in the Army (London, 1689).

Parker, R. (1747) *Memoirs of the Most Remarkable Military Transactions from the Year 1683, to 1718* (London).

A Particular Account from Collonel Kirke of the State of London-Derry and Iniskilling (London, 1689).

Quincy, J. S., Comte de (1899–1901) *Mémoires du chevalier de Quincy*, 3 vols, ed. L. Lecestre (Paris: Société de l'histoire de France. Publications 289, 293, 305).

The Raparee Saint: A Funeral Sermon upon the Death of Monsieur St Ruth, Preached at Gallaway, a little after the Late Fight, by Mac Olero, A Fryer of the New Order, of the Raparees (London and Edinburgh, 1691).

A Relation of Several Signal Victories and Other Considerable Enterprizes lately obtained by Their Majesties' Forces over the Rebels in Ireland (London, 1691).

A Relation of the Victory obtained by the King in Ireland at the Passage of the Boyne on the First Day of this Instant July 1690 and of the Surrender of Drogheda (London, 1690).

A Relation of what most Remarkably happened during the Last Campaign in Ireland betwixt His Majesties Army Royal, and the Forces of the Prince of Orange, sent to Joyn the Rebels, under the Command of the Count de Schomberg (Dublin, 1689).

Richards, Lt. Col. J. (1971) 'Diary of the Siege of Limerick, 1691', in J. T. Gilbert (ed.) *A Jacobite Narrative of the War in Ireland, 1688–1691*, Shannon: Irish University Press, pp. 282–98.

Richards, J. (1888) 'The Diary of the Fleet, 1689', in T. Witherow (ed.) *Two Diaries of Derry in 1689, being Richards' Diary of the Fleet … and Ash's Journal of the Siege*, Londonderry: William Gailey, pp. 1–55.

Shaw, W. A. (ed.) (1931) *Calendar of Treasury Books, 1689–1692*, London: HMSO.

Singer, S. W. (ed.) (1828) *The Correspondence of Henry Hyde, Earl of Clarendon, and of his brother, Lawrence Hyde, Earl of Rochester* (London).

Steele, R. (1910) *A Bibliography of Royal Proclamations of the Tudor and Stuart Sovereigns … 1485–1714*, 2 vols, Oxford: Clarendon Press.

Story, Rev. G. (1691) *A True and Impartial History of the Most Material Occurrences in the Kingdom of Ireland during the Last Two Years* (London, 1691).

Story, Rev. G. (1693) *A Continuation of the Impartial History of the Wars of Ireland, From the Time that the Duke Schonberg Landed with an Army in that Kingdom, to the 23rd of March 1691/2 when Their Majesties' Proclamation was published, declaring the War to be ended* (London).

Tate, L. (ed.) (1932) 'The Letter Book of Richard Talbot', *Analecta Hibernica*, iv., pp. 99–139.

A Third Proclamation by His Grace Frederick Duke of Schonberg, General of all Their Majesties Forces in Ireland, Published at Dundalk, September 14 1689 (London, 1689).

Thompson, E. M. (ed.) (1878) *Correspondence of the Family of Hatton*, London: Camden Society.

Troost, W. (ed.) (1986) 'Letters from Bartholomew van Holmrigh to General Ginkel, Earl of Athlone, 1692 to 1700: From the Huisarchief Amerongen, Amerongen Castle, near Utrecht', *Analecta Hibernica*, xxxiii.

A True Account from Coll. Kirke of the Relieving of London-Derry (London, 1689).

A True Account of the Present State of Ireland, by a Person that with great difficulty left Dublin June 8th, 1689 (London, 1689).

A True and Faithful Account of the Present State and Condition of the Kingdom of Ireland (London, 1690).

A True and Impartial Account of the most Material Passages in Ireland since December 1688, with a Particular Relation of the Forces of Londonderry (London, 1689).

A True and Impartial Account of the Present State of Affairs in London-Derry in Ireland, being a Relation of the late Great Fight betwixt the Protestants and the French and Irish Papists (London, 1689).

A True and Particular Account of the Total Defeat of Coll. Sarsfield and his Party not far from Bellishannon (London, 1689).

A True and Impartial Account of Their Majesties Army in Ireland (London, 1690).

A True and Perfect Journal of the Affairs in Ireland since His Majesties Arrival in that Kingdom (London, 1690).

A True Relation of the Battle of the Boyne in Ireland fought by his Majesty King William in the Year 1690, without Observation or Reflection (London, 1700).

Walker, G. (1971) *A True Account of the Siege of London-Derry* (2nd ed. London, 1689), (ed.) P. Dwyer, Wakefield: S. R. Publishers.

Walker, G. (1971) *A Vindication of the True Account of the Siege of Derry in Ireland* (London, 1689), ed. P. Dwyer, Wakefield: S. R. Publishers.

Witherow, T. (ed.) (1888) *Two Diaries of Derry in 1689, being Richards' Diary of the Fleet ... and Ash's Journal of the Siege*, Londonderry: William Gailey.

SECONDARY WORKS

Ashton, R. (1777) *The Battle of Aughrim: or the Fall of Monsieur St Ruth. A Tragedy* (Dublin).

Bagwell, R. (1916) *Ireland under the Stuarts and during the Interregnum, 1660–1690I*, 3 vols, London: Longmans.

Baxter, S. B. (1966) *William III* (London).

Beckett, J. C. (1976) 'The Irish Armed Forces, 1660–1685', in J. Bossy and P. Jupp (eds) *Essays Presented to Michael Roberts* (Belfast: Blackstaff), 41–53.

Black, E. (ed.) (1990) *Kings in Conflict: Ireland in the 1690s*, Belfast: Ulster Museum.

Bradshaw, W. H. (1878) *Enniskillen Long Ago* (Enniskillen).

Breffny, B. de (1977) *Castles of Ireland*, London: Thames and Hudson.

Burke, J. (2001) 'Siege warfare in Seventeenth-Century Ireland', in P. Lenihan (ed.) *Conquest and Resistance: War in Seventeenth-Century Ireland*, Leiden, Boston and Köln: Brill, pp. 257–91.

Callow, J. (2004) *King in Exile. James II: Warrior, King and Saint, 1689–1701*, Stroud: Sutton.

Childs, J. (1976) *The Army of Charles II*, London: Routledge and Kegan Paul.

Childs, J. (1980) *The Army, James II and the Glorious Revolution*, Manchester: Manchester University Press.

Childs, J. (1987) *The British Army of William III*, Manchester: Manchester University Press.

Childs, J. (1987) *Nobles, Gentlemen and the Profession of Arms in Restoration Britain, 1660–1688*, London: Society for Army Historical Research, Special Publication No. 13.

Childs, J. (1991) *The Nine Years' War and the British Army, 1688–1697: the Operations in the Low Countries*, Manchester: Manchester University Press.

Childs, J. (1996) 'The Williamite War, 1688–1691', in, T. Bartlett and K. Jeffery (eds) *A Military History of Ireland*, Cambridge: Cambridge University Press, pp. 188–210.

Churchill, W. S. (1933–8) *Marlborough: his Life and Times*, 4 vols, London: Harrap.

Connolly, S. J. (ed.) (1998) *The Oxford Companion to Irish History*, Oxford: Oxford University Press.

Costello, C. (1961) 'Irish military surveys of the seventeenth century', *An Costantóir*, xxi., pp. 433–2.

Cox, B. (1995) *King William's European Joint Venture* (Assen: van Gorcum).

Dalton, C. (1892–1904) *English Army Lists and Commission Registers, 1661–1714*, 6 vols (London, repr. 1960: Francis Edwards).

Dalton, C. (1907) *King Charles II's Irish Army Lists, 1661–1685* (London, repr. 2000: De Búrca).

Dalton, C. (1909) *The Scots Army, 1661–1688* (London, repr. 1989: Greenhill).

D'Alton, J. (1997) *Illustrations Historical and Genealogical of King James's Irish Army List, 1689* (Kansas City: Irish Genealogical Foundation).

Davis, J. (1887–95) *The History of the Second Queen's Royal Regiment*, 2 vols (London).

Doherty, R. (1998) *The Williamite War in Ireland, 1688–1691*, Dublin: Four Courts Press.

Ellis, P. B. (1976) *The Boyne Water*, London: Hamish Hamilton.

Garland, J. L. (1949) 'The Regiment of Mac Elligott, 1688–1689', *Irish Sword*, i., pp. 121–7.

Garstin, J. R. (1933)'Some extracts relating to Ireland from the Journal of Gideon Bonnivert, 1690', *Louth Archaeological Society Journal*, viii., pp. 18–21

Gébler, C. (2006) *The Siege of Derry: A History*, London: Macmillan.

Glozier, M. (2002) *The Huguenot Soldiers of William of Orange and the Glorious Revolution of 1688: the Lions of Judah*, Brighton: Sussex Academic Press.

Glozier, M. (2005) *Marshal Schomberg, 1615–90: 'the Ablest Soldier of his Age'*, Brighton: Sussex Academic Press.

Graham, J. (1829) *A History of the Siege of Londonderry and the Defence of Enniskillen in 1688 and 1689* (Dublin).

Ó hAnnracháin, Tadhg (2001) 'The strategic involvement of continental powers in Ireland, 1596–1691', in P. Lenihan (ed.) *Conquest and Resistance: War in Seventeenth-Century Ireland*, Leiden, Boston and Köln: Brill, pp. 25–52.

Harris, W. (1749) *The History of the Life and Reign of William-Henry, Prince of Nassau and Orange* (Dublin).

Hayes-McCoy, G. A. (1990) *Irish Battles: a Military History of Ireland*, Belfast: Appletree Press.

Hebbert, F. J. (1975) 'The Richards Brothers', *Irish Sword*, xii., pp. 200–11.

Hempton, J. (1861) *The Siege and History of Londonderry* (Londonderry).

Henry, W. and King, C. S. (1987) *Upper Lough Erne in 1739*, ed. H. Weir, Whitegate: Ballinakella Press.

Jones, D. W. (1988) *War and Economy in the Age of William III and Marlborough*, Oxford: Blackwell.

Jones, J. R. (1993) *Marlborough*, Cambridge: Cambridge University Press.

Kazner, J. F. A. (1789) *Leben Friedrichs von Schomberg oder Schoenberg*, 2 vols (Mannheim).

Kazner, J. F. A. (1807) *Campagnes du Maréchal de Schomberg en Portugal, 1662–1668*, trans. C. F. D. Dumouriez (London).

Kelly, W. P. (ed.) (2001) *The Sieges of Derry*, Dublin: Four Courts Press.

Kelly, W. P. (2001) 'The Forgotten Siege of Derry, March–August, 1649', in W. P. Kelly (ed.) *The Sieges of Derry*, Dublin: Four Courts Press, pp. 31–52.

Kerrigan, P. M. (1980) 'Seventeenth-century fortifications, forts and garrisons in Ireland: a Preliminary List', *Irish Sword*, xiv., pp. 3–24.

Kerrigan, P. M. (2001) 'Ireland in Naval Strategy, 1641–1691', in P. Lenihan (ed.) *Conquest and Resistance: War in Seventeenth-Century Ireland*, Leiden, Boston and Köln: Brill, pp. 151–76.

King, C. S. (ed.) (1892) *Henry's Upper Lough Erne in 1739* (Dublin).

Lenihan, P. (ed.) (2001) *Conquest and Resistance: War in Seventeenth-Century Ireland*, Leiden, Boston and Köln: Brill.

Lenihan, P. (2001) 'Strategic geography, 1641–1691', in P. Lenihan (ed.) *Conquest and Resistance: War in Seventeenth-Century Ireland*, Leiden, Boston and Köln: Brill, pp. 115–50.

Lenihan, P. (2003) *1690, Battle of the Boyne*, Stroud: Tempus.

Lynn, J. (1997) *Giant of the Grand Siècle: the French Army, 1610–1715*, Cambridge: Cambridge University Press.

McBride, I. (1997) *The Siege of Derry in Ulster Protestant Mythology*, Dublin: Four Courts Press.

Mackay, J. (1842) *The Life of Lieut.-Gen. Hugh Mackay of Scoury* (London).

Maclysaght, E. (1941) *Calendar of the Orrery Papers* Irish Manuscript Commission, Dublin.

Macpherson, J. (1775) *Original Papers containing the Secret History of Great Britain, from the Restoration to the Accession of the House of Hannover*, 2 vols (London).

Maguire, W. A. (ed.) (1990) *Kings in Conflict: the Revolutionary War in Ireland and its Aftermath, 1689–1750*, Belfast: Blackstaff Press.

Manning, R. B. (2006) *An Apprenticeship in Arms: the Origins of the British Army, 1585–1702*, Oxford: Oxford University Press.

Miller, J. (1976) 'Thomas Sheridan (1646–1712) and his "Narrative"', *Irish Historical Studies*, xx.

Murphy, J. A. (1959) *Justin MacCarthy, Lord Mountcashel* (Cork).

Napier, M. (1859–62) *Memorials and Letters illustrative of the Life and Times of John Graham of Claverhouse, Viscount Dundee*, 3 vols (Edinburgh).

O'Callaghan, J. C. (1969) *History of the Irish Brigades in the Service of France*, Shannon: Irish University Press.

O'Carroll, D. (2001) 'Change and continuity in weapons and tactics, 1594–1691', in P. Lenihan (ed.) *Conquest and Resistance: War in Seventeenth-Century Ireland*, Leiden, Boston and Köln: Brill, pp. 210–55.

Petrie, C. (1972) *The Great Tyrconnel: a Chapter in Anglo-Irish Relations*, Dublin: Mercier Press.

Robb, N. A. (1966) *William of Orange, a Personal Portrait*, 2 vols, London: Heinemann.

Sergeant, P. W. (1969) *Little Jennings and Fighting Dick Talbot: a Life of the Duke and Duchess of Tyrconnel*, London: Hutchinson.

Simms, J. G. (1956) *The Williamite Confiscation in Ireland, 1690–1703*, London: Faber and Faber.

Simms, J. G. (1969) *Jacobite Ireland, 1685–1691*, London: Routledge and Kegan Paul.

Simms, J. G. (1986) *War and Politics in Ireland, 1649–1730*, London: Hambledon.

Speed, J. (1995) *The Counties of Britain: A Tudor Atlas by John Speed*, intr. Nigel Nicolson, London: Thames and Hudson.

Sterne, L. (2003) *The Life and Opinions of Tristram Shandy, Gentleman*, London: Penguin.

Taylor, G. and Skinner, A. (1783) *Maps of the Roads of Ireland* (2nd ed., Dublin, repr. Shannon, 1969).

Todhunter, J. (1895) *The Life of Patrick Sarsfield* (London).

Trimble, W. C. (1919) *The History of Enniskillen* (Enniskillen).

Troost, W. (2004) *William III, the Stadholder-King: a Political Biography*, Aldershot: Ashgate.

Wauchope, P. (1992) *Patrick Sarsfield and the Williamite War*, Dublin: Irish Academic Press.

Wheeler, J. S. (1999) *Cromwell in Ireland*, Dublin: Gill and Macmillan.

Wheeler, J. S. (2001) 'The logistics of conquest', in P. Lenihan (ed.) *Conquest and Resistance: War in Seventeenth-Century Ireland*, Leiden, Boston and Köln: Brill, pp. 177–209.

Witherow, T. (1885) *Derry and Enniskillen in the Year 1689* (Belfast).

Wolseley, G. (1894) *The Life of John Churchill, Duke of Marlborough, to the Accession of Queen Anne*, 2 vols (London).

Young, J. (2001) 'Invasions: Scotland and Ireland, 1641–1691', in P. Lenihan (ed.) *Conquest and Resistance: War in Seventeenth-Century Ireland*, Leiden, Boston and Köln: Brill, pp. 53–86.

Index